BUT I'M DIFFERENT NOW

(The memoirs of a Mod with a Punk attitude, who takes you 'access all areas' with his tales of discovery, friendship, and survival)

Pete Eastwood

Grosvenor House
Publishing Limited

All rights reserved
Copyright © Pete Eastwood, 2022

The right of Pete Eastwood to be identified as the author of this
work has been asserted in accordance with Section 78
of the Copyright, Designs and Patents Act 1988

The book cover is copyright to Pete Eastwood

This book is published by
Grosvenor House Publishing Ltd
Link House
140 The Broadway, Tolworth, Surrey, KT6 7HT.
www.grosvenorhousepublishing.co.uk

This book is sold subject to the conditions that it shall not, by way of
trade or otherwise, be lent, resold, hired out or otherwise circulated
without the author's or publisher's prior consent in any form of binding or
cover other than that in which it is published and
without a similar condition including this condition being imposed
on the subsequent purchaser.

A CIP record for this book
is available from the British Library

ISBN 978-1-83975-900-0

For my daughter Emma Leah

CONTENTS

Chapter 1 – Start 1
Chapter 2 – When You're Young 30
Chapter 3 – This Is The Modern World 69
Chapter 4 – Girl On The Phone 81
Chapter 5 – That's Entertainment 89
Chapter 6 – Thick As Thieves 107
Chapter 7 – The Bitterest Pill – (30th October, 1982 –
  Remember the date) 122
Chapter 8 – Absolute Beginners 143
Chapter 9 – The Place I Love 181
Chapter 10 – No Problem 191
Chapter 11 – Boy About Town 204
Chapter 12 – The Paris Match 227
Chapter 13 – A Different Kind of Bird for Jez 236
Chapter 14 – Heaven Must Have Sent You 246
Chapter 15 – Marine Boy 254
Chapter 16 – Confessions of a Driving Instructor 260
Chapter 17 – This is My World Today 266
Chapter 18 – Searching, Looking for Love 276
Chapter 19 – Four Weddings, a Funeral, and a King 285
Chapter 20 – Changes 299
Chapter 21 – We Are Family 312

Chapter 22 – Brand New Start 320

Chapter 23 – A Friargate Return 329

Chapter 24 – Waking up to a Bad Head 338

Chapter 25 – Rock Goes To College 351

Chapter 26 – Nothing To Lose 368

Chapter 27 – Not Very Sound 378

Chapter 28 – A Certain Band 386

Chapter 29 – Five Days in a Field 432

Chapter 30 – No Smoking 444

Chapter 31 – 2010 456

Chapter 32 – Agents Ruined My Life 476

Chapter 33 – It Should Have Been Me 494

Chapter 34 – The Kids All Dream Of Making It,
 Whatever That Means 505

Chapter 35 – Liar 524

Chapter 36 – Pie Man/A Chance Meeting 531

Chapter 37 – 336 Hours 557

Chapter 38 – Happy Ending 579

Chapter 39 – F… cancer Let's Dance 584

Chapter 40 – A Different Kind of Bird for Me 620

Chapter 41 – Fab 624

Chapter 42 – 'What is that Daddy, a plate?' 641

Chapter 43 – Top Ten 646

Chapter 44 – Tough Times 650

Chapter 45 – And In The End 657

INTRODUCTION

The first time I saw a member of the female form naked, I was with my grandma, and the first time I witnessed two people having sex, Bob Geldof was in the room.
I certainly don't want these two facts to set the tone for my story, but things have always happened to me that don't necessarily happen to everyone else.
I used to think that the situations I found myself in were pretty normal, but when I used to ask friends if such a thing had happened to them, they would always say, 'No, Pete!'

On occasions in the past, I have had people say that I should write a book and tell my story, but I have always felt that nobody would want to read a story about me. But now it is 2020, and we find ourselves in the very unusual situation of being in a COVID lockdown. Everyone is stuck at home and maybe, for the first time in their lives, find themselves with time on their hands.

To be honest, there were a few factors that led me to finally putting pen to paper, one obviously being the lockdown situation. But the main one was that my mum had passed away last November, and whilst clearing her house we discovered a box of very old family photos in her attic. Sadly, not all of them had information written on the back to identify the people and places, and I so wished I had had the opportunity to discuss these with her whilst she was still alive.

A few weeks before this, I had been reading an autobiography by Andrew Ridgley from Wham, and realised that just before they became famous, they were basically getting up to the same sort of things as me and my mates. Based on these three factors, I decided to write my book.

The idea was to record the adventures of a group of best friends, living in the same area, who met on their first day at secondary school, and although they took different pathways in adulthood and now have different views and beliefs, at 56 years of age they still remain as close as ever, and have contact with each other on an almost daily basis.

They say that everyone has a book in them, and I believe a lot of people do, so here goes!

CHAPTER ONE

START

My grandma used to say that I was the bonniest baby in Brownhill, and even though I doubt that was an official title, that's grandmas for you.

My first family home was in Darwen, next to Sunnyhurst Woods, but after just six months, we moved to Whalley New Road in Blackburn. It is pretty difficult trying to pinpoint my first childhood memory, but I have always said I remembered being pushed in my pram around the Brownhill area, though I may have imagined that.
Next, the Eastwood family moved again to 63 Bank Hey Lane North, and that's where I feel my childhood really began.
My dad, George H Eastwood, worked at Crown Paints in Darwen, and my mum Margery M, was a housewife, keeping house, looking after me and my brother, and putting delicious homemade meals on the table for when my dad returned home from work each evening. My parents were smart, decent, and well-respected members of the community, and even though it was never intended, it did feel that it had been my role to try and tarnish that image over the years.

We have an old family photograph somewhere of me aged two, sitting in a round plastic bath in the living room (the type of photograph that mums would get out when you brought your first girlfriend home), and not long after it was taken, the living room ceiling fell in on my head. I actually do feel that I remember this incident happening (I mean you would, wouldn't you?), but one thing is for sure: remember it or not, this incident would go on to set the tone for the rest of my story (and my life).

Bank Hey Lane North was a nice, quiet, and respectable street, with St Gabriel's Church at the end of the avenue, and a cherry tree at the end of our front garden. (It's still there today, 53 years later.) Our neighbours were friendly, and everyone seemed to know each other.

For me, the highlight of any day was a visit to Mrs Shorrock's sweet shop at the bottom of the road. The penny tray in particular (as it was probably all I could afford anyway) offered such delights as Flying Saucers, Black Jacks, Fruit Salads, Space Dust, and my absolute favourite, Bazooka Joe bubble gum. The attraction for me was the small comic strip wrapped around the bubbly; I wanted to own every comic, so kept on buying the gum. On the comic strip were adverts for free gifts to send away for, such as Davey Crocket and Wild Bill Hickok Adventure Novels, Exploding Battleship Submarines and Baseball Sunglasses (just like the Big Leaguers wore). But the one I longed for the most was the Real Camera Fun, which would take 127 film and take 16 photos which could be enlarged. To get these, you had to send a certain number of comics and a small amount of money to an address in Westbury in N.Y. (So, not free, after all!) I can't remember ever sending for any of these gifts, but I continued to buy the bubbly anyway.

Money is hard to come by when you are a kid, and to help fund my latest obsession, I would have to help with the gardening from time to time. On one occasion, I spent the whole morning tidying up a flower bed in the back garden, only to be horrified by the 13p wage my dad gave me for my efforts. (No minimum wage back then.)

We had an apple tree, a large greenhouse full of tomatoes (which my dad tried to convince us would grow extra fast the more you talked to them), and grew most fruit and vegetables you could think of. They would always end up in one of my mum's homemade pies, which were legendary.

My grandma and grandad (Edna and Jim Burrows) lived at 19 Roe Lee Park, which was only about ten minutes' walk from our house, so we found ourselves visiting them a lot growing up, and both me and Robin would spend a large percentage of our childhood hanging out in Roe Lee Park in the kids' playground, on either the swings, the slide, or the spider's web. The only problem with the spider's web was that you needed someone to run around holding it in order for it to pick up speed. And you had to stay on it until the person with the most confidence decided it was time to stop, no matter how sick and dizzy you felt.

My first school was St Gabriel's Infant School in 1967, when I was aged four-and-a-half. It was a 20-minute walk from our house, and some of the pupils I shared that first ever class with are still friends today.
Our headteacher was Mr King, and like his name indicates, what he said went. I don't have any memories of him being horrible, just him being a nice respectable gentleman. But he was old-school, (pardon the pun) and he was pretty strict.

My main memories from that school were seeing who could 'wee' the highest up the walls of the outside toilets at playtime. I don't remember ever entering into this boys' activity myself, but I do remember watching with amusement at the more confident members of our class, trying to beat the previous day's target on the red brick wall at the back of the urinal. Obviously, at that age no world records were broken at this chosen sport, but the winner did end up being 'Cock of the playground' for the rest of the day (literally).

At the end of our playground was an old scout hut, and at morning break the dinner ladies would serve us cups of hot chocolate, which was without a doubt the highlight of every school day, and remains the best hot chocolate I have ever tasted.

One day my mum and Graham Duff's mum were invited into school, as seemingly I had cut a hole in his jumper with a pair of scissors from the art class. Looking back, I'm not sure if he had actually been the one who had cut a hole in my jumper, but I do remember being told off by my mum, and receiving a lecture from Mr King,

In 1971, Britain went decimal, and new coins were made and introduced to the public. I remember my dad coming into school to collect me and Robin, and bringing with him a handful of these new shiny coins to show us. There were 2ps, 1ps and tiny 1/2ps, but I don't recall if he gave them to us or simply just showed us them, but I was already planning my next visit to Mrs Shorrock's.

At the back of the scout hut, houses were being built on a new site, and after school a small group of us would search around in all the mud and rubble looking for Cat's Eyes, which were a retro reflective safety device being used as raised pavement markers. I have no idea what they were doing on that site, but they were a cool thing to own, and the latest craze at the time.

The year that man first landed on the moon, St Gabriel's newly-built school was ready to open its doors at Wilworth Crescent, and in 1972 it was our turn to move up to the juniors.

The old school had received its first pupils in 1901, and had served both me and Robin well, so I guess it was about time we moved on. My mum would walk us to the 'spot under the bridge', hand us our lunchboxes and watch us walk up the long path, either on our own or with a bunch of friends. Mr King's new office was situated against the wall in the centre of the main hall – a perfect viewing point to see what was happening throughout the day. Some of the teachers I remember with fondness are Mrs Whitworth, Mr Moody and Mrs Tootle, and another teacher was Mr Sharples, who was Deputy Head, and was the person you were sent to if you had been in trouble.

It is fair to say that education has never been my main priority in my daily life. I attended lessons because I had to, but much preferred all the bits in between. We used to have our PE lessons in the main hall under the watchful eye of Mr King, and it was these lessons that proved to me that I was no athlete. We were expected to run and jump over a wooden horse, and even though I had long legs compared to most, I dreaded doing this whilst all my classmates looked on. Another activity I hated was the ropes, which were hung from the ceiling. We were expected to haul ourselves up to the top of the rope, but as much as I tried, I could never pull myself up that high.

For me, and lots of others, break times were the thing we looked forward to the most. The boys would form gangs and walk around the playground talking about the latest Gary Glitter record (not good), or who had the best conker. The girls would do the same, but they would probably have been chatting about the latest *Jackie* weekly magazine, and Suzi Quatro.

When I look back on the things that use to excite us back then, it is always with great fondness. Our passions and interests were always so innocent, with things such as conkers, marbles, and little boxes of toy soldiers, to name but a few. I know that each generation reserves the bragging rights on the things that they grew up with, but if I was a kid now, I think I would choose these things over a mobile phone or Xbox any day.

Conkering was a big deal back then, and everybody would go to great lengths to own the hardest and biggest conker. The secret was to go hunting for horse chestnut trees which were off the beaten track, so that nobody had beaten you to them, leaving the trees full of conkers. Hours of fun were had as we threw sticks high up into the branches, trying to knock off the green spiky cases, within which lay a beautiful, shiny, brown conker. We would then soak them in vinegar or put them in the oven to try and harden them, but even though I tried both methods, they never worked for me.

Night after night we would visit Blackburn Cemetery, or Lovely Hall Lane, and I remember my Grandma and Grandad taking me and Robin to a secret location one evening. I don't know where it was, but it seemed to be in the country, as I remember a big stately home and a secluded lane lined with horse chestnut trees on both sides. It was wonderful, and I felt like we were the only people who knew this place existed. We spent ages collecting some of the biggest brown conkers I had ever seen, but I wish I knew where this place was now, and that I had asked my grandparents at the time. Every time I hear the Keane song *Somewhere Only We Know* it reminds me of that special place, and that time.

Marbles were another popular pastime, and you would always strive to get your hands on the rare ones with unusual patterns and colours in the glass. Regularly I would go to Ste Dickinson's house for a game after school, which was always good fun. And funnily enough, whilst I have been writing this book, I bumped into him at Brownhill for the first time in over 40 years. I also used to go round to another friend's house some evenings – Michael Downes – who had the best collection of toy soldiers around, and we would play for hours staging our own battles on his parents' living room table.

The new school was situated next to some fields, and during the hot summers of the early 1970s our chosen activity was rushing out of class at break times and heading for the fields to try and secure a den for us and the rest of our gang. We would then run from den to den, trying to rob them of all the hay. It would sometimes end up in a fight, as each gang was desperate to get their hands on the biggest pile, for some strange reason.
One incident that sticks in my mind was when my new friend Jeremy, who had just joined the school from Westholme, swallowed a drawing pin and started choking. Mr Sharples was alerted, and he rang for an ambulance which took Jeremy to Blackburn Hospital. Luckily, he lived to tell tale, but little did I know back then that I would spend the next 43 years having adventures with this person.

Another good friend at Gabriel's was Howard Clayton, whose dad Ronnie had been captain of the England football team and also for Blackburn Rovers. I remember him telling me one day that his dad used to earn about £100 per week, and I remember thinking at the time, *Wow, how can someone earn that much?* Imagine what his weekly pay would be if he were playing in today's game. At the time, we boys didn't appreciate just what an absolute legend Ronnie Clayton actually was; to us he was just Howard's dad, who used to play football.

On the football front, I am not sure what the process was that led us to choosing our favourite football team, but my choice was Liverpool, even though other friends opted for the likes of Leeds, Manchester United, or Chelsea. I put my choice down to the fact that Liverpool was the best; I mean, who in their right mind would settle for second or third best? My local team was Blackburn Rovers, who were not in the top flight back then (or now), so you would always choose a favourite from the First Division to support as well.

Andrew Smith, who I hung around with a fair bit at school, lived at the local newsagents at Roe Lee, and was pretty popular with the other pupils, as his house was full of toys, sweets, and comics. Outside the shop were three red bubble gum machines, which I became addicted to. Yet again, not for the bubbly, but for the miniature joke books that would sometimes drop into the silver flap at the bottom. I think the machines used to take 2ps, but one day at my Grandma's I discovered a bag of old coins which seemed to be around the same size, so I thought it was a good idea to give them a try on my next visit. To my delight – and the delight of my friends, after I had handed a few out – my plan had worked, and we spent the week slotting them into the machines until they finally ran out. When I look back at that incident today, I cringe, as you can bet your bottom dollar that bag of old coins would have been worth a darn site more than the 2ps I was supposed to be putting in in the first place.

At the time, I feel that my best friend at school was Stuart Bradshaw, who used to live on Pemberton Street. I went to his house for tea a few times and remember thinking that me and him would be mates forever. But this was not to be, as one day whilst walking home with him after school, he dropped a bombshell and told me that his family was moving to Adelaide in Australia. I had never heard of anyone emigrating before and was really upset. On his last day at school, I remember saying my last goodbyes to him at the bottom of St Gabriel's path, and don't mind admitting that we both had tears in our eyes. We promised to stay in touch, and to my joy the following Christmas I received a card from him from the other side of the world. Unfortunately, though, communication fizzled out after that. I guess he had simply settled into his new life and forgot about his old one in Blackburn. I still think about him from time to time and wish that there had been social media around then, as it would have been a lot easier to stay in touch.

Living at Bank Hey Lane North was great, but most of the other kids in the area seemed older than me and my brother. There was Martin Brown, who lived directly across the road from us, who I got on with and looked up to, with him being older. At the bottom of the road, just around the corner, lived Cass and his best friend Gino, who certainly wouldn't waste time on the likes of us younger boys. Woody, who was my age, lived just down from us, and like all neighbourhoods we had a local bully. Our bully was Eric, who lived right at the top of the lane on the next estate. He had a brother called Ste, and at a young age, I for one definitely dreaded bumping into him and his gang.

There were two occasions in particular that spring to mind, that had me quaking in my boots.
I don't remember what I was doing at the top of our road on my own, but what I do remember is being surrounded by about five of them, Eric showing me a large bag of maggots that he was holding, and him telling me to put some of the wriggly creatures into my mouth and chew. No way was I going to eat maggots, even though he was twice my size and a bully. So I said I could hear my mum shouting for me in the distance, and politely said my goodbyes.

A couple of weeks after Maggot Gate, there was a knock on our front door, and when I answered it, there stood a girl who I had seen around the area before. Across the road were Eric and his crew, and she told me that he wanted to make up with me and invited me to go for a jog around the block with them. This was the last thing I wanted to do, but how could I say no and look like a total wimp? We had been slowly jogging for about ten minutes when Eric suggested we stop and catch our breath at the bottom of the road, whilst he called at one of the houses for his friend. I started to think that maybe I had been wrong about him, but I was wrong! Eric's friend came out of his house, walked straight up to me, and tupped me in the face. Yes, it hurt. I hadn't been expecting it and I dreaded what was coming next, but all of a sudden the lad's sister appeared, told them off and to leave me alone, and surprisingly this actually worked. They slowly walked off, leaving me extremely grateful and relieved.

Maggots came into my life once again, as my new best buddy at the time, Ian Lucas, lived at Brownhill, and his dad owned a hardware shop next to Candy & Cards. In his shop he sold all kinds of floats and other fishing gear, and I had no idea at the time what a float was. Ian had to educate me in the finer details of the art of fishing, but I was attracted to the floats due to their really bright colours. I don't actually remember ever going fishing with Ian and his dad, but I think I must have at some point, as I became the proud owner of a collection of very brightly coloured floats and a bag of maggots not long after.

Next door to Ken's shop was the wonderful Candy & Cards and, like it said on the tin, it was a card/sweet shop, but the main attraction was having the best selection of different flavoured ice cream in the area. You could spend ages staring at all the various options, deciding which would be your flavour of choice. Orange, Mint, Choc Chip, and mine and my dad's personal favourite, Rum and Raisin. It was always a treat to visit Candy & Cards with my parents, and no doubt for the rest of the Brownhill community back then.

Right across the road, at the side of the Brownhill Arms Public House, was a very tiny hairdressers. Outside the shop was a green parrot in a cage, which would talk to the customers as they were going into the shop for a monthly trim. I had never heard a bird talk before and was fascinated by it.

That little shop was still there up until recently, but unfortunately the parrot vacated its perch many years ago. Just a few yards away from the hairdressers was a row of shops, and I always felt like I was on an adventure when I was allowed on Saturday mornings to visit these shops without being accompanied by one of my parents. I would always buy a bottle of Canada Dry (ginger beer), and felt pretty grown up doing so. I would then rush back home, just in time to watch the magnificent *The Flashing Blade*.

The programme was created from the original French television series made in the 1960s, and was a bit like The Three Musketeers, with horses and swords, and I absolutely loved it. It was a proper boys' adventure, and I can still remember the very catchy theme music to this day.

You've got to fight for what you want

For all that you believe.

It's right to fight for what we want

And live the way we please.

(Not a bad mantra at all, if you ask me.)

Next door to us lived the Fence family, and they had three children – John, David, and Susan. Both the brothers were older than me and Robin, and it is fair to say that over the years, they taught us swear words, told us all about 'big school' and what to expect, and gave us a better insight into the finer details of sex education than any formal sex education lessons could ever have done. Even though we were younger than them, we formed a great friendship, and we would regularly play together in each other's garden, along with their golden Labrador.

John, the oldest son, used to buy a monthly horror magazine, *Monster*, which was really only for 18+ readers, but he used to let me look at it, as I loved anything scary. There were shocking pictures of lesbian vampires, and torture scenes from the latest cinema releases, so what was not to like?
John also introduced me to Bruce Lee, for which I am eternally grateful. Bruce was the coolest human being that ever lived to me at the time, and I was blown away by how he looked and moved. John also collected *Kung Fu Monthly*, which I became obsessed with, featuring David Carradine who played the lead role in the TV series of the same name. *Kung Fu* was first broadcast in the UK in October 1972, and was originally created for Bruce Lee until the powers that be opted for what they considered to be the safer option, choosing Carradine for the role.

As a family we would attend St Gabriel's Church most Sunday mornings, and the vicar was a lovely softly spoken chap called Mr Wynne, who lived in a large house at the side of the shops at Brownhill. One Saturday morning on my way to buy my weekly bottle of Canada Dry, I almost got run over whilst crossing the road. I recall a very angry lady getting out of her car and shouting at me, informing me that she had a young child in the back seat. We were both shaken up, and as it was totally my fault, rushing across the road without paying attention to oncoming traffic, I felt terrible.

The following morning, I was standing in church with my family, wondering what the next hymn would be that I would attempt to mime to, when to my absolute horror, Mr Wynne started to tell the congregation about a very silly boy who had carelessly almost caused a car crash. I was lost for words and wanted the ground to swallow me up. We might have been in God's house, but He obviously chose not to intervene and allowed me to face my deserved humiliation. The only blessing to come out of this incident was that the vicar didn't mention my name, but I was convinced that everybody knew that stupid boy was me, anyway.

My mum had been heavily involved with Brownhill Amateur Dramatics at St Gabriel's Church for years, and as a young girl she would be part of the cast of plays that were put on there. She even played the starring role in some of the productions, such as *The Masque of Christmas Eve* in 1945, and *Babes in the Wood*, also 1945. Now that Robin and I were on the scene, her involvement was backstage, and we would spend hours with her some evenings, offering our services as she worked on the costumes and the décor. I'm not too sure we were much help, but I always remembered how much I enjoyed it, and we got to watch some of the performances from the side of the stage, which was exciting.

For some strange reason, when we were young my mum thought it was a good idea for her to dress me and Robin in the same outfits. Maybe it was cheaper to buy two outfits of the same style and colour, but whatever the reason, I always felt it was her way of letting us both know that she was in charge and would have the final say. It's one thing wearing the same school uniform as everyone else in your school, but to have to look identical to your younger brother every other day wasn't right in my book.

Another daily highlight growing up was the sound of the ice cream van arriving on your street. These were the days before ice cream men sold their customers Ecstasy tablets and a bag of weed from under the counter. Mr Whippy and Mr Softie were fully legit back then, offering the likes of Fab and Zoom lollies, screwballs, 99s, Dr Who lollies, Count Dracula's Secret, and my personal favourite, the Fruit Salad Boat. This was fresh fruit salad, with loads of vanilla ice cream, topped with raspberry sauce and hundreds and thousands, served in a red plastic, boat-shaped dish. These were also the most expensive item on the van, so it really was a treat every time I managed to muster up enough money to buy one.

Growing up, my Grandma and Grandad were a big part of our lives, and I would always enjoy visiting them and our trips out. Grandad Jim would drive us to the sand dunes at Lytham, where we would go to see the windmill and then walk all the way back to the car and eat our sandwiches. Then Robin and I would spend a couple of hours running up and down the sand dunes, having fun and exploring. The day would be topped off with a bag of chips wrapped in newspaper, and would always be eaten outside. Sometimes our trips to the seaside would end up at Fleetwood, which had been their place to visit in the 20s, 30s, and 40s. And sometimes we would go to Blackpool, where we boys would spend all our time and money on the pier or in one of the many arcades. I loved playing the one-armed bandit and slot machines, and one of my dad's favourites, the Penny Drop.

A regular annual event was Blackpool Illuminations; we would never miss it. I seem to remember that it always rained, so we usually ended up driving down the promenade, viewing the amazing spectacle of light through the car window. Again, a chip supper featured, and then the return trip home with me and Robin falling asleep in the back seat, occasionally waking up to ask, 'Are we there yet?'

What days they were, and I remember them with great fondness. Except for the time I had strayed away from my family as we sat on the beach, and ended up waist-deep in sea water, clinging to a girder under the pier. Fortunately, someone rescued me and took me back to my parents, and it was a long time before I went off investigating on my own again.
Blackpool Fun House was another favourite, and looking back now, I don't think the health and safety police would allow any part of it nowadays. But it was proper entertainment, and I don't recall anybody dying before the clipboard brigade showed their faces and closed it down. Also, we didn't realise at the time how actually horrendous Blackpool Tower Circus was during our family visits. It featured lions, elephants, horses, and of course Charlie Cairoli.

My first proper holiday with my mum, dad, and Robin, was to Pontins in Southport. It had a large boating lake in the centre of the complex, and my mum bought me and Robin white, black, and gold sailor hats to wear whilst we were on the boats. We went swimming with my dad in the baths, but my clearest memory was when one day I decided to go for a short walk around the complex on my own. Thinking I had been some time and that my parents would be worrying, I legged it back up the stairs and along the long outside corridor until I reached our chalet with the green door. I opened the door and went to sit on the settee, and was shocked to realise that I was in the wrong chalet, with the wrong family, watching the wrong TV channel. The problem had been that every chalet had a green door (in my defence) and all looked identical to me, but my family found it hilarious on my return, especially Robin.

Back at home, I caught chickenpox and was confined to the house. I was really bored, but John from next door had a brilliant idea to alleviate the boredom, and between us we devised a pulley system reaching from his bedroom to mine. The plan was to send each other personal items, using a small empty box with string going through the top of it. Unfortunately, the box was too small to fit any magazines, but it worked, and kept me entertained until my giant spots had cleared up.

Bonfire night was another family tradition for the Eastwoods, and my Grandma and Grandad would come round to watch the Astra and Standard fireworks my dad had purchased – Roman Candles, Catherine Wheels, Snowstorm, Traffic Lights and, before they were banned, Jumping Jacks. He would always be Master of Ceremonies, constantly telling us that whatever happened we must never return to a lit firework. Sparklers were passed around, along with my mum's homemade treacle toffee which she was rightly proud of. On the nearest Saturday to November 5th, there would always be a huge family-friendly bonfire and firework display at Witton Park, and it always seemed to pour down, but it never stopped us attending.

When we were young, my dad used to travel abroad a lot with work. He was the Research Manager for Crown Paints, and this was an important part of his job. Hamburg was a regular destination, and he visited Canada, New York, and Hong Kong. We used to miss him a lot, but always looked forward to the souvenirs he brought home for us.

On arriving at his hotel in New York, he was welcomed by the hotel concierge, who proceeded to tell him that the previous week a person had been shot dead in the same room that Dad had been allocated. Not the welcome he was hoping for on his first visit to the Big Apple!

On another occasion, my dad travelled to Hong Kong and settled into his room, only to find the following morning, when he had looked out of the window, several black limos at the hotel entrance and a number of men in black suits pointing sniper rifles at the floor above my dad's window. Seemingly, an American Diplomat was staying there, and these were his security men. Another unfriendly welcome party that my dad experienced on his travels away.

No matter how many air miles my dad had notched up, my mum never ventured abroad. I think the thought of flying didn't appeal to her, so she was just content to holiday on home turf.

Sometimes on a Saturday, my dad would have to nip into his office to collect something, and on a few occasions, I remember him taking me with him. I was always fascinated to visit where he actually worked and to be introduced to some of his colleagues. One of them had obviously heard about my Bruce Lee obsession, and had kindly painted me this brilliant picture of him in one of his famous poses. And I am ashamed to say that I still haven't got around to getting it framed.

When Crown Match pots were developed, my dad was invited to Buckingham Palace to advise the Queen on her colour scheme, which must have been an experience. I bet he never smoked a joint in the palace toilets, but I guess it was quite fitting that the Queen would opt for Crown.

On the occasions my dad was working away, my Grandma would sometimes take me and Robin to the Odeon Cinema on Penny Street in Blackburn. Saturday mornings they would have the Mickey Mouse Club, which we loved. Formerly The Rialto, it opened its doors in December 1931, before being taken over by Odeon theatres in 1957. The Odeon was a beautiful old building, but on 23rd March, 1974, some bright spark at the town hall decided it would be a good idea to knock it down and replace it with a car park. (It wasn't.)

The year was 1974, and I was in my final year at St Gabriel's. It had been a really nice school to attend and the teachers had been lovely. To celebrate us leaving, the school had arranged a week away Youth Hostelling at Hawkshead in the Lake District. It was the first time I had spent the week away from my parents, and I was pretty excited. The sleeping arrangements were dormitories, which accommodated six bunk beds each, and I was in the same room as my mates Jez, Shaft, Andrew Smith, and Carl Vickers. This was great, but we had certainly drawn the short straw, as it turned out that Mr Sharples would be sleeping in the bottom bunk of the bed across from me.

The first morning, we were woken early and told to make our own beds (a new concept for me), and after our morning chores were done and we had eaten our breakfast, we were taken on a very long walk around Hawkshead. I remember thinking the scenery was beautiful, but I think we were more appreciative of the Fools Gold which Mr Sharples pointed out underneath some of the rocks he had collected. After the second night, we boys took objection to having to get undressed with the room light on, while Mr Sharples undressed in the dark. Carl Vickers decided it would be fun to shine his torch at him just as he was removing his trousers. This was hilarious comedy timing, and the whole dorm rolled about their bunk beds in fits of uncontrollable laughter, but unfortunately our teacher failed to see the funny side.

As the week went on, we built up quite a friendship with the girls, and I recall Janet Smith standing in a phone box in the town, changing her jumper, and in doing so, flashing her bra to us red-blooded 10-year-olds. It's funny what you remember from when you were a kid.

That night, someone (probably Jez) thought it would be a great idea to sneak into the girls' dormitory after the teachers were asleep. The girls were on the floor above us, so once Mr Sharples started snoring, we crept out of the room without waking him. We made it without any of the other teachers waking up, but like I said, we were only ten, so certainly nothing untoward happened.
We had completed our mission, but now we had to make it back without waking Mr Sharples. Jez had a plan and suggested that we should cover our faces with toothpaste and, with outstretched arms, walk into the dormitory and, if stopped, claim to be sleepwalking. This was a terrible idea, but it was the only one we had. On our return, we didn't need Carl's torch to realise that Mr Sharples was waiting for us when we entered the room. Yet again, he failed to see the funny side of our actions.

During the hot summer of 1974, our neighbours the Fence family went to Wales for their annual holiday. I was going to miss John and David but thought that a week would soon fly by, and they would be back before I knew it.
One day, as I stood on our drive, I noticed that they had left their kitchen window open slightly, and thought to myself that if I somehow managed to squeeze through it and make my way up to John's room, I could look through his magazine collection at my leisure and then climb back through, and no-one would be the wiser. I considered my idea to be harmless fun, as I was no burglar and I had no intention of stealing anything.

My heart was racing, but after making sure that the coast was clear, I somehow managed to climb through and found myself in my neighbours' kitchen. My heart beating even faster at this point, I made my way to John's bedroom, making sure that anything I touched was put back in exactly the same place. If I am being honest, even though it seemed a pretty innocent idea at the time, I did feel as though I shouldn't have been going through with it. I don't even remember if I even ended up reading any of his mags, but I did feel I had outstayed my unofficial welcome and that it was time for me to leave. It had been a very tight squeeze through that small window, so I decided to leave through the front door instead. I stepped into the porch and closed the door to the house behind me, but when I tried to exit the door, to my horror I found it firmly locked. I then attempted to open the door leading back inside the house, but that was also locked.

I felt a panic set in, and I even debated whether to try and break the door window out of desperation, using a large rock I found inside a plant pot. But the inside window had fancy lead patterns in the glass, and there was no way I was about to add vandalism to my list of crimes, as it would clearly only make matters worse. (If that was even possible.)
What a nightmare. I was locked in a boiling hot porch with no way of getting out unless I could attract someone's attention by shouting 'help' through the letterbox to any passers-by. Even though I knew I would be in a whole lot of trouble and had no idea at all how I was about to explain being there in the first place. For over two hours I was stuck there feeling terrible, but eventually a girl who I recognised heard my cry for help and came over. I told her that it was a long story and pleaded with her to go and get my dad from next door, as I had no alternative.

To say that my dad was angry with me is a huge understatement, and I could tell how disappointed he was, which made me feel even worse. It was clear that there was not going to be any happy ending to this situation, and what happened next was even more humiliating. I don't think I have ever seen him so irate.

My dad had to call the Fence family while they were on their holidays, and attempt to explain to them why his oldest son was in fact stuck inside their front porch. Then he had to drive halfway to Wales to meet up with them and borrow the key to let me out.

Because of my irresponsible actions, our family name was no longer respectable with our neighbours, and nothing was ever the same again. To this day, Mrs Fence has never spoken a single word to me since, and even my relationship with John and David was pretty strained.

I am not proud of my behaviour that day, but it happened, and I can't turn back the clock. It is also fair to say that I have had my fair share of embarrassing moments throughout my life, but this one remains at number one.

Even though I'd had some great times growing up at Brownhill, you wouldn't have heard any arguments from me when my parents started to discuss the idea of moving.

We quickly sold our house, and we moved to Lammack, the posh end of Blackburn (or so I was told). The house was a new build, 1 Kestrel Close, and it was only about 15 minutes' walk from my secondary school of choice (my mum's choice) where I had moved to. I was apprehensive about going to secondary school, as I had been told all about the customary initiation ceremonies that new pupils had to go through, like having your head shoved down the toilet. This did not appeal to me, so I decided to keep my head down and lie low.
In the 70s, being the cock of your year or even the school was a sought-after position, and Friargate had its fair share of head cases. There were two skinhead brothers, Smudge and Smize, who also had a reputation of being cocks of the Blackburn End at Ewood Park, as football hooliganism was rife back then.

When I am ever asked about my time at Friargate, I always quote that there were only ever three things I liked about secondary school, and they were – Dundee biscuits, the Thursday night school disco, and Carol Cooper, which I feel is a fairly accurate assessment.

I found the transition from junior to secondary school slightly daunting, and it took me a while to find and remember where everything was. I was based in A block in 1RG tutor group, and at the side of B block there was a tuck shop. Every morning break, I would queue up and buy these large, round chocolatey biscuits called a Dundee biscuit. I had never heard of them before (or since), but I absolutely loved them.

The other pupils in my tutor group all seemed friendly, and our tutor Mr Grogan was really nice, but yet again, like in Junior school, I struggled to concentrate on the lessons and spent most of the time gazing out of the window, daydreaming. Looking back, I struggle to acknowledge a single subject that I looked forward to, which is sad. I would sit in my Geology class wondering why on earth we had to learn about rocks. I detested Maths and didn't understand most of what was being taught. I mean, who needs Pythagoras's Theorem and logarithms in their life? Certainly not me. Our teacher, Mr Lord, was old school and seemed like a nice guy, but I certainly didn't feature on his pupil of the week list.

The only subject that evoked any sense of interest in me was Art, and although I was not the best at drawing, I did sort of enjoy my weekly lesson. Part of the reason for this was down to the characters that were in our class. Mick Fox springs to mind; he was so funny. On one occasion, he produced a crisp £1 note from his pocket and offered it to the first classmate who offered him 10p for it. Someone offered him the money, and we watched as Mick tore the note in half and handed it to the buyer. Mick is still a friend today and is still as mad.

Looking back, it is a toss-up between two subjects as to which I disliked the most. PE lessons were fine, providing you remembered your full kit. But you will struggle to find many of our group who even remotely enjoyed cross country running. As I acknowledged earlier, I was no athlete and was a really weak runner, so could be usually found trailing along at the back. We always had to run all along the dual carriageway (usually in the rain), along Ramsgreave Drive and up Lammack Road, and then back to school.

One week, we thought we would be clever and hide in someone's garden opposite the rugby club, and then re-join the rest of the group on their second lap. The first week we got away with this scam of avoiding the physical aspect of the run, but the second week someone grassed on us, and we found ourselves in detention.

The other contender for my most disliked lesson was Technical Drawing. I was clueless and dreaded every minute in the class. Mentoring wasn't a thing back in the 70s, and if the teacher thought you were stupid, you were called stupid. Our teacher had a special place reserved in his classroom for those like me who failed to demonstrate an aptitude for the subject to the level he was expecting, and fondly named us the Andy Pandy group.

That wasn't all his teaching experience had to offer us lucky pupils, and his punishments ranged from calling you out to the front of the class, handing you a piece chalk and telling you to draw a shaded patch on the blackboard, where you would stand for the rest of the lesson, with your nose pushed up against it. Even worse, if that wasn't humiliating enough, he would sometimes put your head under the cold water tap at the front of the classroom, so that the rest of your classmates would laugh at you.

The outcome of this outrageous behaviour was that we never learnt tech drawing, and he never won Teacher of the Year.

Our new home was one of the first houses to be built on the new site, and construction was still ongoing when we moved in. It didn't take me long to get used to my new surroundings, and I didn't even seem to mind the constant mud. I think I saw it as quite an adventure exploring all the other half-built properties.

I had chosen to come home at lunchtimes from school. One reason was to avoid the likes of the infamous semolina pudding slopped up by the dinner ladies, and the other was to try to avoid getting my head shoved down the bog.

What this daily walk home up the road would lead to was me getting to know the other pupils from my year group who lived near me, who also wanted to avoid semolina. Little did I know back then that this bunch of newfound friends would turn out to be my best mates for the rest of my life.

Eight of my mates lived just around the corner from me on Rhodes Avenue – Waker, Bullinge, Karl, Birchy, Julie, Steve S, Des, and my old mucker Jez.

Ste H, from my class, lived about a ten-minute walk away; Simon (Rama), who was also in my class, lived in a big house on West Park Road; Nick, on the edge of town; and Julie's best mate, Mary, lived in the paper shop at the top of Four Lane Ends.

Our friendship group was formed, and everything we did socially involved each other. My previous life at Brownhill had most definitely faded into the past, and not only did I have a new house and a new set of friends, but I became the owner of my first ever pet – in the form of a blue budgerigar named Perky, who used to fly around the living room and land on the curtains.

Seemingly, my Grandad and Grandma used to have a dog called Sandy that would stand guarding my pram, but I suppose I *was* the bonniest baby in Brownhill after all. (Not my words!)

My Bruce Lee fascination had certainly followed me to Lammack, and the whole of my bedroom wall, including the ceiling, was plastered in his posters. I was still too young to go and watch his films at the cinema, so I guess that would just have to wait.

I also still had a love for Hammer horror films, and on a Monday night on television there was a series called 'Appointment with Fear' which would feature different Hammer Horror films each week. The films featured Boris Karloff in *Frankenstein* and *The Mummy*, *The Werewolf* starring Bela Lugosi, and of course those lesbian vampires in *Twins of Evil*, starring Peter Cushing.

These films were on late at night, but the temptation got the better of me and I devised a plan to sneak downstairs once everyone was in bed, turn the television on with really low sound, and hope that for the next hour-and-a-half nobody would wake up and catch me. This might seem like a simple enough plan, but it was never a given. For one, I had to wait until my dad had gone to bed, as he was always the last to go up. Also, sometimes I would fall asleep by mistake, and would wake up in the morning proper mad with myself. Most of these films were shown in black and white, but it really was a Monday night treat, and I got a buzz out of doing something I knew I was not supposed to.

Another TV attraction for us young lads at the time was the Friday night French films on BBC2. I didn't have a clue what was going on, as the actors spoke in French (imagine!), but the cheap thrills we managed to take from the films were worth it. This again would have to rely on my dad going to bed before the films had started, as back in the early 70s we didn't have the option to record programmes to watch later. We had three TV channels, and If you weren't sitting in front of the telly when your programme came on, you missed it. I think that my dad maybe had cottoned on to what I was up to, as he started going to bed later and later, which was beyond annoying. It's also funny when I look back and remember that there was no such thing as all-night TV back then. Everything stopped being broadcast at midnight, and the only thing that would appear on your screen was the testcard, followed by a very loud, annoying, bleeping sound to remind you to turn your TV set off.

Growing up in the 1970s as a young red-blooded male, there were certain television moments that would stick in your mind and make a big impression. *Rock Follies*, *Logan's Run*, *Twins of Evil*, French films, Carry On films, and of course *Barbarella* (Queen of the Galaxy).

We were all growing up fast, but who would have known that a school PE lesson was about to change my life forever?

We were playing football on the top field just outside our tutor group in A block, and even though I didn't have any football skills to write home about, I was just relieved that we hadn't been told to do cross country. We had been booting the ball up and down the pitch for about 20 minutes when I decided to go in for a tackle. My mate Bullinge had fouled me, and it really hurt, so I decided to get him back and I kicked the back of his legs, resulting in him calling me an 'adopted bastard'.
It took a while for his words to sink in, but I don't really think I thought it was anything more than just a childish retaliation insult. But when I arrived home that afternoon, I found my brother sitting in my dad's armchair crying, which I thought was strange.
Apparently, the jungle drums at school had obviously reached his ears, and he had arrived home before me and brought up the delicate subject with my mum. Well, it was bound to be let out of the bag at some stage, right? Now the cat had been well and truly let out, and once my dad arrived home from work, my parents sat me down and proceeded to tell me that I was special, as I had been chosen from hundreds of other babies. They said that they didn't know much about my past, but would tell me the little they did know, if I wanted to hear it.
I told them I wasn't interested, and to be fair I think Robin seemed to have taken it worse than I had (on the outside anyway), as he was no doubt concerned about maybe losing such a cool brother.

I tried my utmost to brush off this family revelation and act as though it hadn't bothered me in the slightest, but looking back, I don't believe I even allowed this news to properly sink in.

The next day the news about my adoption was playground gossip and had made its way throughout the school. But how did Bullinge even know (before me!)? I simply presumed that he must have overheard a conversation between his parents, as back in those days with that generation, scandal like this certainly did the rounds.

To this day, when I bring the subject up with him, he always tells me he feels terrible and that he hadn't really known. He literally came out with the first insult that came into his head after I had booted him. I always explain to him that he actually did me a favour, as I might never have found out at all, if it hadn't been for him.

I never asked my parents if they were ever intending on telling me that I was adopted (maybe I should have), but I think that if I hadn't had such a lovely upbringing, maybe I would have reacted differently. I certainly had nothing to complain about, and left it there. I also didn't want to risk upsetting my mum and dad by trying to find out more information or even tracing my family, so it was 13 years before I brought the subject up again. Instead, I simply carried on as normal, and for the rest of the week at school I bashed metal in metalwork, sawed pieces of wood in woodwork, struggled to find the geography classroom, and spent my money on Dundee biscuits.

Away from school, I would hang out with my friends as much as possible and leave Robin to find his own entertainment. After all, my mum was no longer dressing us in the same outfits any more, so I felt no obligation to hang out with him. Robin was now in the year below me at school and had made his own friendship group.

One of the chosen activities before we moved to Lammack was garden creeping. Even though it escapes me who actually came up with this evening pastime, most nights we would participate. Garden creeping consisted of a group of friends meeting up once it had gone dark and spending the next hour or so sneaking through everybody's back gardens. I have no idea whatsoever what the actual point in this activity was, other than again, we were doing something that we were not supposed to. We would stumble over garden fences and through muddy flowerbeds, and on the occasions the property owner would appear and question us, we would claim to be looking for our escaped rabbit. Of course, they never believed us, but I guess that was all part of the buzz.

I was now a little older and such pastimes were deemed as childish, so we would meet up and hang around under a lamppost, or inside the half-built houses on our estate. We also had the bonus of Julie and Mary joining us, and I must admit that Mary was my first proper crush, as Jane Fonda and Barbara Windsor didn't really count. I don't know what it was about Mary, but I proper fancied her. The only problem with this predicament was that so did half of my other mates, and unfortunately I was far too shy to do anything about it.

Both Julie and Mary were really nice girls, great company, and we would hang around with them every chance we got. I certainly had rivalry for Mary's attention, as Karl was obsessed, and even though this always fell on deaf ears, he made no attempt to disguise his ongoing love for her.

One night, we had been hanging around in one of the half-built houses on Kestrel Close, and Mary had left her cardigan behind by mistake. Karl took it home with him and slept with it for around three months until we grassed on him, and she asked for it back.

One hot summer's evening, we decided to venture a little further than usual and explore the fields at the front of our house. We were all taking turns on a thick rope swing we had found, when we heard a girl screaming in the background over on the main playing field. We all proceeded to run towards the noise and were confronted by some dodgy-looking bloke trying to attack a girl, who lived at the top of our road. Luckily, Bullinge's older brother Andy was with us, along with his mate Dave, and from out of nowhere Andy produced a bicycle chain and started to wave it above his head. This quick thinking did the trick, and the bloke legged it.

In normal circumstances, Andy would have no doubt been asked why on earth he would feel the need to take a bicycle chain out with him on a night out, especially when – to my knowledge – he didn't own a bike. But on this occasion, he received a certificate from the police for his brave intervention.

Panini football cards, or Panini Swaps, were now the new craze at school. The obvious mission was to collect a complete set or complete the individual members of your favourite football team. If you had any doubles in your collection, you would find someone who was after yours and swap it for one of theirs that you needed. Alternatively, you could take part in the latest activity sweeping the playground where you took turns to throw your card as near as you could against the allocated playground wall, and the person who threw their card the closest got to keep all the cards that had been thrown. Conkers and marbles had taken a back seat, and Panini was the new kid on the block.

A few of my friends had started smoking, but it really didn't appeal to me. The thing at the time was to buy singles, usually No6 from a shop on Revidge. The shopkeeper didn't seem to care about how old you were, just as long as they got your money. One day Simon and I decided to give it a try in an effort to see what all the fuss was about. We bought a few cigarettes and a cigar each, and then went to Corporation Park to smoke them. I thought they tasted horrible and they made me cough, and I can honestly say that since that day neither a cigarette nor cigar has touched my lips (of which I am proud).

Simon lived near the park in a big old house on West Park Road, across from East Lancs Cricket Club. But his dad was a doctor, so I suppose they could afford it. I had never been inside a house this big before; they even had their own music room, which I thought was pretty impressive. The house also had secret tunnels leading to the wine cellar, which happened to be fully stocked and, even better, from their cellar you could climb through a small round hole in the wall and end up in next door's cellar. My brother, Robin, once tried to climb through the hole but got stuck, and for fun Simon tried to set fire to the seat of his jeans. Robin never saw the funny side, and certainly never went back to Simon's house.

By now my grandparents had moved from Roe Lee Park to a house just around the corner (146 Cornelian Street). I always loved visiting them, and even though our new house was now further away, it didn't reduce my visits. My friends also loved visiting Grandma Edna, as she would give us all spending money, much to my Grandad's annoyance. Once he would hear the clasp of her purse opening, he would look over the top of his very large newspaper with a look of disapproval on his face. After a while my Grandma became wise to this and set up a small dish in the spare bedroom, in which she would put her spare 50p coins for us to collect on our next visit. (What a legend!)

I know folk always go on about the summers of the 1970s being the best, but I can't remember bad weather ever affecting our plans, so I guess they must be right. One day, my Grandma decided to take me and Robin for a walk to the local reservoir at the top of Parsonage Road, being a nice day and that. The place was surrounded by pine woods, and on arrival I noticed a small wooden jetty in the distance, with some people sitting on it dangling their feet in the water. As we walked in their direction, I made out that it was a lad and two young girls.

'Alright, Pete,' shouted the male, and to my surprise it was our neighbour Martin from across the road. What was even more of a surprise was that the two girls directly in front of me were sharing a bikini. One girl was wearing the top, and the other the bottoms – and nothing else! My eyes almost popped out of my head, whilst at the same time, I tried my upmost to act like that this was no big deal.

Martin and his two friends hadn't even batted an eyelid, and just acted as though this was simply an everyday occurrence. I was enjoying the view that much that I had forgotten I was even with my brother and my Grandma, and I was gutted when I heard her calling me from a few yards away.

I am not too sure if my brother will remember this educational encounter at Dean Clough, but I for one told this story many times over the following months, to anyone who would listen (even though my Grandma never did take us back there).

I had developed a love of movies at a very young age, and my first memory of visiting a cinema with my family was on holiday in Llandudno in 1974. The film was *Towering Inferno*, featuring Paul Newman and Steve McQueen, and was followed a few days later by *Those Magnificent Men in Their Flying Machines*, starring Terry Thomas. I did enjoy both films at the time, but I think my parents enjoyed them more, and it wasn't until my Grandma took me to see *The Omega Man*, starring Charlton Heston, that a film really stuck in my memory. The film was a sci-fi thriller, where Dr Neville (Heston) had to develop an antidote to a virus that had destroyed humankind in a biological war.

Imagine that happening in real life! A bit far-fetched, if you ask me.

We were extremely lucky in Blackburn as far as cinemas went. The Alexandra cinema in Dock Street was built on the site of the old stables in 1906, and was known as Penks. It is believed that this was the world's first purpose-built cinema. In the 1950s, Blackburn had no fewer than 14 cinemas, or picture houses as they were known back then. The ones I remember were the Odeon (ex Rialto), which was definitely the most luxurious one that the town had to offer – until they turned it into a car park, that is; The Classic on King William Street, formerly the Theatre Royal, which replaced an older theatre where Charlie Chaplin actually performed in 1903, and again in 1905; The Palace, which was on the boulevard; and my personal favourite, the Unit Four at Little Harwood. This was by far the smallest but was the one I attended the most. It had a spell as a nightclub/cabaret club, but reverted back to a cinema in the 1970s.

CHAPTER TWO

WHEN YOU'RE YOUNG

Anybody that knows me, or has ever known me, will tell you that music is my life, and that it was a film that started me on my musical journey. My family and I were on holiday in Bridlington, and my parents had booked a show for us to attend this particular evening on the pier. After we had eaten our evening meal, I decided to take a look in the hotel television room, and found several people watching an old black and white film, which turned out to be *A Hard Day's Night* by The Beatles.
I was totally mesmerised by the songs, the look, and the haircuts... WOW!
My mum, dad, and brother were less enthusiastic, but I loved every second, and when somebody mentioned that they were showing their second film, *Help*, the following night, all I could think about for the rest of the evening and the following day was making sure I bagsied my seat in front of the TV in plenty of time. I somehow knew that what I had just watched was really special, and that it would change my life forever.
The following teatime after our meal, I made sure to get a prime viewing spot in the television room before anyone else sat there. But I have learnt over the years that sometimes when you are looking forward to something that much, things don't always go to plan. Within minutes, several pensioners came in and demanded that they watched *Emmerdale* instead of *Help*, and I was distraught. My holiday had been ruined by the Blue Rinse Brigade, and no matter how many times I politely protested, age had won the day!

One of the first records I ever bought was *Sugar Baby Love* by the Rubettes. I played it to death on our record player at home and must admit I still love the song today. This was the time when folk would stand in front of their mirror, holding their sister's Denman hairbrush, and mime to the lyrics of their favourite chart hit. The problem for me was that I didn't have a sister, so had to wait a little longer before I could carry out this task.

Glam Rock became the Pick of the Pops, and bands like the Glitter Band, Sweet, Mud, and of course the Rubettes, were never off the radio. Some of these groups made a film in 1976 called *Never Too Young to Rock*, which my Grandma took us to see, and even though it never won any awards for acting, I really enjoyed it. One particular scene saw The Rubettes standing on the back of a lorry, wearing red shirts, red suits, white hats, and miming, while driving through the centre of some town. What was not to like? It was all we knew at the time.

The Osmonds were massive, and The Bay City Rollers were sweeping the nation, picking up every teenage girl in their wake along the way. I had deemed these two bands far too sissy for my liking, but remember Nicky and his brother Mick wearing tartan socks to show their allegiance to the cause.

I remember owning some early Elvis tapes of soundtracks from his movies and playing them to death every day on my tiny cassette recorder. Every summer holidays they would show all his films on TV, and I loved them.

Music had started to make a pretty big impact on me, and the must-watch TV programme at the time was *Top of the Pops*. Whichever act was selling the most records that week would be invited on to perform, and every young person at the time would make it their Thursday night ritual to tune in and watch the latest teenage heartthrobs prancing about the stage in shiny suits and polished shoes.
Nobody ever picked up on the fact that none of their guitars had been plugged in, and that everybody was actually miming.

One of the first 7-inch singles I remember owning was *Yes, Sir, I Can Boogie* by Baccara, as glam rock and disco were all we were subjected to throughout the week.

Back at school, I still hadn't found a subject that I really enjoyed, and I continued to stare out of the window during lessons at every opportunity. I couldn't understand why we had to learn how to speak French, even though we did have a young, good looking French teacher in Mrs James, who half the class fancied, which sort of eased the burden of having to attend. I remember my mate Simon being asked to leave the classroom after being accused of putting his hand up her skirt. Shocking really, as if that incident had happened today, he would have ended up in the local paper.

Simon was a ballsy kid, and I recall in one of our classes him going on strike and refusing to work because I had scored more marks than him in a drawing exercise. He argued that I had copied off him, so how on earth had I got more marks? I just found the situation really funny, but refrained from laughing out loud as he was harder than me. He once told me that his family were Quakers, and I couldn't resist making a joke about breakfast cereal, having never heard the term before. But he wasn't amused and nearly broke my arm by twisting it behind my back.

On the subject of breakfast cereal, how come they were far more appealing to kids back in the 70s? They would always include free gifts with every pack back then – a U.S navy frogman with Kellogg's cornflakes, Aristocats stickers with Malted Shreddies, and Dr Who and his enemies stand-up figures with Weetabix. I was always being pulled up by my parents for opening all the packets as soon as they arrived home with the shopping, in order to beat my brother to the free toys.

Dr Who was the hide-behind-the-settee Saturday teatime TV programme that every young kid used to watch. There was a fabulous Dr Who exhibition that arrived in Blackpool that we were lucky enough to visit on a couple of occasions. The exhibition was situated on the famous Golden Mile and was opened by the doctor himself, Mr Jon Pertwee, on 14th April, 1974. On the outside, all you could see was a blue police phone box, but once you stepped inside and walked down a flight of stairs, as if by magic you found yourself surrounded by the most exciting aliens, monsters, costumes, and props from the series. These were the days before you could take a selfie, but you could actually stand next to a cyberman or a dalek. As far as Dr Who's biggest fans go, my mate Nicky is up there. For as long as I have known him, he has had a deep love for the Dr – and no doubt some of his assistants!

Another incident at school I remember is during a home economics class when our teacher told us that we were going to learn how to make Angel Delight. I quite enjoyed learning how to cook, but because I was a boy I wasn't allowed to take it as one of my options. For once, I had followed all the instructions and felt pretty proud of myself as I lifted my offering from the school fridge. I had done something right at school and was excited to be providing my family with that evening's dessert.
Teatime arrived at the Eastwoods, and after our main course my mum dished it out, making sure that we all received equal portions. I remember taking the first mouthful and was horrified to discover that mine in fact tasted of soap powder. Sure enough, my mum, dad, and brother followed, and it tasted that bad that my family couldn't even pretend it had tasted good in an effort to spare my feelings.
The following day, once my teacher had heard about how disappointed I had been, she called all the class back to investigate the matter, and even though it had been obvious that a fellow classmate had put something into my dish, nobody owned up to the prank. The class ended up in detention for the rest of the week, which didn't exactly make me very popular. And even though I never did find out who the culprit had been, I do suspect that Simon may have been trying to get revenge for that picture competition. But I for one wasn't about to accuse him.

We always had rumours doing the rounds about other schools coming down after the bell to kick our heads in, which usually involved the likes of Shad, Everton, or Witton. But they stayed as rumours, as I never actually remember anything happening.

I had been given a chemistry set for Christmas one year, and really loved messing about with it at home. But even though my chemistry teacher at school reminded me of Noel Edmonds, I never really grasped what was going on most of the time.

The teacher with the worst reputation, which certainly proceeded him, was Mr Wary. He taught PE and would take great pleasure in whacking pupils on the backside with his pump at every opportunity. If you forgot your PE kit, or if your parents couldn't afford the full PE kit, he would hit you with it.

I can't really remember what Mr Gregg taught (what does that tell you?), but I can remember his punishment of choice was to sit you on your wooden chair, which he had placed on top of the desk. Then he proceeded to throw the large wooden board duster at you in an effort to knock you off, as if he was at the fairground, trying his luck on the coconut shy. And what was extremely sad was that my brother told me he was still adopting this trademark technique when he was in the sixth form.

I always had a problem with biology at school, ever since our task was to dissect a dead rat and I started to feel faint and fell backwards off my wooden stool in front of the whole class.

I have always had a fear of needles since we were all given our tetanus jabs at school. I waited that long for it to be my turn that I fainted just as I was next in line. It was hot and sweaty in the tiny office we had all been crammed into, and having to stand for ages watching all the other pupils having a needle shoved into their arm proved just too much.

One day, the lesson consisted of each pupil having to prick their own finger with a small needle until they drew blood. I also wasn't a huge fan of blood, even though it is the thing that keeps me alive. (Ungrateful or what!) The task was to then add a sample of your blood to some special paper in order to give you a certain reading, based on how it reacted. Most of my classmates were fine with this, so I just went for it. Mohamed Q, on the other hand, seemed more terrified than me, and had made it pretty clear to everyone in the room that under no circumstances would he be taking part. Our teacher did not agree with his decision and told him in no uncertain terms that he would be getting involved.

After a short debate on the subject, Mrs B jumped from her seat and instructed four fellow pupils to pin him down. At first, I thought this had been a prank, but once I saw Mohamed pinned against the classroom floor with a look of terror in his eyes, I knew this couldn't end well. To my disbelief, she handed each pupil a needle, and I watched as they managed to prick every single finger on both his hands until they were bleeding. For the rest of the day Mohammed just sat outside each of his classrooms on a plastic chair, crying. Imagine if a teacher acted like that today. They would be banged up for sure.

In December 1976, my dad took me and Robin to Ewood Park for the first time, to watch Rovers take on Southampton. I think it may have been a rearranged Saturday match, and the final score was 1-1.
I do remember Mick Shannon coming off the subs bench for the Saints, and that we both loved the experience.
Soon after, Bullinge had discovered that you could catch a bus from Blackburn to Bolton for a mere 13p, and Liverpool were the visitors to Burnden Park, so we decided to go. I was amazed at how electrifying the atmosphere was, and what a step up from our visit to Ewood Park, even though the Rovers match had felt more special to me being with my dad and brother. I still have the Rovers programme today in mint condition, and it is the pride of my collection.

It was around this time that me and my mates started playing football most nights, on the gravel pitches down Lammack. I use

the term playing football very loosely, as we basically used to boot the ball up and down most of the time. Wembley was the game of choice, which consisted of one of us going in nets (usually me), and everybody else running around like headless chickens, trying to score as many goals as they could. It is fair to say that none of us really stood out in terms of footballing ability, even though we all probably thought we did at the time.
Ste H played for the school team and was probably the best, and Nicky had an advantage being the fastest runner, so he used to kick the ball as hard as he could, knowing he would be the first to reach it. I remember Jez being decent, but I was pretty rubbish, so would usually be the goalie.

Simon had not settled at Friargate and had been sent by his parents to attend a boarding school near Middlesbrough. He would join in when he was up visiting his parents, but nobody dared to tackle him anyway.

Julie and Mary never really joined in when we went out with the ball, so we always made sure we would make some time to spend with them.
With Mary living in a newsagent's, she was expected to have a paper round, and luckily for us her route included Rhodes Avenue. It is embarrassing to recall it now, but both Karl and I would usually offer to help her to deliver the evening papers most days. We would wait at the corner of the Avenue and follow her on her round (like lapdogs), trying to make sure we were pushing the correct paper through the right door, and then rushing back so that we would have more time to speak to her. Mary must have known the reason we were so keen to help her each day, but she never let on. I would now like to take this opportunity to profoundly apologise to anybody who received the wrong paper, or no paper, if you were living on Rhodes Avenue in the mid-70s.

I just didn't have the bottle to reveal my feelings for Mary at the time, and the nearest I got was carving her initials, and mine, in the bark of a local tree, as that was a thing back then.

The housing development on Kestrel had become wise to the fact that somebody had been trespassing in their properties at night, so they began to make them more secure. This meant that we would have to find an alternative arrangement in an effort to keep up with our social life. The alternative came in the shape of old, dilapidated, metal changing rooms, across the road from Friargate school, which is where we discovered the rumoured delights of alcohol.

We had managed to get some Skol and Harp lager, and a cheap bottle of cider, and this became an almost nightly occurrence whenever we could get our hands on something to drink. I have to be honest, I thought at the time that it tasted bloody awful, but kept this to myself, as I didn't want my friends to think I was being soft. But like with most things, if you stick with it, you grow to like it... which I did.

Mary had a Saturday job in the town's library cafe, so naturally this became a hangout for us to meet up at weekends. The lady that ran the cafe (also called Mary) was proper sound with us, and didn't mind us hanging around for hours, as long as Mary got on with her work. Every Saturday morning this became a ritual, and it was somewhere we would all meet to share gossip, parade our latest clothes purchases, and show off any records we had just bought.

Around about this time Des had found himself a job at a local chicken farm, so he now had money to spend. We were all jealous and asked him if he could help us to get a job at the farm. He eventually came up trumps, and me and Bullinge were taken on.

The owner of the farm was a little Irish man called Pat, who had one site up Parsonage Road, and another in Knuzden, and I had never known anyone who managed to come out with as many swear words in 30 seconds as him. (It may have been a record!) These were the days before I was passionate about animal welfare issues, so it was just a job in order to obtain some money.

Bullinge and I decided that we would work two weeks of our school holidays at the farm, and every morning at some unearthly

hour, we were picked up by a small white van, driven by a miserable looking guy named Paul, with two rather large, over excited dogs.
On our arrival, we were asked to go and wait in the office, which was a run-down old hut with papers everywhere, a kettle, and a telephone. This was the hub when rain stopped play, or when you were waiting for a delivery. Suddenly, Pat showed up with his bloody this and bloody that, indicating that he was not going to pay us to sit around all day.
Our first job was bagging sawdust. I say first job, but it was our only job that first day, and after eight hours, we found sawdust on literally every part of our body. I remember being that worn out that I went home and fell asleep in the bath.

Each day on the farm the days seemed to become longer, and the jobs seemed to get harder, while our reward for all this at the end of a shift was an old crumpled £5 note. No unions, no health and safety, and abuse all day off Pat – all for a fiver. We kept saying to each other that we would pack it in, but we never did, as it was our only income and clothes and records weren't going to buy themselves.

Pat would sometimes walk around handing out boiled sweets to everyone, and he had this great knack of making you feel really lucky to be receiving them. At the end of each day, you would have to hang around waiting for him to come and pay you, and he always seemed to be late, as if to keep you on the site a little longer. When he did finally rock up, if he had given you some sweets that day, he would always make a habit of saying, 'Bloody hell, and you want paying as well!'

One morning, I arrived to be told that Pat had a special job for me, and I would be working at his house. He dropped me off and told me the job was cutting the massive lawns he had around his estate. Imagine the scene: it was a boiling hot day, I was dressed in jeans, a donkey jacket, and Wellington boots, pushing a lawnmower around, whilst his teenage daughter lay on a large rug in the centre of the grass, dressed in nothing but a bikini, eating cream cakes and drinking beer. It couldn't have been a worse look I was rocking, and I certainly earned my fiver that day.

We now had some money in our pockets, which was originally meant for saving towards a lads' holiday, but as fast as we earned it, we spent it. We still went to the library café every Saturday morning, but we now had more options to include a weekend shopping spree.
For the past 41 years, the two main things I have spent the majority of my money on have been designer clothes and vinyl records. Music and fashion have always been my two greatest passions, and my shifts working on the chicken farm enabled me to start the ball rolling.

Whenever Simon was home from boarding school, I would go round to his house, and he was the only person I knew that owned a copy of both the Red and Blue albums by The Beatles. He would always play them for me on his small record player in his bedroom, which in my eyes was when my education really started.

Eventually, I owned my own Fab Four record; it was their 1963 EP, (the year I was born, somewhere, to someone) and featured the songs *Do You Want to Know a Secret?*, *Twist and Shout*, *A Taste of Honey*, and *There's a Place*. I absolutely played it to death, and remember running into our house one Saturday afternoon to show my mum and dad what I was now the proud owner of, but they didn't seem that impressed by my day's purchase.

Every Thursday night my mates would pile round to my house so we could all watch *Top of the Pops* together on BBC1 at 7.30. The music scene was not great, as the two main musical genres at the time were disco (which I didn't yet appreciate that much) and the horrendous prog rock, which would bore you to death with its 17-minute guitar solos and never-ending keyboard playing. It really was dreadful.

This particular Thursday, after my mates had helped themselves to a handful of my mum's freshly baked cakes, we were sitting watching glittery shiny band after glittery shiny band prancing about the studio, when four young lads from Manchester (Bolton, to be precise) appeared, playing what in my opinion still remains the greatest pop song of all time. I couldn't take my eyes off the screen, as this was one of the best things I had seen and heard on the show to date.

The group was Buzzcocks (not The Buzzcocks, as Kid Jensen had introduced them), and the song was *Ever Fallen in Love (With Someone You Shouldn't've)?* Music had changed forever, and a thing called Punk had arrived like an atomic bomb. We all knew we had just witnessed the future. (My future, anyway.)

When the public were introduced to The Sex Pistols for the first time via their raucous TV debut in August 1976 on ITV's *So It Goes*, it was definitely a game-changer. The programme was presented by Manchester's very own Mr Music in Tony Wilson, and the Pistols performed *Anarchy in the UK*. The second you clapped eyes on frontman Johnny Rotten in his pink jacket and in-your-face attitude, it was like being smashed in the head with a sledgehammer. I still maintain that this moment was one of the defining musical moments of all time (certainly, for my generation). While I acknowledge the importance of that appearance, I had to wait until 1977 for my own personal musical calling.

Mark's (Bullinge) brother Andy used to have a Saturday job at the record exchange on Darwen Street, and I seem to remember Mark showing me an album by The Jam called *In The City*. The Jam were a New Wave threesome from Woking in Surrey, and this was their debut album. I don't think I can emphasise enough the impact that this album cover had on my life. It was the coolest cover I had ever seen, and the three band members were dressed in black suits, white shirts, and black ties, with the band name spray-painted above their heads. I had to own this record as, after all, I hadn't even heard it yet.

After our library café ritual on a Saturday morning, we now made it our priority to visit the local record shops in the town. I always thought that we were extremely lucky to have the likes of Reidy's, Home of Music, and Ames Tapes and Records in Blackburn. Reidy's would be our first port of call, and we would always enter the shop via the ramp at the market entrance at the back. Upstairs, you would find pianos, acoustic guitars, and sheet music, and downstairs you would find rack after rack of vinyl, so that is where we spent most of our time (and money.)

At the front of the shop, I recall a large plastic display on the wall that would confirm the top 20 chart positions, and at the back you would find several personal listening booths, where you could listen to the vinyl before deciding to buy it. Punk singles were the top of our shopping list, and I would always ask Chris (one of the owners) what latest releases he would recommend and ask him to save me the latest Jam display.

It always felt like it was a competition between our group to see who owned the most punk singles; certainly between me and Karl. Bullinge would buy them, but would swap or sell them the following week, as he got easily bored. Steve S had appalling taste in music (in my humble opinion), and was still living his prog rock life, listening to the likes of Rush, Yes, Genesis, and Rainbow. Simon was on the same page as me and would purchase whatever punk offerings the shops had to offer.

My band was The Jam, Waker loved The Police, Karl The Clash, and Nicky was into the Tom Robinson Band. The thing with Jam fans was that you had to buy their new record on the day it was released; this was law. Jam fans got to know other Jam fans, and it became a bit of a social thing. After all, we did have the best taste and were definitely the best dressed.

After spending most of our money in Reidy's, we would walk through the precinct, past the punks hanging around outside the shop, and enter Ames. The girls behind the counter were really friendly, and I used to love the badge and poster section downstairs.

One of the things I did enjoy at school was the youth club, which took place on a Monday and Wednesday night. Also, the school disco on a Thursday, where we used to stand and watch the braver pupils pogoing at the front and getting proper into the tunes of the day. The night was run by one of the French teachers, but I don't think we appreciated his efforts to help stage such an event, and most folk seemed more interested in the wig he used to wear.

At the youth club, it was a little more relaxed, and we used to play table tennis, and sometimes football in the gym. Like at any school, there was always a group of girls who usually seemed to have more confidence than anybody else, and our very own pink ladies included Nicky's sister Jackie, Cathy, Mandy, Wendy, Anita, and April. Us lads thought we were cool, but obviously we were anything but, yet I do feel we were all decent.
I have always looked back and wished that I'd had enough bottle back then to have been the first in the school to have blue hair, even though my mum would have no doubt kicked me out. The first person in our school to have red hair was Anthony Grogan, who was in my brother's year. Anthony was also into punk, and always looked the part, unlike me. I was into punk music and maybe the attitude, but I was never a punk. The nearest I ever got was to attend the Thursday disco wearing black drainpipe cords, a black and white striped fury V-necked jumper, and a dog collar round my neck that I had borrowed off Mark's dog May.

999 were the first live band that I ever saw; somebody had brought their new single *Emergency* into school, and I remember being interested in their raffle ticket-esque logo that was printed on the label. They performed at King George's Hall, and we were all blown away by the atmosphere on the night and how unbelievably loud it was. My ears were still ringing days after the gig, and that live concert really did set the tone for my lifelong passion.

One Wednesday night at the youth club, after a game of table tennis, I was chatting with some of my school mates that we used to hang around with – Conny, Relo, Greeny – and we came up with the idea of starting our own punk band. None of us could sing or play an instrument at the time, which made us ideal candidates.

Whether or not you are a fan of punk music, the one amazing thing that genre taught us was that more or less anybody could pick up an instrument and form a band. This was a major breakdown of barriers in the industry, as before punk we were force fed the likes of Eric Clapton and Rick Wakeman (no thanks), who were extremely competent at playing, or the likes of George Benson. So without having a talent in this field, you wouldn't even consider giving it a go.

Punk was, on the whole, DIY, and a lot of bands just made it up as they went along. It appeared that the record labels at the time just couldn't get enough of it, and basically signed every act that they could get their hands on, so as not to risk missing out on the next big thing.

Our plan was to form the next Pistols, and I came up with the band name 'Innocent Bystanders', which you must admit is a brilliant name for a punk band from Blackburn. We all agreed to buy our own instruments and we were given permission to practise at the Youth Club.
I spotted an ad in the local paper advertising a red electric guitar from a music tutor in Darwen, and when I went to pick it up, he told me that the guitar had once been owned by Peter Briquette, the bass player of the Boomtown Rats (who I loved). And even though this was a great sales pitch, I am not sure that I ever believed him.
I seem to recall Conny getting hold of a guitar, but not long after we split (before we even played any gigs) due to Greeny refusing to buy a microphone, which was an issue as he was supposed to be the lead singer.

The final thing I enjoyed about school was Carol Cooper. And if Mary had been my first crush, then she was certainly my second.

We had been told one day that a new girl was starting in our year, and that she had arrived from South Africa. My Uncle Bill and Auntie Marion had lived in South Africa for a while, so I became really intrigued – and even more so after I had seen her. She had long, golden (ginger) straight hair all the way down her back, and ultra-cute freckles. I was totally in love, or at least that's how I felt. I recall one day taking a photo of her (you didn't have to ask back then) as she was walking home across the back fields, and wondering what she must have thought as she lifted her head to clock me and Nicky giggling to each other. Helped by the fact that getting a restraining order out on somebody was not a thing back then, things were about to get a whole lot sadder.

Nick and I had managed to find out what road she lived on, and in a moment of madness we decided to take a walk up there in an effort to see her. This was a sign of desperation, and even recalling this incident is pretty darn embarrassing. I remember us both walking down the top of her road, only to find her standing in an upstairs bedroom looking at us through the window. We had been caught out, but for some bizarre reason we decided to hang around for a couple more hours, hiding in an empty doorway across the road in the hope that she might take pity on us and come over to have a chat, but she never did. To make our behaviour even worse, we somehow ended up with her street road sign back at Nick's, but those were the days before eBay, so we probably ended up just dumping it somewhere. Not long after this cringeworthy episode, Miss Cooper started going out with my Gabriel's buddy Dec, and that was that.

One of the things I always found strange was that the friendships I had at junior school didn't necessarily remain at secondary school. Ian Lucas was in the same year as me, but I hardly remember speaking a single word to him over the five years. Also, my friendship with Dec was never as tight as it used to be. I have a vague recollection of a bit of a fallout when we were kids, over a tortoise we had both found in a local wood. We had both agreed to share our newfound pet, and the deal was that we would take turns to look after it. After a few days, one of us discovered it was dead in the bottom of its box, and we were both pet-less again.

The one thing I will admit to being pretty good at in secondary school was swimming. My mum and dad had given me and Robin a good head start by insisting that we learnt to swim from a young age, and we had the great pleasure of attending Johnson's Swimming School in Darwen. Johnson's is an absolute Darwen institution, and a fabulous success story for the town. It was built in a disused Co-op building by John Johnson in 1971, and it is still going strong today, 49 years later.

Also, with the school we would go each week to Belper Street baths at Daisyfield, and I remember there was always a group of pupils who would stand under the warm showers for as long as they could, because the changing rooms were freezing, until one of our teachers appeared and told them to get out.
We all changed together, using our towels in an attempt to try and cover ourselves, and also for protection against being towel whipped by our fellow classmates. All your belongings would go into metal baskets, which we would then hand in through a hole in the wall in return for a rubber wristband, which would usually go around our ankle. This was a PE lesson that I actually enjoyed, and I would always pride myself on my ability to swim more than a length underwater. I remember passing my bronze award, by having to tread water in a pair of pyjamas, and then dive under water to retrieve a rubber brick. I have always had a love of water, especially underwater, and put this early passion down to a number of things.

One of my favourite TV shows as a kid used to be *Marine Boy*, which was produced in 1965 in Japan, and was a cartoon about the undersea adventures of a boy and his best buddy, a dolphin named Splasher. Marine boy had to eat special gum to enable him to breathe underwater, helping him to solve the day's mystery. I seem to remember it being on BBC1 every morning during the school holidays, and it being a must watch – for me at least.

Also, when we were young, some cousins we had from down south had been scuba diving in the Great Barrier Reef, off the coast of Queensland in Australia. Just the fact that we had relations that had travelled to the other side of the world was exciting enough, but they visited us once at Kestrel Close, and as a gift had given us a few pieces of coral from their travels.
Ladybird books were really popular, and I recall talking my mum into buying me the underwater exploration one from Seed and Gabbutt in town. I even started watching Jacques Cousteau's Undersea World programme with my parents, and decided that I wanted to become a marine biologist when I got older – although this career goal was not something that I would dare share with my school career advisor, for risk of being ridiculed.

Each year my school would hold an inter-tutor group swimming gala at Belper baths, and I would usually win most of my races. One year we even won the whole competition, and all my fellow classmates started to sing *We Are the Champions* by Queen. I really did feel pretty proud of this achievement, as my mum and dad had just witnessed me do something right for once. My performance that night even led to me being chosen to represent my town in a swimming competition a few months later, even though I didn't win my race.

My dad always used to say that if I remembered my schoolwork like I did my Jam lyrics, I would get straight A's in all my exams. And it wasn't until several years later that I understood what he had meant, and tended to agree with him.

I was never into fighting at school, and only ever recall having one fight in the whole five years I attended. I say fight, but it was over in less than a minute. I have no idea what it was over but remember Michael Dixon from my year confronting me as I was heading into C block for my lesson.
I told him I had no reason at all to fight him, which resulted in him punching me in the face. This really hurt, so I retaliated, and that was it.

As far as school punishment went, I remember getting hit with a ruler one time in chemistry, for something that Simon had done. But throughout my five years, I only ever got summoned to receive the dreaded cane once. Luckily for me, this once had been on the last day before the six weeks' summer holidays. I was given a classroom number on G block and told to meet the year head at the end of the day's lessons. I arrived to find an empty classroom, waited a couple of minutes for him to arrive, then came to the conclusion that if I legged it, he would probably forget by the time we returned to school. So I did, and I was right.

Writing about my memories of my time at secondary school, I wonder if I have been a little harsh and a bit too negative with the incidents that I have highlighted from the late 1970s. But when I started to write my story, I decided to be as truthful and as honest as my 56-year-old memory would allow. Of course, I enjoyed other aspects of my school life, and after all, this is where I made my lifelong friendship group. But it was a different time back then. This is not an excuse for abuse, and there is no doubt that a small percentage of the teaching staff had been outright bullies in my opinion and had taken great pleasure in throwing their weight about and inflicting pain and misery on the very pupils they were being paid to develop, protect, and nurture. Safeguarding rules and regulations had yet to be introduced; after all, we are talking about a time when you were forced to give away your baby to complete strangers, at the risk of your neighbours finding out that you had participated in sex before you were married.

Probably my worst time at school was taking my exams, even though I acknowledge that it was 100% my fault as I had done little revision, even though my parents had strongly advised me to do so. After all, none of the questions had been about my beloved Jam, so I had no interest at all.

To sit in that very lonely Sports Hall used to leave me with a feeling of dread, and despite the room being filled with my fellow pupils, it definitely was a lonely place if your paper remained blank and you had zero idea about what you were going to write next.

Naturally, I failed to receive any kind of CSE grades that my parents had been hoping for, and I really did regret my lack of effort on the day we all gathered to view our results on the school noticeboard.

To end my school days on a more positive note (no, I didn't end up going out with Carol Cooper), my tutor group had managed to make the final of the Inter-Tutor group cricket competition, which took place at the Blackburn Northern Cricket Club, and it was yours truly that made the winning catch just before lunch. I remember the ball being hit in my direction, and me just holding out my hands and being extremely lucky. But lucky or not, I was a hero amongst my fellow classmates, even if only for a few final days.

Finally, our eagerly anticipated last day had arrived, and our school days had come to an end. The great thing about our last day was that we could bring in our choice of games or music. Naturally, I chose records, but the best part of the day was walking across the playing fields on our way home, carrying out the compulsory tie-burning ritual which was expected of all pupils on their final day.

The year was now 1980, and I had no qualifications and no job, and no idea what my next move would be. When you saw your Careers person at school, unless you told them you wanted to follow the usual path of learning a trade, or going to college to further your education, they had no interest. If you dared to express an interest in becoming a footballer or a pop star, or even a marine biologist, they would simply tell you not to be stupid and to choose something proper. If your self-confidence had not been low enough, you could always rely on these folks to destroy it even further.

My brother Robin was the total opposite to me; he was very academic, studying, revising, and reaping the benefits with his exam results. At least, that is what my mum and dad would tell me on a regular basis. I did feel sorry for my parents, as they had done everything that they could to support me and to try and persuade me to do the same, but it just wasn't a priority at the time.

At one stage, they even attempted to give me extra lessons after school to enable me to improve.
My dad was a whizz at maths, and spent hours trying to teach me the benefit of accepting logarithms into my life. My mum was very good at English, and again spent a considerable amount of her time explaining to me about grammar, punctuation, and spelling, but to no avail. I used to try to convince them that I could concentrate better if I had my music playing in the background, but they didn't fall for it, to my disappointment.

Trying my best to put my academic failures to the back of my mind for the time being, I decided to put most of my efforts into making the most of the summer holidays and enhancing my social life with my friends. We had recently discovered the local YMCA, and would visit regularly to play table tennis. Right from the off, I loved playing the sport and was pretty decent at it. Bullinge was my biggest rival at the time, and we would compete against each other for hours.
On a Saturday night, they had a roller-skating event called Star Skate, where folk would skate around the hall in a circle, while they blasted out the latest chart music to keep you entertained. This activity did not appeal to me, and I wasn't sure if this was because I couldn't skate or had no desire to embarrass myself in front of Julie and Mary. Or maybe it was simply that I couldn't stand *Brown Girl in the Ring* by Boney M, which they would apparently play on rotation. But once my mates had told me what a great time they had all had, I did feel I had missed out.

We all seemed to be growing up really fast, but still found the time to hang around together every opportunity that we could. One evening in particular stands out, and I would remember it for a pretty long time after. We had been down on the back fields, and somebody suggested that we had a game of postman's knock. I had heard of the game before but didn't have a clue what was about to happen. The rules of the game were simple: if your number was lucky enough to get picked, you could go behind the nearest bush and snog Mary. (I'm not joking!) Now, I can't remember the finer details of the rules, but I knew I was deeply indebted to whatever person came up with the idea in the first place. This of course was in theory, as for some unfair reason my number was not the one being chosen. So I had to sit back and watch Waker and Karl disappear behind that bush – but never me.

I sort of concluded that the game must have been fixed, and the basic fact of the matter was that Mary had no desire to carry out such activities with yours truly. Suddenly, and to my complete surprise (and delight), I heard someone say, 'Pete, it's No 5, that's you.' Trying my utmost to stay cool and act as though it had been no big deal (alright!), I walked slowly over to the sacred bush to receive my reward, and what happened next did by no means disappoint. Sure enough, Mary had been waiting, and snog her I did. I have no doubt that Mary's experience of the situation was completely different to mine, but it made my night (month, year), and the number five became my new lucky number – and still is.

The next time I found myself in that field was far less pleasurable, as we were joined by a couple of large horses that were sometimes kept there. Neither of them seemed very impressed at having some unwanted humans trespassing on their turf, and they had started to move in our direction. The rest of our group managed to run and jump over a stream at the bottom of the field to safety, but being a weak runner, I found myself face-to-face with this local Mr Ed.

At this point Simon shouted those immortal words, 'Pete, just stand still and you will be alright, as horses don't bite.' Not long after, I found myself in Accident and Emergency, waiting for what I can remember to be a very large tetanus injection, as I had a bite mark stretching from the front of my shoulder to the back. The others were in absolute stitches about Simon's poor advice and what had just happened, while I had learnt a new fact about horses.

I was in no major rush to return to the scene of the crime, which meant I would have to come up with an alternative destination in order to keep us all entertained during our long hot summer. This came in the form of daily adventure trips out, and I came up with a plan to visit local destinations that none of us had visited as a group before. Top of my list was the Pine Woods. I mean, it had been pretty memorable on my previous visit, and even though Martin and his friends had not been there to greet me on this occasion, we had a wonderful time swimming in the reservoir and exploring the woods.

Our second destination of choice was a disused mansion, which involved a long walk up alongside Billinge Woods and over several farmers' fields. The mansion in question was the remains of Woodfold Hall that had been built in 1798 for cotton magnate Henry Sudell. In 1849 it had become the property of the Thwates family, and for many years was home to Elma Yerburgh, the daughter of Daniel Thwates. When Elma had died age 82 in 1946, the contents were auctioned off, and in 1949 the roof had to be taken off as a way of avoiding paying rates and certain taxes. We used to love hanging around in the old remains, probably because we knew we were not supposed to, and we would visit the mansion many times.

China Town was another destination we would visit, although there was nothing oriental about the place, just trees and streams, over the fields at the back of the Brownhill pub.

Karl and Birchy used to go off on their own collecting birds' eggs, until one day an owl landed on Karl's head, and as he ran through the woods screaming, the owl refused to let go of his scalp, to the amusement of Birchy (and us, once he told us the tale).

Only one of our planned destinations managed to elude us, but it wasn't through lack of effort trying to find it. Someone had told me that there was a nudist camp in nearby Ribchester and that they had seen an advert in a naturist magazine for sale in WH Smith. We added it to our places to visit list, and spent hours traipsing around Ribchester peering over dry-stone walls and searching through hedgerows, but found nothing.

My early memories of growing up would always involve lots of family members. Ever-present was my Grandma and Grandad, Edna and Jim Burrows, and one of my fondest recollections is of sitting in front of their fire with Robin at their house on Cornelian Street, toasting pieces of round bread, on the nights we had been staying there. Even today, the smell of freshly made toast takes me back to that place and time; you can't beat it.
My Uncle Bill and Auntie Marion were the other relations we would see the most of, and I thought the world of them. I remember waving them off at Manchester Airport, as Uncle Bill (my mum's brother) had just agreed to a new job in South Africa. They only ended up staying a few months in the end, due to apartheid, as I know they felt really uncomfortable about the situation.

On each occasion they visited our house, just as they were leaving Uncle Bill would come over and shake my hand to say goodbye, and he would always have a hidden ten-pound note folded up for us. This was something my dad would adopt, years later, with Janet.
A lot of family gatherings would take place at the Burrows' residence, and my Grandma would always put on a good spread. I used to love her home cooking, which I think just encouraged her to make more. My family would always end up playing cards for pennies, and even though Las Vegas it was not, it certainly was a much-loved family tradition, with both Robin and me just watching on.

On the occasions that the posh side of our family would come up to visit from down south, we would always meet up at the Saxon Inn where they were staying, which was always a real treat.

Not too many of my family are still alive today, but I have always remembered those get-togethers growing up with such fondness. Unfortunately, my memories of visiting my dad's side of the family are very vague, but I do remember visiting his father on London Road now and again at weekends. My only real recollections of these visits are of him having an outside toilet, and a few tins of Spam in his cupboard.

My dad was originally from Rochdale, so we would sometimes travel over and visit his relatives.

When we visited his Uncle Eric and Auntie Clara, they would always get their home movie projector out for us, and we would be treated to their collection of black and white Laurel and Hardy films, which we thought were wonderful. Also, we were always told the story about his Auntie Polly making a very large kilt for the local politician at the time, but it's not something they would brag about today.

Each Christmas was always enhanced by the extra five presents that my grandparents would buy us. The only downside to this, was that my Grandma would always tell us beforehand what she had bought. As far as gifts go, I have always loved the element of surprise, but no matter how many times I would ask her to keep it a secret until the big day, she always let it slip out. I still own the Kevin Keegan and Kenny Dalglish Annuals that I received back then, as I clearly have an issue with getting rid of stuff.

My mum's mince pies were legendary, and her Christmas cake was to die for, but my Uncle Bill had such a good appetite that he would regularly go back for seconds, and sometimes even thirds. This meant that I would always keep a watchful eye on the proceedings, hoping there would be enough left for us during the week.

As far as family holidays went, we would either go to Llandudno or Bridlington, and stay in a family hotel. We would go to see shows on the pier, featuring the likes of Ken Dodd, but at the risk of sounding ungrateful, I remember always craving a little more excitement than what was on offer.

On one of our Llandudno stays, I recall I had a fascination for pen knives (for some strange reason), and I am ashamed to admit it now, but nicking money out of your father's wallet had become a thing (for me and Jez anyway). I needed hard cash to add to my collection, so when nobody was around, I borrowed a tenner. The rule was, you could only take a note out of his wallet, providing he had three or more inside it. The logic behind the three tenners' rule was that the more notes he had sitting there, the less chance he had of noticing that one was missing. I remember nicking a couple on that holiday, and to my knowledge my dad never did find out (or at least, he never let on to us kids). I would always announce I was going for an early morning walk, and then go off to find the nearest newsagents on my own. These were the days before knife crime was rife, and the shopkeeper didn't care how old you were, providing they made the sale. My knife obsession didn't last for long, and I have no idea where it even came from, but I am sure it was for more than to simply carve Mary's initials into the nearest tree.

During our stay in Wales, we visited Caernarfon Castle, went up the Great Orme in a cable car, visited the Welsh mountain zoo, and I was allowed to drink half a lager and black in the hotel bar. How could you want any more from your summer holidays? But I did.

Back in the late 70s and early 80s, Butlins in Pwllheli had become really popular with a few of our mates' groups, and this was the last family holiday I remember the Eastwoods going on.
One night, I remember going off on my own to check out the camp disco (by that I mean that it was the in-house discotheque, not a music room for anybody camp).
Punk had just recently arrived in Pwllheli, and most young people at the disco were dressed accordingly. I still didn't have enough confidence to go over and talk to the girls at the side of the dance floor, or even to dance for that matter, so I simply stood in the corner people-watching for a while. Times were changing, as was I, and I had a feeling that this would be the final time I would be going away with my mum, dad, and brother.

Football was still a growing passion of mine, and at least once a week I would go around to Jez's house on the corner of Rhodes Avenue to play Subbuteo. Jez was a Leeds fan back then – probably because they were by far the dirtiest team – and I naturally opted for Liverpool, or on occasions Celtic because I liked their green and white stripes.

On a Saturday morning, in between our record buying, we would sometimes visit a football programme shop on Preston New Road, called Bentley's. The guy who ran it was proper sound, which made our behaviour even more out of order. In his shop were two rooms – one was his office, and one at the front with rack after rack of programmes. The plan was always that a couple of us would keep him distracted by chatting to him in the office, while the others would stay in the other room, cramming into our school bags as many footy programmes that we could fit. Even worse, the following Saturday we would go back in and try to sell him back some of the ones we had stolen off him the previous week. One particular week I remember selling him a Rovers v Wolves 1960 FA Cup Final programme, which had fallen into my bag the previous Saturday.

Myself and my other mate Steven, who also had great taste in football teams, had started going to watch Liverpool at Anfield. As soon as you left the train station at Lime Street, the atmosphere was boss. And no matter where you turned, you would see like-minded people wearing the same colours as you. We would follow the crowds to the ground, and I have never seen an end so full as the Kop; we were packed in like sardines, and it took forever to push our way through the standing crowd to claim the best spot we could behind Ray Clemence's goal. I had also never seen as many people wearing the same colours before. It was as if every single person was wearing either a shirt, a scarf, a hat, or all three, displaying pride in their team, and this was the first time I remember feeling part of a gang and belonging to something.

We were absolutely spoilt at that time supporting Liverpool, as they had one of the greatest club sides of all time. The manager was Bob Paisley, and we really did love him. He wasn't cocky, loud, or flashy, as he would do his talking through the way his team performed on the pitch. At the time I remember them having no fewer than seven first team players in the current England team, so I really had chosen well.

There are far too many highlights of supporting Liverpool back then to even attempt to write in this book, but up there must be when they won the European Cup for the first time, beating Borussia Monchengladbach 3-1 in Rome in 1977. I will never forget the look on my mum and dad's faces as they walked in on me jumping up and down in the bath at home, while holding (and drinking) a bottle of Pomagne (only the best).

One Boxing Day my Uncle Bill managed to get some free tickets via work for Liverpool's visit to Old Trafford, and even though it was freezing and it ended 0 – 0, the occasion was really special being with my dad, my uncle, and my brother.

In 1982 Liverpool announced that their new kit sponsors were none other than Crown Paints, and this was fantastic, as surely my dad would be able to pull a few strings, being lab manager and all that. Sure enough, George came up trumps, and on Saturday, 18th April, 1987, he managed to sort us both out with a special hospitality package at Anfield for the visit of Nottingham Forest. It had only taken him five years.

I was proper excited as he drove us down the East Lancs Road, and bombarded him with never ending questions about what we would be allowed to do once we arrived. We were escorted through a special entrance and given a tour of the ground, given a pre-match meal and a welcome pack, and then shown to our seats. It turned out that it had been local boy Gary Ablett's home debut for the first team, and he played a blinder. My dad had chosen well, and 37, 357 – plus two members of the Eastwood family – witnessed a 3-0 victory for the home side. Back inside Anfield after the game, I had my photo taken with Grobbelaar and Ablett in front of some trophies, while my dad stood chatting to some reps. It had been a brilliant day, but the journey home would end it on a sour note.

Believe it or not, I had a massive row with him over the air conditioning (long story), which resulted in him calling me a name that I had never heard him speak before, and would no way repeat in here. I really had been shocked, and had obviously wound him up that much.

1980, and school was well and truly over. Based on the fact that I had not been inundated with job offers, along with being fed up with my parents nagging me about future plans, I agreed to go to college to learn photography. My mum and dad had bought me a Zenit camera, and my tutor Tom seemed like a nice guy.
Unfortunately, though, I couldn't just take photography on its own, and had to choose other subjects to make my hours up. The subjects I ended up choosing were maths (no chance), English Literature (as if), and something called communication studies. This was a new start for me, and an opportunity to gain some qualifications – or so I thought.
Photography was split into two parts: Practical, to learn the art of taking good quality photographs and develop them; and Theory, to learn about the history of photography, which would feature in our final exam.

One morning, I was walking down to college with Karl, when he asked me if I'd heard that John Lennon had been shot and was in fact dead. It stopped me in my tracks, and at first I thought he may have been winding me up, but he assured me that it had been on the news just before he had left the house. Mobile phones had yet to be invented, so I had to wait until I arrived at my maths class for it to be confirmed. On the evening of 8th December, 1980, John Lennon had been fatally shot in the archway of his Dakota residence by an American Beatles fan (or not) Mark Chapman. Chapman had travelled from Hawaii to meet his hero, but apparently had been angered by Lennon's lifestyle. Reportedly, the final words uttered by John at the time had been, 'Yeah.'

Myself, Waker, Karl, and Julie attended his memorial service in Liverpool six days later, after I had felt an overwhelming urge to pay my respects. Thousands of people attended outside the St George's Hall building, and people climbed lampposts and stood on roof tops to ensure that they did not miss anything. On the St George's steps, 80 Beatles tribute bands from all over the world were performing live, and I seem to remember Gerry and the Pacemakers being one of them, but I may be wrong.

It was estimated that 30,000 people joined together that day to honour John Lennon, and another 50,000 congregated in Central Park New York to do the same. At Yoko's request, at midnight (UK time) the two cities linked up for a ten-minute silent candlelit vigil, and radio stations around the world marked the occasion by temporarily halting their broadcasts. And on the journey home in the car, we all agreed that we were so glad we had attended to be a small part of that day.

Back at college, I was thoroughly enjoying my Tuesday night practical photography class, taking photos of models and learning the skills to develop the photos myself in the darkroom. But on a Monday when we were supposed to be learning about the history side of things, we were basically just doing the same.

Our social life began to improve, as we had put all our efforts into trying to get served in any pub that would believe our new made-up ages. The first that had fallen for our lies was The Carlton on Shear Brow, where we would frequent the back room to play bar football and eat Planters peanuts. The landlord at the time was proper sarcastic, and I recall him unplugging the fruit machine because Jez had just dropped the jackpot. He refused to plug it back in until Jez had bought him a drink.

I have never been a big fan of nuts, but these Planters were delicious. Nuts in a pub back then were always hanging on the wall behind the bar, attached to a cardboard display featuring a topless female. Every time somebody would buy a packet, it would reveal a bit more of the picture – a bit like Catchphrase for adults – so naturally we ate a lot of nuts.

The Prince of Wales on Montague Street was another haunt that Nicky and I had found ourselves being able to get served in. On a Saturday night they used to have a disco, so we attended then, knowing that there would be more girls in. A couple of girls in particular that had caught Nicky's eye used to come in both dressed as Gary Newman, wearing all black outfits with a red band across their shoulders. I must admit they did look pretty cool at the time and certainly stood out, but I don't remember even finding out their names.

I recall attempting to get served in The George on the outskirts of town, and remember the landlord telling Bullinge that he could still see his nappy rash, so that didn't go too well.

The main pub that we were all keen to get served in was The Farthings on Rosewood Avenue, just across the road from where Nicky had moved to. Eventually, most of us managed to persuade the landlord and landlady that we had been old enough, and Nicky's mum Jenny even rang up the pub and had a word with the landlord, saying, 'What do you mean you don't believe my Nicholas is old enough?' And it worked.

We had been accepted in our new local, which was run by the legendary Paul and Christine Waterfield, and they ended up not just being our landlord and landlady, but really good friends to us all.

Back to college, and our tutor Tom would always arrange for young models to join us in our lesson, in order to help us develop our photo-taking skills, so I was never going to complain. Also, he asked if we knew anyone that might fancy gaining some modelling experience. My friend Karl had a younger sister called Elaine, who I thought may be photogenic, so I asked her if she would be up for it and she agreed. The following Monday I brought Elaine into college, and everything seemed above board – just a few different posing shots in front of a green background. Tom seemed happy with the session, as did the class, and Elaine also enjoyed herself.

I hadn't mentioned it to Karl, as I didn't think it was a big deal, being her friend, too. But I was wrong. The following Tuesday I arranged to meet Karl after my lesson, as we must have been going out. Karl arrived early, just as I was in the dark room processing the previous week's negatives, and as I stood rocking the developing trays up and down in the relevant solution, to my horror (and also Karl's) the photos I had been developing were of his sister. Karl stood next to me with his eyes fixed on the trays, getting angrier and angrier. I tried my best to explain to him that everything had been above board and with consent, and even though we were good friends, it is fair to say that he was pretty naffed off. It took several weeks for the subject to go away.

The learning at the time from my other subjects was pretty minimal, due to the group consensus that we would get more out of attending the Jubilee pub across the road than we would from attending class. I can't remember everybody's name from my classes, so it would be difficult to blame individuals for leading me astray. And to be fair, it's not like I had to be dragged there kicking and screaming.
My mate Nick was also attending college at the same time, studying electrical engineering, and we would regularly meet up and check out the nightlife. Nick would usually bring his classmate Dwayne with him, who was a pretty cool character and had a bit of a New Romantic look about him, rocking a Phil Oakey-esque hairstyle. I remember us all going to the college Christmas do at Fernando's wine bar, and we really did have a very merry time, even though it had taken place in the afternoon. Apparently, The Smiths had played upstairs in the Elizabethan Suite for 50p, and also the Manic Street Preachers, but unfortunately not on the day we were there.

The briefing we had been given for our photography practical exam had been to go with the theme 'Two's Company'. I had taken some black and white photos of Birchy's younger brother and his neighbour's daughter, and remember It being an absolute mission to get a boy and a girl of that age to hold hands. I took

some of a blind lady with her guide dog, as I thought it had summed up the theme pretty well, and to be fair, I was proud of how they had all come out.
As the weeks went by, the models kept arriving, and if I am honest, I was concerned by the fact that we had not been learning the stuff we were supposed to be. Also at the time, a rumour had started to go round hinting that Tom would take some of the girls out into the countryside on a Friday afternoon for a private session. Sure enough, when the time came around to sit our exam, I didn't have enough knowledge on the subject to pass it, and no matter how many times I tried to explain the reasons for this to my parents, there was only one person who was to blame in their eyes.

Several years later, I remember reading in my local evening paper an article about a tutor at college who had been sacked for setting up secret cameras in the students' toilets and filming them without their knowledge. Guess what the name of that tutor was...!

With my job prospects getting worse by the day, and having no desire to consider a chicken farm return, I signed up to a Government scheme called YTS (Youth training Scheme). The scheme was launched with the aim of offering 16- to 17-year-olds opportunities for training and work experience, but was heavily criticised as a shambolic attempt by Thatcher's government to cover up the unemployment figures at the time. Critics claimed that the scheme enabled employers to exploit school leavers for cheap labour.

My cheap labour exploitation was in Corporation Park, helping to point drystone walls. I have to say It was a pretty pointless experience, as we spent more time sitting inside a tiny wooden shed drinking brews than we did on the job. I recall having a really grumpy supervisor who would basically moan at you most of the time and give you very little training or support.

I even remember one Christmas on our last day at work before the holidays, he ended up pinning me up against the shed wall, because he told me I had been overdressed for the job in my parka and boating blazer. He told me it would look bad on him if his bosses had showed up.

If I was going to be able to keep up my newfound social life, there was only one thing for it – I was going to have to get myself a job, and fast. I felt I was being left behind by the rest of my mates, as they all seemed to have a plan or a career path, which I certainly did not have.

Jez was the first one to start a full-time job, and worked as a trainee chef at Samuel Whitbread in Samlesbury. I know that back then Jez used to love cooking, but I know he liked the female waitresses even more.

My Dad proudly showing off the bonniest baby in Brownhill.

In our Sunday best, with Mum, Dad, and Robin.
(No idea who the random baby is?)

A bit of a mod cut, but matching outfits, at Blackpool with Mum.

In our front garden at Bank Hey Lane North, with Grandma and Grandad, Jim and Edna Burrows.

BUT I'M DIFFERENT NOW

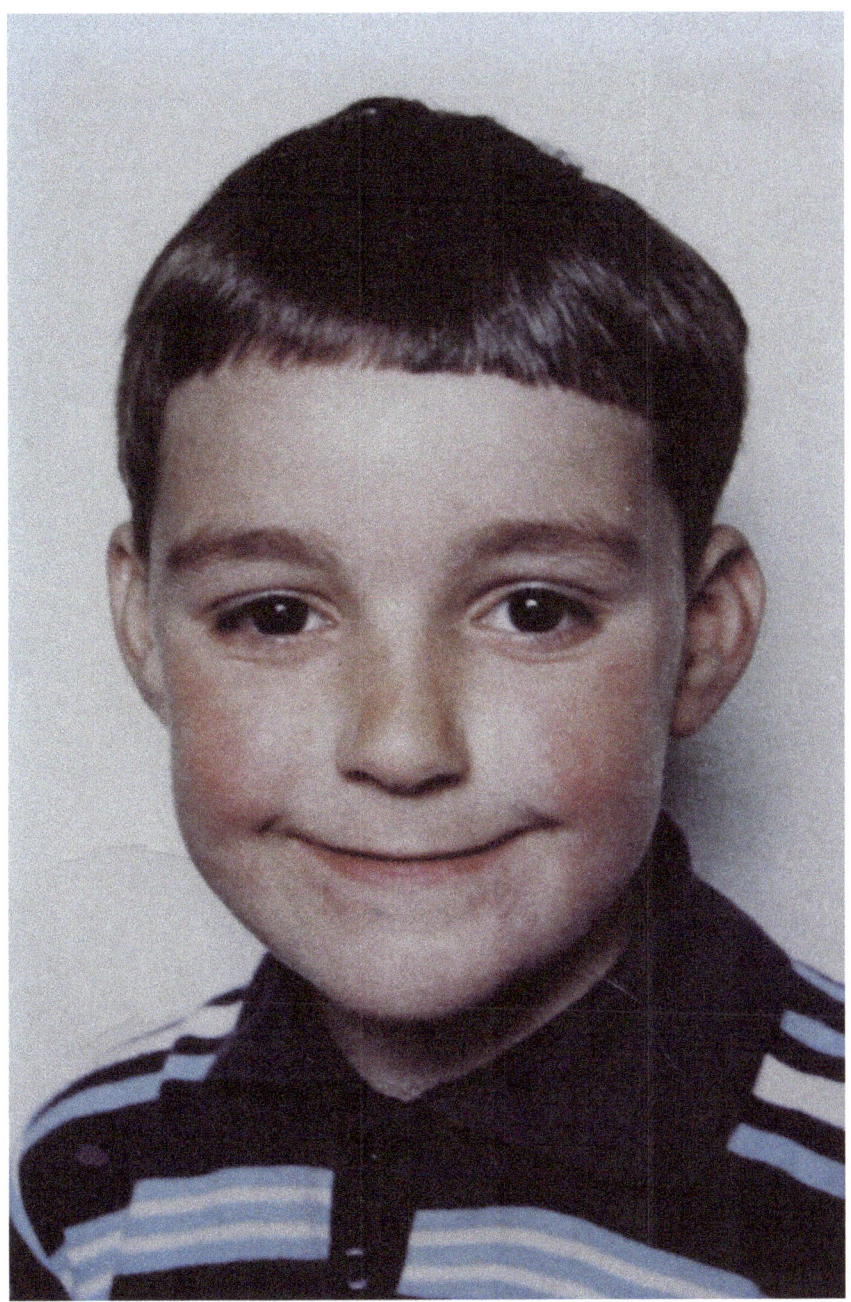

I wish I still had that haircut and shirt now.

Grandad Jim, Uncle Stanley, Auntie Marion, Mum, Uncle Bill, and Dad, after tucking into one of my mums famous spreads.

CHAPTER THREE

THIS IS THE MODERN WORLD

There is absolutely no doubt that watching *A Hard Day's Night* on that family holiday had been a defining moment for me, and certainly the foundation and benchmark for my musical taste. When we lived on Bank Hey Lane, night after night I would be found lying on the floor in our front room, on my own, the lights turned off, listening to Beatles records through my headphones.
I think we only had a couple of albums, and no doubt compilations, but this was my chosen nightly fix.

The only other records the Eastwood family had in their collection that I was even remotely interested in at the time were the *Top of the Pops* compilations that I think arrived on Christmas Day. We had no idea that most of the album tracks were not sung by the original artists, so we just played them to death. In fact, I feel my *Sugar Baby Love* appreciation had arrived via these.
Every year Pickwick Records would churn out these compilations, which intended to replicate the sound of the original chart hits and were recorded by a studio group comprising of session musicians and singers who remained uncredited. These singers did actually include Elton John and Tina Charles before they had become famous in their own right.

Even though these LPs featured the latest chart hit singles, it was the record sleeve that attracted all the attention. Each cover featured a scantily clad female (sometimes two for the price of one), standing in a very suggestive pose (and you didn't even need to purchase any nuts). There is no way that Pickwick would get away with selling such sexist material today, but for a young lad back then who had never heard of the word sexist, they were part of my education. And from a marketing point of view, it was genius.

In the mid-seventies, you were either a Bowie fan or a Ferry fan. My mate Nick would definitely be in camp David and was always trying to get me to listen to his albums every time I called for him (for that, I now thank him). Even though I absolutely love and appreciate Bowie today, at the time I was team Roxy. I had heard the likes of *Virginia Plain*, *Tokyo Joe*, and *This is Tomorrow Calling*, and had loved them.

On one occasion, Jez had lent me a dark red chef's jacket that I felt looked like something Mr Ferry would have worn, and I had planned to wear it on this particular Saturday night, hoping to impress. Nick had called for me, and just as we were about to step out of the front door, my mum appeared and said, 'You are not going out wearing that.' Me being me, I explained to her that I was, and this debate went on for several minutes with neither side backing down. Nicky tried to calm the situation and told me to take it off, but my plan was to go upstairs and throw the jacket out of the bedroom window then finally be allowed out of the front door. However, by the time I got back downstairs, Nicky had left, and my mum had locked the front door. There was no way I was going to miss this night out, which I had been looking forward to all week. So I tried to climb out of the downstairs toilet window, only to find my dad standing waiting for me on the patio. My stubbornness meant that I spent the rest of the night in my bedroom, beyond fed up about what I may have been missing.

The arrival of Punk and New Wave had changed everything, and it was the first time I had noticed the current generation giving attitude to previous ones. The first time I set my eyes on the *In the City* album cover, I knew that things had changed for me. I never considered The Jam to be a punk band anyway; I just thought they were New Wave.
At our school disco, I had heard some new songs that had made me pay extra attention – *My Girl* by Madness, *It's Different for*

Girls by Joe Jackson, *Echo Beach* by Martha and the Muffins, and *My World* by Secret Affair. I liked punk music yet never considered myself a punk. But what this new sound was representing was 100% me. The Mod Revival had arrived, and this was down to two things. The Jam had made such an early impact with their influences taken from The Kinks, The Who, and The Small Faces, dressing in smart suits and with Weller's Marriot-style haircut. When The Who released *Quadrophenia* in 1979, I felt as if I had been sent to watch a public information film telling me how I should live my life!

Quadrophenia was set in London and Brighton in 1965, and the story follows a young Mod called Jimmy, and his search for some self-worth and a need to fit in. The way they looked, the music they liked, the scooters they rode; my benchmark had been set. These factors were responsible for a 60s Mod revival, and I knew for sure that I was a Mod and that this was the gang I wanted to be a part of. After all, Jimmy said, 'You have to be somebody.'

For me to become a fully-fledged member of this new gang, I needed a parka, and not just any parka, it had to be an original Army issue parka. I found my new parka in a shop on Darwen Street called 'Outsider,' and they sold all the current Punk and Mod gear. No parka was complete without customising it with the expected Jam or Who patches, and later Scooter Club patches and badges.
I proper loved it, and really did feel a part of something special when I wore it.

For me, The Jam were everything; their music, and the way they dressed, and everything they said in interviews, would resonate with me. To me, they couldn't put a foot wrong. The rule was that you had to buy their new single on the actual day it came out, and then play it over and over on your record player until you had learned every lyric. When the band were about to release an album, Radio 1 on a Sunday night would play track after track, whilst interviewing the band about their songs. I would have my tape recorder on standby and record the whole show, stopping and starting the recorder to make sure that I missed out all the adverts and the weather report. It really became an art form, trying our best to master this procedure, and by the time the album was released, we had already learnt every single second of it.

Whatever the band would wear for their TOTP performances, we would do all we could to replicate it. I recall finding out where they bought their shoes from, and my mum's face was a picture when I told her I was going to London to buy myself a pair. The thing is, I was serious, and the following week I walked into Shelly's shoe shop on Carnaby Street and became the proud owner of a pair of The Jam's original stage shoes. They were proper dapper, black velvet with a white stripe down the centre, and two white stripes down the side.

The other pointed black and white Jam shoe could be purchased much closer to home at Norman Taylor's shop on Bank Top, under the name of a 'Frank Wright' shoe. Norman Taylor had been an established name in Blackburn for years and was usually where your parents would take you to purchase a pair of school shoes for the new term. The shop wasn't exactly known for being trendy, but I remember going in the day after seeing the band perform *News of the World* on Thursday night's show and asking an elderly gentleman behind the counter if he happened to have a pair of the Frank Wright shoe in size 9. 'Oh, you mean The Jam shoe?' he replied, proving yet again the power of a band.

I even remember buying an old medal from an antique shop in Truro, Cornwall, because Paul Weller had worn one on his jacket on the front cover of *The Face* magazine.

A dark blue Fred Perry, light blue Sta Press trousers, black wraparound sunglasses, and a splendid red and blue striped boating blazer, would be the final ingredients to complete my uniform. Well, almost, as on a Saturday morning I would head down to visit Majestic Hair Salon in town, clutching three small photographs of Paul Weller, showing front, side, and back views of his head.

One evening, my dad arrived home to announce that he had managed to sort me out a temporary job at Crown. He explained that a position had come up to be a Colour Matcher in the Research Lab, and I was shocked. This was surely the answer to all my money problems, so I thanked him and told him I would try my best. I was now confident that I would be able to book a holiday with my mates, now that I was working, and Nick and I managed to book our first summer holiday without our parents – opting for Newquay.

After a 13-hour coach journey throughout the night, we finally arrived at our holiday destination.

We checked into our hotel, feeling all grown up, and after unpacking, set off for the nearest beach. Towan beach was only down the road from where we were staying, and the funny thing was that we had literally been stood on it for less than five minutes when a pigeon had left Nicky a souvenir right in the middle of his flat-top hairdo. It was hilarious watching him discovering the white gooey liquid all over his hair, and I remember him saying, 'If this is what the birds think of me in Newquay, we may as well go home now.'

That night, we hit the town, and I must admit Nicky did look pretty cool, dressed in a black baggy suit, white shirt, and black pointed winkle pickers. His hair looked as though he had used a spirit level on it, and was so flat you could have balanced your pint on top. I was in camp Mod, and we would literally count all the funny looks that we received simply walking down the street. I don't think the place had really caught up yet, in terms of the latest fashions.

I remember walking into the Sailor's Arms, and within the first five seconds of us being there, the DJ had stopped the music and announced over the microphone, ''It's not fancy dress tonight, lads!' We didn't know where to look, but kind of enjoyed the attention.

Whether or not these Cornish folks appreciated our dress sense or not was one thing, but they couldn't deny that Nicky was a really cool dancer. Even though I loved dancing and needed a few pints to give me the courage to even get on the dancefloor, I couldn't dance to save my life.

Towards the end of the night, the DJ had started to play *Queen Bitch* by Bowie, and by this time Nick had drunk enough pints to find himself on the dance floor. No sooner had he started to pull some shapes than he was joined by two confident looking girls, both dressed in shiny red leather catsuits, who were both carrying a leather whip. I stood open-mouthed as Nicky managed to keep his cool, and the three of them took over the dance floor and proceeded to put on a show for everyone in the room. This was a really cool moment, possibly Nicky's finest, and it has been impossible for me to listen to *Queen Bitch* since, without it taking me back to that dance floor in the Sailors Arms on that night.

The following day we decided to visit the world famous Fistral Beach, where people fly in from all over the world (including Hawaii) for the World Surfing Championships. We had spotted a couple of decent looking girls sitting just in front of us on beach towels, but this was the afternoon, and we hadn't had any alcohol yet to help boost our confidence. So, we basically sat discussing who was going to make the first move. Too late. We had waited so long that two young lads beat us to it.

To avoid making our disappointment look obvious, we stayed facing the other way and simply listened in to the smooth-talking chat up lines in Cockney accents. When we finally did turn around, we were surprised to find a couple of right wallies showing us how it was done. And from that day on, I realised that to be successful with a member of the opposite sex, you didn't necessarily have to have the looks, providing you had the chat, and put their success down to their confident Cockney banter.

Nick and I were having a great first holiday away, and the weather had been kind to us. And even though our success rate with the ladies had been minimal, that evening things were about to change… or so I thought.

Dressed in our best Lancashire finery, we headed out for the evening, still turning heads as we walked into town and confident that our luck was about to change. In the second bar that we visited, we started chatting to a couple of girls, who seemed as keen on us as we had been about them. Nick's long nails were certainly a talking point, and they suggested we all move on to a nightclub they had recommended. The nightclub ended up being a room above a pub that happened to have a disco, but the night was going well, and at least the DJ hadn't stopped the music this time on our arrival.

We sat in a corner and carried on chatting when suddenly Roxy Music came on. Nick and I headed for the floor, surprised that our new friends hadn't followed us, so we only danced to that one song and then went to sit back down. We had literally just made it back, when the two girls got up and started to dance to some disco record. To be fair, they had asked us to join them, but dancing to disco was not on our agenda. This scenario happened a couple more times, where we got up to dance to music we liked, and they did the same. Remembering the saying 'Treat them mean, keep them keen', I imagined that they would no doubt see us as a bit of a challenge. But I couldn't have been more wrong. When our song finished, we turned to find they were sitting in a totally different place with a couple of different lads (no doubt who liked disco).

My only other clear memory of that holiday was being invited to a party in a beach house, after the pubs had closed. And I recall a group of young people walking in with Cockney accents and wearing Paisley scarfs, which I thought looked the business. The London Mods had arrived, and they seemed way ahead of us (well, me, anyway). Also, just when I thought that they couldn't have been any cooler, they changed the music and put on *Tired of Waiting* by The Kinks. This was the first time I had heard the song, and I fell in love with it that very moment.

We'd had a brilliant night, and a brilliant holiday, but I knew it was time to up my game.

Back to reality, it had felt strange starting work at Crown under my dad's guidance. Everybody seemed very friendly, even though I knew that my dad, being their boss, may have helped. I was on my best behaviour, and tried my utmost to follow the rules and complete all the tasks I had been given.
I had to wear a white lab coat during the day, and felt at the time that it was a really good job. For lunch I would join my dad over at Crown House, along with other managers and directors sitting on the same table. The food was awesome, and for a three-course meal it only cost around 20p. I did feel as though the lunchtime conversation went way over my head (my fault, not theirs), and I was most certainly a fish out of water.

One of the younger members of my dad's team, Brendon, would sometimes kindly offer to give me a lift back over to Blackburn on the occasions when my dad would have to work late. The problem with this was that Brandon owned a 1000cc Harley Davidson, and I'd sit on the back in my parka, clinging on for dear life, and hoping to God that nobody would recognise me on that contraption – even though I did appreciate his offer.

One day during my morning break, I was looking through that week's NME magazine when I came across a small advert advertising a trip to Paris to see The Jam live for £34. Now that I was earning my own money, this felt as good a reason as any to book my first trip abroad. I just needed to find some likeminded person to come with me.

The highlight of our social activities around this time was our weekly visit to Blackburn Rugby Club. It was only a small function room overlooking the rugby pitches, but what a night. Every Saturday the same crowd (mainly from the area) would queue up around the building, with their membership card in one hand and their chosen vinyl in the other. The great thing was you were encouraged to bring down your own records, and my vinyl of choice was usually Department S/*Going Left Right* (the B side of *Is Vic There?*), The Jam/*The Great Depression*, Dolly Mixture/*Been Teen*, and The Beat/*Twist and Crawl*.

Even though I used to go to the club with my mates, I would meet up with other fellow mods Kev, Kershy, Johnny V, and Cass. Cass was the Ace Face around Brownhill at that time and was the first one of us lot to own a scooter– a blue Vespa P200E.

Paul Ryan was another weekly regular and was a top lad, but it always annoyed me that he not only looked more like Paul Weller than I did, but he was also a far better dancer (not hard). We would always head to the dance floor for the same tunes, and he always had his best mates Roy and Sammy ever-present. Paul was most certainly singing from the same hymn sheet as myself, so I asked him if he fancied coming to Paris with me, and to my delight he told me yes.

After the experience of seeing 999 at King George's Hall, attending live concerts became a regular part of my social life. Through the Students' Union at college, I booked to see The Who at Deeside Leisure Centre in Wales. I went dressed in my parka but felt slightly concerned when I found myself surrounded by Rockers, wearing scruffy biking jackets and covered in beer towels. (What is that all about?) The Who were outstanding, with Kenny Jones on drums, John Entwistle playing the bass like it had been part of his body, and Townsend and Daltrey living up to all my expectations, for sure.

I also attended Lancaster University to watch The Boomtown Rats, who I loved back then. Geldof was on form, with his 'in your face' attitude and stage swagger, but even he was overshadowed by the two people having sex by the side of me. I remember turning my head to check out the audience behind me, only to discover a lad and a girl participating in full blown sexual intercourse standing up, whilst Bob shouted out the lyrics to *She's So Modern* from the stage.

Having a venue like King George's Hall on our doorstep was an absolute blessing, as every touring band worth its salt would add the venue to their list of tour dates. I am not sure we appreciated this at the time, as we probably just took it for granted that at some stage our favourite acts would be playing our town. Having always been a huge Buzzcocks fan, I am sure I would have been one of the first people to purchase my ticket to see them, once their gig had been announced. The pub across the road from the venue, and the one part responsible for me failing college, was always packed on the night of a gig, and was where you would arrange to meet folk for a pre-gig beer. Standing in front of the stage, in the middle, I always buzzed off the atmosphere of all the Punks pogoing, but was never a fan of the spitting, and on this particular occasion, it seemed that I wasn't the only one.

Buzzcocks frontman Pete Shelley, had already warned the crowd a couple of times to 'stop f****** spitting', but the lad who was jumping up and down next to me totally ignored this warning, and had continued gobbing in his direction. Just as the band was halfway through their song *Boredom*, suddenly the drummer, John Maher, jumped from behind his kit and ran to the front of the stage. And with all the energy that he still had left, he proceeded to throw one of his sticks towards the offending moron standing next to me. However, on this occasion, John's aim had been pretty poor, and the next thing I felt was an excruciating pain in the centre of my forehead. Within seconds, a giant lump had appeared directly above my eyes, and I started to feel dizzy and sick. The band continued to finish their song, and I recall Mick Fox helping me to the back of the hall to sit down, which is where I remained until the end of the concert. I remember telling this story to Pete Shelley several years later, and mentioned that if it had happened now, I could have sued John, but I am not sure how Pete had taken it.

On another occasion, Jez and I went into the box office to buy two Stiff Little Fingers tickets for that evening's gig, when a bloke appeared and asked if we would like to work the show. He said we would get free tickets, meet the band, and also get paid. This was a no-brainer, so we said yes straight away.
We were both given access-all-area passes and spent the rest of the day lugging giant amps about and helping the rest of the roadies

to set up the band's equipment. We briefly met the band, and then got a taxi home to freshen up and get changed (and rest). To my disappointment, Jez had decided not to return, saying that it was far too hard work. He had a point but, really, this was SLF we were talking about!

On my arrival back at the venue, a pretty scary looking Punk had noticed my MCP crew pass that had been stuck onto my jacket and asked me outright to give it to him. I could tell by the way he was staring at me that this wasn't a joke, so thinking quickly, I explained to him that I had needed it to get back in, as I was working. But I promised him that I would throw it down to him from the open window at the top of the building, providing he didn't move. Lancashire's dumbest Punk fell hook, line, and sinker for this Mod's tales, but I remember worrying all the way through the show whether a certain Mohican would be still standing waiting for me, in the same spot, after the concert.

When the support band finished, I was called up on stage to move a monitor and can still remember the dirty looks I seemed to be getting from the row of Punks standing at the front. The main act was brilliant, but the second it was over, I was summoned to start carrying amps and monitors (that I could barely lift) as we were told to clear the stage as quickly as possible.

To be fair, a couple of the band members had helped us out with moving the gear, and Henry Cluney even gave me a bottle of beer. I had planned to keep it as a souvenir, but as we were standing in the office waiting to get paid, it fell out from under my jacket, and one of the crew claimed it. While I enjoyed my experience of being a roadie, it's fair to say that this was my first, and definitely my last, time in that role.

The following week The Undertones were in town, and for the weeks leading up to it I had been playing their new album, *Positive Touch*, constantly to get me in the mood. I still had my MCP crew pass from the Fingers gig, so I was sorted, or so I thought.

On the day of the gig, I went down to King George's late afternoon in an attempt to attend the soundcheck. I was sitting in the balcony on my own, when about three songs in, a couple of burly looking security blokes started to make their way towards me from either end of the row. At the time there had been several security rumours going round regarding the IRA and Irish bands, so I presumed it was something to do with that. One of the blokes asked me what I was doing there, and I confidently pointed out my MCP crew pass to him, imagining that would be that. Wrong! What I hadn't realised was that this Undertones concert was not an MCP production, and I was grabbed by the collar of my jacket and booted out of the nearest fire exit (literally) and ended up back on the street.

I was gutted to miss the gig. This certainly hadn't been a positive touch, but I had definitely learnt my lesson.

CHAPTER FOUR

GIRL ON THE PHONE

It was still a couple of months before we needed to pick up our French phrase book and dig out our passports, so life just carried on as normal(ish). I had started seeing a girl who was in my brother's year at school. I use the term 'seeing' very loosely, as the arrangement that we had was that we would see each other during the week, but at weekends we would do our own thing. At first this seemed a pretty good idea, but it felt a little strange on a Monday when she would go into detail about what she had got up to on the Saturday night.

Her name was Yvonne, and at the time my personal preference had certainly been small, blonde, with certain assets. She had managed to tick all the boxes for essentials and desirables, so for the time being the job was hers.

My mum used to have her own ideas about most of my friends, but she liked Simon, as he was a doctor's son. Whenever he called round to our house, my mum would always take him to one side and ask him to make sure that I didn't get into any trouble. Simon would find this hilarious, as he had always admitted to being a bit of a nutter, and if there was any trouble to be had, he would be at the front of the queue. My mate Jez was a no-no, which was funny, as I had always felt that his mum believed me to be the bad influence.

Jez would have this thing where he would walk up and down local railway tracks, searching for these small, round, green detonators, which would explode if you dropped something heavy on them. He also made the local paper for dragging a park bench across a local bowling green, which had not impressed me as my Grandad had been a keen bowler.

Yvonne had been the first female that I had actually taken home to officially meet my parents, and we would spend most of our time locked away upstairs in my room. I would never have been allowed to have a lock on my door, so the routine was to place something heavy behind it and place the latest Jam album on my record player. The snazzy thing about record players then was that you would place your record onto the turntable, lift up the arm, and it would play that side continuously, without you having to go back over to it. My mum and dad were slightly older than a lot of my friends' parents and held pretty old-fashioned views when it came to girlfriends and sex, and I can't believe, looking back, that I got away with as much as I did whilst growing up.

Yvonne used to live with her mum at the bottom of a really steep hill, and I always preferred her coming to ours at night, as whenever I went to her house, the walk back home was a killer. I don't remember what the straw was that broke the camel's back, but my mum decided that I was no longer allowed to spend my evenings locked away in my bedroom with Yvonne, so I needed a plan B, which came in the form of my Grandma and Grandad's house. There was a good chance that my mum would have pre-warned my Grandma about Yvonne, so the first night I took her round to Cornelian Street to meet them, I introduced her as Cathy. Of course, I felt terrible about lying to my grandparents (and feel even worse now writing it down), but needs must. I was a young lad who appreciated my newfound freedom, so who could really blame me?

My Grandma seemed to like 'Cathy' and would more or less leave us alone in the front bedroom most evenings. But just in case, I used to position the large electric fire behind the door as a Do Not Disturb sign.

Around this time, we had started attending the local cinemas more often – soppy films with Yvonne, even though the storyline didn't really matter on the night; and more laddish films with my mates. Unit Four at Little Harwood was our favourite cinema, as it was the most local and it had four small individual rooms. What we tended to do was pay to go and see say a Sinbad movie, and once it had started, sneak into a Bruce Lee film next door. This would almost always work, and I couldn't even tell you how many times I watched each movie by doing this. I remember we would always walk out of the cinema thinking we were really hard, attempting to replicate all Bruce's moves as we walked home.

Eventually we decided to up the ante, and ended up swapping Jeet Kun Do for sex. 'Confessions of...' films, which starred Robin Askwith, became our new choice in celluloid: *Confessions of a Window Cleaner, a Taxi Driver, a Holiday Camp;* you get the drift. These movies were a step up from the Carry On films and played an important role in our adult education.

As far as dirty films go, the one that had the biggest reputation was *Emmanuelle*, starring Sylvia Kristel. We noticed that Unit Four were due to screen it in a couple of weeks, which was just enough time for me and Simon to plan how we were going to blag our way in. We always had to keep our wits about us, as we had to remember one date of birth to enable us to travel on the bus for half price, and a different one to gain entry at the cinema to watch an X-rated movie.

The day in question was glorious and sunny, so my decision to wear my navy-blue snorkel jacket was not one of my best. Just as we were about to enter the cinema, I zipped my hood up all the way (just like Kenny from South Park) so that the staff wouldn't be able to see the whole of my face properly. As it turned out, the cinema staff were unable to see any of my face, as my zip had somehow managed to get jammed. We walked up to the ticket desk, and the lady behind the counter said, 'Let us see your face then.' I tried my utmost to casually pull down my zip, but it failed to move.

The situation was getting more embarrassing by the second, but try as I might, the darn thing was well and truly stuck. By now the two women on the ticket desk had both taken turns at having a quick tug, but there was zero movement. They then resorted to ringing the manager from upstairs, who also came down and had a go. Just as I had given up on any hope of us being allowed in, the manager said, 'Oh, just let them in. At least they'll get a cheap thrill.' I never wore my snorkel jacket again for the cinema.

The first proper nickname I remember being given was Buzby, who was a yellow (later orange) talking cartoon bird, launched in 1976 by the Post Office/BT. His catchphrase (spoken by Bernard Cribbins) was 'Make someone happy with a phone call' which is exactly what I tried to do, mainly Yvonne. And I must admit, I did tend to be on the phone a lot more than the average human being.

No mobiles back then, though. I had to rely on red phone boxes – even though most at the time had been vandalised and didn't work – pub telephones, or our phone at home. The Farthings pub used to have a phone on the wall in the corridor to the male toilets, and I was never off it. At home, we had a cream dial telephone that used to sit on a table right at the end of the hall, next to the front door. I was constantly receiving lectures off my parents about the number of times I was using it, and about the size of the phone bills. Eventually they decided to put a small silver lock on it, which was a bit of a pain, but it didn't take me long to work out that Mum's nail file that she kept in the bathroom would open the lock with very little effort.

I used to wait until my mum was busy baking in the kitchen (at the other end of the hall) then I'd sneak up to the phone, take off the lock with the file, call the number, and then replace the lock. As soon as my mum heard a conversation going on, she would step outside the kitchen. And before she had a chance to question me, I would shout, 'Mum, they called me!' I managed to get away with this blag for several months, until she became wise and purchased a different lock. So I just found a different nail file.

Jez had bought himself a Vespa scooter with the money he was earning from his job at Whitbread, and everybody was impressed with it (in our circles anyway). It had a fantastic custom spray paint design on each side panel and was one of the coolest scooters around. Paul at The Farthings was a huge scooter buff, and had always bought scooters and done them up. His current pride and joy was a Lambretta GC200, with a Bass logo spray paint job on the side panel.

I don't recall why I became a member of the Red Rose Scooter Club in Accrington, and not the Blackburn Moderators, but it may have been because someone that I always used to see at Jam gigs had invited me over to check out his club. Red Rose used to meet at the Greyhound pub in Accrington every Sunday lunchtime, so I would always try to attend. Mainly we would just chat about the latest Jam concert, scooter rally, or Mod release, and I remember booking onto a coach trip they had organised to go and watch The Jam play at Michael Sobel Sports Centre in London.

The date was Saturday, 12th December, 1981, and for just £4.50 we would also be treated to Bananarama, The Questions, and Dept S.

Inside the venue, I noticed a C.N.D. stall giving out badges and leaflets, as the campaign for Nuclear Disarmament was prominent at that time, and even Weller had been snapped wearing the badge, so obviously I grabbed one. The hall was vast, and the sound was nothing to write home about, but I enjoyed the gig. The Jam had started their 21-song set with *The Gift* (probably my least favourite of theirs), and ended with a favourite *When You're Young as* the evening's entertainment had drawn to an end.

The weather had been terrible, with it being December, and there was snow and ice everywhere. But the one thing I will never forget is how cold it was on the very long journey back up North. In fact, I can categorically confirm that it was the most freezing I had (or have) ever been in my life.

Blackburn Moderators would have their meetings in the Galligreaves pub, and the Vulcan pub, which I always though was a strange choice of venue, as it was a well-known hangout for bikers. The scooter club members used to meet upstairs, and I don't remember any trouble between the two groups, but I am pretty sure there must have been at some stage.

I do remember one of their group coming over to me in the library café and threatening to kick my head in, because I had been sat there in my parka. But I was holding the Punk album *Hanx* by SLF, so maybe I had made the right choice after all in pledging my allegiance to Accy.

At the end of the day, I was a Mod (by choice), but I wasn't going to start pretending that I had suddenly stopped loving my old Punk records that I had spent the past few years collecting, because somebody with a crap haircut told me that I couldn't like both.

When it came to The Jam, they had an unbelievably loyal following, and I would bet that anyone who loved them back in the day would still have that love for them now. I feel this had a lot to do with the band doing all that they could to break down the usual barriers between the artist and their audience. They were well known for letting fans into their soundchecks, and they would always take the time to chat to their audience before and after their gigs.

Also, most of what they were singing about was relevant; current issues that young people could relate to. A lot of the acts up until then had gone out of their way to put up a barrier between themselves and the people who paid to watch them. Especially during the Prog Rock phase, as they would prance around the stage in their terrible outfits, thinking and believing that they were some sort of demigods, and their only personal interaction was after the show when one of their road crew would hand-select girls (groupies) to take backstage.

There was none of that nonsense with The Jam. They were our band, who appreciated that without our support, they wouldn't have been doing what they were doing. I would analyse every outfit they wore and every one of their lyrics, listening carefully to everything that Weller had to say. Because for me, I could relate to it, and it all made sense.

I remember reading an interview that Paul had done for some magazine, and the journalist had asked him what he wanted their music to mean to their fans. He explained that if you were a housewife doing the cleaning, hoovering, and household chores, and a Jam song came on the radio, it may make her say 'F*** it' and throw the hoover down and seek an alternative. Sexist as that may seem today, I didn't feel for one second that Paul meant it that way, and I fully got it (and still do).

The band played my local venue in Blackburn three times, in '78, '79, and '80. The first time they arrived at King George's Hall, to perform on the same stage that The Beatles and Bowie had stood on, I remember nicking off school so that I could try and talk my way into their soundcheck. The date was Monday, 12th June, and two English pounds is all it cost to gain entry. I recall standing in a long queue outside King George's, and a couple of Punks coming over and asking me to give them my ticket. I explained that I hadn't bought one yet, as that was the reason I was standing there. I don't think they believed me, but it did the trick and they walked away to pester some other poor sod.

The Jolt were the support on the night, and were pretty good, but The Jam were incredible and almost blew the roof off the venue with their fast-paced energetic delivery. (This was my band for sure.)

Wednesday, 12th December saw the band return to the venue, and tickets were the pricey sum of £3 this time. It was part of their Setting Sons tour to help promote the album. This was actually an MCP production, but there was no way I was about to try my luck again and risk missing out.

I had rushed home from school excited, shoved my tea down, and changed into the smartest outfit I owned at the time. Me, Ste H, Jez, and Nicky, all met at Chris Almond's house on Langham Road, and then headed down to the venue. We heard that the band had been drinking in the Star and Garter on the boulevard around teatime, and I was gutted to have missed out. The Vapors were the evening's support, and they were quality. Their singer,

Dave Fenton, gave me a blue Vapors badge as he entered the building, which I still have and occasionally wear.

The Jam, as always, were amazing and were spurred on by the parka-wearing Northern crowd singing 'We are the Mods' throughout. I managed to take a couple of decent photos of the band, which I still cherish, as I have never seen any others from that night.

During their encore, after they had finished playing *The Modern World*, Paul threw his plectrum into the crowd, and my mate Ste managed to pounce and pick it up before anybody else. Not intending to miss out on this opportunity, I managed to persuade him to sell it to me for 50p. (The best 50p I ever spent.) We waited around afterwards to meet the band, and they very kindly signed both my ticket and my autograph album. Both these sets of signatures from the band of my generation hang proudly on my office wall today, to remind me of when I was young.

Their third visit to Blackburn was on Tuesday, 3rd June, and like the previous year, they had increased the price by £1. I can't actually remember who I went with that night, but for some strange reason I had agreed to go and sit in the balcony with them. The support came from The Expressos, but I can't remember if they were any good or not. I vividly remember The Jam coming on stage to the sound of a ringing telephone in the background. I said, 'See you later' and ran as fast as I could down the stairs to the main hall, just as the words 'Girl on the phone keeps a-ringing back' came out of Weller's mouth.

CHAPTER FIVE

THAT'S ENTERTAINMENT

The first band I remember hanging around with, and trying to help, were locals Faded Image, around 79/80. I already knew some of them from my time spent in the Library café, and I think it was Kershy who had introduced me to them. There was Zolly on drums, Craig (Rooster) on bass, and Kev and Dave Mac on guitar. Dave was the younger brother of Big John, the bass player in Blackburn's very own Power Pop/Punk success The Stiffs, but Faded Image were missing a lead singer. Initially, this was not an issue, as the only song I heard from them up until then was an instrumental version of *House of the Rising Sun* by The Animals. Waker had a school friend called Ash, who lived on East Park Road, and who I felt might be interested. Ash ran a Punk disco at Wesley Hall in town, loved The Stranglers and The Ramones, and although he didn't come across as a full-blown Punk, he had a pretty cool look with his spiky blond hair. Sure enough, my hunch had been correct, and Faded Image had now got themselves a front man.

The first time I saw the band live with Ashley on board was at Zolly's sister's 21st birthday party at the Polish Club. I think I had a crush on Rita at the time, but I managed to keep it to myself. I was impressed and offered to take some photos of them at their next gig. This took place at the prestigious Oswaldtwistle Civic Hall, at the Valentine's disco, and after the band had played, some young girls came over and asked me for my autograph. I tried to explain that I had not been in the band and that I was only the photographer, but it didn't seem to matter. They still insisted that they had wanted it. This was a lightbulb moment for me, and I started to realise that being involved in this music thing and hanging around with bands wasn't a bad idea. I believe that very moment set the foundation for my future passion, and adventures in the scene.

The date was Tuesday, 24th February, 1981, and in two days' time my beloved Jam were performing in Paris. Paul and I were on the train to the big smoke, as the coaches were picking us up at Victoria Coach Station the following day. We had decided to sneak into first class for the journey down to London, but it hadn't taken long before a very bad-tempered guard spotted us and threw us out.

We hadn't booked anywhere to stay for the evening, but if you could show the police your ticket to prove future travel for the following day, they would allow you stay on Euston Station overnight.

I was dressed in a long, dark blue leather jacket, light blue Sta-Prest trousers, a standard Fred Perry shirt, the Shelley's Jam stage shoe, and black wraparound sunglasses. And to this day, one of my favourite ever photographs of myself is lying on a bench that night, sleeping under a plaque of the Queen, using a plastic bag as a pillow on Euston Station.

I don't know what it is about me always managing to attract the attention of Punks wherever I go, but this time was no exception. The first thing I saw that morning once I had managed to open my eyes was a guy with a big Mohican peering down at me. The first words to come out of his mouth were, 'Are you a Mod?' On almost every other occasion, my reply would have been sarcastic, but something told me that in this instance, sarcasm would not have been my best move.

I simply replied. 'Yes, why?' To which he asked, 'Can I have your blue trousers?'

I tried to explain to this rather odd human being the reasons why I needed to keep possession of my pants, and he seemed to accept them. I do remember that him and his mates offered to show us around Carnaby Street, but Paul very wisely declined the offer.

This was my first time on a ferry, and I spent most of it sitting on the floor next to the bar, feeling queasy. The gig had been moved from its original venue of Pavilion on Baltard, to Ouverture Des Portes, as there had been rumours going round regarding French skinheads and possible trouble.

We were absolutely buzzing, as it was our first time abroad, watching our favourite band, and Mods everywhere. Support had come from Guest Star and Bikini, and then eventually, Paul, Bruce, and Rick took to the stage and opened with *Dreamtime*. There had been a bit of trouble before the gig, and I vaguely remember Weller saying something over the microphone and getting the perpetrators thrown out, before starting off again with David Watts.

The gig was brilliant, as was being in a foreign country, watching your favourite band from back home. And when Paul tied a Union Jack around his microphone stand (in defiance of any trouble, maybe), the place erupted, and I really did feel that I was a part of his gang.

After delivering a 13-song set with two encores, *Heatwave*, *Tube Station*, and ending with *'A' Bomb in Wardour Street*, it was all over. I had managed to take a couple of okay photos, which had been tough standing at the front of a very excited crowd, and we both felt that we had just experienced something pretty special. To this day, it remains in my top five greatest ever gigs attended.

Outside, the rumours of trouble had materialised, and the first thing we saw as we left the venue was a large group of short-haired youths walking in line towards us. Without exaggeration, I have never witnessed scenes as violent as what happened next. As we hurriedly attempted to find our coach and take our seats, whilst still in one piece, there was a full-blown riot happening just inches away from us. I would guess that 30-50 French Skins, many with baseball bats, were randomly attacking anyone who they considered to be English.

We somehow managed to find and board our coach, but couldn't believe our eyes when we realised that the coach next to ours had been completely burnt out. We watched in horror as the French police started attacking the coach driver with their batons. They were hitting and attacking anyone they thought had travelled, blatantly ignoring the Skins who had started all the trouble in the first place. I don't mind admitting that both Paul and I were scared to death by this incident, and by what might happen next. I have no idea at all how the people on the burnt-out coach managed to get out, but we certainly didn't need any more hints about not being welcome, and we managed to flee the scene.

As part of our ticket deal, we were supposed to now have a sightseeing trip around the city before heading back to the ferry, but this was cancelled due to the trouble. I did feel a little cheated at the time, but to be fair, we had only really travelled to see The Jam, and I agreed that we had definitely seen enough Parisian sights for one day.

We arrived back to Victoria, and made our way over to Euston, not believing that things could possibly get any worse. But as we were checking the boards for our train time, three police officers came over and asked us to follow them into their station room. We were both baffled, as we stood in a very small police room, being shouted at (what felt like an interrogation at the time) as if they had been filming a scene from *The Sweeney*. I one hundred per cent felt that we were about to be beaten up, as the officers were becoming more aggressive by the minute, but luckily no physical violence took place.

Eventually it became apparent that our friendly Mohican and his two sidekicks were wanted by the police in connection with robbing the fruit machines on the station, and they had been after them for weeks. The police had spotted us on the security cameras talking to them that morning, and thought we were part of their gang. We were shocked, and even more shocked at how long it took to convince them that we had nothing at all to do with it, or them.
We told them everything we knew and were highly relieved when they said we could go. We were sitting waiting for our train back

to Preston to set off when I noticed those very same Punks walking up and down the platform, as though they were looking for us. I remember us both crouching down in our seats, and praying for the driver to set off, back to some sort of normality. We finally arrived home safe and knackered, but what had become apparent (to me, at least) was that going to watch a live band was never quite as straightforward as turning up, watching the show, and then going home. But it hadn't put me off.

Like most locals, The Farthings certainly had its characters, and the more we attended, the more we discovered whose seat we hadn't to sit in, and whose glass you couldn't drink from. We had Stan the man, Ray the cue, and a guy called Graham, who looked and acted like he was a member of The Bee Gees but ended up borrowing some money off Paul (the landlord) and then disappeared, never to be seen again. There were two brothers who used to put all their day's (week's) wages into the fruit machines, and then go out to the cash machine and come back in and do the same again.

I must admit that these machines were pretty addictive, and even though I was never obsessed, I would always make sure that I had enough cash for a few beers and for a few goes on the bandits.
Jez, on the other hand, once sold his beloved Timex watch so that he could have a few more plays.
Matt and Al were well known to all the regulars for getting all the girls. Al had the chat and reputation, and Matt was one of the best-looking lads around. One corner of the pub was named 'Hayley's Corner', as a young girl called Hayley would come in every night around teatime and just sit there for hours, waiting for Al. Sometimes he showed up, and sometimes he didn't, but she would stay seated, just in case.

We had the legendary Ness behind the bar, and of course Paul and Christine steering the ship. Nicky would tell us that he was head barman, but even though he lived about 30 seconds away, he would always be the last person to turn up for work. Bullinge and

Ste also ended up working there, and even though my preference was always on the other side of the bar, I was always invited to join the staff for their after-hours drinks' session. This was fun, because once the customers had left, you would receive a complimentary pint, a bag of crisps of your choice, and would spend the following hour gossiping about which of the regulars was sleeping with who.

Friday lunchtime, like clockwork, the majority of The Farthings' customers – male and female, and including the landlord – would travel up the road to The Ousebooth pub, off St James Road, for their Friday lunchtime entertainment, i.e., the stripper. The secret was always to discreetly stand at the back, or you could find yourself sitting at the front on a wooden stool, covered in baby oil (like Ste did). Friday at the Ousebooth, and Sunday at the Sett End; that was the kind of local entertainment on offer in the 80s.

Tradition would usually dictate that on a Saturday lunchtime we would usually meet at The Clarence pub in town. The place was renowned for its sticky carpets, and your feet would stick to the floor as you walked.

The first club myself and Jez managed to get entry to was the infamous Top Hat Club at the bottom of Shear Brown. The Top Hat had a fierce reputation for trouble and was referred to locally as the 'Flying Bottle' (for reasons far too apparent). Jez talked me into giving it a try, and it certainly was an eye-opener. You would walk inside the door and up a steep flight of stairs, where some nasty looking bouncers would eye you up as you passed. I recall a very dark, smallish room in one part, with several TV sets on the wall showing hard core porn as if it was standard. In the larger room, the DJ was playing a tune to three people, so I don't think we hung around for long.

I remember a guy I used to work with telling me that once he was up there, a lady had come over to him from the bar and asked him if he wanted to dance. Having noticed that she had been with her partner, he politely declined her offer. The next thing he knew, the lady's husband marched over, threatening to throw him down the stairs and asking him what was wrong with his wife. I think that about sums it up.

The Rugby Club was still the hottest ticket our end of town, but the word had spread, and people who had never attended before started showing up. This led to far too many people turning up than could actually fit in the room, so something had to change. Some Saturday nights we would queue up for ages outside, and still not get in.
This new clientele would sometimes cause trouble, which had never happened before, so we started to go down extra early (after *Blind Date*), with our membership card in hand, to even stand a chance of gaining entry.
Ant Grogan was in his bondage pants, Nancy looking like Siouxsie Sioux, with her best mate Christine, and Scouse with his over-stretched sleeves once he hit the dancefloor. The Philips sisters (Claire, Julia, and Karen) would always attend, as would Paul, Roy, and Sammy – Paul looking more like Paul Weller every week, much to my annoyance.
I had got to know a couple of the rugby players, Mick and Kev. A couple of years ago, somebody told me that Kev ended up being Princess Diana's security guy, and that on the day of her fatal accident, he had taken the day off. Whether that story is true or not, I couldn't tell you, as the last time I saw Kev was waking up the morning after a party at Lark Hill flats back in the 80s, both with terrible hangovers. Then he moved to Germany and joined the Army.

My friend Chris Penny was a Punk, but not one of those with an in-your-face attitude or searching for trouble. He was the funniest person I knew, and without him, I would not have appreciated how effective the act of sarcasm can be. Chris – or Chris Crass, as he later became known (due to his love of the band) – was certainly not a rugby player, but would always attend.

I met Chris through drinking in our local, and he was dating fellow Punk, Yaz. They were definitely the Sid and Nancy of

Rosewood Avenue at the time, and I always remember somebody putting *Real Dead Ringer for Love* on the pub jukebox, and the pair of them having everybody transfixed as they carried out the whole lip-syncing video routine, whilst prancing around the pool room. Even now, I always chuckle to myself whenever that song comes on.

Chris really liked a drink, and many a time he would follow me home after The Farthings had closed, in an attempt to try and talk me into nicking a bottle of my mum and dad's wine, which they used to keep in their bedroom. I think the most worrying time was once when I was round at his, and I was just sitting on his kitchen unit chatting to him, when suddenly he opened the washing machine door, and went and fetched the family cat. I recall jumping down and standing in front of the machine, explaining to him that there was no scenario where he was going to end up giving his pet a spin.
He just laughed and told me he was only joking, and to be fair, I believed him.

One particular night at the Rugby Club, I had taken down my S.L.F. album *Hanx*, hoping that the DJ would play the track *Wait and See*. The DJ kept telling me that he would, but it was getting towards the end of the event. I asked my mates Nicky and Karl not to leave without me, as he was just about to play my request. After I left the dancefloor, I couldn't find them anywhere, so I collected my vinyl from the DJ booth and started to make my way up the very dark path that led to the club entrance. I noticed a couple of figures walking towards me, and I think I asked them for the time, to which one of them replied by tupping me in the face and then sitting on me. The two lads had been in the same year as me at school, and one of them was massive (bigger than me in both length and width), so there was no way I was about to just push him off. His sidekick hit me on the head with a bottle, but when it didn't smash, he then attempted to break it on a nearby rock. He dragged my top off and took my wallet out of my back pocket, then they both started taking turns at kicking me in the head.

I remember wondering when the hell they were going to stop, as it seemed to be never-ending. Eventually, a rugby player came out of the club and, seeing what was happening, ran back in to get some more help. Yes, my mates had ignored my request to wait for me; and yes, I was in a bad way. I have no recollection how I made it home.
I remember standing looking at myself in the bathroom mirror, staring at my injuries and crying, as I was such a mess. I had Doc marks all over my head and on my back, and struggled to know what to say once my dad walked in the room.

I found out later that the reason for this unprovoked attack was that the two lads were members of Vausy's gang, and a number of weeks previously, whilst we were playing football down Lammack, Simon had responded to some comments they had hurled at us. But as he had returned to boarding school, I guess I was the next best thing. Wow, Simon had even managed to get my head kicked in, and he wasn't even in the town. Not that my mum would have believed it.

The more folk from other areas showed up at the Rugby Club, the more trouble there seemed to be, and the club finally closed its doors after receiving several complaints, citing fighting and drugs as the reason.

The Farthings was a free house back then, and one day Paul told me that the brewery was planning on selling it. We were all shocked, as it wasn't just our beloved local but Paul and Christine's home. Between us, we managed to devise a plan, and we agreed to make some flyers, asking folk to support us and boycott the place. The majority of the next day was spent avoiding the work I should have been doing, and instead sneaking off to print out hundreds of flyers on the photocopier. I found a guillotine and chopped them up into flyer-sized leaflets, and couldn't wait to head down to the pub that night to proudly show Paul what all my hard work had achieved.
I remember walking in after work and holding out my hands containing a giant pile of the picket leaflets, only for Paul to

explain that they had just received the brilliant news that the brewery had backed down, and the pub was safe (for now). Obviously, I was pleased by this news, as it had been what we had been hoping to achieve anyway, but I was also pretty gutted at having spent most of my day at work printing off leaflets that wouldn't now be needed.

I must admit that things at Crown had started to go downhill for me, and it was 100% my own doing. Remembering this time and writing it down does make me feel a little ashamed, but if I am going to write my story, I am going to be completely honest about the things that happened.

For some reason, after my 20p lunch, I would spend the rest of my dinner hour sat in my dad's office, leaning back in his swivel chair, and using his telephone (when he was out, that is). I would either ring friends or I would call Yvonne, who was doing a hairdressing course at college, so was at home a lot during the week. I knew at the time that other staff must have walked past and thought, *Who the hell does he think he is? Poor George!*

There was also a public phone box outside in the yard, that I used to hog a lot, and staff would refer to me as Buzby. If this wasn't enough, I had got into the habit of sneaking off in the afternoons, which really was out of order. About 2pm, I would find somewhere to hide my lab coat, then take the lift at the back of the lab that took me outside the building. I would then walk sheepishly up the road and wait for the bus to Blackburn, from opposite Johnson's Swimming baths. Once there, I would make my way over to Yvonne's house for some 'afternoon delight'. Then I would head back over to Darwen, up in the lift, retrieve my lab coat, and slide back into work, thinking that nobody would know any different.

After several afternoon visits, Yvonne told me that a neighbour had told her mum that she had been letting a boy in during the day. Her mum had asked them to keep a lookout, so the following day, this boy would make the same journey, but this time I would be wearing my lab coat and holding a tin of Crown's finest emulsion. How I thought I would get away with this behaviour, God only knows, and what made it even worse was that the team were all really nice to me, and it must have been beyond embarrassing for my dad.

Not too long after this, I received a phone call saying that the job had come to an end – something to do with tax purposes, as it had only ever been a temporary post. But I knew I had deserved it. I applied for a job in the factory part of Crown, but that didn't last long. The role was to stand by a conveyor belt and place lids on full tins of paint as they passed at record speed – but I struggled to keep up.

I did feel like I had totally messed up (for the sake of biology), as it was a great place to work, a decent wage, and the chance of it being a job for life. The thing that I did take away from my Crown experience was how much my dad was respected by his staff, and that you didn't have to bawl and shout just because you were the boss. One day, someone would ask if they could finish early, and he would say yes. And on other occasions he might ask them if they were able to stay behind a little later to finish a job. This was give and take, and a mutual respect for each other – and I never forgot it. (Just a shame that I never showed any!)

The 'in' movies at the time (in with us, anyway) were films like *Porky's, Lemon Popsicle, Hot Bubblegum, Animal House,* and *Bachelor Party*. And basically, the storyline was about young lads (mainly Italian American} spending all their time trying to get laid. These movies were never going to take home an Oscar or a Golden Globe, but they were titillating fun for lads of our age. The thing I realised from these films was that when they had a party, they had a party! We had been to several house parties back then, and some had been okay, but nothing at all like the ones we witnessed on the big screen. This seemed unfair to me, and I was determined to do something about it. My initial plan was to hire a local hotel room and throw a mental party, but every hotel I tried to book turned me down. Plan B was to have it at our house when my parents were away, but I had already been warned off such activities, due to previous incidents.

As I have already mentioned, my mum was a very keen baker, and every weekend she would bake all sorts of goodies for the family (and my mates). She would make currant buns, pies, fancy biscuits, and cakes. A favourite of my mates was definitely her chocolate shortbreads, or as Birchy christened them 'Fudgerydoos'! We would have around six tins stacked up in the kitchen next to the back door, and every time my mates would visit, they would help themselves to a handful. My personal favourite was her wimberry pies, hands down. My mum would always make a couple of pies every week – rhubarb, blackcurrant, apple (my dad's favourite), strawberry (my second choice), plum, and wimberry.

One particular Sunday, she had a bowl of plums on the side of the kitchen worktops, waiting for her to return from Blackburn Northern, watching the cricket. My mates had been round playing snooker in our back room, where we had a very small snooker table that would sit on top of our dining table. We were playing a knockout game – one minute you had a shot, and then had to wait until all the others had taken theirs. In between my silky skills, I remember walking into the kitchen and noticing that the bowl that had once been full of plums was now empty. I started to ask everyone if they had moved the plums for a laugh, but nobody owned up. And before I could ask again, I heard my dad's Vauxhall Viva pull up outside the house.

I knew that it was too far-fetched to expect my mum not to notice that the plums were missing, and sure enough the front door opened, and it took her about ten seconds to walk into the kitchen and ask me where they had gone, as she was about to make a pie. Saying the first thing that came into my head, I told her, 'Mum, you are not going to believe this, but we were all in the other room playing snooker, and Mark's dog May must have walked into the kitchen, without us noticing, stood up on two legs against the worktop, and somehow managed to knock the bowl over with her paw and eat all the plums.'

That very second, and with Pythonesque comedy timing, my dad appeared at the kitchen door, and said, 'It must have been a bloody clever dog, it has spit all the pips into the bin!' It's still my favourite story ever.

This was not the only time I attempted to put the blame on a particular golden Labrador. The last time my parents had been away, Yvonne had stayed. This particular evening, we had been winding each other up – no idea why – and it came to a climax after I threw a very small amount of cold tea at her. I would like to say that this spur-of-the-moment action was not something I had ever done before, or since, and I thought she might have seen the funny side. I couldn't have been more wrong. She jumped up, ran into the kitchen, and produced a bread knife from out of the drawer.

We had a downstairs toilet, and I just about managed to run and lock myself in it before Yvonne made it to the door. She appeared to be getting more and more angry by the second, and started to kick the bottom of the door, whilst shouting for me to come out. I tried to reason with her and explain that whilst she had a large knife in her hand, I wouldn't be coming out, but this seemed to wind her up even more. So she just carried on kicking and hitting the door, whilst I stayed put.

Once things had settled down and I had apologised (about 40 times), I came out of the toilet to find that the bottom of the door was covered in kick marks and scratches. My plan was to buy some varnish from John's Cut Price the following morning, thinking this would cover up the marks. Unknown to me, though, my parents had decided to come back from their holidays a day early and noticed the damaged door within seconds of entering the hallway. I explained that Mark had been around with his dog, and whilst he had been using the toilet, May had continuously scratched at the door (with those deadly paws again), waiting for him to come out. No sarcastic comment this time from my dad; just a comment of disbelief from my mum.

Back to the party idea. Learning from my previous mistakes while my parents were away, and astounded that they even trusted me alone again, I promised myself that even though I had intended the party to be memorable, I would make sure that everything would be tidied up before they returned. The thing was that I broke the golden rule of only inviting people that you know to your house party, right from the start. Even though Facebook hadn't been invented back then, it never took long for the news to get out about some free entertainment. My mate Steven was pretty good with electronics and worked out that if he obtained several starter motors from fluorescent lights and attached them to the lightbulbs throughout the house, they would constantly flash on and off all through the evening, giving it a disco effect.

I had purchased some coloured bulbs to replace the boring white ones, and we had all chipped in for as many cans of beer as we could afford. And of course, there was the secret stash of wine in my parents' room. Robin was at university in Newcastle, which made it impossible for me to blame him for anything that may go wrong.

It was a Friday night, and the house was beginning to fill up from early on. Even though I don't recall who was playing the music, we had made a DJ stand by using my mum's sideboard turned the opposite way round with my brother's record player on the top, to encourage everyone to start dancing. I would not recommend it to anyone, but we sort of had an open-door policy, as in folk who were walking past and heard the music would be welcomed in.

My friend, Karl, had grabbed a kitchen knife (not sure if it was the same one) and threatened to slit his wrists over the fact that Waker was now seeing Mary. He had drunk far too many cans of Harp lager for anyone to reason with him, so the way this sensitive situation was handled was that Mark's brother, Andy, and my next-door neighbour Dave lifted Karl up, threw him onto the front garden, and told him that he couldn't come back into the

party until he got a grip. Not very diplomatic, but then again maybe it was, as it seemed to do the trick.
I ventured upstairs to check if anyone had been in the bedrooms and to see if there was any wine left, but felt sick myself. And as I was lying on my bed, a lad I knew, Nick, appeared and tried to convince me to drink a pint of salty water that he had brought me. Foolishly, I took his advice and ended up throwing up all over my bedroom floor.
People would come and go, until there was only a handful of us left at about 6.30 in the morning.

The biggest mistake I had made, though, was to hold the party the night before my parents were due home from their holiday. What was I thinking? We were all drunk and shattered, but there was no time to go to bed, and no time to tidy up (in that state). Somebody (Waker) suggested going into town and waiting for a café to open, so we could have a full English breakfast to help us sober up. Not a smart move, but we made it.

I am ashamed to admit the sight that my parents came back to, and the state of the house that I had just left. They entered the living room to find the door hanging off from its hinges, and to green flashing lights everywhere helping to hide the fag burns on the carpet. Empty beer cans were strewn throughout, and there was none of their wine left. (I blame Chris for that.)
On my return, no matter how much I apologised or grovelled to my mum and dad, I was told that I had to leave, as I was no longer living at 1 Kestrel Close. And who could blame them? Sometimes you don't really appreciate things and realise the effects that your actions might have on others, until you are older and more grown up. And you pray that your own children would never be as disrespectful as you once were at their age.

I moved out of Kestrel Close and moved into 146 Cornelian St, to stay with my Grandma and Grandad. I am not too sure what my Grandad felt about this new arrangement but could tell that my Grandma was happy to have me there. Endless amounts of cooking, a Dansette record player, and an electric blanket on the bed – things weren't that bad after all.

I knew that staying there could only be a temporary arrangement, so I put my name down on the council list for a flat. Being thrown out of my home was one thing, but what I found pretty awkward was that at the time I was still working at Crown Paints, and my dad was still my boss. We were still speaking to each other – we had to – but things were a little strained, to say the least.

The blue Dansette that my grandparents had in the living room under the television was a godsend, and I would play my records on it at every opportunity – mainly The Jam, or The Beatles, as my Grandma pretended that she liked them both. I tried to teach her the lyrics by always singing along loudly, but I reckon she was only saying it to please me. I will never forget the time when a reporter from our local newspaper stopped her in the street and asked her what sort of music she liked. She put herself in line to be nominated for the coolest Grandma around award by answering, '*The Butterfly Collector* by The Jam.' I read the article with such pride, once it had been delivered, and I knew that my constant Chinese water torture of continuously playing my singles must have paid off.

When I wasn't hogging the Dansette, my Grandad would always have the radio on, listening to his classical music, which he obviously loved. But the only time I managed to get him to peer above his newspaper, while I was playing mine, was the time I had put on *Glad to Be Gay* by The Tom Robinson Band. My Grandad went mental, and I had never ever seen him lose his temper before in this way. I don't know if he thought I was trying to tell him something, but he jumped up, grabbed me by my shirt, and physically threw me out of the front door. The only way I managed to get back in was by promising him that I would never play that song again. (Sorry, Tom.)

In those days, folk would always leave their front doors open when they were in, and I always worried that, even though they were my grandparents, one day I might barge in and find them in an uncompromising situation. Luckily, I never did, but I think that was more about how my mind worked, rather than how they behaved. When the front door was locked, I knew that I would usually find them on the top bowling green in Roe Lee Park, as my Grandad Jim loved his crown green bowling and was pretty good at it.

My Grandma's hobby (apart from listening to The Jam) was pottery painting, and she would attend classes every week to develop her painting skills. Every single member of our family was given pieces of her work at one time or the other, and she painted me one plate featuring Bruce Lee, and another of me at a swimming gala.

My mates would still call round, and my Grandma would give them spending money and tell them to spend it wisely. Spend it wisely we did not, and the visits to her local sweet shop (Park Sides) had changed from asking for the penny tray to us asking for boxes of matches.

At this point, can I just deeply apologise to all my friends in the Fire Service for this next section? I am not proud of my actions, but the fact of the matter was that me and Jez were into lighting fires.
Not people's houses or their belongings, but fields and patches of grass.
I remember one time, after we had received our 50p each off Edna, we went straight over to Park Sides and bought 13 boxes of Swan Vesta matches. The shopkeeper didn't even question this, which made it easier for us. Our hiding place was behind a loose rock in the wall at the left-hand side of the gate at 146, and even now I find it impossible to walk past the house without glancing over at that stone that used to cover up all our evidence,

To be fair, we weren't totally reckless. We used to set a small section of grass on fire (usually St Gabriel's fields or at the back of the Knowles Arms pub), but we would always put it out before we wandered off. Sometimes Simon would get involved, if he was home, but it was mainly me and Jez carrying out this moronic act. My Grandma must have wondered why we always smelled of fire and matches, but the 50ps would still be waiting in the secret dish in the front bedroom.

We had a very near miss on one occasion – and we never did it again. I had been lighting bits of grass at the back of the Knowles pub, on the field, and Jez had been jumping on them to put them out. Afterwards, we were walking home up Pleckgate Road when we heard the sound of a fire engine in the distance. We turned around to look, and to our absolute horror, we could see that the field we had just left was ablaze, and what we thought had been put out obviously hadn't! We both felt awful about what we had done, and as it turned out it took three engines to put out that blaze. It was definitely a warning to us both to find a different hobby.

Whilst I was staying at my grandparents' house, they took a holiday to Eastbourne, and I took the opportunity to invite a few friends around on the Saturday night. I knew I couldn't afford to get evicted from yet another house, so I made sure we were pretty well behaved throughout. In fact, the only controversial thing we did all night was to have a game of strip poker, at which I lost.

After I had been living on Cornelian Street for several months, I received a letter from the council telling me that a flat had become available, and I was able to move in. Normally, the waiting list for a flat could take years, but my Grandma told me that she had spoken to someone she knew at the council and had asked them to speed my application through.

CHAPTER SIX

THICK AS THIEVES

My new home would be 90 Livesey Court, at Mill Hill in Blackburn. There were three blocks of high-rise flats at Mill Hill – Griffin Court, Ewood Court, and Livesey Court – and I found myself on the 14th floor of Livesey. On the few occasions that the urine-smelling lift was actually working, I would force myself to use it, as walking up the dark, graffiti-sprayed staircase was arguably more depressing.
At the end of the day, though, this flat had become my new home, so I would have to embrace it.
It had been tough carrying all my belongings up to number 90, but once everything was in, I was pretty settled.

I will admit that I only really concentrated on my one main room – my bedroom, which even though it contained two single beds was used as a sort of living space if folk visited. At times, I did feel like my flat was a bit of a glorified locker, due to the number of times my mates (Jez) asked to borrow my keys, so they (he) could entertain. But it was nearer to my job at Crown, and I didn't really have any other options.

The second weekend I was there, one of my neighbours across the hall called round and invited me to a party at his on the Saturday night. He seemed friendly and looked like Neil from *The Young Ones*. He was clearly a Rocker, and I wasn't too sure if he had been setting me up or not, but I had to show willing, so politely accepted.
Party time arrived, so I made my way across the hall to Neil's flat – and stood out like a sore thumb. I was dressed in my full Mod attire, and every other person in the room had long hair and

was wearing a black leather jacket. I must admit that everyone was friendly enough towards their Mod neighbour, but I did find it a little strange when one of them walked in with a couple of ferrets and let them loose. I initially thought it may have been some sort of Rocker ritual that I was about to witness, but they just seemed to chase them around the room.

The other thing I found strange about Neil's was that against one side of the wall he had a very large stack of speakers, which almost reached the ceiling, but only two of them seemed to work.

A few months later, I read a story in the local paper about a guy who lived in Mill Hill flats, who used to keep all his drugs inside his speakers, and that he had just been sent down. That explained everything, so I guessed I was about to get a new neighbour.

Around the same time, I remember reading about another of my neighbours in the local paper. He had been arrested for having several different bank accounts full of dosh, even though he had been unemployed at the time. A reason for this may have been that at the time the holiday destination of choice (if you lived in Mill Hill, that is) was Switzerland. The wonderful scenic delights of the country were not high on folks' 'to do lists', but shopping was indeed top of their agenda – and in particular sports gear, including brands such as Lacoste, Fila, Ellesse, Adidas, and Sergio Tacchini, which were all sought-after must-haves for any 80s casual around that area.

When I say shopping, however, I use this term very loosely, as no money would actually change hands whilst acquiring these items. Everybody in town was aware of these Swiss trips abroad to nick the latest gear, as half of them would put in orders for themselves.

Even though Jez and I had been best mates from a very young age (same junior school, and both finding out that we had been adopted), he had always been attracted to any sign of trouble. I mean, I was no saint, as you will have already read, but Jez thought that most of my other mates were boring (even though he had grown up with them), and he was always drawn to folk who happened to be up to no good. It didn't take long before

Jez decided that he wanted a piece of the action. After all, he had sold jeans to the Russians during his school trip from St Wilfrid's, back in the 70s, after realising that they had a shortage of denim.

The sports casuals were linked to the individual football gangs of the time. Growing up, the Blackburn End had always had several well-known hard nuts who were more interested in a bit of football violence than actually watching the match. I always remember being round at Jez's one night, having our weekly Subbuteo Challenge, when a 'World in Action' documentary programme came on the telly about football hooligans. They had interviewed a group of Millwall fans, who at the time had the worst reputation in football for kicking off, and to our amazement they said that the only place they feared going to watch their team (or not) was Blackburn.

Blackburn Youth was the group to join in my day, if you weren't that bothered about watching the game, which I was. Naturally, Jez had become involved, so he no longer stood with me on match days, opting to make his own entertainment with his new gang. I would usually have an idea where to find him, though, as I could either follow the sound of chanting 'Youth, Youth, Youth' at the game, or find him loitering down some side street after the match.

A trip to Switzerland was arranged, and Jez's passport had been waiting on the side for days. How it used to work was that one of the travelling group would buy a mate's credit card off them for around £50 (or from someone they knew), and the deal was to ring up and report it missing after about five days. The group would travel first class, drink Dom Perignon, and stay in a top hotel – all of which would be charged to their newly acquired card. At the time, Switzerland did not have any security alarms on their shops, and hadn't yet introduced card machines to check if your card was kosher or not. The group would visit the shop during the day and choose what they wanted, and then return at night with adequate bags for storage. All they had to do was lift the very flimsy metal shutter around the shop, break in, and proceed to fill their holdalls with as much gear as they could cram in. Jez told me on his return that it had been so easy, he could have fallen asleep inside the shop for an hour and still not been caught. They arrived back in Blackburn with their bags full of swag, and sold most of the gear to half the regulars in their local (fulfilling orders). By then, the original card holder had reported it missing, but by now it was far too late.

You'd think that I would have learned from the first house party that I had thrown, but apparently not. I decided to have a party at my flat. The difference this time was that I was determined to stick to my original rule, by only inviting trustworthy people I knew. I was well aware that was the key.

Even though I lived at Mill Hill, sadly I still found the need to visit my beloved Farthings most nights. Getting there on the bus wasn't a problem, but I must admit that on some occasions it was a pretty lonely walk home back to the fourteenth floor. The night before my party I had spent the evening in my local, drinking and having a laugh with my mates. Once last orders had been called, I set off walking on my long journey home.

I walked down Whalley New Road and took a short cut down Whalley Range, past Soko shoes, when I noticed a couple of girls walking on the other side of the road. They shouted something across to me, and not being someone to miss out on an opportunity, I chatted to them for several minutes then invited them to my party the following night. Della and Anne seemed up for it, so I gave them my address and told them that I hoped to seem them there.
Friends +2 had been invited, beer had been bought, and my records were out, so I thought to myself, *What could possibly go wrong?* I had invited whatever neighbours I had managed to contact, as I reckoned that way there was less chance of anyone complaining about the noise.
Mid-evening, and the flat was pretty full, as most of the mates that had said they were coming had actually turned up. Everyone seemed to be getting on, and folk were taking turns putting on the

music. Due to me having a couple of single beds in my main room (the bedroom), it had become quite popular with some of the guests, and Jez was one of the main people using it.

I remember Karl banging on the door and being ignored (due to folk being busy). After a few minutes of this, Jez appeared at the door telling him to go away. Karl would not back down, especially after a beer or ten, and he continued to bang, annoying not only Jez but everyone else. Jez eventually opened the door and proceeded to punch him in the mouth. Karl, being well known by now for causing a bit of drama at a party, said that he was going to kill himself (again), and ran into the bathroom, thinking it was a good idea to put his hand through my Liverpool mirror which I had got off Bullinge's years earlier.

The next thing we heard was a girl I had never seen before, running down the hallway shouting, 'Don't worry, don't worry, I'm a nurse.' She sat Karl down in the middle of the hallway and lifted his arm up in an attempt to stop the bleeding.

Apart from that one incident, I felt that things had been going pretty well, considering. Della and Anne had showed up as they promised, and told me they were just nipping out to go to the chip shop. Up until then, the secret had been to make sure that the lock was on the front door to avoid any unwelcome guests just barging in. Little did I know that after the girls returned from the chippy, they had forgotten to put the latch back on the door. To my disbelief, the front door suddenly burst open, and a line of lads just piled into my flat.

I knew a few of them, but I certainly wouldn't count them as friends. When I questioned what they were doing, I was told that it was all over town that I was having a party at Mill Hill flats, and they went on to inform me that one of them had just been released from prison that day, so was in the mood to let his hair down. I felt at the time that I didn't really have an option, other than to let them stay, as I for one wasn't about to tell them that they had to go.

The music was very loud and everyone, except Karl, had been getting into the swing of things. Jez had finally vacated the bedroom, and as luck would have it I found myself spending some time in my own bedroom with a couple of other partygoers, who were in the next bed to me. It really was like a scene from *Quadrophenia*, so I was loving every minute.

A little later, and to my dismay, the door burst open. But instead of Karl standing there, it was a policeman in full uniform, asking rather abruptly who the flat belonged to. I must admit that the second I saw the officer standing there, I hid my head under the covers, hoping he would go away. I heard him asking the question again and got the impression that he wasn't going to be leaving any time soon if somebody didn't answer.

After debating with myself and the other person who was sharing the bed with me for what seemed like ages, I decided that the best thing to do was pull back the covers and admit to the officer my responsibilities. If I'd had any misguided idea about him maybe seeing the funny side of the situation, this was immediately dispelled the second he walked straight up to my bed, put his face right up next to mine, and said, 'I wouldn't let my dog live here!'

Part of me wanted to ask him about his dog, and part of me wondered what my bed partner was thinking about this embarrassing situation. But mainly I was a little concerned about what the officer was on about, as everything had been fine before I entered the bedroom.

I begrudgingly got out of bed, thinking I had better inspect the rest of the flat, and was shocked to discover foot marks all the way up the walls. How on earth had that happened? I walked into the kitchen and was told that someone had decided to fry a bar of soap, and when they realised that it wasn't such a good idea after all, they had thrown it out of the window. This wasn't the worst of it. The frying pan had hit a car windscreen, and the fact that I lived on the fourteenth floor meant that the driver would certainly need to save up for a new one. Someone had filled my

kettle with Heinz Tomato soup, and covered my heater in rice pudding, for some unearthly reason.
My longing to have a party like the ones in *Animal House* had ended, but I didn't have time for an investigation to find out which moron had been responsible, as I noticed the police rounding everyone up and telling them to leave. I explained that I had promised that several of my friends could stay the night, and that it was far too late for them to make alternative arrangements. But to my absolute despair, the officer pointed to a handful of random people in the corner, and told them they could stay the night then carried on throwing the rest of the people out. The police had only gone and chosen the gate-crashers for the sleepover and told the majority of my friends to leave.

It was awful. I lay in bed unable to sleep, listening out in case I got robbed. I heard a couple having sex in a cupboard next to the bedroom, and at about 2.30 in the morning, I could hear an argument. I found out later that Mark's brother Andy had chased someone around Mill Hill with one of my kitchen knives. (What is it with me and kitchen knives?)
It turned out to be a total nightmare of an evening. Della and Anne gave me some sob story about having nowhere to stay, as they had been thrown out of their home (snap). So, being soft, I agreed to let them hang around. This decision was aided by the fact that they had offered to help me tidy up from the previous night's antics. I must admit that this turned out to be a pretty unusual arrangement, as one night one of them would get in and share my bed, and the following night the other one would do the same. I don't really remember anything sexual taking place during these bed-hopping evenings, but wondered how on earth I was going to explain this situation to Yvonne.

I guessed that the best thing to do was invite her over and introduce her to both the girls, so that she could see for herself that it had just been a case of me helping them out. Early doors, I had been drinking at The Farthings with Yvonne and my mate Simon, who offered to give us a lift back to my flat. I seem to

recall that Yvonne was wearing a pretty low-cut top (that really showed off her personality), and just as we were about to pull up at the flats, I realised that Simon had started to notice for himself just how low it actually was. The problem with this was that Simon was the driver, and within seconds we had mounted the pavement and crashed the car into the nearest lamppost.
Thankfully, no-one was hurt – apart from Simon's pride, that is, and his bumper. But things didn't get any better once we entered No 90. It was a little awkward introducing Yvonne to my newfound flatmates, and she certainly didn't stay long. (Oh well.)

Della and Anne didn't seem to work during the day, so I would leave them inside my flat whilst I went to work at Crown. At first, this didn't seem to be an issue, but as the weeks went by, I started to notice several of my belongings had gone missing. It turned out that whilst I was grafting away cleaning paint dispensers, they had been inviting some of their mates from Mill Hill round, and in the end, I realised that they had robbed me of half of my stuff.

They had stolen money, clothes, photos, and more importantly, my vinyl. If you think that most of my spending money for years had been spent on my beloved record collection, first-day Jam releases, original Beatles vinyl, and a huge amount of Punk and Mod singles, and now most of that had gone. To say that I was devastated was an understatement, and as the years went by, I remembered more and more items that they must have taken.

The one thing that was obvious about these unwelcome houseguests was that they were Blackburn's, maybe Lancashire's, dumbest criminals, as they had written their names all the way through my autograph album. I owned a small blue autograph book, with orange, yellow, and pink pages, as I have always loved a good autograph. And as well as their names, they had written Mill Hill Punks across the cover. Punks they were. And it became pretty clear that my newfound flatmates would be receiving their marching orders with immediate effect.

About a couple of months or so after my so-called party, I received a not very friendly letter from the Council, regarding incidents that had happened that night at Livesey Court. I reckoned the best thing I could do was jump before I was pushed. I mean, two parties = two evictions. So I started to put all my efforts into sweet talking my mum and dad into allowing the prodigal son to return home.

To my amazement, nine months had just been enough time for my mum to back down and allow me to live at Kestrel Close once again, but I do believe that she never really forgave me for my disrespectful behaviour. I waved goodbye to Mill Hill (for now) and returned to Lammack, and I really was on my best behaviour (at first). And although I wasn't happy at all that Robin had now moved into my old, larger bedroom and I was now in the ultra-small boxroom at the front, I knew I just had to put up with it. I also knew that Mark's brother would be disappointed by this new arrangement, as I had sussed him out a long time ago.

When I used to have the bigger bedroom at the back of the house, I had a giant art drawing on the wall called a Doodle Art. They were really popular at the time, and mine was a very large underwater scene with all different kinds of fish and coral to colour in. The idea was that whenever any of my mates called round, they would have a turn at colouring in an area of their choice. Even though we didn't really hang around with Mark's brother that much, Andy and his mate Dave would call round on sunny days just to have a go. I eventually realised that this was in the hope of catching my next-door neighbour's mum sunbathing topless in the back garden, and not because they fancied themselves as budding artists.

The one thing I had not missed during the time I lived away from home was the crazy maniac up the road. Not too long after we had moved into Kestral, we had been hanging out on the narrow path at the back of the garages when a very large, angry, strange looking man had appeared at his back gate overlooking the path.

This man was called Febber and lived in the black and white mock Tudor cottage at the top of Lammack Road.

I must admit that initially we had annoyed him by leaning against his green back gate, and maybe kicking it a little, but from that moment on, this very scary looking bloke would haunt and terrorise me and my friends for years to come.

If I had been returning home from a night out, I had two options to get to our house: one, I could walk along Lammack Road and down Hawkshaw Bank Lane; or two, I could take the quicker route of down the back path and past the garages at two or three in the morning. The quicker route had always seemed the better option, but it was absolutely terrifying daring to walk (or run) down in the dark, as on a number of occasions Febber was standing halfway down, as if he had been waiting for me. It is hard to put into words how crazy this guy seemed to us at the time, and several times we had to call the police on him. Not that that did any good. It turned out that if the police had to visit him, they would only go in twos; they seemed to be as freaked out by him as we were. They once told us after one of their visits that he had some sort of bunker inside the house, inside which he had two large shelves stacked only with tins of Spam. He told the officers that if it had been Palestine, he would have killed us, which only added to our fear of him.

The one thing I always remember about him was that if he managed to spot you, or if we had annoyed him – which happened a lot – he would never run after you. Instead, he would sort of march down the road, but he always managed to catch us up.

There were large nails sticking out of the back door of his Tudor cottage, and I swear on a couple of occasions that I braved that creepy path I heard airgun pellets flying past my head. One time I even saw him standing on top of his roof watching us walk past, which proper freaked me out.

Over the years we saw less and less of him, and there was even a feature in the local paper stating he had turned his cottage into a mini-Colditz to make his home a fortress. He had blocked up his front door, bricked up the windows, built a 10ft high chain link fence at the back of his property, and installed his own electricity generator (like you do!). He told the police that he had done all this because he kept getting vandalised, and claimed he'd had his windows smashed 24 times, and that people had thrown bricks, pieces of metal, and even a baseball bat into his home.

I have discussed this with my mate Birchy from time to time, and he seemed to think that maybe we had terrorised him back then, as he had called the police over a hundred times to complain about vandals. But I never saw it like that, I must be honest. Yes, I kicked his back gate with the back of my foot, and I recall we did knock on his door on the odd occasion, but we really hadn't caused any damage or carried out any of those things that he claimed happened. However, that's not to say that nobody did.

I also remember one time reading in the paper that he had chased a young lad through the streets wielding a joiner's saw above his head, so I knew I hadn't imagined the whole thing. He was a bloody nutter!

I finally left Crown, but knew I needed to get a job to fund my nights out and new gear, and to be able to pay a little towards my board at home. The good thing about being back was that I didn't have to pay rent, just the odd tenner here and there for board. I didn't pay any bills and I loved my mum's baking skills (and the final product), as did my mates. I could also nick my dad's booze out of the drinks cabinet and blame Robin. But I really did miss the independence of having my own place, especially now that parties were out of the question. And bringing girls back was not exactly encouraged – whilst my parents were awake that is.

I ended up getting a job in Darwen, at Darwen Sun Leisure, but it didn't last long. The place was unbelievably cliquey with Darwen folk who had probably been there for years, so there was no way they were going to roll out the red carpet for somebody from Blackburn. Most people there were really unfriendly towards me.

The job was wiring up and assembling sunbeds, and I am embarrassed to admit that at that time I spent a couple of hours each week lying on one myself. I mean, who didn't want to look like Wham back then? And I would go and visit Majestic or Outline gym above Burtons on a Saturday morning.

Nobody really showed me properly what to do at the job; there was certainly no training, and I struggled to grasp the wiring side of it. What I found unbearable was that on my first two days, as I was trying to work out what to do next, this lad walked over to me and shouted for maximum effect, 'Oh my God. You've done it wrong again!' My supervisor, Jasper (as if), had really been okay with me but he was rushed off his feet, so he didn't really have time to train me properly.

At lunchtimes, you were allowed to use one of their sunbeds for free, but I always felt a little strange whilst lying there in the small, designated room. I had noticed at least two man-made holes in the wall and could always hear somebody whispering, so I decide to sack it off.

I had been there a matter of days, and enough was enough, so this time when the village idiot walked over and tried to publicly humiliate me (yet again), to his surprise I pinned him against the nearest wall. The following morning, I walked into work as normal, only to be summoned into the boss's office. 'It's not really working out is it, Pete?' he said. I just replied, 'No, not really.' And that was that.

As I had now joined the ranks of the unemployed, I decided to spend the afternoon in The Farthings with Walker's sister, Lisa. They had a Zamovski vodka promotion on, so I thought why not? Even though I have never liked vodka. Every time you bought a drink, you would get a free branded gift to encourage you to keep on drinking, and I found myself being the proud new owner of a small, silver foldaway address book, which I thought might come in handy for collecting girls' numbers in. After the two of us had downed far too many drinks (for an afternoon, anyway), we both came up with the plan of going to visit her brother in Sunderland, where he was at university. Since nobody owned a mobile back then, it was a bit of a gamble to go visiting unannounced.

Two return tickets to Sunderland, please, and we were off. These days it's really hard to imagine not being able to contact people, and not having your every move tracked, but that was how it was in the 80s – and I feel that in some way it was a whole lot better.

We knew that Mark was sharing a student house with several other lads, so at least someone would be in... or so we thought. Wrong. We managed to get a taxi to the address Lisa had written down, and were looking forward to surprising him. The house they were living in was surrounded by several derelict buildings and rubble, which surprised me a bit. But what surprised me even more was the fact that nobody was at home. I even questioned if we had gone to the correct address, but Lisa assured me that we had.

A Friday night in Sunderland with nowhere to stay and not enough money to book in somewhere, things were looking pretty grim. We hung around the building for a little while, but still no sign of life. My idea had been that, seeing that it was a Friday and Mark certainly loved a few beers, we could walk around the local clubs and hopefully bump into him along the way. Someone with a funny accent directed us to the main area of pubs and clubs, and we spent the next couple of hours walking around aimlessly searching for my mate, and her brother.

Time was getting on, and I really didn't fancy walking the streets all night, so as a last resort I went over and asked the doorman of the local club if it was okay if I could just nip in for a couple of minutes to see if I could spot my friend. No joy there; they thought I was trying to pull a fast one by gaining entry without paying.

The person who directed us to the area had warned us that this particular club had been really rough, and just as we were about to give up, those uncooperative bouncers physically threw somebody out for fighting. It reminded me of a Western film, when the saloon doors open and the cowboy goes flying through the air. This cowboy certainly went flying, and landed in the middle of the road, right beside where we were standing. I thought that we had better move on pretty sharpish, as he looked like a nutter and was definitely not in the best of moods. But just as we turned to go (hoping not to be noticed by this Patrick Swayze-type Mackem), he called us over and it turned out this 'nutter' was in fact friendly (considering). Once we explained our unfortunate situation, to our astonishment he invited us to go and stay at his place.

At the time, I felt that it would be a bad move to turn down his very kind offer of accommodation, even though a small part of me wondered if it was a trap to try and rob us, so we accepted and tried to look grateful.

I can't remember if we walked or got a taxi to Patrick's abode, but things seemed even more strange once we arrived, as he only really had one main room, which featured a double bed occupied by his partner. The wife swapping situation crossed my mind, as I was still totally shocked that he had asked us back in the first place, just after being manhandled into the middle of the road. But thankfully, he told us we could both sleep on the settee across from the bed, which was a huge relief.

I don't recall either of us getting much sleep, and breakfast had not been part of the deal, so at daylight we said our thank yous and goodbyes, and jumped into a taxi back to the student house.

To our relief, this time someone answered the door and directed us straight up to Walker's bedroom. Mark was fast asleep after a hard night's drinking, and still seemed pretty much the worse for wear when he opened his eyes and noticed his mate and his sister standing at the bottom of the bed. His face was a picture; he was in absolute shock. In fact, he told us later that he thought he was still dreaming.

Once he managed to come round, he was really pleased by the effort we had both made to visit him.

We had a great weekend, which you tend to do when its unplanned, and I couldn't believe the number of parties that were taking place. On the Saturday, Mark took us out to a local house party just down the road, and after about 20 minutes he said, 'Let's try another', then another. They were happening all around the area, and you could literally walk from one to the next. We ended up in a really lively pub, and the DJ put The Jam on the decks. At that time, no matter what club or pub (with a disco) I was in, once I heard my band blasting through the speakers, I always made my way to the dancefloor. Mark had mentioned that it was a bit of a rough pub, and drawing attention to myself was not recommended, but sure enough, I was up.

The other thing I was a little concerned about was that I was hoping Mark didn't think there was something going on between me and his sister (breaking the mates' code), but thankfully this was quickly alleviated when she ended up copping off with a dentist called Tim, who Mark happened to know.

CHAPTER SEVEN

THE BITTEREST PILL

(30th October, 1982 – Remember the date)

At 12.45pm (lunchtime), I found myself sitting in Yvonne's house with her and her mate Siobhan.
We'd had a bit of an argument (for a change), so it was a relief when Siobhan called round, as we hadn't really been speaking. I was listening to Radio 1s Newsbeat, when the unthinkable was announced over the airwaves. I almost fell off the settee, when I heard that The Jam were splitting up.

This news had come totally out of the blue, as their latest single, *Beat Surrender*, had gone straight into the charts at number 1. Forget the childish argument, I was devastated, and I don't mind admitting that a tear appeared in my eye.
The Jam had been everything to me over the past five years, and they had seemed tighter than ever to their fans. When interviewed for the national news that day, Paul stood there in his long, flash mac and scarf, on a windy day at the seaside, and declared that he thought they had achieved enough. He added that he thought they had done all that they could do as a threesome and that it was a good time to finish it. 'I don't want to drag it on and go on for the next 20 years and become nothing, mean nothing, and end up like the rest of the groups.' He also said that he wanted what they had achieved over the past five/six years to count for something.
Paul had been the spokesman of our generation – if you were a Mod, that is. But the decision had been made, so we were just going to have to get used to it. More importantly, Bruce and Rick were going to have to do the same, as this had come as just as much of a shock to them as it had to us fans.

I had travelled all over to see my favourite band – to Paris, London, Manchester, and more – and now I was going to have to pledge my allegiance to someone new. I just couldn't imagine it; there would only ever be one Jam.

Back in the late 1970s in Blackburn, we had our own band doing pretty well – The Stiffs. The original members were Phil Hendricks (lead), Ian (Strang) Barnes (guitar), Big John McVittie (bass), and Tommy O'Kane (drums).
I first became aware of the band through my involvement with Faded Image, as Big John had been Dave Mac's older brother. I didn't personally know them as individuals back then, but had certainly followed their progress, with them being local. Phil and Strang had gone to Queen Elizabeth Grammar School (QEGS) (same as Walker and Chris), and apparently, they had been sitting at a local landmark one night (The Tank up Revidge), at the age of 14, and decided to form a band. The next time they visited, they had just been signed to EMI. Punk was in at the time, but they had been described as more of a Power Pop/Pop Punk act.

Formed in 1976, they played several church halls and youth club gigs before they self-released their first single, *Standard English/Brookside Riot Squad/DC Rip* on Dork Records in 1979. But It was their second single *Inside Out/Kids on the Street,* that really started to get them noticed. Legendary DJ John Peel had picked up the record from early on and declared on air that *Inside Out* was the greatest record in the history of the Universe. He even interrupted DJ Mike Read's show live on air, and insisted he played the record.

The band signed a long-term record deal with EMI in 1980, and they really did look like they were going places and about to put Blackburn on the musical map. Communications were so primitive back then that EMI had to contact our local record shop, Ames, in an effort to track the band down.

The Stiffs always used to drink in the Alexandra pub on Dukes Brow, and The Alex was a well-known drinkers' pub (so naturally

Waker could be found propping up the bar on a Friday night). On the few occasions I joined him, folk would always say, 'Oh, that's the Stiffs' room.'

I remember sitting on the floor at the Regent pub watching them, and will never forget them supporting the UK Subs at King George's Hall. I was in the front row, and some fighting broke out at the side of me. All of a sudden, the Stiffs' drummer stopped playing mid-song and jumped off the stage into the audience. I had never witnessed such a thing before and could only guess that he must have seen some of his mates getting punched. Either way, it was certainly Rock and Roll in my eyes, and I recall buzzing at the time about the fact a local band was getting played on Radio 1 every night.

My next job, after my experience at Darwen Sun Leisure, was at a firm in Hoddlesden, called Vernon Carus. And even though Waker had left university with a degree in Biochemistry, I ended up getting him a job with me. Carus was a sort of textile factory, and people on the shop floor would pack nappies, amongst other things. We worked downstairs making Rig Abandonment Suits for the oil rigs, which was pretty apt at the time, as Mark's dad was working on the rigs in Aberdeen. To be fair, it was a decent place to work, but I think the attraction was the 230 women to 19 men ratio (or about that).

It was a bit of a mission to travel there from Lammack, as we had to get two buses and a coach there and back every day. On our journey home, after working overtime, we would spend the majority of the bus ride home just laughing about stuff. We finally worked out that this must have been caused by breathing in the extra strong adhesive we used on the suit zips every day.
The company used to run the best incentive scheme I have ever known, to encourage the staff to work extra hours. Carus would give you an extra 13% of your weekly earnings and put it in a savings account for you – not taken out of your wage, but an additional amount paid by them. And every July, they

would give you this lump sum for you to put towards your summer holidays.

The fact that the females by far outnumbered the males at work meant that at Christmas time it would be totally crazy on the shop floor. It was an unwritten rule that the management would turn a blind eye to any wild happenings by the staff during the two weeks before the Christmas break. During this time, going on to the shop floor was literally like Commando Warfare, and we used to carry a can of shaving foam under our overalls just in case we needed to retaliate. If you happened to be off guard, your fate was usually to be jumped on by several females, half stripped, and tied to a post, always covered in shaving foam, and then left there. I could never believe the type of things that we would be allowed to get away with, but it certainly livened up the long working days.

I got along with everybody in our room, apart from one guy called Dave (there is always one, and usually called Dave). It must have been a local trait for someone to point out your mistakes in order to make themselves look good. Mark was off sick one particular day, and I had had just about as much as I could take from this loudmouth. After our morning break, I returned to our room to notice he had set up his suit on my work bench. I walked over to ask him if he could move it, but he must have thought I had been going for him, as he punched me on the nose. I really hadn't expected this reaction, but I still managed to fight my corner. The door swung open and our supervisor Sandra walked into the room to find me sitting on top of Dave with blood gushing out of my nose. We were both summoned to go and see the big boss, and Dave was told that he would no longer be working for the firm.

After a lecture, making me fully aware of their company policy of never allowing an employee to stay after they had been involved in a fight, I was told that based on my supervisor's feedback, I was going to be the only one to sidestep that rule. I was briefly given a second chance, but that December my name appeared on the list of redundancies, which I felt was no coincidence.

I remember on the day of the incident, I called round at Mark's house on my way home, and before I could explain why I had a bloody nose, he just said 'Dave!' So, I got Mark the job, and he was still working there while I was back in the job-hunting market.

Mark left not long after me, to start a new job at ICI, but his time in Hoddlesden had certainly been worth the effort, as Karen Hutchinson, who was the fastest nappy-packer on the shop floor, later became Karen Walker, as he ended up marrying her.

Back to our social life. Saturday nights at the Rugby Club had been replaced by Monday nights at the New Inns, and more or less the same crowd had moved from Ramsgreave Road to Wilpshire Road, Rishton. The Bay Horse New Inns was a popular place for travellers to stop off in the 18th and 19th Century, as a break from taking their livestock to Great Harwood's Charter market.

In the early 80s, it was a must-night-out on a Monday evening, and the same regulars could be seen dancing to the likes of *Searching* by Hazel Dean and *It's Raining Men* by the Weather Girls, before they had both become chart hits. I even remember one Monday night it had been snowing that bad that even DMC taxis were not running, but we had zero intentions of missing our weekly club night. So we managed to persuade The Farthings' landlord, Paul, to take a break from his shift behind the bar and try to drive us there. And like a legend, he did.
In 1984 a major blaze destroyed most of the building, and that was the end of our weekly Monday nights out.

The same regular crowd found a new weekly club night to replace the last, and we all ascended on Mr G's in Fleming Square every Wednesday evening. The DJ was Mark Grise, and he played some right bangers.
We had maybe the UK's smallest night club in Mia Two, which was situated across from St Wilfrid's School. However, the town's

greatest offering in terms of nightlife was Romeo and Juliet's (the Cav), where we were finally able to gain entry. Known to locals as The Cav, due to its former name the Cavendish, it was on a different level to all other nightclubs in the town. It had a large room with a lower and upper dancefloor, and a smaller room which included several dark, seated booths to sit in, in case you happened to get lucky.

Every time you walked from the small room into the large one, they always seemed to be playing *Celebration* by Kool and the Gang. I recall there being fancy lamps on all the tables in the big room, and also telephones. This was certainly a massive step up from the Top Hat Club, and we soon became regulars. I think it was either Tuesday or Wednesday night when they used to stage the Young Farmers' nights, and they were pretty lively at the time. Sometimes, they would have a live act performing, and the crowd would lap it up.

I will never forget watching Fat Larry's band perform in the small room. They were flying high in the charts with their track *Zoom* at the time. It was a boiling hot summer's night, and the drummer was a pretty big lad. Halfway through their rendition of their hit, I noticed that he had pulled a handkerchief from his top pocket and proceeded to mop the sweat from his forehead. The weird thing was that whilst he did this, the drums carried on playing, even though his hands were nowhere near the kit. I was amazed at how he had managed to achieve such a feat, and this was my first introduction to an act using a backing track. I felt cheated at the time, but this was how a lot of bands performed in those days, especially on the pub/club circuit. I also felt totally cheated the first time I realised that the acts who performed each week on *Top of the Pops* had actually been miming to the track and not playing live.

At first, it was an ambition of every band or solo artist to perform on the weekly chart show, but having achieved that goal, I heard a lot of them in interviews saying that they thought 'Is that it?' and being slightly underwhelmed by the experience. One of the contributing factors to this was that they were not allowed to play live and were told to mime. A few artists rebelled at the time, and Weller in particular would either chew gum or laugh during their performance, as a way of letting the audience become more aware of this restriction. The Clash, in fact, refused to play *Top of the Pops* at all because of this.

Being out of work and having little money was never a barrier to me attending gigs, having holidays, or going to the pub every night. It is fair to say that I have probably lived beyond my means since I was 15, or even before. I have always felt that life was far too short to miss out on the opportunities that it has to offer. I totally respect folk who say, if they haven't got it, they can't do it. That is fine for them, but not for this Mod. And I have always managed to find a way of achieving the things I have wanted to do, somehow. This would sometimes come in the form of my dad lending me money, or me getting a bank loan, but I never allowed being skint to be a barrier.

Another bad habit I had since the age of around 15 was my obsession for designer clothes and labels. I would never just buy anything because it had a certain label on it, if I didn't like it. But I would find what I liked and would usually stick to the same designer brands. We were really spoilt back then in Blackburn for male clothes shops, and my stores of choice were Pelle and Replay on King William Street. Pelle, run by Pelle (not that one) would stock some quality Italian brands and my favourite shirts made by Central Park. Replay, run by Michael Ellis, would also stock some must-have shirts that would always catch my eye – Air Balloon being one. These shops were not cheap, so I really did need to get another job in order to maintain my weekly visits.

Yvonne liked the band Wham, like most girls at that time, and I noticed they were playing Blackpool Opera House as part of their 'Club Fantastic' tour. I was also a bit of a fan, but my main motivation to purchase tickets was that I had noticed that tickets to see The Police (who I loved) were going on sale at the venue the following morning after the Wham gig. I purchased the tickets to see George and Andrew, booked a B&B to stay the night, and was actually in the good books for a while.

I was looking forward to seeing Wham, but knew that if any of my mates had questioned this, I could simply say I was going to please Yvonne. I knew Ste H wouldn't give me any grief, as he used to think that he was George Michael.

I remember the venue being full of young girls, screaming and shouting, and feeling a little out of place. And when Andrew and George got dressed into their Fila sports gear, including shorts, and started playing badminton on stage, with George rolling the shuttlecock up and down his leg before putting it down his shorts, I considered sneaking out.

I must admit, though, I did enjoy their youthfulness and energy, and also their songs, but the highlight for me was when George said he wanted to try out a new song on us, if we didn't mind.

He told us that they had written it a while back and hadn't really sung it live to many people. That song was *Careless Whisper*, and the rest is history. Looking back now, I am so glad I attended that gig and got to witness George Michael live. Unfortunately, that was my one and only time.

The morning after the Wham concert, we headed over to the Opera House to try and buy two tickets to see the mighty Police. Folk had been queuing overnight all around the building, but once the Box Office opened, I noticed there were actually two queues. One for Mr Green Door himself, Shakin' Stevens, and one for the Police. I joined the one for Shaky, and waited until I got closer to the ticket desk, then swapped lines, hoping nobody had seen me. Seconds later, and just as I thought I had got away with it, a little old lady started to hit me on the back with her rolled-up umbrella, shouting, 'People have been here all night for these tickets.' I explained to her that I thought I had been in the queue for Mr Stevens, and she seemed to go away, to my delight. I felt a little bad, but just about managed to secure a couple of tickets for Sting and Co.

The Police gig a few weeks later was brilliant, and in such a small venue for them. Sting, wearing a pair of black Doc Martens and with the attitude to match, did not disappoint whilst blasting out their hits, and we both proper enjoyed it. I remember ringing my dad after the gig and asking him for a lift home.

'Where are you, in town?' he asked.

'No,' I replied, 'Blackpool.'

Anyone who knew my dad over the years would not be surprised to learn that he did in fact pick us up from Blackpool after the concert, because he was well known for always trying to help people. I am not saying that he was enamoured by a road trip to the coast at that time in the evening, but he came.

One evening after work, Dad returned home and told us the unthinkable – he was leaving Crown after over 40 years at the company. His employment there was ending. An American company was taking it over, and he felt that they would no doubt want their own people working there, so had agreed a deal as a sort of voluntary redundancy type of thing. Robin and I were shocked by the news, as he had loved working there and I could never imagine him just sitting at home doing nothing. What I believed saved him back then was his involvement in Blackburn Northern Cricket Club. Cricket was his great love, and my mum's, and his decision to become more involved would give him a focus and a reason to get out of bed in a morning, which I believe is massively important.

Over the years my dad would take up almost every position at the club, whilst my mum helped out with the cricket teas, and my brother Robin would captain the 3rd team. We were a real cricketing family – well, they certainly were. Yet again, I was the odd one out. Don't get me wrong, it was totally my decision, as I was no big fan of the sport, but I did love the fact that they were all involved. And it meant that I had the house to myself on a Sunday afternoon, so I had a lot to be grateful for.

The only time that I would visit the Northern was for their annual Sportsman's Dinner, but being honest, the first time my dad invited me to the event, I wasn't too keen on attending. I couldn't imagine spending a Friday night in a room without any females in it, just blokes. To be fair, though, I really did enjoy these evenings and would make sure I was sorted for a ticket year after year. They had some really good acts perform and after-dinner speakers, and those Northern nights will always remain really special to me, as they were the only real time that me, my brother, and my dad would have a night out together.

I have always been mega unlucky when it comes to winning anything – competitions, raffles, etc; it just doesn't happen. To my astonishment, this bad luck briefly changed at one Sportsman's Dinner and I found myself the proud owner of a crate of Chinese oriental soup. It wasn't something that I had thought I would like, but hey, I did win it. A few weeks later, there was a collection at work towards a charitable cause in China, so I donated it and sent the soup back to where it had originated from.

My parents were good friends with Colin and Julia at the Cricket Club. Colin was the works manager of a local electronics firm, Unilab, which was based at Skew Bridge, just down the road from The Farthings. Colin happened to mention to my dad that the firm had been taking people on, so my dad had mentioned me. I knew that I needed to earn a weekly wage sooner rather than later, so I filled out an application form to work in their Despatch department. Finally, it seemed that my luck had changed, as I was offered the job and they told me that my interview had gone really well. This was a welcome confidence boost for me, even though I hadn't been too sure what to expect.

I started my new job, and soon realised that, like most small factories at that time, Unilab had its fair share of characters and hierarchy, which depended on how long you had worked there. The firm made science teaching equipment for schools and colleges, and on the shop floor you had mainly females wiring up power supplies or soldering circuit boards. There was a test department, a packing department, and a couple of offices – one of which was occupied by the works manager, Colin. His office was in the central position on the shop floor, perfectly placed for him to oversee everything that was going on. At the front of the building were other offices, and at the end of the long drive was where my Despatch department was. Katy and Carol basically ran the shop floor in terms of what was acceptable or wasn't, as they had worked there the longest. And to be honest, I certainly wouldn't have messed with them.

In the Despatch department, I worked with a really nice guy called Don, who was also the works van driver, which meant he spent most of each day on the road. My supervisor was Brian, and even though I got on with him, he was a strange guy, to say the least.

Now that I was working full time and earning a weekly wage, I felt it was time to have a lads' holiday abroad, as opposed to our annual pilgrimage to Newquay in Cornwall.

The year after me and Nick had been on the pull in Newquay, me, Waker, and Nidge had chosen it for our summer holiday destination. Nidge was a mate, and even though I didn't see as much of him as I saw all my other mates, I will always be indebted to him as he introduced me to Tamla Motown, and more specifically *Heaven Must Have Sent You* by The Elgins.

The first time we holidayed in Newquay, it had taken 13 long hours to get there by coach, so this time Waker offered to drive. The other difference was that we had decided to stay in a tent, on a campsite called Hendra. This was my first proper experience of camping, but what made it worse was that my parents and brother had booked to stay at the same time, in the second-best hotel in Newquay.

I managed to sort of get in with a girl called Adele, and remember meeting up with Robin to try and beg and bribe him into letting us stay in his room for the night, as I thought that asking her back to our tent would put her off. Robin being Robin told me no chance, and seemed to take great satisfaction in spoiling my night. No brotherly love there. My date night with Adele ended up not going to plan, but we did carry on hanging around with her and her mate for the next few nights.

I can't remember the name of Adele's friend, but we used to refer to her as BJ, simply because she always wore a brown leather jacket. Adele's parents ran a B&B on St George's Road called Brig House, named after the place in Halifax, where they were from.

Adele and BJ had taken us to a well-known night club called Boom, Boom, and I remember there were always several squaddies in there at the end of each night, usually looking for a fight.

At the end of each evening, it was always a bit of a trek to attempt the 30-minute walk in the dark back to our campsite, and it always freaked us out having to feel our way into our tent in the pitch black whilst drunk.

The days were spent between the Newquay Arms, and Fistral or Towan beach, and our daily routine each evening would be to wait outside the chip shop for it to open, in order to purchase our evening meal (fish and chips). After that, we would head for The Prince Albert pub at the top of the road. On the jukebox there were a couple of tunes that we all really loved, *Pity Poor Alfie* by The Jam, and *Boy Trouble* by Bananarama, and every night we would play these two songs as many times as our change would allow. Eventually, until one evening, the landlord unplugged the jukebox as we were walking through the door. We had obviously left our mark!

At the end of the night doing the pub circuit, we would either end up at the very small nightclub underneath the Prince Albert, called Berties, or pay a visit to either Tall Trees or Boom Boom; on some occasions, all three. Despite the fact that we had been slumming it in a tent whilst Robin was warmly tucked up in bed at the Edgecombe, we had a fantastic holiday. One of my favourite photos from those days is of me, Waker, and Nidge, sitting together in the Prince Albert, all wearing tank tops.

I always carried a camera with me for every occasion, so luckily I have always been able to look back at these memories with fondness, and also to remind my mates about the wonderful times we shared. These days, I am called a visual storyteller on social media, and I have always had a passion for capturing life. One of the things from that holiday that really stands out is that my family had planned to go home a day earlier than us and had offered to take our tent back with them. At the time, this sounded fine, because we had barely had any room in the car driving down.

We spent the night on the town as usual. Nidge had fallen in love with a girl called Debbie, Mark had continued to resist the charms and attention from BJ, and I had started to wonder what we were going to do to keep us entertained throughout the night. We hadn't planned for how bloody freezing it would be from around 2am onwards, and we spent the final hours of our summer holiday huddled up together in the campsite toilets, taking it in turns to press the button on the wall mounted hand-dryer to try and keep warm.

As soon as the shops opened the following morning, we headed down to our regular haunt to spend what money we had left on a full English breakfast and cream cakes. Mark realised that he was flat broke, and he asked me to save him a bean. I would have been skint, too, if I hadn't bumped into my dad the day before, and he had given me 20 quid. Not trying to be tight, but purely because I thought it would be humorous, I took him at his word and saved one baked bean from my plate for him. He didn't find this funny and went mental, and I didn't hear the end of it for at least the next 12 months.

The following year, surprise, surprise, we again opted for Newquay. But this time, Julie and Mary said they were up for coming with us. Things didn't actually go to plan, after Yvonne

announced that she wanted to go, too. To my surprise, once the others heard this, they said it was okay and suggested that we should go away together, and that they would make alternative arrangements.
I must admit that I was pretty gutted at this change of plan and didn't understand why we couldn't all go together, but I know they were only trying to help.
Everybody else cancelled the holiday except for Karl, as he was quoted as saying, 'It's my holiday and I am going on it.' This put me in a really awkward position, as Karl and I had booked before Yvonne even mentioned it, but I was sort of seeing her so I couldn't just tell her no.
I admit that it turned out to be a pretty strange arrangement as what was agreed, to be fair to Karl, was for me and him keep our original booking at Brig House, and for Yvonne to stay in the hotel across the road. The week away became a bit of a nightmare for me, as Karl would want to go to one beach and Yvonne would want to go to another, so I spent all my time trying to keep the peace.

The first day there, we all agreed to go to Fistral beach as it was boiling hot. Karl obviously felt a bit of a gooseberry, so told us that he was going for a walk along the beach on his own. He had obviously been gone a while, and we had forgotten that he was even with us. When he finally arrived back, Yvonne was sunbathing topless, and it was clear that Karl didn't know where to look and was a little embarrassed, due to us all being friends. After the beach we made our way back to Brig House, but even though it was only the middle of the afternoon, Karl climbed up onto the top bunk and said he was having a sleep. This left us sitting on the bottom bunk, but after a while, things started to get a little frisky between the two of us. Yet again, the fact that Karl was on holiday with us had blended into the background, until a very confused mate was awoken by the excitement and was hanging over the top bunk questioning what we were doing.

This most certainly set the tone for the rest of the week, and I even suggested he try and cop off with Adele (which I thought would have helped the situation), but even though he tried, nothing came of it. We made the most of what we could for the final few days, and looking back, I am surprised the three of us actually survived the week together and remained friends.

It had been a memorable week away, and apart from our shenanigans, someone had suffered a fatal heart attack on Fistral beach, three young lads had jumped over a hedge at the end of the bowling green at the top of Towan, and ended up falling off the cliff. And a water skier had been chased by a 12ft basking shark. You could never say that our holidays in Newquay were ever dull.

Learning from the previous visit, our next trip to Newquay was just me and Yvonne, but as always, things didn't really go to plan. We booked a nice hotel which was just up the road from Brig House, and after a very long coach journey (which I vowed never to do again), we checked in, unpacked, then headed to the beach to sunbathe for a while. I noticed an older couple who kept staring at us, and eventually the guy walked over and asked me if it was okay for him take a photograph of Yvonne sunbathing topless, for the lads at work. I couldn't believe what I was hearing! I mean, he was with his wife! He explained that she reminded him of the model Sam Fox, and thought his work colleagues would really appreciate it. I explained to him that he was asking the wrong person, as I was not her agent, so he posed the same question to Yvonne. I honestly can't remember what her answer was, or if he ended up taking any snaps, but imagine if that had happened today! He would be arrested.

The following day, as we were walking back from the beach, we began arguing about something really petty. Yvonne had accused me of being funny with her over some attention she had been getting from a group of lads while she was sunbathing. This ridiculous argument carried on into the evening, and we childishly spent most of the night debating the subject. Just before we were due to go down to breakfast the next morning, there was a loud knock on the door, and to our disgust, the lady standing there asked us both to vacate the hotel, claiming that we had kept half of their guests awake all night with our falling out. This was, and still remains one of the most embarrassing moments of my life – and there have been a few. The shame that we both felt trailing around Newquay in the boiling hot sun, carrying our suitcases, and trying to find somewhere else to stay, will never leave me.

We eventually managed to book into a room across the road from the Brig House. It was where Yvonne had stayed the previous year, so I am not sure why we hadn't tried that in the place first. That night, as we were waiting for our evening meal, I couldn't believe it when we were joined at the same table by one of my scootering friends from back home, Dave Hartley. I realised then that booking a holiday away did not always mean taking a break from the people back home. Well, certainly not for me, anyway.

One of the days whilst we were there it was pretty cloudy, so Yvonne suggested we should pay a visit to the sunbed shop down the road, as there was no way you could return home from holiday without a tan, even in this country. Whilst we were there, we took several inappropriate photographs, just for a laugh. Close by, next to the Newquay Arms, was a photo developing shop called 'One hour developing'. Back then you didn't have the luxury of mobile phones or digital cameras, and you certainly couldn't view your photos without taking them to the likes of Fast Film or Supersnaps to be developed.

After each holiday, you would always be excited and look forward to getting your pictures back, hoping that they had all turned out, and that you wouldn't be given somebody else's snaps by mistake. I had not wanted to risk anything like that happening with our afternoon's shoot, so we took our film to this shop and planned to wait outside whilst they were being developed. What we had both failed to notice was that every single photo that was developed came down a conveyor belt in the centre of the shop window, for anyone standing there to view. We couldn't believe our luck, and although the photos had been reasonably tame, we made a sharp exit to around the corner, and sheepishly returned to collect them about an hour later.

The following year found just us lads returning to stay at Brig House. It was great to have a regular place to stay, and Adele and her parents were always really welcoming. This trip found me, Waker, Bullinge, and Ste H making the journey, and we always had a daily routine before breakfast. One of us would nip down to the nearest newsagent to buy the morning paper. During breakfast we would pick our horses for the day, and once fed, we would head to the local bookies to put on our bets. This would be followed by a couple of games of pool in the Newquay Arms, before heading off to the beach.

On our first day there, I was just walking away from the table in the Newquay Arms, after just beating Waker at a game of pool, when this random guy came over and asked me where I was going. A little surprised, I told him that he was fine to set up a game, as we were heading off to the beach. He explained that I wasn't going anywhere, as Newquay rules stated that if you won your game of pool, you had to stay on the table until you lost.

We eventually made it to Fistral, as there was no way I was about to win another game, and we all decided to try our hand at surfing. It would have been rude not to, seeing as we were on the same beach where the actual World Surfing Championships were held. I always looked at people who could surf and thought what a really cool thing to be able to do, but what I never realised until then was how difficult it was. After spending a couple of hours trying my best to stand up on the board, the guy said to me when I handed it back in, 'Did you make sure you waxed the board first?' Now he tells us!

One thing that always surprised me about Newquay was that within minutes of last orders being called, you would be asked to leave the pub, even if you had only just bought a pint. This was hard to get used to, as in Blackburn most pubs would simply close the front door after last orders and continue serving, using the back.

It was a Sunday night, and due to it being quiet, we decided to go for a meal about 9pm. Last orders had been called at dead on

10.30pm, and our only real options left were to either go back to our B&B, or head to the beach. The beach won, and we found ourselves down on Towan, even though the sun had gone down and it wasn't very warm. I remember Ste asking everyone how much we would give him if he took off all his clothes and jumped into the sea (like lads do). We all agreed to bet him, so off he went, discarding all his belongings in a pile on the sand, and heading off towards the water. Due to the fact that we were still really childish at the time, just as he was about to approach the very cold looking water, we picked up his clothes and ran off in the opposite direction.
He noticed what was happening, and eventually managed to catch up with us, as we struggled to run at speed whilst laughing our heads off.

At the time, one of my favourite ever groups, Everything But The Girl, had just released a new album, but with being on holiday, I was struggling to afford it. It was a total spur of the moment thing, but I announced that if between them they gave me enough money to buy the LP, I would streak back to our B&B fully naked. It didn't take them long to agree to this off-the-cuff challenge, and I recall Bullinge wouldn't even let me keep my socks on, saying that he wanted his money's worth.

We were standing at the side of the Central pub, and I had to sneak around the back of the building, head over to one of the main roads just up from the town centre, and then up St George's Road to where we were staying, hoping that Adele wouldn't be looking out of her window as I ran up the road. At the bottom of the main road there was an Amusement Arcade, where a police car would regularly park, so I knew I would have to be careful.

Sure enough, I stripped off, and my mates agreed to bring my clothes. It was freezing as I crept behind the pub without being spotted. I made my way cautiously up the main road, looking behind me to make sure the police weren't in their usual spot. The coast was clear... or at least I thought it was! As I was looking behind me whilst streaking up the main road, I failed to notice a police car driving down in the opposite direction. I had absolutely no idea how I was going to get out of this, as the car pulled over and asked me to explain my actions.

There were two officers in the car – the younger one who was obviously seeing the funny side, and the older one who definitely wasn't. 'You are not going to believe this,' I said to them both, and explained that I had been swimming on Towan beach when, to my surprise, my mates had picked up my clothes and proceeded to run off in the opposite direction. I was just about to elaborate about me not being a very fast runner, when the older officer no doubt realised that my privates were exactly in line with his wound down window. He told me to get in the back, and when the younger officer handed me his helmet (to cover mine), it began to feel like it was some kind of set-up.

They asked me again where my so-called mates were, and just as I was about to tell them I had no idea, I spotted them in the distance, running across the car park opposite. The older officer called them over, and I heard him say, 'What would you do if I told you we had your mate, naked, in the back of our car?'

I remember Bullinge peering in the back window, to find me with a helmet strategically placed and a grin on my face. As they were being lectured by Mr Serious, they all struggled to keep a straight face, especially Mark. The officer then turned to me and said they could arrest me and take me down to the station, but he eventually let me off with a caution and allowed me to put my clothes back on.

At least I had given them something to talk about back at Newquay Police Station on a Sunday night, but more importantly, I became the very proud owner of *Baby, the Stars Shine Bright* by Everything But The Girl (which is still a part of my beloved record collection today, over 38 years later).

The following morning, I went nervously down to breakfast, praying that nobody from Brig House had seen or heard about the previous night's antics, when Waker pointed out that Adele must have been gazing out of her bedroom window and seen me, because I was the only one at breakfast who had been given two eggs on my plate.

Whilst choosing our daily runners, I noticed that there was a horse running called Peter's Blue (you just couldn't make it up). I told my mates that this must be a sign, and that they were stupid not to back it. To my surprise, when we called into the bookies on our way back from the beach, it was confirmed that Peter's Blue had in fact won, and half of us were in the money, while the other half were kicking themselves.

We finally made it home, and as Waker had dropped me off at ours, Mum and Dad came out of the house and walked over to the car to greet me. They appeared to be in a foul mood, which confused me as I had been looking forward to telling them about what a great week we had just had. But this all went out of the window when they explained that during our week away, my Grandma Edna had passed away.

I was absolutely mortified, but they explained that they hadn't wanted to spoil our holiday and had decided to wait until I returned home before telling me. I felt sick but had arranged to go out that night with my holiday buddies, to reminisce about the week we had just had in Newquay. Still in shock, I told them that I would meet them in The Farthings around 8.30pm. I have no recollection of what my parents' reaction was to my decision, but I had been looking forward to our holiday catch up and didn't want to miss anything.

Sure enough, I got ready and met up with everyone, but after around half an hour, the pains in my stomach became so unbearable that the inevitable happened, and I had to go home to deal with the shock of such terribly sad news. I had always been unbelievably close to my Grandma and was going to miss her massively. When we have conversations today about her, Robin always makes out that he was never that close to her and reckons that she had never liked him. Who knows, but I cannot believe that was true, and certainly don't have any memories along those lines.

Being honest, I do admit that I was her favourite, but that was nothing to do with anything that I had done or said, but simply due to my adoption. My mum had thought she couldn't have children, but after they adopted me, she found herself pregnant with Robin. I know that happens a lot, once the pressure is off and folk stop trying. Apparently, once my Grandma knew about my mum's pregnancy, she asked my mum, 'What about Peter? What are you going to do now?'
This was the story my mum told us, but how much of it is true, God only knows.

CHAPTER EIGHT

ABSOLUTE BEGINNERS

My parents asked me if I wanted my coming of age at 18 or 21, and I opted for the Key of the Door 21, whatever that means. I don't remember what we did for my 18th birthday (maybe my mates can) but we obviously did something.

Folk will tell you that drinking alcohol is not as good once you reach the legal age, but it certainly tasted the same to me. Apart from the dreaded Pernod, that is. When we started to go to the Cav, I always took a small green bottle of the stuff with me, hidden inside my jacket pocket. And just to confirm that the saying is true, one Thursday night I drank far too much of the stuff and was out of my head. The morning after, I felt beyond rough, and can categorically announce that I have never touched the stuff since.

When Paul and Christine at The Farthings had been given only two weeks to leave their job, and home, by Bass Charrington, all the regulars had their photograph taken as a celebration victory once the brewery changed their mind. This photograph appeared on the front page of our local paper (*Lancashire Telegraph*), but the problem was that some of us regulars were underage at the time. Ste received a slap off his dad, as he was on the very front row, holding a pint. Paul the landlord also found out that his so-called head barman, Nicky, was underage at the time his mum, Jenny, had vouched for him. But the main thing was that we had managed to keep our beloved local.

Things had been going well at Unilab, and I had started to make some really good friends. Jean and Martin, who were running packing, seemed really nice (although Martin had a bit of a temper if he wasn't happy). And Katy and Bev were the ones that I chatted to the most. Karen McLeod was great to get on with, and Ste K was fast becoming a mate.

I remember it was the final day before we finished for Christmas, and it had been snowing. As folk do (childish folk, that is), we were throwing snowballs at each other and making the most of the festive weather, when I thought it would be funny to grab a handful of snow and drop it down Karen's back to surprise her. Unbeknown to me, Karen had the same idea, and we both found ourselves facing each other, both holding a handful of snow. Karen attempted to put her cold offering down the front of my jeans, whilst in retaliation, I shoved mine down the front of her top. Suddenly, at that very moment, the heavy metal doors slid open, followed by, 'What the hell is going on here!' Sure enough, our works manager Colin had caught us in the act, and it was one of those very few occasions in my life when I couldn't think of a single word to say to explain our actions, and where he had found our hands – innocent as it may have been.

Tony K was a great lad, too, and he told me that he was the keyboard player in the local band, Bradford. Yes, that's right, Bradford from Blackburn! They were a Skinhead/Indie band from Mill Hill and were starting to make a name for themselves on the local scene at that time.

The date was Saturday, 13th July, 1985, and me and my mates were boarding a flight bound for Corfu in Greece, even though the world's biggest live musical event, Live Aid, was taking place at Wembley Stadium on that same day. Usually, I would have put all of my efforts into attending the London event, but this was our first holiday abroad, and it had been booked before Live Aid had been announced.

Thomas Cook told us that our hotel was double booked, so they had moved us to a private villa on the beach across the road (not something we were about to complain about). Our first morning in Parama, we found ourselves drinking large 30p (in drachmas) bottles of beer at 8.30am. The temperature was 110 centigrade, and I had never known heat like it. Every 15 minutes we had to stop off for a drink, usually orange juice, just to cope. I remember we tried to play football on a hotel roof, but the heat was unbearable. And when some clown kicked the ball off the end of the roof, that was as good an excuse as any to stop playing. A couple of us called into a local bar to try and catch a bit of the concert, but my dad was recording the whole lot for me anyway, on the pile of blank VHS cassette tapes I had left him.

Our first night in Benitses turned out to be surreal, to say the least. We had opted for an open-air nightclub just on the main stretch, and just outside, floating in the sea, was the original Love Boat, from the Sunday afternoon TV series. The DJ for the evening was Christopher Quinten, who played Brian Tilsley in Coronation Street, and his first request announcement was for the Burnley Suicide Squad. it was as if we were in a parallel universe.

Burnley FC happened to be the very arch-rivals of my hometown club, Blackburn Rovers, and the actual, proper members of this delightful squad were well known for attacking rival fans, slashing them with a Stanley knife and leaving a calling card stating, 'You have just met a member of the BSS.' As it happened, these lads from Burnley were okay, so we started hanging around with them at night. One told us he had been a DJ (Mark), and another name I seem to remember was Spam (and you could see why), but that is about it for names.
Even though we were in a villa, we still had the use of our original hotel, and at the end of the night we made our way back to Hotel Frini so that we could carry on drinking. Jez had overdone it on ouzo and fell asleep in Reception. When he woke, he found he was covered in lipstick marks all over his face. Not remembering anything from the previous few hours, he began to brag to us all, claiming that he must have got lucky and added a notch on the imaginary 'Copping Off' chart.

The following night, we bumped into a couple of the Burnley lads, who admitted that the lipstick had come from them. Not only that, but Jez had also been so out of it that he hadn't noticed when they shaved off all his pubic hair for a laugh. (That explained why he had been itching all day!) We found it hilarious, but as expected, Jez went crazy at this news, and was no way prepared to allow Burnley to get one over on Blackburn. He dragged me over to the hotel, intending to find out which rooms they were staying in so that he could get his own back. But when we rang the bell in reception, nobody arrived behind the counter. Then we heard the sound of a bed going up and down in a small side room. The manager was only having it off with one of his receptionists a few feet away from us! It was like being an extra in *Carry on Abroad*. Jez, still beyond angry, failed to see the funny side and went outside to start bricking the hotel. Burnley 1, Blackburn 0.

The 1980s had a lot to answer for in terms of fashion, and Jez embraced this on this holiday. One evening as we were getting ready to leave our villa, he appeared in our bedroom wearing a white vest-type t-shirt with 'No Problem' written in the centre in pink lettering. He wore white pants, and an Olivia Newton-John-style headband to match. There was no way on earth I for one was going to walk out of the front door with him dressed like that (Wham or no Wham).

'It's okay, Jez, we're not quite ready, mate. You go, and we'll meet you over at the hotel in a while.' The second he stepped foot out of the door, everyone just rolled around the floor laughing. I guess that's mates for you.

The following day we hired scooters and made our way over to a recommended beach. I had been on the back, with Bullinge driving, and the views were spectacular. Once we were on the beach, I remember some American guys coming over and asking me if they could have the Blackburn Rovers shirt I was wearing, but I declined their request. Looking back now, I should have just given it to them.

Ste decided to have a go at paragliding, and somehow managed to talk me into joining him. I have absolutely no idea how this had happened, as I was really petrified of heights. I guess I must have thought that if you fall, it will only be into water anyway. But once I got up there, there was no way on this planet I was prepared to fall into the sea from that height; it would have been like hitting concrete.

Once in the air, I recall holding onto the harness so tight that the straps were digging into my arms. Don't get me wrong, the view of Corfu was incredible from up there. But I was terrified and knew that I wouldn't be trying it again anytime soon.

From time to time, I do find myself having ridiculous ideas, and that day was no exception. I had challenged Bullinge to attempt to swim with me to a large rock that didn't seem that far away from the beach. We were both decent swimmers and imagined that it would probably take us around half an hour to reach it. My calculations, though, were totally out of the window. After we had been swimming non-stop for about an hour and a half, we began to question what we were doing, as we didn't seem that much closer than when we had set off.

The rest of our group were just dots on the beach by this time, and the water beneath us had become freezing. We didn't want to abandon our challenge, but felt that it would be stupid to carry on. The decision was made to head back, so we climbed onto some small rocks at the side to try and have a rest, but as I was wearing fins, I fell and managed to cut my leg open (as if things couldn't get any worse). When we finally reached the beach, I was drained of energy. And riding back on the scooter with Mark, I felt so ill that I just wanted to curl up and die at the side of the road. Relieved to finally get back to the villa, I headed straight to bed, which is where I stayed for the rest of the night.

Mates or no mates, there was no way the others were about to miss out on another night out in Benitses, no matter how ill

I was. At about 2.30am, the villa door burst open, and a very drunk group of friends all crashed onto my bed and proceeded to enlighten me on the details of what a brilliant night they'd had. I told them that I was glad that they had not allowed me to spoil their fun, but that I'd had a very strange visit earlier, from a very irate Greek lady. She had called round shouting and waving her arms about, even though I didn't have a clue what she was talking about. I told them that she kept pointing to the balcony.

What came to light was that the previous morning Jez had decided to release some of his bodily fluids over the end of our balcony, not stopping for a second to realise that a Greek family were living underneath us and had put their washing out on the line. How embarrassing! Brits abroad, eh?

On my return from sunny Greece, as promised my dad had managed to record as much of Live Aid as he could on my five cassettes. Shattered as I was after a mad holiday with the boys, I was determined to watch as much of it as my eyes would allow, before falling asleep on the settee. The following day, I watched the remainder of the tapes and thought it had looked amazing.

I had always been a fan and admirer of Bob Geldof, and what he had managed to pull off was just spectacular. Believe it or not, the two bands I had not been a fan of were the ones who absolutely stole the show. U2 and Queen had both put on career-defining performances, and whether you were a fan or not, you couldn't help but appreciate their immense talent. Queen at that time were a bit of a spent force to me; they had been there, done it, and sold a million t-shirts. Folk had started to get a little bored of them, and the fact that they had cashed in by performing at Sun City in South Africa, when a lot of other British acts had pulled out on principle, had not impressed a lot of people.

I was told that as soon as they heard that they had a 17-minute slot at Live Aid, they rented a rehearsal room space in London, and practised playing for exactly 17 minutes, within an inch of their life. So, it is no coincidence that their set at Wembley on that day was one of the greatest musical moments of all time, in my humble opinion.

I recently saw a documentary on Live Aid – Behind the Scenes, and I honestly don't believe there is another human alive who could or would have made that day happen, and raise such an amazing amount of money for an incredibly important cause, other than Mr Geldof.

Paul Weller's next move after breaking up The Jam was to form a new band called The Style Council. He had gone from being an angry young man to a young man who appeared to be enjoying life. I think it is fair to say, that a lot of Jam fans just didn't get it, and were left bemused at the release of their debut single *Speak Like a Child* on 11th March, 1983. The song became a hit, peaking at number 4 on the UK charts, even though there was a noticeable shift from what The Jam had been releasing. But I actually liked the tune.
The Style Council was made up of Mick Talbot from The Merton Parkas, Steve White, one of the best drummers I have ever seen, Dee C Lee of Wham fame, and of course Paul himself. I did prefer The Jam, they were my band, but if Paul wanted to try something new, then who was I to argue? I was happy to carry on backing him.

For some strange reason, I always craved something exciting in the hours when most people were in bed (especially our parents). When we were about sixteen, we had this thing where we would sneak downstairs once everyone was asleep and venture out of the house. There was no logic to these actions, other than it was exciting to do something that we were not supposed to be doing. Rebels or what? All we did was meet up with our mates who had also managed to sneak out, and simply walk around the streets in the dark, hiding from the odd passing car. Bullinge and Karl had been caught out doing this by their parents, and there were occasions when they had been sleepwalking around Rhodes Avenue, where they lived.

By the 80s, the afterhours entertainment came in the shape of bringing girls back from the Cav. The Cav had been called many different names over the years – The Cavendish, Romeo and Juliet's, Peppermint Place, Utopia – and even though my favourite memories were from the R&J time, we still always called it the Cav. It was easier to remember, and I could never imagine saying to my friends, 'Are we going up Peppermint Place tonight?'
We started attending the Cav three times a week – Thursday, Friday, and Saturday – and I am sure that our faces had become pretty well known by the other regulars and especially the doormen. There would normally be a couple of bouncers on the door you had to get past, then you would make your own way down the long, glass corridor until you arrived at the ticket desk, where you would find another couple of bouncers standing looking at you. Nicky's cousin, Manny, worked there on the doors, so we would always say hello. But the one you really didn't want to mess with was a guy called Hussain. Through word of mouth, he was known to be one of the toughest doormen in the town. We witnessed at first-hand when it kicked off in the club, but once Hussain arrived on the scene, things had ended pretty sharpish.

On a night out, we would normally start off in The Farthings, and after a couple of pints (and a go on the bandit) we would get a DMC taxi to the Brewers Arms, then maybe have one in the White Bull across the road, and head over to the Wine Lodge. From there we would always go to Toffs and stand towards the top of the steps, on the right near the door, in order to clock everyone coming in and leaving. Sometimes we wouldn't even need to arrange to meet our friends, as they would automatically know that at 9.30pm, we would be standing on the third step in Toffs (standard). We would then head over to Blakey's and to that end of town, before heading off back to Toffs, due to the Cav steps being just across the road.

These days people find it hard to believe when I tell them that Blackburn had some of the best nightlife around, due to the number of pubs and clubs there were in such a small area. The pub route was known as the Barbary Coast in past years, and it is estimated that a massive 224 public houses in the town have since closed.

In the 1980s and 90s, folk used to get coaches from as far away as Birmingham to visit the Cav, and you could wait for ages queueing to get to the top of the concrete steps on the car park. When I tried to purchase a membership, I was told that they had run out of the official cards, and instead I was given a temporary one. On the back I noticed that it was an old membership card for their catering manager, so there was only one thing to do! I turned it to the front of my plastic wallet, and each week I would brazenly push past everyone waiting on the steps, claiming to be the Catering Manager, and telling them that if they didn't let me pass, I would make sure they would not be getting in. That's confidence for you! Of course, from time to time some bodybuilding type would tell me 'no' and attempt to punch me, but the queue was always that tightly packed that it was a struggle for them to find the space to throw a punch.

One of the first girls I got off with up there was called Wendy, and she managed to tick two out of the three essentials for me to have been attracted to her – small and blonde – so I asked her back.

I don't think I ever made out it was my own pad or anything, and would always warn folk that my parents would be in bed so we would have to keep the noise down.

Things were going well, and I reckon the top she was wearing must have been designed by the same people who invented the Tardis, as the two essentials became three in a matter of minutes. We always used to joke at the time about just how many girls in Blackburn had seen my dad's pyjamas. And sure enough, just as I was about to put my clothes back on, my dad appeared at the living room door and told us both in no uncertain terms to get dressed straight away, and that my guest would have to leave. Things were a little strained at home the following morning, as my mum made it pretty clear that she did not approve of my previous night's behaviour, but I had become used to being a disappointment, and anyway, it had been a great night.

Now and then, if we were feeling adventurous, we would venture to other nightclubs and bars in nearby towns. Burnley had the Cats Whiskers, whilst Preston offered Clouds. Nicky and I had seen Animal Nightlife there, and they were brilliant. They had a brilliant album out at that time called *Lush Life,* which included their hit *Mr Solitaire.*

Accrington had the nightclub, Lar-di-dars, who had the ridiculous rule that you had to wear a jacket at all times, and it was against their policy to even roll up your sleeves up, even on a hot summer's night. (What clown decides these things?) If you wanted to be guaranteed to pull, and weren't very fussy, Sutty's at Mill Hill was the place to attend. Being fussy, I actually hated the place, even though my mates loved it, but in all the times I was dragged up there, I can't remember enjoying a single night.

It's funny really when you think about it. You spend the first part of your life trying not to be weird, and the second part of it going out of your way to be weird. There is no doubt in my mind, though, that I have always been pretty strange, compared to my mates. The word 'normal' has never really appealed to me, and apart from being a Mod and wearing a parka, being an individual has always been more appealing.
Most of my mates would sleep with anyone given the chance, and they did, but I always had to fancy someone or I didn't see the point. There are probably more girls out there that used to think that I was gay (as opposed to straight), because on several occasions I would lie there pretending to snore, or would make up some hard to believe excuse to avoid taking things to the next level, if I had not felt it at the time.

I once started seeing a really nice girl, who I'd met at the Rugby Club, called Jacky. She was good looking with straight, dark hair. She even wrote to me when I lived at my flat, from her family holiday in France. I told Nicky at the time that I intended to stop seeing her, due to her being a little bit tall (not in the job description) and the fact that she kept complimenting me. These two things would have been a positive to most people, I know. But even though it is always nice to hear good things about yourself, I have always struggled receiving compliments, and when she told me that she thought I was a really good dancer, I knew she had been lying and had to go.

Monday, we would go to the New Inns; Tuesday to Clouds; Wednesdays to Mr G's; and Thursday, Friday, and Saturday, up the Cav. Sunday, we would go to Poachers at Bamber Bridge, where every girl behind the bar had clearly been taken on based on their looks. (Paul had recommended Poachers.) And other Sunday options would include Henry Africa's in Standish, Wigan, which was really popular, especially with the Hen and Stag dos, and also over to Chorley, as it has some decent pubs to visit, like the Swan with two necks and The Weird Arms, which I thought was very fitting.

The cool guys from our area were Baz, and Anthony Grogan from Beryl Avenue. I had met Baz whilst I was on my photography course at college, and had known Anthony from school. (He was the first to have red hair.) They had started to go over to Manchester on a Saturday night, to a cool new club called The Hacienda. We decided to drag ourselves away from the Cav one week (me and Nicky, that is) and join them on the coach. I knew a few of the people in our group – Cathy, from behind The Farthings' bar, and Jill – but most of the others were strangers. I am sure that Anthony H Wilson had been sitting behind the desk on the front door (but might be wrong), and did not know what to expect once inside, seeing as it more resembled a warehouse than any nightclub I had been used to.
The experience at The Hacienda was pretty mad. The posts were covered in yellow and black industrial tape, the DJs would be found in small booths really high up, and you had to climb a hell of a lot of steps to get up there. There was a bar downstairs, and as we were walking down, some nutter was letting fireworks off on the stairs (bangers) as we were passing.

The drink that we had been warned about was called a Killer Zombie, and we soon found out where it got its name. Folk had recommended them to us, but advised us not to drink a full one on our own – and at £10 each, we were both happy to share. Less than an hour later, and based on the lack of feelings in my legs, it became apparent why we had been given the advice.
I enjoyed the experience, and did return for a couple more visits, but if I am being truthful, it wasn't really my kind of night (back then). I remember commenting to Nicky that during the whole evening I had only recognised about three tunes, and that it was more his cup of tea than mine. Only knowing three songs would probably be a good thing if it was today, and I am sure that my comment said a lot more about me at the time than the actual club.

People may feel that it would have been cooler to pretend I had enjoyed it more than I had, but I just think that it is cooler to be honest. Back then, I had tunnel vision when It came to music and was only prepared to listen to the bands and artists that were on my Mod/Punk radar. I would like to think that I have widened my antenna a lot since then, and I am really pleased that we at least managed to visit the iconic club when we did.

My dad would always say that Mark might go out on a Monday and a Friday, and that Karl would go out on a Friday and Saturday, and Nicky would go out on a Saturday and Sunday, but I went out all seven. He was correct, and providing the others made sure that I had some company each night of the week, I couldn't see things changing any time soon.

Like most small factories at the time, having a reputation for being a bit of a knocking shop was standard, and Unilab was no exception. A rubbish job, with rubbish pay, the employees (us) would have to find some other way to get through the long, boring days and keep themselves entertained.
The one memorable thing about working there was the pretty prevalent social life that was part of the deal. Almost every weekend we attended a house party or a night around town with

our work buddies. Due to the nature of the job, there was a large number of young girls taking up wiring roles on the shop floor, who were always up for a good time. People always said that it was me who instigated most of the social activities, and they are probably right, but like I said, crap job, crap wage, there had to be something to look forward to at the end of the working week.

We had been told by our boss that the company was moving from its home at Skew Bridge to Hutton Street, next door to the Daisy Dairy and Graham & Brown, as it was a bigger building. I was now the Supervisor of Packing and Despatch, as the original guy had left. The slightly extra money each week came in handy to help finance my seven nights out a week, but I questioned whether or not I had done the right thing in accepting the position, as I felt that things had become a little strained between me, Jean, and Martin. I understood their reluctance in accepting me in this new role, as they had both worked in the packing department for a long time before I rocked up. The thing was, I never had any desire to oversee that area. It was just that the two departments had been merged, and even though I have never been the type to tell folk what to do, gear and beer would have to be paid for somehow, so I decided to give it my best shot.

Another factor which made my role a little awkward was that all the young lads that worked for me at the time were also my mates, and the folk that I would party with outside work hours. They would push me as far as they could, as they knew that I was never going to tell them off.

One Christmas, we were asked to take a delivery in the yard of a couple of pallets of panels that we had been waiting for. A very long lorry turned up, and the driver told me that the pallets were right at the front of the load. I asked the Despatch lads to help, as he had to unload every other pallet first, before he could get to ours. There was snow on the ground, and it was freezing outside, and just to add to the festive authenticity of the situation, all the other pallets on his lorry were full of boxes of Christmas crackers.

Andy, Mick, Baz, and Dave formed a line to help unload the boxes. The driver threw them off the wagon to the person at the front of the queue, and then they would pass them down the line. What I didn't know at the time was that while the driver turned his back to reach for another box, a box of crackers was thrown to someone standing inside the side door of our department. Eventually every single hidden area or empty box in Despatch was filled with boxes of these crackers; there were literally hundreds. There had been that many on his wagon that the driver had been none the wiser. I always wondered to myself if he ever realised once he returned to the depot, but one thing was for sure, the employees of Unilab didn't need to buy any crackers at Christmas for at least the next three years.

The rubbish thing about working there was clocking in. As you walked down the yard and entered the workers' door, there was a telephone on the wall (which I took full advantage of). But as you walked onto the shop floor, there on the wall was an old-fashioned clock machine that you had to place your card in to record the time you arrived at work, and what time you left the building. If you were late, there was no way of getting away with it, but what made things worse was that the whole of the shop floor would witness this, along with Colin, whose office was a matter of feet away.

The company was run by this born-again Christian type, and I will never forget the day he pulled up onto the car park in his Jag and noticed a Mars Bar wrapper lying in the yard. Instead of doing what most humans would have done and simply picked it up and put it in the nearest bin, he went to his office, rang the works manager, Colin, who then called me and asked me if I could get one of my team to go out into the yard and dispose of it. I was speechless. Four people involved in picking up a chocolate bar wrapper; I certainly didn't feel it was very Christian of him.

Now and again, we would be offered the option of earning some extra money by doing overtime. In fact, sometimes we were not really given the option to say no, and were told we more or less had to do it, especially if an urgent order had to go out. The extra money came in handy, but the stumbling block to this was the fact that we went drinking every night, and many a Saturday morning we would turn up unfit for work, just so we could get the hours in. On more than one occasion we had been out to the Cav on a Friday night and invited some girls back to our house. In the morning my dad would walk into my bedroom, notice I was sharing my bed with somebody from the previous night, tell us both to get dressed, and then ask the girl to leave. Then he'd give us both a lift to Hutton Street (providing she worked there, that is). My dad was like that; he would throw someone out (usually on my mother's instructions) and then, when asked politely, would give them a lift home. Legend!

A new girl had started called Angie, and I asked her out on her very first day (before anybody else had the chance). She told me that she would think about it, but for reasons I still can't understand, other girls on the shop floor had warned her off me, telling her that I wouldn't be faithful and that I would mess her around. Not faithful, me? No way. I considered myself to be as loyal and as faithful as you could be, and was genuinely hurt and wounded by this unfounded accusation from people I got on with, or thought I had. I really liked her and wouldn't have messed her around (being a small blonde, and that).

Every Monday morning at work, the gossip on the shop floor would be about who had slept with who over the weekend, and who folk had started seeing. The people at work were pretty tight knit on the whole, and we would attend each other's weddings, birthdays, and any other party that someone might throw.
I don't really remember my 18th birthday in terms of how I celebrated it, but for my 21st we hired a Milles minibus to take my close group of friends to Manchester. My mum and dad threw a bit of a party for us all beforehand, with friends and relations, and my mum had put on a spread. Around 7.30pm, we said our goodbyes, told them not to wait up, and headed off over to Manchester.

I had booked us into the well-known club, Foo Foo Lamars, but once we arrived, we were told, 'Sorry, lads, you're not coming in tonight', despite my booking.

This was a sickener, but it was my 21st so we simply chose another club that we could get into.

We ended up having a top evening at this club, and I vaguely remember trying to talk the doormen into letting me, and the girl I had just met, go outside for a while, and agreeing to let us back in after. They were having none of it, even though it was my special day.

We arrived back at Waker's at about 3am, and he told me that out of all the times we had gone back to his, the only voice his parents could hear throughout our talking was mine. This worried me, and I tried to remember the past conversations we'd had that I wouldn't have wanted them to hear.

I was just about to head over his parents' back fence and make my way home, when one of us noticed somebody was missing. We had only gone and left Nidge in the nightclub! I know Nidge was small and quiet, but to travel back and not notice that he wasn't with us, was unreal.

Believe it or not, the house phone rang at that moment, and our forgotten friend was on the other end of the line. It was a good job that he had remembered Mark's phone number, as none of us had mobiles in those days. Mark came off the phone and, to our disbelief, announced that he had agreed to drive back over there and pick Nidge up, asking if we fancied tagging along. We knew it was a stupid move, but sure enough we all piled into the back of Mark's red Vauxhall Viva and headed back over to Manchester, to collect our friend.

One of my favourite nights out at that time was a Saturday night around Bolton. This was before Peter Kay and Mr DeNiro were on the scene, but for whatever reason, the streets were always packed, and reminded me of being on holiday.

There were two fruit machine-obsessed brothers that were regulars in The Farthings, and if we timed it right and waited until the machines had swallowed up all their current budget, they would do anything for some extra spends, so that they could get back on those machines. We would all club together and offer one of them around £15 to drive us over to Bolton. Not only that, but he would also wait inside his car for hours, whilst we were boogying in the nightclub, then drive us all home at about 2am.

I always felt bad for him regarding this arrangement, and would offer him the chance to join us in the club, but he always declined, preferring to have a quick kip in the back. The nightclub of choice was called Dance Factory, and I recall having many a good time up there, but once I discovered that the former mill town could offer a nightclub with a swimming pool in the middle of it, it was time for a venue change.

I remember a girlfriend of mine ringing me up and saying, 'Pete, I know that you would rather be in Ibiza (she knew me well), but there is a club in Bolton that features an actual pool.' So that was that. The nightclub was called Eden, and it offered a fabulous night. And even though the pool was not in the middle of the club, they had a pool – and we were going in it.

It was situated at the back of the building, which was perhaps just as well, and like a lot of things that you would never get away with now, they had their own unofficial rules before you could jump in. There were changing rooms at the side, but the door would always be left open, so you would regularly find a group of males (Nicky) hovering outside the entrance.

It is hard to believe now but their unwritten rule was that females were advised to remove their tops before entering the water, as they claimed that it would clog up the pool's filtering system. I was half expecting Frankie Howard or Sid James to be the pool attendants, but the surprising thing was that it usually worked. Girls would be in the pool topless, probably thinking that they were doing the club a favour, and I am sure that in some ways they were!

One particular time we went up, a mate of mine had warned me against it, telling me that the night before there had been a shooting outside involving the doormen in some sort of drug gang dispute. I figured that lightning was not about to strike twice, so we kept to our plans. When we were leaving Eden at about 3am, as we walked out onto the street, the entrance was covered up with black and yellow police tape. Lightning had struck twice, and there had been another shooting.

I had repeatedly told Bullinge about this nightclub with a pool, and knowing that he had done his length, I finally managed to persuade him to join me. We chose a night when DJ Trevor Nelson was performing, as we both appreciated his choice in music. Even though it was a really good night, the pool had been closed off, so all the time I had spent trying to talk Mark into dusting off his Speedos had been to no avail. I guess those pesky bikini tops had got the better of the filter system after all.

Going up the Cav on average three times a week, I am sure that there were more 'not so good nights' as opposed to good ones, but we always felt we might miss out on something if we didn't attend. There is no doubt at all that Nicky and Jez were the most successful up there in terms of success rate with the opposite sex (out of our group). Jez would use his gift of the gab and usually walk around in time for the 12 o'clock smooches and ask if he could steal a dance off some girl he liked. I was with him on one occasion when he asked a girl for a dance, and her reply was, 'No. Will you go away and leave me alone?' She was making out that he was some sort of creep. Jez, being ultra-confident of his own abilities and not one to easily give up, carried on pursuing her with his famous chat. And after leaving him to it for a couple of minutes, and half expecting him to get a slap, I turned round to find him necking with her in the corner! I must admit I was ultra- impressed.

Nicky, on the other hand, worked on the law of averages, along with the attraction of his long nails. Around 11.45pm, he would

tell us that he was just going for a walk and disappear for at least half an hour. What he would do was walk around the club several times with his eyes on full radar. If any girl happened to smile at him, or even just look his way, he would go over and ask her to dance. Of course, a lot of the time they would politely decline his friendly offer, but the law of averages says that if he managed to ask ten girls out, then at least one of them was bound to say yes.
The secret is being okay with being turned down, as some of my mates would not try again for months after being rejected. But Nicky had thicker skin, and this meant that almost every time we went to the Cav, he would end up with a girl. Everybody used to joke to Nicky that there was a trench in the carpet up there due to the number of times he would walk around, but he would just simply grin. It is also fair to say that Jez and Nicky weren't very fussy when it came to copping off, which contributed towards their heavy points tally.

The time I was the most grateful for this lack of standards, with respect, was a wet Thursday night in Blackburn. For some reason, Nick had been up the Cav on the Friday and I had not gone with him, which was very unusual. He'd met a couple of girls from London and taken them back to his mum's house. Apparently, they were up to visit some relations on Ramsgreave Drive. Nick bragged about what a good time he'd had and asked me if I fancied going on a blind date with him, as he had arranged to see them again before they returned down South. I told him in no uncertain terms that there was no chance whatsoever you would find me going on any sort of blind date, but eventually I agreed to go out with him that Thursday. I told him, though, that I would not be going out with either of the girls.

I remember sitting in the Brewers, and the weather outside was shocking, when Nick pointed out that the girls walking towards us were our company for the night. I had a quick look and declared that there was no way at all I would be going out with her, as she really wasn't my type, automatically assuming that the one I was attracted to had been spoken for. But to my delight,

Nick told me that it wasn't her that he had been with, but the other one (what a guy). I changed my mind within seconds, and due to our lack of options because of the weather, we decided to stay put. After a while, I suggested that we head back to mine.

My dad kept a drinks cabinet in the front room, and every time I brought some visitors back, I would ask them what they were drinking. I remember one night messing about and inventing the Eastwood Cocktail, but I wish I could remember for certain what the exact ingredients were for these beauties. It was along the lines of Malibu, pineapple juice, and maybe lemonade.

My dad wasn't tight at all, but he had noticed that his liquor supply had been slowly dwindling, so to try and catch the culprits out, he put a black felt tip pen line on each bottle. This was never going to be the deterrent he hoped, as I just got myself a black felt tip pen and amended the line each time. He was also not what you would call stupid, and when I blamed my brother for his missing booze, he informed me that Robin was at university in Newcastle, so this was not possible.

Anyway, back to our little Cockney friends. We had managed not to wake my parents up on our return, and whilst Nicky was in the kitchen with his chosen partner, I was left in the living room with mine. I was getting nowhere fast, and remember poking my head next door to see if Nicky was having more luck than I was. It was safe to say that he was, and I couldn't help but be concerned at what I had seen, as they were both lying on the serving hatch where my mum baked her cakes. She would have had a fit if she had seen them.
There was nothing I could do, and not wanting to disturb them, I returned to the living room to give things one last try. The situation was going from bad to worse and I was beginning to wonder why she had even come back in the first place, but just as I was about to give up, out of the blue she started to take things forward at a rapid speed. I was just starting to savour the moment regarding how fast my luck had changed, when to my absolute

horror she started shouting something highly inappropriate at the top of her voice. And before I even had time to panic, I heard my dad's footsteps marching down the stairs. The living room door burst open for him to see the four of us sitting on the settee, looking very sheepish, and his instruction to me was along the lines of, 'Get those slags out!' Another end of night ruined, and on this occasion, they would not be getting a lift home.

Our next summer holiday destination of choice was Tenerife – Los Christianos to be exact, and this was before Robert Maxwell did a Reggie Perrin at the resort. The plan was for me and Jez to spend the first week at this giant hotel, and then be joined on the second week by Bullinge, his mate Baz, and Dave (Kershy), who were staying somewhere around the corner. They booked the holiday after us and had no idea where they were staying until they arrived, so we were just hoping that it wasn't too far away from us. This was providing that I managed to survive the first week alone with Jez.

As soon as we arrived at our hotel, Jez told me that he had felt really ill, and instead of venturing out to see the sights, he opted to go to bed and try to sleep it off. I was worried that this could possibly spoil our holiday, but luckily the following morning he was fine and back to his usual mad self. We would sit at breakfast and Jez would randomly jump up and wander around the other tables, asking folk if they wanted their eggs or other items on their plate.

The hotel was well known for its sports facilities, so we booked to have a game of tennis the following morning. The famous Playa De Las Americas was only a taxi ride away, and based on its reputation for offering a very lively nightlife, the plan was to pay it a visit each evening. On our first night, we paid to attend a Reps' welcoming event in a local bar, organised for all the new arrivals. Because we had paid a certain amount, all the drinks were supposed to be free. This, as always, was a con. About two hours in, it was announced that to get a free drink at the bar you

had to take your empty glass to put it in. We came up with the idea to walk around the room and collect as many empty glasses as we could find, so that we would be sorted for the rest of the night.
We were indeed sorted, as underneath our chairs and on our table were pint glasses filled with lager and others with champagne. I reckon it was around 3.45am when my body told me 'no more', but when I suggested leaving, Jez said that he was staying a little longer and he would see me back at our room.

I have absolutely no idea how I managed to find my way back to the hotel, never mind our room, but I did. It is fair to say that I was the most drunk I had ever been up to that point, and I finally crashed out, fully dressed on the top of the bed. Normally I would never have done such a thing. No matter what state I was in, I would always hang my clothes up in the wardrobe before falling into bed (must be a Mod thing).

I eventually woke the following morning feeling extremely rough and realised that Jez was not in the room. Stupidly, I thought he must have gone down to breakfast, so I made my way down, but there was no sign of him. After I had eaten as much stodge as I could manage, hoping it would cure my hangover, I went over to reception to hire our tennis equipment, ready for when he finally decided to show his face. I gave the receptionist my booking slip, expecting her to exchange it for our rackets and balls, but to my surprise she informed me that I would have to leave the hotel. Not again! I couldn't believe what I was hearing and guessed that Jez must have really outdone himself this time.

Around an hour later, I spotted him outside our hotel and asked him to explain what was going on. Apparently, he had returned to the hotel at around 4.30am, very much the worse for wear. He had asked the guy on reception several times for our room key, but the man had just ignored him and continued to talk to a local policeman who was there. When Jez started to lose his patience and added a couple of obscenities in Spanish to the conversation, the policeman walked over and started to hit Jez with his baton then told him to get outside.

Jez's version was that once outside, he had called over a stray dog that was hanging around outside the hotel and had fallen asleep leaning on it. He also said that the policeman had kicked our bedroom door open, demanding to see our passports, and apparently, I hadn't moved a muscle and carried on sleeping, oblivious to the situation Jez had put us both in.

Getting evicted from our hotel on holiday after only one day was a new one even for Jez.

No matter what we said to the manager, he told us to leave the hotel, and we stood there for the rest of the day with our Rep as she pleaded with him to give us another chance. But he really wasn't for budging. After a lot of persuading, he begrudgingly agreed with our Rep to give us one final chance, and even though this was a relief, it felt that our every move was being watched for the rest of our stay. When Mark, Baz, and Dave arrived for our second week, and were staying just down the road, things settled down a little, and we spent most nights sleeping at theirs.

The first pub that we started in each evening was called the John Bull, and on our first night there, I told a girl that she reminded me of Barry Grant's sister in *Brookside* (Karen). This wasn't my greatest chat up line, but it worked, as she invited me back to her apartment. She was actually called Karen, and she and her friend Laura were from East Kilbride in Scotland. Their apartment was pretty smart and, to make up the numbers, I had taken Bullinge with me. Mark was going out with Ste's sister at that time, but Laura was really good looking, and we were on holiday after all.

I ended up in bed with Karen (too much info, I know), and I remember her telling me that she couldn't have full blown sex with me as she had promised her fiancé that she wouldn't. I thought that was fair enough, but I reckoned her fiancé seemed pretty understanding anyway. The other two were on the balcony and I tried to listen to see if my mate was getting anywhere, but all I could hear was him talking about his girlfriend back home.

Hence, their conversation didn't last long, and Mark ended up going back to his apartment. Even though at the time I was amazed at how boring he had been, to be fair, he was always the loyal type, which is a good trait to have. So I eventually dropped the subject.

The following morning, we had arranged to visit a water park, and I had asked Mark if they could call round and pick me up, as I had really wanted to go. I woke up in a strange bed, with a strange girl, in a strange place, and I had not had a visit from my friends. I recall swimming up and down in Karen and Laura's private pool and thinking this was the life. The boys had clearly forgotten to pick me up, so I spent the day with Team East Kilbride.

When I eventually returned back to our apartment, I remember strolling in like the cat who had got the cream and was told that they didn't call back for me as they hadn't wanted to disturb me at the time, which I suppose was fair enough.

It was becoming pretty clear by now that it was impossible to come away, anywhere, without another group from our hometown being present. We had barely taken off when we discovered that there was a group of lads on board the plane who were from the Highercroft area of Blackburn. We chatted with them for a while and swapped contact details, as we agreed to meet up. To say that these lads were pretty rowdy was an understatement, and the names I can remember are Stuart, Gash, Molly, Wally, and the maddest one by far, Kirky. He was a Tottenham fan, but everyone else supported Rovers, which meant there wasn't too much rivalry on the footballing front.

The nightlife in Las Americas was absolutely mental and the liveliest I had known up to this point. Mrs T club, for the best British sounds around, Come to the Coolest Disco in Town, Veronica ll, and the famous Sgt Pepper's Cocktail Bar, were about as packed as you could get. Veronica's was an open-air nightclub, and I must admit that I was a little freaked out, dancing under the stars on the dancefloor whilst the local police regularly walked past carrying hand guns. I had not experienced this before. Also, the DJ asked if there was anyone from Blackburn in the club, and several groups of people started to cheer. I ended up kissing someone that I had known from around town back home, and have actually just spent the last 17 years working at the same place as her, but it was certainly in the moment.

We all had an absolutely wonderful holiday in Tenerife, but we (Jez) nearly caused a riot at the airport going home, once it was announced that our plane had been delayed.

The week after we arrived home, I couldn't believe my eyes when I read an article in the morning paper regarding an incident in Veronica's bar. One of those local policemen who had freaked me out back then, had sat down on a bar stool a few days later, and his gun that had been in his holster had accidently gone off as he was taking his seat, killing the person on the next stool.

Another thing happened that had been linked to our holiday in Tenerife. On one of our nights out with the girls, Laura told us a story about her suing a First Division footballer. She told us that she had been on holiday in Ibiza the previous year, and she and her mates had stopped to buy some chips when suddenly this guy who she recognised came over and asked for a chip. When she refused and told him to go and get his own, he punched her in the face and broke her jaw.
To me, this story seemed a bit far-fetched and her jaw looked fine, so I declared that I didn't know whether to believe her or not. This didn't go down well, but I was only being honest.
Several weeks after we had returned home, I was at a friend's house and the television was on, but the sound had been turned down. The 10 o'clock news came on, and to my disbelief, a picture of Laura appeared on the screen, and everything she had told us that night had been true. I felt terrible that I had doubted her.

Jez and I did ring them one evening, using the numbers they had given us, but they were a little sheepish – no doubt due to the fact they were both engaged at the time. That's a holiday romance for you!

VHS video cassettes, back in the day, really changed our lives. Until then, we would have to visit a cinema to be able to watch the latest or recommended films. I will always remember the day my dad brought home our first colour television and the first thing we watched on it that night was an old Jerry Lewis film. But the arrival of VHS cassettes meant that if you could afford a video machine player, you could go to your local video shop to select that evening's viewing.

I had always been a fan of watching the television and going to watch a movie, and started off like most kids, watching the likes of *The Magic Roundabout, Trumpton, The Clangers, The Double Deckers* and *Joe 90*. These were followed by the likes of *Tintin, The Banana Splits, Deputy Dawg*, and of course, *Marine Boy*, especially during the summer holidays.

A little older, and I moved onto *The Flashing Blade, Dr Who, The Tomorrow's People, Kung Fu*, and *Appointment with Fear*. But while I lived at home, my mum and dad would be in control of the TV remote in the evenings, which meant that we were subjected to shows like *The Wheeltappers and Shunters, The Black and White Minstrel Show, It's a Knockout, Love Thy Neighbour, Jim 'll Fix It* (who knew then?), The News, and thankfully, *Morecambe and Wise, Gilligan's Island*, and *The Beverley Hillbillies*.

Once I discovered my love for music, it was every show on TV that happened to feature my favourite bands. *Top of the Pops, So It Goes, The Old Grey Whistle Test, The Tube*, and my favourite, *Revolver* hosted by Peter Cook. *Revolver* predominantly featured Punk and New Wave bands who were just about to break through, but it is interesting watching the old footage of this show and picking out the members of the audience who went on to join well known bands not long after.

Variety Video was our chosen Holy Grail, to go and rent the latest movies. Yes, you had to wait a few months after their cinema release to borrow the latest blockbuster, but we were far more interested in watching the films that we were not supposed to see. Pirate videos and video nasties were what we were after, and we couldn't get enough of them.

Video nasty was a term used in the UK to refer to a number of films, usually low budget horror and exploitation movies that would appear on video cassette but were highly criticised for their violent content by the press, various religious groups, and especially Mary Whitehouse.

The thing was that these video releases had not been brought before the British Board of Film Classification, due to a loophole in the film classification laws that allowed videos to bypass the review process. The better known of these titles included *I Spit on Your Grave, Zombie Flesh Eaters, The Burning, The Evil Dead*, and *The Texas Chainsaw Massacre*, which were eventually given a cinema release with cuts.

The video titles that shocked our senses were the likes of *Island of Death, The Last House on the Left, Nightmares in a Damaged Brain, Snuff, Faces of Death*, and of course the Cannibal titles, including *Cannibal Apocalypse, Cannibal Ferox*, and *Cannibal Holocaust*. The amazing thing was that Variety Video, opposite King George's Hall, stocked the lot, and we would hire them at every opportunity.

I had to wait until my parents were out and I had the house to myself, then ask someone who could drive, usually Waker, to take us to the shop to select the evening's VHS treat. The films were all disturbing in their own way, but the one that freaked me out the most was *Faces of Death*. I had walked down to the video shop on my own to rent the film, as I had heard so much about its reputation, and recall putting it on at home and being so concerned and freaked out about what might be coming next that I rang Nicky up and told him he had to come round and watch it with me.

Basically, it was a documentary about death around the world, and the scene that got everyone talking was at a supposed restaurant in Asia, where the waiter would bring a live monkey to a table of two couples. There was a hole in the middle of the table where the monkey's head would poke through, and the waiter would then, with a sharp knife, slice off the top of the monkey's head and the diners would grab their spoon and tuck into the monkey's brain – considered a delicacy.

This was absolutely horrific, and if that wasn't enough, the film ended with a man in a hole being shot, and watching him slowly dying.

Anyone reading this would no doubt wonder why on earth anyone would want to spend their time watching scenes like that, and I totally agree. But we were young, and we had no idea at all what was coming next in the film, which in a funny sort of way was exciting back then. These days, I am passionate about all animal welfare issues and would never dream of watching a video like that.

The Snuff video had a conspiracy theory surrounding its release, as it was claimed – word of mouth –at the time that some of the actors that 'died' in the film had been killed for real, as they had not been seen since. This, of course, was absolute nonsense and was purely a marketing ploy.

Following a campaign led by Conservative activist Mary Whitehouse and the National Viewers and Listeners Association (NVLA), prosecutions were brought against any individual deciding to trade in these obscene videos. The Director of Public Prosecutions released a list of 72 films which he believed to have violated the Obscene Publications Act of 1959, as a tool to assist the local authorities. The majority, if not all, of these titles were on the hit list, and literally overnight video shops were raided, and the offending items removed from the shelves. I remember walking through the door of my favourite video shop the following day to find that most of the shelves were half empty. It actually looked like they had been burgled.

Years later, with the arrival of the DVD replacing video cassettes, the majority of these titles became available on this new snazzy format, but a number of cuts had been made. To get your hands on the full uncut version, you had to order them from America. So I did. I don't know what possessed me, but I ordered a DVD of *The Dreaded Faces of Death*, and as I was watching it again after all these years, I felt guilty and sick at the fact that I had yet again purchased this upsetting footage.

At the end of the DVD, added as an extra, was included the making of the documentary, which I was glad about, as it explained that the much talked about monkey scene was actually fake. After initially producing a real monkey at the beginning of the clip, it was substituted with a rubber monkey, and the actual brain that everyone seemed to enjoy was dyed cauliflower. Watching this was a massive relief, but there was some genuine footage as part of the documentary, and the result of this second viewing caused me to become a vegetarian for 11 weeks and giving up red meat for just over four years.

As for pirate videos at the time, or any time, they were just as sought after by our group as the nasties. A pirate video could have been absolutely anything, and could always be obtained from someone, if you knew where to look and who to ask. Feature films that were still showing at the cinemas were always popular, and you could purchase these makeshift versions from most places you visited on your holidays. I remember buying about five in Cyprus and having to wait until I got home before I could view them. A couple of the videos were blank, and another was such bad quality that you couldn't make it to the end. The final one actually seemed okay, until the last few minutes. Just as the punchline was about to be revealed, it cut off. It wasn't as if I was going back to Ayia Napa to complain. I had been well and truly conned.

The movies would either have been a really terrible copy of the original, probably originating from someone who had sat on the Oscars or Academy judging panel committee, or had been really badly filmed by some dodgy looking bloke in a movie cinema. Basically, you would be watching a scene when suddenly someone would stand up in front of the screen to go to the toilet. You would always find these kinds of films for sale on the seafront at Blackpool, and at the time we paid a few visits there ourselves.

Dirty films were the other popular pirate format doing the rounds before the internet. These again would not be the best quality, but people would do anything for a cheap thrill, and it was our only way of getting hold of some of these titles. Paul at The Farthings had a mate who ran the Borough pub in town, and it was alleged that he was the proud owner of the muckiest movie collection around. Paul would borrow these off his friend and pass them around The Farthings, so we had to put our name down and place our order, then wait until someone else brought the film back.

I recall borrowing the much-hyped film *Debbie Does Dallas* and being very disappointed by the quality and the lead. It might just as well have been Deidre does Daisyfield to me, as the film was no *Emmanuelle*.

The most memorable time was when Nicky asked to borrow a film, and Paul selected one for him, saying that the girls in it were all gorgeous. Nicky couldn't wait to finish his shift and go home to watch it. At the time he lived on Hardy Street with a couple of male mates and a girl, and he had to wait for them all to go to bed before watching his evening's entertainment.

It is safe to say that what appeared on his television screen that night was not the cheap thrill he was expecting (so he says). Instead, Paul had given him a gay porno film, featuring sailors in the Navy. Nick made out that as soon as he realised what the film was about, he turned it off, but what was hilarious was that he told us he stayed awake all night worrying and thinking that if he popped his clogs during the night, his mates would find the video – which was now under his bed – the following day and that would have been his legacy. Nobody would have believed that this was not the real Nick. Nice one, Paul!

The videos that appealed to me the most at the time were the bootleg concerts of my favourite bands. Someone filming at a gig, and maybe recording the sound straight from the desk, had always been a popular concept between music fans, and even some of the bands. You could normally buy such pirates from a record fair, if you knew which stall to go to, and they would produce a whole extra stock from under the counter. It really was big business done properly, and I used to love my visits to Manchester, as there was always a fabulous selection to choose from.

Even though I have always been extra fussy when it comes to standards and quality, I have always had an attraction to getting my hands on things that were banned or you were not supposed to have. Paul had even started a movie night in our local on a Tuesday evening, and we would poach all the regulars from The Brownhill and The Knowles, as he would usually show either a video nasty such as *I Spit on Your Grave,* or the very inappropriate adult cartoon, *King Dick.*

There was even a time we had been at Baz's house at Mill Hill, and he put on a pirate video called *Down on the Farm,* but I certainly won't be writing about that one!

Even the local nightclub would offer its own form of titillation in the 80s. On a Thursday night at the Cav, they would stage a weekly Miss Wet T-Shirt competition to pull in the crowds. Just to avoid accusations of being sexist, they would also stage a Mr Wet and Wiggly contest from time to time. It really is amazing to look back and realise what was acceptable back then, but which folk would never get away with nowadays. Even at the time I felt that this was incredibly cringeworthy, but it never put us off attending. The format was that halfway through the night, someone would bring out a little paddling pool and place it in the centre of the dancefloor. One by one, a girl (or a lad) would stand inside the pool, whilst some pervert DJ would produce a watering can and pour freezing cold water over selected parts of the body. After everyone had taken their turn, the audience would choose the winner.

Vausey, the one with the gang, lived in a sort of a mansion at the top of Whinney Lane at Mellor.
His dad had made his fortune by inventing a wireless plug, and needless to say, living and partying in this mansion certainly attracted the girls.

Every week, we would pay to go up the Cav and spend a large percentage of our night trying to get off with a girl. But I noticed that Vausey's lot usually didn't even have to attend the nightclub to get lucky. They would simply park their van on the car park around 2am, when everyone was leaving the club, and basically meet girls then to take back to his.

Me and Waker were watching a video at our house one Friday night, when I suggested we give it a go. We only really did it for a laugh, but sure enough about 1.45am, we rang a DMC taxi to take us to the Cav car park, and to our absolute surprise it only took us about five minutes to meet two girls and be invited back to theirs. When we arrived back at Jayne's house somewhere in Mill Hill, to Mark's annoyance, her mate said goodnight to us all and marched off down the street to her house.
Mark ended up crashing on Jayne's settee, whilst I had been given her bed to sleep in.

What I thought had been a mad night was just about to get a whole lot madder. Around 7.30am, Jayne jumped out of bed and said she was going to be late for work. Instead of telling us to sling our hook, she asked me to make sure we shut the front door behind us when we left. Surely, she wasn't about to head for work and leave two strange looking blokes in her house? What was even stranger was that she wrote down her number on a ten-pound note and handed it to me. A tenner was a fair bit in those days and would at least have paid for the latest LP.
It took literally about 90 seconds for us to realise why we had been trusted in this stranger's house alone. The fact of the matter was that we weren't alone; within seconds of the front door shutting, the biggest and meanest looking Alsatian dog appeared

from nowhere and positioned itself inches away from us both. I can assure anyone reading this that my description of this dog is not over exaggerated, as it resembled Zoltan, the Hound of Dracula.

Waker was still lying on the settee, using a very thin blanket to hide behind, and I was wearing a big chunky, baggy jumper, sitting in the chair right next to him. If I made a noise or moved a little, our canine friend would bark aggressively and grab my jumper in its teeth. I remember wondering if this was actually happening to us, and what might have started off as being funny had certainly turned to very unfunny within minutes. Jayne must have known that this would happen, as that's why she had not just asked us to leave when she did.

The longer this situation went on, the more frightened we both were, and I don't mind admitting that at one point I am sure we both had tears in our eyes. It was that scary. This dog was relentless, and just as we began to feel our ordeal was never going to end, I picked my moment and legged it to the downstairs toilet. I managed to climb out of the toilet window, go around the front, and whilst the dog was waiting at the toilet door, Mark made a run for it. We had escaped to live another day, and I recall legging it down her street as fast as we could in the pouring rain.

I must admit, I had begun to wonder why my dates weren't as straightforward as other people's, but that was the last time we ever went to the Cav after it had finished.

When I lived at my flat, I came up with the idea of borrowing my dad's car for the night. But like the rest of my ideas, this did not go to plan and was another disappointment that my parents would periodically bring up as a reminder of things I had done wrong – as if I needed reminding.

A few of us were sat around debating what the night may have in store when I announced that my mum and dad were away, and that their Vauxhall Viva was sitting outside the house doing nothing. Obviously as I couldn't drive, I had been hoping that Nidge would offer – providing I could nick it, that is. The stumbling block was my brother Robin, who lived at home. I knew there was no way whatsoever that he was about to just hand me the keys.

I paid a visit to my parents' house and explained to him that we were planning to go to Blackpool for a drive, and that I would certainly make sure to return the keys the following morning. That way, nobody would be none the wiser. As I had anticipated, my brother laughed at me, made a sarcastic comment, and told me that there was no chance.

I tried again to persuade him to change his mind, but Robin was like my dad in terms of keeping within the law and not doing anything that you were not supposed to do. My dad would drive another half a mile from where he was dropping you off, rather than let you out on a yellow line, and Robin had adopted his cautious traits.

There was only one thing for it. I would just have to take the keys, as the friendly approach had not worked. Even this turned out to be harder than I imagined, and the pair of us ended up engaging in a proper fist fight on top of his bed. Even though he was holding the keys as tightly as he could, I eventually managed to grab them and leg it out of the door. I am afraid that on this occasion the Guardian of the Viva was well and truly beaten.

We hadn't really given any thought to what we were going to do once we got to Blackpool, but the plan was just to drive around for a bit and then park up. I remember peering out of the back window and noticing a police car right behind us, and asking everyone to keep quiet and calm.

I said to Nidge, 'We are being followed by the police. Whatever you do, act normal, and hopefully they will go away.'

But not long after offering this piece of advice, and to everyone's despair, we all realised that Nigel was actually driving down the centre of the tram tracks. Sure enough, the police pulled us over and asked us to produce our documents. I explained to the officer that my dad had lent me the keys to his car as he was away on holiday, and even though he ended up letting us go, he said that they would be chasing this story up. That was me in trouble again!

The only other thing I remember from this occasion is waking up in bed the morning after, to find a girl from my year at school lying next to me, and wondering how the hell did that happen.

They say that if you can't remember a night out, then it must have been a good one, so I reckoned it must have been. And because it was in my flat, some of my mates were in the bed next to me, so I was hoping to ask them for more information once my lady friend had said her goodbyes.

Angie from work moved into a flat at Larkhill, along with her mate, Trish, and even though I visited a couple of times, I always felt I had to be invited, so as not to make it too obvious that I still fancied her. The only way we could contact each other was for her to ring me at my parents' home (still with the lock on) or for me to call the phone in her flats. But unless we arranged the time I would ring, I would run the risk of anyone from the other flats picking up the phone.

It was Christmas time and I hadn't heard from Angie for several days, which I was pretty gutted about. Simon and I had gone to watch Rovers, thinking that this would be my only thrill over the festive period. The match was a boring 1-1 draw, and it was freezing with snow and ice everywhere. When I arrived home, I asked my dad on the off chance if anybody had rung for me, expecting him to say no. But to my surprise he said, 'Oh, yes, someone call Angie rang and asked if you could call her back tonight.' Forget Rovers, I was buzzing. I mean she wouldn't have called me if she wasn't interested, right?

I called her on time, and was relieved when she in fact answered, as it really was hit and miss ringing that phone. Angie told me that she and Trish had rowed, and that Trish had gone off to London for the weekend, so asked if I fancied going over to hers that night. I was even more buzzing and didn't even pretend to check my diary before accepting her invitation, whilst doing my best not to sound too desperate. I told my parents that I wasn't sure if I was staying out or not, but that I had my key just in case, not being too presumptuous.

I really enjoyed my evening round at Angie's flat, as we always got on really well and we shared the same taste in music – Soul and Funk, that is, not Punk or Mod. Just as I was about to bring the subject up regarding a sleepover, Angie told me that I may have to go as she was going to have a bath. Always being one to find a positive out of a negative, I zoomed in on the word 'may', thinking that if she wanted me to leave, she would have used more forceful terminology.
Sure enough, my positivity worked, and she told me that she wouldn't be long, then headed off to the bathroom. I admit thinking at the time that perhaps I should go and join her, hoping that she had a bottle of Matey on the side, but wondered if I should be a gentleman and do the honourable thing and just wait there. Not wanting to jeopardise our friendship in case I had read the signs wrong, I chose the latter.

Still thinking to myself that I stood a good chance of staying, as it was now almost midnight, Ange appeared wearing only her dressing gown. But as proof that you should never take anything for granted, especially not in my life, knocking at the door made both of us jump. Bang, bang, bang at the flat door. Surely someone must have the wrong number, as the timing couldn't have been any worse.

I didn't know whether to hide or not while Angie went to answer the door, but I couldn't believe my eyes, or my luck, when standing there, looking even less pleased than me, was Trish. I recall her first words were, 'I knew you would invite him round.' Why in the world, the night after New Year's Day, would Trish decide to travel back to Blackburn and arrive back home at midnight? It was as though she had been waiting outside the flat door all the time, planning when to make her grand entrance.

The situation reminded me, in some small way, of my favourite joke as a child. I have never been able to remember any jokes, no matter how funny, but this one went along the lines of...

A family of bears decided to go for a picnic in the woods, and on their arrival, they realised they had left the tin opener at home. The walk to the woods had made the bears really hungry and they couldn't wait to tuck in and start munching on their sandwiches.

Not wanting to spoil the picnic, Father Bear agreed to return back home and collect the tin opener, but on the strict instructions that no-one started eating until he returned. They all agreed, and off he went.
24 hours went by and still Father Bear hadn't returned. Baby Bear was dying to make a start on the picnic, but Mother Bear told them that they had promised and that it was only fair they waited for him to return.

A whole week passed, and the same conversation was had. One month went by and still no sign of Father Bear, and the rest of the family were starving. So Mother Bear announced that it might be okay for them to have just one sandwich each to keep them going, when suddenly, a voice came from behind a bush saying, 'You do, and I won't go!'

Back at the flat, I kept quiet, but Angie and Trish had been arguing for a while when Angie suggested we go to my house. I didn't need persuading and rang my regular taxi firm. Taxis at that time of year charged time-and-a-half, but I was more concerned about how I was going to sneak Angie in without my parents waking up. Accepting this damage limitation, so far so good, I even managed to bang on some Jonathan Butler on my music system without any rumblings from next door. But as was becoming tradition in our household, my dad appeared in my box room the following morning and asked my houseguest to please leave. I can't remember if he gave her a lift back, but he probably did. It took me a long time to get my head around Trish's timing on that fateful night, but I don't think I ever discussed it with her.

Our first day back at Unilab, I was summoned to Colin's office at the end of the day, even though I had no idea what I had done wrong. Once there, and to my disbelief, he asked me what Angie was doing wearing my jumper for work. I couldn't believe he was asking me this, but explained that she must have borrowed it the other evening when she had stayed over at ours.
I really liked that jumper, but that was the last I saw of it.

CHAPTER NINE

THE PLACE I LOVE

When I was young, I saw some pictures of this magical place in my Grandma's newspaper supplement. Later I found out the destination was the Seychelles in the Indian Ocean, and have spent my life craving a visit.
After our dysfunctional holiday in Tenerife, me and my mates talked about having a change and maybe trying out the Caribbean, but obviously this was going to take a lot of saving up. Each year my intentions were always to cut down on going out every night and to save some money towards our summer break. This never happened, and I have always found myself heading down to the TSB on Lord St West to get a £500 loan to ease the burden.

The Seychelles were still out of the equation, as my mates told me that there was no way they could afford to go there. Instead, Barbados was the destination chosen, and I knew this time I would need a bit more willpower, as the £500 from the TSB definitely wouldn't cover it all.

I had a bet with Jean at work that I would be staying in for a month so I could put some money away for once, and I started off with good intentions. But after only two nights, I felt I might be missing out on something and scrapped the idea. I had planned to stick to the story as far as Jean was concerned, but my cover was blown when I walked into The Farthings the following night to see Jean and her husband, Alan, sitting near the entrance. I lost the bet.

After a few months, some of our friends decided that they couldn't afford such a lavish trip, so it ended up just being me and Karl heading for the paradise isle. On the actual day we were jetting off, we arranged to meet Bullinge at lunchtime for a drink in Toffs. Mark was on his lunch break from work, so only had an hour. He told us that his fiancée had just been on holiday to Cyprus with her mate, but she had told him she didn't trust him, so he was going nowhere. I thought this was a little tight and proper out of order, so I told him he should come to Barbados with us.

Thinking I was joking, Mark laughed it off, but I told him I was deadly serious and to my amazement he replied, 'Go on then.'

He legged it over to his bank and. luckily, knowing the girl behind the counter, he managed to sort a loan out there and then. Whilst he was doing that, Karl and I headed straight to Thomas Cook and begged our rep, Joanne, to try and find him a last-minute booking on our flight, and a room at Smugglers Cove in Saint James where we would be staying.

Being a person that doesn't do barriers, I knew this might be possible, even though a long shot, and Joanne proved me right. Bullinge was now the proud owner of a return ticket to Barbados, which had been achieved in record time. Even though me and Karl had booked this holiday the previous November, Mark was packed before us. Everything had worked out well, and we felt really pleased with ourselves. There was just one small thing we had overlooked: the small task of explaining to his fiancée that he was off to the Caribbean that evening.

This was one thing that I was certainly not getting involved with, even though I was pretty sure that I would get the blame. As expected, Debbie hit the roof at this very unexpected news; in reality, it was Mark's Capri windscreen she actually hit, and managed to put a crack in it. Bullinge did love his Capris.

I recall standing on the Boulevard that night, with my dad, Karl, and Bullinge, waiting for my and Karl's coach to take us to London, and fully expected Debbie to suddenly appear and attack me for taking her fella away. But luckily it didn't happen.

As the booking was very last minute, there wasn't a seat on our coach for Mark, so he was getting the train and agreed to meet us at Heathrow, where we were flying from. We didn't get any sleep on the coach and were shattered as we sprawled on a bench in the airport, waiting for our holiday buddy to turn up. He finally found us, and as we were waiting for our gate to be called, I couldn't help but notice a girl who was walking up and down just in front of us. The reason she caught my eye, apart from the fact she was really good looking, was that I thought she looked classy. She certainly stood out in a crowd, as far as I was concerned, though I knew the odds of seeing her again were next to zero. To our surprise, the mystery female appeared at the same check-in desk as us! Surely, she wasn't going to Barbados?

The flight to Barbados was about nine hours, and it was the only flight I had ever been on where the bars were all free. It is safe to say that we took full advantage of this, and between the three of us, I dread to think how many Budweisers were supped. We were told that we would be refuelling in Antigua, and as we were walking down the steps of the plane, I noticed a couple of security guys running towards us and waving their arms about. I turned to tell the other two about this commotion, when to my absolute disbelief I realised that Karl had only got a lit cigarette in his hand. He had obviously not noticed the giant Esso truck re-fuelling at the bottom of the steps, and the two very lively security guys were actually running towards us.

Just as we were about to reboard our plane, I noticed my mystery girl in the distance with what looked like her mum and dad. We finally landed in Barbados, and I will never forget the amazing view from out of the plane window as we descended, and the turquoise blue lagoons as *The Living Daylights* by A-Ha was playing through the tannoy.

The beach at Saint James was absolutely beautiful, and our hotel was right on it. We were three hotels away from the exquisite Sandy Lane Complex with its own private golf course and spa.

Apparently, Rod Stewart was staying there at the same time we were there, but we never bumped into the wannabe Scot.

We all unpacked as fast as we could, and within 20 minutes of arriving, the three of us were swimming in the sea, with flying fish jumping out of the water all around us. If that moment wasn't magical enough, the couple strolling beside us on the beach were none other than the parents of that mystery girl from the airport lounge, which proved to me that there is a God after all. It turned out that the mystery girl was called Jenny, and she was staying with her parents, Roy and Sheila Brooks, at the Buccaneer Bay Hotel, just a short walk along the beach from our hotel.

We started talking to Roy and Sheila as they were passing, and even though we had only just met them, they invited us to a barbecue at their hotel that night, encouraging us to hang out with their daughter (go on then!). Not knowing what to expect, we accepted their kind invitation and headed off to get ready. Their hotel was something else, and what we had imagined would be a few burgers and sausages cooked inside the hotel, couldn't have been more different. This ultra-posh barbie was almost on the beach, the chefs were all wearing tall white hats, and it was a six-course meal, which included port.

There were around 20 people sharing a very long table, and even though everyone seemed really friendly, I couldn't help worrying how much this banquet was going to cost. After all, we were three skint lads from Blackburn, and even though our holiday had only cost us £750 each, we had each taken a loan out to pay for it.

After a brilliant evening with our newfound friends, we thought we had better ask for the bill. When it arrived, I remember us all studying it, trying to make sense of the large numbers in Bajan Dollars. We reckoned that paying this would probably wipe out the majority of our spending money, but before we even managed to work out the total cost of the three meals, Roy told us that as he had invited us, the evening was on him. Phew! We couldn't believe his generosity, as we hardly knew the guy, but we were certainly very grateful for his kindness on that occasion.

Luckily, we all got on with Jenny really well, and without a doubt that first night in the magnificent Saint James set the tone for the rest of our stay. I think that we all fancied Jenny, if we were being honest, but even though we hung around with her every day, naturally, she chose the big, muscle-bound waterski instructor to offer her affections to – and certainly not us in that way.

Roy and Sheila originally came from Manchester, where they had a chemical company, before moving to Lichtenstein in Germany. They visited the Buccaneer Bay Hotel several times a year, (alright for some), and it didn't take us long to realise that every single guest staying at the hotel was probably a millionaire. Roy was great company to be in and always held court; Colin worked on the Stock Exchange; Ruth owned her own designer clothes shop in Dublin; and there was a family from Lancaster who owned a few racehorses. They actually gave us a tip about their prize horse, called Cariga Bay, and even though for years I always looked out for it, I never heard the name again. (It's probably still running!)

All these people were on another level to us in terms of wealth and status, but they never made us feel that we were any different. If they'd only known that our holiday friendship had been sponsored by TSB! Roy's generosity was never-ending, and he wouldn't let us go to the bar without him shouting, 'I'll get those!' I didn't want to take advantage of him, so tried on numerous occasions to sneak off without him seeing me, but he always managed to spot me.
When it was Jenny's birthday, Roy hired a 52ft catamaran for us all to spend the day on, out in the Caribbean, which also included free food, free drinks, and free water sports. It felt like we were dreaming, and we could never have imagined that our first trip to the Caribbean would have turned out like this.

Being a fan of water, I really fancied a go on the jet skis that Roy had arranged to accompany our trip. Bullinge was the first to have a go, and he was pretty good at balancing and staying on the machine. Mark had been a keen skateboarder back in the day, which had clearly helped him with his balance. In my case, being 6ft 2 meant my balance had always been terrible, but I was still going to give it a go.

Watching someone riding a jet ski made it look reasonably simple, but it turned out to be a whole lot harder than I thought. My problem was mounting the thing, as the technique was to start off behind it in the water and, once you started the engine, you were supposed to pull yourself up onto the seat. The issue was that every time I managed to start the motor, the pressure hit me in a very delicate place, which made it impossible for me to pull myself up.

This calamity went on for around 15 minutes until I eventually managed to flood the engine. What I didn't realise was that by now I was drifting further and further away from the catamaran and our party, which now appeared like little dots on the horizon. I knew at the time that this wasn't good, but the more I pushed the jet ski forward and then swam breaststroke in order to catch it up, the more I was going nowhere. After attempting these actions over and over again, and not getting any nearer to our boat, I had almost used all my energy up and was starting to feel slightly worried.

What happened next, I couldn't have predicted. It was as if I had been granted one wish and had called for my Fairy Godmother(s). Heading towards me was a really flashy speedboat, and as it got closer, I noticed that along with the guy steering the boat, there were two model-type females in bikinis chilling in the back. They pulled up alongside me and told me to get in, and as I had sat in-between the two beauties in the back, I knew that my return was probably going to feature in the top three list of my most embarrassing moments.

Sure enough, as I climbed back on board the catamaran, everyone was clapping, shouting, and screaming at my comedy-esque rescue, and I remember telling them that the whole thing had been planned so that I could be rescued by two bikini-clad beauties.

Unfortunately, the joking didn't last long, as the guy who drove the boat was in fact the owner of the flooded jet ski, and he was not exactly happy with me. He gave me a lecture, saying I had ruined his pride and joy, and that I was officially the worst person in Barbados to hire one of his machines. At least I was top of a list for something!

Swimming in the sea at Saint James was an amazing experience, as the water was crystal blue and if you put your head under the water you were surrounded by large, flat yellow and blue fish. One night we even went skinny dipping as the Jolly Roger sailed past in the distance, but it wasn't quite the same with just Bullinge and Karl for company.

The following day, we were listening to Roy holding court as usual around the pool, as he insisted on buying a round of drinks every 20 minutes for anyone who was listening to him. Karl and Mark ended up so drunk by mid-afternoon that I had to venture out all on my own that evening and leave them both in bed.
One of the guests at the Buccaneer Bay was there with his two-year-old daughter, Chloe, who was the cutest thing, and we used to play at throwing her in the pool, which she seemed to love. She reminded me of a very, very, young Bridget Bardot, and years later ended up being the star of Sky One's hit series, 'Caribbean Uncovered'. I never forgot her name and almost fell off my chair when she appeared on the screen dancing on a nightclub table all those years later. I guess she had grown up!

The barman was the spitting image of Eddie Murphy, but his name was actually Mike, and one evening he took us to the amazing Baxters Road in Bridgetown. I don't think we would have been brave enough to go there without our wonderful guide, but what an eye-opener it was. I have never experienced anything like it in my life. A massive, long road and a massive, long party. Every few yards there was a giant stack system blasting out Reggae music, and all generations were dancing in the street, on shop roofs, and on top of cars. There was fresh chicken and fish being cooked at the side of the road, and at some point during the evening I noticed an elderly Rastafarian guy lying in the gutter as if he was dead. But what had summed the place up more than anything was, dead or not, he had a huge smile on his face.

We didn't notice any other holidaymakers, just real Bajans having a really good time. The road is described as Bridgetown's Mecca for friendly people, good food, and great rum, and the *piece de resistance* would have to be 'Only Joe's Place' AKA 'Bel Air Jazz Club' ,which was described by Mick Jagger as being 'the best club in the world'. I so wish I had taken my camera!

As Mark had managed to book his holiday at the very last minute, it meant that he had to fly back to the UK a few days before Karl and I were due to leave. We had almost spent up by the final couple of nights, even though our new group of friends had treated us at every opportunity.

Karl and I planned to go out for a pretty posh meal to treat ourselves and had made sure we were going on our own, so that for once we could pay for our own evening. We booked a table, but just before we were about to leave, Karl admitted that he had fully spent up. I offered to treat him, but once we were at the restaurant, the cheapest thing we could find on the menu was a three-course deal for £25 each. In 1987, paying £25 for a meal was a little expensive, but we had already sat down. I remember complaining about my soup being cold and feeling extremely embarrassed when they explained to me that summer soup was served cold.

I have no idea what the origin of my main course was, but knew there was no chance of me eating it. For dessert, we were given what resembled an After Eight mint, which was the only thing I enjoyed, but at £50 it was the most expensive mint I have ever had.

During our final week we were invited to join a game of Trivial Pursuit with a lot of the guests at the Buccaneer Bay. We graciously accepted, only to find that this was no ordinary game. It was the

American Genius version and not only that but the inventor of the game, Chris Haney, had sent it to the hotel as a gift. We were playing for a couple of very expensive bottles of champagne, and my partner was a very intelligent American gentleman, who told us all that he was responsible for all the water in New York. The game was taking hours and we were still no closer to finishing, but we realised how serious everyone was taking it when my partner, who was due to fly home that evening, made a couple of phone calls to alert folk that he was now staying an extra day in Barbados just so he could finish the game. I suppose you could argue that his change of plans was worth it, as we won the game, despite me not answering a single question.

Our time in paradise was finally over, and we could never have imagined how incredible it was going to be. My only observation at the time was that our experience would have been even better if we, especially me, had met more girls. We did meet three girls from London during the first week, but Bullinge just talked to them about his fiancée, which kind of put them off. At least no-one could ever accuse him of being disloyal, despite us agreeing that what happened in the Caribbean stays in the Caribbean.

Karl and I said our goodbyes and made our way to the airport. On arrival, I noticed a couple of girls getting out of a taxi and remember joking to the guy behind the check-in desk about him seating us next to them, but I don't think he saw the funny side. Just before we were due to set off, to my astonishment and delight, the very same females came and sat right behind our seats. Unfortunately, my excitement didn't last long as the girl I fancied started to chat to a young lad who was sitting across the aisle from her, so I guessed that was that.

Thirty minutes into our flight, Karl went to the toilet, and just when I thought I had used up all my luck over the past two weeks, the girl I'd had my eye on since her taxi exit came over to me and asked if I minded if she came and sat next to me. (I couldn't make it up.) A couple of minutes later, Karl returned from the toilet, wondering why someone was in his seat. 'Err, what's going on?' he asked. I asked him if he didn't mind sitting behind us with her mate. He didn't, and spent the next hour trying to chat her up. But even though they seemed to be getting on, it was pretty obvious that chatting was as far as things were going to go.

The two girls were from Leicester, and the one I was sitting with reminded me a little of Sally from *Coronation Street*, but it is safe to say that Sally from the Street never got up to what her lookalike did – not whilst I was watching it anyway. The return flight from Barbados was beyond memorable, and even though I didn't officially become a member of the prestigious Mile High Club, I had certainly qualified for a temporary member's card.

We must have finally nodded off around four in the morning, and I remember being woken by the sound of people eating breakfast, and that we were the only two people on the plane who hadn't been served food. I could tell myself that it was because the stewards didn't want to wake us up, but I knew it was down to our inappropriate behaviour throughout the night.

It had been the perfect end to a perfect holiday, but I must acknowledge I felt embarrassed and ashamed about the things we had got up to, plus the fact we were surrounded by a sea of empty Budweiser cans. We didn't swap contact details at the time, due to the fact she said she had a boyfriend, who was obviously another very understanding member of the male species from another town.

A number of weeks after we returned from our Bajan adventure, we received a letter from Roy and Sheila, thanking us for being tremendous company and inviting us to visit them in Liechtenstein so they could take us skiing. But not being great letter writers at the time, we never replied – something I have always regretted.

CHAPTER TEN

NO PROBLEM

Before everything was available online, comics and magazines were always something that played a part in my life growing up. In the 1970s the first weekly comic I remember collecting was called *Whizzer and Chips*. *Beano* and *Dandy* were then replaced by the likes of *Spider-Man* and *The Fantastic Four*. As I got a little older, my reading choice would then include *Kung-Fu Monthly*, which I absolutely loved, and the glossy, colour posters of my hero Bruce Lee were plastered all over my bedroom walls, including the ceiling.

From 1976 right up until it ceased in 1982, *The Beatles Monthly* was my bible. Originally, available in the 60s, it ran for six years and 77 issues (63-69) and then re-published in the 80s which included new content. A must, for sure, for any Beatles fanatic or collector like myself, and my Grandma subscribed to them each month from our local newsagent. They are an important part of my memorabilia collection today, made even more special due to the fact that it was my Grandma that bought them for me.

Football magazines then followed, with the likes of *Shoot* and *Goal* being personal favourites of mine before music took over everything.

In the late 1970s, we were spoilt for choice with the music papers on offer, and I would find myself purchasing most on a weekly basis, in the hope that they would feature my beloved Jam, which they usually did. *Sounds, Melody Maker, New Musical Express, Look-In, Smash Hits, Flexi Pop,* and *The Face*. Everything we needed to know about the current music scene, our favourite bands, and the latest gigs, were to be found within the pages of these music papers. At one point the NME was the music bible for any budding fan, before it sold out and became a commercial advertising joke.

Most of my best friends were not really into their music as much as I was. Simon was always a stalwart, but he had been away for most of the time. Nicky was really into his New Romance stuff, to be fair, and would preach about the likes of Bowie, Gary Newman, Japan, and Bauhaus. Ste H stopped at Wham, and to this day still hasn't moved on. Steve S was happy to make the odd appearance at our local sweaty hangout for fans of Motorhead, Rainbow, Queen, and Rush, Pipas.
Bullinge was always a Soul boy at heart, and even though he pretended to like the Punk singles that we would all buy, the fact that he would sell them the following week exposed his fickle side. Waker would still be buying records and attending the odd gig, and Karl would still think that it was a competition amongst us to see who could own the most Punk singles.
As for fully committing to a scene, apart from my own Mod allegiance, to his credit Birchy had been a full-blown Punk, dyed spiky hair, the right gear, even down to sniffing glue, and for a short period of time he was the full package.
I remember the time when he was reported missing after a Punk gig at King George's Hall. The following day I happened to spot him just outside the Jubilee pub in town. I no sooner started to ask where he had been hiding, when all of a sudden, his mum, Kath, appeared from nowhere. I was worried that I would get the blame for her son's disappearance, but before anyone could say a word, she grabbed him by his jacket and marched him across the road to the local police station, where she asked the Desk Sergeant to lock him up.

The gigs continued for me on a regular basis, and I would travel all over the UK to get my fix of my favourite artists live. Bullinge and I went to Lancaster Poly to watch Haircut 100, where I tried to convince the security that Mark was in fact Nick Heyward's brother so that we could get backstage, and it worked. I saw the Style Council several times, but the highlight for me was our trip to London to watch them at the Royal Albert Hall.

I went with Bullinge, and I seem to remember Waker driving, but I might be wrong. We had time to kill before the gig, so decided to pay a visit to Soho beforehand. Taking my style inspiration from Paul's new love for anything French, I was dressed in a khaki green flash mac and a black beret, which may have looked okay at the concert, but had a different connotation altogether in Soho.

We chose to take a look in one of the many entertainment booths on offer, and then realised that we would need to get a pocket full of change if we intended staying for more than just a few minutes. We were each given a very small booth to stand in, and once you placed your 50p in the slot, a letterbox would open for you to feast your eyes on a chosen girl (by them, not us) who was stripping.
It was no coincidence that just as she was about to remove her bra, the money ran out and the letterbox would close, like in the Madonna video. I reckon you got around one minute's viewing time for your half an English pound, which meant it was literally like playing on a slot machine, putting in coin after coin so you could carry on taking part. It wasn't until I looked back on the photos of us that I realised how dodgy I must had looked in that outfit. It was time to move on, as we had all run out of 50ps between us.

The gig itself was wonderful, and we managed to stand right in front of the stage throughout. I recall looking round and thinking what an incredible venue and being so glad we had made the effort.

Back at home, our weekly visits to the Cav continued, and I remember myself and Jez taking a couple of girls we met back to the Eastwood residence after it had finished. One of the girls was from my class at school, and Jez expressed an interest. This left me with her mate, who told me that she was the manageress of Dorothy Perkins in town. Those two were on our living room settee but had turned it around facing the wall, for more privacy. This left me and Miss Perkins making our own entertainment in the centre of the room. I was concentrating so hard on the task in hand that I failed to hear my dad's footsteps making their way down the stairs. He walked into the living room and, not being very impressed with what he discovered, he told me I was out of order and asked my guest to leave. He failed to notice Jez and his friend for the night up to no good on the turned-around sofa.

My mum certainly wasn't a fan of either my houseguests or my behaviour, and had her own unconventional way of shaming me. On one occasion, she found a copy of *Mayfair* magazine underneath the chair in the living room one morning, but instead of throwing it in the bin or asking me or Robin who it belonged to, she just left it on top of the settee. It was a Saturday and the offending item sat there the whole day, despite what visitors called round. She had waited for the culprit to come and claim their belongings, but that didn't happen. I considered blaming my dad at the time, but I guess that would have been going too far.

On another occasion, which was ten times more embarrassing, one of our elderly neighbours Mrs Rosenberg was round visiting my mum. I walked into the living room to hear my mum complaining about my actions the previous night. Suddenly, to my absolute horror – and I am sure Mrs R's too – my mum marched upstairs, picked up my brown bedspread, and threw it in the middle of the living room floor, along with the comment, 'Is this normal??!!'

The things that folk got away with at Unilab were unreal, and I was physically evicted from our Work Manager's office at least three times. He once lectured me about something that I had done out of work's time, and I retaliated by calling him Fred Flintstone. He told me that he didn't mind me speaking my mind, even though he didn't agree with me, but he did object to me calling him a caveman and went mad. He even called in another member of staff from the next office to physically remove me at the time. That evening, I felt a little bad about how things had gone with my boss and that I may have gone a little too far, so I decided to apologise to him the following morning. No sooner had I opened my mouth to say that I might have been a little out of order, but he stopped me flat and told me I didn't need to apologise, as he respected me for speaking my mind, which I really respected him for.

I was given a young apprentice called Rob to help us out in Despatch. One morning I saw him arrive at work, but then didn't see him again for a couple of hours. I presumed that he must have gone home for some reason, but it turned out that my team had only gone and put him inside a large export container and taped it up, as some kind of initiation to working in our department.

In Despatch, we packed a lot of circuit boards into something called an MFA case. They were large black cases and were stored on top of the toilets along the corridor next to the stores. I noticed that more than usual, some members of the team were offering to go and fetch these cases from where they were stored, without me even having to ask. It seemed a little strange at the time, but I guessed they were just using their initiative. It turned out that the real reason for their willingness to bring the cases was a whole lot more sinister, and I have a feeling that if these kinds of actions happened today, folk would be in a whole lot of trouble.

What had happened was that some unidentified member (or members) of my team had climbed on top of the works toilets, where the cases were stored, and thought it was a clever idea to drill a number of holes in the toilet roof. It turned out that each hole was exactly in the middle of each female cubicle. From Despatch, you could see right through the stores, ending at the toilet entrance, and when certain females were spotted going to the loo, the folk who knew about this ridiculous scam would then offer to go and get some cases, and in turn play their own personal version of 'What the butler saw'. You just couldn't make it up.

This was eventually exposed when a very angry Jean asked me to follow her into the Ladies – me being her supervisor and all that.

She explained to me that she had been sitting on the toilet, minding her own business, when she noticed a few pieces of plaster on the floor by her feet. She looked up and was mortified to discover a small round hole peering down at her. At the time, I felt highly embarrassed and didn't quite know what to say to Jean regarding the incident, so I went and reported our findings to Colin at once, but no-one owned up to this prank and no-one got in trouble for it.

I was socialising a lot with Ste from work, and he was the hardest lad I had ever met. He was softly spoken and didn't look handy, but boy could he look after himself. He slowly got to know my mates, as we had been going on nights out together more and more.

It was our Unilab Christmas do at The Palace nightclub in Blackpool, and I invited Karl along as my guest. I introduced him to Ste but didn't get the chance to give him the heads up about Ste being handy. We returned from the dancefloor and Ste noticed his pint of golden (lager and bitter) was missing. Back then, nightclubs were notorious for anyone just picking up your drink, and Ste asked our group if anyone had taken his beer. But he didn't receive the reply he was hoping for.
He noticed that Karl had been sitting there, and asked him in no uncertain terms if he had nicked his drink. Karl by this time had downed quite a few beers of his own. Not being a person to back down, despite his size, he grabbed Ste round the top button of his shirt, dragged him down so he was a little closer to him, and spelled out that he had already said that he had not touched his drink.
I couldn't believe what I was watching, and before I could intervene, both my mates were fighting. It took less than a minute for the bouncers to show up and throw them both out of the nearest fire exit. I knew at the time that if I followed them out, there would be no way of getting back into the club, so I hoped that they would sort stuff out and I would see them at the end of the night.

As far as sorting things out, Karl had approached Ste again outside and eventually woke up in a Blackpool hospital, minus his shoe and the shirt he had been wearing. After this incident at the seaside, Ste and Karl put the night behind them and became good friends, which I was glad about.

That evening at the Palace also became pretty significant for another reason, although little did I know it at the time. I noticed a girl I liked called Alison, who was going out with one of Ste's mates, and who had occasionally visited The Farthings. Having lost the two mates I was with, I thought it might be a good opportunity to ask her if she fancied a dance. I waited ten minutes to finally get the chance to talk to her, but the lad she was chatting to just wouldn't shut up. Not wanting to lose out on an opportunity, I noticed that the girl Alison was with was standing a few feet away on her own. Feeling reasonably confident, I walked over to her and asked if she fancied a dance, and I was a little taken aback when she simply replied, 'No thanks.'
Little did I know back then that I would end up marrying the same girl who had blatantly fired me off that night at the Palace.

Janet Whittaker was her name, and we started bumping into her and Alison, her sister Elaine, and her schoolfriend, Tracey, more and more around town. Me, Ste, and Karl all got on really well with them and some Friday/Saturday nights we agreed to meet up with them at about 9.30 on the Toffs steps. We invited them back to Kestrel Close a number of times after the Cav had finished, but even though they got to sample an Eastwood Cocktail on more than one occasion, everything stayed above board and they never got to witness my dad's pyjamas.

When discussing our next mates' summer holiday, the same thing happened as the previous year. The Seychelles was initially mentioned as a possible destination, but my mates said they couldn't afford it. They then admitted that they probably couldn't afford a holiday at all that year – aye alright. Everyone except Simon, that is. The truth was that the partners my mates were

seeing at the time had clearly put a stop to them travelling, unless it was with them.
As the Caribbean had offered such an amazing experience the year before, we agreed to try it again, but this time our destination of choice was Jamaica.

I had just started to see Janet officially by then, after months of just being friends and hanging about with each other's groups on nights out. She actually went out with Ste first for a while, but I guess you need to try on a few pairs of Levis before you find the pair you really want to commit to.

Simon had just started seeing a girl called Amanda, who was really nice, so we did wonder at the time if we were doing the right thing, due to the timing of everything.

Anyway, we landed in Montego Bay, and the place looked beautiful. I don't remember if we were given free drinks on our nine-hour flight or not, but I was certainly better behaved than the previous time I had been on a plane. We arrived at our hotel, unpacked as fast as we could and hit the beach to catch some rays. I would say we had been lying there for no more than 30 minutes, when I heard a female voice asking Simon if he fancied having sex with her. I had my eyes shut at the time sunbathing, and there was no way I was about to open them to be asked the same question.
The female in question didn't use the exact words 'do you want to have sex?', but her exact words were far too inappropriate for my story and she was clearly a prostitute. So, even if he had felt the urge to take her up on her offer, he would have had to pay for the privilege, and we hadn't taken that much spends with us. It didn't take us long to realise that maybe this holiday had been a bad idea after all.

There were two Army ships stationed at the beach, and with us being two 6ft white males with short hair, we struggled to even walk down the street without somebody shouting, 'Get back to the ship, white boy.'

Our holiday was beginning to turn into a bit of a nightmare, whereas in Barbados the only real hassle you got was now and again when some young, smooth-talking Bajan asked if you wanted to ride the jet ski for some 'motion in the ocean'. And based on my previous experience in that field, I would never take them up on their kind offer.

Here in Montego Bay, you couldn't walk more than a few yards without a local calling out, 'Buy me a Red Stripe.' It ended up with us not feeling safe to do anything other than go for a meal together each night, but it was not very romantic being just me and Simon.

I admit to ringing Janet a few times whilst there, just to help me through the weeks, but what I didn't realise at the time was that it cost around £35 per call, which was a huge amount of money then, despite being told by Buzby, 'It's good to talk.'

Every time we tried to exchange our travellers' cheques, we were told that they weren't able to do it, and even our hotel was unfriendly and unhelpful.

The Upper Deck was the nicest restaurant that we found to eat at, and Simon being a thousand times more adventurous than me in the food department, would always ask for curried goat just so he could prove this fact. But everywhere he asked for this local delicacy, he would be told that they had just run out of it.

On at least two occasions we were approached during our nights out by local prostitutes, and even though we politely declined their advances, saying that we had girlfriends back at the hotel, they still insisted on following us back, making comments such us, 'What's up, you not like Jamaican girls?'

For a change, we booked a trip via one of the reps for an evening on the Big River, and although we were looking forward to it, nobody arrived to pick us up.

The saying in Jamaica was, 'No problem.' But based on our short time on the island, everything seemed to be a problem. We planned to visit Kingston on the Saturday morning, but as we were sitting around the pool deciding what time to set off, we heard on someone's radio that earlier that morning three men had attempted to break into a shop and had been shot dead by the police, so we decided to give Kingston a miss.

Nicky's mum, Jenny, originally came from Jamaica, and I remember her concern at the time when I announced I would be going. She told me that whenever she returned there, she always hid any jewellery instead of wearing it in public, so maybe we should have listened to her and chosen somewhere else.

Anyone reading my account of our holiday in Montego Bay might think that I haven't got a single nice thing to say about the place, which isn't true. Jamaica itself was thoroughly beautiful, and we did have some enjoyable trips as part of our stay.

We visited and climbed the famous Dunn's River Falls in Ocho Rios, which was spectacular. The waterfalls were extra popular due to them being featured in the Tom Cruise blockbuster movie, *Cocktail*, but Simon was no Elisabeth Shue, and even though the experience was extremely enjoyable, I wasn't about to recreate that memorable scene from the movie.

Rick's Café, a Caribbean restaurant in Negril, was also a wonderful place to visit, offering Caribbean food, cocktails, cliffside jumping, and fabulous sunsets. Also, Negril boasted the most magnificent beach I had ever seen.
We visited the Crocodile Park, where a scene from *Live and Let Die* was filmed, but I felt uncomfortable about how cruel the confined spaces were where the crocodiles were kept.

One night we were having a drink in a seafront bar and started chatting to a lady who was sitting across from us. She told us that she was the owner of a pretty exclusive golf course and restaurant and invited us to go for a meal the following night. We booked a taxi to take us, which turned out to be a mission in itself, and we struggled to even find the place, as it was totally off the beaten track and not a place you would just stumble across.

We were impressed with the place once we found it, but as I was eating my meal, I noticed that a lad on the table in the corner was staring at us. I mentioned it to Simon, but he probably thought I had been imagining it. All of a sudden, we heard the words, 'Are you from Blackburn?' We literally couldn't even come to the outback in Jamaica without bumping into someone from back home.

It was a lad who was known around Blackburn as Bryan Ferry, due to his likeness to the singer. His real name was Derek, and he actually lived in Larkhill flats, the same as Angie. I think he was on his honeymoon, but what were the odds of us being in the same building in Montego Bay, especially with it being a private club?

The Red Stripe begging continued every single time we went out, and initially I am sure we gave some money to the first few people who asked, but this hassle was relentless and, let's face it, we were on our holidays. What I feel summed it up the best, happened on the final week. An elderly gentleman came over to talk to us as we were walking through a market. Simon, by this time, had very little patience left and just walked off. The man asked me if Simon didn't like Jamaicans as he had walked away, so I tried to explain why. The gentleman explained to me that not everyone in Montego Bay was like that; some folk just wanted to be friendly and have a chat. Simon, who was way ahead, started looking at me as though I was stupid to fall for it again. After around ten minutes of me listening to this chap telling me not to judge everyone the same, to my disappointment at the end of our conversation, he said to me, 'Now, are you going to buy me a Red Stripe?'

We were staying in a very tiny room with two single beds pushed together. Simon had a photo of Amanda by his side of the bed, and I had one of Janet. One morning, Simon woke to find himself covered with midge bites from head to foot, yet I didn't have a single bite, despite us being inches away from each other. It has always amazed me that no matter where I have travelled in the world, for some strange reason I am always the one that has never been bitten by anything.

By the second day of our holiday, I was that fed up I started to count off the days on a blank postcard, like you do on a prison cell wall. So you can imagine our faces at the airport when it was announced over the tannoy that our flight home was delayed. Neither of us said a single word to each other; we just sat there, looking and feeling extremely fed up.

Overall, our trip to Montego Bay was a bit of a disappointment, certainly compared to the previous year's holiday. I know it didn't help the situation that we had both started seeing someone just before we left, but I feel you go on holiday to relax and feel safe, and neither of those things happened during our time away.

A couple of situations occurred on our return from holiday, which I felt pretty awkward about.
I was sitting in The Farthings one evening chatting to Ste's girlfriend at the time, Julie, and she asked me what Jamaica had been like, as she and her mate were due to fly there the following weekend.
I tried my very best to stay positive; after all, our experience had been individual to us, and the last thing I wanted to do was put a downer on Julie's holiday.
Julie could tell that I was hiding something so pushed me to tell her the truth. Despite what I told her, they still went on their holiday, but it turned out that they had a worse time than we did. They also booked an evening on the Big River, but their transport actually turned up. Julie told us that they were sailing down the river on a wooden raft, and once they turned a corner to a more secluded part of the river, the guy who was steering the raft stopped it moving and asked them to both take their clothes off. Luckily, another raft appeared in sight, so he started to move again as though nothing had happened. She said that both she and her friend were terrified.
Just when they thought things couldn't get worse, Hurricane Gilbert arrived on 12th September in 1988, causing death and destruction throughout Jamaica, and as a result their return flights home were cancelled. They ended up being put up in an emergency

shelter for two days, until they were eventually rescued by an Airtours shuttle.

The other incident happened whilst I was in Reef, buying a shirt. The deputy manager, Vince, was serving me and said he was off to Jamaica for his honeymoon. He knew that I had recently been and asked me how it was. The exact thing happened as with Julie; I tried to give him the positive bits and play down the rest, but again Vince sussed me out and pushed me to tell him the truth. Once I had described our experiences, he disappeared into the back of the shop for several minutes, and on his return explained that he had called his travel agents up and cancelled Jamaica and re-booked for Barbados instead. I felt terrible that through what I had told him, he'd changed his honeymoon plans, and I wished I hadn't gone into the shop, as he would have been none the wiser. But to be fair, he seemed grateful for the heads-up.

As I am writing this, I recall sitting around a pool in Jamaica one day, and needing a drink as it was so hot. I walked over to the bar and stood waiting for over five minutes in the boiling sun for someone to come and serve me. I heard a noise from behind the bar, looked over, and found the barman sitting cross-legged on the floor, eating what looked like chicken and rice. I politely asked him if I could please have a drink and he simply said, 'When I finish my dinner, I will serve you, no problem.'

CHAPTER ELEVEN

BOY ABOUT TOWN

My first day back at Unilab after my holiday, I was summoned to the boss's office. There, Colin told me that both he and the works director wanted to know how on earth I could afford to go to Jamaica on holiday, as both of them had only managed to take a break in this country. I couldn't believe what I was hearing and told him politely that it was nobody's business where I decided to go for my holidays. He even told me that he knew about the five £35 phone calls that I had made home, which left me even more speechless. I explained that it was up to me how I spent my money, and the conversation ended with him telling me that work must be paying me too much.

The nights out with Ste and Karl continued, and so did the fighting. I have never been into fighting or any kind of violence (except Bruce on screen), but it was getting to the stage that almost every time we went out, we would end up having a scrap. I have never started a fight in my life, but being over 6ft 2, I have always been a target for someone's random punches, which has always baffled me. Karl is certainly not a troublemaker, but to be fair, after one too many beers, he always found a new confidence. Over the years, Karl has probably had a fight with most of us, and even though he has never won one, he will never back down, no matter how big his opponent might be.

I started to realise that Ste had a bit of a reputation for looking after himself, as every time we bumped into a well-known hard nut during our nights out around the town, they would always know him and say, 'Alright, Ste?' I never saw Ste start a fight, but I never saw him lose one; he would always finish them off, once put

in that position. On the nights when it was me, Karl, Ste, and Simon, I always felt extra confident of coming off the better of any idiots we might bump into.
We were off to the Cav, and called into Blakeys, part of King George's Hall, for a few beers beforehand. We were in the toilets when some very cocky young lad slammed the door open, and it hit either Ste or Simon on the back with the force. Ste questioned his actions, expecting the lad to apologise, and that would have been that. Instead, this Rocky wannabee did the opposite, and made some derogatory comment then walked over to Ste. Two punches were all it took for this not-so-hard nut to end up unconscious on the floor, surrounded by blood, then the bouncers came into the toilets and told us to leave as the police were on their way.

A week later, we were in the Wine Lodge having a drink, when one of the members of the Blackburn Youth came over to Ste and told him he had been out of order, as one of their members had ended up in intensive care for the past 4 days. Ste, not prepared to be threatened, simply laughed at him and told him to go away, knowing that there was absolutely nothing they could or would do about it.

As karma would have it, the lad who Ste hit that night in Blakey's was the same lad who had robbed my flat and plastered his name all the way through my autograph album. Even though I would not have wished any violence against him, I did and still do believe in karma.

It was a Thursday night, and I had decided to wear a new cream coat that I had recently purchased from Replay/Reef, for the first time. Karl commented on whether it was wise to wear my new pride and joy up the Cav, but I explained that we were unlikely to get into any trouble on a Thursday night, so I kept it on. We had only been up there for about half an hour when a fight broke out involving us. I have absolutely no idea how it started or who threw the first punch, but I established pretty early on that it was a coach load of Blackpool bouncers we were scuffling with. I looked over at Karl, to see him literally jumping in the air trying his best to reach the doorman that he was trying to punch.

I recall two blokes were trying to lay into me, and I remember shouting, 'Watch the bloody coat!' (or something to that effect) as they were dragging it over my head.

The DJ even stopped the music and turned all the lights on, so maybe I should have taken Karl's wise advice after all.

I could never get my head around why complete strangers would just walk up to me in the Cav and think it was okay to randomly punch me in the face, but it seemed to happen on a regular basis back then.

One night I was dancing to *Never Too Much* by Luther Vandross, minding my own business, when out of the blue, two lads ran over to me and proceeded to punch me in the mouth – both at the same time. As I hadn't been expecting this intrusion on my worship of Luther, I was caught off my guard and ended up sprawled across the dancefloor. Within seconds, I was joined by some weedy looking guy in a bow tie, who was lying next to me but was fully unconscious.

Ste and Simon, witnessing what had happened, joined in to protect me, but I didn't even get the chance to explain what had happened before two of the Cav's doormen appeared and threw us both out of the nearest fire exit.

Standing in the car park, feeling sorry for myself and receiving some very strange looks from Mr Bow Tie, who had come round by then, I resigned myself to getting a taxi home. I knew I wouldn't be getting back into the club. Before I could flag down a taxi, Simon, Ste, and even Jez joined me in the car park, followed by about ten of the lads who had first started all the trouble. Jez was with about three other lads and suggested going to get some extra help from inside his car. Not being quite sure what he meant by this, I watched as he and his entourage walked over to the boot of his car and, one by one, grabbed themselves a weapon. Someone had a car jack, another was holding a hammer, and so on. I had no intention of choosing a personal weapon for myself, as it was not my thing, but as luck would have it, before anyone had chance to cause any real damage, several police cars came screeching into the car park. And I remember everyone walking off, sheepishly holding their weapons out of sight.

Being involved in fights each weekend was becoming so frequent that we were summoned to go and see our works director to explain the situation. The problem was that every Monday morning when we were clocking on at work, the whole of the shop floor, including Colin, would notice that we had black eyes, cuts and bruises, or a dented head, yet again. Three weeks in a row this happened, and Colin must have felt that it needed addressing and couldn't just be ignored. The girls on the shop floor simply burst into laughter, as they had been expecting it anyway.

We stood in our director's office, trying to convince him that we were not troublemakers in any way, despite the cuts and bruises all over our faces. I told him that strangers would just walk up to me and inflict violence against me for no apparent reason. I am not sure I managed to convince him, and to be honest, I don't think I would have been convinced if I'd been standing in his shoes.

The fact that Janet and I were friends before we started seeing each other was a good thing, I think, as we knew a fair bit about each other from the start. The downside to this might have been that as a mate, I would no doubt have told her about some of the funny situations from my past, whereas being a partner, I would probably have left a few things out.

I have always considered myself to be a pretty loyal person (for obvious reasons), and my advice has always been to 'start as you mean to carry on'. What I mean by this is, if someone likes you for who you are, then why would you feel the need to change, or let someone change you. I have never got my head around the situation when someone settles down or gets married, and they start to lose touch with their mates, and all the things they loved before this relationship, such as football or music, cease to exist in their new life anymore. They throw away their football programmes, get rid of their vinyl collection, and in some cases just happen to lose the phone numbers of all their friends that they have grown up with. I think it is mental, and have never understood it.

I won't name them, as they are mates – or so I thought, but four of our group seemed to disappear off the face of the earth as soon as they met their partners. I found this beyond sad at the time, and naturally their relationships didn't last, and they came crawling back. Well, at least two did.

Obviously, I know that if you commit to someone, you can't and shouldn't carry on behaving the way you have always done when you were single. I also acknowledge that I am probably an exception, and don't expect folk to carry on the way that I have, keeping all my interests and friends to the extreme.

I remember being in the Wine Lodge with Janet and her sister Elaine, on a night out not long after we started seeing each other. Whilst they were in the toilets, apparently Elaine asked Janet, 'Does it not bother you when Pete is talking to other girls?' The thing is, I would like to think that I would be the exact same person no matter what the situation was, or whoever I was talking to. To me, that is being genuine and not fake. I choose my own mates and who I choose to talk to, and could never imagine ignoring somebody just because of who I was with.

It was 1989, and as I hadn't been away that year, I suggested to Janet that we visit Paris, which would give me the opportunity to see the sights I had missed on my previous visit. She agreed it was a fabulous idea, so we booked a hotel just off the artist area of Montmartre. The hotel was decent, and even though there wasn't a full English breakfast on offer each morning, I filled up for the day on an endless supply of croissants and pastries.

Montmartre was beautiful, and I bought a water colour painting of a Parisian autumn scene from one of the artists, which still hangs on our bedroom wall over the bed today. Just down the road from the hotel was Paris's very own red-light district in Pigalle, but thankfully this time I had left my flash mac and beret at home. We only had to walk along the street for locals to try and drag us into their local live sex shows or Triple X movies, but we always declined their invitation.

I don't remember if it had been my intention to propose to Janet while in Paris, before we arrived, but I knew it needed to be special. My initial plan was maybe to pop the question at the top of the Eiffel Tower, but the second I stood underneath the giant structure, I knew there was no way on this earth that I could climb something that tall, as I was terrified of heights.

Plan B was to propose as we were sailing down the River Seine, but realising that the sightseeing cruise I was booking had three rows of tourists sitting next to each other, I bottled out.

We both loved what we saw in Paris, but found it unbelievably expensive, and our funds started to run out by our second to last night. We went for a few drinks in various wine bars and then decided to buy a bottle of champagne, a few bottles of beer, and a cooked half chicken and head back to our room. I must have had a few too many beers, because I could tell I was annoying Janet. And when she said that she would love to pour her glass of French bubbly over my head, I guessed that this was as good a time as any to ask her to marry me.
Not the most romantic proposal, I guess, but maybe it was. Janet had naturally said yes (ha-ha) and things were okay with the world again, apart from the very small matter of breaking the news to my parents, which I certainly wasn't looking forward to.

The relationships between my mum and the females I had invited back over the years had always been frosty at best. And even though Janet was a godsend, as far as my parents would eventually realise, things hadn't got off to the easiest of starts.

I was never one to invite a girl back and introduce her to my parents, as I had always chosen to bring them home when I knew Mum and Dad would be in bed. I had known that this relationship with Janet was different, and that it was definitely more than a one-night stand. So I eventually plucked up enough courage to introduce her to them, after I had been seeing her for several weeks. After the introduction, Janet went to the downstairs toilet in the hall and heard my dad, in a loud voice, blurt out, 'I thought you were seeing Heather.' Janet had clearly heard this, but luckily it didn't cause much of a big deal.

When we announced our engagement to them both, my mum fell silent and made it blatantly obvious that she was far from impressed. Eventually, when she did speak, she simply looked at Janet and asked her if she knew what she was letting herself in for! Not a single word to me! It was as if I wasn't in the same room as them.

Looking back now, it might have been a sensible question to ask Janet, and maybe she did have very good reasons to think like that, based on my previous experiences with the female form. What I do know was that their reaction put an absolute downer on what we thought was positive news, and at the time I felt really angry with them, as Janet did not deserve that, even if I did.

Anyway, whether they liked the news or not, it was happening, so they would just have to get used to it.

My plan was to hold onto my football programmes, certainly keep hold of my record collection, but stop inviting girls back for an Eastwood Cocktail. Like the majority of my other mates partners, Janet was not overly impressed by the constant Unilab social activities and regular nights out. I always invited her to our events, though, and eventually she got to know the people I worked with – a large percentage of whom would end up being friends for life.

One morning at work, I noticed a new girl sitting outside Colin's office, so I decided to say hello and check if she was okay. It turned out that Sarah was starting a new summer job in R&D, and her mum was Norma on Reception, who was really wonderful. After we chatted for a few minutes, I established that she was a fan of Joe Jackson, loved the band Squeeze, and that her favourite Beatles song was *Hey Bulldog*, which cemented our friendship for many years to come.

The workforce at Unilab, excluding the managers – although Colin was okay – were the reason that we all stuck at the job and put up with a rubbish wage, and a bit of a rubbish role, to be honest. Even though I was Supervisor/Team Leader, I felt that the job in Despatch was not really a long-term one for me. I did question whether I would ever find a role where I felt that I had something to offer or that I was any good at, but I guess that I had become more and more institutionalised over the years I had worked there. I felt I would need to be pushed as opposed to me deciding to leave the job of my own accord.

As for my other friends' career paths, Bullinge was working for the Post Office counter in town, whilst Ste opted to stay on the other side of the counter and become a postman. Waker was now a Shift Manager at ICI, and Kershy was part of his team. Steve was working for Shorrocks in Blackburn, whilst Jez was a wood machinist in Darwen, as he was fed up with unsociable hours at Samuel Whitbread, and had no doubt worked his way through all the waitresses that worked there. Nicky had left university in Nottingham and, after applying for around 100 jobs, finally secured his dream job working for the Environment Agency, as Dr Who's assistant role didn't pop up very often.

I use Nick's positivity and persistence when I am talking to young people, as an example to never give up on the things that you really want in life. I know that at the time, Nicky found it tough applying for job after job and only receiving a 'no thanks' or sometimes no reply at all. I recall that he felt really down about the situation and like giving up, and that he would never get the job he had set his heart on. But it is credit to him that he never gave up, and in the end his patience certainly paid off.

Simon went from Friargate School to a boarding school in Middlesbrough, then to university in Sheffield, before landing a management accountancy role at the Royal Free Hospital in London, sort of following in his father's footsteps.
I reckon that Birchy was the biggest surprise, though, as he went from playing soldiers with a stick in the fields next to Rhodes Avenue and the Tank, to joining the Military Police in Germany, and even having his very own Rottweiler as his partner.

Karl went down the engineering route, after serving his apprenticeship at Training 2000, and I was making sure that science teaching equipment was despatched in boxes in time to meet their orders.

As for Julie and Mary, well, Mary had been engaged to Waker during the time he was in Sunderland at university, but he was a big drinker, and I am not saying that this was the reason, but they eventually split up. Mary went to train as a nurse, and the minute she signed up at college, we never saw her again. She moved out of town and met a male nurse, got married, and settled down. My first true crush was now officially off the radar.

The move away amazed me. Not the fact that she had gone, but that she chose not to keep in touch with anyone and to cut all ties. She didn't even keep in touch with Julie, who she had grown up with and been best mates with. I don't know how Julie felt at the time, as she never really said, but it was Mary's choice and obviously what she wanted.

I clearly liked a drink by the fact I was out every night, but I never considered myself a big drinker. What put me off was when we first started our Unilab nights out, one of our group – Ian, from Stores – would always get wasted in the first few pubs we visited, and before we had even made our way up to the Cav. He was always in a pile on the floor, looking a right mess, and I never understood why he got himself in such a state where he wasn't even capable of chatting to any girls. That was if he even made it to the club, which he usually didn't. Not for me. That is not to say that I have never been wasted, but I would generally prefer to know what I was saying and who I was saying it to.

During the Two-Tone scene, I tried to see as many of the bands that I could, as I loved them all. Unfortunately, I was a little too young to attend when The Specials and Madness played the Golden Palms (Mecca) in Blackburn. But I did go and see The Selecter, The Beat, and Secret Affair, at King George's Hall with Nicky. At the time, I wasn't impressed by Secret Affair live, but I did like them on record so maybe they just had an off night. The Selecter with Pauline Black were brilliant, and I borrowed a trilby off my Uncle Stanley on Rhodes Avenue, who I used to go to the Rovers with and stand in the Riverside.

Nicky wore the hat throughout the gig, as it suited him better than me. We walked home up Shear Brow afterwards, chatting about how great the gig had been, and when we arrived at the top outside The Sportsman's pub, I asked him for my hat back, as I needed to return it the following day. But as Nicky removed it from his head, we both realised that his Afro haircut was now in the shape of the trilby that he had worn. I thought it was hilarious, but Nicky just legged it home without stopping, trying to avoid bumping into anyone on the way.

At the time of The Selecter gig, we were both still at school, so money was tight. I really wanted to go to the gig but hadn't enough money for the ticket. On Clayton Street, there was a printers where you could buy any colour or type of paper you could think of. And at home, my mum owned some pretty fancy scissors which left a jagged edge when you used them to cut anything.

My idea was to somehow buy a ticket, buy the same paper it was printed on, and make a few myself to hopefully sell at school, as *On My Radio* and *Three-Minute Hero* were played regularly at the school disco/youth club.

I purchased a ticket at the box office, went straight to the printers, and selected some light blue paper which was the nearest match. I can't remember how I photocopied the tickets (maybe the printers), but I did, then borrowed the snazzy scissors off my mum, and hey presto, I had made my own forgeries for the Selecter gig (sorry, Pauline).
To be honest, I didn't want to take things too far and push my luck, so I think I only sold about four.
The deal was that I would walk in first with the original, and then my customers would follow suit.
I was extremely nervous imagining what on earth would happen to me if I was caught, but to my absolute amazement it worked, and everyone made it in. (Phew!)

The Beat also performed at KGH, and I loved them. I bought their debut album, *I Just Can't Stop It*, in 1980 (aged 14) whilst on a family holiday in Bridlington. Dave Wakeling, Ranking Rodger and Papa Sax – they have remained to this day one of my favourite bands, and that is one of my favourite albums.

My first Scooter Rally was an experience. I went with Jez, a lad called Tin Head, and a few of the lads from Red Rose Scooter Club. The destination was Colwyn Bay in Wales, and as I didn't own a scooter, I had to jump on the back of someone else's vehicle for the journey down there. I used to ride on the back of Jez's magnificent machine every now and then, and also on a scooter owned by my mate, Dave from Belthorn. But for this road trip, I was offered a ride off a guy I used to bump into at Jam gigs.

I really buzzed off riding through the towns on a Vespa, or now and again a Lambretta, and loved the looks we used to attract off passers-by, and especially bikers. When we arrived in Colwyn Bay, it was literally like the scene from *Quadrophenia*, where all the scooters pulled up on the front near the beach and you kept recognising faces from back home. There were parkas everywhere. It looked great and most of them included patches of The Who and The Jam, and from previous rallies, or just simply a Union Jack target sewn onto the back.

There were a fair few Mods about, wearing two-tone suits and either Jam shoes or desert boots, but always a thin, black tie. The rest were scooter boys and girls, who were totally different in my book. Yes, they both shared a love of Italian scooters, but that was where it ended. Being a Mod was about looking sharp and standing out in a crowd, for wearing the best suit or the best shirt. But scooter boys looked proper scruffy to me, on the whole, and they would wear the likes of Army trousers and a lot of camouflage gear. In my opinion, they might as well have been riding motorbikes. Also, a lot of them were not even into the same music as the Mods, and were more likely to jump around the dancefloor to The Exploited, The Ruts, or the Cockney Rejects.

The day was brilliant, and the weather had been kind, but the journey back home was a lot less glamorous. The lad's scooter I was riding on the back of broke down, which was a regular occurrence on runs out like this. There was always a van around for this eventuality, so both me and the knackered scooter were shoved into the back of the van for the return trip. If that wasn't bad enough, it appeared that every broken-down scooter during the journey back had also been thrown into the van, and I found myself lying on the floor in the back of this mucky looking vehicle with no seats and no windows, with four scooters on top of me, and not knowing when we were about to stop again and add another one to the mix. It certainly wasn't my idea of fun, and I was more than relieved to be finally let out, with the odd bruise and a few patches of oil on my parka.

I say I've never owned a scooter, but I actually did – for a few weeks at least. I was walking home from The Farthings one night, with I think Karl and possibly Waker, when I noticed a gold Vespa 90 dumped at the entrance to Rhodes Avenue, near the bushes. Being the only one present who was wearing an original US Army-issue parka, I felt that it was only right for me to stake a claim on this wonderful mode of transport. I took it back to our garage at Kestrel Close and gave my mate Cass a call the following day to come and take a look at it, him being a whizz on all scooter faults.

It ended up needing new gears, so Cass worked his magic and sorted it for me. We also found out that it had originated from Guernsey, and for the next few weeks I rode it as much as I could. At the end of Richmond Terrace in Blackburn there was a well-known scooter dealership, Victor Bernards, where I bought myself an open-faced black helmet, and ended up spraying the peak silver. It was rumoured that Sting's scooter in *Quadrophenia* was sourced and registered at Victor's, having the initials VCB on the front visor.

The issue was that without any tax and insurance for my Vespa, I was limited to only using it at night, as there was less chance of me being pulled up. I practised riding it on the long path in Corporation Park, and remember having a couple of close shaves on it.

I was riding around Rhodes Avenue, and it wasn't my brightest idea (literally) to wear my black wraparound sunglasses while driving, as I could hardly see through them in the dark – even though they did look cool. I took the turning on the corner next to where Waker and Bullinge lived, and out of the corner of my eye I noticed Waker's mum, dad, and sister on their front doorstep a few feet away. I took the corner so sharply that I was 100% convinced I was going to crash into Mark's dad's car parked outside. Amazingly, I managed to stay on board my vehicle and lived to tell the tale, but I always wondered if they knew it was me.

The other incident happened on Meins Road in Billinge. I was with Jez, and we decided to time each other riding the length of the road and back. I had only just turned the corner away from him when I lost control, and following a massive bang/crash, I found myself lying in the middle of the road with my scooter on top of me.

I recall a very posh family ran out of their very big house to see if I was okay, and it was one of those occasions when you stand up, dust yourself off, and make out to everyone present that everything is fine. But the second they returned indoors, I collapsed on the road again, as I was in absolute agony.

Eventually, I picked the scooter up, minus a couple of mirrors, and wheeled it back around the corner to play down my accident to Jez. Not only was my scooter damaged, but also my pride. I still have the scar on my side from that evening, as a reminder not to be a complete idiot in the future.

About a month later, a few of my mates were round at our house – Kev, Rooster, and their mate Nick – when Nick asked me what I was doing with his scooter in our garage. I tried to explain that I had found it abandoned on the corner of Rhodes Avenue and that I hadn't stolen it, but he seemed pretty wound up by my explanation and ended up taking it home with him. So I was left without a scooter once more.

The A Team, Birchy, Waker, Bullinge, Ste H, Mary, Karl, Julie, Steve.

Me and Cass in all our mod finery, visiting Bulling at his new house in Kendal.

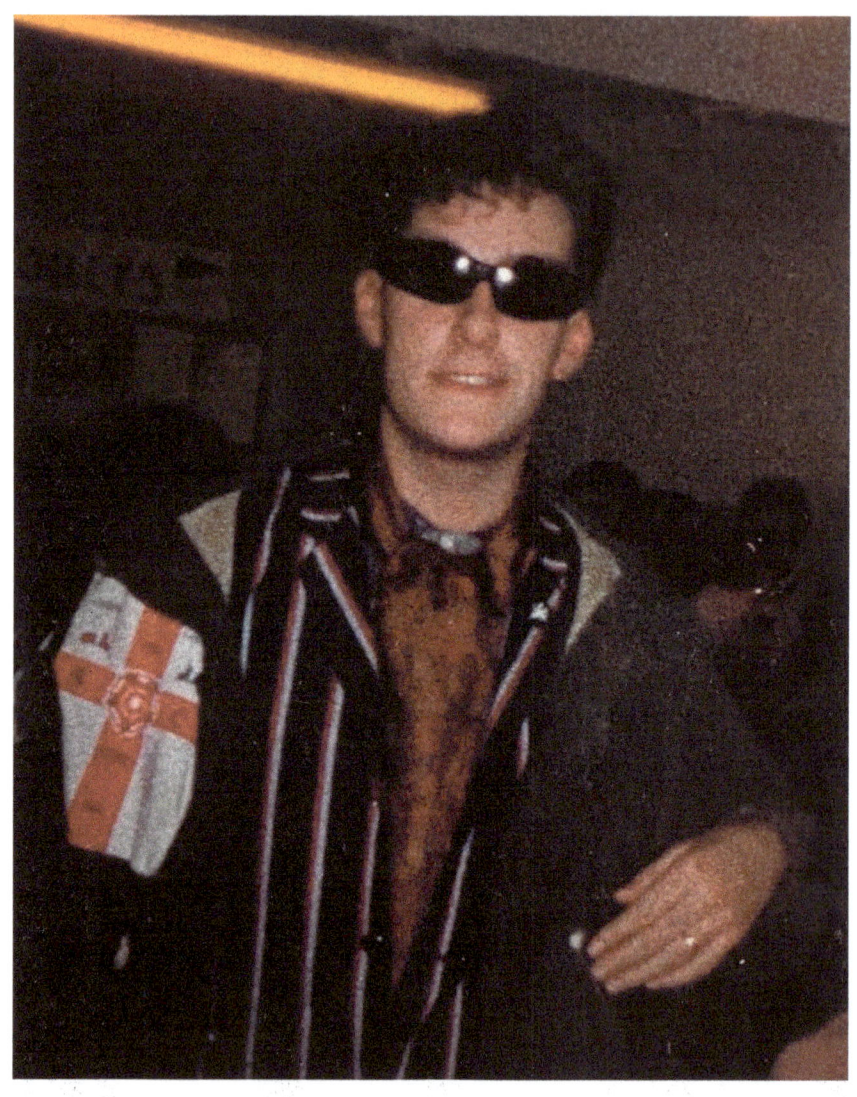

Mr Mod

All Mod Cons

On Fistral Beach in Newquay attempting to surf,
with Ste H and Bullinge.

With Nidge and Waker in the Prince Albert Pub in Newquay.

With Bulling, Jez, and Baz, on their balcony in Tenerife.

At Montego Bay Airport in Jamaica after discovering our flight home had been delayed. (No words needed)

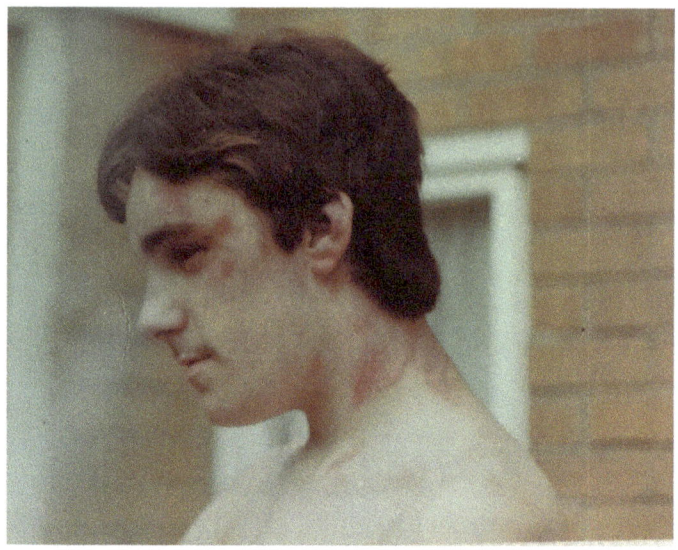

The results of my Rugby Club beating.

Playing Pool with Nick in the Farthings,
wearing our favourite shirts from Pelle.

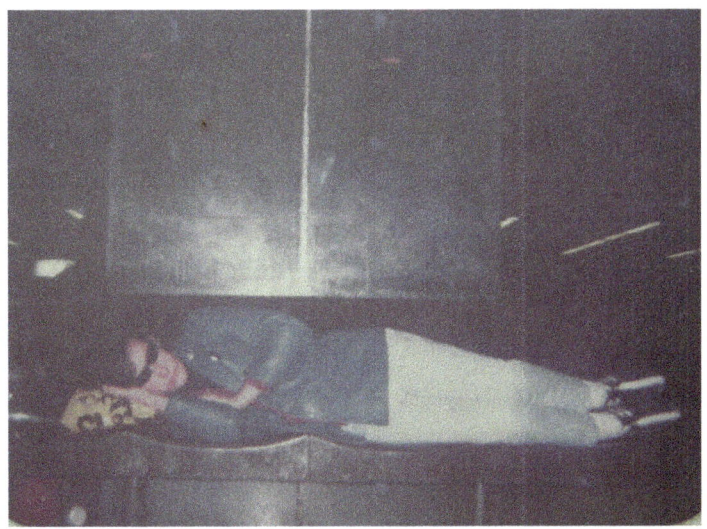

Sleeping rough on Euston Station, before going to see The Jam in Paris.

The Jam performing at King George's Hall, Blackburn.

Meeting Paul after their Blackburn gig.

CHAPTER TWELVE

THE PARIS MATCH

Janet and I officially got engaged on Christmas Eve, and booked to stay the night at the Millstone Hotel at Mellor. I remember it being a typical winter's night and that there was snow on the ground. We attended the evening church service at the local church, to add to the festivities. We naturally stayed in the honeymoon suite, and I was told that a few weeks later The Beautiful South stayed in the very same room, and had trashed it.

So, after coming to the conclusion that Janet was a keeper, we set our wedding date for Saturday, 16th June, 1990. Again, initially, my parents frowned upon this commitment, but eventually came around to the fact that it was going to happen anyway.
My mum told me that there was no way they would be paying for Jez to come to the wedding, hoping that I wouldn't invite him, but I made it perfectly clear that he had been one of my best and oldest friends for the majority of my life, and he would be coming – even if I had to pay for him myself.

The engagement ring was ordered from Preston's of Bolton, but it ended up getting lost in the post (some dodgy postmen about), so we had to order another one. And I was on tenterhooks worrying if it would arrive on time or not.

Because of this, Janet's wedding ring was sourced from Peter Jackson's in town, just to be on the safe side. I asked Bullinge to be my best man, but it was a tough call, as I was lucky enough to have a few best mates that I could have asked. The fact that I had been Mark's best man in 1989, when he made an honest woman of Debbie, probably helped to make my choice. I asked Nick to be my usher, but that was a little awkward, because he thought I meant best man, which made me feel bad. My brother-in-law, Warren, and my brother, Robin, were chosen to be groomsmen, and Janet had her sisters, Pauline and Elaine, as bridesmaids, along with her niece, Claire, who she was godmother to, and her cousin Lorraine's daughter, Vicky.

Like any wedding, making arrangements was a stressful affair, with my mum and dad (mainly my mum) deciding who we should invite and who should be left out. My mum was even of the mindset that the eldest members of the family should be sat in order in the church, having the oldest at the front. I thought that this kind of Victorian tradition was nonsense for our big day, but the main thing I was thinking about at this point was my dreaded stag do. I say dreaded, because back then it was tradition for the groom to be stripped naked and either tied to a lamppost, or left alone in a strange location to find the largest leaf they could lay their hands on, and somehow make it home.

As it was ultra-popular at the time, I decided on Bernard Manning's Embassy Club in Westbourne Grove, Manchester. Bernard was always a controversial comedian, and even at that time, he was deemed to be sexist, racist, and in fact probably every word that ended in 'ist'. But it was a well-known choice for stag and hen parties, so I guessed it would be fine.

I hired a minibus, and attending were my best mates minus Jez, some work friends from Unilab, my brothers-in-law Warren and Martin, my future stepfather-in-law Fred, and my brother Robin.

As we walked into the Embassy, it reminded me of those proper 1970s working men's clubs that would have a cabaret on a Saturday night. The Wheel-Tappers and Shunters Social Club would regularly feature on the television, and my parents would watch it religiously.
We were given a number of tables and told not to go to the bar, as there was a table service in place. So everyone would throw a

tenner into the kitty, and the people who worked there would bring our drinks – barrel glasses only – to our table. Initially, this sounded fine, but the waiters were obviously taking their tips every time we ordered a round, and it meant that everyone had to keep up with the fastest drinker, and as soon as they wanted another pint, it meant that you had to have another.

I say waiters, but they were actually the club's security men, and every one of them had arms like Popeye, so obviously there was no way you were ever going to argue about the drinks bill.

There were a couple of cheesy club acts on first, and then the main host, Bernard, appeared on stage to the words, 'Get 'em in, Get 'em pissed, and Get 'em out!' A charming welcome, I thought, but even though I have never been able to remember any jokes, he was really funny on the night.

At one point in the evening, Bernard called anyone up onto the stage whose stag do it was, and even though I planned to stay put and keep my head down, there was no way my group was about to let that happen. I stood, very embarrassed, on the stage with about five other unfortunate males, whilst I was asked to sing a song that I didn't know the words to. Then he turned to me and said, 'I bet your mother puts your sandwiches up for you!' and the whole room burst out laughing at me – none louder than the people off our minibus. But how did he know?

Later in the evening, during Bernard's second slot, Nicky said that he was just off to visit the toilets.
I strongly advised him to try and wait until Mr Manning had done his bit and left the stage, but Nicky was bursting so ignored my advice. On his return, Bernard spotted him – being only the second black person in the room – and a couple of minutes later, Nicky was on stage under the lights, singing *Old Man River* with him. Imagine if that happened today; it would make the newspapers for sure!

At some stage in the night, I have memories of a fight breaking out on the table behind us, and that was the night over with. The club's very own Charles Atlas changed from waiter to bouncer and threw everybody out, and there was nothing at all we could do about it, stag do or no stag do.

The journey back was pretty good natured, considering that everyone on the minibus was drunk. And it seemed like it was going to be uneventful, until I heard a voice saying, 'Let's strip him.'

Damn! I'd thought I had got away with it, but not a chance. My so-called friends started to take off my clothes, and I knew there was no point trying to fight them off, as it was tradition. One minute, my future father-in-law, Fred, was helping to undo my trousers, and the next thing he announced that there was no way Janet was going to see me in this state and ordered everyone to get my clothes back on.

As it was my stag do, they obviously felt it was my 'rite of passage', so they ignored him and simply carried on. By this time, Fred was getting pretty angry, but I was already naked, and was thrown off the bus and left on a grass verge right outside Walkers Steel. My plan was to act as though I was a lot more drunk than I actually was, in the hope they would somehow take pity on me and allow me back on the bus. To add to the effect, I had my eyes closed. By that stage, two groups had formed: my mates who wanted to leave me there; and my imminent family members – Fred, Warren, Martin, and Rob, on Team P, who argued that I should be allowed back on the bus, as I was far too wasted.
I am glad to announce that my family won, convincing the others that I was in no fit state to find my own way home, so my plan had worked.

Even though I was now safely back on the bus, tensions got worse, and at one stage Fred attempted to throw a punch at Ste. However, Ste ducked, and Fred managed to hit Karl right in the face instead. I couldn't believe how things were turning out, but I couldn't intervene as I was supposed to be really drunk. To my disbelief, Fred ended up being thrown off the minibus. But unlike me, he was left to make his own way home.

Janet was on her hen night at the same time and had opted to take her entourage to Tiggis Italian restaurant, and then up to Manhattan Heights nightclub. She arrived back home at some unearthly hour to find Fred sitting in his chair waiting for her, and announcing that 'no bums like that will be going to any wedding of ours.'

I was taken back to Mark and Debbie's new house down Lammack, but I had never seen their spare room before, so when I woke up in the morning I didn't have a clue where I was.

Stag and hen nights used to take place the night before the wedding, but due to the large number of males who failed to attend their own big day, it was eventually changed to at least a week before, to give the groom (or hen) a chance to recover, find their way back, or even allow their eyebrows to have a chance to grow back. This was a blessing to me, as it gave Fred just enough time to calm down and relent on his wedding ban for most of my mates.

Our wedding day arrived, and we tied the knot at St James's Church at the top of St James's Road in Blackburn. Everything about the day was perfect, apart from the fact that my Grandma and Grandad were missing. Our wedding reception was at a place called The Vineyard in Bamber Bridge, and when Jez and I went to Poachers on a Sunday night, we used to call at the Vineyard for a drink on the way. I always found the venue to be classy, with its white piano and that, and had made a comment at the time that if I ever ended up getting married, I would like the reception to be there.
When Janet and I started to discuss possible venues, we both amazingly mentioned the place as our first choice, so it was a given.

My mum and dad loved being the parents of the groom, even though they had initially had their doubts, and particularly that I was the groom. They even chatted to Jez, who for once was on his best behaviour. The only thing we hadn't taken into account while planning our big day was that England were playing Holland in the World Cup at Stadio Sant'Elia in Italy. I got a lot of stick for choosing a World Cup match day to get married on, and even though I don't think it put folk off attending, I did notice several guests making regular trips to the car park throughout the evening to check the score on their radios.

The game ended in a 0-0 draw, and I recall our DJ Ste playing *World in Motion* by New Order five times during the night. I can't hear that song now without thinking of our special day, despite *Endless Love* by Lionel Richie being our official wedding first dance song.

I was 26 years old, and even though I felt a little too young to settle down, the day was perfect. Janet looked beautiful and had even turned up on time. Bullinge didn't lose the rings, and did a splendid job with his best man's speech. The weather was spot on, which enabled the photographer Paul Daville to capture all the shots he required, and the evening bash stayed trouble-free, which is always a bonus on someone's wedding day.

Our first ever property together was Number 9 Cloverfields, which was just off Peter Street in Daisyfield. We chose the plot at the end of the road, and watched it being built.

When I lived at home with my parents, my mum was a really good cook, but we always more or less had the same meals on the same day growing up. The problem with this was that for example on a Wednesday we always had liver, which I didn't particularly like, then every single Wednesday I would never look forward to my tea, no matter how hungry I might have been.

The first thing that I thought of after I said the words 'I do' (or maybe the second) was that now I was married I could have whatever meal I fancied on whatever day I wanted it on.

Even though 9 Cloverfields was our brand-new marital home, Janet was not the first person to stay the night there, other than myself. Jez somehow missed my stag do, which was no surprise, and arranged for me to have another one, but this time it was just me and him. We went for a few beers around Preston, and we planned to jump the taxi once we arrived back to Blackburn. But for most of the journey our driver told us about how tough the job had been, with people always ripping her off, so we ended up not only paying the fare but also giving her a tip.

We arrived back at Cloverfields and just sat there for hours chatting and attempting to watch a film. It was around 4 in the morning, and I couldn't understand why I wasn't even remotely tired. But what I hadn't realised at the time was that whilst in Preston, Jez had only gone and spiked my drink with Wizz (Speed). We were about a quarter of the way through the film *Nine-and-a-Half Weeks* with Kim Basinger, when Jez asked me to turn it off, telling me that there was no way he could watch a film like that with just another bloke. He admitted to spiking my drink while I had been at the toilet, which explained a lot, but as I had always hated drugs, I remember being proper naffed off and told him I thought he was totally out of order.

The only time I had taken drugs – not including Pro Plus, beer, or poppers – was on a night out at Mr G's nightclub. A group of us arranged to go downtown after last orders in The Farthings, and as the evening progressed, one by one my mates bottled out and chose not to go, leaving me with the local drug dealer. I only really knew him to say 'alright' to, but had told him I was going to Mr G's so wasn't sure how to get out of it.

John was driving and offered me a lump of something to take, maybe cannabis. Until then, I had always had the willpower to say no and turn down any offer of illegal substances, or even cigarettes, but he kept on pushing me to eat whatever it was. So eventually I did, just to shut him up. I spent the whole evening at the club expecting to start feeling strange or experience something different, but nothing whatsoever happened, and I still felt the same. That's maybe the reason I never bothered with it again.

Around the time I started seeing Janet, I was into Soul, Funk, and R&B – Luther Vandross, Freddie Jackson, Teddy Prendergrass, Jonathan Butler, and Anita Baker, to name a few. For our honeymoon, we chose to return to Paris, but agreed to delay it for a week so that we could go and watch Anita Baker in Birmingham. I loved her album *Rapture*, but remember being a little disappointed with the gig and regretted changing our honeymoon plans for it.

As it turned out, we both felt that booking a week in Paris might have been a mistake. We had really enjoyed our short break there when I proposed to Janet, but it was so unbelievably expensive, and we'd only stayed for a long weekend on our previous visit.

We were recommended a restaurant to try, telling us that if we chose to eat where a lot of the locals ate, we shouldn't get ripped off. When we found the place, it reminded me of an old stately home, with a really large dining area and what seemed like around a hundred tables. There was only one other person in the room, so we chose our table and sat down, only to find that when someone else entered, they were directed to sit at our table by the waiter, even though the whole place was near enough empty. Apparently, that had been their way, filling it up from the back, so myself and the new Mrs Eastwood found ourselves having a romantic meal on our honeymoon, alongside some strange Parisian geezer.

After a short time, we were joined by another bloke, and the two of them ordered a dish which wasn't even cooked. Raw, minced meat topped with a raw egg! It looked horrendous, and surely must have been a mistake? Apparently Steak Tartare was a local delicacy, but it certainly wasn't for me.

Another weird thing about the place was that on the tables they had plain white paper tablecloths, and it was down to the customer to add up their own bill as they went along. You wrote on the tablecloth, and when the waiter appeared at the end of your meal, you told him how much you owed him.

England managed to avoid getting knocked out of the World Cup at Italia 90, and whilst we were on our honeymoon in France, England were playing their quarter final match against Belgium. We found a local bar to watch it in, and it was pretty obvious that we were the only two people present who actually wanted England to win the game.

The atmosphere was really tense, and the match went into extra time. In the 120th minute, David Platt banged in a goal for England, to put them through to the World Cup Semi Finals. I was ecstatic and found myself jumping up and down whilst running around the bar, much to the annoyance of every single local.

CHAPTER THIRTEEN

A DIFFERENT KIND OF BIRD FOR JEZ

Living on Cloverfields was great, and right up Janet's street, pardon the pun. She had grown up in a house full of very loud females – three sisters – so was used to the noise and the fact that there was never a dull moment. Almost everyone on our road got on with each other, and when someone had a party or a BBQ, we would always be invited. It was a bit like *EastEnders*, where everyone would leave their door unlocked, and folk would sometimes just barge in without even knocking, which took a little bit of getting used to for me.

There were only two people who were not included in this equation. One was a young girl who had been a prostitute, rented a house at the end of the road, and kept herself to herself – as far as the neighbours were concerned anyway. And across from her was a very unfriendly Cockney builder who, on a weekly basis, would arrive home drunk from his local and threaten other people on the road. He had a very high gate, which obviously was meant to keep people out, and at the same time keep his very large dog in. And even though he lived with his wife, he would usually be seen on a Sunday night, shouting through that girl's letterbox across the road, asking for a free one!

I even heard him shouting up at one of the neighbours and threatening them with a gun. On another occasion, he threw a massive brick right through the window of his next-door neighbour, whilst the family were in. The funny thing was that if someone had a party and failed to invite him, which they always did, he would call the police and complain about the noise and that he had been left out. A complete nutter.

I may not be good at a lot of things, but one thing is for sure, I know how to throw a party. I realise that my description of Cloverfields up to this point sounds a little like describing the Chatsworth Estate off *Shameless*, but on the whole it really was a nice friendly little road.

The first party we threw on the road was a celebration BBQ for Rovers winning the Premier League, only four years after being taken over by local entrepreneur, Jack Walker. We had planned to invite around 20 people, but ended up having 86.

We had recently been on a family holiday to Spain, and whilst there had bumped into a work colleague of Janet's called Julie, and her husband John. Julie worked at BT, and John was a huge Liverpool fan, so we naturally hit it off straight away. I happened to mention that we were planning a BBQ on our return home, and he told me that he worked for a frozen food company in Oswaldtwistle and might be able to help out with a few burgers.

On the day of the do, John called round in his car and I couldn't believe what I was seeing. Every single part of his car was packed full of every kind of frozen food you could think of. That was the food sorted, and even though we were catering for 86 people, we ended up with so many boxes of burgers and sausages left over that the next day we ended up banging on everyone's doors on the road to make sure nothing was wasted.

The party was a huge success, with plenty of food, drink, and fantastic music. A couple of musician friends, Ian H and Pete B, had brought their acoustic guitars, and provided us with the evening's entertainment. Also, unlike my previous parties, the Old Bill managed to stay away, which was a bonus.

Even though my first love was Liverpool, due to the cost and the fact it would take all day travelling there and back, I decided to show some support for my hometown team Blackburn Rovers, as they had been in a separate division from Liverpool anyway.

Like anything that I would commit to, it had to be all or nothing. So I would never miss a game at Ewood Park, whether it was a sunny Saturday afternoon or a freezing wet Tuesday night.

I started off attending with my Uncle Stanley, who lived on Rhodes Avenue near Jez, and each week we would stand in exactly the same spot on the Riverside, along with some other people he knew. These were the days when you would stand on the terraces, and I soon realised that attending a football match was a little like visiting a pub. The regulars had their usual seats, and their usual place at the bar where they would stand. And some even had their own personal beer glass, and woe betide anyone who sat, stood, or drank from what they thought was rightfully theirs. A football match was pretty much the same; the regulars would attend week after week, and always stood or sat in the exact same location. My mate Jez would also attend with me the majority of the time, and eventually we ended up moving over to the Blackburn End.

A few of the lads that we knew from around town drank in the Adelphi Pub on the Boulevard, and for away matches we would on occasions go with them. It didn't take me long to realise that most of them were more interested in a pint than in a game of football. I remember travelling to Wolves, and it was almost half time, and we were still sitting in the pub. By the time we made it to Molineux, it was half time, and we struggled to talk them into letting us into the ground. Within a minute of the second half starting, Rovers scored, and as we were celebrating, a policeman walked over and threw Jez out for jumping up and down. All that way for less than two minutes.

I remember persuading Ste to drive to Grimsby, but he was reluctant, having just purchased a brand-new car which was his pride and joy. He eventually agreed to take us, but after the match a group of Grimsby supporters started to chase us and were throwing bricks at the car. That was the last time he offered to drive, which I sort of expected.

It was Waker's turn to drive, and this time the destination was Plough Lane to watch Rovers play Wimbledon. As before, we spent so long in the pub after our long journey down that it was half time when we finally made it to the ground. This time we found that every turnstile was closed, and we could see no way of getting in. There was no way at all I was prepared to travel hours to get there and not watch any of the game, so I suggested climbing over the wall that just happened to be covered with barbed wire. Somehow, we all managed to make it over and ran into the crowd. What we didn't realise was that the *Match of the Day* cameras had spotted us, and within a matter of minutes we found ourselves standing in a police room at the ground being questioned. I remember at the time being the only one out of our group that gave them the wrong name and address, and I couldn't believe my ears when every one of my mates gave their correct ones. The outcome of my very bad idea was a lecture off the police officer, followed by being told that we were now officially banned from Wimbledon Football Club, followed by, 'If you pay to get in, it will be okay for you to stay.'

One thing that always happened during our trips away with the Adelphi lot was when we would stop and visit a service station for supplies, not many things would get paid for. On most occasions these shops were so packed that they didn't even notice that half of our coach was stuffing their pockets with Mars bars, pork pies, and crisps. Or if they did notice, they were not about to challenge this behaviour – safety in numbers and all that. I must add that on no occasion did I ever steal anything myself. Maybe the shelves had already been emptied by the time I entered the shop.

Talking about nicking, it wasn't long before Jez arranged to take another holiday in Switzerland.
I remember him ringing our house phone at 12.45am from his hotel in Zurich, to ask me the name of the song that we used to sing in the Blackburn End.
Money was no object, especially when it was someone else's, and when he arrived home, he came round to our house in Cloverfields

with all his bags full of swag. He told me he had taken £29,000 worth of gear, including Iceberg jumpers, nine Cartier watches, and a number of leather jackets. He spread it all out on our living room floor, taking up every bit of space available, and I must admit for a few seconds I wondered if I should have gone with them.

Like anyone in this kind of situation who finds themselves getting away with stuff, you become greedy. And even though you vow to cut your losses and never to return again, you end up not sticking to it. On their third trip, Jez and his Blackburn Youth cronies visited the country on what was becoming their regular shopping spree, but this time they were seconds away from getting caught, which really shook them up. He told me that the Swiss police arrived on the scene whilst they were hiding on the roof of one of the shops they were trying to rob. He told me that no way would he be going back to Zurich, and I said I thought this was a wise decision.

At weekends Jez would never really come out with me and my mates, as he found them boring. He would always be more attracted to the people in the pub that had some sort of reputation, such as Al, Matt, and Wayne, so he would choose to spend time with them instead. He also used to play for The Farthings' football team, along with Ste, and I arranged to go and watch them play on the local fields one Sunday morning. I was standing talking to Christine, Jez's girlfriend at the time, when at the end of the match he stupidly took off his shirt to reveal half of his body was covered in love bites. I didn't know where to look, and when Christine asked me if I knew what Jez had been up to – knowing full well that they hadn't been given by her – I assured her that I didn't have a clue. Even though I can't remember if The Farthings ended up winning the match, one thing was certain, Christine ended up being an ex-girlfriend.

Jez told me later that he had been on his own in the Balaclava pub in town the night before, and had met an older woman – maybe a prostitute, he said. Despite the Balaclava having the best juke box in town, he went back to her house up Shadsworth and said she had blown his mind! We definitely moved in different circles.

Just down the road from the Balaclava was a favourite stopping-off place at the end of the night, The Khyber Café on Whalley Range. Not being a fan of curries, I detested ending up there, but it was a famous local landmark for a lot of people I knew, especially Jez, Birchy, and Knotty, so I would sometimes be dragged along.
We were in there one Saturday night, and one of our group was playing bar football with one of the locals. I am not too sure what happened, but an argument broke out between the two of them. Dennis, who was with us, and who was a very handy lad, kept warning the lad that it was just a game and advised him to leave it. But this lad stupidly ignored him, and ended up getting punched for trying to cause some trouble. The next thing I knew was the guy who was working behind the counter produced the largest knife I have ever seen, and proceeded to chase us out of the café. Everyone legged it, running as fast as they could down Whalley Range away from this nutter, but what worried me at the time was that I was the slowest runner, and this guy was still chasing after us, waving his bloody big knife above his head. He was literally inches away from me when a blue police van showed up, and the police started throwing everybody into the back, ignoring the headcase with the weapon. Every single person who was with us that night ended up being arrested, and spent the night in the cells at Blackburn Police Station. Everyone that is, except me. So I guess being a slow runner does have its advantages at times.

I often wonder how on earth I even managed to get myself in all these situations back then. I have always hated fighting, but I always seemed to be around when it happened.
On another occasion I found myself in the middle of a full-blown street battle, when I had planned for a quiet night. We were in the Borough Pub one Friday night, and I started chatting to Nicky's brother Mick and a few of his mates. Suddenly, some lads came in

and walked over to the bar and started threatening Mick. It was totally out of order, as Mick and his mates were not troublemakers, but he told me that there had been some beef over something to do with the Mill Hill lot (these lads) and the Little Harwood lot (with whom Mick and his mates were friends). They told me they were due to meet them in the Jubilee pub in 20 minutes, and being someone who would always back a mate if needed, I offered to go with them, as there were only three of them and around 15 from Mill Hill.

To my amazement, when I tried to recruit support from Nicky, he refused, even though it was his brother who was in a bit of a scrape. Jez, who was there at the time, also refused to help, which really surprised me. Just me then. So I followed Mick, Gaz, and Dave to the Jubilee, not realising what was about to happen.

As we were waiting inside the pub, we were joined by several other lads from Little Harwood, which evened up the numbers on both sides. Minutes later, I found myself being a part of what resembled a riot scene in a movie. Everyone was standing outside the pub in two very large groups, facing one another, some holding pool cues, some holding pool balls and various other weapons. Maybe Nicky and Jez had made the right decision not to get involved after all, although a little soft in my opinion. People started to throw bottles towards each other, followed by sticks and bricks, then everyone began fighting each other in the middle of the road. I found myself facing a lad I had seen before from Mill Hill, both waiting for the other to make the first move. I started moving towards him, feeling that *acting* hard was just as effective as *being* hard in some situations, and to prove my point he started to run away. We threw a couple of punches towards each other, then he dived under a parked car to hide. Others had seen this and dragged him out. I was wondering how long this was going to go on for, but before anyone ended up being seriously hurt, and like a Saturday night scene from *Starsky and Hutch*, police cars came screaming up the road from every direction and everyone had scattered within seconds.

I had managed to leg it over to some spare land, where I ended up in Zanzibar, and managed to meet back up with Nicky and Jez, the two traitors.

Zanzibar was the coolest pub in town at the time, and I remember fancying all three girls from behind the bar back in the day – before I met Janet, that is. Freda had been a witness to the colour of pyjamas my dad was wearing the night I invited her back to mine. I had taken Gillian to a Pelle fashion show at the Saxon Inn (Moat House), but I only went on the one date with her, even though she was really nice. And I sort of messed things up with Jacky. I had been with her on a Christmas do, but when I attempted to introduced her to my friend, Martin, I somehow managed to forget her name. However, she introduced me to the BBQ band, of which I was (and am) grateful.

On the walls in the pub, there used to be several music memorabilia-framed pictures, and I always had my eye on the Bryan Ferry/Roxy Music one. It has a photograph from the Flesh and Blood album cover, several concert tickets surrounding it, and a packet of French cigarettes named Roxy, which Bryan himself had signed. I loved it, and when the pub closed and was looking for new ownership, my dad's friend and neighbour at Lammack saved it for me, being the Area Manager of the brewery who had owned the pub. I may not have ended up with any of the bar staff, but my Bryan Ferry rarity would be the Zanzibar keepsake that I would cherish.

Bullinge would always travel around a lot for the Post Office, and he told me about a girl that he had worked with whilst on the counter in Lancaster. He told me that she was like a model, and apparently resembled Catherine Oxenberg from the TV series, *Dynasty*. He mentioned that she was absolutely obsessed with Bryan Ferry, and reckoned she would do anything at all to get her hands on my wonderful picture, even though there was zero chance of me letting it go.
Mark showed me a photo of her, confirming he had used the correct description, so I guessed that going on a date with her would surely do no harm – even though it would be based on false pretences. He got in touch with her and told her about the picture, and the next thing I received a letter from her with an enclosed

photo, asking me out. I felt a little bad, but she was fit, and it's not like I was about to turn her down.

We went around town together on the following Saturday, and to be fair, we had a pretty good night. I spent the evening trying my best to avoid the subject of the picture every time she brought it up, but at the end of the night she needed to get back to Lancaster on the train. After making up excuse after excuse, eventually I came clean and admitted to her that, due to it being a present, I would feel far too bad if I let it go. Needless to say, we never saw each other again, but I have always subscribed to the saying that 'it is better to have loved and lost, than never to have loved'!

Jez, being Jez, was not very good at following people's advice, including his own, and did the opposite of what he told me he was going to do, by visiting Switzerland for yet another time. The same old deal had taken place: he bought a credit card off someone he knew for £50, and used the card to pay for his travel, accommodation, and refreshments whilst away. The only difference this time was that the lad who sold it to him had bottled it, and instead of following the four-day rule before reporting it missing, he did so after just one day. This lad's actions led to the lot of them being caught on only their second day, and in turn they were all arrested and thrown into a Swiss prison.

When I received the call from Jez – probably his only call of the day – asking me if I could let his mum and dad know what had happened, I knew that no amount of Iceberg jumpers or fancy watches were worth his freedom. Letting his parents know was tough, and I was dreading making the call. The days of playing Subbuteo round at his house were long gone, and even though I felt his mum had seen me as a bad influence back then, she certainly couldn't blame me for this. Sure enough, his mum answered, and I did everything in my power to break the news gently to her. But after she fell silent at my news, she simply thanked me for letting her know and put the phone down.

Jez would ring me from time to time, and he told me he was stuck in his cell for 23 hours a day, which he shared with a Mexican guy who couldn't speak a word of English (and why would he?).
I would write to him every couple of weeks, and he would regularly reply, letting me know how he was getting on. He told me that receiving a letter was the highlight of his week, and even though he appreciated the *Quadrophenia* paperback I had sent him, he complained that it was far too depressing at that time, and in future would prefer if I could send him something a little more light-hearted. (Ungrateful, or what?)

Whilst Jez was in prison, he managed to get himself involved with some pretty dodgy characters who were in a different league to him. Obviously, everyone was baying for the blood of the lad who dropped them in it, but rumour had it he had gone into hiding. I was in our kitchen when the phone on the wall rang, and I answered it to find a couple of lads from Kent on the other end, who Jez had been in prison with. They started the conversation thinking I had been the person that had led to everybody getting arrested, and the more I tried to explain to them that they had the wrong person, and that I was in fact a mate of Jez, the more they ignored what I was saying and carried on threatening me.

The main problem was that I was taking this phone call from these idiots only feet away from where Janet and her mum were washing up, so I was trying really hard to be careful what words I was using. I was just about to hang up when, for some reason, their attitude changed, and they realised they had made a mistake. They told me that they were due to get out in a couple of weeks and wanted to meet me in Darwen, as they would have a bag of fake passports which they wanted me to look after for them. Yet again, how the hell do I manage to get myself into these bloody crazy situations? Honestly, I really don't know.
All in all, Jez ended up serving one year and three months in prison, and it is fair to say the experience changed him forever.

CHAPTER FOURTEEN

HEAVEN MUST HAVE SENT YOU

I don't recall me and Janet having a single row in the first two years of being married, so the indications were that it was going to last. I don't remember ever wondering what it must be like to have kids, but that doesn't mean to say I hadn't.
We started to discuss having children and I was never one to take things for granted, but there was no harm in trying. After all, my mum had obviously tried to become pregnant and struggled, but not long after they adopted me, she became pregnant with Robin.
I seem to think it was around three months after we first engaged in the conversation about adding another member to the Eastwood household, that Janet fell pregnant – no messing around here.
Our world was about to change more than we could have ever imagined. I was 29, and maybe this was finally my time to grow up… just maybe.

Baz, who I worked with at Unilab, wasn't only one of the nicest lads you could ever meet, but he was a superb musician and artist – the two things I would have loved to have a talent in. He very kindly offered to paint some murals on the wall of our spare bedroom to help us turn it into a nursery, and what an amazing job he did. He would come round to ours, night after night, whilst I would sit downstairs, playing Super Mario on the Nintendo, leaving him in peace to work his creative magic. He painted pictures of Pebbles and Bambam from *The Flintstones*, and various Disney characters ranging from Mickey Mouse to Bugs Bunny, and both Janet and I loved it. Janet will always say that one of her memories of the time during her pregnancy was the sound of a Yoshi trying to make it from one land to the next.

When it came to telling our parents about our massive news, my mum – yet again – put a downer on the situation with her negative reaction. It made me really angry at the time, as Janet did not deserve it. Maybe she felt that I wasn't the ideal father material, and maybe she was right, but being honest, who is until it happens? I recall Mary telling me when we were teenagers that she thought I would make a really good dad one day (not with her), which I thought was a very nice thing to say, and I've always remembered it. We hadn't done the usual thing discussing possible baby names, as most couples apparently search through name books looking for inspiration. We both agreed on Daniel Jake if it was a boy, and Janet had always loved the name Emma for a girl, as she had found it classy after reading *A Woman of Substance*.

I remember having the conversation as to what other name would go with Emma – Emma Jane, Emma Jade? Then suddenly I had an idea. At the top of our stairs was a bookcase full of CDs, and I ran up and selected Paul Weller's first solo album, *Paul Weller*, which was released on 29th April, 1992. It stuck in my mind that he had dedicated the LP to his two children, Nathaniel and Leah, so I legged it back downstairs excitedly holding it in my hand and said, 'What about Emma Leah?'

On Wednesday, 24th February, 1993 at 11.22am at Blackburn Hospital, Emma Leah Eastwood entered the world, weighing 7lb 5oz. The original due date we were given was 4th March, which I commented was Kenny Dalglish's birthday – very apt. But when Janet was told she would be having a caesarean section, the date was changed. It was a really weird feeling knowing the exact day and time that our baby was going to enter the world, but I suppose it meant that we could plan for it a little better.

As Janet was having a section, I would have to dress in a green gown, green wellies, and a mask, as if I was an extra in the TV series *M*A*S*H**.
I was pretty worried, as normally the sight of needles, blood, or even a hospital, would leave me feeling faint, and on this occasion

Janet would have her stomach cut open just inches away from me. To be fair, though, it wasn't as gory as I imagined, as they put a small screen up so that I wouldn't witness the whole procedure. Thankfully, I managed to avoid passing out, and I wasn't even the one having the baby.

Janet did an amazing job throughout, but when the nurse walked over to me holding our baby, I couldn't help but think, 'Where did that come from?' as I had not actually witnessed the birth.

It took me a fair few weeks to properly get my head around the fact that I had just become a dad, but you don't really have the luxury of having time to get used to it, as the second you leave the hospital with your bundle of joy, you are on your own – or at least, that is how it felt.

Once our Emma was born, my mum and dad instantly came round to the idea of having a grandchild and were amazing in their support, as was Janet's mum, showing us the ropes and giving us tips on how to cope and what to do. I don't remember Emma Leah sleeping all the way through for at least the first two years, and I would be lying if I made out that it wasn't tough. But you cope because you have to, and not because you necessarily know what you are doing. You take advice, pick up tips, and do what you feel is right, but mainly you wing it and hope for the best, as I'm sure most folk will admit.

You are always advised by the midwife to just act normally when your child is in bed, and if you want to watch TV, then do so; if you want to do the hoovering, then do the hoovering. But in reality, you still end up being as silent as you can be, having spent ages getting her off to sleep in the first place.
I used to lie on the floor next to her cot, holding her hand through the bars if she had woken up. Eventually, and I mean eventually, she would appear to nod off and I found myself crawling on my stomach commando-style, slowly, inch by inch, out of the room. Many a time those efforts were in vain, as she would wake up

again before I could even reach the door, so I would have to start all over again.

Biased as I may be, Emma was beautiful, and it was hard to understand that I had helped create a little human being like her. As she got a little older, she worked out how to throw herself over the side of her cot, which would always worry me. We would be watching TV, when suddenly we would hear a thud from upstairs, and I would run up to find her standing on the landing just staring at me, as if butter wouldn't melt. As she grew, we ended up putting one of those baby gates at the top of the stairs, but it was a waste of time, as she soon worked out how to fling herself over that.

I tried to do my bit in terms of nappy changing, winding, and giving her a bottle, but there is no doubt that Janet would do the most. She would be the one getting up in the night to go and see to Emma, as I was the one working in the morning; that is what we agreed.

Janet always reminds me that when I would bath Emma at night, I would also try and entertain her at the same time. I would stand in the bathroom strumming my acoustic guitar, whilst singing along to the likes of *Wonderwall* and *Don't Look Back in Anger*, trying to encourage her to join in. The thing is, I can't sing a note for the life of me, and I certainly cannot play the guitar, but when you are performing to a two-year-old, they aren't about to tell you that you are rubbish, so you may as well believe that you are Noel himself, playing at the M.E.N, even if only for a few minutes.

I had taken a week off work as part of my paternity leave. On my return, I was called into the office and criticised for being soft, and asked why I wanted to be present at the birth, as I should have been in the pub like a real man would have been (and he wondered where the name Fred Flintstone came from!). His comments reminded me of the story I had been told by one of the lads, Paul in the machine shop, when his wife was expecting. It was weeks away from the due date, and Paul's wife had said to him, 'Is it alright if Kev is present at the birth?'

'Kev who?' replied Paul.

'Kev from our local,' was the reply. And the rest, I feel, folk can guess.

For the first couple of years before Emma was old enough to go to nursery, my parents would have her at their house in Kestrel Close. And as well as spoiling her with constant trips to the seaside, the latest toys, and children's TV, they would also attempt to teach her things. My dad would use his knowledge of maths to help her get interested as well as clued up on the subject, and my mum would do the same for English. A regular haunt they would take her to was the sand dunes at St Anne's, where they had taken me and Robin many years before. And a favourite activity there was the miniature train that you could sit on and go around the track. If the truth be known, I think my mum and dad enjoyed it just as much as Emma, and there was no doubt that they both lived for seeing her when she was little.

It was a tough decision to send her to nursery, and even though my parents had taught her a huge amount, we felt that it would be better for her to mix with other children. The nursery we chose was Oscar Bears, which was a bit mad, as it had been a nightclub in its former life; in fact, the smallest nightclub I had ever been to. Looking back, Oscar Bears was brilliant, and we had no doubt that we had made the right decision. Emma really benefited from her experience there and thought the world of all the staff, especially Claire and Sandra.

At the beginning, Unilab was owned by a guy called John, who owned a motorbike shop on King Street. From time to time, he would come and pay us a visit at random times in the day. It was literally like a scene from *Are You Being Served?*, as he would walk around every department telling us we had 'all done very well'. (Yes, for him.) If we were lucky, he would offer us a boiled sweet from his pocket, which was usually covered in fluff. So I tended to thank him, but say no. On more than one occasion, a member of my team would try and throw him out, thinking he was just some random guy who had walked in off the street.

I'm not saying he was tight or anything, but he would walk around our Despatch department, picking up paper clips he had noticed on the floor, telling us every time that he didn't get where he was without looking after paper clips. He was a character, if nothing else. I imagine if he had got to know about my telephone calls from Jamaica, no doubt he would have docked my wages!

Even though we still only ever called it Unilab, we found ourselves taken over by the Philip Harris Group (science equipment and resources for schools), and in theory things became a little more sophisticated. Several people were made redundant, noticeably Colin, our works manager, and to be fair, I certainly missed him. I had liked the guy, although we did have several run-ins. He was replaced by a younger guy called Gary, but the problem was that Gary was more of a mate than our boss.

The new overall boss originated from Wales, and he brought with him all sorts of new-fangled ideas.
Firstly, the Supervisors would now be called Team Leaders, and would be invited to weekly team meetings so that we could solve all the problems of the company within an hour, as well as bitch about each other. Also new on the agenda was ongoing training, which is something I don't ever remember receiving before. Every now and again the Team Leaders would be sent off to a really posh hotel in Darwen, Astley Bank. You wouldn't believe that you were in Darwen, as it was situated just off the main road, down a country lane, which made it feel as if you were in the middle of the countryside. I heard that Paul Weller would stay there if he had been playing a gig in Manchester or Blackburn, but I couldn't confirm it as being true.

Philip Harris would pay for us all to stay for the weekend, full board for Thursday, Friday, Saturday, and then leave Sunday. My mate Ste was a Team Leader, and my friends Bev and Cindy had been invited along, so I knew it was going to be eventful, if nothing else.

I remember the evening meal on our first night's stay. Nobody had asked what we wanted, and when the food arrived, it was a high-quality meal for sure. But as the most boring diner on the planet, I found it far too fancy and couldn't eat it. Noticing I was having a problem with the food, our manager apologised to me and kindly offered to get me something else. Again, I wasn't consulted on what I would like, so when the waiter came with my second meal, my heart sank. It was salmon, which I really don't like. I didn't have the heart to say anything, so just sat there forcing it down bit by bit. I suppose it is better in the long run to be honest and come clean, but I would never choose to hurt someone's feelings if I didn't have to.

Every Friday, Jean from Packing would walk around our department, handing out these chewy toffee sweets in shiny blue wrappers, which I couldn't stand. The problem was that after around two years of saying thank you and taking one off her each week, I ended up with a drawer full of them, and never did have the heart to tell her. Sorry, Jean!

To be fair, these weekends away were certainly not a Jolly, as we would work from first thing in the morning until around seven at night. After that we had 15 minutes in our room to shower, change, and freshen up, before the evening meal was served.

It had been a long day, and we were still in the bar at three in the morning. One by one, folk would say goodnight and stagger back to their rooms, and I knew that if I didn't do the same, I would be in no fit state for the following day's learning. There were three of us left, and not wanting to appear a wimp, I had managed to hold on up to this point. My plan was to say that I was going to the toilet and then just sneak off to my room. But as soon as I mentioned nipping to the loo, I was told I had better return and carry on our conversation. Based on the fact that the girl instructing me had just told us a tale about her taking a shotgun to her husband, after he had been threatening her, I decided that it might be best if I returned.

The following day I felt rougher than I had in years, and Damian, who was the other remaining drunk, didn't even manage to turn up for breakfast, never mind the morning's training. As rough as I felt, I soon came round in the afternoon when we were told about the internet for the very first time. Gary had been taking the training, and he started to tell us about this new thing that was coming in, called the worldwide web. He had a large pull-down screen and asked us to shout out any subject. I called out John Lennon, and by magic, after he had typed the name into the keypad, a photo of Mr John Lennon appeared on the screen. I think we were all pretty impressed at the time, but little did we know the significance of that afternoon's training.

CHAPTER FIFTEEN

MARINE BOY

One day at work, we were told that because Philip Harris had been keen on staff development for all the staff, the company had put a pot of money aside for everyone to choose an area or a subject that they felt they needed to improve on. We were allowed £50 each, and to my knowledge, everyone else chose something that was relevant to their particular job. I chose scuba diving.
Even though I knew I was pushing my luck, I was deadly serious, and no-one was more surprised than me when my request was accepted.

Paul, who I used to work with at the chicken farm, was involved with Diver Services at Glenfield Park, and I enlisted my brother-in-law Martin to join me. I thought there would be safety in numbers, so we both signed up for the PADI Open Water Scuba Diving Course.
I learnt from day one about the massive rivalry there was between PADI (Professional Association of Diving Instructors) and BSAC (British Sub-Aqua Club). I was led to believe that BSAC were a lot more thorough with their training, and they would look down on divers from PADI, making out that they were rushed through their training to a level that BSAC deemed unfit. Personally, I found the rivalry to be childish, as we were all doing the same thing after all.

We had to take a theory test before we could step into the water, and even though I found it challenging, both Martin and I did our revision and managed to pass. Our first lesson in the water took place at Belper Street Baths, which was just down the road from our house, and where I would often go as a kid. The difference this time was that our lessons would be underwater, and you had

to stay under for around 15 minutes each time, whilst the instructor communicated with us via hand signals. It was freezing every time we surfaced, but we still managed to complete each test.
After a couple of weeks at Belper, we moved our lessons to Bank Hey pool on Heys Lane, and the first thing said to us once we arrived was, 'Right, lads, I want you to swim 20 lengths of the pool nonstop to prove that you are fit enough to carry on.'

Our next challenge was to dive at a disused quarry called Capenwray at Lancaster, and this was certainly a step up from the pool, as you had to dive to various ledges underwater, navigating around an old helicopter and a statue of a horse reading a newspaper, which had sunk there.
The final part of our qualification was an 18-metre open water dive up at Wastwater in the Lake District. The location was beautiful – a giant lake, half a mile across and surrounded by snow-capped mountains. This was to be the final part of our exam, and if we successfully completed this, we would be fully qualified scuba divers. I felt I had come a long way from collecting coral as a child, watching Marine Boy, and reading my Underwater Divers Ladybird book.
Due to the poor conditions in the UK, we were told we would be qualified to dive anywhere in the world if we completed this. Wastwater and surrounding area was like a picture postcard, but I understood what they meant, as the temperature of the water was five degrees, and it only had one metre visibility.

We got changed behind a rock and were told that if we got into any trouble in the water, the only option would be to call the RAF helicopter to come and rescue us. Our diving instructor for the day was Clive, who I had worked with at Unilab, and he needed us to pass in order for him to get to the next level as an instructor.

As we were learning and didn't have any of the gear ourselves, we had to rent equipment from Diver Services – dry suit, fins, snorkel, and mask – and had to make do with the best condition ones they could find that fitted. At Lancaster, I had found the kit really restricting when underwater, and when I came out after my first dive, my mask was full of blood and I had bruises all over my body, which had been caused by the pressure. Janet thought I was mad and couldn't understand how I found this new activity pleasurable in any way. And at times, I admit, I wondered that myself.

The first task at Wastwater was to dive to 18 metres, but the first thing they had pointed out was a number of metal plaques attached to rocks as we were descending, in memory of divers who had died. Once we reached 18 metres, which to be fair didn't really feel that much further down than our normal dives, we had to take off our masks so we couldn't see a thing, and take the regulator out of our mouths and throw it behind us. Then, as we slowly made our way to the surface, you and your diving buddy (Martin, in my case) had to take turns at taking a breath out of one of the regulators, all the way up to the surface.
Our next task was to navigate between two points underwater, using a compass. But I had always struggled to navigate on dry land, so I wasn't confident at all.

We had just started to submerge when it appeared that something was wrong with Martin. He seemed to be in trouble, and made hand signals to Clive indicating that he wanted to return to the surface. But before Clive could react, to our horror, Martin made a bolt to the surface, which is something they teach you to never do. As you ascend, pressure decreases and the air in your lungs expands. This can make the air sacs in your lungs rupture, which in turn makes it hard for you to breathe. At higher pressure underwater, nitrogen gas goes into the body's tissues, which doesn't cause a problem down in the water.

By the time I reached the surface, I could see that Martin was panicking. He was coughing and spluttering, and I noticed that his lips had turned blue. Everyone's efforts now were to get him out of the water as quickly as possible and to make sure he was safe. He ended up in the back of the diver service van covered with a silver foil blanket, often used after a car crash to keep folk warm. It transpired that the dry suit he'd rented had a small hole in it, which let water in, and the longer Martin was in the lake the faster his body temperature dropped, unbeknown to him. He felt ill and panicked, and ended up hyperventilating.

This was certainly a very scary incident, and it was such a relief that he was going to be okay. The incident shook him up more than you could imagine, and he vowed never to go into the water again. The instructor tried his best to talk him round, as he needed him to complete the course, but Martin was having none of it and was clearly still very upset.
Clive eventually backed off, knowing he was fighting a losing battle, and his attention then turned to me. I must admit the incident had shaken me up too, and I saw it as an excuse for me to call it a day and get away with not having to go back into the water. But Clive and some of the others told me that was the worst thing I could do. Like riding a bike, it was important that I went back into the lake that day. They reckoned that if I didn't, I would never go back in again and finish my course. Even though I found it really hard, I knew their advice was correct, and I was just going to have to push myself to do it.

I somehow managed to complete and pass my underwater navigation task, but I surfaced right in the centre of the lake. By this time, I was absolutely shattered, but the more I used what little energy I had left to try and swim to shore, the more it felt like I was going nowhere. I was a quarter of a mile out and surrounded by snow-capped mountains everywhere I looked, which made it difficult to find my bearings. Feeling slightly panicked, I started to swallow mouthfuls of water, and the weight and tightness of my equipment made me feel really restricted. I knew this wasn't good, and began to feel that it was possible for me to drown if I carried on like that.

I started to wave to Clive to alert him to come and help me, and he made his way over to try and calm me down, allowing me to hold on to him as he helped me to the side. He told me that I only had the weight belt task left, and then I would be fully qualified, but right then I couldn't have cared less about passing the course, and told him in no uncertain terms that I just wanted to get to dry land. After a rest at the side of the lake, though, I forced myself to go back into the water and complete the final part of my qualification.

Thanks to Philip Harris, Diver Services, Clive, and not forgetting Martin, I was now a fully qualified PADI Open Water Diver, and for once I felt really proud of myself. As for Martin, he stuck to his word and never ventured into the water again. He even told me he suffered from nightmares for months about our day trip to the Lakes.

A number of years later, we were on holiday in Ibiza – my favourite place – and I decided to put my skills to the test and have a go at scuba diving in more sunnier climes. I found a local diving centre in Sant Antoni, but just as I completed all the paperwork required for me to go diving with them, they realised that I was PADI affiliated and told me that it was far too choppy to take the boat out. I couldn't believe it, but it simply confirmed how childish the rivalry was between the two diving organisations. I eventually discovered another centre further down near Port D'es Torrent, and to my relief, they agreed to take me out.

The instructor only spoke a little English, and the rest of my group were German, so I was definitely the odd one out. We were taken out on a motorboat to the spot where the instructor recommended we should dive, and as usual I was having trouble submerging. I mentioned this to the instructor, hoping he would give me a little support. But he simply said, 'You're qualified, aren't you? Well, just get on with it.' (nice)

Eventually I managed to sort my buoyancy out and joined the others underwater. Once I got the hang of it, I found the experience to be magical, compared to the UK, because the water wasn't freezing, the visibility was superb, and even though I hadn't spotted a horse reading a newspaper this time, it was just what I had hoped diving would be. There were fish and coral everywhere, and it was a great underwater adventure for sure.

Unfortunately, the journey back to the beach was so choppy that I started to feel sick. Everybody was talking in German, so I knew I wouldn't get any sympathy on this occasion. When we got back to the shore, I collapsed on a rock, feeling so rough that I thought I was dying. Thankfully, after a couple of hours back at the hotel, I started to feel a bit better, so I didn't ruin our holiday after all.

CHAPTER SIXTEEN

CONFESSIONS OF A DRIVING INSTRUCTOR

Unlike most members of the male species, I have never had an urge to learn to drive, or even own a car. I rode the scooter I had found for a while, and I ended up driving a forklift truck at work, but unless it was a silver Austin Martin, I had zero interest in buying a car.

I think one of the things that put me off was when my mate Ste purchased his first car. It was his pride and joy, which was fair enough, but every time I asked him if he was coming out, he would tell me that he couldn't afford to, as he had to spend his money on his car. I knew that wasn't for me. I would much rather go out every night and get a DMC taxi than spend most of my wages on my own vehicle.

As time went by, and I was now in my thirties, I started to feel guilty about not being able to drive for the family, and felt it might be time to pay back all my friends and family for all the lifts they had given me over the years.

Now and then back in the day we used to hitch-hike, especially when we had been on our daily adventures. We would always try to flag down a lift from some random stranger to avoid walking home. On the majority of occasions, though, I always had the ability to talk a mate into giving me a lift, or to persuade my dad to drop me off somewhere.

I'll always remember the time when I suggested to Ste and Karl that we spend the day in Blackpool. We were in the pub having a few drinks when they started to ask me how we were going to get home. I have always had this problem where my priority is to go places, while most of the time giving very little thought into how I could get back home. I'm sure there must be a name for it. Around that time, we'd started hanging around with Janet and her mates – Tracey, Alison, and her sister Elaine – but I hadn't started going out with her at this point.

I remembered that at least one of them could drive, so came up with a plan to see if they wanted to join us for the rest of our night out. I gave Janet a call and suggested we meet up for a few drinks, and when she agreed to join us, I suggested that for a change we should meet up in Blackpool, as it would be a laugh. Sure enough, about an hour and a half later, they turned up at the pub we were at, and later that evening we ended up getting a lift home.

If someone was to ask Janet or any of the others about that story today, I have no doubt they would say that they knew we were in Blackpool all along and that we wanted a lift, but I am not too sure. At the end of the day, I can only rely on my memories for any given story, and my version played out like that as far as I am concerned.

Guilt finally got the better of me, and I decided to learn to drive. My mum offered to help me out with some money towards the lessons, and June from work was already taking lessons so I planned to get the details of her instructor. The thing about this decision was that I had decided to keep this a secret, as I could only see myself going through with it providing Janet and my mates didn't know. It's not like they would have believed me anyway, but what actually motivated me in the first place was to fully keep it a secret and surprise everybody once I passed.

My mum agreed to keep it quiet, and I booked a number of Friday afternoons off work, planning to sit in our back garden, away from the world, and revise the Highway Code each week on my own. When I say I was starting from scratch, it couldn't have been more true, as I didn't know the first thing at all about the workings of a car, or even about staying safe on the roads.

For some strange reason, I was never allowed a bike whilst growing up. As a toddler, I had a little tricycle, and remember riding it straight into the pebbled back wall of our house. I still have the scar on my forehead to prove it. But surely that couldn't have been the reason? Whatever it was, it had prevented me from learning any road sense at a young age, and was my excuse why I had never felt confident to learn up till now. My take on it was that as a teenager you ride a bike until you get to know the roads and learn the rules, and then a natural progression was to move on to a car.

Week after week on Friday afternoons, I sat in the hammock in our back garden, studying everything I needed to know about the Highway Code. I can't remember how Janet found out, but someone told her that I hadn't been working for the past few Friday afternoons. I made up a number of excuses at first, as I really wanted to keep it from her, but when the conversation went along the lines of 'Are you having an affair?', I had no option but to come clean.

Even though I still didn't feel overly confident, I managed to book my theory test at a centre somewhere in Preston. It took me ages to find the place, but I remember noticing several people dressed in Army uniform on Preston station, which I felt was a little strange. With minutes to spare, I was rushed to my chair in front of a small computer, as the test was via touchscreen, and I remember giving it my best shot. After I finished, an elderly gentleman approached me and said, 'Who's a clever boy then?' (this was a first!) and proceeded to inform me that I had only managed to pass my test with full marks – 34 out of 34. I was actually stunned, and couldn't wait to get home and tell Janet.

As I was making my way back towards the town centre, a jet flew over my head, and I smiled to myself that it must have been commissioned to celebrate me achieving full marks on my test. I noticed that there was a huge crowd of people in the direction I was walking in, and asked a couple what all the fuss was about. They just pointed to a wooden stand a few yards ahead and told me that a Rock FM DJ was there.

I took another few more steps forward and started to push my way through the crowd, when none other than the Queen and her husband, Prince Philip, just walked past me – literally a few feet away. This certainly explained why so many police and Army had been on the station when I arrived, and I must have been the only person in Preston that day who wasn't aware of the Queen's visit.

Back at work, June told me the name and contact details of the instructor she was having lessons from. His name was Tod, so I gave him a call and booked myself in for the following week. I dreaded my first ride out in Tod's car, and must have looked as white as a ghost by the time he picked me up.
I explained to him that I didn't know a single thing about cars, in the hope that he would break me in gently, but the opposite happened. He needed to get the girl who was sitting in the back seat back home to Accrington, so he told me to start driving.
I was extremely nervous, and every time I asked him for directions, I had to constantly repeat myself, as Tod's attention was on the girl in the back seat, and not on me. By the time we dropped off the girl, it had eaten into 25 minutes of my paid lesson. Even though I felt pretty proud that I had managed to drive to Accrington and back in one piece, I couldn't help but feel I was being ripped off.
The following week, the same thing happened, and I even heard him say to our young lady friend, 'I have been a driving instructor for over 25 years now, and the only reason I took up the job in the first place was because I thought it would lead to me having some affairs!' This was totally out of order. On top of being highly unprofessional, the girl was a lot younger than me, and Tod was at least twice my age.

The following day at work, I approached June with 'You know that Tod…,' planning on blowing his cover and telling her all about what I had heard, when she had stopped me in my tracks. She told me that she didn't have lessons with him any more, as he put his hand on her leg or fondled her ears whenever she was stopped at a traffic light. I decided to follow her lead and sent

Tod packing, but to be honest, I really should have reported him, the dodgy git!

Two weeks passed and eventually I found myself a new instructor. This time, he concentrated on teaching me how to drive and seemed a really nice guy. At weekends and sometimes at night, Janet would take me out and let me have a go in her car, driving around secluded local industrial sites to help me gain confidence behind the wheel. I felt that I had come on leaps and bounds over the past couple of months, and my instructor had even hinted I was close to booking my test.

I took a break from lessons for a couple of weeks as we were going on holiday, but when we arrived back at the airport after our well-earned break in the sun, I had a problem with my left eye, with loads of floaty bits swimming around which affected my sight.

I didn't mention this to Janet or Emma, as I thought it was because I was over tired, but the following morning there was no change, and I started to worry. As my job involved driving a forklift truck, I told Janet that I couldn't go into work and that I needed to see a doctor. My doctor told me that he couldn't see anything untoward, but to be safe he sent me to the Eye Clinic at Blackburn Hospital, to get thoroughly checked out.

I hated hospitals at the best of times, and after waiting for around four-and-a-half hours, I was finally called in to have an eye test via the chart on the wall then told to take a seat outside in the waiting room. Just then, I spotted a couple of doctors coming towards me in a panic. Before I knew what was going on, I was being told by the Eye Specialist that if I didn't have emergency laser eye treatment that day, I could lose the sight in my left eye within the next 48 hours.

To say I was in shock was an understatement, but he explained that I had a partially detached retina, no doubt due to the number of times I had been punched in the face up the Cav, and that I also had three small holes in my retina that needed to be sealed immediately.

To be fair, the fact that he told me I was having the treatment there and then was obviously a wise move, because if he had told me to go home and return at a later date, I would have no doubt started searching for my passport.

The procedure itself was pretty unpleasant, as I had to rest my chin on this plastic contraption whilst they lasered up the holes in my eye to repair the damage. I remember it hurting, and I do recall noticing a burning smell as they were carrying it out. Thankfully, it didn't last more than a few minutes, and my consultant told me that if I ever experienced a flashing sensation in either of my eyes in future, it would be an emergency, and I should make my way straight to the Eye Clinic at Burnley Hospital.

I guessed that this would be the end of my scuba diving, due to the pressure. And even though they never told me it would affect my ability to drive, I used this situation as an excuse to stop my driving lessons. So it was now back to cadging lifts off family and friends again, but at least nobody could say I didn't try.

Even though my eyes have been reasonably okay since that day, I did read in the paper a couple of years ago that the same veteran Eye Specialist had been suspended, due to irregularities, leading me to question if anyone could actually be trusted.

CHAPTER SEVENTEEN

THIS IS MY WORLD TODAY

The one thing I noticed, or even imagined, from almost day one of being married, was the extra attention my new role seemed to attract from members of the opposite sex. Nothing really major, but it did feel as if, now that I wasn't trying to meet anyone, I would find myself in situations where I wouldn't have to try at all if I wanted to be unfaithful. It's like most things: you try too hard at something and you obviously come across as being desperate, which in itself is a turn off. But as soon as you relax and act as though you are not bothered, it must be seen as some sort of attraction or challenge.

I am not going to mention every incident, as I have always been happily married, but one incident stands out as illustrating how easy it can be to end up in a situation with no idea how it happened.

I was round town with a few of my male mates and said 'hi' to an ex-girlfriend of one of my friends from years back. We were in O'Neill's Irish bar at the time, but we left and made our way to Mr G's. I was at the bar getting a drink when the same girl appeared and started chatting to me. It seemed innocent enough, but later that night I was sitting at the back of the club when she appeared again. Like with the blue sweets from Jean, the longer the conversation went on, the more stupid I would have felt if I had suddenly just thrown into the mix that I was happily married. After all, we were only talking, and maybe I was imagining things. However, to leave me in absolutely no doubt, she managed to grab my hand and attempted to put it down her top – attempted being the operative word. Then she leant over and tried to kiss me.

So I quickly made up an excuse and hurried off to try and find my mates.

Thinking she had taken the hint, I was standing at the door at the end of the evening, waiting for everyone else, when a taxi pulled up just outside. The rear door swung open, and she was lying across the back seat, telling me to get in. She shouted, 'Come on, we are going back to your house.'

I was almost lost for words (almost), but instead of just coming clean, I made up some elaborate story about my mate not being in a good place and me having to make sure he got home safe.

I don't for one second think she believed me, but my words worked, and she slammed shut the door of the taxi, not looking overly impressed, and it zoomed off up the road. Phew! That had been a close call, even though I had no idea how I had found myself in that situation.

The following Thursday, I was out with Janet for a few drinks. Again, we were in O'Neill's, and I went to the bar to order our drinks. To my horror, I turned round to see Janet deep in conversation with the very same girl I had met at the club the week before. I couldn't believe my luck! I mean seriously, what were the odds of this happening?

At that point, neither of them looked like they wanted to kill me, which was a huge bonus, so I sheepishly took our drinks over, worried sick about what might happen next. When Janet told me she was going to the toilet, I was left alone with this girl again.

Before I could think of any small talk, the girl said, 'I guess that's your wife then,' as they didn't actually know each other and had just literally started chatting.

I told her that she was, that I was happily married, and apologised for not mentioning this fact to her the previous week. I also thanked her for not mentioning anything to Janet, and to her total credit, she was really cool about the situation and told me that it wasn't a problem and that she understood. I couldn't believe how lucky I had been, as things could have gone either way. Thankfully, the incident was forgotten about, and Janet and I carried on with our night out, and also our marriage.

As far as parties go, I feel our next party at Cloverfields was definitely our best. We decided to throw a 70s party, and what a party it was. As always, I went absolutely overboard and ended up dressing the majority of our house. We had a mirror ball hanging from the ceiling in the living room, a 70s DJ stand and lights, giant posters of Shaft, Abba, and Starsky and Hutch plastered on the walls, along with my old *Top of the Pops* album covers anywhere they would fit. I spent weeks sourcing official 70s sweets – white mice, Black Jacks, Fruit Salads, Space Dust, Anglo Bubbly, Bootlaces, and a box of Curly Wurlys – which were all left in dishes in the kitchen. We even had an original 1970s Triumph Stag motorcar parked across our front lawn, thanks to Andy and Vicky from next door.

As Emma was a little too young to attend, she was staying the night at my parents' house. To get into the mood for the evening's entertainment, our neighbour Andy drove us around town in the Stag, gathering strange looks along the way – no doubt down to our giant afros. We also stopped off at Kestrel Close so that Emma would get the chance to see me in my light blue safari suit, stacker shoes, fake moustache, giant medallion, and of course an afro wig. But I'm not sure Emma knew who we were when we popped up at the living room window, as Andy looked even more authentic than me.

Every single person put in the effort to dress up, and it was hilarious watching taxi after taxi pull up outside, trying to work out who was in the John Travolta suit or who resembled Huggy Bear. Our friends at the end of the road, Julie and Steve, were away, leaving their parents to babysit. And when they returned home, Julie's mum told her that she'd thought there was some sort of cult going on with the amount of crazy-looking people turning up.

Most of our neighbours were invited, apart from the obvious two, and it really was a fantastic night with everyone dancing the night away to the best 70s bangers we could find. We ended up having to redecorate the house afterwards, but it was worth it.

The next party we threw was a Caribbean beach party – yes, at Daisyfield – and a similar effort was put into that. We told Emma she was okay to attend, so arranged for her to wear a fruit headdress and a grass skirt, so that she looked the part. I could be found at the end of the garden running Pedro's Cocktail Bar that took me weeks to make. I made it out of an old wooden bench, as many bamboo canes I could get my hands on, and then spray painted everything in Rastafarian colours – green, yellow, and red – to finish the thing off. I spent the afternoon sitting behind it in my yellow Hawaiian shirt, making and serving cocktails to all and sundry. We even had fake palm trees, a mini beach, and I organised a limbo competition. But when it started to rain, we ended up taking the party indoors, and the kitchen was rammed full of colourful people drinking Red Stripe and getting down to Reggae. Zero trouble, zero police visits and, like I've already said, we know how to throw a party.

I have already mentioned that when I went to see Secret Affair at King George's Hall in Blackburn in the early 80s, I wasn't that impressed on the night, but there had been an announcement that they were playing in Accrington, and I got quite excited. My friends Colin and Dave's band The Itch were supporting, so I rounded up the troops for what promised to be a fabulous night.
During the week leading up to the gig, I played their albums and was really looking forward to their set. On the night, Ste from work talked me into calling at a local cocktail bar just before The Itch were due to be on. I wasn't sure what to order, so I told him that I would have the same as him.
I had no idea what the cocktail was called, but it looked pretty fancy with what looked like thick cream on the top, and was then set alight. Ste suggested downing it in one as we didn't want to be late to watch the band, but as we were walking away, I heard the barmaid say, 'You must be brave. You'll be on your back in half an hour.'

The Itch were great, and I remember dancing all the way through their set. I was dying for the loo and figured I would have just enough time before Secret Affair came on. I did what I went to do, then I heard the sound of guitars warming up on stage. The problem was, I was so drunk that I wasn't able to work out how to get out of the toilet cubicle. The girl who had served me the drink clearly had a point, and even though I wasn't on my back – not that there was enough room anyway – I was well and truly stuck in the cubicle and I couldn't work out where the handle was to let myself out.

Everyone must have wondered where I was, because I was the one who had been looking forward to the gig the most. And even though I could hear every single song, I didn't manage to find my way out and missed their entire set. Gutted wasn't the word, and to this day I have no idea how I finally managed to escape and, more importantly, make my way home back over to Blackburn. Janet found it hilarious and did say it was the most drunk she had ever seen me, but she clearly hadn't been in Tenerife.

Back in those days, things were totally different to what they are now. No mobile phones to take footage of your every move, very little CCTV, very few Health and Safety rules, and club doormen seemed to be above the law half the time. The lad I had my only fight with at school, Michael, tried to break up a fight at The New Inns involving his friend, only to find himself badly beaten up by the bouncers. He later tragically died from a twisted windpipe and other injuries he received on that night. In Blackburn, it was general knowledge there were at least a couple of coppers down at the station who had a reputation for beating up kids in the cells, and I still remember their names!

One of the most incredible programmes I have ever watched on DVD/TV is a 1976 documentary called 'Juvenile Liaison', made by Nick Broomfield, who had attended our local college. The documentary was a look behind the scenes of the Juvenile Liaison Department at Blackburn Police Station. The result was supposed to be an indictment of how the British authorities treated who they considered to be juvenile delinquents in the late 1960s.

A total of two films were shot overall, and the first examined a series of local children and their run-ins with the law over very minor wrongdoings, such as stealing an apple, robbing a cowboy outfit off a mate, nicking sweets from Woolworths (who didn't?), or basically nicking off school.

Juvenile Liaison 2 revisited some of the families in an attempt to try and measure the success of the scheme. But it had been reported that before the film crews started filming, the families had been visited by the police, in an effort to shut them up. This 'gentle' persuasion clearly worked on some of the families, as several of them suddenly refused to take part. After its production, the first film was banned by the BFI for fifteen years, and was referred to as 'the film the police arrested'.

In 1968, the Lancashire Police adopted the Juvenile Liaison Scheme, designed to keep young offenders out of court, and deemed it being good for public relations. It operated on close contact between the police, parents, schools, and social workers, and the young people taken on the scheme were first-time offenders. The main character, Sergeant Ray, had the mannerisms (as well as the dress sense) of one Gene Hunt from *Life on Mars*, but with kids.
If a young person told their parents they had felt ill, hoping to get the day off school, their lovely parents would call the police, and before they knew it, Sergeant George Ray showed up at their house and proceeded to drag the little liar out of bed by their ear. You had to watch it to believe it!
A young Asian girl from a local school was interrogated by CID for allegedly stealing her friend's apple. But the hardest clip to watch was that of an eight-year-old boy who, without his parents' consent or knowledge, was thrown into the police cells and questioned about not giving back his friend's cowboy outfit, which he claimed he had borrowed.
Watching it, I had feelings of disbelief. Parts were hilarious; parts were uncomfortable to watch; and some scenes were extremely sad. It also turned out that some of those so-called caring parents had been absolute wrong-uns.

It was alleged that by the time the second film was released in 1990, Sgt Ray had been demoted to doing playground duty at one of the local schools. But if it had been up to me, he wouldn't have been within a mile of any young people, even though he no doubt thought he was doing the right thing at the time.

I feel that both of Nick's documentaries were an accurate glimpse of life in a Northern town back then, and showed the types of behaviour that would be acceptable if you were an adult or wore a uniform. I would urge everyone to either try and get your hands on a copy of these documentaries, or at least view as much as you can on YouTube.

When I look back on the large number of celebrities who appeared on our television as we grew up (certainly in our house) from TV presenters, radio hosts, politicians, football coaches, film directors, and even our local weatherman, many turned out to be abusers of children. It is frightening to even contemplate how folk could turn a blind eye to what was going on, enabling them to get away with their horrific crimes. Some of the prime time shows and adverts that were never off our TV set at home when I lived with my parents were presented by paedophiles, not to mention my dad's aunty making enormous kilts for a certain someone.

I remember walking home from The Farthings one night with the usual suspects when one of us, maybe me, came up with the ridiculous idea of placing some traffic cones we had found across the middle of the road at Pleck Farm Avenue, blocking the street off for a laugh.
A car tried to drive past, noticed us in the background, and reversed as fast as they could, driving in our direction up onto the grass verge, *Dukes of Hazzard*-style. We all legged it into one of the back gardens on the road. Bullige, Des, Waker, and Karl managed to hide behind a bush or fence, leaving me standing in the centre of the garden, holding my *Setting Sons* LP by The Jam.
The people in the car told me they were police officers and that I had to follow them. Once we reached their car at the end of the

avenue, they made me spread myself across the bonnet whilst they searched my pockets. There were two males and two females, and every time the male who was lecturing me about how stupid we had been, said a word, he would follow it by hitting me in the face with my beloved Jam LP.

They told me to get into the back of their car, and it was then I noticed that they had all smelt of alcohol. I started to worry, and as they drove off with me in the back, I questioned if they really were police officers. I don't know what made them eventually stop and let me out, and to this day I still have no idea whether they were real police or not, but I do know that they appeared to be highly dodgy, and our childish actions had led to me having the life scared out of me.

Like any other Thursday, Friday, and Saturday night, that particular Saturday we had pushed our way past all the 'out of towners' queuing up on the Cav steps, but as we arrived at the door the bouncer simply slammed it in our faces, saying, 'You're not coming in tonight, lads.' This was unusual, as we were regulars and all that, so I questioned this through the glass on the door. I didn't threaten anyone and certainly didn't swear; I simply asked why we were not being allowed into the club. After all, I was wearing a brand new Van Gils suit I had just bought from Pelle, and looked the business, even though I do say so myself.

Without even replying, the guy opened the door, and three of them dragged me in. But instead of taking me down the usual route, down the glass corridor on the right until you got to the ticket office, they dragged me over to the left side, next to the lift. There, the three of them started to punch and kick me, when I had done absolutely nothing at all to warrant this violent and unprovoked attack. I didn't even fight back, knowing that there were three of them and that it would probably have made things worse.
I was really shocked that this had been allowed to happen, but my main concern was for my suit, and I remember shouting out loud, 'Watch my f*****g suit!' as they dangled me upside down whilst

continuing to kick and punch me. I have no idea at all what had made them stop attacking me, and even though my suit seemed okay, my shirt was ripped to shreds, my tie was still round my neck, and no doubt I had numerous cuts and bruises all over my body.

I was still in shock and had no idea if they were planning on coming back, so I panicked and ran towards the lift to avoid any further violence against me. The lift took me down to the Lord Square entrance, where I found the door to be locked. I started to feel trapped and was worried in case the doormen had decided to follow me. So in desperation, I kicked in the doors and made my escape.
I ran back up to the car park and was shocked to find Ste and Simon both covered in blood. It turned out that they had taken a break from hitting me, and had started on Simon and then finally Ste.

I had never known Ste to come off worse in a fight before, but this hadn't been a fight. He told me that two of the doormen had held his hands behind his back, whilst you-know-who had punched him with his ring. There was a police car in the car park near to the entrance, and I am sure we told them about what had happened, but they did nothing.

The following day, after we had all had time to lick our wounds, my dad took us down to the police station to report what had gone on, and we were interviewed and had some photographs taken of all our injuries. The CID guy told my dad that it was one of the worst cases of an unprovoked attack he had ever seen, and told us not to worry, as they would be taking this to court.

The CID visited our house a couple of weeks later to check my statement and to see if there was anything I wanted to add to my story. They also visited Simon and Ste, to go over things again. I felt that I had received a pretty bad beating, but out of the three of us, I had come off the best. Simon was so rough that for at least a week after his beating, he had to eat liquidised food through a straw at mealtimes, and his dad was a doctor.

Weeks went by and we heard nothing, so we presumed that no news was good news. But finally, after a couple of months, I received a letter from Lancashire Constabulary, which I had to read twice to make sure it was not a mistake. It said that they had taken both sides into consideration and would not be taking the matter any further. Was this a joke? None of us could believe what we were reading. Three blokes had beaten us up, one by one, in an unprovoked attack, and they were getting away with it. How was that possible?

We didn't have a clue what made-up story the doormen had given, but taking both sides into consideration and ending up siding with the attackers was proper out of order, and proved beyond doubt that back then the bully bouncers were seen as saving the police a job, therefore the incident had been dropped. I really lost faith in the law after receiving that letter, and have kept hold of it ever since as proof of what folk were allowed to get away with in those days.

As if things couldn't have got any worse, not only had we been used as punchbags, but we were also banned for life from the Cav for the privilege. Banned for life, and no matter how many times over the years we tried to get back in, we would always be recognised at the ticket desk and accompanied back to the entrance – even though Ste wore a disguise on at least a couple of occasions. Simon's mum was a magistrate and was so disgusted by what had happened that she resigned to make a stand.

These days, nothing happens without someone capturing it on their mobiles; where there is a blame, there's a claim. We now live in a culture where even if you trip up whilst walking down the street, someone can be sued. How much would we have been entitled to if things had been like that back then? I reckon we would have at least ended up with a holiday out of it.

CHAPTER EIGHTEEN

SEARCHING, LOOKING FOR LOVE

From that day on the football field at Friargate when I discovered I was adopted as a baby, I never brought up the subject with my parents. From time to time my mum would mention to Janet that if I ever wanted to know a few more details about what had happened, they would be happy to discuss it with me – even though they didn't know much anyway.
However, I always chose to ignore this. It was no big deal to me growing up, even though subconsciously I am sure it affected a massive part of who I was and what I did. But I guessed that bringing up the subject would only risk upsetting my family, so I chose not to pursue it.

In my mid-twenties, just before we got married, I started to wonder what the reasons or circumstances were that had led me to being given away. Naturally, from time to time you wonder whether your birth father was a famous footballer or musician, because if you don't know for certain where you originated from, the possibilities could be endless. I brought this conversation up with Janet on a couple of occasions, about the option of trying to trace where I came from, as I didn't want to leave it too late.

I decided that I needed to do It before everyone had passed away, and felt that if I went on to have a son or daughter, I would like to be able to answer any kind of questions about my background, if they ever wanted to know. Janet agreed with me, and we started to look into what we needed to do. There was no way that I was going to run the risk of hurting my parents, so I decided that they could never find out about my search.

Anyone adopted before 12th November, 1975, had to attend a counselling session with an approved Adoption Advisor via Social Services before they could apply for their records. Their job was to make you aware that the result of their searches may not mean a happy ending. You could discover that your birth parents were both drug addicts, they might be disabled, or may even have passed away. No mention at all of a possible footballer or rock star!

Once they were convinced that you had understood these possible outcomes, you could apply for a copy of your original birth certificate from the General Register Office. So I started that ball rolling, knowing that what I might find out could actually change my life forever.

On 1st March, 1990, just three months before we tied the knot, our postman dropped my original birth certificate on our mat. And for the first time in my life, I was about to learn the details of my birth.

At the time of my interview, Social Services vowed to chase things up for me, and to try their best to find out some information about my past. But it's a good job I didn't rely on them, as I haven't heard a word from them since.

Born on the 20th September, 1963, in Billinge Hospital in the Borough of Wigan, my birth mother was a Wages Clerk who lived with her parents on Martin Street in Atherton. The birth father's name was left blank, meaning I still had a chance of it being George Best or someone else like that. But there was one piece of information that knocked me for six. For some reason, it hadn't entered my head that at some stage in my existence, I would have been given a different name. I had to read it several times for it to remotely sink in, and since finding out this revelation, I think I have only ever told around three people, including Janet, what my birth name is – even though my mates have asked from time to time. I felt I had only ever been known as Pete, and that was how I wanted it to stay.

As fate would have it, Janet working at BT was extremely helpful, as she managed to find a phone number for the address on Martin Street. Knowing it was a little too far-fetched to expect my birth mother to be still living at the property, I nervously dialled the number. And even though I was right, the family that occupied the house put me in touch with one of my mother's relations who was still living in the area.

Uncle Jock sounded like he had been a right character back in the day, and though he was polite and friendly, he was also a little cautious. I felt he didn't know whether or not to believe that I was who I claimed to be. It ended with him writing a letter to me, inviting me over to Atherton to meet him, which was a really strange feeling. I was about to meet a member of my birth family for the very first time.

It was a beautiful sunny day, and Janet's sister Elaine, and my brother-in-law, Martin, offered to drive us over to Atherton and were going to wait outside the house, once we found it. The minute I walked in, Uncle Jock told us that he knew I had been telling the truth, as he could see the family likeness and similarities. He was a lovely gentleman, and once he was convinced that I was who I claimed to be, he seemed as happy to meet me as I was meeting him. He told me that my mum was called Kathleen, and that she was now living in Canada. But unfortunately, her mother, my grandmother, had only just recently passed away.

Jock was clearly not a fan of my birth father, and when he informed me that Dennis was an alcoholic wife-beater who he believed had been married around five times, I could see why. Before we left, he gave me a piece of paper on which Kathleen's phone number in Canada was written.

As we were heading out of Atherton, I suggested stopping off at the nearest pub for a drink, as it was beyond hot sitting in the back seat. The others weren't really keen to stop for alcohol during the day, but I managed to persuade them, suggesting we'd just have a quick half. I remember looking around the bar as we entered, and said, 'Just think, one of these bums could actually be my dad!'

This had been a joke (sort of), as I was referring to all the daytime drinkers, but within minutes of us buying a drink, two blokes walked in and, unbelievably, I heard the barmaid say, ' Alright, Dennis.'

What were the odds on my birth father walking into the same random pub where we had chosen to stop off, at exactly the same time?

We watched them go and stand at the end of the bar, and when one of them took a pair of black sunglasses out of his pocket and put them on, Janet and Elaine cracked up laughing, saying we were definitely related, because wearing sunglasses indoors was one of my well-known traits. I knew they were only joking, but when I noticed they had supped up their pints and were now walking out of the pub, I knew I had to do something.

On entering the pub, I had noticed a red phone box directly outside. There was only one thing for it; if I didn't act now, it would be too late. I went outside to the phone box and rang the pub, asking if they had seen Dennis Blah, Blah, and to my astonishment, they told me he had just left. I had been a matter of feet away from the person who had got Kathleen pregnant back in 1963, and even though we had glanced over at each other for no more than a split second, we never spoke a word.

If I was being honest, I had no desire to track down and meet this Dennis bloke, after Uncle Jock had told me what he was like, other than to maybe confront him about why he thought it was okay to throw his weight around and be violent against women. Whether you believe in fate or not, though, it was extraordinary that the randomly chosen pub we stopped at for no longer than 20 minutes, led me to my first and only sighting of my birth father. A lucky escape, if you ask me.

For the first time in my life, I had the phone number for my birth mum. I held onto it for about a week, knowing it would be a huge step to call her, and that I would have to choose my moment with care.

It was a Sunday afternoon at Kestrel Close, and the rest of my family were at their beloved cricket.
I worked out the time difference between Canada and the UK, and guessed there was no point in putting it off any longer. My stomach was churning because I was so nervous, and from the moment someone picked up the phone at the other end, I knew my life would change forever – and not necessarily for the better.

After a weird dialling tone and about seven rings, a lady answered. I apologised for disturbing her, and said I was sorry if what I was about to say would be a shock, but I believed that she was my birth mother. Complete silence followed, and at the time it felt as though her whole house had collapsed around her. Not having a reaction to my call that had taken me a week to make, left me feeling terrible. Eventually the voice returned on the line, but sounding a lot more timid than before. She asked me a few details about how I'd found her number, and how sure I was that I had got the right person. Kathleen told me that this had been a massive shock to her, and that she needed some time to properly take it all in. So I gave her my contact details and address, and hung up the phone.

A short while after, I received a letter from Kathleen, explaining the circumstances that had led to her giving me up. Basically, she hadn't had a say in the matter, and unfortunately the person who was responsible for the decision – her mother – had not lived long enough to witness me getting in touch after 26 years. At the age of 16, Kathleen found herself pregnant by the village idiot, who she had been seeing. She had been brought up in a strict mining family, so it was not an option to let the cat out of the bag and make her situation common knowledge, due to the fact she was not married.

Her parents sent her to a Mother and Baby home so that the neighbours were none the wiser, and I was born at Billinge Hospital, and given the name Andrew Neil Wainwright, where my mum managed to keep me for five whole weeks before I was taken away by two strangers, without her ever having a say. In the letter, Kathleen apologised for allowing this to happen, and said that I must hate her, which was never the case.

If I had ended up in care, or having a difficult childhood, then I might have felt differently, but I don't necessarily think that blood is thicker than water. Tell that to Fred West's kids! And she had only been 16 years old anyway. I have never let being adopted bother me or used it as an excuse for anything; after all, I had been extremely fortunate ending up with parents who cared for me and who were decent people. And even though my mother (Margery) hadn't always agreed with my choice of females I brought back, and we were given the same meals on the same day (sometimes), I always knew how lucky I had been.

It always seemed such a cold and cruel generation that allowed a parent to force their daughter to give away their new-born baby to strangers, rather than run the risk of neighbours discovering the truth about the most natural thing in the world. And I can never get my head around such a Dickensian mindset.

It turned out that Kathleen ended up marrying Dennis, and even though it didn't last very long, she gave birth to Sandra a year after me, but this time she was determined to keep her baby, despite the feelings of her parents. So, it turned out that I had a full-blown sister who was now living in Canada. Unfortunately, up until this day, I have never spoken a single word to her.

Then my brother Steven arrived. Unlike me, he became an established athlete, a really good runner and a pretty decent footballer, and lived in Buffalo in New York State.

Eventually, Kathleen escaped Dennis's alleged violence and emigrated to Ontario, Canada, five minutes away from Niagara Falls. She got married again and gave birth to my half-sister Michelle.

Kathleen sent us a wedding day card, wishing us all the best for our big day, and also a card at Christmas, which was nice, being my first. And even though we chatted from time to time over the phone, I managed to keep this secret from my parents.

Then one day, Kathleen announced that she was coming over to the UK to see me. I remember part of me feeling excited, as I had always wondered what she was like. The other part of me was terrified at the thought of my mum, dad, and Robin finding out, and what she would actually think of me.

The day arrived for her visit to 9 Cloverfields, and even though the plan was for me to meet her at Blackburn train station, I bottled out and asked Janet to go instead. I am finding it really hard thinking about how I felt when she eventually walked into the room for the first time, but I do remember being extremely nervous. I tried to hide it, hoping that I wasn't a disappointment after all these years, but I am sure that she must have felt the same. Looking back, I am not too sure if it was a good idea to have had Janet present for the whole of our meeting, or whether I should have spent some time on my own with Kathleen, but I'm sure Janet stayed more out of support for me. Safety in numbers, and all that.
Kathleen seemed to be a nice lady, and her life had certainly been very tough. The situation felt strange to me and I was nervous throughout, as up until that point, I had always been happy with my lot and never had a desire to include anyone else into my life.

I have no idea what Kathleen made of me after our meeting, but I am really glad that it happened and that I finally met the person who had given birth to me all those years ago. We both kept in touch with each other from time to time, either via the odd phone call or receiving the odd Christmas or birthday card. I still have the photographs that she gave me of my family in the States and the Canadian souvenirs she kindly brought over for me, but I never realised at the time that this would be our one and only meeting.

My brother Steven contacted me, saying that he was very excited to meet me, and that he had arranged to visit the UK to come and see us. The same thing happened as with Kathleen. He came round to our house and we sat chatting for a couple of hours. But again, this was a very strange experience for me, as I am sure it was for him. And even though I tried my best to be as friendly and polite as I could be, I don't believe that I really opened up and let him see the real me.
He told us the story of when he'd accidentally met Dennis in a pub in Leigh. Initially Dennis had been all over him, buying him drinks, but once they went back to Dennis's house, Steven saw his dad being violent towards his current partner, and decided there and then that he didn't want anything to do with him, which I think was very wise.

The one thing I do regret about our meeting was not taking him along to the Rovers match the following day, as he was a keen football fan. I think I made up some excuse at the time, but the truth was that I couldn't take him as I didn't want to risk my bother Robin finding out, because seemingly we vaguely resembled each other. I did end up telling Robin about tracing my past and he was cool about it, so looking back, I wish I had been more hospitable.

Over the years, Steven agreed to stay in touch, but even though I feel his intentions were good, the communication always fizzles out. I guess he just has his own busy family life to get on with, as do I, so there is no judgement there.

I have been in touch with Michelle a couple of times, and also other members of the family, and even though it would have been nice to chat to my full sister Sandra at some stage, it has never happened so far. One day maybe.

There is no doubt that social media, especially Facebook, has made our world a whole lot smaller, as it was through this medium that I was told several years ago that both Kathleen and Dennis had passed away, which left me feeling a little strange. At the end of the day, my intentions from the start were always to try and discover where I came from and a little bit about my background, and I certainly achieved that. I also achieved my wish of making sure that my parents never found out about what I had done and discovered, which I was glad about.

I guess things happen to us when we are young that we don't have a say in. Families split up and things don't always go to plan. But I reckon the important thing is how we handle it, deal with it, and move on from it. I have no doubt at all that being adopted and feeling that I had been given away, even though it probably did me a huge favour, has affected large parts of the way I act and behave, such as struggling to handle rejection, and being extra loyal with my friends. But I believe things happen for a reason, and I have had a blessed life, so no complaints from this Mod.

CHAPTER NINETEEN

FOUR WEDDINGS, A FUNERAL, AND A KING

After my Grandma passed away whilst I was on holiday in Newquay, it took a long time for it sink in that I would never see her again. It was the first time that someone so close to me had died, and it definitely left a huge hole in my life. It happened just before my 21st birthday, and my Grandad gave me some money that she had been saving up to buy me a present. I decided I was going to purchase a ring with the money, as an everlasting keepsake to remember her by.

Not long after I found a ring, I was working overtime on a Saturday morning at Unilab. After my shift, I went to the toilets as normal to wash my hands, before heading off home to enjoy the rest of the day. Up until then, I had never taken my Grandma's ring off, but for some reason, this time I had and placed it on the side of the washbasin. Not long after arriving home, I realised the ring was missing and started to panic.

At first, I racked my brains trying to remember where I had seen it last, and then remembered. I knew I had been the last of the workers to leave the building, but as I was walking out of the toilets, a contractor who had been working on the roof all week walked in, so it could only have been him who had taken it.

On Monday, I explained to my Works Manager what had happened, who in turn had a word with the boss in charge of the project. But for days the lad denied knowing anything at all about it. I was adamant that it could only have been him that had taken it, and I was so desperate to get it back that I even offered to pay him a reward for its return, even though in reality he had probably sold it over the weekend and it would be miles away.

I refused to let it drop and, to be fair, his boss continued to pile pressure on him until eventually the lad came clean and admitted taking it. To my amazement, he hadn't sold it after all, but had hidden it in the roof he was working on over the break. I was eternally grateful to both bosses for supporting me on this, and the lad was sacked from that job – or no doubt just moved to another site. But one thing was for sure, that ring never left my finger again.

After my Grandma passed away, I always tried my best to visit my Grandad every week. He would always be as dapper as ever each time I visited, always wearing a suit and tie, even though it was daytime and he wasn't planning on going anywhere. No matter what time I called, he would always have his classical music playing on the radio, which he clearly loved, but I have no idea what happened to his Dansette record player after he passed away. I had always loved spending hours playing my singles and LPs on it as a teenager. I do know that him dying left yet another big hole.

When I look back on how involved my Grandma and Grandad Burrows were in our young lives, I knew that things would never be the same ever again. They took us on regular trips to Blackpool to visit the Fun House on the Pleasure Beach, where the majority of the rides then would certainly breach today's Health and Safety rules. We also had our annual pilgrimage to the Illuminations and the sand dunes at St Annes, Lytham, and Fleetwood. These were the foundations for all the experiences that my parents would give our daughter, Emma, and they were all places that created special feelings and memories for both her and me.

Out of our friends' group, Steve S got married and seemed to disappear off the face of the earth. In fact, I don't even remember being invited to his wedding. Needless to say, it didn't last.

Bullinge married Ste H's sister, Debbie, and even though I was his best man and was pretty proud of my speech on the day, that marriage didn't last either.

Waker got married to Adrienne, who he met in The Farthings, and also asked me to be his best man.

The thing about being a best man is that of course it's an honour, but apart from making sure the rings don't go A.W.O.L., your duty is to stand up and make a speech. Standing up in public and speaking is difficult enough for anyone, but when you are the best man, your job is to tell stories about the groom and hopefully make people laugh, without offending anyone. Taking into account that at a wedding you have different generations from both families present, it's a tough gig.

I had known Mark and his family for a very long time, and thought a lot of them, so I remember it taking me ages to write the speech because I really wanted to do him proud. The wedding reception was at the Woodlands Hotel, Preston New Road, and it was getting closer and closer to my turn to stand up. I have always felt that wedding speeches should be made before you sit down and have your meal, so that the people making the speeches can get it over with and try and enjoy their food, as opposed to worrying themselves sick throughout, trying to remember everything.

I was no exception. And just as everyone was tucking into their dessert, I sneaked off to the toilets to read through my speech for the final time. I locked myself in a cubicle, and no sooner had I taken the folded-up piece of paper out of my jacket pocket than the whole toilets were plunged into darkness.

It was pitch black and I struggled to even get out of the cubicle (again). I wasn't sure if it was a power cut or someone playing a prank, but it ended with me and a very small boy feeling our way around the walls to find the door and get out.

When I got back to my seat, it was time for the speeches to start, and I hadn't managed to revise a single word. Everyone told me that my speech was good, which was a huge relief, but due to the situation being so intense, I ended up with a migraine headache. Up until then, when folk used to go on about having a migraine, I always felt that they were exaggerating; it surely couldn't have been that bad. But now I realised that it was as painful as they all claimed, though luckily, it was to be the one and only time I experienced one.

We had all purchased tickets to see The Style Council in Birmingham, and I seem to remember we hired an Intack van, and that Waker was our designated driver. The gig was memorable for someone out of the crowd throwing a plastic bottle at D.C. Lee, and Paul went mad. Paul hadn't officially been seeing Dee at this point, as far as the fans knew, but the way they were acting and the way Paul threatened to jump into the crowd and hit the guy over the head with his guitar, made me question if something was going on between them. I even thought I spotted them holding hands at one point in the night, but I could have imagined that.

Not long after the concert, it became general knowledge that Paul and Dee had become a couple. They ended up getting married and having children together, without which my daughter Emma would now have a different middle name.

During our journey home, as was standard when we hired a van, I was sitting in the passenger seat with the job of talking to the driver to help keep him awake, whilst everyone else crashed out in the back. It was taking us ages to get out of Birmingham, as we had run out of petrol, and every garage we stopped at seemed to be closed. I am not saying that the place was rough, but it was the only place I had been where you had to pay for your petrol before you filled up your vehicle. Everyone was asleep in the back, and even though it was my job to keep Mark awake, I was struggling myself. Suddenly he said he had something to tell me, which certainly kept me awake.
He hit me with the bombshell that he was seeing Karen from work – the fastest nappy-packer at Carus – so I guessed that

even though I had been given positive feedback about my best man speech, this would be another marriage that was about to break up.

To be fair, and not an excuse, Mark and Adrienne went through a really difficult time, having lost a child to cot death, and I could never even try to imagine what they must have gone through at the time. Anyway, Mark ended up marrying Karen, and they are still together today.

One of the lads at work, Tony, turned to me one day and asked me if I would be his best man, which surprised me. He was one of the nicest lads you could meet, but I remember saying, 'What's up? Do you not have any mates?' It was an honour being Tony's best man, though, and it was my job to plan his stag do.

Audley House club was the venue, and I booked a comedian and a stripper to add to the evening's entertainment. The comedian was a local lad called Tacky, and he went down a storm. My problem was that there was no sign of any stripper, and the natives were getting restless. I tried calling the agency several times from the payphone in the entrance, but nobody picked up. Someone came to me, advising me to do a runner, as there were eighty blokes upstairs who would be baying for my blood if she didn't turn up. Things started to get desperate, and I resorted to asking every female that came through the door if they were from the Agency. One of them was so insulted that she slapped me across the face! Thankfully, the stripper eventually showed up, and everyone was happy.

Needless to say, Tony's marriage to Carol didn't last, and I was starting to gain a reputation for being the kiss of death for any couple who asked me to be their best man.

Simon had started seeing Karl's sister Elaine, and apparently I had set them up, so naturally he had asked me to do the honours. Simon and I were regular supporters of the Rovers, and on a Saturday afternoon you would find us sitting halfway up behind the goal in the Blackburn End. Even when he moved to London, he would regularly make 466-mile round trips to visit his beloved Ewood Park, with the company of his budgerigar, Rocky, in his cage on the passenger seat. What was even more surprising than Simon and Elaine getting hitched, was the fact that they had chosen the day of a Rovers' home game to do it! Not that I've got any room to talk.

Rovers were playing Norwich at home, and it was the first Alan Shearer home game I was going to miss. I was taking my best man duties seriously, but I was a bit gutted and was hoping for a 1-0 win so that we didn't miss out on too much.

The wedding car was a little late picking me up, and by the time it took us to get from our house up to St James's Church, Rovers had already scored three goals. So, the one home match that I missed that season, had only gone and ended in a 7-1 victory to Rovers. I was devastated to miss out on eight goals and ended up buying the match on video just so I could feel even worse.

When Waker got married, I bought him a giant box of Mars bars, as they were something he absolutely loved. But on the confectionery front, Simon's love was for midget gems, and when he moved to London, he always struggled finding anywhere that had sold them. When he was visiting up North or going to the Rovers, he would always make it a priority to visit his favourite sweet shop in Whalley to stock up on supplies.

Even though Simon really appreciated the giant box of midget gems I bought him when he tied the knot, it wasn't enough to save his marriage either. And I now had a track record of 4 out of 4 marriage break-ups after I had been their best man – worst man more like.

When Karl first got engaged, he did another Steve, and disappeared off the face of the earth. And when it didn't work out, he appeared back on the scene with his tail literally between his legs, as though he had never been away. Years later, Karl met Kerry, and

I remember him explaining to me that he wasn't even allowed to have me as his best man, even if he had wanted to, as she had heard about my best man reputation and my terrible track record.

Karl and Kerry's wedding do was at The Pines Hotel in Clayton-le-woods, and like a lot of posh venues at the time, they would stage more than one wedding reception at the same time.

Karl said 'I do', and managed not to lose the rings, and I remember us all being on the front lawn outside chatting, as it was a gorgeous day. When you are standing with a group of people at an event, you can't just wander off to the bar on your own without asking everyone what they would like to drink, as it would be rude. I knew the prices at The Pines wouldn't be cheap, but I offered to go and buy a round.

The bar was heaving, and I had just taken a load of notes out of my pocket, not knowing how much it was going to cost, when the girl behind the bar told me that it was a free bar. I couldn't believe it, as Karl had always been pretty tight, so it really was a shock. I took the drinks back and went round everyone whispering that I was astonished Karl had actually put his hand in his pocket and put on a free bar. We drank our 'paid for' drinks and I offered to go again, and the same thing happened.

Not wanting to appear to be taking advantage of Karl's generous gesture, Janet offered to go and get the next round, but returned with a completely different story.

Janet had ordered the drinks and, not wanting to presume that they were free, she asked how much she owed. The person behind the bar said that it depended on which wedding party she was with. It turned out that Karl hadn't been providing free drinks after all. We had been getting drinks on another person's wedding tab, and Janet's honesty had led to us having to pay for our own drinks for the rest of the day. I knew it had been too good to be true, but at least I had got my rounds in. Karl's marriage to Kerry lasted longer than most, and when they eventually did split up, I knew that this time I couldn't take any of the blame.

It is fair to say that over the years Karl has always been a little gullible, to say the least. When we used to try and outdo each other about who could buy the most Punk singles back in the 70s, I wound him up on a couple of occasions. I got my Grandma, who was a decent artist, to draw me up a fake record sleeve for a band name and song that I had made up. 'Midnight Flashers' by the Lamp Posts was the name of the amazing new Punk song I had 'heard', and Karl fell for it hook, line, and sinker, spending weeks trying his best to get hold of a copy.

I also told him that the hottest Punk track around was called *Toast* by Streetband, and without listening to it, he headed down to Ames Tapes and Records store to ask for it, only to be told that there had been a bread strike, which there was at the time, in 1977. Karl managed to purchase a copy from Reidy's the same day, but was so disappointed when he got it home and found out that it wasn't a Punk record, he took it outside and smashed it to pieces in the middle of the road.

There was the time when we were in Barbados, when Bullinge and I decided to go for a walk along the incredible beach at Saint James. Karl was still sunburnt from the day before, so had opted to stay on the beach fully clothed. Me and Mark were approached by two Bajan guys trying to sell us a coconut, and even though they persisted, we politely declined, knowing that coconuts just fell off trees for free around those parts.

We manged to get rid of them by saying that we weren't really keen on them ourselves, but we knew someone who was. We told them that he was all the way down the beach and that they wouldn't be able to miss him, due to him being the only person sunbathing wearing a t-shirt and jeans, with a towel over his head.

When we finally arrived back, we had both forgotten about the incident, but sure enough, Karl was sitting in the exact same place that we had left him – the only difference was, he had been joined by a very expensive coconut on either side of him. You couldn't write it, and we couldn't stop laughing when he told us that the men wouldn't take no for an answer and he had ended up paying around £25 for the pair.

Another time he was standing at a local cash machine when he was approached by a couple of Iranian guys trying to sell him some leather jackets. Karl ended up drawing out hundreds of pounds and giving it to the men, only to find out the next day that the jackets were in fact plastic. I don't think he's been able to off load them to this day.

But I feel his biggest mistake was when he discovered a Get Rich Quick scheme on the internet. He applied for a £5000 loan and then send it to a stranger in America. The promise was that he would receive weekly phone calls and tips from an advisor, to coach him through setting up his own business online, selling household items. Surprise, surprise, the advice soon stopped, and he didn't ever hear from them again. I did feel really sorry for him, as I could have given him advice for half the price.

I reckon that everyone has a mate like this, and I have not told these stories to embarrass him in any way; they were simply too funny to leave out. Karl has always been a great lifelong friend, and incidentally he now earns more money than any of my Blackburn mates, so he must have done something right. Who would have thought it?

The greatest footballer I have ever seen live, and certainly my all-time favourite, is Kenny Dalglish.
I feel so privileged to have had the chance to stand on the Kop and watch him perform his magic back in the 1970s. The way he handled himself as a person and the way he never criticised his players in public, once he had moved into management, made him not only a legend but a hero in my book.

Over Kenny's footballing career, he had the misfortune to be involved in three of the worst disasters that the game has ever seen, and the way in which he conducted himself throughout each one is a testament to how professional he has always been, and how impeccable he is as a human being.

On 2nd January, 1971, Kenny was in the crowd at Ibrox Stadium when 66 people were killed in a crush, while supporters tried to leave the ground. The match was an Old Firm game, with Rangers playing Celtic, and was attended by a crowd of over 80,000.

On 29th May, 1985, Kenny was sitting in the players' dugout when the Heysel Stadium disaster took place. Liverpool had been playing Juventus in the European Cup Final when tragically a wall collapsed before the kick-off, and 39 supporters were killed and 600 injured. I was watching the match at Jez's old girlfriend's and was in total shock at the live scenes I was witnessing on the television.

On 15th April, 1989, the Hillsborough disaster happened, which saw 96 football fans, young and old, lose their lives due to overcrowding in the central pens of the stand, and led to a further 766 people being injured. Football fans left their homes that day, looking forward to supporting their beloved team for the semi-final of the FA Cup in Sheffield, between Liverpool and Nottingham Forest, but so many of them did not return.

It was said by his family that Kenny never dealt with witnessing three of footballs biggest tragedies, as he was more concerned with the victims and the bereaved than sparing a moment for himself.

I was at Ewood Park that day, and the first I knew about it was seeing it on the news back at Janet's mum's house on Lytham Road. Yet again, I was shocked at what I was watching, and it felt a little strange knowing that it could have easily been me and one of my mates attending at the time.

The way I saw Kenny handle himself, attending funerals and supporting bereaved families for months and years after, is something that I have never forgotten. What a role model!

The date was Saturday, 12th October, 1991, and I was due to attend Nicky's brother Mick's stag do – a day at York races. Under normal circumstances I would never consider backing out of something I have agreed to and wouldn't dream of letting a mate down. But I had a massive dilemma on my hands. On the Friday night before our day out, a rumour was going around that Kenny Dalglish was about to be unveiled as Blackburn Rovers' new manager, and that he would be making an appearance at their home game against Plymouth the next day.

I wrestled with this dilemma for hours, but at the end of the day it was Nicky's brother, not Nicky, whose stag do it was, and there was no way on earth I could miss the arrival of my hero to Ewood Park. I knew that Mick wouldn't even notice if I was there or not, but I would never forgive myself if I wasn't there for Kenny.

The anticipation in the ground that day was electric, as nobody knew for sure if he was about to show up or not. But the moment arrived, and I wouldn't have missed it for anything. The game ended in a 5-2 victory to Rovers and the rest, as they say, is history.

All in all, I supported the Rovers for 28 years through thick and thin – just not against Liverpool – and I still have a drawer full of season tickets to prove it. I attended Ewood at the height of their success, and hardly missed a match when they were in the Second and Third Division. I even stood in the Blackburn End when there were just over 4,000 fans there, on a wet freezing Tuesday evening.

Back in the day, apart from local derbies, the only real matches folk would get excited about were when they drew a bigger team in one of the cup competitions, and to be fair, they usually did us proud. Away matches were a mission, especially with the people I chose to go with, but they were always fun, even if we were dodging bricks and fists for some of the time.

I was at Wembley for the Full Members Cup, the Millennium Stadium for the Worthington Cup, and at Anfield when they won the Premiership. It was a proper rollercoaster for the nerves, and for proof of us attending, if you watch the Sky footage from that day, as soon as Henning Berg lifts the trophy, the camera zooms in on me and Simon chatting on the terraces.

Over the years I have had the pleasure of watching some absolutely wonderful players, and it is hard to pick my favourites. Scott Sellars and Matt Jansen were certainly up there. I loved Graham Le Saux, and he once sold me a jacket at the Originals shop in Ossy. Simon Barker, Big Col, and Super Stu would never let you down, and the King of Ewood Park, Noel Brotherston, most certainly gets a mention for all those Saturday afternoons he kept us entertained back in the day. Damian Duff would appear on any budding Rovers fans list, I'm sure, and is without a doubt towards the top of mine.

Managers came and went, from Jim Smith at the time I started attending, to Jim Iley, who thought that giving out free packets of Wotsits to the crowd would be enough. It wasn't. Howard Kendal had his moments, and Don Mckay should really get a mention for his efforts. He was also really nice, as was his wife, who I had worked with at Unilab. But when King Kenny and Ray Hartford arrived in 1991, we could never have dreamt of the wonderful times they would bring with them and the memories they would leave us with.

They used to train every day just up the road from me on the school fields, the same field where I found out I was adopted. I couldn't believe my eyes watching King Kenny and Big Al gracing the same pitch that I had tried playing football on as a young boy. Janet remembers the time we took Emma with us to watch. She was only young, and ran over to Alan Shearer calling him Daddy, because he was wearing the same shirt that she had seen me wear on many occasions.
I have seen some memorable forwards over the years at Ewood Park, and Simon Garner was the greatest goal scorer I ever saw, never to make the big time or play in the topflight. But the greatest player I ever saw putting on a Rovers shirt is without a doubt Alan Shearer. From day one, he was a different class from anyone I had seen before. Not only was he the greatest goal scorer I ever witnessed at Rovers, but he could also possibly be the greatest goal scorer I have witnessed anywhere, and I have watched Rush,

Dalglish, Lineker, etc. If he was given two chances to score a goal, he would score two goals; he was like a machine. And I feel so lucky to have seen him play so many matches for my home team.

On the goalkeeping front, it was Paul Bradshaw guarding the goals when I started to follow them, and he was a really good keeper. If I was choosing my top four, it would include Terry Gennoe, Shay Given, and the magnificent Tim Flowers, having watched the majority of his appearances for the club. But my number one spot would have to go to Mr Brad Friedel in terms of consistency and quality. And I feel it is only right to pick him as my number one.

When Rovers won the Premier League under Kenny and Ray, people said that they had bought it, but I disagreed. Of course, the financial support from Jack Walker put them in the market to approach quality players, but Kenny didn't just go out and pay millions for every squad member. He was a genius at building a squad that had the right blend to be successful together. Homegrown talent like Jason Wilcox was in the team, and he brought in Alan Wright from Blackpool, who most people hadn't heard of, but did a wonderful job. People raised their eyebrows when he signed Gordon Cowans, as they felt he may be a little too old, but Kenny knew what he was doing. And in total, I think they spent £29million to enable them to lift the trophy. These days, teams would spend double that on a single player.

Not long after my dad took Robin and me to our first game, against Southampton, he stopped going to football matches. I remember wondering at the time how on earth he could possibly just stop going after all those years of loving it. But the truth is he had found something that he enjoyed even more than watching 11 blokes running up and down a field chasing a bag of wind. His main love had always been cricket, and once he got involved in Blackburn Northern and supporting them in every way – on a weekly and sometimes daily basis – football naturally took a back seat, and I never in a million years thought for a minute that the same thing would happen to me. But one day, it did.

I cherish the memories of the times that I physically followed the sport, and even the time when I played it a little myself. I played goalkeeper for Bay Horse Saab Garage in Blackburn, and think we played on Tuesday evenings down at Witton Park on the AstroTurf in some sort of league. I enjoyed being part of the team, but when they started to be managed by an ex-Charlton Athletic player who wanted to take things more seriously, I decided to jump before I was pushed, as I wasn't really very good anyway.

I don't miss going to football matches these days, if I'm being honest, and haven't for a long time.

The fact that everything is about money, and the huge amounts spent on players and paid to players turns me off. In fact, some of my favourite memories supporting Rovers are from the Second and Third Division. Yes, it was upsetting to see their dramatic fall from grace after Kenny left, and of course I still look out for their results on a Saturday. I also buzz at the fact that my first love, Liverpool, are back on top and have just won the league again for the first time in 30 years.

Will I ever attend a match at Anfield again? Who knows? I would like to think so, even if only once. Sometimes I'll watch a match on the TV, but not very often, so I guess I just found something else that I loved even more.

CHAPTER TWENTY

CHANGES

People say that your 30s are the best years of your life. Apparently, this is down to the mental shift that takes place. It not only shows that you're an adult, but that you no longer give a damn about what everyone thinks and are happy doing what you want without seeking out anybody else's approval.
To be honest, I have personally loved every decade, and every one has been better than the last, but the one I feel had the most changes was when I was in my 30s. I have heard it referred to as the Spiritual Thirties, and that was certainly the case with me.

At 18 and 21, I never felt the need to have a party or a do of my own, instead opting just for a night out with my close mates instead. To celebrate my 30th birthday, I agreed to have a joint party with Nicky in The Farthings, and really enjoyed everyone making the effort and turning up for us both.
For the life of me, no pun intended, I can't remember what triggered it off, but I developed a fascination for the subject of life after death. I bought every book I could find on the subject and was intrigued by the research that had been done regarding 'near-death experiences and past-life regression' – *Embraced by the Light* by Betty J. Eadie, *Life after Life* by Raymond Moody, *The Tibetan Book of the Living and Dying* by Sogyal Rinpoche, and *Glimpse After Glimpse* by the same author, to name a few.
What really fascinated me were the medical accounts from around the world in all different languages, reporting similar things. Someone lying in a hospital bed is deemed clinically dead, because the heart has stopped beating, and after the medical staff have worked on the body, eventually the patient has been brought back to life. It was sometimes reported that while the patient had been

in the clinically dead state, they recalled seeing a bright light, seeing people they had known in the past who had died, and in some instances, recalling conversations and procedures in the operating room or even in other rooms of the hospital. Whether this happened in Canada or India, the patients explained the exact same experiences. There is a saying that all crows don't have to be black – meaning you only need to see one white one to prove that not all crows are black.

I ended up buying and reading every single book on the subject I could find, as I found it hard to imagine that the medical records and reports by doctors, physicians, and surgeons from around the world could all be fake. The idea that all these medical professionals would lie seemed a little too far-fetched.

I even went as far as persuading Liam, my mate from work, to come with me to have a past-life regression done, as I was intrigued at the time on what it might bring up. I had seen an advert in the local paper for an ex-medical professional who lived in Darwen, and who carried out such a procedure. Liam thought it might be interesting and talked a couple of his mates into coming along, too.

We arrived at this large, old house and were welcomed in by the doctor (not that one). The deal was to have a one-hour consultation and then agree to return for him to carry the procedure out, providing he was happy with us. A past-life regression is a method that uses hypnosis to recover what practitioners believe are memories of past lives or incarnations. It is typically undertaken either in a pursuit of a spiritual experience, or in a psychotherapeutic setting.
Even though the whole thing was my idea in the first place, on the night I was definitely the most scared to go through with it, thinking that if something did actually happen, it could change my life forever – a terrifying thought.

Three of us were sitting on the settee and one on a chair, and the guy asked us to look and concentrate on a frisbee-sized wooden

disc that was placed on the wall above his fireplace. The disc had a dot in the centre and had circular spirals from the centre to the edge. It started to spin slowly, and we were instructed to keep our eyes fixed on the centre.
After a while staring at it, the plastic flowers in a vase in the corner appeared to begin to melt, and it felt really weird. At this point we were asked to close our eyes, and he concentrated on us one by one, asking us relevant questions regarding any possible past memories. He came to me last, and I remember shaking a bit as I was so nervous about what I might see. I'm not certain if we were fortunate or unfortunate, but it turned out that none of us regressed to any memories of a past life. Surprise, surprise!

I am sure people reading this will think, 'No surprise there then' and think that he was just a conman ripping us off. But he did appear to be really shocked and told us that we were his first ever group where no-one had experienced anything. Because of this, he told us that he wasn't going to charge us. So basically, he had given us three hours of his personal time and not made a penny from it, so I'm not sure how he could have been ripping us off.

I don't know what had motivated me to go in the first place, as I have never had any strong feelings of a previous life, not even a king or anything, but I suppose even if there is any truth in it, everyone must have had a first life at some stage, so maybe we were all just starting off.

What was really freaky, though, was that Liam's mate Kev, who was with us that night, tragically lost his life the week after our visit. I know the two incidents were not linked, but it felt a little strange and made us think. Kev had been standing outside a local nightclub when he was attacked for no apparent reason. It was so shocking, and left Liam devastated, as were the rest of us.

I was brought up attending St Gabriel's Church at Brownhill, and even got confirmed there (in my judo suit!). But the more I discovered about organised religion, the less I supported the concept.

Wars, murders, greed, abuse, and bullying are all carried out in the name of religion, and always have been. And even though the Catholic church is one of the wealthiest organisations on the planet, kids are still dying every ten seconds through hunger, so how can that be right?

I used to work with a born-again Christian (not the Mars bar wrapper guy) who went to visit starving children in Africa, but instead of taking them food, he took them each a Bible.

I feel that religion is a personal thing and that you don't have to go into a church to pray.
You should do whatever gives you comfort, and what you believe in, without being judged. Some of the most Christian people I have met have never set foot in a church, a mosque, or a synagogue.

I myself pray for family and friends, not for myself, as it feels like the right thing to do, but I am certainly not religious. I probably subscribe to the teachings of Buddhism out of any religions, and I respect anyone's religious beliefs, providing they are peaceful and treat everyone as an equal.

I would like to think that there is an afterlife, as would most people, and that this is not your lot – enjoyable as it may have been. But I guess that believing and hoping in the afterlife is just an insurance policy, just in case you got it wrong the first time. Nobody has ever offered any proof of its existence (ever), and when I observe people who dedicate their whole lives to following a certain religion or God, even though I respect that, I always think that if it is just all made up and nothing really exists, they will have wasted their one and only life following something that someone once wrote in a book, which someone else found. But then again, I guess that is their choice, and who knows anyway? They might be right after all.

In my world I feel it is sensible to side with evolution and believe that everything in nature really does happen for a reason.

I definitely believe in karma, as it totally makes sense that the actions of an individual (cause) influence the future of that individual (effect). This philosophy makes perfect logic to me, and even if there ends up being no truth in it, I believe it is good to be nice anyway. I mean, why wouldn't you?

When it comes to the question of 'is there life on other planets?', I would like to think there is, and feel it is a bit too far-fetched to think we are the only ones. I have witnessed UFOs on two occasions in my life – once when I was about ten years old. I was standing in my neighbour Martin's garden, on Bank Hey Lane North, when a frisbee-sized object flew into his next door's garden and then flew off across the backs. To be fair, it could have been anything, as it was far too small to contain any life, but neither of us had a bloody clue at the time what we had just seen.
I have always been interested in UFOs and the thought of extra-terrestrial life, so for me to tell somebody I had seen one would probably not be seen as very credible or even be believed. That is why my second sighting stands out to me as being genuine, because it was Janet that pointed it out to me.

I would like to think that these days I am always on time if I have arranged to meet someone, but back in the day this wasn't always the case. Anyone who knows me well will know that I would always arrange for my mates to meet me at my house before a night out, and that they would always have to wait for me to finish getting ready. They remind me that they would always find me standing in front of the mirror on the wall in the hallway, messing with my hair. (It must have been a Mod thing.)

On this occasion, that is where I was standing when Janet shouted on me. She had been waiting on the doorstep for me to finish getting ready for our night out and I thought she was trying to hurry me up so ignored her. I was struggling to get my hair right, but she kept shouting my name, so I thought I'd better go and see what she wanted.

When I had joined her outside, she said, 'What is that?' and pointed to this round object that was hovering above the lamppost across the road. That time I saw something as a young boy, the object could have been a flying toy or remote control something, but this was, in my opinion, 100% a full-blown UFO.

It was a frosty winter's evening, and it was difficult to establish the exact size of the object. The best way I can describe it is that it was round and flat, but it seemed to have an luminous ring all the way around it, like the pictures you see of Saturn. It was literally just hovering for what seemed like a couple of minutes, but I remember just staring at it, as if I was in a daze, not actually believing what I was looking at.

Eventually, we both watched it slowly fly off over the houses and down Lammack. I quickly grabbed my jacket and we rushed down Lammack Road to see if we could spot it again, but unfortunately there were no more sightings. I expected to see a story in the following day's local paper, as surely we couldn't have been the only ones to have witnessed it. But there was nothing.

I have absolutely no doubt that what we saw that night was a UFO of some kind, as I certainly couldn't explain it, and the fact that Janet noticed it first, really added to my story. She had no interest in UFOs, and it was no big deal to her, but she can confirm my story that we both saw one.

After serving one year and three months in prison, my mate Jez flew back to the UK to make the most of his freedom and vowed never to return to Switzerland again. What Jez failed to mention was that whilst he had been locked in his cell for the majority of his year, he had developed an addiction to heroin. He couldn't tell me himself, so he asked his girlfriend at the time to give me a call and break this horrendous news to me over the phone. I went to his house in Wilpshire to visit him and was shocked to find him so bad that he had needed to use crutches to get around.

Personally, I have always avoided taking non-prescribed drugs. I mean, I even turned down a line of coke from a Happy Monday one night, and over the years I have begun to detest them more and more. If I had been a teenager in the 60s, would I have taken purple hearts and some of the other pills associated with the Mod scene? Who knows? Maybe.

Drugs always had a strong link with the culture and music scene at that time. But when I became a teenager, all I remember being associated with the Punk scene was sniffing glue, which certainly didn't appeal to me, although I had friends who did.

When Ecstasy was hand-in-hand with the Rave scene and the famous Acid House parties of the late 80s and early 90s, Blackburn was a major player in the scene, but I disliked the fashion, the dancing, and the music, so at no point was it ever on my radar. Maybe if I had loved the scene then, possibly I might have sampled them, but I have never seen a positive outcome through taking drugs and believe all they are good for is ruining or ending lives. They are detrimental to a person's health and wellbeing. I have known friends take four or five Es in a night and been able to handle it, whereas another individual could take one and it could end their life. It's not worth it to me; I prefer living.

Once Emma arrived and we became parents, any chance of me going down that path was never going to be an option, even if I had loved the scene. When you have kids, it is not just you that you have to think about anymore, so in my opinion it should never be considered. I know I may sound like the drug police with my opinions, but I have only known them bring misery to every situation, with Jez being no exception. You don't have to be an expert to know that heroin is always a big no-no. I was both shocked and worried for my friend, and I would like to think I was there to offer him help and support at the time, when needed.

The Class A drug around that time was sweeping through Blackburn, and I always remember going along with Jez to a friend's child's birthday party at the Brownhill Arms, and being stunned that seven out of ten people sitting in the back room were on heroin. Luckily, Jez somehow managed to survive his addiction, even though it has taken him 16 years to kick the habit. There is no doubt that his choices cost him a lot, but hats off to him, as he always managed to hold a steady job down as a wood machinist throughout, which has been a blessing, as it meant that he was never in a situation where he would need to rob anything to fund it.

2001 was a very challenging year, and not one that I would want to repeat in a hurry. My dad had become ill, and initially his doctor told him he was depressed and prescribed him anti-depressants, only to discover he was actually suffering from pancreatic cancer. To add salt to his wounds, his doctor didn't break the news to him sitting in his surgery, but on Little Harwood car park, asking him to wind down his window as he and my mum were driving off. Hard to believe, I know!

This was the first time that someone close to me had been diagnosed with the dreaded 'C' word, and the following months were very tough. If I am being honest, due to all the medication he was on, my dad was never the same person from the minute he was admitted to the hospital. Sometimes we would visit and were able to have a reasonable conversation with him, but other times he was somewhere else. At no stage during his illness did he acknowledge to me that he knew he wasn't going to get better, but I'm sure he knew. When my dad was on the high dependency unit at Blackburn hospital, I remember calling in with Simon to see him on our way to the Rovers. He seemed pretty chuffed that I had brought Simon in with me.

On September 11th, 2001, the single deadliest terrorist attack in human history took place, when a series of four co-ordinated attacks by the Islamic terrorist group, Al-Qaeda, happened against the United States, causing 2,977 fatalities and leaving more than 25,000 injured.
At 8:46am on Tuesday morning, American Airlines Flight 11 – after being hijacked – crashed into floors 93-99 of the North Tower of the World Trade Centre, killing everyone on board and

hundreds inside the building. If this hadn't shocked the world enough, at 9:03am, only 17 minutes after the first attack, hijackers crashed United Airlines Flight 175 into floors 75-85 of the South Tower.

Whilst I was in the bath that morning, oblivious to everything that was happening, the planet's eyes were fixed on New York City. I was still upset from visiting my dad the previous day and I had called up work and taken the day off to think about the situation. I had been in the bath for hours, having little motivation, when my work colleague Cindy text me to say a plane had crashed into a building in America. But even that didn't encourage me to rush and turn the TV on.
By the time I finally got dressed and put on the news, I was speechless. Every one of the news channels was showing the footage on a loop, and I just couldn't get my head around how I had been in the bath and none the wiser to this horrific tragedy taking place. I am sure that like most people even after 19 years, it doesn't matter how many times I have watched those clips, I still can't take my eyes of them in disbelief.

One of our regular nights out at work was a night around town on a Wednesday or Thursday night, always ending up at Bentleys, until it closed. These really were great nights out, and sometimes as many as 30 people form Unilab would attend, even though we would pay for it the morning after.
One of the reasons that these nights were so special, I feel, was the contribution from Bentleys' resident DJ, Smith. I didn't know Gareth (Smith) before our Bentleys' days, but from the minute we walked into the room, the music would change to fully suit our taste. Stone Roses, Oasis, Northern Soul would be the evening's agenda, and one thing would always be guaranteed, the evenings proceedings would always end with Jimmy Radcliffe's Long After Tonight's All Over, with me pulling some shapes on the floor.

The usual suspects would be weekly regulars – Ste, Martin, Carol, Bev, Cindy, Sue, Liam, Little Tracey, Walshy, June, Tee, Cath, and so on – and having our own personal DJ blasting out the tunes kept us coming back for more, week after week.

Thursday, 20th September, 2001 was my 38th birthday, and I had planned to celebrate me entering the world with the usual get together and everyone meeting in Bentleys. With my dad being ill in hospital, and the aftermath of 9/11, going out to celebrate was the last thing on my mind, but I had arranged it, and everyone convinced me that it would do me good and take my mind off things for a few hours.

I called in to see my dad before I was due to head into town, and when he asked me if there was anything to report, I remember telling him that the world had gone mad and that he certainly wasn't missing much. But before I left, and to my amazement, he told me to make sure I had a good night, with it being my birthday. This comment might not sound like anything out of the ordinary, but the way he said it made me feel as though my dad was giving me his approval to go out, have a few beers, and let my hair down. In the past, due to my constant craving to be entertained, my parents would normally act on the side of caution and tell me not to overdo it or to be careful. But the fact that my dad had remembered and came across so genuinely about wanting me to have a good time, even though he was really very ill in his hospital bed, meant so much to me – and still does.

I arrived in Bentleys determined to make the most of the night. After all, my dad had almost instructed me to do so. As it turned out, what a fantastic night I had. The music was wonderful, the company was wonderful, and I remember loving every minute.
I had learnt a magic trick so that I could show it off to friends and customers during the night. Afterall, it was my birthday. It remains the only magic trick I have ever properly learnt, even though I was bought a David Copperfield magic set as a child.
I mixed up a pack of cards and asked a randomer to pick one out without showing me. I then proceeded to reveal that the very same card they had randomly chosen had in fact been tattooed to part

of my body, usually my upper arm or stomach. Luckily, the trick worked every time, to the amazement of the people (or person) watching.

As always, Jimmy Radcliffe ended the evening, and I am sure I was the only person left on the dancefloor. That birthday night out in Bentleys has always been one of my favourite nights out ever, and that was down to the people I was with and the fact that, for once, I had my dad's blessing to let my hair down. The only downside was that Janet had stayed at home looking after Emma, who was eight years old at the time.

My dad was getting worse in hospital and had made it perfectly clear that he would like to come home. My mum was against this, as I think she was struggling with the severity of his illness. I remember being invited to a meeting at the hospital, so that family and medical staff could make a decision on this. It was an awful time, and I did all that I could for my dad to be able to be granted his wish.
I strongly believe that if you are in that situation, it is down to the individual to choose where they would like to die, even though I fully acknowledge how hard that must be for the person or people that are left living in that house.
To my delight, the medical staff gave permission for my dad to come home. So the following day I went with my mum and brother to pick him up, and we parked across the road in the Moorings pub car park. We made sure that my dad had got all his stuff together, and helped him to the entrance of the hospital, whilst Robin went to get the car and drive it to the entrance. But once he got to the car park, he found a big yellow metal clamp attached to the wheel. We couldn't believe it! We had been gone for less than ten minutes and this had happened.

Second to me nicking my dad's car keys that time, I don't think I have ever seen my brother so angry. We had to phone a number and wait around 25 minutes, once we had paid, to get someone to come and remove the clamp. When the lad showed up, I recognised him as being a well-known hard nut from around town, so quickly tried to advise my brother to calm down. We explained that my dad had terminal cancer and that we had only come to pick him up, but he wasn't having any of it. Total scum! It was a proper scam running on the car park, but our priority was to get our dad home, so we begrudgingly paid it and did what we had to do.

The problem was that once my dad was back at home, he was eating very little. We explained to him that he would need to eat to keep his strength up, but it made him sick, so he always refused. I remember sitting with him and Robin on the settee watching England v Greece, when David Beckham scored a stunning free kick in the dying seconds of the game to allow England to qualify for the 2002 World Cup. I knew that my dad had not been properly watching the game, as he was drifting in and out of sleep, but I did notice that he had seen the goal and even commented on it. I couldn't help wondering at the time if that was to be the very last goal that my dad would ever see.

A couple of days later, Janet and I visited my dad on the Monday night to see how he was, and if there was anything that we could do to support both him and Mum. He seemed pretty troubled that night, and we struggled lifting him onto the bed after changing it. He kept going on about being a burden, which really upset me, and it was still on my mind when I woke up the following day.

I called up work on the Tuesday morning and explained that I was concerned about my dad, and that I had a strong feeling that I needed to go and see him. To be fair, work had been really supportive of my situation, so we headed up to Kestral Close.

When we arrived, my mum told us that she hadn't been in to check on my dad yet, so asked me to go and see if he was okay. At first, I thought he was sleeping, but soon realised that he had passed away. It is very difficult to describe the feeling of finding one of your parents after they have passed away, and it was the first time I had seen a dead body.

Our dad, George Hinchcliffe Eastwood, died on October 9th, 2001, aged 74 (incidentally, John Lennon's birthday), and there was one thing for sure – he would be hugely missed.

The hardest thing for me at the time, by far, was having to break the news to Emma, as she idolised him. My parents had played a massive part in Emma's upbringing. In fact, I don't know what we would have done without their help. The truth is that both of them lived for Emma from the moment she was born, and spent their whole time planning how to enrich her life in every way, so I knew it was going to be really tough for her.

Up until then, I had always felt that folk deciding not to go and visit a loved one in the Chapel of Rest was a cop-out, citing that they would rather remember them how they were. But the sight of my dad lying in Talbots Funeral Parlour took years to leave me, and was like a barrier to being able to remember happier times. From that moment, I have never judged anyone's decision whether to visit or not, and fully respect each individual's wishes on the subject.

I know it may seem strange to make out that the funeral was enjoyable, and I know that is not the correct word to use to describe it, but I really did take a lot of comfort seeing the people who had turned up to pay their respects to him. There were old work colleagues from Crown, his friends from the Northern, and my mates who had made the effort. It meant a lot to me, and the day went as well as it could have.

I don't remember planning to stand up in church and say a few words about my dad, but I did. I recall saying that he showed me that you didn't have to shout and bawl and not treat someone well, just because you were their boss. And that I had witnessed the respect he'd had from his team at Crown Paints – something that had always stayed with me.

CHAPTER TWENTY-ONE

WE ARE FAMILY

Even though we still referred to it as Unilab, Philip Harris had now become Novara. Apart from the name, nothing much had changed: we still did the same boring jobs, still took home the terrible wage packet, and still made up for it by having an active works social life.

However, Philip Harris had enabled me to become a scuba diver, introduced me to the internet, and proved to me that there was actually a posh hotel in Darwen.

In 2003, all the team leaders were summoned to the office to be told that everyone was being made redundant, as the business was moving to India. Even though it would mean that I would have to buy my own Christmas crackers from now on, once the news sank in, I actually saw it as a positive move. After all, we were all institutionalised up until that point, and if we hadn't been pushed, I reckon we would still have been working for them today. It was still scary for most of the employees, as that was all they had known for years, but as Mr Ferry always says, 'nothing lasts forever', so it was time for a new challenge.

Novara (Unilab) planned to get rid of people in a three-stage plan, and even though I was earmarked for one of the early exits, I managed to blag my way to being added to the final stage. The funny thing was that even though they were about to get rid of us, they needed us to work overtime to get their final orders out on time.

I remember on my final day asking our Works Manager at the time, Cindy, if I could have my redundancy cheque at lunchtime, and her saying no, because if she handed them out at lunch, nobody would return to work in the afternoon. I explained to her that I wasn't that kind of person, as I had worked at the firm since 1985, and eventually won her over.

Cindy very kindly went and brought me my redundancy cheque to the value of £8,500, for 18 years' service, and exactly 27 minutes later I was sitting in O'Neill's Irish bar, with two pints of lager and a plate of fish and chips and absolutely zero intention of going back. I did feel a little bad about lying to Cindy, as I am usually a very honest person and I considered her to be a friend, but they were firing me off anyway, so I wasn't prepared to be a mug.

There is one thing for sure, I spent my new-found wealth wisely, purchasing two things that I had always wanted – a palm tree and a beer fridge. Thank you, Unilab! The beer fridge was only ever used to store my CDs, and I actually ended up giving it away about a couple of years ago to a very good home, but as for my palm tree, well, that's a completely different matter.
My splendid palm tree is not only the pride of our garden, but most certainly the pride of Pleckgate. It was tiny when I first purchased it, but after years of nurturing, it is now so big that I could possibly climb the thing. Each year, I buy a couple of coconuts from our local market (and pay a lot less than Karl did) and place them under the tree. When my mates call round, at least one of them will ask if they have fallen off the tree, to which I always reply, 'Of course they have, where do you think they have come from?' I always tell Janet that if we ever decide to move to a new house, the tree will most certainly be coming with us or I won't be moving.

Over the eighteen years working for the same firm, I made some friends for life, and of that I will be always grateful. And there was no doubt that wherever we all ended up moving onto, we would most certainly be staying in touch.

Back in 2000, and after living at our first home together on Cloverfields for ten years, Janet decided that she wanted to move.

Some of our neighbours on the road had tried to sell their houses for years, so we knew that we couldn't take it for granted that we would sell ours quickly. As it turned out, less than 20 minutes after the For Sale sign went up, a car appeared on our drive, a lady stepped out and told me that she wanted to buy our house, and buy our house she did (just about). I was pretty settled there, but a number of our friends had already moved onto pastures new, and Janet had made her mind up that she wanted a change. We had both enjoyed living on Cloverfields and it was a really friendly place to live, most of the time, but it was time to move on.

Apparently, we had a supermodel staying next door at one stage, but I never even had the pleasure of introducing myself, and she moved out before I even knew she lived there. However, I wasn't going to miss the crazy builder, and I would definitely not miss the mini-rail crossing around the corner that always seemed to be down whenever I was in a rush to pass.

Our new family home was on Regents View at Pleckgate, just across from The Farthings, and on the same road as my brother and his wife, Fiona.

When Emma was two, we went on a family holiday to Ibiza, and gave her her first taste of the Balearics. Ibiza would become a popular haunt for us in the summer, and quickly became my favourite place to visit. I have a thing about sunsets, and there is no finer one than at my favourite bar, Café Mambo. The first time I visited it was in the morning, and to my amazement the beach in front of the bar was packed full of people chilling, still there from the previous night. Later, that morning, Zoe Ball was running a Radio One live session, and she came over, thinking that the doll Emma was holding was a real baby.
We also bumped into my friend Bev from Unilab on that holiday, and every time Emma has met Bev's son Craig since, he has reminded her of the time in Ibiza when they shared a bouncy castle together.

On another trip to Ibiza, I remember getting up really early and getting a taxi down to Mambo for Pete Tong and Judge Jules. After I had enjoyed the atmosphere for around two hours, I felt that I had better get back to the hotel, as Janet and Emma would be wondering where I was – only to find them both still in bed on my return, which meant I could have stayed longer.

The Sunset Strip is definitely my favourite part, with Café Mambo, Café Del Mar, and Savannah. And the latter was the venue for one of my favourite nights there. Legendary Soul DJ Trevor Nelson was resident DJ for the evening, and Rick James had just passed away that day/week. Trevor was impressed by my request to play something by him, *17*, and he asked us to join him in his private area that included a group of his friends from the Brit Awards. Mr Nelson was delightful company all evening, not forgetting the mint tunes, and told Emma that she was the coolest 11-year-old that he had met.

My other favourite place in Sant Antoni is Kumharas – a meeting place for different cultures, and is as chilled out as you can get. I really do believe it is a bit of a hidden gem, as it is slightly hidden away from the main area, and a lot of people I have mentioned it to have never heard of it. I really would recommend it.

For a change, we decided to have a family holiday with two of Janet's sisters, Elaine and Pauline, and my brothers-in-law, Warren, and Martin, along with my nieces Beckie and Rachel and my nephew Matt. We hired a private villa in Benalmadena Pueblo and life was good.
After we had been there for several days, it was decided that the following evening we would spend a couple of hours at an amusement park somewhere in the mountains. It was only fair on the kids to go somewhere that they would enjoy, rather than to visit the usual restaurants.
We had a really good time there, but we had been at the park for over three hours, and I was dying for a cold drink, due to the heat. I mentioned this to the others, and they agreed to leave and find a

local bar. We found ourselves down on the marina and at a pretty cool bar to have our long-awaited pint in. I have always been terrible at getting served; it's as though I am invisible at 6ft 3, and I am obviously not assertive enough when trying to get served. Eventually, though, I was holding my cold pint of Spain's finest lager (well, the bar's anyway), but I had not taken more than a couple of sips when Elaine asked if everyone was alright to head back to the villa as the kids were tired (they didn't look that tired to me).

At first, I thought she was winding us up, knowing that it had taken me ages to even get a drink, but no, she was deadly serious. I politely made my point that we had only just got there, and that I thought we were going to have at least a couple of drinks, having just spent hours at the amusement park. But Elaine was determined to head back. It wasn't long before the rebel in me came out, and I told Warren that there was no way at all I was going anywhere until I had at least finished my drink. And to my surprise he agreed.

We told the group that we were at least going to finish our drinks and would meet them back at the villa in a while. What made it even better was that Janet and, I think, Pauline, both said they were okay with it and agreed to take the kids back to the villa. I remember saying to Warren that I felt we should have a couple of beers and then head back, so that we weren't pushing our luck.

For a change of scenery, we agreed to have our final drink in a different bar, and as we were looking around trying to find the nearest, a couple of girls handed us some flyers, obviously trying to promote their venue. I tried reading the flyer, but it was impossible as it was written in Spanish, and I struggled with English the majority of the time. The one thing we did work out was that the silhouettes on the flyer seemed to be of naked people, but straight away we noticed that the bar we were just about to walk into had the same name as on the flyer.

The plan had been for me and my brother-in-law to have a couple of quiet drinks before heading back to our families. But knowing that not everything goes to plan, I found myself lying backwards on the front of the stage, with a dollar bill hanging out of my mouth, dreading which part of the dancer's body would be picking it up. We had only gone and found ourselves in a Spanish lap dancing bar, totally unplanned, and I ended up being part of the act.

Luckily the bar was pretty quiet, as it was early, but that meant that as the only two males in the place, we were the ones getting all the attention. And when we were offered a private dance in a separate room, we knew it was time to say our goodbyes (meaning, try and sneak out). We found a way out of the bar without getting any hassle, though I half expected some dodgy looking bloke to come after us saying that it had cost more than a dollar. Luckily, that didn't happen, much to our relief.

The next drink was definitely going to be our last, but we found ourselves in what seemed like a very lively local disco. The atmosphere was fabulous, to be honest, but I knew we were in trouble when we were joined by a couple of very friendly girls. Having zero intention of taking things any further with our newfound holiday buddies, we were friendly and polite (I think) but really struggled to have a decent conversation. We didn't understand a word that they were saying, and I am sure it was the same for them. Not being overly stupid or naïve, I felt we didn't need to speak their language to realise that they were trying to get us to leave with them – as I am sure lesser men would have. We knew that was our signal to leave.

We really struggled to find a taxi back to our villa, and by this time it was around 3.30am so I knew that we would have some explaining to do. Our plan was simply to say that we had waited hours before we could get a taxi, but luckily for us, everyone was fast asleep on our return. I managed to carefully climb into bed without waking anyone up, or so I thought.

The following morning, we were all sitting around the table having a family breakfast that I hadn't prepared for once, and it was pretty obvious to all and sundry that Warren and I looked like we had been dragged through a hedge backwards. I was starting to think (hope) that we had got away with our late-night shenanigans, when Elaine said, in what I thought was a pretty smug tone, 'I bet you both wish you had come back with us last night.' So I replied, 'Well no, actually. Once you left, we went to this lap dancing bar and had a couple of dances, then we went and found a local disco and copped off with a Colombian girl and a Mexican girl,' to which Elaine replied, ' Aye, alright, you wish.' Everyone started laughing, leaving me thinking, *Wow, I tell everyone the truth and they still don't believe me!* At least I couldn't be accused of being a liar.

A couple of years ago, we were out in a local restaurant with friends, and as I was holding court in the bar, I told this same story, thinking that I must have mentioned it to Janet before now. But judging by the force of the slap she gave me, I could tell that I clearly hadn't. It proper hurt. So maybe some things are definitely better left unsaid.

I think it was on our final night of our holiday, Emma, Beckie, Rachel, and Matt had all gone to bed, and the adults were sitting next to the villa pool, having a few final drinks. Janet said that she was tired and was heading off to bed, but I tried to talk her into staying up and told her not to be boring, due to the fact that it was our final night of our holidays.

She said her goodnights and headed off indoors. But a few minutes later, I was chatting to Pauline when Janet suddenly reappeared and started to remove her clothes. What happened was, she had gone indoors and sat on the bed, thinking, *He is not going to call me boring.* Then she came straight back outside, took her clothes off until she was as naked as the day she was born, and – to our disbelief – jumped into the pool, apparently thinking, *I'll show him who's boring.*

I remember saying to Pauline at the time (and in mid-sentence), 'Sorry to be ignorant, but I'm going to join her in the water.' Obviously, drinks had been downed that night, and before I could sing the lines to *We Are Family*, I found myself naked in the pool alongside the Whittaker sisters. I had not seen that one coming!

Warren couldn't swim and wasn't keen on water, so although I'm sure he would have been keen to join us, he made do with watching from the side. Martin finally joined us, and we must have been making one heck of a noise, as we managed to wake the kids up with all the noise we were making. They were banging on their bedroom window and shouting, obviously concerned about what they thought was happening. So, that was that. We all found ourselves going off to bed, but it did make me think before calling Janet boring anytime since.

CHAPTER TWENTY-TWO

BRAND NEW START

Eighteen years working for the same firm had ended, and I found myself standing in a queue at the Job Centre for the first time, which I didn't find to be a very pleasant experience.
Eventually it was my turn to go and see an advisor, who talked through all my work experiences to date. She told me she was going to be my new job coach, and that she would contact me every time a relevant job came up... I never heard from her again!

If I was being honest, all the jobs I had worked at up until this point had not really felt like they were for me, and they certainly hadn't been very rewarding. I actually wondered if I would ever find a role that I felt I was any good at or, especially, had something to offer. For the life of me I really cannot recall who suggested or recommended trying my hand at voluntary work, but I am extremely grateful that they did.

Janet had worked at British Telecom for the majority of her working life, and always told me that nobody ever left because the pay was really good. One night, she returned home and informed me that one of her work colleagues had handed in her notice, as she had been offered a job working in a school as a Learning Mentor. I'd never heard of a Learning Mentor before, but once Janet explained that it was along the lines of engaging and supporting students and pupils who were underachieving at school for a number of reasons, I felt that this role was specifically made for me.
I have no idea why I felt this, as I had really disliked the majority of my school time, and the thought of working with young people had never crossed my mind, but I replied 'wow' and the seed had most certainly been planted.

The first thing I did was to arrange an interview at the Prince's Trust offices on Strawberry Bank in Blackburn, and agreed to be a Volunteer Young Persons Mentor for them. I would be supporting young people from the area who had found themselves having really difficult starts in life and had challenging backgrounds.

After several weeks, I had thrown myself well and truly into the deep end and had committed to support on a weekend away with the staff and young people at Coldwell Activity Centre in Burnley. I was really nervous, wondering if I had been kidding myself in thinking that I would be any good at this mentoring role, but there was only one way I was going to find out, and that was by attending this weekend away. It turned out to be a real eye-opener and definitely took me out of my comfort zone, which had to be a good thing.
To keep a group of young people with different backgrounds and interests constantly engaged for three days was certainly a mission, but I feel that I managed to achieve this pretty well. And the feedback I received from Nigel, my Mentor Support Worker, was extremely positive, which really helped my confidence in the situation.

I have always been absolutely terrified of heights, but found myself abseiling backwards down a giant rock, because if the young people had given it a go – and most did – I couldn't very well back out myself. Looking like a total wimp, I was almost in tears, but I did it, and when several young people clapped and told me well done, I knew it was worth it, even though the praise felt a little like a role reversal.

Trying to get some sleep in a room full of crazy young folk, and some old, was also a mission, especially when it was our group's turn to cook everybody breakfast. Naturally, we didn't manage to wake up on time, and found one of the other groups already hogging the kitchen. You would think that this saved us a job and that we would have been relieved, but they had not been keeping an eye on the grill, and the bacon had been so burnt that it set off the centre's fire alarms, which resulted in a visit from a big, red, shiny fire engine. We had to take the blame for oversleeping, and we all received a lecture about how much it had cost the Trust for the fire engine to pay us a visit. So you could say that the other group certainly did not manage to save our bacon!

The minibus dropped me off on Whalley New Road, near Brownhill, on the Sunday teatime, and even thought I was completely shattered as I walked home, I felt that I had really achieved something that weekend. Maybe this supporting young people lark was for me after all.

The Prince's Trust observed which young person engaged the most with which mentor during the weekend, and then suggested them being a mentee for them to support. Nigel suggested that I could mentor a young girl called Pam, and as I respected his judgement, I happily agreed to this. And for maybe the first time in my life, I felt that I was making a difference (outside of my family).

Pam lived in a children's home and had been subjected to an horrendous upbringing, along with her siblings. Before I could start the role of Pam's mentor, I had to undertake a huge amount of training on the subject (rightly so). The most important thing that it teaches you is you are not the young person's friend; you are purely there to support them, to listen to them, and to the best of your ability within your remit, to make sure they are safe.
The other important thing that the Trust taught us was how important it is whilst working with a young person to be consistent and reliable, as this is the total opposite of what they have been used to all their young lives. Even if you could only volunteer for an hour per week, the Trust would rather that you didn't commit to anything rather than you not being able to make it, and letting the young person down.
I would visit Pam's house once a week, and on one occasion as I was leaving, a staff member shouted after me, 'You'll get your reward in heaven.' So I guessed I must have been doing something right. I also supported with the weekly Arts and Crafts sessions at

the YMCA – the place where I had previously gained a love for table tennis – and at a Saturday morning football session at Bangor Street. My role as a mentor did not mean that I had to be a whizz at art or football. My job was to support and encourage the young people, as these were things that the majority of them had not been used to.

Working for the Prince's Trust as a volunteer at the time most definitely felt like the best decision I had ever made, and during my time there I met some really nice people, who felt as passionate as myself about supporting vulnerable young people and contributing to keeping them safe with the knowledge we had gained from our Child Protection training. Little did I know that in my time of need, the beloved Prince's Trust I dedicated my time to would end up not supporting me, and in fact stabbing me in the back.

Nigel had said he was so impressed by my mentoring that he had recommended me to work for a few hours a week for a Youth Inclusion Project – Y.I.P. – over at my old stomping ground at Mill Hill. The role was to work with the targeted most vulnerable young families in the area, and it turned out that I already knew and worked with a number of them via the Prince's Trust, which turned out to be really helpful. To say that some of these young people were challenging was an understatement, but I always treated them with respect and just talked normally to them, which I'm sure helped my relationship with them.

It doesn't matter if a young person is not regarded as very academic, or they are against the world, they know straight away if you are patronising them, and can always suss out if you are not being genuine with them. I felt that this was one of my strengths when working with them, and it helped to reiterate my theory that if you treat someone with respect, whoever they are, you will usually get respect back.

Y.I.P. was run by Groundworks/Young People's Services/Positive Futures, and we would have numerous trips out, run football teams and sessions, and weekly arts and crafts and games sessions, or basically put on anything that we could come up with in an effort to keep the young people engaged and try to limit their chances of getting involved with crime.

We came up with the idea of staging a talent competition which we called Y.I.P. Idol, nicking the idea form ITV's *Pop Idol* show. The majority of these young people might have been regularly told that they were useless by parents and teachers, but it didn't mean to say that they didn't have a talent, which we hoped we would be about to prove. There was loads of interest in our competition, especially with our younger people, and we ran weekly audition sessions in the back room of the building. It was an absolute pleasure supporting and witnessing some of the hidden talents that they clearly had, and seeing their confidence grow week after week. My own daughter Emma even entered and found herself in the Grand Final, which took place at St Bede's School, performing *Underneath Your Clothes* by Shakira, which blew me away.

During one of our first auditions, a young girl turned up and amazed everyone with her incredible rendition of *Tomorrow* from the musical *Annie*, and I knew from that minute that she would no doubt win the whole thing, which she most certainly did. I couldn't help but wonder if she was that incredible at only eight years of age, what her potential could be given support and encouragement to develop her skills. A clip of her in the Final was posted on YouTube and has received more than a half-a-million views.

My experience of working at the Y.I.P. was really valuable in aiding my mentor role, but I had an issue with the number of times that it would end up closing. Sometimes, I would make my way to work, travelling from the other side of town, only to be told on arrival that I would not be needed that night as they didn't plan to open (why couldn't they have contacted me?). Several of the young people also found themselves being barred for what I considered to be minor reasons. I obviously don't condone attacking the building with pool cues or a fire extinguisher, but what was designed for inclusion spent a lot of the time excluding, so I did have some sympathy for the young people's frustration.

One of the most rewarding projects I was involved with during my time at Mill Hill was a project working with Action Factory, helping to produce an anti-drugs film called 'A Perfect Night.' The young people would be involved in the storyline and more or less every aspect of the filming, with the plan being to show the final edited movie at a local cinema, putting on a big red-carpet event for the young people to showcase their brilliant work. After taking over a local nightclub, Cubes, to carry out a lot of the filming, the director Neil very kindly called round to our house and spent around half an hour of his time teaching me how to edit using a timeline. Looking back, the knowledge I managed to gain in that 30 minutes literally changed my life, giving me numerous options in one of my new roles as a film maker.

I bought myself a small camcorder from the Panasonic shop in town, and even though it was small, it was really high quality for its size (a bit like Janet, haha!). My love of capturing life had started off in the 80s, taking my own photographs and developing them myself in a dark room. Now and again, I would borrow my dad's very large movie camera, but the quality was quite poor and even though I loved videos, they were known for being temperamental at the best of times. The invention of DVDs really was a massive game-changer in terms of reliable quality and the ability to enable you to produce your own.

My main passion was to film a concert or a local band, but as the word got out that I had this extra string to my bow, I found myself being approached for a number of filming jobs, including weddings. Weddings were the last thing I intended to film, as I always felt that you can't re-do 'I do', and if I had made a mistake whilst carrying out this task, I had the potential to ruin someone's day, month, year.

The problem was that when a work colleague asked me if I would film their daughter's wedding, I found it really difficult to say no, so I agreed. I was pretty nervous throughout the day, and only managed to relax a bit once I had managed to capture enough footage to make a decent DVD for them. Doing a decent job and making sure the bride and groom were happy with their product was a ginormous relief, but it led to problems when they recommended me to their friends, and I ended up filming five weddings in total.

Sometimes, I would be asked to sit in the bar area to eat my meal whilst the wedding meal took place, which was fair enough, and sometimes I was very kindly invited to join the main party. The key when filming a wedding was to remember that you were there to do a job, and not to let your hair down, which I have to admit slipped my mind on one occasion.

It was a really posh do, and I was convinced that I recognised one of the bridesmaids that was sitting next to me. Towards the end of the meal, it turned out that the one I thought I recognised was one of the main characters in *Coronation Street*, which explained why I thought I knew her. I was having such a great time, chatting and laughing with the people on my table, that I had forgotten that I was not actually a wedding guest and was in attendance only due to my role as the videographer for the day. As a result, I almost missed the beginning of the speeches.
What made the day even more awkward for me was the fact that the lad who had taken great pleasure in booting me in the head that night outside the Rugby Club was the couple's wedding singer for the evening. I couldn't believe my eyes when he walked through the door, and I am unsure who felt the most uncomfortable. At the end of the day, though, I was there to do a job. So I had no option but to remain professional, and politely said, 'hello', and proceeded to film him murdering Frank.

The Rugby Club incident wasn't even the only time he had attacked me for zero reason. One Christmas, we were having a few drinks around town before planning on heading on up to the Cav. We were in O'Neill's when I noticed my mate from Unilab, Tony, sitting in the back room. I wandered over to say hello to him, and noticed he was sitting next to an unfriendly looking skinhead. I also noticed somebody else out of the corner of my eyes, standing in the corner behind me. I was telling Tony that we were on a Christmas night out, when the guy with no hair stood up, walked over to me, and tupped me in the mouth so hard that I was convinced he had knocked some of my front teeth out.

Suddenly, the guy who was stood in the corner – Mr Wedding Singer – started to punch me, and tried his best to drag me through the bar and outside. The pub managed to capture the whole incident on their CCTV cameras and passed the footage on to the police, but like before, nothing at all became of it.

Two totally unprovoked attacks, and on both occasions, it had been two-on-one, which led me to the conclusion that just because you sing the odd Frank Sinatra tune doesn't mean that you're a gangster (in fact, far from it).

One of the lads I helped to mentor probably had the worst reputation out of everyone for getting in trouble and kicking off, but to be fair he was always okay with me. One night, him and his mates, obviously bored, decided to nick a double decker bus and take it for a ride, but one of the lads jumped off the moving vehicle which then ran over his leg, breaking it. Not exactly Cliff Richard. The story was in the local paper, so there was no chance of them getting away with what had happened.

The young lad told me that he was fed up with getting into trouble and that he was going to try his very best to keep out of it, to which I told him well done. The next thing I heard, he had been sent down, so obviously he didn't try hard enough. A couple of years later, I bumped into him one lunchtime in HMV in town, and he told me that he had been in trouble again and was about to be sentenced. When I asked him what on earth he had been up to this time, he very casually explained that he'd kidnapped a young male and locked him in a garden shed. Almost lost for words (almost), I remember having a long conversation with him, explaining that he could not go around doing stuff like that, and how much better his life would be if he managed to keep out of prison. At the time, I felt as though he had actually listened to me, and it seemed like he meant it when he told me that he knew I was right and assured me that this would be his final time on the wrong side of the law.

Several months later, I noticed his name mentioned on the front page of our local paper. He had been involved in a suspected armed robbery, and ended up getting eight-and-a-half years, so maybe this mentoring lark wasn't for me after all. The advice I had tried to give this young person had clearly gone in one ear and quickly out of the other.

CHAPTER TWENTY-THREE

A FRIARGATE RETURN

A job was advertised in our local paper that seemed too good to be true as far as I was concerned, when Janet pointed it out to me. The post was for a Learning Mentor at Friargate School, which was my old secondary school, and was about five minutes' walk away from our house. By this time, I had undertaken a large amount of mentor training, along with all the hands-on experience I had gained, and I was feeling quietly confident to at least end up with an interview. Fifty people applied for the post, and I ended up getting down to the final five before the interviews took place. They were pretty intense, with all five candidates sitting in the same room for ages and finding ourselves being called through for our interview one by one. I have always been weird about interviews in the fact that, unlike most people, I actually enjoy them, and have always been reasonably confident if it involved a role that I felt I could do.

Even though I had been a rubbish pupil, the fact that Friargate had been my secondary school might go in my favour, along with the fact that I lived locally. But there was one thing that was worrying me. Where we lived, there was a walkway for the school pupils heading to Roe Lee to catch the bus to town. A couple of months previously, I had been standing at the end of our garden when a number of pupils passed by onto the next road. To my absolute astonishment, a young lad took what looked like a flick knife out of his pocket and proceeded to wave the blade about, right in my face. It might have only lasted several seconds, but I was stunned, and by the time I wanted to challenge this behaviour, he was already walking down the next street, laughing away with his mates.

I have never been someone who wants to get young people into trouble, as my roles had been to try and keep them out if it, but I have always felt strongly about young people carrying knives. So there was no way I was about to let this go. I rang the school and explained what had happened to me, and even though the person on the other end of the phone didn't seem very interested, I managed to push for someone to see me. I met with one of the Year Heads, who sat down with me and went through a book of photos of each pupil in the year, to see if I recognised any of them. When I pointed one of them out that looked very familiar, he told me that I must have been mistaken, as it had probably been a flick comb and not a knife I had witnessed three inches away from my face. I couldn't believe what I was hearing. I explained that I wasn't stupid and that I knew the difference between a comb and a knife, but even though I took this incident seriously, I was made to feel that the school was not really interested.

My worry was that someone from the school might remember my visit, and this would go against me getting the job, due to me being seen as a bit of a troublemaker. Towards the end of the morning, and after I had been suited and booted for hours, I found myself being called through to see the headmistress, and to my absolute delight, I was told that I had been successful. Out of 50 people, I was offered the job as a Learning Mentor at Friargate School. The headmistress told me that what had swayed it for me was the fact that I had done voluntary work with the Prince's Trust, which proved that I was dedicated to supporting young people.

As I was walking away from the school, the only thing I could think of was what a massive shame it was that my dad was not here to see me get a job working in a school. He would never have believed it. Maybe for the first time in my life, I felt he would have been really proud of me, working in education, as he had been really into learning and would have approved.

I arrived on my first day, wearing my finest suit, shirt, and tie, and was delighted to learn that the other person who had been offered

a mentor's job was a girl called Chrissie, who I had got on with the best, and thought that she had seemed genuine.
At first, we had a meeting with the Head, and it was hilarious as she ran through the routine. She had written about what it was like to be a headmistress of a secondary school, but she read it in the style of Victoria Wood.

We were then taken on a tour of the school, which I found really strange, as not that much had changed since I had left in 1980. Unfortunately, the tuck shop was no more and there was no sign of Carol Cooper, but familiarity breeds confidence, so I guessed it would be okay. We were then taken to our new mentor office and introduced to the rest of the team. Everyone seemed really nice and came from various working backgrounds, which I felt was great.

The Learning Mentor role was the first time I had noticed a job not being about how many qualifications you had – which in my case was a good job – but about the type of person you were.
I fully subscribed to this philosophy, and it was a refreshing change to the norm. Just because you have a shed full of 'O' levels doesn't mean that you would be effective working with disaffected young people.
Our office was a tiny box room situated next to my old RG tutor group; in fact, I think it had been the old toilets. The way things worked was we would be given a caseload of students, arranging one-to-one meetings with them in the hope that, as their mentor, we would be able to raise their achievement. I loved the idea that raising the achievement of a young person was the main aim of the new role I was entrusted to carry out, as I feel that all young people have a talent. I believed that the barrier was convincing them that they could achieve, as not everyone is given support or encouragement, unfortunately.

The one difference that I was surprised at was that the pupils on my caseload did not necessarily have difficult backgrounds or were on the verge of being involved with crime. Some were merely underachieving at school, and a couple had even been 'gifted and talented', which came as a shock to me, based on my experience at the Trust and Y.I.P.

Having said that, my first pupil that I was assigned to came from a pretty tough background, as his father had spent some time in prison for killing the family dog in the back yard, in front of his son. My first reaction was to suggest that someone else might be better mentoring him, as I might have struggled due to my strong beliefs on animal welfare. That evening, this moral dilemma went around and around in my mind, until I came to the conclusion that me not mentoring the pupil was the totally wrong decision, as it would be really unfair on him. His father's cruel actions were certainly not the boy's fault, and the only way to change someone's way of thinking was to work with, support, and educate them, and to offer alternative options.

We had weekly meetings with our line manager, who had been a teacher when I attended the school and was now also a school governor. In one of our first meetings, she gave us extra roles to carry out in addition to our mentoring, and when she discovered my love of photography, she gave me the role of taking photos of several sporting activities that were taking place at that time. One of these included male boxing sessions in the sports hall, and once I had printed them out, I was asked to display some of them around the school, along with others I had taken, to showcase the positive work that pupils were carrying out. I also gave up several of my evenings to film the Christmas pantomime, *The Wizard of Oz*, and gave it my all to get the best footage possible, in order to make a DVD of the performance as a keepsake for the school, pupils, and parents.
Some mornings, I would even call home on my break and make myself a butty. I couldn't believe how lucky I was to land a job that I loved, and that was on my doorstep.

One thing I couldn't get my head around was sharing a staff room with some of the very same teachers that had taught me. It was mental, and in some cases I found it impossible to address them by their first names. I just couldn't do it. My old maths teacher in particular, who I had spent five years calling 'sir', was the hardest. So I would just say 'Good morning' or 'Good afternoon' and avoid giving him any title.

Once a month we would have a Learning Mentors' meeting at an outside location, usually another school, where we would meet mentors from the other local schools to share good practice and offer each other support regarding our caseloads. That was the plan, and on paper it seemed a really good idea, but the reality was that most of the time was taken up listening to other mentors whingeing about how Friargate was the chosen school, as we had been the only mentors to be given our own personal laptops to use, and our actual role as a mentor was what it was supposed to have been.
The spending of the funds was down to the Head, which meant that a mentor's duties varied from school to school. At one of the schools, one of the mentor's roles was to act as security at lunchtime and breaks, preventing the pupils from leaving the gates. I had witnessed this for myself during one of our visits, as one minute we were sitting chatting to our fellow mentors, and as soon as the bell went off, they jumped up in mid-conversation and legged it outside to carry out their duties. It just confirmed how lucky we had been.

This was the first time in my life that I had actually looked forward to going to work each day, no matter how sad that may sound. I really did feel that I was going above and beyond what was expected in my efforts to support all our pupils. Most mornings I would be first to arrive in the office, and most evenings I would be the last one to leave, not realising how annoying this might have been to the other members of the team. They probably thought, *Who does he think he is?* But I was only trying to help. I even arranged for members of the Prince's Trust to come into school to help me run sessions in the hall, and ended up running a photography class along with a music production class a couple of lunchtimes a week. Me teaching a class – who would have thought it? Certainly not my old teachers, and probably not my dad.

Even though I was running a couple of lunchtime sessions, I certainly had no desire to be a teacher (imagine!) like a few of the mentors did, possibly because it offered more money. I saw teaching and mentoring as two different roles and was more than happy with the one I had. A teacher would hand out discipline, which was fair enough, but many a time I would see the usual suspects bawling and shouting at a pupil on the corridor, which wasn't something I was prepared to do or even believed in. It seemed that in some respects things hadn't changed that much since I had been a pupil at the school.

A mentor's role was to help break down barriers to learning, in an attempt to allow the teacher to concentrate on what they did best – teaching. And we would usually have background information on the pupils, to equip us to better support the young person. For instance, a young carer may get into trouble for arriving late for lessons, as the teacher might not be aware of their home circumstances. Perhaps they were supporting family members, maybe taking their younger siblings to school and then getting themselves ready. So the truth of the matter was that it was a miracle they arrived at school at all, never mind being a few minutes late.

One of my mentees was a pupil called James, and I always found him to be both friendly and polite, at least with me. Over the weeks, I noticed a change in him and was convinced that all was not well. The problem was that although I felt I had a good professional relationship with him, and that he trusted me, it didn't matter how many times I asked him if anything was going on, he was adamant that he was fine. I was convinced that he was being bullied, and what had fuelled my suspicions even more was when his mother rang me, telling me that when it got to Saturday night, James would start to say he was feeling ill, so that he wouldn't be able to go to school on the Monday. I tried everything within my power to support him with this, but felt I was getting nowhere.

The great thing about a mentoring team was that everyone had different strengths and ways of doing things. Not everyone hits it off with every pupil, and I had absolutely no ego asking other mentors to intervene or even add someone to their caseload if I wasn't convinced that things were working out.

I approached a fellow mentor Dan (ex-CID) and asked him for his assistance. What followed blew me away, by the fact that doing something in a slightly different way would lead to a totally different result. Dan came into the room with me and James, and simply gave him a couple of pieces of blank paper and a pen, then told him that we were going out for a walk and if he felt like writing anything down whilst we were away, he was more than welcome. We were out of the room for no longer than half an hour, but on our return, we found that James had written on both sheets of paper, explaining exactly what had been happening to him.

He exposed that a small group of lads were picking on him on the way to school each day, and I was amazed how such a subtle change had been so effective. I learnt that some people find it a lot easier to write about something, as opposed to talking about it. So I had now gained an extra tool for my toolkit.

Working with young people can at times feel like a thankless task, and even though I was over the moon by the fact we got to the bottom of James's bullying issue, I personally felt as though my contribution had been pretty useless and that I hadn't helped him at all. Several years later I bumped into James on the street, and he told me that I had changed his life. Initially, I thought he was joking, but he explained that I was the only person who did not give up trying to find out what was happening to him. That meeting with James was really powerful to me and helped reiterate that just because you feel you haven't really helped someone, doesn't mean to say that you haven't. Sometimes it might take years before you realise it.

The one thing I have found from my experiences as a mentor is that schools need to improve on the way that they deal with the issue of bullying. I found that some schools would never admit to having a problem with bullying, to make the school look better, but sweeping the issue under the carpet means they are simply not doing justice to their young people, which is their job.

At Friargate, we had a big anti-bullying campaign, and the mentors were given the task of visiting all the tutor groups and giving a talk on the subject, along with leaving them a very glossy poster on the campaign. The deal was that any pupil who was experiencing bullying was encouraged to come and speak to one of the mentors. The day after I gave my talk and left my poster, a young Asian girl knocked on our office door and told me that a gang of young people had been throwing stones and bricks at her family home and had shouted insults at her and her mum on a nightly basis, leaving them both petrified. She also told me that on one occasion they had taken her into a local wood and tied her to a tree. No matter how many times I passed on this information and brought the subject up, to my knowledge nothing at all was done, citing that because it was happening out of school, it was nothing to do with school and there was nothing they could do – even though it was happening to one of their own pupils.

On my first day at work in my new job, I had set off walking when a small group of pupils started chatting to me and asking me questions along the lines of, 'Oh, are you the new Sir?' I always felt uncomfortable being called 'Sir' and always will, and the great thing was that as a mentor we were told to use our first names. The funny thing was, though, it didn't matter how many times I explained this to some pupils, I would still be addresses as 'Sir', and still am after all these years.

The first pupil who started a conversation with me that first morning walking was called Sonia, and I ended up mentoring her, because she had started to get a bit of a reputation for being disruptive in class. Her main distraction was her hair, as she spent the majority of every lesson brushing and messing around with it. It ended up that I would meet her just before she was going into

class so that I could confiscate her beloved brush, then return it on her way out of class. Such a simple intervention really was effective, and I ended up making Sonia my student of the week.
At the time, gel pens were all the rage, and we kept a supply of them in the office to hand out to our improved pupils, along with a certificate.

Another of my roles was to help invigilate the school's exams in the very same sports hall where I had sat as a pupil with a blank sheet of paper, not having a clue what to write next. Maybe the fact that I had been in their shoes, and struggled at school, enabled me to have some empathy for the pupils and have a better understanding of ways to support them. But who would have thought that 23+ years later, I would actually be the one marching up and down the hall making sure there was no cheating going on? Certainly not me.

CHAPTER TWENTY-FOUR

WAKING UP TO A BAD HEAD

In a way, the timing for me starting my dream job was pretty poor, as not long after my appointment, it had come to light that the Head of Maths at the school had allegedly been having an affair with one of his pupils from his class. What this revelation meant was that the local media's spotlight was focused on the school, and we even had rumours of death threats towards the teachers, mentors, and the Head, but luckily they were just rumours, and nothing actually happened.

Every morning we would have a staff briefing, updating us on the situation and advising us not to speak to the Press, and in the event that this happened, we were told what we were supposed to say to them.

What surprised me was that a chunk of the conversation was directed towards supporting the teacher involved, which left me feeling a little strange. On my first week at the school, the Head had asked me if I was okay to walk the pupil in question home after the school day, as she lived quite close to me, but I politely declined this request due to the current situation, and was surprised that I had even been asked to do this after only two days at school. I thought this was highly inappropriate, to say the least.

Most of my week was taken up supporting young people, and I couldn't have been happier, feeling as though I was actually achieving something and that for the first time in my life I had managed to find a job I was hopefully good at. My five days a week were taken up working at the school, Saturday morning and Tuesday evenings were committed to Art and Crafts and football sessions with the Prince's Trust, and Thursday evenings I was working on the anti-drugs film for the Youth Inclusion project.

Sometimes it was tough working on these projects, as the support and encouragement we were giving these young people seemed as if it was only coming from us and nobody else. During a singing session, a family member barged into the Project, interrupted the lesson in mid-flow, and proceeded to drag one of our very talented young people out on to the street at Mill Hill without even letting them put their shoes on.

On the football team I was helping to run, there was one young lad who really stood out as being a little bit special at the sport. However, on a Sunday morning during our matches at Witton Park Astro Turf, his parents would sometimes show up, but were usually pretty drunk from the night before and seemed more interested in the can of Stella they were holding than their son who was scoring all the goals.

We started filming 'A Perfect Night' at a nightclub in town called Cubes, and it was a pleasure to witness how excited everyone was, and to see their confidence grow a little more each week. We were short of young people for several scenes, and I was asked by my boss if I could see if any of my Friargate pupils were up for getting involved. As I felt it was a really positive thing to be involved with and it had a really positive message, I asked my line manager at school if this would be okay. There were a number of pupils interested, and I was happy when she gave me the go ahead.

Another task I was given was to try and find out why a large proportion of Asian males at the school were under-achieving and to come up with some strategies to try and help them improve in this area. Having met the identified group of males a couple of times, I established that most of them were big cricket fans. I decided that as a reward (dangling a carrot) for any improved effort in class, and through my family's contacts, I arranged for an international cricketer from India to come into school and give them some coaching lessons. This seemed to go down really well with them, and they all said they were excited.

Things couldn't have been going any better for me, and at times I had to pinch myself, as I couldn't believe my luck. Just to reiterate my feeling, I arrived at work one morning and was handed a bottle of red wine by our headmistress (my boss) for my good work, which Janet certainly appreciated. I actually don't think there was a day went by where I didn't think to myself how lucky I was to end up in a job that I looked forward to attending every single morning.

The day after my bottle of wine gift, I was catching up with paperwork in the main hall when my line manager came over and asked me to go and see the Head in her office. But just as I was about to enter her office, a member of staff asked me if I wanted anyone with me, in terms of representation, and I didn't have a clue what she was on about. I had nothing to hide, so I simply said no, I was okay.
I opened the door to her office and was dumbfounded to see a long table with four people sitting behind it, and a chair at the other end that I was told to sit on.
The other people were the Head, the two School Deputies and my Line Manager. The Head started off by saying there had been some very serious accusations made against me, which left me totally bewildered. Then, to my absolute horror, she asked me if I got off on the photos I took of children/pupils. This left me stunned and almost speechless, and I tried to explain that I took photographs at school because I had been asked to by my Line Manager during a Learning Mentors' meeting, so I took photos of school events to help highlight the positive work that the pupils had been doing. I also explained that every single photograph that had been taken was given to the people involved, pupils and staff, and were also in display cabinets around the school, and had been for months. I told her that I'd had the same role at the Prince's Trust and Groundworks.

The next accusation made against me was about me showing a photograph of a skinned cat around the office, and I was questioned about whether it was appropriate as it showed cruelty to animals. At first, I had absolutely zero idea what she was referring to, but tried to explain that I was passionate about all animal welfare and that I was a member of the League Against Cruel Sports, along with making a monthly donation to the RSPCA. It turned out that several months before, I had received a joke email of a cat that had had its fur shaved in order for it to look funny. I hate stuff like that and certainly would call it cruel, but at the time I received it, there was only myself and a fellow mentor, Pauline, sitting in our office first thing in the morning. Pauline had asked to see the picture that I had been cringing over, and when I showed it to her, she agreed it was horrible and I deleted it straight away off my computer. How this private incident with a fellow member of staff led me to being accused of being inappropriate regarding issues of animal cruelty and a skinned cat, I struggled to get my head around. Added to that was the fact that a fellow colleague, who I'd always felt I got on with, had lied about me and stabbed me in the back.

And still the accusations kept coming. Yet every time I tried to answer them, I was told to shut up, to stop being rude, and to only speak when I was told to do so – all this by the same person who had given me a bottle of wine the day before for my supposed good work.

It was like I was in a bad dream, and my next interrogation question was whether I thought it was appropriate behaviour for a member of staff to involve pupils in a film project that I was involved with. I tried to explain that I had asked two separate members of staff – one being my line manager – if it was okay, as it was being run by Blackburn with Darwen Groundwork Trust and Action Factory. I said I had been told that with it being an outside-of-school event, I was okay, as the school did not have the insurance to cover it. She asked me if I had obtained their parents' permission, to which I explained that of course I had, and that everyone involved had needed a signed consent form from their parents or carers.

I tried to explain that I had nothing to hide and that I had done nothing wrong, and that I was an honest person who was simply trying to tell the truth and was not trying to get out of anything. Throughout the meeting I kept being called rude for interrupting and was criticised for my answers, at which I kept apologising. I felt completely numb and could not comprehend how or why this was happening to me. I thought of all the times I had seen similar incidents on TV dramas, when the accused just sits there and hardly speaks, and you shout at the telly in frustration, 'Speak up, stick up for yourself!', thinking that if you were ever in their shoes, you would act completely different. Well, let me tell you, you probably wouldn't. I was so shocked by what was happening to me I was just in a daze.

My next question the Head asked me was if I had heard of the word 'paedo'. This was very upsetting, and I felt very hurt by it. Again, I tried to explain that this was my dream job and the best thing to ever happened to me. I told her I had put my heart and soul into the job, and always tried my best to be professional, honest, and helpful, and that I had never had a wrong word with anyone – pupils, parents, or staff – and I had never acted inappropriately in any way, ever, within my role. I told her that I did not believe in self-praise or have any big ego, but I felt I needed to stick up for myself. I explained I had three police clearances, and I had worked with young people for three separate agencies, but no matter what words left my mouth, they fell on deaf ears and were treated with contempt.

The Prince's Trust had told me on more than once occasion that I was one of their best workers/volunteers they had working for them, and the YIP I worked for at Mill Hill had voted me their top worker by staff and the young people. So how on earth was this happening?

I was then asked if it was true that I had bought a female pupil a present, which yet again left me feeling bewildered and confused. What she was referring to was the gel pens that a fellow pupil out of Sonia's class had passed onto her, along with a certificate, because Sonia had been chosen as my pupil of the week due to her improvement. The gel pens were purchased by the school, and it was the idea of my line manager to reward positive pupil behaviour, within our remit, as every other learning mentor did.

I knew there and then that if this had been twisted that much to insinuate that this was a personal gift from me, then I was being set up, for some very strange reason. I was just wasting my breath trying to be honest in an attempt to defend myself, as the accusations kept coming. I was asked to go and wait in the nurse's office down the corridor whilst they would discuss everything. I don't know how long I was left to sit there on my own, but it felt like an hour, and all I could think of was how extremely hard it was to understand why someone would say such hurtful lies about me. Sitting there, I felt the loneliest I had ever felt. It seemed like an eternity, sitting feeling shell-shocked, waiting to be summoned back in so that I could learn my fate.

After what seem like forever, one of the Deputy Heads came to take me back into the Head's office, where I was told that I was being suspended with immediate effect. I was told that an investigation would take place, by both the school and Social Services, and I was then escorted to our office so I could collect my coat and phone. I noticed that my laptop and bag had been removed, and I was not allowed to access any of my personal belongings out of my drawer. The Deputy Head told me that he knew it must be hard for me and that he was not allowed to discuss it with me, but I should try not to worry. Was he for real? He escorted me out of the building, and that was that. I didn't even get the chance to burn my tie!

The walk back home was unbelievably tough, as I remember walking slowly across the fields, calling both my mum and Janet to try and somehow explain what had just happened. I don't mind admitting that there were tears rolling down my face.

This incident happened on a Thursday, and by the time the Suspension from Duty letter dropped onto our doormat on the

Saturday morning, the original seven accusations of alleged child protection issues had changed to three, proving that in just over a day they had found four of them to be absolute nonsense.
The three that were left were:

I might have developed a potentially inappropriate relationship with a Prince's Trust client (as if).

That I had developed an inappropriate relationship with a pupil at Friargate High School. (No, I am not the maths teacher, who incidentally received more support than me, and was found guilty of the accusation.);

The taking of a significant number of photographs of young people at the school, and there were questions as to whether I had obtained appropriate permission. (I had).

What made things even worse – if that was even possible – was that the terms of my suspension stated I must not communicate with any employees of the school, any governors, pupils, and parents at Friargate, or Mill Hill Youth Inclusion Project. I was not to attend any council buildings within Blackburn with Darwen, and was unable to take on any sort of paid work anywhere. I also had to make myself available for any meetings which would be arranged as part of my investigation.

What these devastating conditions meant to me was that I had zero support from anyone, and my actual work colleagues that had witnessed my role with the young people and who had the potential to support me challenging these claims, had been blocked. Apparently, we were one of only two local councils in the country that had adopted such unfair regulations, and it just made me feel a whole lot worse about getting through this and the truth coming out.

Other than the odd conversation with the Head, I heard nothing from anybody for months, and it was certainly the loneliest time of my life.

The Headmistress would call me from time to time, but I felt that she was out of order and inappropriate on several occasions. The first conversation she had with me was along the lines of, 'I am just checking if you are okay.' Oh, yeah, hunky dory, never been better. The second time she called me she told me that she thought that I had been grooming young people and that I was probably a paedophile, which left me feeling isolated and numb.

The day I was suspended, I had driven with my brother Robin to the Spread-Eagle car park in Mellor to explain to him what had actually happened, and the first thing he asked me after I finished ranting was, 'Is there any truth in this?' That floored me, but I guess I suppose he felt that he had to ask.

I wondered if the Head, and Pauline, who was a fellow mentor, and my line manager, had any inclination as to what their bizarre lies had done to me, and how it came close to ruining my life and my family's lives. I fully appreciate that if someone has a concern about someone else, especially in this field, then it needs to be investigated. But the way in which I was being treated, and how I was spoken to, was very unfair and extremely inappropriate.

I was sat at home in limbo, day after day, for months, seeing nobody and not knowing what would happen next. In fact, things were that bad that I felt paranoid, and it made me feel scared to leave the house, thinking that every single pupil would know about what had happened. Even a few minutes walking to the shop to buy a daily paper or a butty for my lunch, was timed carefully each day, to avoid bumping into any pupils who might have been on a school break.

I always had the theory, that if I, or anyone else, went over to a group of young people on the street, pointed at a random house, and told them that a paedophile lived there, they wouldn't have questioned or investigated if what they were told was right. They would have simply taken it as read, and maybe put the person's window through and start to terrorise them, innocent or not.

After months of this nightmare, my school investigation was complete, and nothing had been found. Throughout the process they discovered that all the accusations were unfounded, but they had obviously clutched at straws and tried to dig up something else to accuse me of. I was accused of making personal phone calls from our office, which frankly was laughable. Every single member of the team used the office phone for their own personal use on a daily basis, especially Pauline, who would constantly be talking to her partner. Whenever I used the phone, it was either to ring Nigel at the Prince's Trust to arrange for them to come into school and help run some sessions for the pupils (for free), or at worst to quickly call Janet to let her know what time to expect me home, or for a lift. The writing was well and truly on the wall as far as I was concerned, and they were clearly doing everything they could to try and stitch me up and get rid of me.

While I was off work rattling around the house, I had a lot of time to think. It's funny when you look back and remember little things, like a strange look there or an odd comment, then you start to put stuff together in an attempt to try and make some sort of sense out of the situation. I hadn't seen it at the time, but looking back, it must have been annoying for the others with some new bloke arriving and being first in, last out, running this and that, and being over enthusiastic due to the love for the job. I am sure that in their shoes, having been in the job a lot longer, I might also have thought, 'Who the hell does he think he is, trying to take over?' But that had never been my intention. I simply thought the world of my job role, and also my team, and was passionate about trying to support and help to raise achievement in young people.

A couple of days before all this had kicked off at school, I had attended a Multi-Agency Support meeting at Witton Park School, to offer support to Pam, who I was mentoring via the Trust. The meeting was full of social workers and support workers, and I was just honest at the time when speaking about Pam and all the positive things she was involved in, and the effort that she put into her work.

That very evening, my mentor support worker Nigel had called me to make me aware of the positive feedback he had received, in terms of my attendance at the meeting. He told me that one of the social workers who had been present at the meeting, had commented afterwards that I seemed to know Pam well and to support her more than anyone else there. So, Nigel was ringing to tell me well done. But the following day, another person who was present at the meeting (from that school) had called the Trust and also my school, to ask them if they were aware that they had a member of staff that seemed overly keen to work with young people. And these calls had actually triggered this whole process off. WOW!

The thing that I was most disappointed and shocked about was that the people who I felt I would be able to rely on the most to tell the truth and support me, had actually run a mile and turned their backs on me. I received a letter from the manager of the Prince's Trust, saying that they would be having nothing to do with this case, and that I was not to contact any Trust member or young person at all. So, the agency I had given up my time to for free, and had told me that I was one of their best workers, dropped me at the time I needed them the most. I was deeply hurt and stunned by this.

Years later, I bumped into Nigel, who profusely apologised to me for what had happened. He told me that they had been wrong, but that it had been out of his hands at the time as his boss had told the staff not to get involved.

After about three months of doing nothing, I was invited into school for my Investigation hearing by Social Services, and my friend Waker attended with me as my representative. I found the experience of returning to the school to be interrogated pretty tough, but as I had nothing to hide, I welcomed the fact that something was happening. Mark did a good job in representing me, and I felt that the hearing had gone well. I had to wait for the results of the finding, but naturally Social Services found nothing against me, and my biggest crime was to maybe have been too

naïve at times, and a little too passionate in the role that I'd felt passionate about. How sad.
Still not knowing what my future would hold, and still having a feeling that I would never work in this field again, the Head's phone conversations went from calling me a paedo to telling me that she was looking forward to my return to school, and she was going to organise for me to have my own mentor. Unreal!

I discussed this situation long and hard with Janet, looking at my possible options for moving forward, and even though it had been my dream job and I had looked forward to it every day, my integrity had been questioned. Also, the people who I worked with and for, had told lie after lie about me and without a doubt stabbed me in the back. So how on earth could I go back and trust these people? I couldn't.
It was a difficult decision to make, but I decided to give my notice in, as my integrity was more important to me. But to prove a point, I arranged to go into school for one final time for a leaving lunch with my mentor team. I must have been mad to put myself through this trauma, as I found it very, very tough, especially when the first person I bumped into at school was my line manager, who had failed to support me at any level, and had actually made things worse by failing to admit to the things that she had agreed to. However, I felt it important to hold my head up high, as I had never had anything to hide.

Looking back at this time in my life, I would like to think that all my family and friends believed my version of events at the time. During the most difficult part of this situation, I felt confused, low, paranoid, and isolated, but there was never a stage where I considered taking my own life. However, I remember saying to my friend Mark that I understood why people did.
Investigating me over concerns was one thing, but the way I was treated was a very bitter pill to swallow. What was ironic was that I had spent most of my time trying to improve and boost young people's confidence, and then mine was totally destroyed by the very people who had employed me to carry out that task.

The night that all this had started, I was due to be involved in the filming of 'A Perfect Night' film, taking place at Blackburn Hospital. As a result, I was stopped from taking part, and I was absolutely devastated by this ban as I really believed in the project and had been involved from day one. The school also decided to fully delete the whole of the *Wizard of Oz* footage from the school pantomime which I had spent hours filming in my own time, and for which I had promised to give all proceeds to charity.

All of this was hard for me to swallow, but the thing I would find the hardest to forgive them for was ruining my experience of seeing a Beatle for the first time. For my whole life I have had an obsession with the Fab Four, and for the first time in my life I was in possession of a Golden Ticket to actually go and watch Paul McCartney in concert at Manchester M.E.N. I had been looking forward to this from the second I received my ticket, but little did I know that the concert would fall in the middle of my investigation.

When everything was going on, I toyed with the unthinkable option of maybe not attending, but I was due to see a Beatle for the very first time, so in all honesty that was never going to happen. But even though Macca was incredible and performed for over three amazing hours, I couldn't get my situation out of my head, going over and over it, and I found it impossible to concentrate. For robbing me of what should have been a magical, personal experience in my private life, I will never forgive them.

Not long after I left the school, the Headmistress herself moved on, and I heard that there had been investigations about the way she had handled the maths teacher revelation, so I couldn't help but wonder whether what happened to me had been a tactic to divert the attention from herself.

Just before I started to write this very personal chapter in my story, I went searching in my attic for all my original paperwork and letters from the time this happened to me, so I am going by what was recorded at the time, and not just relying on memory.

Whilst rummaging around I came across a local newspaper, which I had obviously kept from 2011, with the front-page headlines reading 'School Head struck off'. Allegedly, my former boss had been struck off from her role as Head of another local school for serious misconduct after being described as 'dishonest' by her Professional Body. According to the paper, she had paid £17,000 of school cash into her own bank account. Unlike me, she failed to attend her own hearing, and even though I would never wish anything bad to happen to anyone, I felt for the first time that folk would now finally believe me that I had been set up.

I feel it is only right to end this chapter with the mention of one person. During and throughout my suspension from the roles that I loved, the fact that I was not allowed to meet up with anyone left me feeling that I had very little support at the time. Not only did these accusations have the potential to ruin my life, but what they put my family through was extremely unfair. Whilst I appreciate that accusations of this nature have folk running for the hills, these are the times that you need support from your friends the most.

I really appreciated the support from Mark (Waker) in representing me, and I had no doubt he believed my version of events – that's what friends are for. But the person who I felt showed me unwavering belief from day one, outside of my family, was my fellow work colleague at Mill Hill, Mark Ashcroft. I had only known Mark for a short while, but the important thing was that he had seen me work with vulnerable young people several times, unlike my friends and family, so he was better qualified to make a relevant judgement. The fact that he made me feel he 100% believed me right from the start, meant the world to me and is something I will never forget. Cheers, Mark!

CHAPTER TWENTY-FIVE

ROCK GOES TO COLLEGE

I was still unsure what my next move was going to be in terms of my career, or on the job front. Even though nothing untoward had been found against me during my investigation, most folk would rather not take that risk, so I felt it was unlikely I would be working with young people again, which was a shame.
After several weeks of not doing very much, to my surprise I received a phone call from my boss at Mill Hill Y.I.P. asking if I would like to work a few hours over summer for the project. She was aware of everything that had happened to me, as she would have been questioned. She told me that she was glad the investigation was all over – as was I – and I agreed to start some work with them the following day, thinking it would be helping to run sessions like I had been doing before.

When I arrived at the Project the following day, I was told that we had a special task to do that day, and me and another worker were driven to someone's private house, asked to remove everything that we could see, and to start filling the waiting van outside.

What had happened was that my boss's sister was leaving her husband, as she said he was violent towards her and the kids. The plan was to remove everything that wasn't nailed down in their house, apart from the bed, whilst he was attending a meeting at work. If I am being honest, I felt highly uncomfortable about this ask, and didn't feel it was right to be involved in someone's personal life. It was not something I had signed up to. But the reality was that my boss had offered me a much-appreciated lifeline and a chance to carry on working within this field that I didn't think I would get back into. So I guess I would just have to grin and bear it, hoping that my next task would be a lot more appropriate.

What was wonderful, though, and a huge relief was that I was able to attend the red-carpet screening of 'A Perfect Night' film at our main cinema in town. The young people loved it, and the Project had even arranged for them to arrive in stye in a long, white limousine, as a reward for all their efforts. I had been given a lifeline, and it was something that I really appreciated.

A job appeared in the local paper for a mentor's role at my local college, so after a lot of thought I decided to fill out an application form. Unfortunately, I wasn't successful in my application, but I received a phone call from the Vice-Principal, who told me that she had looked at my experience and that she would like me to work for the college. This was amazing, and my confidence grew by the day. She told me that there wasn't a specific job role for me at the moment, but she would sort something out and let me know.

In 2003, I was offered the role as a mentor in the E2E department at the college, but the only problem was that she had forgotten to mention this reasonably important information to the current manager of the department. When I showed up for work as arranged on the Monday, not a single person in the room was expecting me. It was highly embarrassing, and I felt really awkward, as I am sure they all did. The manager kept repeating that they hadn't got any work for me, so I felt like I wasn't really needed. I worked for E2E for several months, and even though I got on with both the staff and the students, I always felt that the manager didn't want me there.

In 2004, I noticed a mentor post advertised for a project called the Year 11 Project, but when I handed in my completed application form at the old Courts Pub reception, the girl who took it from me was the same girl that used to rant about the Friargate mentors at the multi-mentor meetings, so I felt I wouldn't stand a chance. Surprisingly, she actually put in a positive word for me, and after an interview I was offered the job.

On my first lunch break, I nipped into town to do some shopping and called into the library on my way back. I was waiting so long for some information on a book that I realised I was about to be late back, which was never an option on my first day. I immediately started running towards the exit, thinking that the door was open, but it wasn't, and I ended up smashing head first into the revolving glass door panel.

They might have had a good window cleaner, but I almost knocked myself out. The pain in my head was excruciating, and people started to look my way at the sound of me hitting the door. I did the usual thing and proceeded to get back onto my feet, and to slowly walk away as if nothing had happened, but I made it about two metres around the corner of the building, and out of sight, before I collapsed into a pile on the ground, struggling to cope with the pain in my head. How could this happen to me on my very first day in my new job? If it had been my second or third day, I would have without a doubt made my way home to spend the rest of the day feeling sorry for myself.

The Cubes nightclub that had been the location for a lot of the 'Perfect Night' filming had closed its doors and reopened as a lap dancing bar called The Velvet Lounge. The same couple we had got to know through our work there owned and ran both ventures, so on the odd occasion when we had been on a night out around town, we would sometimes end up there. It was somewhere to have a late drink, because we would usually end up on the guest list and get in for free.

I came up with the idea of starting a monthly club night event at Blackburn Rugby Club called Punks Reunited, and asked my mate Waker if he fancied being involved and to help me run it. Our first event was successful, and a week later we were sitting in The Farthings on a Thursday night, wondering where we could go for another drink, as it was time for last orders. One of us mentioned the Velvet Lounge – providing we could blag getting in for free – as you didn't have to have a dance. We got a taxi down there and, luckily, they recognised me standing in the queue and told us to come to the front as we were their guests.

Mark went to the bar to get our drinks and I nipped to the loo, but when I got back and sat down, he informed me that he had booked us both a dance. 'What do you mean?' I asked, thinking we had only come in for a couple of beers. I knew it had only been a tenner to cover a dance, so a fiver each wasn't too much of a deal, but the problem was Mark hadn't attended before and had absolutely no idea how much things cost. I thought he was winding me up when he told me we owed £45, but before I could question him about this, our entertainment for the evening came over, and it was too late to do anything about it. Mark had only gone and agreed for us to have a triple lesbian dance (whatever that is) for four-and-a-half times the usual fee, and it was fair to say that he had been well and truly got.

I could pretend that it was not an enjoyable experience and that I had hated every minute, but at the end of the day I was in the toilets when it was booked, and we decided to put the cost down on the Punks Reunited expenses, as it had been pretty Punk of him, after all.

The following day, I was walking down the corridor at college, when I noticed two Beauty students walking towards me in their uniforms and carrying their work. The closer they got, I was sure that I recognised them from somewhere, then it suddenly dawned on me. To my absolute horror, they were only the two lap dancers from the night before! I could have died, as it was obvious from the way I was dressed and wearing my lanyard (for once) that I was a member of the college staff. I felt sick, imagining some sort of newspaper headline, after all I had been through already. As they passed, they sheepishly said 'hello', and I even more sheepishly replied with the same.

I spent the rest of the day worrying about the incident, but thankfully it didn't come back to haunt me. One thing was for sure, though, I never visited the Velvet Lounge again.

The team I worked with on the Year 11 project were brilliant, and we were all passionate about giving our young people a second chance and supporting them to hopefully enable them to have more options in life. Although mentoring was more or less the same no matter who I worked for, I noticed a difference between working at the Prince's Trust, secondary school, the Y.I.P., and working for a college, in terms of the remit. At the Trust and the Y.I.P., staff would sometimes store young people's phone numbers on their phone so they could contact the person they were mentoring, but at secondary school they would be horrified by this. At college, mentees phone numbers were stored on the works mobile phone, and this was the way to contact them and for them to contact us. It was important that you recorded every bit of contact you had with the young person, to cover your back. And you had to get used to each specific mentoring remit depending on where you worked.

Working in this type of field, you would find that on some days after work you couldn't just switch off from the day's events. I worked with girls who had been raped by their 'so-called' fathers, and I was horrified to discover that these were not isolated cases. They were regular occurrences, and sometimes had gone on for years. I worked with students and pupils who were abused by family members, victims of grooming gangs, kids that were neglected, and on one occasion I was left speechless to discover a young person I was mentoring had been injected with heroin as a child, by their parents.

Some young people went on to commit suicide, and some ended up serving time in prison. One young person told me she had been suspended from her previous school for attempting to hang herself in the school toilets, which made me feel both angry and speechless. She should have been offered support, not shown the door and punished for her actions. (What is wrong with people?)
You are never not shocked by the stories that they tell you, and in most cases, it just makes you want to support them even more, and try to show that despite what happened to them in the past, it

doesn't mean that it will happen to them in the future, and that there are people who believe in them.

I have always felt that it was a privilege to be given a role with somebody who had been told that they were rubbish, useless, thick, and crap all their life, and tell them that they weren't, and being able to work at highlighting their positives and improve on building that young person's confidence. Many a time I appreciated where they were coming from, as I'd had very little interest in schoolwork as a youngster, because I did not find it relevant to my life or interests. At least at college you would get to pick your own subject/course to attend, along with the fact you would be supported and encouraged, and not just called 'thick' and left in the corner, like we had been. I do feel strongly that it takes a certain type of person to work with vulnerable young people, and the job wouldn't be right for everyone. The majority of the tutors/teachers I worked with whilst in my mentor role were brilliant, and in a lot of cases they went above and beyond to support the young people in their class.

In my dad's day, when he attended Technical College at night, the induction process was a lot tougher, rightly or wrongly, and I feel that folk only signed up for a course because they actually wanted to learn. Nowadays, the majority of young school leavers are either told or strongly encouraged to attend college in an attempt to cover up the Government's unemployment figures, just like the Manpower scheme in the 80s, and most certainly, in some cases, to get them out from under their parents' feet.

There is absolutely no doubt that a number of students these days attend college in order to enhance their social life, and have very little interest in their actual course. They sign up in an attempt to be able to obtain a student loan, or their parents tell them that they have to attend college in order for them to qualify for benefits, and even in some cases to prevent them being sent to prison.

Part of our remit was to attend Blackburn Magistrates Court, to offer support to any of our students who found themselves on the wrong side of the law. These visits were certainly an eye-opener, and what struck me was that all the young people knew each other and would be laughing and joking together before they were called into court. It was as if they knew that they would be getting away with whatever they had done.

On one occasion, a friend of my student's was standing in the dock, and I was shocked by the long list of crimes that the judge read out – 19 in total. Just as it looked like the judge was about to send him down, which he had already stated that he wanted to, the young person's Youth Offending Worker stood up and told the judge that the lad was about to start a course at college, which I'm sure made the judge begrudgingly give him another chance.

What all this meant, though, was a college tutor who had taken on the job a number of years before, when most students wanted to learn, was not necessarily equipped to handle a class full of kids that would maybe not have that same standard or enthusiasm.

I had only been in my new role for a couple of weeks when I was asked to offer my support in a Motor Vehicle class that I had a Year 11 student in. We did this differently than in school, as we didn't always sit right next to our mentees, in order not to highlight that they needed support. Instead, I would discreetly sit somewhere in the class and offer my student help, or anyone else who may need it, if they were struggling. I was also there to support the tutor, as the theory was that if at some stage things kicked off in class, I would try to deal with the incident, leaving the tutor to do what he did best – teaching.

As it was one of my first classroom support sessions, I was asked to sit in class and observe how things were going, so I found a spare seat towards the front of the room where I could sneakily keep an eye on my student. The tutor started to write some work on the whiteboard and seemed to be writing for ages without turning round to check on his group, although he was talking to them about what he was writing. I found this really strange, but not wanting to make it obvious, I slowly turned round in my chair in an effort to see the students behind me and check if they were okay and that they were understanding what the teacher was saying. To my utter amazement, two groups of students were sitting on their desks playing cards, a couple were lying back in their chairs with their feet on the desk, listening to music on their phones, and to be fair, a small handful were sort of listening – thankfully including my student, although he hadn't written much down. This made me feel uncomfortable, so I made my excuses and headed back to my office to check if this was the norm, but thankfully I was assured that it wasn't.

Another class I was asked to support was a Sexual Health Awareness session run by Brook. Knowing our students that would be attending, I was dreading it. I mean, I consider myself to be very open-minded, but where students were involved, I was expecting to be embarrassed. The girl taking the sessions was barely older than our students and had in fact known some of them, which I wasn't sure was appropriate. My line manager at the time wanted to shield the students from this session and maybe even pull it, but this would have been out of order based on her own personal views.

Things, I felt, were going okay until she told the class that she was not supposed to tell them this, but a prostitute had once shown her how to put a condom on in the dark with your mouth. I almost fell off my chair and thought my line manager would be having a fit if she knew what was going on. After displaying to our students this highly technical skill she'd picked up, she produced a model of an erect penis with the idea of passing it around the class to give everyone a turn at showing how competent their condom applying skills were.

Prudish, I was not, but there was no way on earth I was prepared to set myself up and give a demonstration of my own in front of the group. A number of students apparently found this task to be funny, and the model was moving closer and closer to me by the minute. I turned around to see what the noise was in the corner, only to find three students, trying to avoid their turn, blowing up condoms like a balloon. One of the lads had even managed to pull one right over his head. I saw this as the excuse to enable me to miss out on having a go, and headed to the back of the room to try and bring some calm back to the class.

Once back in our office, my line manager, with a worried look on her face, asked me how the session had gone. I replied that everything was fine and the students had enjoyed it, knowing that some things are definitely better left unsaid.

Attending Open Evenings at college was another duty we were expected to carry out, and on at least two occasions I remember being surrounded by college security guards in the toilets, as I might have resembled Frank Gallagher out of Shameless standing there in my green parka. It took me a while to convince them that I was actually staff.

For some strange reason, I have always had this inside rebel in me, where I struggle with being told what to do. I always say that I will do anything for anyone if they ask me in the correct manner, but it's a different matter if I am told I have to do something. At college we were constantly told to wear our lanyards on display around our necks, and even though I would do this at times, the majority of the time I would just carry it around in my hand or my pocket, claiming that wearing it around my neck ruined a good shirt. I was never sure if folk believed my explanation for what I am sure was very annoying behaviour, but I was deadly serious. It did ruin a good shirt.

My colleague Linda was on the team that interviewed me, and was a co-ordinator on the Year 11 Project, so was involved in almost everything I did at work. One of our early trips with the students was to visit Walton Prison, and the idea was to attempt to give our targeted students – that were on the verge of crime – a short, sharp shock of what life would be like it they carried on the path they were already on. During our minibus journey, the students I was sitting near were certainly not fazed by the prospect of spending time in a prison, and the two behind me on the back seat were bragging between themselves about sneaking some weed into the prison, up their backsides. I'm sure this very childish conversation was purely for my benefit, but I didn't know for sure, and felt slightly worried.

Once we arrived, the security was unbelievably tight, and even staff had to endure being patted down and sniffed at by a very large Alsatian dog. Thankfully, they found nothing untoward on the students (or the staff), which was a huge relief, and we were escorted inside as a group representing our college. As part of the visit, there was a section where they would lock students who had the worst reputation inside a prison cell, in the hope that this would shock them into – hopefully – thinking twice about getting into any future trouble. However, once we arrived, we learnt that this had now been stopped for Health and Safety reasons, which was a pity as it was one of the main reasons we had chosen this visit in the first place.

We were shown a wing that housed 100% lifers, but even that didn't seem to faze the majority of our students. We were then invited to watch a play which was produced and performed by the inmates who had spent most of their lives in and out of the place. The performance was really hard-hitting, as the prisoners acted out their own personal stories about losing everything through getting involved with heroin and other drugs. After the play, there was an opportunity for the young people to ask the prisoners some questions, which everyone hoped would be relevant to what they had just seen and the message they were trying to put across.

A couple of young people from another college asked reasonably sensible questions, then I noticed one of the boys in our group put their hand up, and I started to feel worried. To everyone's horror, the question was along the lines of 'Does it not worry you when you have to bend down in the shower to pick up the soap?' Linda and I, and no doubt everyone else in the room, were speechless, and it was fair to say that the question hadn't gone down too well with the inmates. Beyond embarrassed, we took this as our cue to leave and quietly make our way to the entrance.

The journey home was a nightmare, packed on board our small, rickety college minibus. Linda and my line manager, who was driving, sat up front and I was at the back, trying to keep my eye on the students and keep the peace whenever it kicked off. It was fair to say that some of them had been getting restless, and unfortunately some damage took place to the seats and roof. A student in front of me started to threaten me, whilst the student behind me was attempting to set my coat on fire.
I have never been as relieved to end a journey as I was that day, and I know for sure that Linda, my line manager, and me fully questioned to whether we were in the right job, and whether or not it was time to look for another career.

From the minute I started at college, our Year 11 budget seemed to be never-ending; everything we asked for was okayed by the Finance Department. This was fantastic and enabled us to plan all sorts of trips and activities with our students. Weekly snowboarding sessions at Ski Rossendale, theatre visits, Blackpool Pleasure Beach days out, Lightwater Valley theme park, Tower Wood activity days in the Lakes, and an Army day out at Fulwood Barracks to see what the students were made of. Linda enjoyed these trips almost as much as our young people and certainly led by example, trying her hand at the Army assault course, jumping around in all the mud, climbing to the top of the Leap of Faith at Tower Wood, and being first in the queue for all the scary rides at Blackpool and Lightwater Valley. She really led from the front and showed the students and the rest of the staff, especially me, how it was done.

When I turned 30, my mate Simon very kindly bought me and Janet West End theatre tickets to go and watch Willy Russell's *Blood Brothers* at the Phoenix Theatre in London. Simon has always been generous, and even though I had never heard of the play, I absolutely loved every minute of it. It still remains the best thing I have ever seen in a theatre, and since that day I have been doing *Blood Brothers* missionary work to anyone who will listen and have organised at least five trips to educate folk on how incredible it is.

I suggested this play as the perfect theatre trip to take our students on, as I felt that some would relate to it. The last theatre trip we had taken our previous students to was *Joseph and the Technicolour Dreamcoat*, which was my line manager's choice, but the majority of the students were bored and became restless. The year later, when we took the students to *Blood Brothers* in York, it is fair to say that the majority of them, if not all, had never visited a theatre before and had absolutely no idea what to expect. It was worth the trip alone just to witness their faces staring mesmerised towards the stage, as if transfixed by what they were watching.

In an effort to enhance my working experience in mentoring and youth work, I decided to take a Level One Counselling course which was run by one of the college counsellors. I enjoyed the course and hopefully learned something from it, but we shared an office with my tutor, and even though he was a really nice chap, I couldn't help but feel that he actually needed counselling more than us, due to all the things he was going through at the time.

I then agreed to study for a Foundation Degree in Positive Practice with Children and Young People. Me, sitting a degree? Just imagine, and who would have thought it? The course was over two years, and I had to write 54,000 words, which for me was an absolute mission. Janet always reminds me that she took the degree as well, because it was her that very kindly agreed to type up my pages of scribble, so she did feel like she had been through the experience, too.

Anybody will tell you that taking on a degree is a bumpy road, and even though you usually choose a subject you have an interest in, you will go through stages where the workload is getting too much and you need a work buddy, preferably on the same course, to support and reassure you that you will get through it. My work buddy was Waker's wife, Karen, who was also taking the course. There were a number of occasions when I considered packing it in, due to the never-ending workload, but those late-night phone conversations with Karen offering support and encouragement did the trick, and convinced me that it was all worth it after all. I would also like to think that I offered Karen the same kind of moral support in her times of doubt, which is really why you need a Learning Buddy so you can support each other in what sometimes seems like an unachievable task.

We had a long wooden kitchen table at the time, and every single inch was taken over by my course paperwork for months, adding to Janet's despair. One area that was a learning curve for me right from the start was the amount of the course that you were expected to self-teach. In school, your teachers give you all the information you require, but on the course there were many times when we would turn up for a lesson, only to be sent away and told to learn about a particular subject by ourselves.

My course covered every subject that you would need to know about when working with young people – counselling, advocacy, child protection, youth offending, child development, and mentoring. To be fair, it wasn't the most reassuring of starts, as the tutor who was supposed to be taking us for child protection was off sick, and on entering the classroom, the stand-in tutor said to me, 'Alright, Pete, you probably know more about child protection than I do!' which is not what you want to hear.
Then, to make things worse, the following week the guest speaker was only the same bloke whose house I had helped to clear out, based on being told he had been violent to his own partner and his kids. I actually could not believe what I was listening to, and spent the whole of the lesson keeping quiet, wondering and worrying in case he knew what I had done.

For counselling and mediation, our teacher John was not only one of the best teachers that I had ever had, but he was also one of the nicest people I have met. One week he was unable to take the class and asked one of the other counsellors to take over. The guy seemed nice, but had tried to convince us that if a counsellor ended up having sex with his client, in some cases you could argue this action was okay, as it led to the person feeling more positive about themselves.

At first, I thought he must be joking, but once I realised he was deadly serious, I told him strongly that in absolutely no circumstances could this be seen as acceptable, as it was highly unprofessional and highly inappropriate. Thankfully he only took us for one lesson, and I really enjoyed the learning with John.

Our child development classes were taken by Collette, who I knew through my social circle going back to the New Romantic days, as she was a friend of Nick's. I recalled swapping an earring with her at a party in Darwen when I was around 16, and I was still wearing the earring that day, but I refrained from sharing this information with her in case she thought I was being weird. As it turned out, I considered Collette to be one of the teachers who impacted on me the most. I felt she pushed the boundaries in her class, which always kept it interesting and encouraged you to participate in classroom discussions. She taught us to question everything and not just to take things as read. Even if you had seen something in a book by someone with a posh name, you should research things for yourself.

As part of my coursework I read a book entitled *Just a Boy*, the true story of a stolen childhood by Richard McCann. Richard's mother, Wilma, was the first victim of a serial killer who became known as the Yorkshire Ripper in 1975. I found Richard's story to be riveting but also heart-breaking, as it described the experiences he had been through, being thrown into care as a consequence of the actions of Peter Sutcliffe. I decided to contact Richard via email: one, to let him know how much I enjoyed the book; and two, to invite him to come into college to give a talk to our Child Protection Class and maybe the Criminology class. Richard replied that he had only ever given one talk before, but he eventually agreed to come and visit the college.

He was really nervous beforehand, which wasn't helped by the fact that the whiteboard projector was not working. But he plodded on and ended up giving a really interesting talk, which everyone thoroughly enjoyed. Richard is now a full time professional motivational and inspirational speaker, and I would like to think that his talk at our college gave him some confidence to start the ball rolling in some small way.

Doing my degree had a pretty profound impact on me, and changed the way I would approach a situation and how I would view certain things. I don't just take things for read, and I understand the impact a counselling session can have. When I went through that horrendous experience at Friargate, Occupational Heath referred me to see a counsellor to help me deal with how unfairly I had been treated. I turned up to a council building just off the Boulevard and told my story to a complete stranger who I had never met before and would probably never meet again. For the first time, I just fully offloaded what had happened to me and how it had made me feel, and that was it. I found it to be really powerful, and never felt the need to visit her again once I had told my story.

A counsellor's role is simply to listen, not to judge or offer advice. Listening, I feel, is one of the most powerful qualities you can have, but no doubt the hardest. And I believe very few people have the skill to be a good listener – me included. To listen to someone without feeling the need to interrupt, or to start to plan what you are going to say next, is a very rare skill, but the result can be extremely rewarding. When working with a young person, the length of time that you manage to stay silent can be crucial to your young person potentially opening up. But it is remarkably difficult to overcome that uncomfortable silence and wait for the other person's response.

Another important thing that I have learnt is the importance of not stealing someone else's thunder. If someone is telling you about an experience they have had, it is not a very good move to interrupt them and declare that you have done that, or that you have been there, as this can be seen as you trying to take away their glory. After all, it is their story to tell.

Anyway, a miracle happened, and my two years of hard graft paid off. Not only did I manage to pass my degree course, but I somehow managed to end up with a distinction. Wow!! It turns out that my dad had been right after all. If I had learned my schoolwork like I had learned my Jam lyrics, I would have passed with flying colours, proving that if you are given a task in a subject you are interested in, there is a really good chance you will achieve it. At school, I had very little interest in any of the subjects that I had to study, but this didn't mean I was thick, like I had been told. Hopefully, gaining this qualification would help to prove this.

They told me that having a degree could add an extra £10K on to your salary, but it didn't even add an extra 10p onto mine. To be fair, that was never the reason I did it, and I never used it in terms of progression. But the skills I learnt whilst doing the course are ones I can use forever, in life or in a job role.

The day of my King George's Hall graduation arrived, and even though I felt pretty proud of myself, and of Karen and the rest of my colleagues who had also passed, I couldn't help feeling a little out of place wearing that rather silly gown and hat. I asked my mum if she wanted to order a photograph of me receiving my certificate, and was really surprised when she said, 'No, it's okay.' However, she did attend my ceremony, and I am sure she was proud.
The one thing I found to be sad was the fact that my dad was not around to see it, as I don't reckon I did too much to make him proud whilst he was alive. Getting married to Janet and having Emma would have obviously impressed him, but I guess he would

never have believed that I would end up working in education and gaining a degree.

I spent the whole day thinking about how proud he would have been, silly outfit or no silly outfit. But I must admit that the only thing going through my mind when I was called up on stage to receive my award, was that John Lennon had once actually stood on this very stage.

CHAPTER TWENTY-SIX

NOTHING TO LOSE

Who would have known that I would go from standing in front of my mum's mirror at home, with Yvonne's brown and orange Denman hairbrush in my hand, miming to *Sugar Baby Love* by the Rubettes, to one day actually working with one of them. I use the term 'working with' very loosely, as when I started working at college, a real life ex-Rubette was working in the music department. The students used to tell me that he was always harping on about this old band that he used to be in, but to be fair, if I had been going through the streets on the back of a lorry performing *Tonight* from the *Never Too Young to Rock* movie, I myself would be telling anyone who would listen.

Anyone who has ever known me would no doubt tell you that music has always been the main thing in my life (outside family). From my early cassettes of Elvis, discovering The Beatles on holiday with my family, to being a 13-year-old teenager when Punk broke out, and seeing The Jam for the very first time, nothing has given me more pleasure or meant more to me. Hanging around with and taking photographs of local band Faded Image gave me a buzz like nothing else had ever done, knowing I had been in some way part of a music scene, even though it was only on a local level.

Punk and New Wave had broken down all the barriers, showing that you didn't need to sound like Jean-Michel Jarre to be a musician and be in a band. I had learnt from a very young age that my future would not be in singing or playing an instrument, as I was lousy at both. I started a Punk band, Innocent Bystanders, for about ten minutes at school, and even purchased an electric guitar, but I didn't have the balls or confidence back then to give it a proper go.

I think it was around my eighteenth birthday (may have been before) and I had spent months hinting to my mum and dad that I would really love a musical instrument, preferably a guitar, only to wake up on my birthday morning to discover the instrument they had bought me was a small brown recorder. At the risk of sounding ungrateful, I was truly devastated, as it had literally been the least Rock and Roll thing they could have chosen. I am sure it had been impossible for me at the time to fully hide my disappointment, and even when I thanked them, they must have sensed my absolute dislike of this item. I felt so embarrassed that I hid the offending item deep under my bed, but just like the *Mayfair* magazine previously, every time I arrived back home from school it had miraculously re-appeared on top of my bed again. I think the only thing I learnt to play on it was Three Blind Mice, just to show willing, but eventually I found a better hiding place and that was the last I ever saw of it.

When we were younger, I recall my Mum suggesting that Robin and I take up piano lessons, which I flatly declined, thinking it was far too gay. Then Elton John, Billy Joel, and George Michael proved to me that it was actually a cool thing to be able to do, and I have regretted it ever since.

From seeing my first ever live gig, 999, at King George's Hall, Blackburn, I became addicted to watching live music. And since that night, I very rarely went a week without catching some band or artist perform, usually several times a week. I reckon there are two types of concert-goer: those who expect the songs to sound like they do on the record; and those who don't. I fall into the latter bracket. Don't get me wrong. When I used to go and watch acts like Luther Vandross, George Benson, and a lot of the incredible Soul artists of the 80s and 90s, I fully appreciated how professional they were and how every note sounded perfect. But nowadays (even though there is still a place for that) I crave something a little more exciting.

The reason why live music is so popular and can never be replicated is because you are investing in a completely one-off performance by an artist or artists, where anything can potentially happen. And even if mistakes are made during the set, that on its own can add to the excitement, as you were one of the few people to witness it that night, which makes it unique. I mean, if you want it to sound exactly like the record, why don't you just stay in, save your money, and spend the night playing the record?

All, or certainly most of, my pocket money as a kid was spent on vinyl records, and ever since the age of 12, I have had an obsession with the format. I remember the very first time my daughter Emma Leah discovered one in our house and said, 'Daddy what is this? Is it a plate?' Now she is a vinyl-only DJ in Manchester, so I must have had some influence on her, which I buzz off.

Certain musical moments over the years have had a massive impact on me: watching *A Hard Day's Night* for the very first time, and discovering The Beatles; looking at the cover of the Jam's *In The City* album, and thinking they were the coolest band I had ever seen, and the rest is history; witnessing Buzzcocks on *Top of the Pops* performing *Ever Fallen In Love with Someone, You Shouldn't've,* the greatest pop song of all time, in my opinion; and watching the Libertines on Jools Holland for the first time and thinking 'wow' who on earth are they? Then ringing my friend Simon to ask if he had just seen what I had seen.

I guess my passion started off like a lot of people's as a part of growing up, by sneaking a small transistor radio under your pillow at night in an attempt to listen to the wonderful Radio Luxembourg once the lights had gone out. Barry Biggs' 'Side Show' always springs to mind, but I would fall asleep most nights whilst getting my nightly music fix over the airwaves.

In 1999, I was shopping for some holiday clothes in Leeds with Janet, when I heard that Blackburn Legends The Stiffs were playing a reunion gig that night at Cob Wall Working Men's Club on Daisy Lane, only two minutes away from where we were living. As soon as I heard, I decided I was definitely going and was unbelievably excited, as it was the original line-up who would be performing. I didn't know the band personally, but I certainly knew all their songs, being a local success story who signed to EMI in 1979. The gig was absolutely brilliant, and I knew a lot of the people attending. Blackburn band, Boredom, were the support, and I remember spending most of the night pogoing around the dancefloor with Dave and Colin from The Itch.

The promoter who put the event on was a local lad done good, Alan Parker, who I sort of knew from the time he worked in 'Our Price' in town. Alan, who was originally from Mill Hill, had been involved in music from a very early age, predominantly the Punk scene, and he had made the deal for them to release a live CD before the actual gig was booked, having already sorted a Stiffs' Best of CD, courtesy of Captain Oi records. Initially, Alan wanted to put the gig on at King George's Hall, but the venue was booked solid. It was his dad who suggested Cob Wall, as he knew the Concert Secretary, so the venue was booked.

I arrived to find folk queueing all the way around the building, and the anticipation for the show was electric. Up until this point, it had never entered my head that I could put a gig on or have anything at all to do with working in the industry, as I had always considered it to be out of bounds. I don't know exactly what it was about that night, but I remember gazing over at Alan as he was standing at the bar and thinking, *God, I wish I had put this gig on*. The gig was recorded, and around 16 months later EMI officially released the live album.

I recently explained to Alan that it had been this event, and that moment, that kick-started my idea/belief of actually putting on events for myself. And the fact that it was at Cob Wall Club helped it to seem possible. He told me that he was really chuffed and flattered that it had been that evening that had started me off, which was nice.

As far as line-ups go, it really does need to be the original line-up for me, where possible. It is fair to say that I am not a big fan of cover bands or tribute bands, with the exception of The Bootleg Beatles, especially if the original band is still around. I always wonder why on earth folk would not just pay a little bit extra and go and watch the actual act. Having said all this, I guess it was pretty ironic that it was in fact a tribute act that led me to booking my very first gig.

Each year, Blackburn Council would stage an event called Arts in the Park, for the good folk of this town. It was a family-friendly arts and music festival which started off at Corporation Park (where most folk preferred it), and then moved to Witton Park, due to less neighbours complaining and having car park facilities. In 2004, I took my video camera along to capture all the highlights from the day's event, and I had just read that a Blondie tribute act was about to perform on the stage I was standing on. I was about to walk off when Colin from The Itch told me that it was in fact Phil Hendrik's wife Michelle who was playing the part of Debbie Harry in their band Blondied.

Phil was the front man of The Stiffs and was also playing guitar for his wife in the band, so I decided to watch them for a couple of songs. To my surprise, they were actually really good, and Michelle not only looked like her but also sounded like Debbie Harry when talking between songs. I was enjoying it so much that I ended up hanging around for their whole set, and even filmed a number of songs. I introduced myself after the gig and told Michelle that I would send her any footage I had taken, once I had edited it. I kept to my word and Michelle was happy with it. She invited me along to a video shoot that she and Phil were involved with, which was being shot at the old Blackburn Sawmill up near Tesco.

I asked my friend, Martin (from Unilab) if he fancied coming along, and we both booked the day off work. When we eventually found the right building, we realised that wearing one coat was not enough – it was absolutely freezing. It had snowed for most of the morning, and the snow was blowing in through the broken windows. The band was made up of several other musicians from the Punk era: Phil and Tommy represented The Stiffs; Dave Philp was the frontman from The Automatics; Michelle helped with the vocals; and Ricky Rocket used to be the drummer in Sham 69.

Like with any video shoots, it took hours and hours before everyone was happy with the footage, and even thought it was the coldest I had ever been in the name of Rock and Roll (after The Jam coach journey, that is), we put up with the temperature and had a really fantastic day. I had never met Dave before, as he lived in L.A, but I thought he was highly talented, as we had witnessed him making song parts up on the spot.

Another great thing about the day was that I actually got to know Phil, and in between takes I asked him what the chances were of getting The Stiffs back together and allowing me to put them on a local gig. Phil told me that there was no chance of my idea happening, as he and the lead guitarist had not spoken to each other for years. I knew there had to have been a pretty big reason, so I decided to drop it at the time.

Not being one to give up, though, I planned to bring the subject up again at a later date. I mean, they had been lifelong friends, so you never know. On the occasions when I chatted to Phil over the next few months, I always managed to drop it into our conversation, but the circumstances were still the same, and so was the answer.
I appreciate the idea had been pretty corny at the time, and I had nicked the concept from V.H.1' s Bands Reunited programme, but I found the record sleeve from their *Goodbye My Love* single, and each time I saw a member of the band, I pitched my idea of a gig. Once they agreed to play it, in principle, I asked them to sign the

cover, knowing that if I ever managed to secure all four signatures on their own front cover, the gig would be happening.

I had Phil's, Tommy's, and Big John's, but Strang's was the missing link of my jigsaw, and not knowing him personally limited my options. A few months later, I was due to film The Wasted Punk Festival in Morecambe, and we had just parked up on the nearest car park to the event, when Phil, who was playing, spotted me and came over. He said, 'I have some good news for you, Pete. I was on the phone to Strang last night.' This news was just what I had been waiting to hear, and my mind started running overtime, trying to work out how I was going to make it happen.

At last, my plan had come together, and I managed to get all four signatures written on my record sleeve, even though Strang must have thought I was some sort of weirdo.

I had never put an event on before this, and decided to call Steve Stanley, who had been programming mainly Punk gigs at King George's Hall for years. Steve was based in Grimsby, but his Solid Entertainments company had put on events throughout the country. I asked him if he would be interested if I managed to get The Stiffs back together again. And due to the band's brush with success in the late 70s, he confirmed he was very interested.

Steve had all the contacts and the knowledge to make this show happen, but he told me it was my gig, and it was down to me who I would choose for the line-up. Dave Philp (Automatics) actually lived at Beverly Hills 90210, but offered to pay his own fare in order to come over and play for the event. Phil told me that he would like his pals, Fast Cars from Manchester, to have a slot, so this left me with one more act to book.

Another local band that had certainly made their mark on the music scene from when they formed in 1999 were Tompaulin. Jamie, their front person, had been the media tutor from college, and when I told him about the gig, he recommended a young Punk band from Acton in London, called Dustin's Bar Mitzvah. He told me they had been on the same record label, and felt they would be right up my street. Even though it was the maddest band name I'd ever heard, Jamie's judgement was correct. I played the demo CD he gave me and was properly impressed, so now I had my full line-up booked in.

The date of my first ever gig was November 11th, 2005, at King George's Hall, Blackburn, and I had spent months trying to sell tickets to everyone I knew or bumped into. I sorted out the posters and then flyers, which Strang designed, and the band had held practice sessions every week in a shed at the bottom of their friend Bob's garden in Billinge. But with Phil living in Lincolnshire, the rest of the band had to rehearse without their front man up until the night before the show.

The night of the gig finally arrived, and I was incredibly relieved that the Windsor Suite had started to fill with people excited to see the overdue return of their local power pop, Punk heroes, The Stiffs. Fast Cars did a great job, but I still hadn't heard from Dustins, who were due on next. The plan had been for all the acts to do a soundcheck before we started to allow the public into the venue, but the problem was that Dustins had failed to turn up for theirs. And when I chased them up, their manager told me they were stuck in traffic near Birmingham, which started me panicking.

The band was now due on stage in less than 15 minutes, and I had heard nothing at all from them for over an hour. I was really worried, but with literally minutes to go before they were due on, they burst into the room. And before they even introduced themselves, they barraged me with requests regarding where their beer rider was, even though it was obvious that another beer was the last thing they needed. If I was to be honest, their set was pretty chaotic, to say the least. Their frontman, Dave Laser (what a name), spent a large part of their set debating with the audience about his flatmate, and by the time he managed to break the third string on his guitar, they had to call it a day, as he couldn't carry on without a guitar.

As they were walking back to the dressing room, no doubt to search for the rest of their rider, Dave turned to me and asked me if they had played a particular song. He had been literally that much out of his head at the time that he hadn't a clue what songs he had just performed. At that point, it is fair to say that at least 98% of the audience thought it was one of the worst performances by a band that they had ever witnessed. I, on the other hand, had just found my new favourite group. I can't really speak for anyone else, and maybe more had actually enjoyed it, but me, Strang, and my friend Sarah, had bloody loved it, and we were already looking forward to watching them again. Cheers, Jamie.

I was backstage with The Stiffs boys making sure everything was okay, when literally a couple of minutes before they were due on, Phil asked me if I would like to introduce them on stage. I was flattered by his suggestion, and even though I didn't have a pre-planned speech, I felt it was an honour. So I just went out onto the stage and gave it my best shot at trying to big them up, and make sure the crowd were up for it.

I have always loved the part of a live gig just before the band you have come to watch takes to the stage. The main lights are turned off, the smoke machine kicks in, covering the drum kit, the amps, and monitor in dry ice, the whole audience (on the whole) stops talking, they turn to look at the front and start to cheer, clap, and chant in anticipation that they are about to see their musical heroes for the umpteenth time – or maybe the first. Naturally, the band like to keep their public waiting, but as soon as the manager or guitar tech peers from around the curtains and has deemed there are enough people in, he lifts his hand to signal to the grumpy git behind the sound desk… and it's showtime.

The Stiffs appeared on stage to the cheers of the audience, and I had already jumped off the stage into the crowd just before their opening song, *Volume Control. Let's Activate* was next, and then my personal favourite, *Nothing to Lose*. After belting out seven of their songs, they then welcomed their special guest from L.A., who treated us to a mixture of Automatic tunes and ones from his solo catalogue. Then the Stiff boys were back on stage with another seven fast-paced bangers, ending the night's proceedings with the fans favourite, *DC R.I.P.* (apparently, about a former teacher of theirs at QEGS, who had passed away) and then finally, Mr John Peel's favourite, *Inside Out*.

As I had been loving every minute, the gig seemed to fly by, and eventually everyone began making their way out of the hall, hot and sweaty, but most importantly looking like they'd had a thoroughly good time. I shook a few hands and thanked them for coming, made sure I grabbed a copy of the set list taped to the stage, and rushed backstage to pat the band on the back and to tell them how wonderful they had been. That is what you are supposed to do, but this time I really meant it.

I was proper buzzing that I had managed to carry it off, and even though I had passed the event over to Solid Entertainments, it had been me who'd had the initial idea, booked all the acts, sorted out all the promo, and sold most of the tickets. So I was feeling pretty proud with myself. The only downside from the event was when I handed the fruits of my labour over to Steve the Promoter.
Even though this had never been about making any money for me, the gig was the venue's third most successful show that year in the Windsor suite, and after I had put in all the graft in order to make it happen, to hand over all of the cash was a hard lesson to learn.
Yes, I had been naïve, and no, I wouldn't do that again, but I had got my first gig under my belt and already had a craving to put on my second (learning from this). So the 11th November, 2005 will always mean a lot to me. After all, on that occasion I had nothing to lose.

CHAPTER TWENTY-SEVEN

NOT VERY SOUND

In the media department at college, we were lucky enough to have the use of a professional TV studio right next door to the classroom, and from time to time, the media tutor Jamie invited musicians and bands into the studio to perform a live set. The media students would all work in the session and carry out the roles like camera work, editing, and floor manager, to give themselves experience. The selling point for the band or artist – apart from helping the students – was that they would end up with a free, professionally edited video of their session.

The day after Dustins appeared on The Stiffs line-up, they were booked to play one of these sessions. What I don't believe Jamie had in fact realised at the time of booking them in, was that it was the College Open Day, where parents, students, staff, and the public were welcomed in to have a look around the campus. So, having a Punk band in from Acton at the same time might not have been the best of moves.

It had been explained to the band that no alcohol would be allowed, but true to form they refused to go into the studio unless they were given lager. They had also been asked not to swear, which obviously they ignored. I was lucky enough to be in the studio for this session and absolutely loved it. At one point, the College Principal showed his face and seemed to be okay with how things were going, but to be fair he only hung around for a couple of minutes, which is just as well. My love affair with Dustins was blossoming, as I had found them to be chaotic, edgy, exciting, in your face, and you never knew what was about to happen next. A proper band.

My musical contact list was growing, and a lot of it was down to my camcorder and the filming I had been doing. The more bands that I filmed, the more doors started to open. I had started off just filming local gigs as a way of getting to know the band and getting my name out there. Then to my delight, I found the acts getting bigger and bigger.

When Buzzcocks played our local Darwen Live Festival, I managed to film the majority of their set, despite being in the middle of a drunken crowd who were bouncing up and down. I uploaded a couple of clips to my YouTube channel and received an email from their drummer Phil, asking me if he could have a copy. Initially, he messaged me asking if I had permission to film the band, but a few sentences below he made out that he was only joking, and told me the band had loved Bootlegs, as they had played a pretty big part in their career.

Buzzcocks have always been my third favourite band of all time, and even though it was not the original line-up, to get the chance to meet Pete and Steve was too good an opportunity to turn down. Phil asked if I fancied filming the band at their upcoming Scottish gig, performing at the Wickerman Festival. I had never had the pleasure of visiting Scotland before, so what better time for me to find out if it really was bonny?

I asked my friend Birchy if he fancied a road trip north of the border, and to my surprise and delight, he accepted my offer. I looked on the internet to book us into a hotel for the night, as near to the festival site as possible. And even though I called them to check the location and was told it was around 20 minutes away, we discovered when we arrived that it was bloody miles away. The festival itself was held in a field in Dumfries and Galloway, but the hotel we were staying in was in East Kirkcarswell.

As we were setting off that morning, the sun was shining in Blackburn. So, me being me, I didn't feel the need to take a jacket. That would have been fine, apart from the fact that it was absolutely throwing it down by the time we found the field – one of the worst storms I had ever seen. Birchy offered to lend me his spare jacket, and even though I was in no position to turn him down, I did resemble Norman Wisdom wearing it, as it was about three sizes too small.

We were slightly late making our way to the site and fighting the elements, but to my surprise, Phil, (Buzzcocks drummer) had been waiting for us at the side of the stage with our AAA passes. I had only ever really filmed local bands before, so being in the pit at the front of the main stage, filming one of my favourite bands, was an absolute buzz – no pun intended.

Little did I know at the time that my involvement with the band, and also the festival, was only just beginning.

I sent the edited DVD out to Phil, and he was happy with it, which led him to inviting me to film the band again. I ended up filming Buzzcocks' gigs for the next few years, and it was an absolute pleasure to sort of get to know them. Pete Shelley and Steve Diggle had been the originals in the band, and to find myself backstage after the gig and invited to their after-show parties was amazing, particularly when I look back at that incredible moment when I had seen them on *Top of the Pops*, and the effect it had on me.

When I started my first Club night 'Punks Reunited', folk would say to me, 'You must know Punk Julie.' But I didn't. Julie had been a well-known local Punk from back in the day, but with me not fully subscribing to the Punk scene, our paths had not crossed. Through Punks Reunited I got to know her, and she would be ever-present at the backstage parties after a Buzzcocks' show.

I learnt where Steve's saying 'No Moet, No Showie' had come from, as you very rarely found him without a bottle of Moet Chandon in his hand. And basically, if the promoter did not provide him with a number of bottles of his favourite tipple on the band's rider, they would not be performing.

Backstage was like a small community. No matter where you would travel to see them, the same chosen fans would be granted access to their aftershows.

As for the Wickerman Festival, Sid the organiser had been giving a talk at a music conference at The Ruby Lounge in Manchester, and was explaining to the listening crowd that festivals and events like that would not happen without a large number of people volunteering and giving their time up for free to help make it happen. I was with my brother-in-law Warren, and he suggested that I should go and offer my services as a videographer. And when Sid finished speaking, Warren encouraged me to go over and have a word. I explained to Sid that if they ever needed somebody to do the filming for them, then I was happy to offer my services and volunteer. I didn't think for one second that I would ever hear from him again, but like the saying goes, 'If you don't ask, you don't get.' To my astonishment, about a week later he called and offered me the role.

My love affair with Wickerman had started, and I was over the moon to be visiting a field in Scotland again, but next time I would be taking my own jacket (learning from past mistakes).

Even though I had been volunteering, the festival contributed towards my expenses for the weekend in Dumfries, as by then I had invested £2000 in a new, professional video camera, and there was no way I was about to sleep in a tent with it.

So, every July, me and a couple of mates would book into our usual hotel in East Kirkcarswell, and basically, I would be running up and down a field for two days, trying to capture a bit of all the performances on all the different stages, while my mates would just chill out on the grass, drinking beer and loving every minute. And to be fair, even though I was working hard, so did I.

I loved the fact that all the press who were next to me in the pit would generally only have permission to film or take photographs of the standard first three songs, and then be thrown out, leaving me to film what I wanted, as I worked for the festival and my AAA pass was my passport to stay.

Even with the right authority, I must admit it was still a mission trying to get backstage sometimes, depending on which security person was on the gate at the time. The year that Gary Newman headlined, I had never seen as many photographers in the pit in my life. And even though my job was to make the official video for the event, the press did not care who I was, and I was getting knocked all over the place while folk scrambled to get the best shots. But at least by the fourth song, I had the last laugh.

The night before, KT Tunstall had headlined, but we had been told that under no circumstances was anyone allowed to take any photographs of her, which was a new one on me. And even though the pit was empty for her performance, how on earth were they going to stop people in the crowd from taking terrible quality photos of her on their phones?

One year, I was excited to film the Human League from the front of stage, and even though Phil Oakey had lost his trademark lopsided haircut and was now fully bald, and Joanne and Susan (close up) more resembled the Liver Birds than the two young girls out of the *Don't You Want Me?* video, the band sounded brilliant. And Philip might have lost his hair, but his voice sounded as good as ever.

On the Saturday night around 11.45pm, all the music would stop on the various stages, and everyone would make their way over to the top field where a giant Wickerman statue would be set on fire, followed by a fireworks display. It was magic.

Once everything had burnt out, the stages all started up again, which was usually our cue to try our best to flag a taxi down, in order to return to our hotel bar in time for a nightcap.

On Friday, 15th April, 2005, me and Waker put on our first Punk's Reunited event at Blackburn Rugby Club, and the night was a huge success. The idea was to capitalise on people's love of nostalgia, and to basically play the records we had loved and bought growing up. I felt we put in the effort to attempt to make the room look authentic, and even though looking back now it was a little cheesy and not what I am into now, folk seemed to love it, and It was great seeing so many familiar faces from back in the day.

I was starting to acquire a little more confidence with each event, and I got an absolute buzz out of planning and organising an evening of entertainment and being able to fill a room with people simply letting their hair down and having a good time. I was also doing more and more filming and loved the whole process of producing a DVD, which would usually lead me to picking up more contacts and opening new doors for me, in terms of music.

They say a photograph never lies, but when you are editing video footage, folk only see the bits that you want them to see. I really loved the editing process and would sit in my office at home every opportunity I could find, spending hours going through all my footage. This was the very first time I had ever felt remotely creative, and I would take great pleasure out of creating the final product.

Each year Wickerman would ask me back, Birchy would usually drive, and I would also ask another mate along, depending on who was available and up for it. Spending that weekend in Scotland every July with a couple of chosen friends was really special, and it was the first thing I would put in my diary ever year, to make sure I didn't double book. My friends would always love the weekend away, but once we arrived home, I felt the pressure of having to produce a promotional video of the whole weekend and cutting hours' worth of footage down to about three minutes. Also, being honest, I felt they were very hard to please, which was fair enough, and it would always take me several attempts before the main man Jamie was happy with it.

I don't reckon I was a great filmmaker; I was just okay. But I was cheap, which had always gone in my favour. The one thing I have always been proud of is the ability to hold a camera still while filming, and it actually winds me up when I see other people at gigs, moving their hands up and down, as it is obvious the footage will end up being naff.

Even though I had no doubt that Sid had offered me the role based on how cheap I was, and not because I had necessarily been the best candidate, I managed to get my footage on the Discovery Channel in America, and in the UK. I received a phone call from their producer, who told me they were making a programme on ancient methods of torture and murder (nice) and needed some footage of a burning Wickerman, which I had. Naturally, I sent it to them, and it was surreal watching my name go up in the end credits, once the programme aired.

I also ended up with my promo footage being used on a primetime slot advert on ITV, for Visit Scotland. Fair enough, it only lasted about 19 seconds in total, but I managed to see it several times and was over the moon.

A similar thing also happened to me with The Selecter and Pauline Black, as with me filming Buzzcocks. When The Selecter performed at the festival, I happened to film their entire set, and the next time I went to watch them, I gave Pauline Black a copy of the DVD I had made. Sometime after, and out of the blue, I received a call from her, thanking me for the footage and giving me her contact details.
When Pauline called my mobile, I happened to be sitting on the toilet at the time (too much info, I know), and my dilemma was whether I should offer to call her back or just carry on chatting as though everything was normal. It just didn't feel right having a deep conversation with the Two-Tone legend, whilst sitting on the loo.

Pauline invited me to go and watch her perform at a jazz festival in Nantwich, and I offered to film her set. A friend of a friend had accepted my invitation to come along, and insisted on recording the sound for me, as he had the right equipment. Pauline was marvellous and sang from the back catalogue of Nina Simone and Billie Holiday. I spent extra time on editing the footage, making sure I gave it my best shot, hoping not to disappoint. About a month after the show, I received an email from her, saying that she was confused about the invoice I had sent her, as I had told her that there would be no charge.

I ended up having a phone conversation with her, to try and get my head around what had happened. It turned out that the lad who had recorded it for me, along with his mate, had tried to pull a fast one and sent her a bill for over £300. I was absolutely furious that somebody I knew had gone behind my back to try and con Pauline out of some money, and I did everything I could to try and convince her that I had known nothing at all about it. Pauline didn't know me well enough to realise that this was not my style, and that money was never my motivation when offering to film something.

To my relief, she believed that the mystery invoice had been nothing at all to do with me, and when I did question my so-called friend about the incident, he tried his upmost to blame it all on his own mate, making out he had known nothing about it. This was clearly nonsense, and we have never spoken since.

CHAPTER TWENTY-EIGHT

A CERTAIN BAND

If you happen to Google what your role would include as a band manager, it will highlight four key areas that you need to be successful: one, a babysitter; two, a mediator; three, an interrogator; and four, a shrink. I was about to find out how true these observations were, even though managing a band had never been on my agenda.

In 2006, I noticed a feature in our local paper about a young local band called The Torrents, who had just started out. When I read that their influences were The Beatles, The Jam, and The Libertines, I knew that I had to check them out.

The first time I went to watch them live was at King George's Hall, and I knew from the very first note they played that they were right up my street. Fast-paced Rock and Roll with bags of attitude, decent tunes, and a splendid set of haircuts; I knew I would be going to watch them again.

This band really made an impression on me, and I found them to be a breath of fresh air. At their second gig at Marigolds in Darwen, I noticed what a good following they had, and that everyone at the front was singing along to the lyrics, which was impressive. After their set, I recall chatting to their bass player Joss and asking if they had any flyers to promote their upcoming shows, and was really surprised when he told me 'no'. I explained to him that while they had a room full of people who liked them, there would be no better time to promote their upcoming gigs, and Joss agreed. I think he made a comment along the lines of 'You should be our manager', which I felt really flattered by, but didn't know if he was serious or not, so simply laughed it off.

Joss had clearly been serious about his request, as he asked me again after their next gig, but this time he had asked all the other members, too. The band members had all agreed, but when he asked their lead singer Neal, he half-heartedly mumbled 'yeah'. I did not really know how to take it at the time, but the more I got to know Neal, I realised it was something he would never have asked me himself, even if he had wanted me to.

I really appreciated Joss's request, but managing a band had never featured on my radar. Not wanting to sound ungrateful, I simply thanked him and agreed to give it some thought. The following morning, I remember lying in bed considering his request, and debating with myself what I could actually bring to the table. I guessed it would be better to give it a go and fail than not to try and always wonder. After all, I was loyal, trustworthy, I loved live music, and more importantly, I believed in them as a band.

I came up with the idea of asking my brother-in-law Warren if he fancied coming along for the ride, feeling that having someone to share the experience with me would be better than doing it on my own. I told the band that we didn't want any money, as there was no money coming in, and that it was our job to prove our worth after all.

I was now joint manager of a band and it felt great. Janet and Emma agreed to back me, and we told the band to concentrate on what they did best, writing songs and performing, while we would sort out the rest.

Our very first gig in charge was at The Cavern, on Wednesday, 6th June, 2007, and because we had sold the most tickets, we were given the headline slot out of six bands. That was how venues worked it back then (and probably still do) with emerging bands. You were told you needed to sell as many tickets as you could, and despite who was the better band, the one who sold the most tickets would go on last. As it happened, we managed to put on a coach from Blackburn, and it felt pretty special getting dropped off at the end of Matthew Street and carrying all our equipment down to the world-famous venue.

Once the gear had been dropped off, we all hit the nearby pubs to grab a few beers and to chill out before the gig. I was asked to call back to the venue a little later so they could let me know our stage time, and to find out if we were having a soundcheck or not.

I remember standing outside The Cavern around 7pm and giving my brother a call to see if he had any news. After years of thinking that they couldn't have a baby, my brother Robin and his wife Fiona had found themselves expecting, and the baby was due on this very day. I knew it was good news, as Robin answered in a really good mood, and he was delighted to announce that at 5.26pm on 06.06.07, Matthew George Eastwood had entered the world. It was fantastic news, and only added to the night's excitement for me.

We eventually managed to drag the band away from the pub, as I felt that it was only right to go and show some support to the other bands on the bill, hoping they would reciprocate for us. By the time we walked onto the stage, the room was pretty busy. I was nervous, but buzzing at the same time, watching The Torrents from Blackburn racing through their short set list of tunes. After the gig, the band put all their efforts into attempting to carve their names into the dressing room wall, and I just sat there thinking about all the amazing acts who had done the same before them.

During some of our early gigs I dragged a few of my mates along, knowing that they weren't really their thing, but in order to make up the numbers. All I tended to hear from them (especially Bullinge) was that they couldn't hear a word the band were singing. And it didn't matter how many times I tried to explain the difference between a lead singer and a frontman, it would always fall on deaf ears.

On stage, Neal would come across as if he had an ego the size of Peru, and to be fair, sometimes he did. But the more I had got to know him, the more I realised it was mainly a front, and deep down I never believed he had enough confidence in himself, even though I did.

The coach journeys back from a gig were always mental. The beers would come out, the poppers would also appear (proper hard core), and with the band still being on a high, it was fair to say that our coach drivers would have to put up with a lot. While the band were jumping up and down the bus on our way back from The Cavern, I asked Neal what the tape was that the coach driver had been playing for him. That night he introduced me to The Cribs from Wakefield, and they have been my favourite current band ever since, so I am indebted to him.

I never realised until I worked in education that I suffered from OCD. Linda gave me an online test for a laugh, and the results – based on my honest answers – indicated that it was certainly an issue. What this meant with me managing a band is that it was all or nothing. I would spend the majority of my working day (and night) striving to find them new opportunities, without ever switching off, which is never a good thing.

Looking back, my family put up with a lot, as I couldn't just do half measures. The main plan was to record the three songs they were most proud of, in order to have a product for us to promote. Mark Jones in Ossy was our chosen Producer, so we all ascended on Dudley Avenue, with the mission of recording a demo CD.

Several weeks before, Neal had called into my office at college and told me he had come up with an idea for a song, entitled *A Certain Girl*. These were the days of Myspace, and he had been inspired by a skinhead girl's profile of the same name. I remembered a student telling me about this new social media platform, where you could have your own profile page. It ended up being a really important tool for the music industry, as every band or artist at the time used it to make their own page, to promote their own music, and to help get their name out there. Previous to this, it was unthinkable to attempt to contact a group or musician direct, other than through their fan club. But with Myspace, a lot of the artists actually ran their own websites themselves, and would sometimes reply directly if you bothered to get in touch with them. This really was a game changer in my opinion, and for the first time it attempted to break down the barriers that had always existed between artists and their fans. People on Myspace would be judged by how many 'friends' they had on their page, and I think Lily Allen bagged herself a record deal by the fact she had been one of the first people to have 100,000.

The band decided to record a free demo CD that we could give out at gigs and I could post out to folk, in order to get their music out there. There was always an argument at the time as to whether or not we should release it and charge for a copy, or whether to simply hand it out for free to as many people as seemed interested. I agreed to back them with whatever they decided. The reality was at that stage the only folk likely to pay for a copy would be family and friends, and some of those were so tight they would have expected to be given a free copy anyway. Whereas we could produce hundreds of copies for very little cost and get them out there to all the relevant people, so that is what we did.

Arctic Monkeys were discovered when some of their fans uploaded their demos online, without the band even knowing. The word spread, and the rest is history. It also helped, I have to say, that their tunes were pretty amazing in the first place, but there was no doubt that the online demos certainly speeded things up.

Our time in Mark's studio was thoroughly enjoyable and was a marvellous experience for me. Mark did a superb job, and everybody really liked him, which always helps. The tracks we ended up recording, were *A Certain Girl*, *Red Brick Town*, and the song they'd had before my involvement, *Czechoslovakia*. The session was a triumph, and I was proud to represent and promote the product. Night after night I would spend hours in my office at home, producing copy after copy, so that we could give them out to anyone who wanted one, and even to some folk who didn't.

As for the artwork, which everyone had agreed was important, we had a band meeting to discuss the options and everyone's ideas. I mentioned the fact that every single Beatles record for the first five years had featured a photo of the band on the cover, and Joss highlighted how important branding was for a product, so we all ended up siding with him.
The front cover consisted of a black background with a large red megaphone taking up around ¾ of the cover. Underneath was written The Torrents, and that was it. I really had to push to get them to agree to have their photos on the back, as they weren't overly keen, but I explained that a good set of haircuts like theirs deserved to be out there. And eventually, I got my way.

My friend Sarah obliged with a photoshoot, which happened to be against a red brick wall at Roe Lee, and the band had their first ever product. What surprised me about Neal was that as soon as the recording was finished and mastered, that was it. He wasn't even interested in taking the product home and was ready to move on to the next thing. I had to talk him into having a couple of copies, even if only for his family, but at the end of the day it was my job and Warren's to actually get it out there, so I guess it was fair enough.

Jiffy bags were purchased, and I researched a list of all the relevant people to target, promoters, venues, DJs, radio stations, contacts, record labels, Myspace fans – you name it, I made sure they all received a copy.

If you were fortunate, or unfortunate, enough to bump into me on the street or at the bus stop, you would find yourself being the proud owner of the new mint CD by The Torrents from Blackburn. Some even appeared for sale via eBay, which amazed me.

I attempted to get us a gig at every live venue I could for bands that were classed as emerging; some I was successful with, others simply told me they would think about it. The band performed at The Attic in Accrington, along with Franky's Bar and Marigolds in Darwen, King George's Hall and The Cellar Bar in Blackburn, but our favourite venue we played at, and the place that had the most impact on the band up until then, was Night and Day Café in Manchester. I had bigged the boys up to their promoter Richard and was offered a slot on Saturday, 15th December. Again, we put on a coach, but I learned the hard way how unreliable folk can be. Several friends who had said they were coming, either called me at the last minute with an excuse, or simply just didn't turn up, leaving me with the stress of still trying to find the driver's fee, as he still needed to be paid.

The gig did not have the best of starts, as Neal had done his usual by upsetting the majority of the audience with derogatory comments regarding their local hero Liam Fray. But the set itself went down really well, and I was confident we had picked up some extra fans, which was what it was all about.

After the gig, the promoter asked if he could have a word with me just inside the entrance. He told me that he had enjoyed the set and thought they were a decent band, but asked if I realised that Liam Fray was a good friend of theirs and didn't think it a wise move to slag him off at the venue. Neal had not directly slagged him off, as he was merely quoting some graffiti he claimed to have read on the toilet wall. But as I had no desire to annoy Richard, I said I was sorry if folk had been upset but explained I hadn't written Neal's speeches for him.

Standing outside on Oldham Street getting some fresh air, I was approached by some guy called Dan, who said he was impressed by the band and that he was the producer of the local TV station

Channel M, whose programme City Centre Social had featured the likes of Everything Everything, Twisted Wheel, and Django, Django. He offered The Torrents a slot on the show, which was beyond exciting, and the band were buzzing once I told them about it.

Dan and I had swapped contacts, and he said he would be in touch. And even though they had managed to upset any Courteeners fans that were in the room, the trip to Manchester had been extremely fruitful and well worth the effort.

Just when I thought the week couldn't get any better, I received a phone call that was a real game changer for the band. I had been about to leave my office at college one Friday afternoon, when my mobile rang. The voice on the other end told me he had been Steve Lamacq's Producer on 6 Music, and that Steve really liked our CD. He said Steve had chosen us to be his Unsigned Band of the Week, and that he wanted to interview one of the members that evening, live on the radio. No words could describe how excited I was; I really was over the moon. Steve had been my favourite ever DJ (after John Peel, of course) and 6 Music my favourite radio station and the only one I would listen to. I can honestly say that out of every CD I sent out, Steve would have been my first choice to be impressed by what he had heard, and to get in touch.
I couldn't lock the office up fast enough, and all I could think about was calling up each of the band and sharing this incredible news with them. One by one I attempted to call them, and one by one they were engaged. I tried constantly to try and break the news to them, but nobody was answering, which started to stress me out. There was no way we could miss this opportunity of being interviewed on our favourite show.

Eventually I managed to speak to each member, and the people standing next to me at the bus stop on Penny Street must have thought I was crazy, as they witnessed my very enthusiastic telephone conversations. It's fair to say the band were impressed by my latest good news. Naturally, Neal did the interview with

Steve, and he told me he was so nervous at the time that he had to lie down on his settee at home throughout the chat.

One of the really positive feedbacks I received from folk to whom I posted our CD was The Selecter's Pauline Black, who messaged me saying that *A Certain Girl* was the best song she'd heard in a long time. I insisted that the quote, along with some others, was included with the CD, and Steve told Neal on the radio that at first he had been drawn towards the cover art with the red megaphone, then by the fact they had a nice set of haircuts (essential), and finally the Pauline Black quote had caught his attention and persuaded him to play it.

Steve very kindly gave the song its first 6 Music Airplay, alongside the likes of XTC, Richard Hawley, and Lilly Allen, so we were certainly in good company.

The Torrents' name was starting to get out there, and even I was surprised by the impact that Mr Lamacq's endorsement had on the band. I obviously dropped it into every conversation that we had been 6 Music's Band of the Week, and promoters who had previously hummed and haahed about offering us a gig, suddenly told me to pick a date for when we wanted to headline.

Not being one to do barriers, I called up Fred Perry's head office in London and told them I had been managing the coolest band since the Arctic Monkeys, and asked if they were interested in sponsoring us. They told me that they didn't usually sponsor a band, but if I sent them a promotional pack containing their music and a few photos of the boys, and if they liked what they saw and heard, then they might consider endorsing us.

Sarah was called on again to carry out another photoshoot, and because they wore Fred Perry anyway, they weren't trying to be someone that they were not. My confidence and proactiveness paid off, as they were so impressed by what I had sent them that they invited us down to their head office in London. To complement our trip and justify the very long journey, I did the same with the Merc shop on Carnaby Street, and managed to sort out a gig at the Water Rats venue. All the usual suspects who were in attendance at most of our gigs – Jo, Lucy, Kerry, John, and Joss's girlfriend Rachel – boarded the minibus, and all seemed excited about our latest adventure to the big smoke.

Haircuts fresh, and feeling like it was Christmas Day again, the band, me, and Warren arrived at Fred Perry's offices, which were more than impressive, with the brand's history plastered all over the walls, from tennis rackets to photographs of all their iconic endorsements throughout the years. We were greeted by this goddess named Natalia, who proceeded to walk us over to their main shop in Covent Garden. She told us we could have two items each (including band management), and invited us to just take our time looking around the store and to simply help ourselves if we saw anything we fancied (which didn't include her – to the band's disappointment).

I took great pleasure in watching Neal, Joss, Austin, and Swanny scrutinising all the garments really carefully, and witnessing the looks upon their faces as they walked in and out of the dressing rooms, their hands full of their individually chosen gear, knowing that I had made it happen with simply a phone call and a whole lot of belief.

Eventually, our new wardrobes had been chosen, and Natalia explained that she would arrange for them to be posted out to us. So we thanked her for everything, and headed off to Carnaby Street to do the same thing at the Merc Store.

My mate Simon met up with us for the Water Rats gig, along with ex-Mill Hill promoter of that Cob Wall Stiffs reunion, Alan Parker, who insisted on taking me to a private members' drinking club in the West End before the show.

Our first London gig was decent, and for once, instead of alienating all the audience like he usually did, Neal gave his usual introduction, 'We are The Torrents from Blackburn', and proceeded to drop into the conversation between songs that we had just been chosen as Steve Lamacq's Band of the Week, which was much more effective.

The set went down pretty well, and it was nice to finally meet our new Myspace friend Shona (Whattsie). But after a long day of happenings, the one thing I was not looking forward to was the very long journey back up North.

One of the venues I had not managed to get a gig at was The Castle in Oldham, but when I called up their main guy Steve with our Lamacq news, we agreed on a date for us to headline. Like a lot of renowned venues at the time, it was reasonably small, but with the likes of Kasabian and the Inspiral Carpets performing at the place previously, it had built up a reputation, so we were more than happy to be playing there.

The gig was brilliant, helped by the quality of the sound, which Steve had a reputation for. After the set, the band were surrounded by a group of girls asking for either an autograph or a kiss, or in Neal's case, both. I was standing at the back of the venue with Warren, feeling like a proud dad, taking pleasure out of the fact that things just kept getting better on a weekly basis, and that the hard work seemed to be paying off.

Because I worked on the cause 24/7, I took it personally when gigs didn't go well, and found myself in the horrible position of observing our audiences' every move during our set. If they were bobbing their heads, I noticed it; if three people left the venue, I assumed they had not liked the band. I never considered that they might just have had somewhere to go, and might have been leaving anyway, even if they had been impressed. This was emotionally draining for me, and I knew I would have to learn to chill out more during our shows and to avoid taking things so personally.

Two things also happened in the band that I found really difficult to deal with, but as their manager, I knew that nobody else was going to. The first had apparently been coming for a while, and it was brought to my attention that maybe Swanny needed to leave.

Swanny was our lead guitarist and original member from the start, and even worked with Neal, but it was felt that the direction the band had started to go in might not have been right for him. He was a top lad and everyone really liked him, so this situation was going to require my very best mediation skills to avoid any big fall outs, which I didn't really want.

I arranged to meet Swanny in our usual place, and very discreetly discussed the subject of him being in the band. I am not sure if Swanny had worked out that there might have been an issue, but he told me that he hadn't fully been into the new songs, and that he felt the direction they were going in wasn't for him. This was a really sad moment for me, but nobody had been sacked, nobody had fallen out. The upshot was, though, that The Torrents now needed to search for a new guitarist.

If I'd thought that Swannygate had been a tough one to deal with, my next task was on another level.

When I had agreed to manage the band and asked Warren if he fancied coming along for the ride, he'd suggested we attended a management course, which I hadn't felt was necessary. One thing that concerned me was that I noticed when any gigs had not gone that well, Warren had offered negative feedback to the band before they had even left the stage. I brought up the subject with him, suggesting that this might not be the best way of dealing with the issues. I explained that even if he had a point, it was all about timing. I knew that the moment an act ended a gig, and for a period of time after, they would still be in a zone and usually still on a high. So, to bring them down at that moment, was not the best tactic.

I noticed the band members' facial expressions after being told they had sounded rubbish, sometimes before they had even managed to pack up their gear. But I had hoped that having a word with Warren would have put the issue to bed and no more would be said about the subject. Yet even though I mentioned it several times, it seemed to have been ignored.

Enough was enough, and the band summoned me to attend a meeting with them, which had been awkward enough in itself, and to not include Warren. They told me in no uncertain terms that they did not want him as their manager, because he would always bring them down with his negativity. They also mentioned that they only wanted me to manage the band, and that they wouldn't be changing their mind.

It was the day after New Year's Day when I went round to Warren's house and broke the news to him about the band's decision. From day one, I had vowed to do whatever was best for the band and not what was best for me or any other individual, but I was really dreading this moment, and he obviously did not take it well. The hardest part for me was that Warren was family, and I felt that my sister-in-law Pauline and my niece somehow blamed me for what had happened, as though I had stabbed him in the back or something, when it had been my decision to bring him on board in the first place. Things were strained between me and Warren's side of the family, which made me really sad, but I had agreed to do a job for the band, and I was determined to give it my best shot.

Managing a band that I fully believed in felt like the most natural thing in the world to me, and was the first time in my life that I had found something where I felt 100% confident that I could make a difference.

There was a young band from Morecambe at the time called The Heartbreaks, who had been hotly tipped to become the next Smiths, and I recall being in the Night & Day toilets at the same time as them before our gig. I was just about to go over and introduce myself, when their bass player Deaks actually walked over to me and said, 'You're Pete, aren't you? You manage Torrents.' I was really surprised by this introduction role reversal, and remember thinking at the time that I must be doing something right.

After a lot of discussions on the subject, we decided to offer the ex-Exorsisters guitarist, Gus, the available slot in the band. I remember telling Jamie in Media at college that we had chosen him as we knew him and he was brilliant on guitar. Due to Gus's heavy rock influences from the likes of Led Zeppelin and the like, Jamie questioned if he would fit into the band's Mod/Indie image, and I remember telling him not to worry as we would have him wearing Fred Perry's before he knew it. As it happened, it took about a week for him to cast aside his black leather jacket and welcome a more 60s look.

Gus was a great added talent to the band, and fitted in really well from day one. But the great thing for me was that Swanny had been cool with this move, which I was extremely glad about. The Torrents' first gig with their new line-up was at our beloved Night & Day, supporting NME's current darlings, These New Puritans. True to form, Neal appeared at the microphone and said, 'You don't look pretentious, do you?' alienating every single person in the room before he had even started their first song. I was now used to this strange method of trying to win over an audience, but I had known what I was taking on board, and part of me had actually grown to like it, in a funny kind of a way. The Torrents' set clearly made an impact, as a music journalist came and introduced himself, asking if he could interview the band and take some photos, so he could write a feature on them for In The City magazine.

Our invitation letter for Channel M arrived on my doormat, proving that Dan had kept his word, and invited us over to the studio on Thursday, 21st February, 2008, for an interview with the City Centre Social presenter Gerry McLaughlin, and to perform three of our songs live.

The studio was about a minute's walk from Manchester Victoria Station, and the day itself was a fantastic experience. Emma and my niece Beckie came along for the ride and found it interesting watching the show being put together. Frank Sidebottom was a regular guest on the programme, but to be honest, I found him annoying the way he kept interrupting everyone. The boys were great and clearly revelled under the spotlight, and I managed to nick a couple of Channel M mugs before we left, as a souvenir of the day's antics.

The show was aired on the same evening on Sky channel 203, and I buzzed off hearing my mate Dave had got them to put it on in The Farthings for the regulars who had still been in drinking at 10pm.

The band recorded their second CD demo with Mark again, but this time chose to take a keepsake home with them, in the form of the street sign at the end of the road. *I Ain't Blind*, *Dudley Avenue*, and *The Royale*, were the track listing, and as a memento they stole the whole Dudley Avenue sign. I didn't know what to say when Mark informed me the following week about their street burglary, but deep down I am sure he knew who the culprits were. The sign ended up gracing the band's practice room in Darwen, along with a framed photo of Lady Diana on the wall. But to this day I have no idea where it came from, who put it up, or where it ended up.

One of the hardest things for a band to sort out is finding somewhere decent enough to practise. I say decent, but most would be happy with anywhere, as they are so hard to find. When I first got involved with The Torrents, they used the small, dark basement of the Charles Napier pub to rehearse in, and over the months (years) we used various pubs throughout Blackburn and Darwen. The daughter of the landlady of the Fox and Hounds told her mum they were going places and persuaded her to let us use the back room for our rehearsals, but whenever we turned up at the place, she would have a rant about how much we owed her towards a new vacuum cleaner, because every time she started to clean up, hers would get jammed with broken guitar strings that had apparently been left all over the floor. It was time to move on.

Through my filming, I had received a request to go and film a local band called The Scene, in a recording studio in Whitworth (Studio Studio). In all honesty, I hadn't heard of them up until that point, and had no idea how they had heard of me. The band's drummer Paul was the one who had chosen me to shoot a video for them, and it didn't take long before we became good friends.
Paul's mate Dave was running The Hordens pub up Livesey Branch Road, and the place had been struggling on a Saturday night. Paul talked Dave into allowing him to erect a stage and to put on live gigs every Saturday night. It really was a great idea, and within a short period of time the venue had gone from three men and a dog to being busy every weekend. All the local acts would get in touch for a chance to play, along with bands from further afield.

The Torrents played the opening night on 3rd June, 2007, but it was their second appearance at the venue in February 2008 that proved to be a massive learning curve for me. Up until that moment, the band had started to drink their drinks rider from the moment they arrived at a venue. I had spent weeks giving out the flyers and texting everybody I knew to come and show their support. Knowing that a number of people had come to support me, even when it wasn't really their thing, I was slightly concerned at the state that some of the band had managed to get in before the show.
They were hardly a few songs into their set when, to my total horror, Austin lifted his bass drum above his head and hurled it into the surprised crowd, hitting at least a couple of people on the leg.
Now don't get me wrong, if this incident had happened during a gig that I had not been involved in, I would probably have thought, *Wow! When on earth are they playing again?* But the fact of the matter was that I was their manager and was responsible

for their behaviour. I had visions of the parents of one of the girls who had been hit knocking on my door the following day threatening to sue me. I simply wanted the ground to open up and swallow me. What would all those friends who had given up their Saturday night to support me think.

The landlord Dave started to walk over, and I was expecting him to go mad and ban us. But, to my astonishment, he told me he thought it was great. After it happened, the other band members were so disgusted by what Austin had done that they stormed out of the venue and were all kicking off with each other when their manager/mediator had arrived on the scene.
What had apparently happened was that once Austin started playing, his drums on the little bit of carpet had started to move forward. And after a number of times attempting to pull them back, he had lost his patience and decided to throw them.
This was the first time I had been angry with the band, and I told them that folk had paid to see them and so they should get back in and finish the set, or I would be standing down as their manager. Even though they knew I was serious, it still took all my efforts to get them back onto the stage and attempt to finish their set. This, though, was a huge mistake as they sounded terrible, and just to prove that lightning does sometimes strike twice, Austin repeated his earlier performance, and his very large bass drum ended up in the audience again.

At the time, I had no idea at all how we were going to come back from that, but what I did decide was that it was the last time they would receive their drinks rider before their set.

On the home front, The Cellar Bar on King Street was a regular haunt of the band, and had started putting on regular gigs, both outside in the courtyard and inside in the basement. A couple of their bouncers had been proper dodgy and were getting a reputation for selling drugs to some of the bands, then reporting them to the Police for having drugs on them – as we found out first-hand.

The Cellar Bar's finest hour happened on Friday, 28th September, 2007, when they somehow managed to book The Courteeners from Manchester, and The Torrents were on the bill. It was rumoured that the venue had booked the band for as little as £300, and it was just before they had properly taken off – so, perfect timing.

It was a perfect summer's evening, and the courtyard was packed to the rafters with a mix of Mancunians and regulars. I had naturally taken my camcorder to film some of the gig, and just knew by the buzz around the band that we would be hearing about them again.

NME had written, 'Remember how you felt when you first heard Oasis? or The Libertines? or The Monkeys? *Cavorting* is like all those moments rolled into one.' So this really was a massive coup for the venue. The funny thing was that we were actually booked to perform after The Courteeners, downstairs in the basement, so I would always tell people that it was in fact them who supported us, though I am not sure many were convinced.

The massive shame for the scene locally was that just at the time when the venue showed potential and should have capitalised on the success of that event, the opposite happened, for whatever reason. And that was as good as it got (in my humble opinion).

Another thing I noticed around that time was the amount of backstabbing from other local bands. Certain band members would be overly friendly with the band in public, but slag them off behind their backs, no doubt jealous at the fact they were actually doing something and not just playing pubs in the local area. I always found this jealousy sad and tried to explain that folk needed to realise that if a band did well in the town, it could only be a good thing for the local scene, as it put an extra spotlight on all the other artists. It was a no-brainer to me.

On one occasion, Dave, the Hordens' landlord, asked for a signed poster of the band to frame and hang up in the venue. But it wasn't long before the lead singer of another local band had smashed it out of spite, which I found beyond childish, particularly as it was Dave's property and not ours. (We know who you are.)

Not everybody was like that, though, and the band had a fantastic relationship with The Underdogs from Preston, along with Morning Call from Blackburn, and India Mill from Darwen. When they were playing a gig, we would always put in the effort to go and show our support. And many a time Neal would be invited up on stage to join them on a song, by either Mossy, Alistair, or Tony, when they were performing.

I always found it really positive when bands would support other bands, as too many times the acts you had been on the same line-up with, wouldn't even bother watching your set. As a manager, I would always try to encourage my lads to show their support to other bands we had been playing with.

I always remember the time we were playing Moho on Tib Street in Manchester, and I put on a coach for everybody wanting to attend. After we had played, I remember asking one of their mates what he thought of the gig, and he told me he hadn't bothered watching The Torrents as he had been in another room watching somebody else. I couldn't believe what I was hearing. He actually had the cheek to get a lift over on our coach and not even attempt to support the band! I was tempted to let him walk home.

Pay-to-play was really prevalent back then and was really tough on all the bands. No band I knew had any money; in fact, it was hard enough trying to prise loose change off them most of the time to contribute towards the practice room. Some venues would only offer you a gig if you took a certain number of people, and that was hard, expecting folk to give their night up and shell out a number of times per month.

Night & Day had a policy where you had to bring 25 people before you got paid a penny, then you would only get £1 for every person over that number. I had to pay for the posters we were expected to put up, the flyers we were expected to give out, and the transport there and back. And even though we always put in the effort to try and take as many people as we could to every show, we always played at a loss.

What was really frustrating was that we had been playing at Night & Day, and I'd spent the week delivering flyers to the people who had been coming, so that we would get paid at least something. We took a coach with around 30 people, so at best we would only be given £30, but it would help towards the costs. What happened was that only 24 people bothered to remember the flyer, despite me dropping them off, and we ended up getting nothing, despite taking over a full coach from Blackburn.

We played a gig in Newcastle, and the so-called promoter put zero effort into promoting the night and didn't even put up a poster in the venue we were playing. After our set, I tried to find him to get the expenses that he had promised us, only to be told he had sneaked out of the back entrance and gone home.

We played The Music Box in Manchester, and not a single person was in the venue apart from our crowd, the other band, and the sound engineer. Both bands felt obliged to support each other, despite being completely different types of acts, and I could tell they were dying to head off home after they had played. Hats off to them for hanging around, even though it didn't stop it from being naff.

We turned up to one gig in Wigan only to find it was more like a kids' disco, and I struggled to find anybody over the age of 14 in the room.

We supported The Clone Roses again at King George's Hall, and it absolutely freaked me out how a tribute band managed to pack out the venue, and that the crowd were going crazy at the front as though they thought they were actually watching Ian Brown and Mani. Very strange.

The Zanzibar Club in Liverpool had built up a reputation for having a great sound, along with hosting the likes of The Coral and The Zutons on their road to stardom. The problem was that you were expected to pay a cash sum of £230 before you even entered the building. Luckily for us, we managed to fill a coach to help cover this cost, but we would still have had to pay this fee even if we had taken nobody. To be fair, I was really keen to secure a gig in my favourite city, and it ended up being arguably our finest show, based on the crowd's reaction.

Saturday, 29th March, and we had been supporting a band called Hujan from Malaysia. During our soundcheck I noticed that they seemed to be loving what they were watching, and when we finished, a couple of their team came over and told me we had been incredible. What we didn't know at the time was that Hujan were Malaysia's version of Take That. Not in terms of sound, but in popularity. From the second The Torrents walked onto the stage, Hujan's very enthusiastic crowd went crazy for them, even listening to Neal's ramblings between songs. They were cheering and shouting, as if we were famous, and Neal and the others were certainly in their element.

When a gig would go well, it helped you forget about the rubbish ones. The set ended with the song *Please Leave Right Now*, which had been written about my friend, Punk Julie, (after I had introduced her to the band one night at The Hordens), and the crowd went mental as Neal rolled around the stage, somehow still managing to play his guitar.

A few Torrents' gigs stand out as being memorable, but I actually watched the DVD last night with the footage that the Hujan team filmed of the show, and it does confirm that this was my favourite of ours.

Through that gig in Liverpool, I had kept in contact with a really nice Malaysian guy called Wan Appy, and we were invited to support another of their bands at Moho Live. The event was run by Clint Boon of Inspiral Carpets fame, and was sponsored by Bench. They invited us to a hotel room across the road to have a band interview and they filmed our set, in order to make a feature on the band. Also, thanks to our newfound love of everything Malaysian, we were offered a tour in the country, supporting their beloved Hujan. Tempting as it might have been, we simply could not afford the expenses, but what an experience that would have been.

Another thing we learnt along the way was that just because we had a decent gig at a venue did not necessarily mean that the same thing would happen the next time we played there. I booked another show at Zanzibar, but this time we ended up going on about 11.55pm, once everybody had gone home, and were booked to play with a couple of bands that were a completely different genre. So we ended up having a woeful time, even though the £230 had still been handed over.

The second time we played Water Rats, the promoter had hounded me about how many people we had brought, not taking into consideration we had travelled 233 miles in the back of a transit van. The gig sounded terrible, but once the headline band came on, the muffling sound somehow disappeared and, somehow, they managed to find some stage lighting. I had obviously been naïve to the fact that sometimes venues would purposely hijack your show in order to make other bands look better, which amazed me. All that way for six songs, and then back in the van to do the 233 miles all over again.

By that time, we had secured our own driver in Ash. He was a friend of Joss's brother, growing up, and he had access to his works van most of the time. He kindly offered to take us to every gig, providing he wasn't working. I would be in the passenger seat, being manager of the band and the oldest, whilst the band would be rattling around in the back, with no windows, and spending the majority of their time trying to stop their amps from sliding around.

We also had our own photographer, to my delight, as there was no point in having a good set of haircuts if you didn't show them off in a photoshoot from time to time. We had been rehearsing in the practice room at the end of The Stiffs' mate Bob's garden, when out of the blue I received a call from some guy called Clive, who asked if I was The Torrents' manager. Clive was a local photographer who had spent years photographing local bands, along with more well-known artists. Apparently, he wanted to find a new local band that was going places, and King George's Hall had given him my name.

Demo Two and Three were recorded with Mark, and we had absolutely no reason to think that our Fourth would not be recorded there. What happened was I had been waiting to film The Futureheads at 53 Degrees in Preston, when I presume it was the manager of the support band, The Enemy, came over and asked me to film their set. He took me backstage to meet the three members, and I couldn't believe how young they looked. The Enemy were ace, and obviously went on to bigger things, but after I sent the footage to John, who discovered them and was their manager, we were recommended to go and record at the studio they had been using in Stratford-upon-Avon. This put us in an awkward position, as we had all been happy with Mark. But as their manager, I felt that I wouldn't be doing my job if I denied the band this opportunity. I don't think Mark took it very well and wondered what had gone wrong, which I understood, but it was simply a case of experiencing something new.

Ash offered to drive us, and we booked into the band cottage that John had recommended to me, which also included the use of a B&B across the road for breakfast. We were booked into Vada Studios for the following two days and decided to hit the town on our first night away. Ash had gone home, so it was just me and the band. The thing I liked about The Torrents was that they looked like a band, which was important to me. I always felt that if you are on the stage, then you should look like you deserve to be there, and not just blend in with the audience. Whether it was their haircuts or their attitude, you could tell they were in a band. I used to buzz off the amount of people on the street who would turn their heads at Neal's Indie/Mod haircut.

We had literally been out in Stratford for around five minutes when some guy came over and asked if we were in a band (not me), then insisted we allow him to take us to the pub and buy us all a couple of drinks. It also didn't take long before a group of girls joined us, and they ended up taking us to a local nightclub. What I had found really amusing was that as we were sitting in an alcove chatting to our new female friends, another group of girls stood a couple of metres away, waiting to have their turn – as though they were on the substitutes' bench.

No matter how crazy things would get, and no matter what temptations came their way, I was always really impressed by how loyal Joss was to his girlfriend. And even though he was in a band, which obviously created interest, there was never a time where he even looked remotely tempted.
Joss had been going out with Rachel when I first met him, and they are still happy together as I am writing this, which is extremely impressive. For sure, his loyalty has paid off.

By the time we made it back to the cottage, everyone had been drinking for hours, and I started to feel I was outstaying my welcome. I decided to go to bed and leave the partying to the younger ones. The thing about managing young people was that for a lot of the time it felt like it was helping to keep me young, but there were certainly times where the situation gave me a reality check and I would definitely feel my age, or even older. Neal had been getting rather friendly with one of the girls, called Victoria, and all I could hear whilst lying in bed was The Kinks song by the same name playing on repeat. The smooth devil.

It was a mission attempting to wake everybody the following morning (Babysitter), and looking at their faces over our full English had me worried to say the least. I ordered a minibus to pick us up and take us to the studio and just hoped they would come to before it was time to record.

Vada Studios was in the heart of the Stratford countryside, and the views driving in were beautiful. (at least, I thought so). Once we arrived at our destination, we were greeted by this mad professor-type guy wearing a smoking jacket, who introduced himself as Matt, our producer. He escorted us inside, and as soon as the lads noticed the settee, they made the most of its comfort and each one chose a spot.

Austin put down his drum parts, and Joss and Gus recorded their parts, but at one stage Neal was sprawled out on the studio settee, as if he was trying to catch up on last night's lack of beauty sleep.
This did not impress Matt, and he told us that if they decided to come in tomorrow in that state, he would not be recording them. The band took offence at his abruptness, but I loved his honesty, and there was no doubt this was a much needed, wake-up call. I told them I agreed with him, and that if they intended to go to the next level, they would need to up the ante and start acting more professionally.

Even though we still enjoyed a couple of beers, I suggested that we just stayed in the band cottage that night and prepare ourselves for the following day's work. To my surprise, I seem to recall that is what we ended up doing (Babysitter).

Not being a person who does barriers, and strongly believing that if you don't ask you don't get, I emailed Pauline Black and invited her to come down to the studio to let me introduce her to the band. To my absolute delight, not only did Pauline accept my invitation, but incredibly she offered to help with any backing vocals if we fancied it. True to her word, Pauline turned up at Vada looking as elegant as ever, and indeed recorded her vocals for the track *You Make No Sense*. She had never heard the song before, and to be fair, the song wasn't really the best for her to sing backing on, but I thought she did brilliantly and was blown away by her attendance.

When Matt was working on the mix, the band (Neal) requested the vocals be very low, which absolutely astounded me, and I worried how Pauline would take it. But she was so humble and supportive, saying she understood and didn't blame them – even though, I didn't, and did.

Looking back, I have always felt that their judgement call at that time was one of their biggest mistakes. I am not sure if it was ignorance or arrogance, or both, but even though I expressed my opinion, I allowed them to have the final say. I feel Pauline's vocals should have been far more prominent on the track, and we should have definitely highlighted on the sleeve, 'Featuring Special Guest Vocals by Pauline Black', but there was zero mention of it. But what do I know? Maybe I should have been more of an Interrogator. The other track on the CD was my favourite by the band, *These Things To Bring You Down*, and it still gets me today when I play it.

The thing about a Torrents' gig was it was just as much about the social occasion, because the same group of people would follow the band all around the country. Sometimes Janet would come along, and when they had a local gig, Emma and her mates would blag it in. I always appreciated the support folk would show us, but after all, we *were* the coolest band in town, so why wouldn't they? (Ha!)

In terms of promotion, I might have gone a little overboard. Apart from the required posters and flyers, I sorted out branded badges, t-shirts, pens, fridge magnets – you name it, we had it to help get their name out there.

What the band (Neal) then decided to do was change their name to just Torrents, not The. This might seem pretty pointless to most people, but I assure you it was a big deal to them (Neal).

I remember Pete Shelley telling me that it used to really wind him up when folk referred to the band as The Buzzcocks, which most do, as they were only ever simply called Buzzcocks. Since he shared that bit of insight with me, I find myself getting annoyed when I hear folk using The, when talking about them, and even find myself correcting people if they mention them in a conversation. Sad but true.

Torrents were no different, and pretentious as it might have seemed, Neal would be the first to point out other people's mistakes during an interview. However, I was the one with a reason to be properly naffed off, as it meant me having to reorder all the merch, and spending my time constantly explaining what the new band name was about, even though I hadn't a clue why.

I managed to get the band t-shirts for as little as £2.50, so decided that we might as well just give them out to anyone who wanted one, as at least it would help spread the gospel. Nothing gave me greater pleasure than when a stranger from another town, or even country, would message me on Myspace to thank me for the Torrents' stuff I had sent them. My favourite was from a girl in China, who told me the t-shirt, CD, and badges I had sent her had made her week and cheered her up, which I really buzzed off. I always shared this information with the lads, but being honest, I don't think they really appreciated it, though they should have.

It has always absolutely intrigued me the impact a group of people (or person) can have after making the decision to learn an instrument and start writing songs. How four lads from Blackburn could affect somebody in China, is amazing to me. I mean, four skint lads from Liverpool started a band and changed the planet, which I still find incredible.

From day one, the band's mate Wigan would show up to rehearsals and just sit watching or playing Oasis songs on his guitar, and I suppose it was inevitable that he would end up joining the band. Wigan was our new keyboard player, and he added another dimension to our sound. Vada Studios was booked again, but this time I was unable to get any time off work. I was proper gutted, as up until then I had attended every single gig, every rehearsal, and every recording session. But I decided it might be a good thing to leave them to just get on with it for once.

I was in the office at college when Joss called me asking if I could ring them a taxi to pick them up at the band cottage and take them to the studio. I obliged, after pointing out that I was actually at work in Blackburn. My work colleagues thought I was simple and couldn't get their heads around why the band could not have sorted out their own transport (Babysitter).

As if that wasn't enough, around 11.30am I received a call from our drummer Austin, complaining that they hadn't been given any sausages with their breakfast that morning. I was almost lost for words (almost), but I bit my tongue and explained to him that I was at work, and suggested that the following morning he simply just asked for sausages with his meal (Babysitter).

My third phone call from the band came mid-afternoon, when Neal complained that the way Matt had been recording them was not what they had planned.

The next recordings to come out of Vada were *Waiting For Sunday*, *21 (But Not For Long)*, and *He's A Victim*, and we had started getting a fair bit of radio play. *21* would become a fans' favourite, and the band would end every gig with it.

I really wanted to make a video for *A Certain Girl* at the time, and even came up with the whole storyboard, featuring an old double decker bus which my friend Dobo, had promised to source, being a bus driver himself. I can't remember why it never happened, but we were determined to finally make one for *He's A Victim*.

During one of our shows at Night & Day, my mate Ian introduced me to an old friend of his, Tony, who told me he thought that

Torrents had been the most exciting band he had seen in years. We hit it off from minute one, and Tony told me about a friend of his who was a filmmaker. Me and a couple from the band went over to Manchester to meet Alison, who told us that if she liked the song, she was happy to pull her team together and make us a video. Luckily, Alison liked the tune, and it was all systems go.

Tony was cast as the main character, and Emma and Beckie wangled a part in it, too. The song was about the drudgery of working a 9-to-5 job, and the video was to show Tony snapping under the strain of office life. Our first day's shoot was in Salford, filming the office scenes and some shots of Tony and Neal on the streets. All of a sudden, this skinhead appeared from his house, waving a baseball bat above his head, and proceeded to threaten every single member of our crew. He accused us of filming his kids riding up and down the road, which obviously we hadn't (Mediator). It was literally as though we had been filming a scene from *Shameless*. This was my first experience of the place, so I was thankful that the second day's filming was in Blackburn.

We talked about filming at a number of locations, but the band wanted to be genuine about where they came from, so we chose some flat land at the bottom of Daisyfield flats for authenticity. Like anything that you had wanted to do in Blackburn that was out of the norm, the Council made a big deal out of us wanting to film. Instead of supporting talented young people from the town who were trying to do something positive with their lives, all they did was moan and put up barriers. We were told we had to flyer every single flat to let them know that it was happening, which we did, but they still accused us of not doing it. How different would they have been if we had been a big, signed band from the town? They would have done all they could to try and cling onto our coat tails, of that I have no doubt.

Like I said, I don't do barriers and there was no way this wasn't going to happen, so I did whatever I could to meet all their demands and not give them a reason to complain, even though they did (Interrogator/Mediator).

The shoot was a great day, a sunny Sunday, and we invited family and friends to either take part or simply just watch. The band set up all their equipment, as the plan was for us to play the song for them to mime along to, as though they were playing it live. My niece Rachel and her mates were positioned behind the orange amps, in the hope they would start the dancing off, along with my mate Nick in his baseball cap doing all he could to be down with the kids.

Just before we started to shoot, the manager of the Nicholas Deakins shop in Leeds pulled up and opened his car boot to reveal a car full of new shoes and jackets for me and the band, which was our third clothing endorsement. We had got to know Mark and his mates from when we played The Northern Monkey in the town, and they would always put the effort in and just turn up and surprise us at shows.

The filming went really well, and Alison and her team did us proud. But what gave it that extra touch, for me, were the characters in the flats. Several of them just watched, clearly wondering what was going on. A couple waved down at us, no doubt just happy that something was happening to brighten up their Sunday morning. But the money shot was this lady who obviously lived in one of the top flats and spent the whole time shouting down insults at us, saying, 'Get rid of that, play some chart music!' which was absolutely hilarious. We loved her ramblings that much that we included her on the end of the video, and even if the song is not your cup of tea, I urge you to go onto YouTube and type in *He's A Victim* by Torrents (not The), as it is worth it just to listen to her at the end. (A classic.)

Janet had always got on with the band, which was a good job really, as I was spending a large part of my life with them. But after a certain incident happened, I feel they were a little wary of her, and maybe even a bit scared (as I was) of getting on the wrong side of her.

It was my birthday, and Janet had come to pick me up after band practice at Bob's. As I was getting into the car, she asked me if they had given me a birthday card. When I said 'No,' she went mad, pointing out to me everything I had done for them, and that they couldn't even be bothered to get me a card. She was so angry by their tightness that she burst into the practice room and told them exactly what she had felt. Janet said even Neal did not try to argue with her, and they all stood open-mouthed, no doubt gobsmacked at what was happening.

The next time I arrived at band practice, I had barely walked through the door when they plonked a belated birthday card into my hand, followed by several gifts. Neal gave me a signed vinyl by The Rifles, Austin gave me an old set of his drumsticks that had clearly seen better days. Even though I found this hilarious, despite being grateful, I thought maybe Janet should be managing them if this was the effect that she had.

Opportunities for the band were coming in thick and fast, and at least once per week I would have sorted them something new out – sometimes every day – whether it was a radio play/chat, a magazine feature, or simply just another gig. We supported The Rifles at 53 Degrees in Preston, which was pretty special, as they were a band we all loved. Then we were chosen to play the bands' club night the Narrow Minded Social Club at Proud Galleries in Camden, and Dave Laser from Dustins called down to show his support, which we all appreciated.

We were also chosen to support From The Jam at the 2,350 capacity Carling Academy in Sheffield, and it pleased me that both Bruce and Rick were really friendly with the boys. (08.12.08.)

We played with Catfish and the Bottlemen in Winsford, but to be fair, they hadn't made a name for themselves at that point. We also supported both The Paddingtons and Twisted Wheel, who we all loved, at The Live Lounge in Blackburn.

My friend Paul had managed to turn The Hordens pub into a music venue on a Saturday night, but clearly had ambitions to take things further and decided to take over the old Moist venue on Northgate.

On 29th May, 2009 (Bank Holiday Weekend), The Live Lounge opened its doors for the first time, and on the line-up that night were Torrents, New York Tourists, and a DJ set from Ex-Smiths' drummer Mike Joyce. Helping Paul run the venue was his mate Julian, former promoter of The Attic in Accrington, and Curtis, who had been the sound engineer at The Hordens.

Torrents played the venue several times, and always managed to pack it out, which was no doubt the reason we kept being asked back. The atmosphere at a home gig was always special, as the room would be full of our mates who turned up to have a great time. Neal would start by declaring 'You know who we are,' which sometimes he would open with at gigs further afield, even though they hadn't had a clue. He would then proceed to splash the crowd with water, no doubt trying to wind them up from the beginning.

In Manchester he had made derogatory comments regarding their local son, Liam Fray, along with establishing the audience were pretentious. And in Liverpool, he announced that we had a better football team than their football teams. So, on stage he'd have the confidence of Liam Gallagher, but off stage I always felt that this wasn't the case. Don't get me wrong, I had been his biggest fan and had seen how he wrote a song in the dark outside the practice room, with a bookie's pen and a piece of beermat that he found on the floor, in literally minutes. He was a great frontman and a great songwriter, in my opinion, but I don't believe that he would agree to either. The fact that he never wanted to take home any of his band's CDs or the videos I had made, or by him making sure everyone left the room in the recording studio when it was time to do his vocals, seemed strange. But the really baffling one to me was the times when he had written a new song that everyone seemed to like and that had gone down well at gigs. No sooner would it appear in their set than it was dropped a couple of weeks later. I never understood that.

All these observations proved to me that he wasn't the cocky, big-headed git that he sometimes came across as on stage, but no matter how many times I tried to convince him of his talents, I don't think he ever believed me (Shrink).

I received a call from somebody who worked at MUTV. They had a Saturday morning show on Sky called Good Morning Manchester, where they invited up-and-coming bands along to play live at the start of the programme. We were invited on, and even though they were all Rovers fans (except Wigan), I accepted, thinking that it would be fun.
We headed over to Manchester to pre-record *A Certain Girl* in some sort of office/factory building, and the footage went down well when it was broadcast the following week. I remember a *Coronation Street* actor, who had been a guest on the show, bigging them up as he enjoyed it.

What we didn't know at the time was that it was actually a Battle of the Bands they were running, as we probably wouldn't have entered if we had known. What was even more of a surprise was when I was watching their Christmas show, and out of 11 bands, the presenter announced the winners were: 'A four-piece act from the north side of Lancashire, described as enigmatic Northern upstarts, and having infixions energy. Congratulations to Neal, Joss, Angus, and Austin, as Torrents are our winners of our Battle of the Bands.'

I really couldn't believe it, and neither could the band when I excitedly called them. The prize for winning this very prestigious competition was to play live at Old Trafford, and I could sense that Neal was already planning his opening insults.

I can't remember the reason now, but the prize of playing at the ground somehow changed to me and a couple of the band being invited to Old Trafford for a winners' interview, along with a signed team shirt by a player of their choice to give to our biggest fan. Ronaldo was the player of choice – not by us, but by Jo (Joanne), who supported us everywhere we performed, but it ended up being off Michael Owen.

The dilemma we had at the time was which band members were going to attend; everyone wanted to, and nobody was prepared to back down. Neal ended up having to work, which I was gutted about. No disrespect to the other band members, but Neal was always the natural talker in interviews, and I felt he portrayed the attitude of the band.

The tricky one I felt a little bad about was that Wigan actually supported United, even though he hadn't been involved at the time of entering the competition. But rightly or wrongly, I decided that I wanted to go. After all, it was me who sorted everything out for them anyway. In the end, I arranged for me, Joss, and Austin to attend, and the experience was amazing. We shared the green room with Mani from Stone Roses/Primal Scream, who said after watching the song footage, 'That was good, nice and raucous guitar rock, which I am a big fan of.' Mani was friendly and cool with us and showed no attitude of grandeur at all.

I recall nipping to the toilets and struggling to find my way back to the green room. I walked onto the stand, and the only person I could see in the whole of Old Trafford was the groundsman cutting the grass. Even for a Liverpool fan, I appreciated that experience.

The *Manchester Evening News* sent one of their journalists to cover a gig we had been playing at Night & Day, and had written, 'Torrents bring a welcome energy and change of pace with their up-tempo Jam-meets-Libertines ditties. They jump, sweat, and gesticulate on stage, clearly enjoying themselves immensely…

Their energy is infectious. They can boast a charismatic frontman in Neal, and a vicious wall of guitars that evoke the angry young man thrashings of one Paul Weller.'

I was pretty darn happy with this review, but they added just one slightly negative line at the end, which unfortunately was all Joss zoomed in on. I tried explaining to him that 95% of it had been positive, so take that and don't simply concentrate on the negative, but he still wasn't happy with the review. I told him that if he struggled reading negative comments about the band – something every artist gets – maybe he would be better not reading any at all, as a lot of musicians had adopted that attitude (Shrink).

As a change from recording at Vada, the boys decided to record their next demo at Fly 2 Studio in Sheffield, and it was mad to see the Gold Disc on the wall of the Arctic Monkeys first album. They had recorded a lot of it there, apparently.

The day after we played Proud Camden, I got us a slot at the 2009 Wickerman Festival, sharing the bill with the likes of The Human League, The Zutons, The Magic Numbers, Candi Staton, and Billy Bragg, to name a few. The travel to London in Ash's transit van in order to perform a handful of songs was a mission in itself, and the journey back was a nightmare. I shared the front passenger seat with my mate Birchy, and being over 6ft 2, my legs were halfway up the dashboard, making the journey seem never-ending. (The things we do for Rock and Roll!)

We had barely made it back before we had to all meet up again outside Bob's practice room, in order to pile back in Ash's van and make our way over to Bonny Scotland. As usual, I travelled in Birchy's car, and all in all, I think around 17 of us descended on a field in Dumfries and Galloway. My daughter Emma travelled with us, along with her mates Fallon and Whitney, and my mates Sarah, Tony (Mr *'He's A Victim'*), and Jo and the usual crew.

As usual, due to me still working at the festival and being on filming duties for most of the weekend, me, Birchy, and Tony had booked into our usual hotel, leaving the others to put up their tents in a windy, wet field, which they didn't seem to mind – or not then, at least.

Torrents played the following day on the Scooter Tent stage, and the set seemed to go down well, based on the fact that a group of girls joined us backstage afterwards, requesting the bands' autographs and a few photographs with them. Emma and her mates had hidden cans of lager down their shorts in an effort to get past the site security who were working on the gates, and all in all it was a really special weekend. A group of friends all partying together in a field in Scotland, and this time I remembered my coat (result!).

We planned on getting up early on the Sunday morning to drive over to the site and meet the others before heading back to Blackburn. But anybody who has shared a bedroom with Birchy will know that getting a decent night's sleep is a mission, so we overslept. Knowing the others would be waiting for us put on the pressure for us to hurry up and pack, but there was absolutely no way we (I) were (was) about to turn down our fully cooked Scottish Breakfast. We casually ate our breakfast and drank our tea, planning to make up some excuse for arriving late, but as we drove in the festival gate, we could see Ash standing outside his van, waving his fist in the air. I guess it didn't help the situation that we all burst into uncontrollable laughter at the sight of this, and the fact it had been pouring down and they had only eaten soggy crisps for breakfast.

Birchy pulled up outside the van, and as I slid open the door, with 'You are not going to believe how bad the traffic was,' Jo used words on me that I couldn't possibly repeat in this book. And you know when your own daughter stares at you as if she wants to murder you, it's time to shut up and accept you're in the bad books, with everybody. Despite the breakfast-gate incident, everybody in our group had the time of their lives, and to this day Ash will say it was the best weekend he has ever had, despite the fist-waving.

If the Pauline Black episode was one of the band's big lack of judgements (in my opinion), what happened next was by far their biggest. I received an email from a contact of mine, who forwarded me a message he had been sent from an A & R guy he knew at Warner Music. The message read: 'Torrents are exactly the type of band that my MD is looking for.' This was followed up with a note showing that himself and another guy from Warner had booked their train fares from London, along with their hotel booking, and planned to come and check us out at our upcoming headline show at Night & Day.

This was a huge deal to us, and for sure our most important gig to date. I knew that opportunities like this only come around once every blue moon, and I knew I needed to do whatever it took to make sure we gave it our very best shot. Gus was working for Fish from Marillion on tour, but assured me he would be able to get the time off. However, around a week before our showcase, he called me saying that he couldn't have the night off, and I was absolutely gutted. Did he not realise how important this show was? Was he not bothered about being signed?
It didn't matter what I said or how much I tried to persuade him to play the show (Interrogator) and not let his fellow band members down, the answer was still the same. We even had a conversation about playing the gig with someone else, maybe Swanny, but the rest of the band were adamant they weren't prepared to play it without their current line-up. Also, it would have been a bit rich expecting Swanny to stand in for just one show.

I think this was the first time I really questioned my position. I mean, did they not appreciate the amount of work I put in to make things like this happen? I really did not believe in pulling gigs, and now I was about to cancel our biggest one. I found it extremely difficult to contact the guy from Warner, knowing that we had blown it and that he wouldn't be giving us a second chance. And I was right. That was the last we ever heard from them.

Not long after, we were offered a record contract by a local(ish) label and met their representatives in the Bulls Head pub to discuss the terms. Anybody who has been involved in a band will know that once potential money comes into the conversation, and the members start to put their own case forward as to who contributed what in a song, that is when the arguments start. In fact, it's the reason a lot of bands split up. Everyone knows that the band's main songwriter will be the one who makes the most of the money, and very few groups end up agreeing to split all the profits equally between all the members.

That is why I always loved Paul Heaton. One day Jacqui Abbott was working behind the till in her local Spar type shop, and the following day she was on the same salary as Mr Heaton himself, apparently. Even though Paul wrote most of the songs in The Beautiful South, and in my opinion is one of the greatest songwriters the UK has ever seen (or anywhere for that matter), I believe he always insisted on everyone getting an equal share.

The meeting went well, and luckily I tried to steer the conversation away from who had come up with a particular idea as part of a song (Mediator) to avoid getting bogged down. Thankfully, I insisted on taking the contract home before signing it, as we all know the saying, 'If it seems too good to be true…'

A contact of mine in Manchester had experienced chart success with the act he managed and ended up at No 2. So he was more knowledgeable on how the industry worked, and had seen a fair amount of record contracts in his time. Paul very kindly offered to take a look over ours and advise me on whether to move forward or not.

I remember him calling and telling me to find a pen and some paper, then spending over an hour of his time going through every single aspect of it. 'That bit is fine, Pete. Do not agree to that. This part is standard. Under no circumstances sign that part.' Paul's advice was invaluable, and the upshot of it was that we said

'Thanks, but no thanks' to the deal, as it would have meant that everything the band or individual members produced in the future, for ever, would be owned by this company. A lesson learnt.

From almost the minute I agreed to manage the band, things had been a bit of a whirlwind, and barely a week would go by without something new happening or being offered. We had built up a decent fan base and reputation, good and bad, and would bring people together every time we put on a gig. My issue was that we hadn't been playing enough live – something I believed we should be doing at least two or three times a week if we were to give ourselves a chance of taking things to the next level. The more you play, the better and tighter you become, and the more you manage to get your name out there. I understood it was pretty tough to try and achieve this, as usually everybody is working, and it costs money to transport yourself about for very little financial reward. But like him or not, it is no coincidence that Ed Sheeran had to play over 500 live gigs before he was eventually noticed.

I once heard an early demo of his and he sounded absolutely awful, but he got out there, slept on mates' sofas, and played, played, played, until he honed his talents and went from performing at the Mad Ferret pub in Preston to headlining Glastonbury on his own. I recall reading a tweet by him in 2011: 'Is there anyone near the Mad Ferret in Preston that can give me a cup of tea and a shower, in return for a tune.' Imagine! And he didn't even stipulate it had to be a Yorkshire teabag. He did whatever it took to get out there and play live to folk, and to be fair, we should have been doing the same.

It had been clear for a while that the band's (Neal and Joss) listening tastes had gone from The Libertines and The Cribs, to be replaced by The Editors and Foals, and Neal had made the decision to actually rename the band. 'What Torrents were splitting up now,' after years of effort for them to get to this stage. I was in shock, but what did my head in the most was that in his wisdom he had taken it upon himself to delete the band's Myspace page. So, all the friends and contacts I had spent over three years building up had now been lost forever into hyperspace, without even as much as a discussion (no more amazing feedback from China). I was furious.

I eventually managed to talk the band into playing a final show at The Live Lounge, explaining that it was the least we could do to thank the people who had supported us.

Saturday, 19th February, the poster advertised Torrents' final gig, with support on the night from Danny Connors and The Ladders, and a great new band named The Shaiyans. Neal introduced me to a band from Northampton who he loved, called The On Off's, featuring Andy Crofts (now with The Moons and Paul Weller) and Danny Connors (who now plays guitar for Tom Grennan). We had contacted Danny via Myspace, and he liked what he heard so agreed to play the show with us.

One of the best shows that The Torrents ever played was at The Hordens, around New Year. The venue was packed and was enhanced by the appearance of Tony from Manchester, Wan Appy, and the Leeds Lads, all making the effort. Throughout their set, the crowd had gone mental, jumping up and down, and singing along to every lyric, including my daughter Emma and her mates, which I buzzed off. Danny and The Ladders had also been on the bill with us that night, and they agreed to play our last show.

I felt a little strange on the final night, knowing that everything I had worked towards was about to end. The gig was a good-tempered affair, and even Swanny got up on stage to join them for a couple of songs, and actually looked like he enjoyed it. I thought it was a nice touch hearing the crowd chanting his name to get him up. Naturally they ended with *21*, and Neal's final words were, 'Right, this one is for everybody who has supported us. Cheers, thank you very much. We'll see you soon, I suppose.' And that was it, Torrents were no more.

Imagining this would be the end of my management role, the band assured me that they planned to carry on, but they would have a different name, different songs, and different haircuts. So I wasn't sure if it would be for me. We spent weeks trying to come up with a new band name, and something you would imagine would be easy, it proved extremely hard to come up with something that hadn't already been used and did not sound naff.
Finally, Neal announced that their new band name would be Mondays Arms, and I thought he was winding me up, as it was something you were more likely to read on a pub sign. He loved an album by The Harrisons from Sheffield and got the name from one of their songs. Eventually everyone agreed to go with it – not that they had a say in it anyway.

Even though the songs were different, they sounded okay, but he now sounded like Tom Smith from The Editors, which absolutely was not my bag. It's fair to say that the majority of the people who had supported us over the years, including family, were bemused by these dramatic changes, and who could blame them? To spend years building up a brand then end up flushing it down the toilet was beyond me. And it didn't take long for my patience to run thin, after spending a large part of my time trying to explain to folk what the band name meant.

My main problem was that I kept attending band rehearsals, and still believed they were the best band in the town, so why wouldn't I want to manage them? One of the things that had attracted me to The Torrents was their attitude and swagger as a band, but I didn't feel it was the same for me with Mondays Arms. However, I had worked with them for a long time and believed in them as people, so I decided to stay in the role – for now, anyway.

Sandhills recording studio in Liverpool became the studio of choice, and I attended the first recording session but left them to it on the second. I also arranged with Jamie for them to do a college studio session, and that night he messaged me to confirm he thought they were the best band in Blackburn. (So, it wasn't just me.)

We played our regular gigs at The Mad Ferret, which went down really well, but I still had my doubts as to whether I could still give them 100% and keep my life on hold to support them in their new direction. I loved *End of the Pier*, and some of their other tunes were okay, but they didn't match up to *A Certain Girl, He's A Victim*, or any of The Torrents' tracks, as far as I was concerned. If I was undecided about what to do, a couple of incidents certainly made up my mind for me.

We were offered a gig with Dave and Toby's new bands (out of Dustins) at The Flowerpot in Camden. On the night before we planned to set off, I felt really ill, and was debating if I was fit enough to go. Even though I was also properly skint at the time, I decided it was only a cold – man flu at the worst – and agreed to go, as I never normally missed gigs.

Austin's cousin Martin lived in London, and Austin told us he was happy to put us up for the night, had plenty of food, and would arrange a meal for when we arrived. The minibus picked us up about 9pm, and I chose to sit at the back on my own, being unsociable, due to how rough I felt. The boys stopped off at the first services and filled up on hamburgers, and also at the second, to treat themselves to a selection of doughnuts. On both occasions I stayed on board the bus, knowing I was skint and planning to make do with the couple of chicken sandwiches and bottle of water I had brought with me.

I was freezing and starving (man flu) and put off tucking into my butties for as long as I could, knowing I only had two. No sooner had I taken them out of the silver foil than Austin came over and asked me if he could have one. Then, once he noticed my water, he asked if he could have that, too. The greed and selfishness of these requests really wound me up. I'd watched them all stuff their faces at the previous stops, and at no point had any of them asked if I wanted anything.

The longer the journey took, the rougher I felt. Normally, their bus antics would amuse me and keep me entertained, to an extent, but I had very little tolerance for them on this occasion and was beginning to realise that I had made the wrong decision about going.

We arrived in London at about two in the morning. First, we struggled to find Martin's address, and second, what made things even worse was that for some strange reason he wasn't answering his phone, which I found pathetic when he was expecting us.

It was 3.30am before he answered and we managed to be let into his flat. Just as I was thinking that this nightmare couldn't possibly get any worse, it did. The promise of a meal on arrival had been a fantasy (lie), as not only had he no food in, but he didn't even have enough milk for us to have a brew.

Sleeping arrangements had clearly been sorted out in advance, and while Joss and Rachel disappeared into the bedroom to claim the double bed, I was told that the kitchen floor was to be my resting place for the rest of the night (morning). It's not as if I had expected a bed or anything, but I wasn't even given a blanket, a pillow, or a cushion; I was literally lying on the kitchen floor with my head where people had walked. And despite the fact I was ill and was also their manager, I wasn't given a second thought. Needless to say, I didn't manage to get a second's sleep, and once everybody else had finally risen, I found it impossible to even be in the same room as them. I headed out of the door, telling them I would see them at the venue later that day.

I ended up getting the tube over to my mate Simon's house, and surprised myself by managing not to get lost, which is normally standard. It was a relief meeting up with Simon and his partner Karen, and as per usual, Simon was the perfect host and treated me to a full English at a nearby pub. Then he, Karen, and his beloved dog Rufus, took me on a tour of Hampstead Heath, which was just what I needed to enable me to calm down.

I had never done anything like that before, just walking out and leaving the band, but I felt I needed to, and hoped it might get them to think about things other than themselves. Simon gave me a lift on the back of his scooter through the streets of Camden, and we turned up at The Flowerpot early evening in time to catch our soundcheck. I was standing chatting to him at the bar, when Joss, who was sitting across from us perched on his orange amp, shouted for me to get them some water from behind the bar, and a pen and paper for them to write down the set for the night (Babysitting).

Usually this would have been second nature to me to sort these things out, but before I had chance to reply 'yeah, no problem', Simon literally said in a very concerned voice, 'Why the fu... can't he just get them?' This really was a lightbulb moment for me, and I can't express enough the impact that those simple eight words had made on me. Don't get me wrong, I had agreed to manage the band – The Torrents, anyway – and I had always been happy to do whatever I could to help them out, but that moment made me realise that there was something sadly wrong if I was still wiping their backsides after four years of being involved.
I am not writing this to slag anybody off. For a lot of it, I blame myself for my own actions, but I am merely writing down my honest account of how I felt at the time, based on my memory. Also, I figured that if I had been that good a manager after several years in the role, they should have been sorting out stuff like that for themselves.

The night itself was really good, and the sound guy told me they were one of the best bands that had performed there in a while. It was great meeting up with the Dustins boys, and we managed to get another Camden gig under our belts, but for me things were never the same after that London trip.

My main issue with the band was that in my opinion they were still not playing enough live gigs, and out of four new offers that I got them to play, they would turn down at least two. We had played 22 gigs in the past year, and it should have been 122.

My final decision was to set them a challenge, and depending on how it went would determine if I was prepared to stay involved or not. Without them knowing, I arranged a seven-gig tour for them in places they hadn't played before, and with really decent support and headline bands. Cumbria, Liverpool (X 2), Manchester, Workington, Lancaster, and Blackburn, were all booked in. I booked the gigs, sorted out the posters, and put it all on a plate for them. All they had to do was turn up and play.

We were due to perform at Mowbray Music Festival in the Lakes on Saturday, 13th August, and I chased up their promoter all week in an attempt to talk him into giving us a better slot, which paid off. On the Friday night I was working at The Live Lounge, and at 11.45pm I received a text from Joss, explaining that they couldn't make the gig in the Lakes, as he and Neal were going to the Rovers match.

I knew from that very second I was no longer prepared to manage them, and if I didn't stand down now, I would end up resenting them, which was the last thing I had wanted to happen. I knew I could have gone and offered any other band a tour that was all booked and all the promo sorted, and they would have been more than grateful, and no doubt appreciated my efforts. But I guess like in a long-term relationship, people sometimes take others for granted, even though they have no intention of doing so. It was best for both me and them that I called it a day.

The following morning, I called up each member of the band and explained to them I had decided to stand down as their manager, and everyone told me they understood. Maybe they knew it was coming, or maybe they wanted me to leave. Who knows? But they broke up the following week anyway, which spoke volumes to me.

The important thing to me about the end of this chapter in my life is that I had originally agreed to manage the band because I liked them as human beings. And thankfully, all these years later, I still think the world of them.

My daughter Emma was sharing a train journey with a lad out of a local band we knew, and he questioned why I bothered still managing a band as nothing ever seemed to happen, in his opinion.

I am not one who believes in self-recommendation, so I guess the band should really reply to that, but what I do know is that the reason that The Torrents' story in my book is so long, is because so many things happened and almost all of them were positive.

Also, my time managing the band was some of the best time of my life, and I would like to think that the same could be said about theirs. We might not have signed a record contract, but we have some brilliant memories from back then. And the fact that I helped to make those memories is good enough for me.

CHAPTER TWENTY-NINE

FIVE DAYS IN A FIELD

After attending my very first gig in the 70s, live music became a massive part of my life. But as far as festivals went, our local Arts in the Park event was as exciting as things got up until my invitation to Scotland in 2004. There's no doubt that the Wickerman Festival gave me the taste for something bigger.

I had always heard tales about Glastonbury and read about it in the press, but in 2007 we made a conscious decision to attend. Five days in a muddy field in Somerset might not be everybody's idea of fun, but it had always sounded magical to me to have the majority of your music collection performing in one field or another (maybe not the mud).

Long gone were the days when you could get into the festival site for free by jumping over the wall, and the problem was that tickets were like gold dust, as people would travel from as far as Australia to party in Pilton each year. Me, John from Unilab, my brother-in-law Warren, and his best mate Dave, made it our mission to try and get our hands on a golden ticket each. As luck would have it, 2007 was the first year that the festival introduced a photo ID system requirement on the ticket, which ended any option of attempting to buy from secondary ticket sites as a last resort. Tickets always go on sale first thing on a Sunday morning, so we all shared our bank and registration details with each other, and I sat in my office with two computer screens open, along with my mobile phone, refreshing the screen every five seconds.

By 10.45am, all 137,500 allocated tickets had been sold out in record time, at a cost of £145 each, and to our absolute delight,

Dave had somehow managed to secure ours, while in an hour-and-a-half of trying, I hadn't even managed to access the site even once. We had given ourselves a better chance by agreeing to go for the coach + event ticket option, and luckily this strategy had paid off.

The coach picked us up at Lime Street in Liverpool on the Thursday, and it took hours to finally arrive in Somerset. By the time we made it to Glastonbury town, the roads were absolutely gridlocked, and you just witnessed a row of coaches up ahead for as far as the eye could see. We were moving so slowly along the country lanes that a group of us managed to jump off the coach, visit a local pub for a pint, and literally just stroll a few yards further down the road to reboard our coach. I kid you not.

As it was our first Glastonbury and we didn't really know what to expect, I took far too much baggage. It was a real pain, standing holding it for hours as we slowly shuffled our way through field after field until we finally reached the entrance gates. Both Dave and John were dab hands at putting a tent up, so Warren and I appreciated their skills and contributed very little to the task of erecting our new homes for the next five days. The sheer scale of the festival site amazed us all, and no sooner had the tents gone up than we headed off to investigate and see what entertainment we could find.

On entering the site, we were all given a couple of free toilet rolls, but what we hadn't been given was a warning about how horrendous the toilets would actually be. I had heard rumours and read about what sort of thing to expect, but nothing had prepared me for the reality of the situation once you were actually there. Just in case anybody is eating while they are reading this story, I will refrain from going into any further details on the subject, but needless to say, I spent the next few days trying my best to avoid them, to the best of my ability.

We stumbled upon a giant tent calling itself The Queen's Head, and I was buzzing that the first act we saw was a London band called Underground Heroes, who Neal had told me to listen out for.

Unless you have actually been to the festival, it is almost impossible to get folk to appreciate how big it really is. And with 177,000 music fans attending that year, the odds on finding your tent at the end of the night were extremely slim. Dave told us he had planned ahead, and had brought with him a large yellow flag, advertising Preston Fire Service where he had worked. His idea was to put it up outside his tent, so that we could find it amongst all the other tents. In theory, this was a brilliant idea, but once it was dark, we realised that almost everybody else had come up with the same idea. Finding it became a real mission, even on a Thursday.

One of the first acts we were lucky enough to see on the Friday was Amy Winehouse on the Pyramid Stage at 3.10pm, and little did we know at that moment how lucky we were, and that this would be the first and last time I would get to see her live.

We tried our best to try and discover all the different areas throughout the day, but mud and rain were certainly on the menu, and we found it a proper struggle simply trying to walk from A to B most of the time. At one stage the mud was literally less than one inch off the rim of your wellies, so a very slow shuffle was required in order to prevent it from ending up inside your boots as you were walking.

If the normal toilets were bad, they were nothing compared to the long drops. The secret was not to look down, if you found yourself in the position of having to use them. We even heard the story about people actually falling into them on previous occasions, which to be honest doesn't bear thinking about, true or not.

Before you go to Glastonbury, each person makes a list of all the acts they are hoping to see – maybes, hopefully, and definite. I use different coloured highlighters so that they stand out once I am on site. Obviously, nothing really goes exactly to plan, and everybody has different ideas about who they are hoping to catch, so rather than just wandering off on your own for the majority of the weekend (which would be done for everybody highlighted 'definite') you would need to compromise with your festival buddies. After all, we had all gone together. Also, you needed to give yourself enough time to get to your chosen area, taking mud levels into account, and on some occasions it just wasn't worth the effort.

Over 700 acts played on over 80 stages in 2007, so you really did have to plan your wish list wisely. What always amazed me was, whether you were performing on the Other Stage, John Peel Tent, or even on the Band Stand on The Common, you would always have an audience. Even when the headliner was doing their stuff on The Pyramid, folk would choose to check out some of the more obscure performances, which was great.

That evening (Friday), we chosen our positions in front of The Pyramid Stage to gain the best view that we could for the night's entertainment. Our wish lists had all been the same from then on, and read: The Fratellis, Kasabian, and Sheffield's finest Arctic Monkeys. I sneaked my camcorder in and was capturing as much footage as I could, despite being knocked all over by the exceptionally exuberant crowd.

The Fratellis warmed up the crowd, but if the truth be known, the majority of folk were mainly waiting for Chelsea Dagger. I've never been a huge Kasabian fan, but appreciated what they brought to a live performance. Arctic Monkeys were something else, opening their highly rehearsed set with *When the Sun Goes Down*, followed by hit after hit, to the delight of the crowd. The audience went mental for *Dancefloor* (rightly so) and for my personal favourite at the time, *Mardy Bum*.
The encore was incredible, starting off with *The View from the Afternoon*, followed by a tip of the hat to Dame Shirley Bassey who was performing on the Sunday, with a superb version of *Diamonds Are Forever*. There was a mesmerizing performance of

505, with his invited special guest and mate Miles Kane, and after we were treated to 21 songs, *A Certain Romance* ended our first Friday night at Glastonbury.

I had been standing in the same spot for the best part of seven hours constantly filming, and found myself unable to move once they had finished. The problem was there were 100,000 people all attempting to make their way out of the field, and I had no option other than to hobble my way in the same direction. My back had gone, and I was in complete agony, bent over and unable to stand up straight. Warren and Dave made their way off somewhere, and to be fair, John's patience was hugely appreciated as he stayed with me and supported me as it took over an hour to find our way back to our field, when it would usually take about ten minutes.

We finally arrived back at the site, but by now thousands of extra tents had pitched up, and all with the idea of placing a flag at the side, so we didn't have a clue where our two-berth was. It had been a really long day, managing to cope with all the mud and all the elements, and with my back in agony all I wanted to do was crash out, but we needed to find our tent first. I recall falling over guy rope after guy rope, in an effort to find my bearings, as it was two in the morning, pitch black, and I was freezing, in pain, and lost in a field in Somerset.

Somehow, I even managed to lose John (my carer), but heard some voices in the distance, so was drawn towards them. The closer I got, I realised it was a group of people sitting around a campfire, chatting and playing some songs on an acoustic guitar. I introduced myself and explained I was lost, but felt as though the way I was stumbling around they would probably think I was out of my head. No sooner had I started to explain to them about this great new band I had seen the previous day in The Queens Head, than I suddenly realised it was actually them! I told them I had managed to film most of their set, and George from the band wrote his contact details down on a minute scrap of paper using an eye-liner pencil. (Rock and Roll, eh?)

When I eventually found our tent, I noticed John sitting outside, no doubt kindly waiting for me, but even then it took me another 15 minutes before I managed to bend down enough to let myself in. In all honesty, I had been in so much pain once Arctic Monkeys finished that I was convinced I would end up having to visit the nearest hospital. But thankfully, with John's support and patience, I managed to avoid such a journey.

The years of filming and putting all my efforts into keeping as still as I could for long periods of time have taken its toll, and now if I find myself standing in the same spot for any length of time at a gig, I can feel my back starting to go, which is a signal for me to try and move around a bit more.

By the Saturday the weather really was dreadful, and what I found the hardest was having to carry your bag or all your stuff for the day without being able to put it down for a while, or also to sit down, due to the mud being so bad. It blagged my head walking into a disco tent in the middle of the morning, witnessing a full-blown rave taking place as though I had got my timings wrong.

I was looking forward to Lily Allen later that afternoon, but just before she was due on stage, the rumour was that The Enemy were about to play a secret gig around the corner in The Guardian Lounge. Both Dave and I legged it over and joined the queue, and once in, managed to push our way right to the front. Tom, Liam, and Andy took to the stage, and I was literally about two feet away from the singer's mic. From the first energetic notes, the packed-out crowd were proper up for it, and when they got round to performing *Aggro*, the whole tent erupted. I managed to film most of the set, and it remains to date one of my favourite ever gigs. (Top 10 maybe.)

That night, The Killers were headlining the Pyramid Stage, and I knew for sure that I wouldn't be found there. I had heard about this magical part of Glastonbury, named Lost Vagueness, that only came to life after dark and when all the stages had finished. The others didn't seem as interested in it as me, so I agreed to go and check it out on my own, as I was sure they were planning on attending The Killers gig anyway.

As I was making my way towards the old rail track, I noticed some band performing on the Other Stage in the distance, and tried to work out who they were, as I watched their front man half-hanging off the front of stage. As it turned out, that band and frontman was Iggy Pop and The Stooges, and I could have kicked myself for not taking the time to go over and check them out. When will I ever get that opportunity again to see the Godfather of Punk and his band?

Even though the place I was trying to get to was at the end of a very long path, it was proving more difficult to know which actual turn-off I needed to take once I was near the end of it. I walked into an area that featured half a jumbo jet aeroplane just situated on the floor, but once I attempted to board it, I realised it was actually a cocktail bar.

I eventually arrived at my destination, and I cannot express enough how crazy and mental the place was. There was a makeshift wooden chapel where folk could get married, and I believe Peter Andre and Jordan had done so there that weekend. I noticed a wooden prop that resembled the front of a hotel, and, intrigued, I stepped inside to find a giant jacuzzi being occupied by several bikini-clad females. Wherever you looked, craziness was happening, and it was certainly the strangest place I had ever visited. My only complaint was that no matter how hard I tried, I couldn't find anywhere where I could buy a beer, or even a normal drink for that matter. Just to add to the madness (literally), there were rumours that the band Madness were due to be helicoptered in at 2am to play a secret gig in the giant circus tent. It actually happened, but the tent was so packed with folk trying to get a piece of the action (so they could spend the next few months bragging 'I was there') that I couldn't even make it to the entrance, and had to watch the gig the best I could from outside.

Around 3am, I felt shattered and had given up on any chance of finding a drink, so I figured I might as well start to make my way back to our tent. I made my way to the entrance and attempted to start to walk back along the same path, but could hardly move as thousands of partygoers were all walking towards me. It actually felt as though I was in some weird dream where no matter how hard I tried, I just couldn't reach my planned destination. I'm not sure what it is supposed to mean, but growing up I would regularly have a dream where I was trying to reach somebody, but never quite made it. If I was trying to walk or run somewhere, it would always be in slow motion, or if I was desperate to ring someone, the phone box would always be vandalised and not working, or the 2ps would run out before I managed to say my bit. A bit like *Life on Mars*, I would always wake up without getting to my destination or talking to the person I wanted to.

It really was surreal trying to walk in one direction when everybody else was walking towards me en masse, and it felt as though it took forever to move forward just several metres. It turned out all my efforts were for nothing, as I was stopped and pulled over to the side of the path, only to be told by the police that I couldn't go back the way I had come because they had cordoned it off. I explained I needed to go back in that direction as that was where I was camping, but they couldn't have cared less, so I ended up walking in the opposite direction.

At least now, I was heading in the same direction as everybody else, but then some guy in a hi-vis jacket (obviously important) directed me into a field full of tepees. I really couldn't imagine the evening (morning) getting any stranger, but found myself stumbling around a pitch-black field full of giant tents, and could hear voices and music, but couldn't see a soul. I guessed I might as well take my chances and venture into one of the tepees to see what was going on, and to my amazement I'd stumbled upon a full-blown party taking place. It was literally like the Tardis; inside the tent seemed to be about ten times larger than it looked on the outside. It hosted a proper bar inside, and everybody was acting as though they had just arrived from another planet (a real flower power moment).

Still craving a drink, I headed over to the bar and asked if they had any lager, only to be told by some strange looking, hippy guy, 'Sorry, man, we only serve Love Potion here.' I explained I was sharing my tent with another bloke, so I decided to leave it, and resigned myself to the fact that I would not be drinking alcohol for the foreseeable. I don't really know how I managed to make my way back to our tent, but somehow I did, and no matter how much I attempted to describe my previous night's experience to the others, I knew I couldn't possibly do it justice or get them to believe how mad it had been.

Sunday morning, I watched The Coral and The Cribs in the rain (my two favourite current bands), but the terrible weather certainly hadn't put off most people, and many folk were covered from head to foot in mud, dancing. Some were even diving in it. The Enemy performed on The Other stage, ignoring the elements, whilst the audience had brought their own form of entertainment to the party by providing a display of frisbee throwing, no doubt in an attempt to keep themselves warm.

We had been really lucky with where we had ended up pitching our tents, as some fields were so waterlogged that the tents had simply floated away.

Sunday afternoon, I decided to go off on my own and explore some of the smaller stages that the festival had to offer, but once I heard the vocal tones of one Dame Shirley Bassey, it was impossible not to hang on for a while and appreciate how incredible it was. Her performance at Glastonbury 2007 was very nearly her final one, as no sooner had her private helicopter set off than the weather conditions had forced her pilot to perform an emergency landing. The decision was taken after the pilot discovered that the Battersea heliport had shut down due to the bad weather, and he was forced to touch down at Collingwood College in Surrey, along with her fellow passenger, world renowned music promoter Harvey Goldsmith.

After potentially cheating death, the 70-year-old singer – dressed in a Mac and a pair of wellies – emerged from her aircraft declaring to the group of already gathered locals that she did not need a cup of tea, but could really do with using somebody's bathroom. (Imagine.)

We had all been looking forward to The Who headlining the Sunday night, but we hadn't put any effort into fighting for a place at the front. Instead, we opted to sit on top of the hill, underneath my large umbrella, not looking forward to the prospect of having to take down our tents in only a few hours' time.

The Who were marvellous, but it was difficult to take in all the atmosphere being so far away from the stage. They opened as always with *I Can't Explain*, and despite the terrible weather affecting the sound quality at times, they ended Glastonbury 2007 with a six-song encore, including *The Kids Are Alright*, *Pinball Wizard*, and *Amazing Journey*, before we made our way back to our tents in an attempt to try and get dry and maybe grab a few hours' sleep.

Glastonbury Festival is renowned for its poor weather conditions, and a part of me had wanted to experience the complete thing, but by the time Monday morning came around, we were all sick to death of it.
Attempting to take down our tents whilst it was throwing it down was certainly not my idea of fun, but the biggest challenge was to try and keep hold of our belongings during the journey from the campsite to where the coaches were supposed to be picking us up. I struggled to keep everything I was carrying out of the mud and felt as though my arms were about to drop off, but letting go was not an option.

We'd had a fantastic weekend but now I just wanted to get home. So imagine our disappointment when we eventually made it over to the coach park only to be told that all the coaches had been cancelled. Unbeknown to us, the weather had been so extreme throughout the country that a number of towns and roads were completely flooded, meaning coaches had struggled to get anywhere near the site. It literally was a nightmare, and after five days in a field, it was the last thing we wanted to hear.

The car park itself resembled an accident scene, with folk walking up and down looking exhausted, covered in large, silver foil-type cloaks to keep them warm, and thousands all congregating, not having a clue how they were about to get home. After what felt like ages, an official showed up to explain that it wasn't possible for individual coaches to make it onto the site. So, throughout the afternoon, if a coach turned up that happened to be heading anywhere near the town you were trying to get to, you would just have to do your upmost to push your way onto it. Basically, it was a free-for-all, with a first-come-first-served policy.

We managed to jump on board maybe the third coach that showed up with the name Liverpool written on the front, and to our relief we were dropped off back at Lime Street, only to find we would have to wait at least another hour before our train back to Preston was due. I was so fed up at the time, cold, hungry, and beyond shattered, that I offered to pay £100 for us to hire a taxi straight back to Blackburn. But the other three opted to go and find a pub, thinking it was far too much to spend for the sake of an hour. All I could think about was that boiling hot bath that would be waiting for me on my return. Not Rock and Roll, I know. But true.

I had got my first ever Glastonbury under my belt, and despite all the challenging elements, I was hooked. I am not sure if it was all the mythology relating to the place, regarding Joseph of Arimathea and King Arthur and the Holy Grail, or even the story that Jesus himself had once visited the legendary town, or that it is said to be built on ley lines, but whatever it is, I really did find it to be a truly magical place. I think the fact that anything goes is a huge contributing factor. I mean, if a 65-year-old bloke walked past you and was wearing a wedding dress, hardly anybody, if any, would even bat an eyelid. Thousands of like-minded people just turned up in a field in Somerset once a year, simply to be themselves. No matter if you were a bank manager, a lawyer, or a window cleaner, you could simply lose all your inhibitions, dress how you like, and act how you want, in order to escape the pressures of the real world and simply let your hair down for those five days out of 365 – and be entertained on top of it.

Who wouldn't want to experience that? And I would urge everybody – even if music is not your main goal – to add it to your bucket list and experience it at least once. It is certainly the first date I look out for every year. And along with Ibiza, it has become my favourite place to visit, and is a very special place for me.

CHAPTER THIRTY

NO SMOKING

From the moment I discovered The Beatles on that family holiday with my parents, music has always been a major force in my life, and I truly could not imagine going any length of time without it. From the second I started to receive spending money, music-related items have been the main thing I spend my money on. Vinyl records, CDs, concert tickets, festival passes, band t-shirts, books, magazines, posters, badges, and any other relevant memorabilia I can get my hands on. But I never imagined that I would go from watching *Top of the Pops* each week with my mates, to working with some of the very same artists that I took great delight from watching on my TV screen back then.

Before Punk, working in music had seemed totally out of reach, but even though I never had a desire to be a roadie (too hard), my one experience in the role with SLF had given me a taste of being on the other side of the stage and hanging out with the band, which I loved and felt at home with.

From starting off taking photos of Faded Image at aged 16 to filming some of my musical heroes in later life, opportunities have just got better and better. My decision to buy myself a camcorder, after being taught how to edit, was a door-opener, as I have ended up filming for the likes of Buzzcocks, The Futureheads, The Enemy, Pauline Black, Dodgy, Ghosts, and for members of The Who, The Jam, and The Specials, to name a few.

I feel it is safe to say that up until I started in youth work and then in music, I wasn't really open to the idea of making new friends or letting people in. I had always felt as though I had by far enough friends already, so I never really felt the need to make any new ones. I am sure at times I may have come across as ignorant, which was never my intention, but while my mates would return from their holidays saying that they had met up with Dwain and Debbie in Benidorm, and they planned to meet up with them in a few weeks to share their Super Snaps Prints, I never had the desire to know anybody new and would usually just keep myself to myself.

All this attitude changed once I started to work with young people, as It was all about sharing good practice in order to best equip yourself in supporting that individual, even though that sometimes only ever happened in theory and not practice. And once I started to dip my toe inside the music industry, my attitude changed even more, because the whole thing was about networking and getting your product to as many people as you could. Managing a band introduced me to a large number of new, like-minded friends and contacts, as did filming.

Paul at The Live Lounge asked me if I fancied being a promoter/booker for them, and remembering how I had felt after putting The Stiffs on, I accepted, and joined the team of him, Julian, and Curtis. The Live Lounge had started with a bang in Blackburn, and like anything new, had attracted a fair amount of people attending most of the early gigs. It was a welcome edition to the local music scene and would offer most of the local acts a chance to perform there on a regular basis. Ju was managing local band New York Tourists, so when any well-known acts performed at the venue, they would usually find themselves added to the line-up, along with Torrents, as they both usually brought a crowd.

The Paddingtons gig was a standout one to me, as they were a great band and very underrated, in my opinion. I remember pogoing at the front with Curtis's mum Louise and loving every minute of the chaos. Twisted Wheel was also memorable, having attended some of their early gigs before they signed to Columbia (one of which had been in the Cellar Bar Basement). Simon and

Oscar from Ocean Colour Scene performed an acoustic show at the venue and they were brilliant, but the biggest crowd that the venue ever had was when Tim and Mark from The Charlatans performed.

It's a miracle that the gig even happened, as a Fire Chief had told Paul that unless he expanded the entrance doors at the front of the building, it would not be allowed to go ahead, as the capacity would have to remain at 150 people. We had sold a lot more tickets than that, so Paul had no option but to sort out the alterations.

On the night, Paul told me that there were over 300 in, and to be fair, even I struggled to get a decent view of the stage, and I am over 6ft 2. Even once the gig started, three fire officers had been standing outside the front doors, debating with Paul about how many people were inside, and even though he invited them in to count everybody for themselves, it was almost impossible to step foot inside the place because it was that rammed. We ended up getting away with it, and Tim and Mark continued entertaining the masses, totally oblivious that the gig could have been pulled at any minute.

If you are someone who has never put on a show on your own, it is hard to appreciate how much work actually goes into making it happen. It is never just a case of booking a band and then waiting for them to turn up on the night. I would spend hours during the week checking out new bands, before selecting two or three for a line-up. Then once I had given them all the venue details, explained to them what back line we would be providing – to avoid having a room full of drum kits and amps – I'd arrange with them what they needed to bring.

Then a poster and maybe some flyers need to be planned, designed, and ordered, and I would spend the rest of the week promoting and pushing the event. A couple of days before, I would contact all the acts to let them know what time their soundcheck would be – once the sound engineer had confirmed a time when he was due to arrive – and I would feel obliged to make it down to the venue early to meet the acts that I had booked, and to be there while they set their stuff up and for the soundcheck. Most bands would be offered, or demand, a rider, so that would have to be negotiated, purchased, and dished out, and we would usually let them make use of the band room upstairs so they could chill out before their set.

One of my favourite bands that played the venue were The Crookes from Sheffield, and along with being a splendid bunch of chaps, their style and their songs were a breath of fresh air for me and a change from watching indie band after indie band trying to stake a claim to be the next Oasis or Arctic Monkeys, which was never going to happen. I had never heard of the band at the time, as it was Ju who had booked them, but what impressed me the most and was impossible to ignore was how they adapted to a not very interested Blackburn audience.
They had performed two or three songs on stage, and being honest, most folk in the room were not really paying attention, preferring to talk through their tunes or just mess around on their phones. Suddenly, the band jumped down off stage, gathered in a circle in the middle of the crowd, and proceeded to sing an acapella version of their incredible song *Yes, Yes, We're Magicians*, which literally blew everyone away. And once they returned to the stage, they found themselves with a captive audience listening to every lyric. I likened the moment to a comedian being heckled and how they would respond in an attempt to win over the crowd. I just thought it was genius, and proved how talented they really were (along with proving they had balls).

The Crookes ended up signing to Fierce Panda Records, and I know Steve Lamacq had been a fan and had even put them up at his home one night. But I never felt they got the recognition they deserved, and I'd urge anybody reading this book to go and check them out – especially that song. I still maintain that their lead singer George has one of the best voices I have heard in music.

Certainly, one of my favourite bands (if not the favourite) that I managed to bring to the venue was The Tapestry from Manchester.

Following a tip-off to check them out, I liked what I had heard and booked them to support a Brighton band called Munich. It was early evening, and all of a sudden a minibus pulled up outside the venue and an army of people wearing red prised themselves out and burst into the room in an explosion of colour (red), declaring that the band had arrived. Apparently, The Tapestry used to pick a theme before every show in order to get their friends, family, and fans involved, and to make things more interesting. Grown-up blokes were wearing dresses, and The Live Lounge was full of red balloons. Being partial to a bit of chaos myself, I knew whatever they did next, I would love it.

Their live performance that night certainly didn't disappoint and was even madder than I was expecting, calling everybody on stage towards the end of their set, and only stopping once it became impossible to carry on performing. The guy in the red dress must have been punched in the nose at some point in the mayhem, and the blood on his face matched his outfit, but he was having the time of his life, dancing and jumping about the stage.

Paul had been out for the night with his wife Sharon, and they both arrived at the venue just as the stage riot was happening. I could tell by their reaction they were unsure what they were witnessing, whereas I knew I had just discovered my favourite new band.

Our Emma ended up getting a job at the place, and at the start was only 15 so was limited to glass collecting, but as soon as she was old enough (ish) she ended up behind the bar. This was great, and at least she got to see all the bands for free, but it became pretty annoying on the times I found myself talking to members of the opposite sex, only to be interrupted by her coming over and asking me, in a rather loud tone, what I thought Mum would be doing.

When she first started working there, several friends, and even members of my own band, warned me against it, telling me that it wasn't safe. But Emma told me she had been cool with everything, and I knew that Paul and the team would definitely have her back, if anything happened. As it turned out, it was the best thing she could have done at the time, as it really helped with her confidence and brought her out of her shell, along with giving her life skills, teaching her how to deal with the general public and how to handle drunks. And I really do believe that this education at Live Lounge has put her in good stead to carry out her job in retail today. Along with that, she has very fond memories of those times and the people she got to meet.

On one occasion, Emma was working when somebody she knew, and had obviously fallen out with, apparently just walked over and went for her, attacking her out of the blue. Paul was upstairs in the office watching the incident on CCTV, and told me he was just about to rush down and offer some assistance to his employee when he watched Emma spin this girl around – despite her being twice Emma's size – and wrestle her to the floor. So, he ended up staying put in the office, assuming that Emma didn't need any help sticking up for herself!

On one occasion, I was having a pint in the Irish pub across the road and was gazing out of the window, when I noticed Emma on her break, standing outside the venue chatting to the doormen. Suddenly I noticed she was holding a cigarette in her hand, and as smoking has always been one of my pet hates, I remember feeling sick. Obviously, it is up to my daughter whatever she chooses to do in life, but I was mortified. It had never entered my head that she would ever smoke. I never mentioned it to her on the night, but recall waking up Janet when I arrived home. She in turn discussed it with Emma the following day and was assured it had been a complete one-off. Even though it is really nothing to do with me, and for all I know she might be a chain-smoker behind my back, but it was the first and last time I ever saw her holding a fag.

Around the same time I had been working at The Live Lounge, a new venue was due to open in Preston, named Blitz. The owner, another Pete, contacted me and asked if I was free to meet up to discuss the possibility of me booking for them. I was honoured that he had even considered me for that role, and agreed to meet him and his daughter Jenny to discuss the idea. I knew of Jenny from being the drummer in a band, and got on well with Pete. So despite not being able to drive, and the fact I had been booking for The Live Lounge, I guessed if they were kind enough to think of me, I should give it a go.

Opening night was Thursday, 27th September, 2012, and I helped secure The Sunshine Underground from Leeds to headline, booked The New York Tourists, and a band from Accy called Moral Panic. And believe it or not, the bottom of the bill, and first on, was none other than Catfish and the Bottlemen, who Jenny had known and booked. I felt the night was a complete success, and I guess Pete was happy as he asked me to start booking in some more nights.

I booked The Crookes to perform along with an artist I had been managing, called Miranda, but after I had been booking for them for around three weeks, I realised that it was actually costing me to put all this effort in and decided to ask if there was any chance of getting paid. Pete explained that there had not been any money coming in yet, but said he would look at the situation as soon as they started making a profit. I fully understood where he was coming from, even though I was a little surprised he expected me to lose out for helping him. I ended up explaining that I couldn't give up that much time for free, especially at cost, and wished them luck, but decided to leave the venue.

I really liked Pete and his family, and even though, luckily, we never fell out over it, I was gutted to leave. A few months later, somebody accused me of being greedy, referring to my decision to leave the place. That really upset me, and was the first time I had ever been accused of being that. It was also ironic, as up until that point my friends had always challenged me for putting events on and not making any money, and this was the first time I had actually been assertive and stuck up for myself, in terms of cash. I have never been financially motivated, but at the end of the day, I was spending hours per week attempting to book a line-up, paying to get some promo designed and printed off, paying for my own transport from Blackburn and back, and even having to buy my own drinks. So something had to give.

It is funny when you think about it. If I am representing an artist, or artists, I am confident I will get them the best deal I can, but when it comes to being that assertive for myself, I just can't seem to manage it. And I end up undervaluing myself on every occasion.

I recall putting The Stiffs on at Witton Park for the Arts in the Park event, and told the person from the council I was dealing with that the cheapest they would go out for was £1000, and not a penny less. They begrudgingly agreed to my demand, but a little nearer the time, they made out that they couldn't afford the full amount agreed. (Aye, alright!) I eventually agreed on a slightly lower fee but told them I wanted a hotel room included for the Saturday night. I remember ringing Phil from the band and telling him I had sorted a room out for him and Michelle, and even though they didn't actually need it, I explained that I had demanded it on principle.

When I arrived at the festival site on the day, I was just making my way backstage to say hello to Pauline Black, who was also performing, when I was stopped and warned against doing so. Apparently, the hotel room I had insisted on for The Stiffs was in fact the very same room that had been promised to The Selecter on their rider (so I was told), and the news had only just been broken to Pauline that it was no longer available. So, I was advised to leave things for a while, which I did. I have always felt bad about that hotel room incident, and have never explained my version to Pauline. So if by any far-fetched chance you are reading this (as if), I would like to offer my sincere apologies (sorry), even though it wasn't my decision.

After I stood down as manager of Mondays Arms, I had no real desire to make that commitment again, even though I had loved my time in that role. Now I was concentrating on filming and booking acts. A few people asked if I had heard of a local singer/songwriter called Miranda and told me I should check her out. I knew her brother through being in a local band, and agreed to go and watch her perform.

At the time, she was playing mainly covers in a local pub, but I could tell she was really talented and driven. And even though the gig was nothing at all to do with me, I remember asking the landlord if he minded turning down the volume on the TVs around the room, showing football, while she was performing. At the end of her set, I watched him come over and ask Miranda if she could carry on playing as the regulars were loving it. But I asked him if she was going to be paid any extra money for this, as she wasn't a performing monkey.

After the performance, Miranda asked if I could watch her perform some of her original songs, to give me chance to listen to her own compositions, so I arranged for her to play a private gig at The Live Lounge for me and my friend Sarah. Sarah had a really varied taste in music and a lot of it was not necessarily my cup of tea, but I really valued her opinion and knew she would be completely honest and not simply tell me what I had wanted to hear, which I appreciated.

Miranda performed about six of her own songs, and both of us were impressed. That night I was asked if I would consider managing her, and even though it was a world away from the chaos of The Torrents, I saw it as a challenge and agreed to take the role on.

I arranged a weekly practice at The Live Lounge for her and her brother Rory, and pulled Clive in to carry out a couple of photoshoots for her. One was at my old stomping ground, the pine woods, at some ridiculous time in the morning. And for the love of art, I found myself standing in the reservoir with water just below my knees, absolutely freezing, holding one of Clive's flashlights in the exact correct position. That is dedication.

We played a gig with The Crookes at Blitz, and she went down really well. She performed a song I rated, called *Escort*, which she had written with her brother and local rap artist, Rob. I felt it was certainly her standout track at the time and had good potential.

Because of the way I work – full on or not at all – I was always paranoid that things were going too fast. And even though I was not totally convinced, both Miranda and Rory assured me that was how they liked it. She had planned her solo album and even written the sleeve notes for it, then one day, completely out of the blue, I received a text from her mum telling me that she no longer wanted a manager, as the pressure of going to Uni, along with how fast everything had been happening, was getting too much. I was at a music conference at the time, and to be honest, I was totally gutted. I think mainly due to the reality of being rejected, but also the thought that I might have put pressure on somebody I had been trying to help. That was the last thing I had intended to do, as my only motivation had been to try and support a local artist who I believed was talented.

After that experience, I vowed never to manage anybody again. What it taught me was to always go with your gut feeling; you have it for a reason, and it will usually be right.

Even though I was determined to stick to my No Manager pledge, it didn't prevent the number of requests I received, and still do. Local bands and musicians would ask me outright if I fancied managing them, and I would get weekly, sometimes daily, requests online – something which has always amazed me.

Once, I received a digital package from a band, including their songs, their photos, and a folder with everything they had achieved so far. They expressed that they were really keen for me to manage them, and asked if I would consider their offer. Even though I had no intention of taking them up on this, once I finished reading the band bio, I was shocked to discover they were based in Mexico.

How on earth could I manage somebody from another country? And how on earth had they even heard about me? I messaged them and politely turned their request down, but did ask where they had heard of me. I received a reply explaining that they'd liked what I did with The Torrents. I was astonished that my promoting had travelled that far.

Somebody only really needs to look at my social media profiles to see that I have passion for everything Mod, yet I have lost count of the number of requests I have received to manage full-on Heavy Rock bands. I reckon over the years I have been asked to manage well over 100 times, and even though I appreciate every single one and take it as a compliment, I could never just put my life on hold again if I didn't 100% believe in the individual act, and if they did not excite me musically.

I once received a request from a Wakefield act called The Incredible Magpie Band, and after I thanked them but explained I was not planning on taking on such a role anymore, they asked if they could send me a copy of their upcoming album. After I had listened a couple of times, I realised that every single song on it was brilliant and questioned whether I had jumped the gun with my decision.

The Tapestry was a band that I loved enough to maybe make that commitment to manage, and even though I represented them for a short period of time and helped them get some high-profile support slots, I chose to never bring the subject up. I felt they were at a level where they needed somebody who had more time and could offer them a lot more than I could. They were another very underrated band, in my opinion, and I was always surprised they were never signed and offered a record deal. I went to watch them a lot live, and on every occasion the room would be packed and going mental throughout their set.

I remember one of their gigs in Wigan where, after their first couple of songs, most of the room was just sitting around and only half listening. But by the time they started to perform their fourth number, everybody was on their feet and going crazy. I once talked my mate Bullinge into coming with me to see them perform at Band on The Wall in Manchester, even though he was not really into new bands, or anything since the 1980s, to be honest. Towards the end of their set, he turned to me and said, 'I am not sure if they are ever going to make it,' to which I replied, 'To sell out a gig at Band on The Wall, and have everybody in the room going mad, dancing and singing along to all your songs, I reckon, they already have.'

CHAPTER THIRTY-ONE

2010

Just as 1961 is considered to be a good year for wine, as far as live music consumption goes 2010 is unlikely to be beaten – certainly as far as I am concerned.
In 2008, we failed to secure Glastonbury tickets, but attended the festival again in 2009. There was no way we were risking going on the coach again, and thankfully John offered to drive. Dave and Warren set off on the Wednesday and very kindly offered to put up our tent, which allowed us to casually drive down on the Thursday and meet up with them. Dave's mate Roni had sorted us a really good spot to camp, just down from the old railway lines near the entrance, and not only were we across from the Other Stage, but it was also really easy to find our way back. The weather was rubbish as usual, but we expected nothing less so didn't let it bother us too much.

I shared a two-berth with John again, and was beginning to realise that ours was probably one of the smallest in our field. I also made the decision to hardly eat throughout the weekend, in an effort to avoid those horrific toilets as much as I could, having learned from my previous visit. My routine was to take a packet of Rice Krispies and have a couple of bowls first thing each morning, which would hopefully last me until at least teatime.

That year there were rumours that whilst folk were asleep in their tents, a gang was going round slashing the bottom of their tents and nicking what they could, without folk waking up. The only things I had with me of any value were my phone and my camcorder. The video camera slept with me inside my sleeping bag, and I thought it was a good idea to hide my phone inside my

box of breakfast cereal, assuming that there was no way anybody would want to steal a half-eaten box of Rice Krispies.
I only just managed to fit in our tent, and certainly couldn't stretch out my legs, so I really was roughing it. Dave, on the other hand, really had his head screwed on and, compared to ours, his tent was more like a palace, with at least three separate rooms for everybody to spread out. Another thing was that there was no way Dave was about to settle for a plastic dish of cereal, and every morning he would get out his stove and cook bacon and sausages, which I found really hard to turn down – though I did.

The headliners that year were Bruce Springsteen, Neil Young, and Blur. I certainly had no intention of checking Springsteen out, even though Sarah told me that she wouldn't speak to me again if I didn't. I guess it was just a risk I would have to take.

As it turned out, my favourite act of that weekend was Ray Davies, in the Acoustic Tent, who I think was on at the same time as Springsteen anyway (sorry, Sarah). It was the first time I had seen the Kink, and I loved every minute. I seem to recall that he was wearing a pair of wellies on stage, even though I am not sure they had ever come into contact with any mud, as they looked as though he had only just purchased them from backstage.
He ended his incredible set with *Waterloo Sunset* (Paul Weller's favourite song), and *Lola* (second encore), and my lasting memory was when we were making our way out of the giant tent after the gig and the whole crowd joined in a communal chorus of *Lola*, which sounded magic. So you can stick your *Born in the USA*. We chose well.

I was standing in front of the Pyramid Stage on the Sunday, as Blur were about to come on, but didn't really fancy two hours of Park Life. So I made my way over to John Peel, in order to check out Jarvis Cocker. Jarvis was wonderful and stuck to his solo material, despite members of the crowd constantly calling out for Pulp tunes. I managed to film most of his set but reckon I must have somehow left the tape in the tent that night, as no matter how many times I have searched for it since, it has never been found.

Dave and Warren had planned to set off back on the Monday, like everybody else, but John worked out that the best time to attempt to get off the car park was just before the Sunday headliner finished – providing you hadn't wanted to watch them, that is. So, we said our goodbyes to Worthy Farm for another year, and somehow made it back to Blackburn in four hours, which was a record for us.

As far as benchmark years go for attending live music, I doubt 2010 will ever be rivalled – not for me anyway. From the second I heard that Stevie Wonder was booked to headline Glastonbury, being anywhere else on the planet on that date was not an option. I don't remember how I managed to secure my ticket, but I did. John had decided to take a year off, so I would have to find another way of getting there and back. Dave and Warren were going, but their car was full, so I told them I would see them there. Being honest, I was starting to worry, but at the final minute I was offered a lifeline in the form of Beth, who worked behind the bar with Emma at The Live Lounge. I didn't really know her that well, but there was no way I was about to turn a lift down to go and witness Mr Wonder perform, so I accepted her very kind offer.

Once we set off, Beth explained that we were stopping off in Liverpool first to pick up her friend Sarah, who was apparently coming with us. The thing was that the ticket Beth had secured for Sarah, had a photo of somebody else on the front, and once she joined us inside the car, in my opinion it looked nothing like her – they both had different hair colours. The two girls didn't seem remotely concerned by this small observation, but I worried about what she was going to do if the people on the gate were as observant as me and she ended up being turned away. Would this mean none of us could go in? I mean, we couldn't simply leave her there.

The plan was to spend Tuesday night on a car park in the town, and then on the Wednesday morning once the gates opened, we would attempt to find Beth's other mates that she had arranged to meet inside.

Glastonbury Festival in 2010 was taking place during the FIFA World Cup Finals in South Africa, and England's final group game against Slovenia on the Wednesday was being shown on the Pyramid Stage screens at 3pm. So I knew we would have to get in and put up our tents in plenty of time to catch the kick-off.

I have no idea how, but Sarah managed to get in without even being questioned, which was a huge relief. We then met up with Beth and Sarah's other mates, and agreed to watch the match once we had got sorted. Beth had taken so many bags that we agreed to carry all their belongings in first, and then head back to the car for mine. That was the plan anyway, but by the time we carried everything in of theirs, and pitched up both their tents, everybody was knackered. So we agreed to grab a beer and go back to the car for my stuff a little later.

For once at Worthy Farm, the weather was boiling, and one drink led to two and so on. And while I was keen to go and collect my stuff, Sarah was completely out of it, unconscious on the grass, and Beth was enjoying her drinks far too much to listen to me going on about making another journey. So I guessed it wouldn't be happening anytime soon.

It was a great atmosphere watching the football on the giant screens in the sunshine, with everybody in a fantastic mood, and especially once Jermain Defoe managed to score England's winner to put them into the last 16. As I was watching the match, Beth's mate Helena came over to chat. I must admit that when I had been first introduced to her earlier in the day, I had felt she was a bit of a diva, and even though the diva assumption might have been correct, after talking to her, I found her to be really nice and not what I had imagined.

After the game, I finally managed to nag Beth until she agreed to help me go and collect my gear from her car. That meant I could now let my hair down and relax, without worrying about not having a sleeping bag or a box of my trusty breakfast cereal. Even though I was camped in our usual spot, next to Warren and Dave's tents, I felt I couldn't just get a lift down with Beth then tell her that I would see her later. So I found myself hanging around with them for the whole weekend.

I noticed that Boy George was due to play in the Wow Tent over in the Dance Village at 8.30pm, and had always fancied seeing him live. I wasn't sure if the others would be up for it, but they told me they were and agreed to come along. This was great, but I was beginning to realise that it took them about ten minutes to simply walk a matter of yards, as every time a group of lads walked in our direction, Beth and Sarah would stop and talk to them. This went on for over an hour and we had barely moved, so I had more or less given up any hope of catching the gig, as It was now around 9.30pm, and we were still a way off the dance tents.

We finally made it to Wow, and I just assumed the gig would be over. It was so packed that I couldn't get anywhere near the entrance. Only a few acts had performed on the Thursday night back then, so those that did were guaranteed a large audience. I asked a bloke nearby how the concert had been, and to my delight he informed me that Boy George hadn't even come on yet, due to the overcrowding. This was fantastic news, but by then I had managed to lose everybody, and it looked pretty doubtful that the tent would have room for anybody else.
Out of the blue, Helena appeared, grabbed my hand, and proceeded to drag me the whole of way through the crowd until we were eventually standing at the front. For once, I was that annoying git that barges past you at the last minute at a gig, after you have been standing in that same claimed spot for hours. This action had not gone unnoticed, though, and I received punches to the back of my head and was booted up the backside, and even

though these attacks were not pleasant at the time, I feel they were probably justified. I did feel bad, but it was not as if I had planned it. And I did find myself standing at the front of the stage waiting for Mr Culture Club to show up.

It was 10pm before he finally graced us with his presence, and he was wearing a black suit and a bright yellow hat (he knows how to pick a good hat), and was rocking glittery green eye shadow – we were that close. The crowd was clearly getting restless by this point and he addressed them by saying, 'One benefit of not having a career is that you don't know what the fuck I'm gonna do now.' Then he performed a version of Louis Armstrong's *Nobody Knows The Trouble I've Seen*.

It was barely a year since George had been released from prison, and the audience went wild during a rousing version of *Karma Chameleon* (my dad's favourite), in which he changed the lyrics to 'I'm a man with three convictions'.

The gig really was fantastic and certainly worth the effort, but by the time it finished it is fair to say that the beers that Helena had been drinking throughout the day had started to take effect. We couldn't find anywhere in the Dance Village to get a nightcap, so we stopped at one of the stalls for her to buy some chips – no doubt to soak up the alcohol. No sooner had she been tucking into her night-time snack than she realised her mobile phone was missing, so we legged it back over to the stall, but they assured us they hadn't seen it.
By this time, I was starting to take the blame for what had happened, and even though I'd only known her for a couple of days, she was convinced it was my fault for her misplacing her mobile. Under normal circumstances I would have simply walked off and left her to it, but we were in the middle of a field in Pilton, and the chances of Helena being able to find her way back to her tent in that state were pretty slim. So I put up with the earache a little longer and did the gentlemanly thing, making sure she made it back to her tent safe and sound.

I woke up early on the Friday, as the tent was really hot with the Somerset sun shining on it, and I had to get out and grab some fresh air. The first sight I witnessed was about 50 people walking past along the old rail track just up from us. They were all wearing Rolf Harris masks and generally excited because he was opening the Pyramid Stage that day, but I'm not sure they would want to brag about the experience today, or if they might still be in possession of those masks.

Due to the phonegate incident, I made a conscious effort to stay clear of Beth and her mates. So I watched The Courteeners with Dave and our mate Jo (Torrents' No 1 fan), and danced with Jo in a field throughout Snoop Dogg's performance.

Someone who Sarah knew was apparently a well-known ticket tout, and he and a couple of his mates were selling fake AAA wristbands outside the gates, which both Sarah and Beth used to blag getting backstage for Snoop. Rumour had it that the two other touts were nicked backstage during his set, allegedly having in their possession a bag containing £35,000 in cash.

Irish rockers U2 were booked to headline the Pyramid on the Friday, but luckily for me they pulled out at the last minute, citing Bono's recent back surgery as the reason. They were replaced by Damon Albarn's band Gorillaz, which I found astonishing. In my eyes, there was no way on the planet that they warranted that slot, and to back up my theory, even folk who liked them said they were disappointed having watched them.

Earlier in the evening I had opted to go and see Carl Barrat perform on the Leftfield Stage, and received a text from Helena, apologising for the previous night. She was honest enough to admit she had ended up finding her phone at the bottom of her bag that morning, so all was well with the world and I agreed to meet up with them later that evening, after I had watched The Flaming Lips headline the Other Stage and avoided cardboard cut-outs of monkeys.

Lost Vagueness had now been replaced by Shangri-La, which aimed to expand minds and open hearts and had a deep history in outsider art and underground culture, but was just as crazy as its previous incarnation.

Dustin's manager Pete had previously contacted me from their tour of Japan, asking me if I could find them a squat to stay at after their North Bar gig in Blackburn, as they'd spent every penny of their budget on tour. I ended up sorting them out a luxury flat in a decent area for the night, despite being warned against it. He was now managing a band called Depot, who I'd already booked for a Live Lounge gig. He contacted me to let me know they were playing at a secret part of Glastonbury on the Saturday night.

The late Joe Strummer first set up camp backstage at Glastonbury years ago, and it soon became a hidden gem, word of mouth institution called Strummerville. Since Joe's death in 2002, the area has been maintained by the charity of the same name, which was set up by his family, and it's located in the Unfair Ground area, next to the Joe Strummer memory stone. There is a campfire that is lit all weekend long in front of a very small stage that encourages folk to simply have a jam, regardless of their musical background or taste. Throughout the weekend, the stage hosts a mix of the latest new talent, along with more established names.

Depot were due to play a Campfire Session that evening, and even though I hadn't got a clue where the area was, I told Pete that he could rely on my support, and I would be there.

That morning I watched, and filmed, Sting's daughter's band, I Blame Coco on the Park Stage, and naturally The Cribs, later in the day on the Other Stage. Muse were the evening's headline act, so you would see me nowhere near there. But I fancied checking out Shakira – I mean, who wouldn't? – but my phone had run out of battery, and I was keen to phone home.

I made the decision to queue for ages at the Orange Charge Tent, but this was in fact a terrible choice, as I found myself unfortunately standing behind the planet's most selfish young person. I ended up in one of those catch 22 situations where I had been waiting that long for a chance to charge my phone that I figured it would be stupid to give up now. I had been there well over an hour and was half watching Neil Young's performance from the previous year on the wall TVs, and to make things even worse, it was announced that none other than Miss Kylie Minogue had been special guest for The Scissor Sisters on the Pyramid. At this point I wanted to perform physical violence on this kid in front of me – and I'm a pacifist.

The thing was, his phone was around 90% charged already, he knew I had been standing there for over an hour, and (even worse) the whole of the time it was charging, he was playing stupid games on the phone. So he really did deserve a slap. A voice came over the tannoy announcing they would be closing in ten minutes, so I thought surely this little freak would call it a day and give someone else a turn... but no chance. He waited until the very last second before he unplugged the lead and threw it onto the counter. I was fuming. I can't remember or repeat what I ended up saying to him, but it had zero effect.

This lad had proper wound me up with his lack of thought for anybody else, but I should have just forgotten about my phone and stuck to watching the live performances. By that time, I had no idea where anybody would be, and it wasn't as if I could call them. So I decided to make my way over to the path that would hopefully take me to Strummerville.

As I was walking through the gathered crowds, I realised that The Pet Shop Boys had just taken to the Other Stage. My plan was to check them out for about ten minutes and then carry on my way, but they were so magnificent live that I ended up watching their whole set. I really did enjoy them, and even today when I hear *New York City Boy*, it reminds me of that magical moment at Glastonbury.

It was an absolute effort trying to find my way to Strummerville and I almost gave up, but after about my fifth attempt I came across the campfire. Pete was a real character (crafty cockney), and from the moment he spotted me, that was it. He put his arm around my shoulder and for the next hour (at least) he proceeded to introduce me to everybody he knew, and a lot he didn't, including Sting's daughter Coco Summer (Eliot Paulina). I remember sharing with her that her birth had been one of the first things I had watched on MTV. At the time I had been gobsmacked by the fact that a music channel was broadcasting actual childbirth, Sting or no Sting. But unless I dreamt it, I really did witness it. Luckily, the camera had been at the opposite end to all the action, and had spared Trudy's dignity.

The Drums turned up and performed, and I was sitting on a settee with The Mystery Jets, amazed that no matter who had been performing, folk would sit around the campfire the whole of the way through the night. I didn't even see anybody leave. I remember asking Pete several times what time Depot were due on, and he kept telling me 'soon', but I realised that the stage listings were not really going to plan and they never knew who was going to simply turn up, which I sort of loved. You had to be there in order to catch all the hidden gems, which was probably why nobody left.

Depot came on at 5.30am, but I was on that much of a high that grabbing some sleep was the last thing on my mind. I enjoyed their short set and figured it was a good time to say my goodbyes and head back to my tent, before the others woke up. As I was walking down the path, I witnessed one of the most beautiful sights I have ever seen – a Glastonbury morning twilight. The large round moon was the largest I had ever seen in the sky, and it looked incredible. A low mist surrounded the thousands of tents and tepees, resembling some kind of festival postcard beauty. This moment was just before the morning sunrise, and the light from the sky appeared diffused, making the background a kind of pinkish. Added to the individual festival lights surrounding every area, it really was a sight to behold.

The majority of people were still fast asleep in their tents, which made it seem even more special, and there was a very faint buzz in the air, along with some bird song, indicating that this was the calm before the storm. It would only be witnessed by very few humans who were lucky enough, or mad enough, to still be awake.

Every other day and night I had taken my camera with me, but for the first time I had chosen to leave it in a security cloakroom, not knowing how crazy Strummerville would get. So there I was, literally looking at probably the greatest sight I had ever seen, and I had nothing at all to capture it on.

I think I managed to grab about an hour's kip before the sun on my tent made it unbearable to stay inside. I started off watching the England V Germany game with all the others that afternoon, but it was clear there was only going to be one outcome, so I spared myself the final half hour of the usual humiliation and decided to leave the field. I am not proud of what happened next, and in fact it is a wonder I have even admitted this decision in words, but I guess if you are writing a book, you need to be honest.

Keane were performing on the Avalon Stage, and I don't care what everybody says, I think that Tom Chaplin has got an amazing voice and that the band's debut album *Hopes and Fears* is one of the finest albums ever made. I wish I had written it. The dilemma I had was that even though I was keen to check them out (no pun) as I had never seen them live at that point, their stage time clashed with none other than the mighty Ray Davies, who was performing on the Pyramid Stage in the Legends slot. Now I know that this should have been a no-brainer, and I feel terrible remembering it even now, and any fellow Mod reading this will have no doubt already put the book down (and I don't blame them), but my plan was to leg it over to the Avalon field, watch about ten minutes of Tom and the boys, then head over to the main stage. After all, I'd seen Ray perform at the festival the previous year, I kept telling myself.

I have to be honest, though, once I managed to fight my way into the beyond packed tent, I thought that Keane sounded incredible. They even had to wait a while between each song in order for the audience applause to stop, as it seemed to be never-ending. My plan to only watch part of their set went out of the window, as the crowd was so tightly packed in that it was impossible to even put my hand in my pocket, never mind attempt to leave before the end.

I am not proud of missing Ray's set, and have had to live with that decision ever since. But try not to judge me too much, as we all make mistakes at one time or another.

My next artist to be lucky enough to have yellow highlighter through their name was Julian Casablanca's from The Strokes, who was down to play in John Peel. I agreed to meet the others after his set, just in time for Stevie, and headed off to find my spot in front of my favourite stage. In all honesty, I was disappointed by his performance and was in fact pretty bored, which surprised me. Maybe my mind was far too set on seeing Stevie Wonder to be able to appreciate anybody else.

My main mission now was to somehow manage to make my way over to the Pyramid for the weekend's finale, as the usual route I planned to take was closed due to thousands of like-minded people everywhere I looked. I really should have known better, but by the time I finally made my way all the way around the site to where I had arranged to meet Beth and the others, it was like trying to find a needle in a haystack. Begrudgingly, I decided to watch the gig from where I was standing, as folk had now been in position for hours and I didn't fancy any more punches to the head.

The time was 9.45pm and a musical legend was about to take to the stage. There were no spaces in the crowd for as far as my eyes could see; it was well and truly packed out. Suddenly, the lights came on and the great man himself appeared to deafening cheers, screams, and shouts. Then he started his headline set with *My Eyes Don't Cry*, followed by the outrageously good *Master Blaster* (Jamming) and a cover of The Beatles *We Can Work It Out*. The audience were absolutely lapping it up, and so was I, even though I had ended up watching it on my own.

The woman next to me started to make some small talk, so I presumed she was simply being friendly, but the more I tried to concentrate on the stage, the more questions she asked me. Thinking nothing of it, I explained I had lost all my mates, and felt a little freaked out when she told me they had come from Blackpool and kept offering to give me a lift back to the seaside town that night, after the gig. She explained that her husband was away with the Army, but the more we chatted, the more I noticed the two very large blokes standing on the other side of her, staring at me as though it was me chatting *her* up. She told me they were her husband's brothers, which would explain the death stares. But on top of feeling pretty naffed off by the fact she was interrupting the concert of a lifetime, I had a really weird feeling about them and couldn't wait to move away.

All of a sudden, my fairy godmother appeared! To my amazement, Beth arrived from nowhere, grabbed my hand, and dragged me through the exited crowd (it must be a trait with that lot) until somehow we ended up at the spot with all the others, waving their glow sticks around, and dancing like their lives depended on it. I was buzzing, and once I found out that Beth had spent the past 35 minutes fighting her way through the crowd in an attempt to find me – even though Stevie had already come on – I knew she was a true friend for sure.

The atmosphere was unbelievable, everybody dancing in a party spirit to all the expected hits, with flares and fireworks; it really was magical. He ended his 19-song set with *Happy Birthday*, and dedicated it to the main man himself, Mr Michael Eavis. Then to everybody's delight, Stevie welcomed him on stage to join in the chorus, with it being the festival's 40th year and that. The crowd went crazy, and all joined in with the lyrics, and in a touching moment Stevie handed Michael a harmonica as a gift, saying he had also given one to Barack Obama. And he made a plea for all events to be inclusive to all, despite someone's disability.

Stevie really was a musical genius and I loved every second of it, but to watch him headline Glastonbury in a field with over 80,000 people, partying with a group of mad friends – despite them being new ones – was as good as it gets. And it's in my five top favourite gigs of all time.

As soon as Mr Wonder left the stage, me and Beth's friend Carrie made our way as quickly as we could over to the Glade stage to catch the end of The Levellers set – both being huge fans. And that was it for another year.

Glastonbury 2010: Thank you, you were everything I hoped for and more. The weather – from start to finish, the Somerset sunshine was shining bright, and there was zero sign of mud-drenched fields, like in previous years. The acts – we had been spoilt by the weekend's entertainment for sure, and what a finale, wow! Certainly the benchmark for everything to come. Also, the company – old friends and new without doubt contributed in a huge way to making these six days and nights in Pilton ones to remember.

I finally arrived home, and despite the fact that I was drained of all energy, I was on such a high that grabbing some sleep was not an option. It would have been impossible anyway, with everything going around in my head. My voice had almost gone, I had glitter all over my face, and other parts of my body, and the previous morning's face paint on my cheek. I remember thinking to myself, *Who needs drugs when you can feel as high on life as this, without even taking anything?* I walked down to our local Tesco with a permanent smile on my face, and they must have thought I was simple, first thing in the morning, looking like that.

It took around a month for my body to fully recover from those six days in a field, and as always, I was booked to film the Wickerman Festival again.

Birchy was providing the transport, and I invited my mate Dave along, as his favourite band Ocean Colour Scene were headlining the Saturday night. I booked the three of us into our usual hostelry, but the day we were setting off I noticed a post on Facebook from one of the locals in The Farthings, offering two free passes for the festival to anybody who wanted them. Normally I wouldn't have taken much notice or even seen posts from him, but it was on The Farthings page, and I did know that one of his mates had worked on the stage crew the previous year, so it could have been genuine.

I knew that spending hours on end in a field would certainly not appeal to Janet, and even though it was ultra-short notice, Beth and Sarah were up for taking the passes. I was at work at the time, so had a taxi take me to The Farthings, bought the guy a couple of beers, and collected the wristbands. I had always found this lad to be a bit full of it, and my concerns were proven right when the security on the gate told us that the passes were a year out of date, and took them off us. I should have known not to trust him, and I felt terrible, as we had just arrived in Kirkcarswell Farm. We couldn't just say 'See ya' and expect them both to somehow make their way back to Blackburn. So after several minutes of debating their options, Dave very kindly offered to lend them the money for two tickets, and I suggested sneaking them into our hotel for the next three days.

I remember standing outside the front door of our hotel for ages for the chance to sneak them into our room without anyone on reception noticing. We finally managed it, and I begrudgingly gave up my double bed and agreed to sleep in the small box room with Ian. I honestly thought we had got away with it, until the following morning when I went down to breakfast and the waitress said, 'A table for five, is it?' I couldn't believe they knew, after all our efforts to hide both girls, but at least this meant they could now tuck into a fully cooked Scottish breakfast, and not simply make do with the toast I was planning to sneak back to the room.

Buzzcocks and The Charlatans played on the Friday, and I did my usual, running up and down the fields attempting to capture everything, whilst the others just drank and chilled in the Scottish sunshine – hence, me deserving the double bed.

I was standing in front of the main stage on Saturday afternoon, when I happened to notice my old friend Rooster (Craig) from Faded Image. I couldn't believe it; I hadn't seen him since the 80s. He introduced me to his wife Tracy, and I explained that I was working for the festival as their filmmaker. Being a fellow Mod back in the day, I asked Craig if they were planning on watching Ocean Colour Scene that evening, to which he replied, 'Watching them? We are with them.'

Apparently, they were good friends with the band, and had even been given lifetime passes to go and watch them. I had watched the band several times before, and remembered them in the early days playing with and being championed by Paul Weller.

Craig asked if I wanted to meet them, and I knew Dave would love it, so agreed. He escorted us to their mobile unit backstage and introduced us to the band, who were really nice. Steve Cradock told us if we wanted anything signed or any photographs, to wait at the bottom of the ramp just before they were due on stage. They took us onto the backstage area with them, signed what was asked, and let us take as many photos we wanted, so the thousands of fans packed into the field had to wait a little longer for their Saturday headliner to begin their set.
After Dave headed back into the crowd, Craig, Tracy, and I were invited to watch the concert from the stage. Not only that, but their manager Chris (Steve's Dad) also told me I was okay to film from the front if I wanted. It really was surreal to be standing at the side of the headline band, watching, and capturing the huge Scottish crowd appreciating every song. And it's the closest I will ever get to understanding what Liam Gallagher must feel like, gazing down on everyone, feeling privileged to be in that position. This really ended a wonderful day, but the best thing of all had been bumping into my old friend Craig again and agreeing to stay in touch. (Of all the fields…)

This almost didn't happen, as the following day we were sitting on the grass grabbing something to eat when I managed to get something stuck in my throat. Not wanting to make a scene, I wandered off on my own in an attempt to somehow cough it up in private, but this didn't happen and I honestly started to acknowledge that this wasn't good. Birchy asked Beth where I had gone, but when she told him I was over there on my phone, Ian glanced over and knew I was in trouble. By the time he joined me, I was leaning over a fence and starting to panic as this item had been stuck now for far too long. The next thing I knew, Ian had wrapped his arms around my body and performed what I believe is known as the Heimlich Manoeuvre.

He wasn't messing about, and the force of his thrust actually hurt, but it did the trick and managed to dislodge whatever was stuck there, to my relief. Ian told me afterwards that he had picked up these skills whilst serving in the Military Police in Germany, and I for one was glad that he had. Now I know when I tell this story that most people will think I am exaggerating when I say that my time was running out, and that Birchy probably saved my life that day in a field in Galloway, but as far as I am concerned, I am not, and he did.

Due to us staying at the same hotel every year, we had got to know one of the girls that worked there and would always attempt to talk her into joining us at the festival site to let her hair down for once, as opposed to serving us breakfast. But she always had to work. This particular year, she warned us about her current boyfriend, saying that he was jealous and that he had a really bad temper. The lad behind the bar told us that even though he was his best mate, he really was the village idiot.

Birchy, Dave and I arrived back at the hotel bar around midnight and were having a laugh with the two staff who were serving us a nightcap, when we were informed that the guy had heard we were chatting up his girl (his words, not mine) and he was on his way to sort us out. We found this highly amusing and simply carried on chatting and drinking.

The next thing we knew was some complete maniac was banging on the front door of the hotel as though they were trying to knock it down (obviously him). Mr barman went to let him in before he woke all the guests up with the racket, and just like a scene from a John Wayne movie when the saloon doors burst open and the gunslinger barges in, the boyfriend marched straight over to Ian and asked him what was going on.

So, if you can, imagine the scene. There's me, who is not into violence and who has never considered himself to be hard, leaning back in my chair, drinking my drink, and doing all I could to hold back from answering his ridiculous question. He could have chosen me to come over to and maybe have fancied his chances. Oh no! He could have gone over to Dave, ex-Navy, fireman – but no. Instead, he chose to inflict his drunken threatening tones on Ian, ex-Military Police Arms Response Officer, and a guy who – like the script states – has a particular set of skills acquired over a long career, and who you would back in most situations. (And he saved my life!)

Not too sure what was about to happen next, I suggested hitting him over the head with his favourite bar stool (unlike me, I know), but Birchy responded with a sudden burst of uncontrollable laughter, which confused him. What was even funnier was when his friend behind the bar said to me, 'Mate, I know I have been having a chat with you and getting on, but if a fight breaks out, I will be on his side.' That started me off laughing.

On this occasion, Ian and Dave opted for the sensible option and persuaded me to follow them up to our bedrooms: one, in order not to put their professional careers at risk; and two, to enable the bar stool to stay in one piece.

Another festival under my belt, I planned to avoid spending time in a field for the foreseeable and to spend some quality time at home. I know I always say that Janet is the planet's most understanding wife, but even I know when I am pushing my luck.

In 2010, Kendal Calling was awarded The Best Small UK Festival Award, and even though one of my favourite bands, The Coral, were headlining the Sunday night, it was taking place only a week after Wickerman so I forced myself to give it a miss.

On the Thursday evening, Beth called me in an effort to talk me into attending, and I tried to explain why I couldn't and how skint I was. But, like me, she didn't take no for an answer, and within an hour of our conversation, she had driven round to our house, told me that she and Sarah had bought me a ticket, and shoved £100 into my hand, so it would have been rude not to have agreed. Janet was present and, to her credit, told me she was cool with this (Legend), but to be fair, she had been put on the spot. Anyway, I packed my stuff again in record time and was off to Penrith with a couple of very generous nutters.

A guy in a party dress helped me set up my tent, while at the same time the tent across from me was being raided in a supposed drug bust by the police. It was certainly different from Glastonbury, as you never really notice the police there, and when you do see them, they are usually laughing and joking, wearing silly hats, and proper getting into the spirit of things. I once even witnessed them walking past folk who were smoking a joint, and not bothering, and I never saw them raiding any tents. Don't get me wrong, I am not saying that this is how the police should behave at festivals, but it clearly works at Worthy Farm.

As always, Beth met up with a group of her mates, and as always, Sarah put the P into Party. I remember making my way back to my tent about 1am, but being unable to sleep, around an hour later I heard Sarah falling into their tent, which was next to mine, and wondering how on earth she even found her way back in that state. The thing was, though, Sarah hadn't come back to finally catch up on any much-needed shut-eye. Oh no. She merely called back so she could pick up some more supplies, before heading back into the site so that she could carry on raving.

The weekend was fab, and mad, and without a doubt the highlight for me was The Coral's performance on the Sunday night. They were superb, and performed the majority of the tracks from their new album, *Butterfly House*. Not only is it one of my favourite LPs of all time, but that gig remains in my top 10 favourite gigs. So cheers, Janet, for being cool about me attending – and, of course, Beth and Sarah for making it happen.

Janet and I had a weekend in Edinburgh watching The Fringe, which happened to be great, and we saw John Bishop in a really small gig for him, and also went to watch Beth's mate Carrie (my Levellers gig buddy) in a play she was performing in.
So, that meant that in 2010 I attended no fewer than seven festivals in nine weeks! Even for me, that is some going, and a personal record I am sure I will never beat.

CHAPTER THIRTY-TWO

AGENTS RUINED MY LIFE

One day in 2011, I was at work when I received a random phone call from a lady called Karen, saying that my name had been given to her and that she was doing a survey about the local music scene.

I receive many random calls throughout the day, so I almost hung up. Also, to be honest, I initially felt she was just some random person with a clipboard, and that I would never hear from her again.

However, I am glad I didn't put the phone down that afternoon, as I was wrong. I did hear from Karen again, just like she promised, and she didn't even own a clipboard. Karen, I discovered, was in fact a straight-talking Salford lass who was great friends with Alison, who filmed and produced Torrents' *He's A Victim* video, which explained where my name had come from. After spending time working for London Records, she ended up working with Tony Wilson at Factory and The Hacienda, so I couldn't not take her seriously.

When Tony passed away, his wife Yvette (who was originally from Blackburn, I believe) invited Karen to carry on his work, bringing everyone who worked in music throughout Pennine Lancashire together in some kind of network. I liked Karen from the start, was honoured that she ended up contacting me, and was more than happy to help or get involved in whatever project she was running.

As it turned out, the initiative was named 'Oh To Play Sound City', and the group of local music people who were brought together met up on a regular basis, attending a music promoters course at Burnley College, gaining tips and meeting industry folk who shared their stories, and with the task of putting on a series of gigs at local venues, selecting the acts of our choice to perform in a heats competition, and the winning act was offered a slot at Liverpool's Sound City Festival.

I attended the course in Burnley, which helped me network, gave me an industry insight, and helped with my confidence in staging events. Also, working on this project with Karen introduced me to and began my love affair with this newfound festival in my favourite city. Cheers, Karen.

Karen told us about a young singer/songwriter she had been managing and invited us to go and watch her performance at the event. When her artist had played at The Mad Ferret in Preston, Karen had managed to somehow persuade five record labels to attend the gig, which was amazing. Getting the likes of Atlantic to make the long journey up north is almost unheard of. Karen's efforts paid off, and London-based Atlantic Records agreed to sign the very talented Rae Morris from Blackpool, in a small venue in Lancashire.

I was lucky enough to book Rae for a performance at The Live Lounge, which really was a coup. Supporting on the night was Karen's other artist, JP Cooper, who has just gone from strength to strength, and a young local artist called Caroline Eve who I had been trying to help. The night itself created a really nice vibe at the venue, and brought in a completely new crowd, which was great.

It was Rae's birthday that night, and her mum and dad planned to surprise her upstairs in the band room with a special birthday cake and champagne after her set. I remember Karen gave me the bottle and asked me if I would open it, but asked me to make sure it didn't go everywhere (obviously not cheap bubbly!) Not really liking the stuff myself, or being experienced at uncorking a bottle, it actually did go everywhere, but I managed to salvage enough to fill Rae's glass, which I feel she appreciated – which is probably more than the person who paid for it.

In 2009, I was at Glastonbury when the news came through that Michael Jackson had died. It was the Friday night and, as we were walking back to our tent, I overheard somebody mention it. I didn't believe it, but as my phone had zero reception, I had no way of checking at that time of night. John and I woke up to my phone receiving non-stop texts reading 'Pete, Michael Jackson is dead. Pete, Michael Jackson is dead.'

In 2011, I was working at The Wickerman Festival in Scotland when the devastating news appeared on my phone that the extraordinarily talented Amy Winehouse had been found dead at her flat in London. I was stunned by this shocking news, even though I am sure that not everybody was surprised. I found myself just wandering up and down the main field trying to share my horrible news with every single person who walked past me, even though they either didn't believe me or weren't that bothered, to my frustration. I noticed that one of Scotland's main music presenters, Jim Gellatly, was standing against the front barrier, and I felt the need to go over and break my shocking news to him. But no matter how many times I tried to convince him, he really wasn't having it.

I always thought that if I ever ended up sending him a Demo CD in the future, I would introduce myself as that guy who told you about Amy, as there was no way he was about to forget that and would play it for sure.

Also, what was really surreal about the situation was that around that time there was a battle of the bands-style programme on Channel 4 called Orange Unsigned, presented by Alex Zane and Lauren Laverne. That particular year, the winning act was called Emma's Imagination, and she was actually part of the Wickerman crew. As a reward, she was given a slot on the main stage. This was the last performance I watched, and believe it or not, she ended her set with an Amy Winehouse cover (*TDOTO*), literally around ten seconds before I received the news about her death. I can only imagine how she must have felt as she walked backstage and was told the news about her musical hero.

I was starting to feel paranoid and wondered if this festival malarkey was a good thing. After all, it seemed that every time I was in a field, a musical legend popped their clogs (a slight over-exaggeration, I know, but you get my point).

Watching The Libertines on Jools Holland for the first time had a pretty big impact on me, as I loved the tunes, the performance, and also their attitude. At the time, there was barely a day went by where one newspaper or another – or all – hadn't had some sort of feature about Pete Doherty. Whether it was his bust-up with Carl, his time spent doing bird, or an opinion about his friend Amy, he was never out of the news. Paul and I came up with the idea of bringing him to Blackburn, and because The Live Lounge was far too small to consider staging such an event there, King George's Hall was our venue of choice. We knew it was going to be a massive mission to pull it off but, like I always say, I don't do barriers. So I had no reason to think that it wouldn't happen. The plan was for Paul to somehow find the finances, and my job was to deal with his agent and book him.

When I had dealt with music agents previously, I found them on the whole to be pretty difficult to work with, and many seemed to have a bigger ego than the artists they were representing. But at the end of the day, if you wanted to book musicians at a certain level, going through their agent was the only way. The strangest part of this process is when they ask you to make them an offer, but you haven't booked their artist before, how on earth are you supposed to know how much they are expecting? Normally, when you buy a product, it has a price tag on it, so you make the decision whether or not you believe it is worth it, or if you can afford it. The dilemma with booking artists was that if you don't offer enough, in some cases you wouldn't even receive a reply, and you risked being blacklisted by the agent for clearly offending them (as if I am a mind reader). On the other hand, if you naively offer too much, you highlight the fact that you don't really have a clue, and of course they are going to snap your hand off. After you have been booking for a period of time, and especially if you keep up-to-date with the current music industry, you eventually gain some rough idea about what sort of offer to put in. But I have to say that I don't think I will ever fully get my head around why they couldn't just give me a price.

I had learnt that the secret to booking an act was around timing. As with anything, it really does pay to do your research, and not simply go in there blind. Check if the act you are after is on tour or even performing close to your area, as this could determine whether you will get them or not. If they have already planned several shows, most of the time it is not that big a deal to simply add another date to the list (in theory) – providing they are happy with your offer, that is. To simply ask or expect somebody to play a one-off show doesn't just narrow your chances of getting them, but will increase their fee considerably. Sometimes, them already having a gig around your area might go against you, as they may not be up for performing there twice or could have even signed a contract to agree to this not happening. Either way, do your homework and just ask the question.

Another thing you will need to get used to when booking artists, is riders. A band rider or artist rider is a given added extra once the artist reaches a certain level. For anybody who is unfamiliar with the term rider, it is a set of requests or demands that a performer sets as the criteria for their performance, and this is expected to be fulfilled by the venue or the promoter/booker hosting the show. Riders can vary, but usually include hospitality (hence The Stiffs hotel room) and technical requirements.

I have always told folk I would love to write a book on riders, as I find it both interesting and hilarious the type of thing that individuals ask for. When you are an upcoming band like The

Torrents and performing at the small venues around the UK, you can usually expect a few beers and maybe some water, if you're lucky. And in most cases that will be your payment for playing the gig. It used to be that acts would just state the number of beers they expected, but nowadays they let you know what beers they don't want (usually Carling, Fosters, Carlsberg) and name the exact ones they do want (good quality, strong lager, and always the most expensive). At times they even state the alcohol percentage they require (at least 5%).

The higher up the industry ladder you find yourself, the more outrageous items you can ask for, and everyone knows the diva-like demands that the likes of Mariah Carey is believed to have insisted on. From puppies and kittens in the dressing room (how cruel is that?) to pink rose petals scattered wherever she walks, and her alleging that she doesn't do steps.

On occasions, a band's rider requests may come across as unreasonable and excessive, and just basically taking the mickey. But this is generally the agent trying to blag as much as they can for their client, and sometimes no doubt pushing to see how much they can actually get away with. Sometimes the artist is unaware of this (sometimes), and on occasions you will be sent a standard tour rider but not necessarily be obliged to go out and purchase everything on the list. I recommend discussing this with the agent if unsure.

As I have been booking now for a long time and would like to think I have become more experienced in that area, I am now reasonably confident about what I need to buy, what I need to negotiate on, and what to ignore. After all, it is important to me that the people I book have an enjoyable experience and that they appreciate I have put the effort in.

Some requests I have been sent over the years, though, have been laughable, and whilst I generally do all I can to meet their needs, there are just some rider items that I simply ignore and move on.

I was once asked by a band to provide them with five pairs of white socks, and I wouldn't have minded but there were only four of them in the band. As if I'd be responsible for keeping their driver's feet warm.

Warm towels is always one that makes me laugh. I don't mind providing towels for established artists, but where on earth am I going to warm them up and, more importantly, keep them warm? Fridge magnets and postcards containing local scenes? They have clearly never visited Blackburn. An ironing board, a fan, a trouser press, Pink Himalayan rock salt, and even a box of tampons, have all been requested.

Even though I had been booking acts for The Live Lounge, I had a desire to put some gigs on myself, and discussed this with Paul, who agreed for me to have any Thursday nights. I was watching an interview with Paul McCartney in which he was explaining that The Beatles had been sitting in their practice room one time, tuning up all their instruments, and based on the distorted sound they had made, he and John had looked at each other and both said the word 'Fairground'. From then on, that was the name they would give to these rehearsal sessions.

I remember thinking, *Wow! There is no better name to give a live event than that, based on all the different sounds you get from various levels of acts.*

My own club nights were born, and even though I would tell folk that the name had some kind of cool Beatles link (tip of the hat), I refused to explain to them what it was. To me, this just added to the mystery, and friends would contact me at all hours for months (years) trying to guess the connection to the fabs. The guesses would always be the obvious ones (as if), and most people would opt for 'Being the Benefit of Mr Kite,' as though I would go down the easy route. Friends would actually take it really seriously, trying to find out where the name had come from. In fact, some even offered to trade me something for the answer, but I never caved in, knowing that they would never work it out in a month of Sundays.

At times I even questioned myself whether I had randomly dreamt it, as no matter how many times I have trawled YouTube or fast-forwarded through my very large collection of Beatles-related DVDs, I have never been able to find that Macca interview again.

My first Fairground night (Fairground 1) took place at The Live Lounge on Thursday, 2nd June, 2011, and The Moons were my chosen headline act. The Moons are fronted by Andy Crofts, who was previously in The On Offs from Northampton, with Danny Connors, and is currently a member of Paul Weller's band of extremely talented merry men. I was really happy to get them to perform on my opening night. Smith was my DJ and was requested to play *Mr Kite* just before the headline band took to the stage, along with playing his usual Mod/Motown/Northern Soul classics. Even Andy commented that he didn't play a bad song all night, which he was buzzing about.

The evening was a success and The Moons went down really well. They were ace, and I guess for the bargain price of three English pounds, everybody went home happy. Strang from The Stiffs had designed my wonderful event poster (still pride of place in my office today), and Andy must have enjoyed the night and liked the poster, as he asked me for one on his way out.

My thing was, and still is, to bring new acts and emerging talent to perform in the town for the first time, and what I always attempted to do was to kill two birds with one stone and try to arrange with Jamie in Media for the acts to come into college and play a session for the media/music students whilst they were in the area. This would be a positive experience for the students, working with an industry-level act opposed to some local pub band, and be a good thing for the artists, who received a high-quality DVD of them performing a number of their tunes.

How it used to work was that I would arrange to meet the act outside college just before lunchtime, introduce myself, take them and their gear into the studio, and then take them for lunch in the swanky college restaurant, Scholars. The food was high quality (most of the time) and the catering students would work on the day's service. Most did a great job, but the fact that they were training at the time meant that on some occasions it would end up feeling like a scene from *Fawlty Towers*, and I found myself having to explain these actions to the artists I was having soup with.

The Moons' session was tremendous, but not long afterwards James and Tom ended up leaving the band and starting Temples, which instantly made the footage out of date. I recall looking at James in the studio and thinking, *I bet he ends up with a solo career*, as he seemed to be that talented.

After sending several emails and staying as patient as I could, I finally received a reply from Pete Doherty's agent, Don, indicating that bringing him to Blackburn for the very first time, and no doubt the last, might be an option. The fact that he was due to perform at Leeds Festival certainly helped our cause, as he would be in the area anyway, and naively we ended up signing a contract stating that we would pay a very large sum of money for one man with an acoustic guitar to perform a one-hour set at King George's.

Due to the constant media obsession with him, we were convinced the show was going to sell out, and if that was the case, Paul, Ju and I stood to make a tidy profit. This was the first time I had staged an event at this level, and from the second we announced it, I was inundated with requests to support. Literally, day and night my phone would constantly ping with messages from bands, solo artists, and managers, asking me to consider them for a slot.

I chose The Tapestry to be Pete's main support on the night, as in my opinion they were the best unsigned band I knew, and they would be relevant to the line-up. The other support acts were eventually booked in, but little did I know that our problems were only just about to start.

I constantly heard negative comments from folk questioning if Pete would even turn up, but to be fair I did not doubt he would show his face up North, especially after the tragedy that had happened to Amy, his friend. I was confident enough, but what concerned me was that all these negative folks going around spreading doom and gloom were bound to affect ticket sales. Also, one of the support acts that had almost begged for a slot started to mess us about. They asked us to post them out some tickets to sell, saying it was not a problem, but apparently they had gone missing in the post and they told us they never received them. Not one to disbelieve folk (unless on holiday or up The Cav), I might have believed them but for several people regularly telling me that they had given them to their mates and had no intention of selling a single ticket.

Asking artists to sell some tickets has never been my style, as I book an act because I like them and rate them. But when you need to find a fee amounting to thousands, something has to give, and in order for the event to be a success for everyone involved, every single person needs to do their bit.

Paul ended up driving to where they lived to deliver some extra tickets, but rumours kept coming in and they still hadn't sold a single one. As Paul was financing this concert and doing everything within his power to find the money from somewhere, he decided that enough was enough and told me that I had to pull the artist. I found this tough, as I got on with them (or so I thought), and that should have been it. *Should have* being the operative words, but somebody I had helped out previously, and obviously a mate of theirs, lied and contacted Pete's agent, telling him to be aware of these dodgy promoters from Blackburn, which I found astounding. From that moment on, I noticed that their agent's tone completely changed when communicating with me, and I received an email demanding I put the artist back on the line-up.

So, you jump through hoops to book an act, and agree to pay them thousands of pounds (no doubt a lot more than other people paid), agree to spend hundreds of pounds on their rider, and now they are trying to tell you who you should book on your own line-up. This was getting ridiculous, but the problem we were facing was risking being blacklisted by an agency, through no fault of our own. This was the first time I had booked at this level, and of course they hadn't heard of me before, so even though I consider myself to be honest and genuine, as I do everything for a deep love of music and not money, if the people who I was dealing with thought I was messing them around, not only would they refuse to work with me again, but probably warn others against it. I knew I had to do what they said or pack in putting gigs on altogether.

If that wasn't enough, I was in a meeting at work the following day when I received a call from somebody I knew in the industry, explaining that they weren't sure if I was aware or not but Mr Doherty sometimes surrounded himself with some pretty handy people down South. They had apparently heard about us changing the line-up and were planning to make a trip up North to try and track us down.

All I was trying to do was put on an event to hopefully entertain the good folk of Blackburn and put it on the musical map for one night, and now I was receiving threats! To be honest, I was highly stressed, and at that point all I wanted to do was throw my phone in the canal and pack it all in, seriously. Luckily I was nowhere near any canals and I had committed to the gig, so even though I was in the middle of work, I arranged an emergency meeting at The Live Lounge with Paul and explained that whatever he thought or felt about the situation, we would need to go back to our original line-up. If I had received that call from anybody else, I might have simply laughed and brushed it off, but I really respected the person who made it, and knew 100% that they were deadly serious. So we had to act.

The even bigger issue we had to try and overcome was that tickets for the show were not selling as we had hoped. What we thought had gone in our favour – booking him whilst he was in the area – had actually gone against us, as all the Indie kids around Blackburn who liked Pete had already set off, or planned to set off, to Leeds Festival before our event. This was a huge blow, and out of desperation, I ended up contacting somebody I knew who happened to know the agency who put in a word for us, and the upshot of it was we ended up swapping the gig from upstairs in King George's with a capacity of 1800, to the Windsor Suite downstairs, reducing it to 750. After a lot of begging, we amended the fee to a few thousand, but this meant that even if the event sold out, we would stand to make a pretty big loss.

Now, if we had been those dodgy promoters from Blackburn that we were accused of being, no doubt at this stage we would have pulled the show, as it was costing us to put it on and bringing us a whole lot of aggro and stress. But I wasn't the type to pull gigs unless it was out of my control, so we agreed to carry on and make it the best that we could, knowing that we were about to make a loss for our efforts.

As the date grew nearer, we were getting more worried, and we ended up paying around £2000 extra for an advert on a local radio show, which in my opinion ended up having zero effect on our ticket sales.

Purchasing all the rider requirements took us the best part of a week to track everything down and tick it off our list. Then the night before the show, I received an email asking if, on top of the giant fee and hundreds spent on food, drink, and other hospitality requirements, an extra £2000 in £50 notes could be left in the dressing room for the evening's float. We didn't really know if this was standard at this level (highly unlikely) or if they were really taking the piss (no doubt the latter), but we reckoned we had managed to get that far so it would be stupid to mess things up now.

At the bottom of the email, it insisted on one of us being at the venue car park at 3.30am in order to meet the coach. I had no intention of it being me, standing there freezing at some unearthly hour, and seem to recall Paul dealing with that one.

By the time the evening arrived, we had more or less sold all the tickets. It was a relief to witness a reasonably packed room, as I'd spent months promoting it and attempting to sell a ticket to anybody I came into contact with, even though half the people had never heard of him. The support acts had done their thing, and The Tapestry had proved yet again why they deserved the slot. The lights went down, the crowd were excited, proving my theory right about Pete turning up, even though I admit I felt massively relieved once his arrival was confirmed. Mr Doherty took to the stage and the audience showed their appreciation for him. I was thankful he had made it onto the Windsor Suite stage, but felt a little disappointed that he hadn't put more effort into his appearance. He opted to present himself in a dark, long-sleeved t-shirt that was creased, as though he had just woken up on his tour bus (which he obviously had), as opposed to some of his usual dapper uniforms we were used to seeing him in. But I suppose it was a wet Thursday night in Blackburn.

Acoustic guitar or not, we were witnessing a songwriting maestro at work (in my opinion), and the audience participation was proof to me that folk were enjoying themselves, singing along to the lyrics to all his well-known tunes. *Death on the Stairs*, *Music When the Lights Go Out* (I wish I had written it), *Don't Look Back Into the Sun*, *F Forever*, *What a Waster*, teasing the crowd with his performance of *Albion*, by mentioning the towns Burnley and Bolton, before eventually dropping Blackburn into the mix, to the room's delight. Pete even introduced two Parisian ballet dancers for *Last of the English Roses* (probably why his fee was so high), and just one of the dancers for his version of *What Katie Did*.

The gig was a success, in terms of enjoyment and entertainment – not profit – and my favourite part of his set was when he ended the evening with a tip of his hat to his friend Amy, by leaving us with a couple of choruses of her classic *Tears Dry On Their Own*. At first, when he started strumming the intro, I don't think people had worked it out, but as soon as his heartfelt tribute became clear, the crowd erupted – and his hour was up.

I filmed as much as I could of the gig, taking into account that at times the audience was pretty raucous, then I uploaded a compilation of the show onto YouTube. I do really buzz off watching it now and again, knowing that we brought a Libertine to Blackburn, even at a fairly big loss.

To the best of my knowledge, Pete didn't even step foot in his dressing room throughout all the time he was here, and he seemed to come straight from his bus onto the stage, and then straight back afterwards, so I have no idea who ate the food and drank the drinks we provided and, come to think of it, spent the 2K! He ended up sleeping two nights on the venue car park, and I was determined to meet him, after spending months trying to make it happen. At first I struggled to blag my way onto his bus, and I felt I was invisible as one of the support bands just pushed right in front of me to get on themselves, even offering him drugs in loud voices on the car park which, to be fair, was turned down flat.

The guy who was looking after him eventually spotted me amongst all the commotion, and realised that it was me who had booked him. He told the others who were blocking the steps to move aside and then literally dragged me on, which meant that my perseverance had paid off. I found Pete to be really nice, and we chatted about when he had stood in the Darwen End at Ewood supporting QPR in their away match at Rovers. He told me he had enjoyed the gig, and I was given a signed t-shirt. I was happy that I'd met him and chuffed that he was nice, but I was gutted that Paul missed out because he'd had to shoot off back to The Live Lounge once the gig finished.

I didn't want to outstay my welcome, and was struggling to get heard anyway above the support band constantly telling him that he knew them, so I went to join the others and check out the Indie disco Paul had put on. I felt pretty popular, as folk kept coming over and thanking me, telling me how much they had enjoyed it. But what surprised me was that my mate Jez had attended the show. He wouldn't normally be seen at live events, but I was proper chuffed that he'd made the effort.

When I look back on everything we put up with in order for the concert to happen, it was certainly a learning curve about shows at that level. And one thing is for sure, there is no way on earth I would put up with that nonsense, or somebody behind a computer screen telling me what to do, and especially who to have on my own line-up. No chance. It had been stressful and we made a loss (Paul), and at that point I was considering packing it all in. But at the end of the day, I don't regret doing it, and I really enjoyed the gig. After all, I managed to book a Libertine, of which I am proud.

Having just about recovered from the solo Libertine gig, I put all my efforts back into my own nights and staged two more Fairground events at The Live Lounge that year. The first was on Thursday, 27th October (Fairground 2), when I booked a great young band I happened to love from Norwich, called The Kabeedies, to headline. To complement their quirky Indie pop tunes, they had a charismatic front person in Katie, and I could never work out if her constant dancing throughout their performances was either brilliant or naff. Either way, my eyes would be transfixed watching her moves, and I loved them that much that I wasn't able to take my eyes off her pulling some shapes.

As always, I booked them in for a college session with Jamie on the afternoon of the show, and remember them all piling out of the back of their van on arrival. Katie asked if she could use the toilet to freshen up, and less than ten minutes later, she reappeared looking more like a goddess about to appear on *Top of the Pops*, and certainly not as though she had just fallen out of the back of a transit.

My Fairground 3 event was on Thursday, 10th November, and I was extremely chuffed to be able to bring Starsailor's James Walsh to the town. Starsailor originated from Chorley, not far from me, and had enjoyed chart success with their single *Silence Is Easy*, reaching Number 9 in 2003. They went on to have ten Top 40 hit singles in the UK, and ever since I saw them support The Police on their massive final tour in 2008 at Manchester Arena, I had been keen on booking James for one of my shows.

Supporting on the night was the very talented Darwen band Outsider, but their lead singer Danny ended up having his car broken into outside while they were performing, which clearly took some of the gloss off the occasion for him. I also booked the multi-talented Seamus McLoughlin from Preston as James's main support.

A couple of days before the event, Paul called me to say he was unfortunately going to miss the night, as he had just booked a family holiday in Tenerife. But he assured me that he would leave James's fee behind the bar for me for on the night. When I arrived that night, there was zero fee for anybody, which was a huge problem for me, as I was told that James required his full fee in cash before he would perform.

Totally stressed, I roped both Janet and Emma into working on the door, for free, and we were still selling tickets right up to the last minute, as until we had taken a certain amount, I couldn't be sure that it was going to happen. I remember being called to the front door to be asked if three dodgy looking blokes were okay to come in. I know I have no right to judge folk, but they really didn't look like music fans – whatever they look like – and seemed pretty out of it anyway. But the truth of the matter was that at the time we were not in a position to pick and choose, as we needed every penny, so I begrudgingly told Janet to let them in. Big mistake.

Literally about half an hour before James was due to take to the stage, Janet came over to tell me we had managed to take enough to pay his fee, which was a huge relief to me – and to his tour manager, once I handed it over. By this time the room was so packed that I had to walk all the way around the outside of the building in order to reach the toilets, or backstage.

James went down a storm with the packed-out audience, with an emotional performance of *Alcoholic*, and fans' favourites *Poor Misguided Fool*, *Lullaby*, and *Silence Is Easy*. Looking around the room and seeing the enjoyment on people's faces was confirmation again why I go through all this stress in order to make it happen.

The next day I arranged to meet James again, as he had agreed to play a session in the college studio that morning. I took him for lunch in the restaurant, and one of our students who just happened to be serving at the time, was obviously told that somebody famous had been in. He kept coming over to our table and repeatedly asking him if he wanted the same thing, over and over. I had to explain that the students were in training, and James was cool about it, but I did find it amusing.

Fairground 3 had been another success, but no sooner had it ended than Seamus came to me with a distraught look on his face and told me that somebody had stolen his guitar from upstairs. This wasn't just any guitar; he had owned it for the majority of his life, and it had travelled all over the world with him, so really it was irreplaceable. Initially, I thought it must have been misplaced, but everyone had searched high and low, and it was nowhere to be seen.
Seamus was becoming more and more anxious at the thought of never seeing his prized possession again and we stood for ages in the office, trawling through all the CCTV footage from the night, until the culprit was finally identified (thanks to everybody present). I had been right to have concerns over the three blokes I'd agreed to let in, as one of them somehow made it upstairs and was captured on the screen walking out of one of the rooms, clutching the missing guitar case.

We froze the image and I took a photo on my phone so that everybody could share it on social media. Sure enough, the magic of Facebook came to the rescue once again, as one of the staff members in a local music shop, Rimmers, saw the post, and when the thief visited the shop the following morning and attempted to sell them the item, they called the police, who ended up chasing him down Darwen Street before thankfully capturing him and reclaiming Seamus's guitar.

Later that day, the local paper printed a feature on the incident, although they claimed it was the Starsailor frontman who had been robbed. But at least the guitar had been returned in one piece to its rightful owner – to the relief of Mr McLoughlin, and me!

CHAPTER THIRTY-THREE

IT SHOULD HAVE BEEN ME

Ever since I have been blessed enough to work in my passion – music – there have been times where I think to myself, *How on earth did this actually happen?* And I have often felt guilty about the fact that one person could have such an amazing time. The thing is, though, things haven't always gone to plan, and the phrase 'It was good, but it could have been better' springs to mind.

Through my live filming work, I was asked by Simon Townshend of The Who (Pete's brother) if I fancied filming when The Who were performing in Liverpool in 2006. The very thought of being on The Who's guestlist and possibly having Access All Areas was incredible, as I have always considered them to be the greatest live band of all time. This was an opportunity that I just couldn't afford to miss!

The gig was due to take place in a giant tent on Liverpool Docks, and I was beyond excited at the prospect. I told Simon that I needed to bring a mate to help me carry my camera equipment (that old chestnut), and asked my friend and fellow Mod Kev, who didn't need to think twice about it.

On the day of the concert, the plan was to work in the morning at college, and book the afternoon off. This would allow us to make it over to Liverpool in plenty of time, in the hope that by some miracle we would get to meet the band beforehand. What happened next didn't just ruin my day, or month, but my whole year (and probably beyond).

I had literally just left college when I received a call from Mr Townshend, who had some devastating news for me. The Who had also been performing on the docks the previous night, and Simon very apologetically explained that somehow the organisers had managed to reserve our guestlist tickets for the two seats at the front on the wrong night. Unfortunately, every single seat had now been taken for that night's performance. He told me he was so sorry, but there was nothing at all he could do.

Initially I was buzzing that a member of The Who had called me, but the excitement didn't last long, and I was mortified by this news. I'd spent the whole morning dreaming about meeting Roger and Pete, and now it definitely wasn't going to happen. I appreciated that he had taken the time to call me personally, even though it was the last thing I had wanted to hear. I also felt terrible for Kev, as I knew he was looking forward to it as much as me, and now I had to ring and let him down.

For anybody that is not really into music and doesn't appreciate The Who, I am sure they will think I was overreacting, but I can tell you I was gutted for months, and it was a massive disappointment.

Simon, to be fair, kept in touch, and as a way of making up for what had happened (or hadn't) he sorted me out with guestlist passes for The Wireless Festival at Harewood House in Leeds, at which The Who were headlining. I was excited again, and gave one pass to my brother-in-law Warren, and the other to my mate Martin. Our wristbands had been left on the gates as Simon had promised, and we watched The Super Furry Animals, Eels, The Zutons, and were blown away by the magnificent spectacle of The Flaming Lips, with their performance involving 100 Father Christmases, aliens, giant balloons, and streamers. They certainly did put the P in Party.

I was determined to make sure we had a prime slot for The Who, but that meant pushing and fighting our way to the front, claiming our spot, and not moving from there for hours and hours. This included putting up with not going to buy a drink or visiting the loos, but it was a sacrifice that just had to be made. It was the closest I had ever been to the band, and they thrilled the crowd with a 24-song set, treating us to a string of hits from their back catalogue, opening with *Who Are You?* and *I Can't Explain*, and an encore including *Substitute* and *Won't Get Fooled Again*. But to my surprise, and disappointment, no *My Generation*. All in all, the three of us had a pretty fabulous day at Harewood House. The weather was kind to us, I was introduced (not personally) to the craziness of The Flaming Lips, and I stood at the front for The Who.

We started to make our way to the nearest entrance with the rest of the crowd, but just before we were about to step foot out of the gates, I noticed a small doorway in the hedge right across from us. For some reason, I found the need to walk over and ask the security guy what was through the gap, to which he replied, 'Where people can go if they have that wristband on', pointing to mine.

Even though the event had finished, I was intrigued enough to walk through the gap in the hedge, as if I was visiting the secret garden. The view that welcomed me reminded me of that moment on *Bullseye* with Jim Bowen, when he tells the contestants, 'This is what you could have won.' Apparently, it was a private area for The Who's family and friends, with posh toilets, a chill-out area and private bar, and even a Head Chef wearing a tall white hat. I couldn't believe what I was looking at.

Not being one to purposely take advantage of somebody's goodwill and the situation, I presumed that Simon's offer of three wristbands had been enough, and that the passes were simply to get us into the festival site for free. But it seems the passes that Simon kindly left us on the gate had actually entitled us to use a separate entrance once we arrived, rather than queueing up for ages with everybody else. We would have been granted access to the private artist area, which provided clean toilets, freshly cooked cuisine, a private bar, and the option to watch the acts from the side of the stage, as opposed to slumming it in a field, eating rubber chicken, going hours without using a toilet or buying a drink, and fighting our way to the front to claim our spot.

If there was ever a case of 'It was good, but it could have been better', this was it. All three of us had enjoyed a good day, but I would be lying if I said I wasn't totally gutted about such a wasted opportunity. I ended up thanking Simon again for his kindness, but didn't have the heart to tell him what we had missed out on.

In 2012, Paul at The Live Lounge told me that he was looking at taking over an old club in Preston and turning it into a live music venue. He asked if I wanted to be involved and be their booker/promoter for the place, and once I had seen it with my own eyes, I was really excited about the prospect and its potential. Formerly The Honey Lounge, it needed a fair bit of work to transform it into a venue again, but it was doable, and both Paul and I saw it as a challenge.

Paul attended various meetings in order to secure a late licence, and to get the go-ahead to turn our plans into reality. I was given the task of booking a line-up for our opening night. I felt it was only right to choose local bands as support, but set my heart on booking Sam Duckworth of Get Cape Wear Cape Fly. This was not an easy booking, but eventually I signed a contract to secure him for our opener.

Unfortunately, all our efforts were wasted, as the local police officer who was responsible for licensing decided at the very last minute that it wasn't going to happen. He quoted that the venue was literally situated several metres outside some sort of trouble exclusion zone, and refused to grant the venue a realistic late licence, making it impossible for us to go ahead with any of our plans.

Paul fought this decision the best he could and ended up losing a large amount of money over their questionable (dodgy) last minute change of heart. It seemed clear to us that for some reason, they did not want out-of-towners taking over the venue.

I had to go back to the booking agent with my tail between my legs and try to explain that after all my efforts convincing them how much I wanted to book their artist, now I was about to cancel the booking. I could only hope for dear life that it wouldn't lead to me being blacklisted for messing them around. We had even renamed the venue The Gate, being in the Friargate area of Preston, but its life ended before it even had a chance to begin, which was an absolute sickener.

This incident had well and truly put Paul off attempting to spread his empire further afield and scuppered any future chances I had of booking Sam again. The intervention of this officer had been clearly personal, and out of order, as less than a year later someone else took it over and it opened its doors with a late licence, which just added to our bewilderment and disappointment.

Also in 2012, one of the organisers of Kendal Calling contacted me asking if I was interested in working on a very exciting event they were planning to put on at Jodrell Bank. Sunday, 24th June was the date, and the line-up featured none other than my musical hero Mr Paul Weller, along with Graham Coxton from Blur, Gomez, and Craig Charles. My job was to spread the word and help promote the event, in exchange for guest and hospitality passes. I was putting posters up for weeks in any spare time I could find, along with promoting it on social media and spreading the gospel to anybody who would listen. Elbow were headlining the night before, and the weather was pretty bad.

I woke up on the Sunday morning – the day of the event – only to receive a message that due to the high levels of mud from the Elbow concert, the decision had been made to unfortunately cancel that day's Paul Weller event. I couldn't believe my luck. I had spent the majority of that week planning what I was going to say to Paul, if I was lucky enough to meet him. The event I had spent months shoving down everybody's throats, was now not happening, and yet again I was beyond gutted.

The following month, Kendal Calling Festival was happening, but I didn't plan to attend the event as the line-up wasn't really my cup of tea that year. On the Thursday evening, I received a message from a band from Liverpool I knew, called The Hummingbirds, who explained they had kindly added me to their guestlist for the festival. I knew my mate Karl was planning on going to the Lakes that weekend for one of the Wainwright walks he was passionate about, so I managed to talk him into dropping me off at the festival site. I remember watching The Hummingbirds' performance in the Calling Out tent, but can't really recall any other acts that I watched that day.
My problem was that even though I knew people attending, I was camping in the artists' field, away from everyone I knew. That evening, I remember lying in my sleeping bag, unable to get to sleep, absolutely freezing and hungry, thinking, *Sack this, I am not putting up with another night like this!* So I messaged Karl the following morning, asking if he was alright to pick me up.
It hadn't helped that the people who set up their tent next to mine during the night were acting stupid and being pretty loud in the process. When I emerged from my tent that morning, I realised that my camping neighbours were none other than The Lancashire Hotpots who, to be fair, were really sound once I went over and introduced myself. They were acting in the same way as they would have been if they were on stage, which made me laugh.

That evening, after his walk, Karl very kindly called and picked me up, and all I could think of during our journey back to Blackburn was a warm bath and a comfy bed, as the Cumbrian weather was anything but warm.

As I had been lying there freezing that morning, waiting for my mate, I heard a conversation from another artists' tent, about a Mod band from Manchester, named The Gramotones. Even though this young, no doubt jealous, band was slagging them off at the time, The Gramotones sounded right up my street. And not only that, they also possibly had the greatest band name I had ever heard.

That Saturday evening at home, just before I planned to go to my bed, I decided to go onto the Kendal Calling website to check out all the acts I would be missing on the Sunday, when I noticed that The Gramotones were due to perform that afternoon in the Tim Peaks Café. I couldn't believe my luck, and that I was about to miss the opportunity of checking them out.

As I was somebody who hated to miss out on something I was interested in, along with the thing about not doing barriers, and am totally off my head sometimes, I made the executive decision to send Karl another text, even though it was 1am, asking that if he was planning on going walking again, could he please give me a lift back to Penrith.

Janet thought that I was mad, as I had literally only been back for several hours, and now I was talking about returning. Even though I agreed she had a point, Karl picked me up around 6am, and dropped me off back at the site. It was so early when we arrived that the gates hadn't even opened, so I found myself just hanging around on the street outside until they did.

The first thing I did once they had finally let me in was find the nearest tent where I could buy a brew, and as I was sitting there chatting to some Rastafarian guy who was running the tent and a couple of members from The Tea Street Band, also from Liverpool, I started to feel a dull ache in my stomach. It was something I had not experienced before. As I was chatting, it seemed to be getting slightly more painful, so I said my goodbyes and thought it might help if I went for a wander around the fields.

I had a spare pass for the day, and as I hate things going to waste, I had posted on Facebook, offering it to anyone who was in the area. My old mate Chris Penny ended up getting in touch, asking if his mate Mick could have it. I had gone to junior school with Mick and hadn't seen him for years, so I agreed to meet him outside the festival gates. As kids, I would go around to his house after school and play with his awesome collection of toy soldiers. We were both into them, but he had a much better collection than me.

I was looking forward to catching up with him after all this time, but Mick was really late turning up, and I was waiting for the best part of an hour for him, across from somebody's garden. Time was getting on, and it was only around half an hour until The Gramotones gig.
All through the afternoon the pains in my stomach had been getting worse, and by this time I was in complete agony. I found myself leaning over the house's garden wall in an effort to somehow ease the pain. Mick eventually showed up, but by that time I could hardly stand up, so literally said hello, passed him his wristband, and told him I needed to catch a band so I would see him later. I hobbled back into the site and started making my way across the fields to Tim Peaks, in order to catch the band I had come to see.

It was around five minutes before the gig was due to start, and I was about a minute away when the pain was so bad that I ended up collapsing in a heap in the middle of the field. I had never known pain like it in my life, and as a result, I couldn't have cared less who was staring at me or what I looked like. I noticed my new Rastafarian friend standing a few feet away, but felt so rough that I couldn't even acknowledge that I had spotted him.

Suddenly, a couple of paramedics appeared beside me, and the next thing I knew I was lying in some medical centre bed, while folk were examining me. Believe it or not, the medical centre was right next door to Tim Peaks, and just to rub salt into the wounds, if I listened hard enough, I could actually hear The Gramotones performing their set; I just couldn't see them.

Maybe I should have just listened to Janet and stayed at home, as this was anything but fun. Whatever position I managed to put myself in, I felt excruciating pain, and had no idea what was causing it. I managed to text Karl saying, 'Whatever you are doing, please can you come and pick me up?' He replied that he was currently up a mountain, but would start to make his way down and set off to collect me (proper mate).

The medical staff were discussing sending me to Penrith Hospital, and I had to really talk them into letting me go home. I reassured them that my friend was collecting me at the gates, and promised them I would visit my local hospital the next morning.
After what felt like ages, Karl messaged me that he'd arrived, but the medical staff insisted on dropping me off at the entrance, in some kind of medical-type open jeep. As we were driving through the grounds, I spotted the band I had come to see, walking through a field carrying all their equipment. I nodded acknowledgement to them as we drove past, no doubt confusing them as to why I was sitting in the back of a medical vehicle, after not attending their set.

The following morning, I visited Blackburn Hospital and was told that I had in fact got kidney stones, which explained the pain. When I tell anybody this story and explain the agony I was in at the time, I always tell them to Google kidney stones as proof, because it describes the pain as the nearest a male will ever come to understanding what childbirth feels like. I rest my case.

In 2017, as part of Liverpool Music Week, Nile Rodgers and Chic were performing at the Echo Arena, and it was their first performance in the city since 1979. I considered Nile to be a complete legend within the music industry, so there was no way I was about to miss out. For once, Janet also wanted to come, as she loved Chic, so I purchased a couple of tickets and booked us into the Holiday Inn Express on Albert Dock, right across from the venue.

I went over to the arena in the afternoon on a mission to attend the soundcheck, and found myself second in a very large queue.

As we stood there freezing and making small talk with the lady on security at the front, she told us that the people who were lucky enough to be in the front few (me) were in for a very special treat, as we were about to be given a really special wristband.

The soundcheck was fabulous, and as I was standing against the barrier at the front of the stage, I couldn't believe I was witnessing a Chic rehearsal, with Nile Rodgers literally a matter of feet away. Nile even asked us at one point if they should include *Like A Virgin*, *Lost in Music*, and *Notorious*, as part of their set.

After they finished, we were taken into a room, where Nile chatted to us about some of his experiences in music and life. Then, to my absolute delight, I was given the chance to meet the great man, and of course I asked him for a couple of autographs and a photograph with him. The photo actually came out really well, and after I had done the expected thing and posted it to social media, I was flooded with messages and comments asking how on earth I had managed to meet such a legend. I replied, 'Got Lucky.'

As I was talking to him, I noticed a very large queue forming behind me, all hoping for a chance to say a few words to him, and no doubt ask for a selfie. There were so many things I wanted to ask him, but it was only fair I gave the other people a turn. After contemplating re-joining the queue, I decided not to outstay my welcome and I went back to meet Janet at the hotel.

I consider Chic with Nile to be one of the best live acts on the planet, and on this occasion, they certainly lived up to that accolade. They were superb, with hit after hit, and even the members of the audience who had opted for seats found themselves hardly sitting on them. I challenge anybody to stay seated to the likes of *Le Freak*, *Everybody Dance*, or *Good Times*. In fact, I consider *Everybody Dance* to be an instruction, when coming from the mouth of Mr Rodgers.

As is standard for a Chic concert, during their grand finale for *Good Times*, the band allow family and friends to come up on stage to join them dancing and singing along. This was the perfect way to end the evening and the atmosphere in the arena was electric. But after a few minutes watching these celebrations, I began to realise that the majority of the people who were dancing away on stage and having the time of their lives were the same people who had been at the soundcheck and in that room with me. Suddenly it dawned on me that those special wristbands the security lady was talking about included a stage pass for this very moment, and I had missed out. They must have handed them out to the people in that room just after I left.

Gutted wasn't the word, and every few seconds I kept interrupting Janet's mum-dancing to repeat out loud, 'IT SHOULD HAVE BEEN ME! I can't believe it! I can't believe it! I should be up there on stage with Nile.' I was proper sick that I had missed out on yet another magical opportunity in music, and one I will never get the chance to do again. If only I had re-joined the queue and waited just a little longer.

I have seen Chic perform on TV a few times since that evening, and when it gets to the end of the show and they invite everybody up, I find myself telling whoever is in the room at the time, 'I could have done that.' And the disappointment of that night comes flooding back to me again.

CHAPTER THIRTY-FOUR

THE KIDS ALL DREAM OF MAKING IT (WHATEVER THAT MEANS)

I enjoyed some really great nights at The Live Lounge, and in my opinion brought some really great acts to perform there, but I was finding my role as artist booker and promoter more soul-destroying by the week. Like any new venue, when it first opened its doors to the fine folk of Blackburn, almost every live night would see the room busy. But I guess the novelty had kind of worn off, and it became clear that the majority of people in this town would rather spend their Saturday night watching a tribute band in a pub, or engaging in a local karaoke, than choosing to check out an up-and-coming band they had never heard of.

Week after week I used to stand outside the venue chatting to the bands I had booked, and being asked the same question, 'Where is everyone?' I tried to explain that this was Blackburn, and that our once very bustling night-time economy had ended years ago.

Then there was the argument about whose role it is to promote an event. The answer to this question, in my opinion, is everybody involved – i.e., the band/act performing, and also the booker/promoter, and the venue – because it is in everybody's best interest to help make the night a success.
As a promoter, as far as I am concerned I do everything I can at my end to promote the gig, but strongly believe that the bands/acts should do the same. I can't remember how many times bands turned up, having not even mentioned the gig on their social media pages, yet expecting to perform to a packed-out room. And at the same time they want us to pay for the posters/flyers, provide

them with a back line (or more, in some cases), provide them with drinks, and sometimes food, on top of paying them for their lack of effort and terrible attitude, while I have to endure 25 minutes of someone trying to be Oasis. Well, I am sorry, that is just not living in the real world (not mine, anyway), and it's certainly not the ingredients to make a successful show.

I would always give the same speech to bands every week and explain that it didn't really matter how many people were in the audience, what mattered was *who* was in the audience. I explained that The Police once came out to about three people, but decided to play the best possible show that they could, which is what I believe in. It turned out that one of those three in the crowd that day was some bigwig in American radio, who was really impressed. The Police ended up playing The Shea Stadium and being the biggest band in the world, so it sort of proves my point. Mind you, it helps if you are a bloody great band to start with.

I have known bands listen to my rant, nod their heads in agreement, and then spend the whole of their set in between songs, which weren't that good anyway, moaning and complaining about the empty room, having done zero promotion themselves. There is also a matter of respect to take into account. Even if there are only three people in the room, you don't know how far they have travelled to be there, or what sacrifices they have made to come and watch you play. So that alone is a good enough reason to go out there and give it your best shot.

I personally have always had a policy of making sure I always watch the acts I have booked, unlike a lot of promoters. My belief is that if they are good enough for me to book them, why wouldn't I want to see them perform? The problem was, though, that I was the only person from the venue who would show support to the acts performing most weeks, which really was soul-destroying for me. I booked an act that I considered to be high standard, and who had travelled the length of the country to play a set for me and a handful of other folks, and that was it.

In my opinion the main downfall of The Live Lounge, and certainly me working there, was coke. A number of years previously, heroin had been the town's drug of choice (not the whole town!), but cocaine was the current narcotic folk were using. Nobody seemed interested in the live music anymore, and the music-loving audience that we'd had at the start had changed. Now it was anybody from around town just ending up there in order to get themselves another late drink, when they had clearly had enough drinks already, judging by the state they were in when they arrived.

The final straw was when I attempted to break up a fight one night in the corridor next to the toilets, between two travellers. The bouncers who were getting paid to sort out these issues were upstairs in the office, no doubt coked up, and I thought to myself, *I am the music promoter, and I find myself breaking up fights? No chance.* And that was it. I decided to leave, there and then.

The Live Lounge closed its doors on 30th April, 2015, and yes, at the time it was a huge shame for the people of Blackburn and another nail in its lack of night-time economy. But I guess if you don't support a venue, you will inevitably end up losing it. At its best, it was a great thing for the town and hosted some splendid acts. I even watched Catfish and the Bottlemen perform there, to around 15 people. Friendships were made there, and I am grateful to Paul for not just offering me a job there but putting our Emma through her apprenticeship of learning how to deal with annoying people, at a pretty young age.

Even though my role mentoring young people at college has always been a subject that I am passionate about, I would have worked in the music department supporting their students for free, if I could have afforded to. On several occasions, senior members of staff promised to make the most of my knowledge, experience, and contacts in the current music scene, and find me a role in that area, but nothing ever came of their comments. Just words. But the music tutor at the time, Dave, asked me if I would be up for delivering a lecture to his music students on artist management, and even though I hadn't done anything like that before, I considered it to be an honour to be asked. So I thanked him, and agreed to do it.

To try and keep the attention of a class of music students for around 45 minutes is a mission in itself, and I attempted to make my talk as interesting and as honest as I could to achieve that. I always introduce myself as a Mod with a Punk attitude, and explain that by the end of a session the audience will hopefully understand the importance of a Pink Jiffy Bag. I explain why I feel I am qualified enough to deliver the lecture to them, hopefully proving that I am not just some randomer reading a textbook, and that music no doubt helped to save my life, which will be expanded on in the next chapter. I also point out that all my events sell out in advance now, that I have been given over £50,000 from people I have never met, and that I am proud to say I had turned a line of coke down from a Happy Monday.

Walking around college wearing a black t-shirt and carrying a guitar case doesn't make you a musician, so you need to decide if you want your love of music to try and become a career for you, which is unbelievably hard, or if you are happy for it to simply become a hobby. Either way, there is nothing cooler, in my opinion, than being in a band with your best mates.

Everybody knows, or should do, that practice, practice, practice, is key to learning your craft (not just a textbook), and playing live as many times as you get the chance is vital to becoming tighter as a band or an artist, and to getting your name out there, which is a given.

I appreciate that without having a manager or somebody to represent your band, it is difficult to book loads of gigs in before anybody knows who you are. But each band member needs to do their bit and utilise their individual strengths. If somebody is a whizz on the internet, then get them sorting out and running the band's social media platforms. If someone is confident at speaking on the phone and meeting people – no doubt the lead singer – they should be booking the gigs and doing the networking.

When you are starting off as a band, I would suggest playing as many places as you are offered, as it is not until you become a little more established that you are in a position to pick and choose. Everybody starts off at the bottom and builds up their name in a pub before moving up to perform at more well-known music venues.
Don't expect to get paid at the start, but if you do, it's a bonus. However, it is reasonable to ask for expenses, especially if you make the effort to take people along to the venue.
Be aware of Pay to Play, and if you do end up with some money, I strongly suggest that it goes towards your next recording session, and not on beer.
If you can bank on picking up a handful of new fans at each gig, then eventually you will build up a fan base, which is so important. Put in the same effort if there are 100 people watching you, as if there were only 10, even though the motivation may not be the same. Treat the venue and the audience with respect and be nice, as it is unlikely you will be asked back otherwise. Generally, you must earn the right to have an attitude and get away with it.
You want folk to remember you for the right reasons, as building up your contact list is vital.
I also strongly recommend attending and playing selected Open Mic Nights (The Ferret, The Deaf Institute, or relevant to your area), which will help to get your name known at the venue and could lead to you building up a relationship with other bands and artists.
Another thing I am a huge fan of is gig swaps with other bands. They will agree to put you on when they play in front of their crowd, in exchange for you doing the same. I have even known bands getting a mini-tour out of this arrangement.

Having a product to promote is what it is all about, and I always recommend that if you have one really good track, and a few that are okay, only put the good one online to represent you, because standards are important, and first impressions are everything. If someone from a label or a venue or radio station attempts to check you out, they might end up listening to your sub-standard recording and trust me, if they are not impressed by the first 15 seconds, it is highly unlikely they will wait until the end of the song. They certainly won't waste time searching for anything else you have available. FIRST IMPRESSIONS.

Once you have a product that you are all proud of, and are happy for it to represent your band, the important thing to remember is to spend time and effort targeting the relevant labels and radio stations that you would like to hear it. Don't just send it out willy-nilly to all and sundry, because you will be wasting both your time and your money.

If you are promoting an Indie track, for instance, there is no point in sending it to a station or a label that specialises in Rap music, as it will end up in the bin. Research the relevant DJs and labels that are right for your genre, but make sure you get all the correct information, as I believe that if you spell Steve Lamacq's name wrong, it will again end up in the bin. Why should he put in the time and effort, if you haven't? I even heard of a case where a band researched a specific DJ and found out that he liked doughnuts, so they sent him a box with their CD attached. This may sound really stupid, but I don't think so. I can guarantee that particular DJ would 100% give their CD a play.

The key to me is to be different, in order to stand out, and this is where the Pink Jiffy Bags come in. A supporter of new music like Mr Lamacq must receive a large amount of jiffy bags and envelopes on his desk every day, and there is a very good chance that the majority of them (if not all) will be either white or brown. If yours is the only pink one, not only will it stand out from all the rest, but there is a good bet that yours will be the one that is selected to be played.

Several DJs have said that sometimes they have received a CD from a band or an artist and the only place that has any information was the cover, leaving the CD face blank. If a DJ takes a number of CDs to play, they will not have the time to spend working out what disc goes in what wallet. So I strongly recommend making sure your name and contact details are written on your product. Imagine if they liked it but had no idea who you were or how to get in contact. WASTED OPPORTUNITY.

It's a bit like if you are playing a gig, where it is important to let your audience know who you are and where they can check you out. If you can't afford a banner to help to spread the gospel, then tell them the information in between a couple of songs, and certainly at the end of your set. I have actually watched a band and thought they were decent, but left at the end not having a clue who they were. TOTAL MADNESS.

Standards and quality control are important in anything you do, and it absolutely amazes me the amount of artists online that are happy to post, and share, really poor quality phone footage for the world to judge them by.
Even if you don't fancy going down the route of t-shirts, fridge magnets, pens, etc, in order to help spread your name, it is easy enough to order some decent quality posters and flyers from the likes of Awesome Merchandise, Vistaprint, and Solopress. I have used all three for the past 15 years now, and they have never let me down.

Once you have your posters and flyers, other than the venue you are performing at, it is a mission to find places you are okay to put them. I don't believe that simply handing out flyers in the street to folk walking by is worth the effort, unless you have thousands; most people will not be interested, and the flyers are sure to end up on the ground. This is where targeting comes in again. Stand outside, or inside, a relevant gig with an audience similar to your own. Also, it is a good idea to have some flyers at your gigs advertising the next time you are going to play, because your audience (some anyway) are all in one place, so it makes sense.

Don't expect the promoter who booked you to watch your set. In my experience, most don't. Either they were not even at the venue or they chose to spend their time standing outside talking to the doorman. Some will, though. Also, don't expect the other bands on the same bill to watch your set. Some might, and you may get a couple of members checking out a couple of your tunes, but don't expect it.

If you are planning on putting on a coach or minibus to one of your shows, I suggest you collect the money up front, as you will get people who say they are attending then back out, usually at the last minute and on the day. But the driver will still expect to be paid the same amount, whether there are 30 of you or 3, so money will need to come from somewhere.

I understand that bands may require a few beers before they appear on stage, to calm their nerves and help them get in the mood. But at the beginning of your quest, it might be a good idea to save the majority of your drink's rider (if you have one) until after you have played (as you don't want to witness your bass drum flying past the crowd).

If you find yourself playing a few gigs and getting some radio play, it is important that you sign up to PRS (Performing Right Society), as every time you perform live or receive a play, you will get paid for your efforts. The amount you receive will depend on the level of the venue you perform at and the radio station that plays your track, but this all mounts up and is certainly worth it.

I would also advise artists sign up to PPL (Phonographic Performance Limited), as it collects and distributes money for the use of recorded companies and performers, where PRS collects and distributes money for the use of the musical composition and lyrics, on behalf of songwriters, composers, and publishers. I have always advised bands and artists to look at signing up to these organisations, but it amazes me the amount that do but can't be bothered to chase up any payments still owing to them.

Once you find yourself with a recording you are happy with, definitely upload it to the BBC Introducing uploader for your area. It is easy, free, and could lead to several new opportunities, including radio play, a live session, and even a festival slot (providing your face fits, and they like it).

I found it really hard in the early days getting on at a festival, due to the number of like-minded acts all trying to achieve the same, but you should still give it your best shot and apply. What I've learnt is that a promoter booking for such an event will want to see what you look and sound like live, as anybody can make themselves sound good in a music video. Sometimes I would suggest maybe opting for a couple of minutes of high-quality footage (studio or gig) as opposed to making a polished music video, because I for one would never book an act without seeing what they were like live.

If you do find yourself lucky enough to get on a festival line-up, just enjoy the experience, but be aware that you could end up on a pretty obscure stage somewhere, performing to three people and a dog. But hopefully not.

There has never been an easier way to promote your brand, in terms of the number of social media platforms. I would suggest using them all to help you get your name out there and communicate with fans and promoters. Having a good relationship with your audience is really important and to keep them onboard. After all, you don't have an excuse not to, as all you have to do is sit in a room on your own and use a keyboard. You don't even have to leave your front door these days.

I would mainly suggest that you try to enjoy every minute, and if you believe in something, stick to it. Write your songs for you and not what you think people are going to like. I recall Ed Sheeran saying that he spent ages trying to write a hit and getting nowhere, but the minute (not literally) he changed that philosophy and just wrote songs for himself, and ones he wanted to write, things started to happen.

Networking is so important for any band or artist, and I suggest somebody representing you – or yourself – should attend relevant music conferences in your area(ish). This will give you the opportunity to meet and chat with industry folk and for them to know who you are. You can also pass them a product, and listen to their advice. I attend these regularly, even if I am not representing anybody, and two I would recommend are Sound City in Liverpool, and Un-Convention in Manchester.

My friend Mike swears by sitting on the front row at any conference, as you have more chance of getting noticed by the panel, and you will be at the front of the queue to speak to them afterwards.

I have spent the past 15 years plus watching young Indie bands trying to be the next Oasis or Arctic Monkeys, and I must admit it became really boring. Try and find your own sound and be different and unique. In my opinion, you will stand more chance of standing out and not simply blending in.

Try not to give yourself too many barriers, as if you don't ask, you don't get. But be realistic. I mean, I managed to secure my band free clothes endorsements from three well-known brands by simply ringing up and selling to them what I believed in – basically asking.

Finding a manager or somebody to represent you can be a great thing, providing they are right for you and doing it for the correct reasons (because they believe in you and your potential, and not for money). And unless they have a proven track record supporting artists, I would suggest they need to prove their worth before any money changes hands. I mean, you have to be earning it in order to pay it out.

I am a huge fan of the benefits of volunteering, and if you are passionate about working in the industry, getting your feet in the door is key. Offer to volunteer at a local (or not so local) festival or independent label, or venue. They can only say no. I offered my services as an average filmmaker and ended up working for The Wickerman Festival for over four years, which was brilliant. Also, I was once at a conference listening to a session run by this Rap label, who explained they had 13 people working at the label, 12 of whom started off as volunteers, including their MD, which kind of proves my point.

I mentioned earlier that I had been given over £50,000, which is true. And if you know what you are looking for and who to ask, there are pots of money out there with the potential of supporting your cause.

When I was managing the band The Torrents, we played gigs all over the UK, but I always struggled to find out what other bands had been in that particular town. Based on this, I came up with the idea for a new website, initially using the name TownBand, but once I discovered that some surfing dude from California owned that domain and wasn't prepared to sell it, I changed the name to TownBandit.
The idea of the site was to be able to select the name of a town from a drop-down menu, which would result in all the music information in that area being shown, including every band and artist, music shop, recording studio, venue, etc. I felt that offering this information all in one place would be really handy if planning a tour, or even simply a gig in that town, as it would make more sense performing with a local band, as opposed to taking your own that nobody had heard of. I couldn't believe such a simple idea hadn't been done before and, in my opinion, still hasn't. I thought it was a good idea, but wasn't too sure if anybody else would agree, until one evening I explained the concept to Elbow's manager Phil, who convinced me it was worth chasing up.

Anyway, I ended up winning an Innovation Award and being given £3000 towards a website being built. Web companies put in their tenders to me, but unfortunately I feel we might have chosen the wrong one, as we didn't get it completed in the timeframe we were promised and they didn't do what they said they would.

Arts Council funding can also be a fantastic lifeline and support option when putting on an event or planning anything creative within the industry. I won't pretend that applying for this help is easy, and you are up against thousands who are asking for the same thing. But I have been extremely lucky on that front, and if you apply and they deem what you are planning to be worthwhile, to yourself and to your community, they are a wonderful option for help. (If you don't ask…)

I believe it is important to create a bit of hype around your band to get people interested, but even more important, don't start believing in your own hype.

It might sound an obvious statement, but a band has more chance of making it if they stay together, as most bands end up splitting up over stupid reasons or simply giving up far too early. The band Elbow were together for around 17 years before they finally got recognised for their talent by winning the Mercury Music Prize, which was certainly a game-changer for them. At one stage the band James sold more band t-shirts than they did records, due to the lack of proactiveness from their label, but they stayed together, and nobody is sitting down now when they perform.

What I have written in this chapter is obviously not written in stone, and some folk may not agree with it, it is merely the ramblings (and maybe the gospel) of a Mod with a Punk attitude, not attempting to be negative, but simply sharing my experiences and my opinions to possibly try and help others in some small way. The music industry is a really small place, and whilst it can take you years to build up some sort of reputation (if at all), you really can lose it overnight.

Another thing I would suggest is only playing a reasonably short set at the beginning, as opposed to boring folk to death or not knowing when to pack it in. Leave your audience wanting more. But that's only a thought.

I always ended my lectures with two things: one, I would play them a short YouTube video on the whiteboard, called Band V Promoter, which I feel accurately sums up some of the things I have been saying. And two, I handed out some compilation CDs I have made, featuring a chosen track from five bands from Blackburn that managed to get signed, and almost made it – whatever that means. I use this CD as a benchmark of the level that they need to be at if they are serious about what they are doing.

I really enjoyed these lectures, and hopefully the students got at least something out of them in some small way. Each year I feel I improved on my delivery, and was even told by the tutor that I could have been an after-dinner speaker, which was kind of him. He even commented on the fact that I received a round of applause from the class at the end, which was more than he ever got – or so he said.

There is no quick fix or magic formula to making it in the music industry, but I would suggest it comes down to four ingredients (maybe five):

1) Be different and find your own sound, as the more unique you are, the more chance you have of standing out and getting noticed.
2) Luck. Even if you get everything else right, you will 100% need some luck on your side. Almost every well-known musician I have chatted to or have listened to has a back story involving a whole lot of lucky breaks or coincidences, no matter how big they are.
3) Timing. Timing is key; doing things at the right time or at the relevant time is essential.
4) Be bloody good. Even if you manage to get every radio station, every record label, and every DJ to listen to your track, if they are not impressed by what they are listening to, it is sort of pointless.

When you have a couple of songs, it can be really tempting to send them to every Tom, Dick, and Harry, and upload them to your webpage. But if they are sub-standard, it will be doing more harm than good.

5) Oh, and I almost forgot, a good set of haircuts.

Going down the route of a TV talent show, such as the *X Factor*, or *The Voice*, or even *Orange Unsigned*, is certainly not my cup of tea, or to be fair the chosen route of the majority of the musicians that I have known. But I guess it comes down to horses for courses, and it definitely works for some folk.

I would argue that Diana Vickers was (I believe) stacking bananas in Marks and Spencer before her time on *X Factor* (not that there is anything wrong with stacking bananas), and since then she has released two albums, had a couple of UK tours, appeared on various TV programmes and in West End shows, made a movie in Australia with Clint Eastwood's son (no relation), and no doubt lives in a luxury flat in London. So who am I (or you, for that matter) to say that route didn't work for her?

In 2014, our local, and quite magnificent, music shop Reidy's was running a music talent competition called Reidy's Exposure (Get your music heard) at King George's Hall in Blackburn. The idea was to hunt out the best emerging talent from across Lancashire, and beyond, and there were a variety of prizes on offer, including the opportunity to perform at the venue, a music video, a recording session, and £1000 voucher to be spent on musical instruments in Reidy's itself.

I was asked to be a judge on the panel, and I brought in Karen and Alison. Along with a local radio presenter, we were given the task of deciding who we felt was worthy of going through each round. I thoroughly enjoyed the experience, and we really did see some wonderful young talent.

One of the local musicians who entered was a singer/songwriter from Langho, called Grace Davies. I was already aware of her talent but knew she would need to be extra special to impress the likes of Karen, as she was managing Rae Morris at the time, who was incredible. After we had watched all the evening's acts, the judges were ushered into King George's Hall's office to make up our minds as to who we were putting through. I argued the case for putting Grace through, but even though the others admitted she was talented, I was outvoted and they cast their vote for someone else.

We had to then go back out into the main room again and announce the acts we were putting through. This was tough, and at one stage I found myself surrounded by a band's family, asking if they could have another audition, based on the fact that one of the judges had arrived late and missed one of their songs. I noticed that Grace was upset at not going through, so I went over to explain to her that it was only a local talent competition and not something that would define her career, and that I thought she had been really good.

A while after that disappointment for her, I noticed she was doing a live session for Radio Lancashire, involving an audience. It was during the day, and I was working at the time, but I managed to sneak out on my break in order to offer my support. Once I arrived at the station, I realised that out of 150 seats, I was the only one who had actually turned up. I really felt for Grace and could see that she was clearly upset by the lack of support. So just before she was due to go on air, I did all I could to try and reassure her that this was no big deal, as it was only the start of her career and she should simply enjoy the experience.

She managed to pull off the live session regardless and performed a great cover of Bowie's *Life on Mars*. The point of my story is that Grace believed in herself and her ability and, like her or not, she managed to stick to it. Less than three years after that Radio Lancashire session, we saw her on prime-time TV, performing a duet she had written with none other than Paloma Faith. I am the first person you will hear slagging off the programme, as it is more about the celebrity judges than it is about the music, but I feel Grace changed the show's ethics for that year. Throughout, she insisted on performing her own songs, for the first time on the show, as opposed to the cheesy drivel that the programme usually churns out. So hat's off to Miss Davies.

Also, millions of people now know who she is, so not getting through in that local competition or having an audience for her radio session made no difference at all in the grand scheme of things. In fact, it probably made her stronger. Grace ended up being a runner-up that year, which is not bad for a girl from Langho – or anywhere for that matter.

Everybody knows that as far as Blackburn bands go, we have to go back to 1964 to brag about any major chart success, when The Four Pennies reached Number 1 with *Juliette*. Certainly, in my generation there are a handful of groups that have achieved great things, but unfortunately never just quite made it in terms of major success. The CD that I always hand out to students at the end of my talks features the five bands who I consider have come the nearest, out of the ones that I have been aware of.

The Stiffs need to get a mention and to be considered in any argument about who is the best band from the town. Starting in 1976 and described as Punk or Power Punk, they played their first public live performance at East Lancs Cricket Club in 1977, after learning their trade during several church hall and local Youth Club bookings. They went on to release their first single *Standard English* on their own Dork Records Label in 79, but it was their second offering, *Inside Out*, that managed to grab the attention of legendary DJ John Peel, who not only played the song on a regular basis on his Radio 1 Show, but invited the band to perform two John Peel Sessions, which was a goal for any new act at the time.

Inside Out was reissued by EMI's Zonophone subsidiary label in 1980, and features on a number of Punk Compilation albums. Also, in that year, the band signed a long-term deal with EMI.

They later signed to Stiff Records and released *Goodbye My Love* (Glitterband Cover) which became a turntable hit, spending several weeks in the National Airplay Charts. The Stiffs went on a national tour with the UK Subs and Anti- Pasti, and still manage to pack out a room whenever they perform today.

Bradford (yes, Bradford from Blackburn) started making waves in the town in 1988, with the release of their debut single *Skin Storm*, which incidentally was the first independently financed recording to be released on Compact Disc. Fronted by the multi-talented Ian H, the band signed to The Smiths Producer Stephen Street's Foundation Label, and Street produced the majority of their material during their two-year association. They ended up being signed to Sire Records, and opened for Morrissey at his first post-Smiths concert at Wolverhampton Civic Hall. They released two singles in 1989, which both ended up being hits on the UK Indie Chart, and Street and Sire helped Bradford release their album *Shouting Quietly* (great name).

Morrissey ended up recording a cover version of *Skin Storm* which he released as a B Side. Bradford toured extensively, supporting the likes of Primal Scream, Joe Strummer, James, and Sugarcubes, and at the time were tipped to be the next Smiths. Original members Ian and Ewan, along with Stephen Street himself, now make up the current Bradford line-up, and have recently completed their first new album in over 30 years, entitled *Bright Hours*, to be released in 2021.

The Burn consisted of mainly local lads who went to school together in Blackburn (with the exception of Lee,) and chose their band name as an abbreviation for their hometown. Their first demo was recorded at Badly Drawn Boy's studio and was heard by Dave Boyd (the manager of Hut, a Virgin Records subsidiary) whilst he was shopping in a vintage clothes shop on Carnaby Street. He was so impressed that not long after he made the journey up North to meet the band and ended up signing them in 2001. Their debut album was recorded at The Chapel Studio in

Lincolnshire, entitled *Sally O Matress*, released in 2003 (a fine piece of work).

The Burn toured with Oasis, with Liam Gallagher watching their set stageside every night, Ian Brown, The Coral, The Music, Paul Weller, and performed at Glastonbury, V Festival, and The Isle Of White Festival in 2003. The highlight of the band's adventures came when they were spotted by the agents of The Rolling Stones, while playing The Isle Of White, and they were so impressed that The Burn from Mill Hill Blackburn were invited to support The Stones in Paris, which would be the highlight of any band's career. I even heard that Robert De Niro and Johnny Depp were in the audience that night.

Local band **Tompaulin** were formed in 1999 and named after the Irish Poet Tom Paulin. The band released five singles on the Action Records Track & Field and Ugly Man labels, before releasing their debut album *The Town and The City* in 2001. The band were often compared to the likes of Belle & Sebastian, and *The Times* described them as 'Exactly the right balance between grim reality and the chord sequences that lift you out of it'. Tompaulin released five singles and three albums, played Glastonbury Festival, performed on Granada Reports, and recorded two John Peel Sessions for his BBC Radio 1 Shows in 2000 and 2001.

The band was fronted by Jamie, who was the Media Tutor at college and who I worked with putting on those live studio sessions for the students. And *The Boy Hairdresser*, off their first album, is one of my favourite songs.

Having written down the achievements of those four local bands that I would argue did make it in some way, I admit that even though I included my own band The Torrents on the CD I handed out, I could never try and claim that what they achieved was on the same level as the ones mentioned above. But as far as the past 15 years go in this town, I would argue that they were definitely up there during that period. The Torrents, or just Torrents, played at various known venues around the country, including Sheffield

Carling Academy One. They were named Steve Lamacq's Band of the Week on 6 Music, MUTV Band of the Year, featured on several TV programmes, had several magazine features, radio play, and clothing endorsements.

Granted, we didn't mate around with Steve Jones, share a brew with Morrissey, make small talk with Mick Jagger, or record any John Peel Sessions (unfortunately), but we did get our name out there and had a wonderful time doing so.

I have no problem admitting to being star-struck when I find myself lucky enough to meet the musicians whose vinyl I have purchased and played over the years, despite the fact that on many occasions our Emma tries to convince me that they are only human beings and no different to anybody else.(as if).

CHAPTER THIRTY-FIVE

LIAR

In 2013, ex-Hacienda DJ Dave Haslam was doing one of his brilliant In Conversation events at The Albert Hall in Manchester with Mr Punk Rock himself, John Lydon. (Thursday, 9th October) John had just brought a book out (near Christmas, and all that), entitled *Anger Is An Energy*.

I had never visited The Albert Hall before, but there was no way I was about to miss the opportunity of meeting a Sex Pistol. The deal for anybody who purchased a ticket was that you would listen to Mr Lydon putting the world to rights for about an hour, and providing you spent your hard-earned cash on buying a copy of his autobiography, he promised to sign it for you at the end.

The questions and answer session with Dave did not disappoint, even though you could put your money on who did most of the talking. My mate Gav had been a huge fan, and even though he didn't attend, he told me that if I managed to get John's autograph for him, he would get it framed and put it up in his kitchen.

Rather than just ask him to sign a boring piece of paper, I always like to be creative, and in the past I have bought birthday cards and got them signed for folk. On the afternoon of the gig, I called into our local Tesco Express at Roe Lee to attempt to find a card suitable for a Pistol to sign, but the choice was really limited. The one I opted for in the end had a photograph of Les Dawson on the front and read, 'I went to my Doctor and asked for something for persistent wind. He gave me a kite.'

I guessed everyone liked Les Dawson, so thought I'd be fine. But the bad news was that we had been told that John would only sign one copy of his book each, as sometimes events like this would attract fans who brought their entire record collection of that artist in order to hog the time and ask for every item to be signed, not sparing a thought for how many people were still waiting in the queue behind them. However, the good news was that, unlike the usual protocol at these events where you get a matter of seconds to get a signature and move along, we were told we each had five minutes with the artist, which was amazing.

Folk patiently queued for hours, and it was about midnight before it was my turn. Once you were next in line, you would go over to his table, leaving everybody else a fair distance away. Next to John was some official(ish) looking guy sitting on the next table, watching everybody to make sure they were sticking to the rules of one book only.

I don't know why, but I was a little nervous walking over to this menacing looking guy with spikey hair sitting in the corner. I walked up to the table and told John it was really nice to meet him, to which he responded by hurtling forward, putting his head about two inches away from mine, and shouting in a really loud voice, 'LIAR!'

I hadn't been expecting that, and wasted the next minute (of my five) trying to convince him that I actually meant it. Even though the (fun police) guy on the next table was staring in my direction, I thought it was now or never, so decided to push my luck. And as soon as John had kindly signed my copy of his book, I produced the card from my back pocket and asked him if he would do the same for my friend who couldn't make it.

For a few seconds he just slightly stared at me, making me even more nervous. Then suddenly, and out of the blue, he shouted, 'I bloody love Les Dawson!' I had chosen well, and he proceeded to write 'Les is Brilliant, John Rotten Dawson, Hugs & Kisses'. I was buzzing (and I knew so would Gav be).

Little did I know at the time, that John had had some sort of past encounter with Les, so as for choosing a relevant card went, I did well. I thanked him for taking the time to spend hours meeting folk and signing their books for them, to which he replied, 'Why wouldn't I? They have paid to come and see me, so it's the least I can do.' That made me think he was a real top bloke, as I had never known anyone hang around for that long before.

My mate Tony was also in the queue with his partner Kay, and he told me it was 2.30am before they got the chance to meet Mr Lydon, which was incredible to me. But he said they ended up doing the bumps with him at one point, so I guess it was worth the wait.

The following morning when I woke up, I debated with myself whether or not I was going to give the card. Everybody else who had attended had merely had their book signed, although many were selling for around £100 on eBay a matter of hours later. However, the card was totally unique, and I knew that nobody else on the planet would have a signed Les Dawson card with a private message written in it by a Pistol. I am sure I would have done the right thing anyway, but it was Emma who told me that I had to give it to Gav, as it was him I had sorted it for. And to be honest, I knew she was right. Gav loved it, got it framed, and it has pride of place in his kitchen to date.

The council-run music and arts festival 'Arts In The Park', which Blackburn folk had been treated to annually since 2000, was axed in 2007, but in 2013 a small dedicated group of volunteers – including me – drew up plans to bring it back in some form. Witton Country Park was the destination, and the team met weekly to discuss budgets, barriers, and line-ups. Volunteers were sought on a weekly basis, but instead of giving them a role that was more befitting their skillset, the powers-that-be decided it was only fair that everybody giving their time up on the day should be given the experience of a number of roles, which I felt was ridiculous.

I was given the role of Main Stage Manager and Artist Booker, and Part Fundraiser, as I was working at the local college at the time and felt they may support the event in some way, especially if we tried to involve some of the students. I made an appointment to meet with the College Principal and asked if he would consider sponsoring us. Luckily for me (us), he told me he had been a musician in his earlier life and had been forced to choose between going on tour as a drummer or going down the route of education. He told me that he had chosen the more boring route (his words) and that he loved the idea of what we were trying to do for the town, so committed to giving me £10,000.

I had literally been in his office less than ten minutes and had managed to talk him into giving us £10K. I was buzzing and knew that the rest of the team would be as well. When I mentioned this commitment to my work colleagues, they seemed a little shocked, and sort of made out, 'Well you haven't got it yet, so we will believe it when we see it.' The following afternoon I received a phone call from the finance department, notifying me that my cheque was ready to collect. I couldn't believe it was that easy, but if you don't ask... And sure enough, I walked over to collect it without so much as 'Can you keep the receipts' or 'What are you going to spend it on?' A less trustworthy person might have found themselves lying in a hammock in Barbados, with a pina colada in their hand; I mean, who would have known?

The main problem we found ourselves with was trying to open a bank account with NatWest; it was absolutely unbelievable the amount of red tape and fobbing off we received. I completely understand that these things don't happen overnight and that they take time, but six months to open an account is beyond incompetent by anybody's standards. Day after day, week after week, month after month, I would go into the branch and listen to excuse after excuse as to why the account had not been set up yet. This situation became really serious in the end, and came within a day of threatening the event all together.
The issue was that the cheque was due to go out of date, and I worried that if I went back to college and asked them for another one, they might realise how bloody generous they had been in the

first place and changed their mind. Also, when you apply for funding and are successful, you need to have the relevant bank account set up (Business/Non-Profit) in time for it to be paid in on the date of the transfer, or else you lose it.

We actually reached one day to go before this happened, as it really did go right down to the wire.
I remember I visited the branch just before lunchtime and asked to speak to the manager, making her fully aware that I would not be leaving her office until the account was set up. After leaving me standing next to her desk for around 20 minutes, she finally returned and assured me that the Event Bank Account was now okay to pay some money into. (Emily Bishop, eat your heart out!) I had never known it that difficult to give somebody £35,000 in my life, and I certainly won't be rushing back to open any more accounts with them.

Blackburn Festival took place on Saturday, 15th June, 2013 (from midday until 9pm), and the weather was decent, on the whole. I had booked Twisted Wheel to headline, and a young talented Soul musician I had spotted in Liverpool, called Esco Williams. A number of local acts were on the bill, and I also put on The Tapestry, knowing that they would never let anybody down live.

I had never managed a main stage before, but felt confident that I would somehow blag my way through it. I asked my mate Birchy, who was an Arms Response Officer in London, if he would be my right-hand man on stage (minus the weapons), as there was nobody I trusted more if things went wrong. But the Event Chairman wanted to put him on car park duties, enabling all the volunteers to have a go at all the different roles. I was speechless – almost – and refused to allow it to happen, trying to get him to understand how a 17-year-old stranger with spots and zero experience in this field, would be of no help whatsoever to me on stage.

The thing I have learnt about putting on an event, especially a Festival, is how important timing is to the smooth running of the day. Everybody has a time slot for their set, and if somebody fails to meet that, everybody else will suffer. If a band showed up late or overplayed their performance, this would lead to the headline band being given less time – and that was not an option. Also, we had a 9pm curfew.

One of the R&B acts we had booked from Birmingham didn't turn up for their soundcheck, and when I eventually got through to their manager, he told me they were stuck in traffic. The closer it had got to their set, the more concerned I became, especially after someone who knew them told me they had a reputation for always arriving late for events. When they eventually showed up, they were already ten minutes into what should have been their slot. As stage manager, I was given the unenviable task of letting them know that their planned 45-minute set was now down to 25 minutes, and believe me this did not go down very well with the Brummie divas. I recall being fully surrounded by the artists' entourage, about 15 in total, but I managed to stick to my guns and 25 minutes is what they got.

The day was going well, I felt (apart from Brummiegate), and even though it wasn't packed, the main acts had a decent crowd watching them. Twisted Wheel took to the stage and were going down well with the crowd, but with only three songs left of their set, a bit of trouble broke out in the field across from them. What we didn't know at the time was it was a handful of teenagers from Preston (maybe footy fans) who kicked off, but to be fair, it did look like handbags from where I was standing. Security went mad, and ended up chasing them around the field like something resembling the opening scenes from Benny Hill, whilst in great Titanic fashion the band carried on playing, as if they were oblivious to all the commotion in front of our stage.

The next thing I knew was our chairman (or whatever name he gave himself that year) urgently ran over to me and told me to pull the gig. This was something I was never going to do – or not because of five 16-year-olds anyway. I tried to explain to him that our headline band, Twisted Wheel, had literally two songs left, that all the crowd in front of the stage were waiting for their grand finale of *You Stole The Sun*' and that if I pulled the gig now, he would have a mini-riot on his hands. After a few more minutes arguing with him, their set ended, and he took great pleasure in telling me that I was sacked.

'SACKED?' I said, laughing out loud. 'I am a volunteer, how can I be sacked?'
I thanked the band, thanked Ian and the people I had been working with, and casually walked away with Janet, shaking my head. I was also putting on two bands at The Live Lounge that evening, and needed to make my way down there.

I was literally in the venue for around 30 minutes when the chairman walked through the doors and made his way over to me, apologised (to be fair), and attempted to give me a hug. I appreciated his comments (and actions), but I knew if I was to carry on putting on gigs, something would have to change. I wasn't going to do it and answer to anybody else; from now on I would be doing it on my own terms.

CHAPTER THIRTY-SIX

PIE MAN A CHANCE MEETING

Back at college, the studio sessions came to an end, due to our brilliant Sound Engineer leaving (Joe), and Jamie eventually moving over to Art (as opposed to Media). This was a huge shame, as over the years we had brought in some quality acts, but I guess that nothing lasts forever. (BF)

At college, the highlight of any day for most members of staff was a trip to the College Bakery at lunchtime. Not only was it run by the friendliest baker in town, but he would make his prices up as he went along (in your favour,) and even if you selected about five items, he would say, 'Oh, just give us a quid.' When I say friendly, that is probably an understatement, as no matter how many people were waiting in the queue, he would ask how you were doing, and how your weekend had been.

On this particular day, I was waiting for my turn, looking forward to some leek and potato soup (not that I like leeks), when I heard John ask the two girls in front of me how their band was going. To be honest, I hadn't paid too much attention to them as I was full of a cold and the warm soup was my main priority at that moment, but I presumed they were music students, because that department was at the bottom of the ramp where we were standing.

That would have been that, but just as they were about to walk away, our friendly baker John threw a spanner in the works and said to them, 'He is the one you need to talk to.' And he pointed to me. I thought, *Here we go*. And at that moment, the two students both turned to face me, and said, 'Why, what do you do?' That was it, my leek and potato soup became a distant memory, and I spent the next ten minutes asking them questions and answering theirs. They asked who I was into, no doubt expecting me to give them some cliche answer based on my age or maybe my haircut, but as soon as I mentioned Temples, we started off on common ground. Believe it or not, they were due to go and watch the band the following week.

Talking to them, they knew more about 80s Synth music than I did, and I had lived through it (thanks to Nicky). Without being disrespectful, I had worked at college for over ten years by then, and in that time had met and talked with a number of music students. But none were anything like these two; they really did stand out, and they impressed me with their level of knowledge and their cool persona.

Eventually, we said our goodbyes and they hurried back to their class, while I took my cold soup back to our office. But I must admit that throughout that afternoon I couldn't get our chat out of my head. They were the coolest girls I had met in a long time, but I knew there was a really good chance that I would never see them again, so that was that.

As I finished work that afternoon, I was walking through the campus when one of the music tutors I knew thanked me for chatting to two music students in his class, Keely and Courtney, who hadn't stopped talking about me all afternoon (which I am sure was a slight exaggeration). He asked if I didn't mind calling into their practical lesson the following day, to offer them a bit of advice.

When I walked into their class and saw them both sitting at a piano, in the process of writing a song, I remember thinking, *Wow!* I told them both I was impressed, and even though I dropped into the conversation that I had promised I was never going to manage anyone again, they invited me to come and watch them perform the following week at their end-of-year showcase for family and friends. (11.12.14.)

I accepted the invitation, but I can't lie, I was hoping that they wouldn't be very good then I wouldn't have the temptation of what should I do next. Up until that point they had sent me a couple of rough demos which sounded decent enough, but they were instrumentals, so I had no idea what their vocals sounded like. On the night, each music student got up and performed in front of a small audience, and most sounded okay, but they went down the usual route of performing Whitney covers and so on.

When it was Keely and Courtney's turn, I knew I was in trouble. Yes, there were parts out of tune, but they sounded good, and from what I had seen and heard there was clearly potential. But the thing that impressed me the most was their set choices, which were amazing, from the likes of Chvrches, to Bauhaus, to Imogen Heap, and Crystal Castles. Nobody I knew, or had known, would have chosen a set list like that.
I sat there knowing I had a problem. No matter how much I was impressed by them, I really couldn't risk going back on my word and committing to help someone again. But I also knew that it would be hard just to ignore them. At the end of the event, I went over to the studio to tell them I had enjoyed it and explained that I would love to try and help them in some way. Even though managing them was not an option, I told them I was happy to represent them, and after I explained what this would mean, we all agreed that would be the plan.

What had I just committed to? And how was I going to explain my latest venture to Janet and Emma? It was not going to be easy. I decided not to hit them with this news all at once, but to drip-feed my involvement over the coming months (damage limitation).

We used the studio at college to rehearse, and every band meeting was at Liz N Lil's (the old Grapes pub), accompanied by either vanilla or chocolate milk shakes, or hot chocolate on a colder day.

Even their band name was something that no other act would have chosen – Pax and the Scarlet Field. Scarlet Field was apparently taken from The Horrors' song *Scarlet Fields*, and the Pax part had no doubt some sort of Goth overtones – being a couple of proud Goths, as they told me every day. Keely and Courtney were great company, a little mad and certainly unique, but their passion and knowledge for music was a breath of fresh air, and there was never a dull moment when they were around.

As part of their music course, they had to plan and perform at their own event, so my first official Pax gig was 22nd February, 2015, at Two Gates Bowling Club in Darwen, and it was the first time I properly met their parents. After my experience at Friargate, and the fact they were both 16, it was important to me that I always received their parents' permission to support them in the way that I had offered. Keely's dad had actually worked with Waker, and both Mark and Karen had known them for years, which really did help, as I am sure Mark had put in a good word about me when he was asked, 'What about this Pete?'

Courtney's dad approached me and introduced himself, then told me that I better not be filling their heads up with nonsense, with talks of record deals and fame, which I assured him was the last thing I was about to do. I was glad to get that awkward conversation out of the way.

I dragged some of my mates along to offer their support, and even though I knew they weren't really into that sort of thing (music since the 1980s), I regretted giving them the invite, as I almost ended up falling out with them for being ignorant and talking at the bar the whole of the way through the performance.

As for Pax themselves, they did a really good job pulling everything together, and even though in their words they would say they were awful on that afternoon, it was really early days still. And I definitely saw enough from their performance to know they had potential.

We were offered a slot on the main stage at Darwen Live, once the word got out that they were a band and had someone representing them. But a couple of days before we were due to play, I made the decision in the practice room that they were not ready. I was honest with them about my opinion, and even though I am sure it was something they did not want to hear, they took it in the right way once I explained my reasons for it, and agreed that I should pull the gig.

Like I have said before, I hate pulling gigs, and it was something I very rarely do, but my priority was them, and there was no way I was about to agree for them to give people their first impressions of them, if they weren't ready or at their best. Keely and Courtney could easily have taken my comments the wrong way, and that would have been the end of that. But instead, they worked their socks off for the next couple of months by rehearsing and song writing, and their improvement was clear to see.

My friends Jamie and Patricia, who had booked The Torrents for Frankie's Bar when they were promoting at the venue, were putting on a local Festival in July called MooFest at Wellybobs Farm, also in Darwen, that would showcase the local bands. And Pax were offered a slot. Even though the weather conditions were pretty grim for them to perform on the back of the lorry, what stood out to me was watching both of their dads filming it on their phones and hearing the words, 'Blimey, I didn't realise that they were this good!' That proved that their hard work had paid off, even though Pax both told me that they had sucked.

I was really impressed with their efforts and the fact that a local label tried their best to sign them. So I had decided to throw caution to the wind and offered to manage them. Agreeing to represent them was more or less the same thing anyway, and had really just been a blag to make out to folk (Janet and Emma) that I had not fully committed.

As always, I called a meeting at Liz N Lil's for the Monday lunchtime, put forward my proposal, and thankfully they both said yes, as I would have felt pretty stupid if they had turned me down after all that. I had gone against my word, but I guess sometimes you have no idea what life will throw at you or who it will pair you up with, so if my passion of trying to support young people was the only thing I felt I was any good at, how could I turn this down? I was just going to have to put up with the earache, which I obviously deserved.

No sooner than I had made the decision to manage them, it almost all came crashing down – in a pretty dramatic fashion.

I noticed a post that Karen had made online, advertising a special event taking place in Manchester, at the old Granada Studios site. The event was called 'An Ode To Anthony H Wilson', and was to launch a tribute single to the Factory Records legend who passed away on 10th August, 2007. The single was due to be released the following day by Skinny Dog Records, featuring artwork by Peter Saville, and a remix by Andy Weatherall. The poem in the song, which was due to be performed at the launch party, was written by Mancunian poet Mike Garry. Tony's name had been king in the Manchester music scene since he first launched Factory Records in 1978, and he went on to sign the likes of Joy Division, New Order, and The Happy Mondays to the label.

After reading about the event and imagining it would no doubt be full of music industry folk, I felt it might be a good introduction for Keely and Courtney to attend, and it would enable me to introduce them to some of my contacts, getting their name out there. They seemed keen on the idea, and I made sure that both sets of parents were happy for them to go, just to cover my back.

The three of us got the train over to Victoria and made our way over to Atherton Street. Once we arrived, we weren't too sure which was the correct building for the event, but we started chatting to this random guy in the street, who just happened to be the photographer for the evening, so we followed him in. We were only inside the venue for around five minutes when we bumped into him again, and he asked if he could take a few photos of the girls outside. They were up for it, and I guessed there would be no harm done. After all, my job was to try and get them noticed. So far so good.

My friends Tony and Kay were at the event, and I bumped into Karen, so introduced them both to her. I remember attempting to nick one of the event posters off the wall (I mean, how else are you supposed to get them?), and getting pulled over by a bouncer who told me to put it back, which just added to Tony's amusement.

We watched the warm-up acts on stage. Clint Boon was the DJ, and the premiere of the music video was shown to us. The main act appeared on stage – Mike Garry and Joe Duddell – and as they started to perform their showpiece, I looked in front of me just below the stage and noticed Keely slowly swaying from side to side. Knowing I had only bought them a Coke, I was concerned, especially once she started to collapse in what seemed like slow motion at the time. She actually fainted, and I seem to recall that somebody caught her before she hit the floor, which was a relief.

Tony noticed what had happened and ran over to one of the doormen to ask for a chair for Keely to sit on. The doorman obliged, and we sat her just outside the entrance inside the foyer. I remember Rowetta from The Happy Mondays coming over to check that she was alright, which was nice of her, and Keely herself seemed to be in a bit of a daze. She told us she was okay, even though she didn't have a clue about what had just happened. I explained my concern to her and suggested that we started to head back to the train station. Even though Keely told me she was enjoying herself (apart from the last 15 minutes) and wanted to stay, I managed to convince her that getting her home safe was my only priority.

We said our goodbyes to Tony and Kay and took a taxi back to Victoria. Once we arrived, we realised we had only just missed our train going back to Blackburn and needed to wait another hour until the last train arrived – if it hadn't been cancelled.

Let me tell you this, my friends, that hour was one of the longest hours of my life. As the minutes went by, Keely was clearly getting worse and worse. At the same time, Courtney started to have some sort of panic attack and was hysterical at the state of her best friend, and started to cry.

Imagine the scenario: I had duty of care of two 16-year-olds, along with the trust of their parents; we were in a different city; Keely was acting as though she was out of her head on drugs; and Courtney was almost hyperventilating and was in tears. Whichever way you looked at this, the situation was not good. Maybe if I had been a builder or an electrician or something, and hadn't worked in Child Protection, I might not have felt so sick. And maybe if I hadn't been through all those accusations at Friargate School, I would not have worried so much about what might happen. But the fact is, both these things were true, and once Courtney called her dad and asked him to meet us at Blackburn Station in an hour, I not only imagined losing my job but knew my intention of managing the band after this night was never going to happen.

The train journey back was no better, and I was totally freaked out by watching Keely staring at herself in the train window with a look of confusion on her face, and chatting to herself in a language I certainly hadn't heard before.

We arrived back on home soil, and I nervously escorted the girls over to Courtney's dad's car, where he was waiting for us. I remember saying, 'Hi Chris, can I just say, I know Keely looks as though she is out of her head on some drug, and I know you don't know me, but I am actually anti-drugs. I hate them, I have never taken any, and all Keely has had tonight is a drink of Coke.' He simply replied, 'Ok,' and I think he thanked me for bringing them back, then got in his car and drove them home to Darwen.

I felt terrible and woke Janet up once I arrived home. I said, 'I need to let you know what has just happened.' I couldn't sleep properly, worrying about how Keely was, and hoping she was alright.

Saturday morning was the same, and I worried myself sick about what was going to happen after our trip to Manchester had gone so horribly wrong. I can't remember what time it was, maybe about 11am, I received a call from Keely, and even though she sounded rough, thankfully she told me she was fine. She told me she'd had a great night (on the whole) and thanked me for looking after them both. This was wonderful to hear, and such a relief, but I wasn't out of the woods yet, as she informed me that her dad was going to ring me soon.

It felt like hours before he actually called, and I was ultra-nervous about taking the call, knowing it could go either way. But once he had thanked me for looking after Keely and making sure they both got back safe, he told me that he believed my story of events, and I could finally relax and know that everything would be okay.

To this day, it still remains a mystery what happened to Keely that night in Manchester, and we have discussed it on many occasions. Keely assured me that she hadn't taken anything herself, and I believe her, so all we can really put it down to was that her drink must have been spiked. At some stage in the evening somebody must have slipped something into her drink, without any of us being aware of what was happening. It is hard to imagine that at an industry event with so many like-minded people and friends, somebody attending would do something like that, but I am afraid that is our only explanation.

My friend Sarah was the person I would always go to when it came to asking her opinion on anything I was doing in music. I knew she would always give me her honest opinion on what I was asking her, and not simply tell me what I was hoping to hear. I met Sarah in Liz N Lil's and let her listen to their early demos through my headphones, and she was impressed, which I was pleased about.

Jamie at college was involved in putting on a media event at Blackburn Museum and Art Gallery, and I was invited to attend.

The event was a talk given by an ex-media student who, amongst other things, had recently shot a video for none other than Johnny Marr. So I talked Sarah into coming along, as it sounded like it would be interesting. We both enjoyed the evening, but towards the end I started to get a little bored and found myself gazing around the room, conjuring up old memories of when I used to visit the museum with my Grandma as a kid. I remembered always being freaked out by the stuffed birds and the Egyptian Mummy that they seemed to have had forever.

I am not sure what made the idea pop into my head, but I recall turning to Sarah and whispering, 'Imagine putting a gig on in here, as if they would let me.' The room was stunning, and all four walls were completely covered in very old, expensive artwork, and even though I knew it was a bit of a crazy idea and more or less a non-starter from the off, my mind wouldn't let it drop. All that night and again the following morning, it was all I could think about.

Sticking to my 'If you don't ask, you don't get' principle, I felt it was a too good idea to just forget it, and decided to email Rebecca, who ran the building. I had got to know her a little through my involvement with Blackburn Festival in 2013. My email read along the lines of 'Have you ever had somebody put on a live gig in the museum's 140-year history? And if not, would you consider it?' To my astonishment, Rebecca replied confirming 'No,' which only made me more determined. She said that she was happy to meet me and discuss what idea I had in mind. Result.

Before attending our meeting, I put a lot of thought into what my selling point was, and what I could say to win over her trust in me, and actually let me do it. My philosophy was to only sell advanced tickets for any event, as that way you could sort of vet your audience and know who you were selling tickets to. This in turn would avoid any drunken idiots simply showing up on the night.

I couldn't believe my luck when Rebecca actually listened to my idea without turning it down flat. I also explained that it would help to raise the awareness for the museum itself as, no disrespect, half of my mates weren't even aware that we had a museum in the town.

In theory, it was agreed that I could put an event on that year in the main room, providing we could agree on how we were to do it, and that Rebecca was informed about every aspect of it. I happily agreed because, after all, she was responsible for millions of pounds worth of artwork, so I knew I would have to tread carefully and fully respect her wishes.

The obvious but only name I felt I could give my event was Night At The Museum Live – Live being the operative word, to avoid being confused with the film of the similar name. And I had no desire to be linked with Ben Affleck in any way.

After months of negotiations, meetings, and plans, Night At The Museum Live 1 (NATM) took place on Thursday, August 14th, 2014 (7.30pm-10.30pm), and the line-up read: Jamie Brewer (from Preston), Bad Cardigan (from Blackburn), The Gramotones (from Manchester), and The Hummingbirds (from Liverpool). My mate Strang designed the posters for me, which looked classy, and we not only had an incredible Apothecary Cocktail Bar on the night, but we named one of the cocktails after the headline band, a Hummingbird – which went down really well with our audience, along with the artists. The seats were set out in rows in the main room, with only 120 advanced tickets sold, and a very small guestlist.

The tickets sold out within a couple of weeks of announcing it, and my mate Smith was the DJ for the evening, playing a mixture of his usual Soul/Northern Soul/Indie Mix, and of course *Being The Benefit Of Mr Kite* lined up to put on just before I was due to stand on stage and introduce the evening's entertainment. I don't know what it is, but I am happy to get up and stand up on any stage and give a speech to the audience, providing it is about a subject which I know something about. But add a microphone to the mix, and I become a little nervous, which is strange.

Even though I had previously put on three separate Fairground events, I hadn't been able to make all of the decisions and do things exactly how I had wanted to do them. Attention to detail was my thing, and putting in the effort, in the hope that everybody including the acts, the audience, the staff, and the professional cocktail waiters, fully enjoyed the complete experience.

Rebecca and her team at the museum were a magnificent help, along with Janet and Emma, who creatively dressed the stage in sunflowers and lighting.

When I first met Sid, who was the organiser of The Wickerman Festival, he told the story of the time they were just starting the festival. He said that he contacted Michael Eavis to ask him for some advice and was invited down to Glastonbury to take a tour of the site. After walking around with Michael for a couple of hours, and just before they said their goodbyes, Sid asked again if he had any advice for him. To which Michael replied, 'Be different.' There are hundreds of music festivals throughout the UK every year, so for you to stand a chance of standing out, and basically surviving, doing things a little differently and being unique made a lot of sense to me.

That was it. I had a new tagline for my Fairground events: 'Putting Amazing Acts in Amazing Buildings,' was born. I had already established that putting a gig on in a gig venue wasn't enough in this town, but if you offered something unique to folk, at a high standard, you stood a far better chance of it being a success.

Jamie Brewer opened the proceedings, using his magical fingers to produce a pretty incredible sound from his much-strummed acoustic guitar. And Tom and Jack, from local act Bad Cardigan, took the honour of being the first ever band to perform at Blackburn Museum in 140 years, which Jack still boasts about even today (rightly so).

I feel it is fair to acknowledge that our next act, The Gramotones, won over the hearts and ears of the audience and absolutely delighted the crowd with a fantastic cover of *I Heard It Through The Grapevine*, as well as my personal favourite of theirs, *Daltry Street*.

Even though The Hummingbirds were one of my favourite new bands at the time, I really did feel for them having to follow The Gramotones, and even though they were brilliant and their vocal harmonies sounded wonderful in that museum room, people were still talking about the previous act, so it was tough for them.

Leading up to the event, I had received the usual lectures from a couple of my friends, asking why on earth I was putting something on at a loss. But halfway through the night, I remember looking across at the sold-out audience clapping and cheering on a school night in Blackburn, and thinking to myself, 'That is why I do it.' The pleasure I got at being the one responsible for making it happen (along with a great team), meant more to me than making some money, but my mates never did get that.

My first NATM had been a magnificent success, and the main thing was that Rebecca was happy with how things had gone, so I knew there was every chance she would allow me to put on another, which was brilliant.

When I had first discussed my idea with a friend of mine called Gav, he was so blown away by the prospect of having a concert in such a beautiful room that, as a gift of his appreciation, he ordered me a very creative feedback book, so that the acts, along with the audience, could leave their comments about how much they had enjoyed the experience (or not). He even gave me a special pen to go with it, which was designed to look like one of those ancient quill pens, which was really good of him.

Reading people's comments a couple of days after the event was really special for me, and just confirmed the reason I had put in so much effort, despite not making a penny. 'Fab unique night, can't wait for the next one.' 'Absolutely awesome.' 'Fantastic line-up, magical setting.' 'A bold and brilliant venture.' And from Gav, 'Brilliant night, biggest four-hour grin ever.'

NATM 2 took place on December 4th that year and featured a young talented artist I had discovered from Liverpool, called Sophia Ben-Yousef, the very brilliant Seamus McLoughlin (who never let his guitar go out of his sight this time), and the multi-talented Steve Pilgrim, who not only is the main sticks man for Mr Paul Weller, but is a magnificent singer/songwriter in his own right. Again, everybody loved the event, and this time we moved the bar into a separate room to keep the noise down while the acts were performing.

Our third event took place the following May, and not long after the event I received a phone call from Rebecca, asking me if I still wanted to put a gig on in a church, as she had found me one. Previous to this I had attended a music conference in Preston that had taken place in a large church, and put on by the joint nicest man in music, Jeff Thompson. As part of the conference, Karima Francis performed, and the idea of putting on something like that had never left me.

The church that Rebecca was referring to was the Grade 2-listed Holy Trinity Church at Mount Pleasant, literally about a five minute drive from our house. The church was built between 1837 and 1846, but closed its doors in 1981 and had just been left to rot ever since, which was a huge shame.

I was excited by Rebecca's phone conversation and almost bit her hand off at the chance to go and look at the Gothic revival building. I couldn't believe my luck at being offered a museum and a church to put on my events, and I agreed to put on its first ever live performance, providing it could be an all-day music and arts festival, and providing it could be called 'Confessional'. To the best of my memory, I recall the name simply coming into my head at the thought of putting on an event in a church. But my friend Jon tells me it was him who thought up the name, even though

I really don't remember that. Either way, I (we) couldn't have come up with a more relevant name to represent the event.

The funny thing was, the church had actually been a Christian church (C of E) and the fact that our name had connections to the Catholic church meant that various people had to have a meeting in order to decide if permission would be granted for us to go ahead with our plans, which was mental.
Luckily, we were given the go ahead, so I had to try and pull a bit of a team together. Emma agreed to help with the art side of things, using her creative mind to come up with a few ideas of how we were going to make it special. Keely and Courtney agreed to get involved, as it made sense giving them the experience and chance to network with other acts.

One thing I decided from the start was that I didn't just want to put a gig on in a church. My intention was to make sure that everybody who walked through the church doors would have the wow factor from the second they stepped in. The museum stage had been pretty straightforward to dress, but a church of this size actually took months to dress it in a way where it would have an effect on people.

It has to be said that the star of the show in the build-up to putting it on was my art guy Kev. Whatever ideas we would come up with, he somehow found a way of making them happen. I hadn't known Kev before, but he was an art student who offered his services via the college art technician Ste, who also offered to help from the start.

One evening we were all in church, and Emma and I were gazing at the ceiling, trying to work out how on earth we were going to hang several coloured lanterns we planned to have. Kev just appeared and ended up building some sort of makeshift fishing rod with a weight on the end, and came up with the idea of hooking them over the very high church lights, which actually worked. And I knew from that very moment that we would need Kev involved.

Confessional Festival first opened its doors to the public on Saturday, 26th September, 2015, after months of hard work, and the church itself looked magical, especially at night. I was happy with the line-up I had booked, with The Tea Street Band headlining, and the Howling Rhythm DJs, including a full brass section, ending the event. Their final tune – Stevie Wonder's *Superstition* – evoked memories of sunnier nights in Somerset, for me at least.

James and Katy, who had now taken over running the bar at my NATM events, installed a large bar, and James even dressed up as a priest, as befitting his surroundings. During the event, a lady came over to me to thank me for putting it on, and she told me she had just seen the vicar, to which I replied, 'That is not the vicar, that is our barman.'

We had the wonderful Matt Abbott as our compere, introducing all the acts and performing his own material from the pulpit. I knew Matt from booking his old band, Skint And Demoralised, a few years previously, and once he went down the poetry route I couldn't think of anybody who would do a better job, and I was right. My friend Joe Martin was our stage manager, as he had toured with Twisted Wheel as their guitar tec. And we had a 7ft selfie coffin (long story).

Several weeks before the event, I had my hair cut at Vidal Sassoon in Manchester, because I had always wanted to give it a try. Anyway, I was making my way back to Victoria Station after paying for the most expensive haircut of my life, when I received a text from Joe, inviting me to go and watch him perform at Manchester Food and Drink festival, literally ten minutes' walk away. I had got to know Joe because we always seemed to be attending the same gigs and would notice each other in the crowd, but the most we would ever communicate with each other was a slight nod of the head. No doubt both of us were attempting to hold onto our cool demeanours. Over time I got to know him, and vaguely knew that he played guitar, so I decided to walk over and show my support.

I just happened to have a bag full of Confessional flyers with me, as I never left home without them., As I was waiting for Joe to appear, I started to put some out on the table in front of me, when I noticed a girl sitting opposite pick one up and read it. 'Is this your event?' she asked. Once I told her that it was, she told me that she was an artist from Leeds, and she asked me if there was anything I needed. I explained that I already had an art team and that we had been working on stuff for months, but admitted the only thing I needed at that point was a 7ft coffin. Erin ended up building me such coffin, and I asked Torrents' old driver Ash to do me the favour of going over to Leeds to pick it up, which I am sure was his strangest request that month.

Joe eventually appeared on stage and blew me away with the handful of songs he performed. After he finished his set, I wandered over to him and said, 'Bloody hell, mate, I didn't realise that you were that good.' Half-jokingly I said, 'You don't need a manager, do you?' and was surprised when he told me that he would love me to manage him.

How do I get myself in these situations? The problem was, though, I was that impressed by him that surely I had to at least consider the idea? This time, I wasn't worried about how to approach the subject with Janet and Emma, but how I was going to drop this into the conversation with Keely and Courtney. I had assured them that I would only ever manage one act at a time and that I wouldn't be managing anybody else after them, so this was not going to be easy.

All three of us were in the church one afternoon, when I decided to mention my dilemma. I genuinely asked for their opinion, and Courtney half-heartedly told me pretty quietly that if I wanted to manage him, it was up to me. Keely, on the other hand, made her thoughts perfectly clear, even before she opened her mouth. After knowing Keely for some time now, I had picked up on the fact that if she wasn't happy with something (or someone), she developed a kind of death stare (her trademark), and I just knew that I had got my answer right there and then.

Little did they know at the time what an absolute favour they did Joe. A couple of weeks later(ish), Joe formed the band Cabbage, so I could have ruined his life if I had started to manage him that week (a lucky escape).

Confessional Festival was a huge success, and the feedback was unreal. All the arts décor was awesome, and I was proud of the team. Smith entertained in between acts as our DJ, and I received the approval of the local councillor (which was important). He told me that he had always had a vision to turn the disused church into a music venue, and I had proved it could be done.

When I was first given permission to stage an event in the venue, I was told that the church group who were responsible for the building were fine with me putting on live music into the church, and were okay with us selling alcohol in the place. They were even alright with us having a 7ft coffin at the event, even though I am not quite sure what they thought we were going to do with it once it arrived. Their only stipulation had been 'No lap dancers'. (Drat!) I was told that I could go ahead with all my plans, providing I promised not to book any lap dancers, so I agreed.

Despite all the wonderful feedback from all the good folk who attended the event, there is always one. And on this occasion, the one came in the form of one of the neighbours, who made three complaints. One, he wasn't very happy at the fact that you could buy alcohol in a church. What does he think red wine is? Two, he was very concerned by the sight of a coffin being carried in. Where does he expect to see a coffin, if not in a church? And Three, and to be fair I agreed with him on this one, he really wasn't happy at the sight of women weeing in the bushes.
I couldn't believe what I was hearing. What about the portable toilets we had provided? This wound me up, as time after time I had been working in church for hours leading up to the event, and

had been dying to use a toilet, but we didn't have any. Yet I still couldn't bring myself to actually relieve myself within the church grounds.

The one thing I hadn't planned for, though, was receiving an email from Erin, asking me if she could have her coffin back. She needed it as part of her Uni project, and I had only two days to work out how I was about to get a 7ft selfie coffin back to Leeds.

Anyway, I had got my first Confessional under my belt, and despite the fact that people had been drinking in one room for up to 12 hours, there was zero trouble. In fact, I didn't even see as much as an argument take place, which was special.

I think the thing that had stood out to me the most about the event was where else on a Saturday night, or any night for that matter, would you find a 16-year-old dancing next to a 65-year-old, with both of them looking like they were having the time of their lives (Cue the music from *Dirty Dancing*)?

Ringing in sick at work has always been something that I hate to do, even when it's genuine. I always feel like folk think I'm simply putting on my sick voice in order to get an extra day off. To the best of my memory, I have only ever told a white lie (or a proper lie) on the one occasion, but it was for a really worthy cause. The date was 3rd October, 2013, and from the second I heard that The Kinks frontman Ray Davies was doing a book signing in Manchester, I knew I had to be there, one way or another. I really can't remember if I had already used up my holiday entitlement, or if I had recently had some time off, but leading up to the sacred date I remember having the dilemma of whether I should come clean and risk getting turned down, or keep the matter in my own hands and simply just call in sick that morning.

I hated being dishonest, even though I can't remember what I said. But it was Ray Davies, and I always worked to live, not the other way round.

Hoping that nobody would see me looking sheepish on Blackburn station, I boarded a train to Manchester, excited by the hope of meeting such a musical legend, but still feeling bad about nicking off. I joined the massive queue outside Waterstones, thinking to myself that knowing my luck I would probably end up on Granada Reports or something, as that type of thing happens to me. The book signing event was the usual deal: you must purchase the artist's book, and then go and stand in line until it's your turn to tell him how much you love him and what a legend he is, which he already knows.

There were hundreds waiting to meet him – no doubt all skiving off work – and finally it was my turn to stand up at the table. I have to be honest, I found him to be a bit miserable at the time, but I guess you can only put up with 'Can I have your autograph? Can I have a photograph?' so many times, not all day and all of the night. Boom! He signed both my books (one for Emma), and I had my photograph taken with him, even though I was a little gutted that it was a really bad hair day for me.

My mate Tony was also in the queue, and I took his obligatory meet-and-greet snap, then basically got the train from Victoria back to Blackburn, yet again hoping I wouldn't bump into anybody, especially from college. Part of me wished he had been a little friendlier, and all of me wished my hair had looked better, but I had achieved what I had set out to achieve and met the person who had written *Waterloo Sunset* and *Tired of Waiting*, so it was worth it.

Later that evening, Tony gave me a call, and once again pointed out my latest Tom Chance moment. Apparently, a guy who had travelled up from London had decided to sell his book on eBay, not long after getting it signed. But instead of posting a photograph of him getting the book signed, as proof in the listing, out of the hundreds of people who had turned up that afternoon, he had decided to take (and post) a picture of Ray signing mine, with me at the front – in clear view. Now I know that the chances of my line manager at work going onto eBay to search for some literature by The Kinks was pretty slim, but come on. Does stuff like this just happen to everybody?

As a concept, I have always believed in karma: how can it not be a thing when it makes such sense? The following day after my encounter with Ray, I felt really ill and knew that I probably deserved it. I remember forcing myself to go into work but being sent back home not long after. I was standing in my boss's office (Ann) with her and Keith, and being asked how ill I felt. I found myself in an awkward situation, as Ann was battling cancer at the time, and I remember feeling absolutely terrible. I had no idea at all what was wrong with me, but I knew it was nothing compared to what she was going through, so felt really guilty even discussing it.

The outcome of our meeting was that I was told to go home by Keith and was advised not to return until after Christmas in January 2014, as to make sure I had fully recovered.

I had worked with Keith for several years at college, and the more I got to know him, the more I respected him. When I first started the job, being honest, I used to listen to his stories and the things that he used to say to folk, and think there was no way that somebody could be that perfect, but as time went by, I realised that everything he was saying was actually true.
Keith had a pretty tough upbringing, and had gone from being a very successful barber to finding himself at rock bottom. But for as long as I have known him, he has dedicated his time, and passion, into supporting the underprivileged, young people, and basically anybody with a problem or who needs his help. A true inspiration, in my eyes.

The problem was that he was so popular at college that it was impossible to put a timeline on him going from A to B, because no matter where he went, somebody would stop him and ask him if he could help.

One day, Keith came into the office and showed us all a letter he had just received, saying he had been awarded an MBE, and he needed to respond to confirm or not if he would be attending the Palace. Before working with us, Keith had worked in the Learning Support Department, and they were constantly playing practical jokes on each other, so I didn't feel it was too disrespectful at the time to imagine that this was just another of those wind-ups. He showed me the letter and asked me for my honest opinion, and to my shame, I recall telling him that you could buy stuff like that on eBay, and to avoid looking silly and allowing his jockers to win, he should probably just ignore it and throw it in the bin.

Anyway, Keith visited Buckingham Palace and collected his award from the Queen, thankfully ignoring anything I had said. It made me feel bad for not believing it, as the award was well and truly deserved.

As a child I vaguely recall my mum telling me that I'd spent weeks in Blackburn Hospital with a suspected brain tumour, which is mental. What is more mental, though, is the fact that for some strange reason, I never chose to question this later in life. So I still don't know the proper story.
What is certain, though, is that I don't do things by halves, and when I'm ill, I am really ill.

I was brushing my teeth one evening when I happened to notice that one side of my mouth had dropped a little, and the toothpaste was starting to run down my chin (not a good look). Luckily, Janet had heard of this happening to somebody at BT, and insisted on me going straight to hospital, ignoring me saying that it was alright. It turned out I had something called Bell's Palsy, which is a temporary paralysis of the facial muscles, and the secret to avoid any long-lasting effects was catching it early, which I managed to do thanks to Janet.

Learning to drive was halted by the need for me to endure emergency eye surgery, and collapsing in a field in Penrith, due to having kidney stones, indicated that me simply getting man flu was a very unlikely option.

A couple of local musicians, Phil and Steven from the bands Scar, Into The Black, and Anhadonia, had opened up a local Music Tuition Studio (MMT) on Symonds Street in Blackburn, which was a marvellous new addition to the town. I was attending one of their student showcases with my band one afternoon when Torrents' old producer Mark came over to say hello. Being perfectly honest, I didn't recognise him at first, and it took me a couple of minutes before it twigged who he was. I always really liked Mark (a proper decent chap), and it was great to see him after so long.

What I didn't know about him was his fanatical love of anything synth, and as he'd heard that I was managing a young synth band, he invited us to his studio for a chat. I introduced him to Keely and Courtney at our first Confessional, and decided to take him up on his offer, because they were both really up for it.

Once Pax realised that the original machine that New Order recorded 'Blue Monday' on was in Mark's studio, they were won over, and especially once he produced original Moog after original Moog for them to have a go on. That was it; we had committed to record their debut EP there. We visited the studio in Ossy at least once every week, and it was great watching their confidence grow. Mark not only helped with recording duties and synth stories from the 80s, but with advice, ideas, and he even contributed towards the songwriting, which was highly appreciated.

During the start of 2016, I noticed I had a problem with my hearing, and for the majority of the time it was slightly muffled, like before your ears pop on a plane. I knew that out of everybody, I would be the prime candidate to develop tinnitus at some stage, because I had spent more than half of my life standing next to speakers, watching and filming live gigs, so basically put my ear problem down to this.

Having an issue with my hearing was a bit of a problem, especially working in music, as not only was I managing a band, but I was often sent artist demos on a regular basis and asked to give my opinion. Another thing I had developed was a dull headache on the right side of the back of my head. Not being somebody who would normally suffer from a headache, unless it was a hangover, I was slightly concerned by the length of time it went on.

As always, not wanting to worry Janet by talking about my ailments, I mentioned this to Linda at work. I didn't make a big deal out of it, but I am sure it was obvious to her that I was concerned.

For some strange reason (which I really can't remember), we decided to move Confessional from September to April, but this wasn't the greatest of ideas, as the temperature in church was bloody freezing the closer we were getting to the date.

On Wednesday, 10th February, 2016, we all received the monumentally terrible news that David Bowie had passed away, and this time I knew I wasn't to blame, because at that point I had avoided fields. I was obviously into Bowie – how could I not be? – but I had chosen Ferry, while Nick would preach to me every week about David's latest album. It wasn't until he died that I really started to appreciate what he had in fact brought to the table, underlining the saying, 'You don't know what you have until it's gone.'

Keely and Courtney were proper into him and were gutted by the news, but at the time Keely quoted me something that I found wonderful, saying, 'Don't cry because it's over, smile because it happened.' I loved this, and have adopted it as one of my mantras.

I came up with the idea of ending that year's Confessional event with a Bowie Hour, as it was the least we could do. And from the second I thought of doing it, I started to get excited by the prospect. The likes of Jeramia Ferrari, and Bang Bang Romeo were booked, and the décor in church looked as good as ever.

BUT I'M DIFFERENT NOW

To put on a successful event, of course you need somebody like me to come up with the idea and book the line-up, but just as important (if not more) is having a trustworthy, talented team that you know you can rely on. And after years of working in this field, and learning as I went along, I had finally put together a team that certainly was passionate about putting it on, and everybody brought something to the table.

I always book the same sound engineers for all my events (Blake and Si), and they are brilliant at what they do and have never let me down. One of the most important ingredients of this event, in my opinion, is the lighting of the church. In the daytime we have the sunlight shining through our stunning stained-glass windows, and with the magnificent skills of my lighting guys, Steven and Barry, the venue really comes alive at night, and without a doubt offers people the wow factor.

The weeks leading up to the festival, we found ourselves spending longer and longer inside the extremely freezing building, but for a number of weeks now my headache had been getting a lot more painful. I was going into work and moaning to Linda about it, but finally came clean to Janet as it was impossible to hide it any longer. In fact, the pain had started to become so bad at night once I put my head on the pillow that I ended up only being able to sleep on my left side, which was annoying.

I visited my doctor at Little Harwood who, after checking me over, told me they couldn't find anything. And I also visited the dentist twice, convinced it was an abscess because the pain had spread to the front of my mouth, but the results of his X-ray showed nothing.

After my second visit to see my doctor, he referred me to a local private hospital, Beardwood, hoping that they would finally give me a diagnosis. But after Linda dropped me off, and the physician put a camera up my nose and partially down my throat, all he ended up giving me was a prescription for some sort of nasal spray, which I didn't even bother getting. I knew it was nothing to do with my nose.

Our second Confessional took place on 30th April, and from the minute I arrived at church that morning, I was literally shivering because the temperature was so cold. Being highly concerned about the comfort of our congregation on the day, we borrowed some emergency patio heaters at the last minute, but the room was so big that unless you were standing directly underneath them at the time, they had made no difference whatsoever.

I started to panic early on at the event, as I noticed that a large number of the people were heading towards the entrance, but I was highly relieved to see them reappear a little while later, wearing coats, hats, scarves, and in some cases gloves, to make sure they were warm enough while they were being entertained.

The event was fantastic, and Bowie Hour was everything I had hoped it would be, thanks to Fergal, who travelled up from London to DJ and be Ziggy for the evening.

I was absolutely buzzing about how well Confessional had gone and about the amount of magnificent feedback I had received. But little did I know that in just nine days' time my life was about to change forever.

CHAPTER THIRTY-SEVEN

336 HOURS

Monday, 9th May, 2016, I woke up at some ridiculously early hour for work, as always, and no sooner had I walked into our office and logged on, then I noticed we had all received an email informing us that we had been placed into a redundancy pool. It looked like we were about to lose our jobs.

I told my team that I was going to treat them all to lunch, as I know that is what Keith would have done if he had not been off sick. Myself, Linda, and Louise visited Kings Court on King Street, and all ordered a Full English (standard), but what was really unusual was I hardly touched mine, and Linda even commented on the amount of food I had left.

After work, I called into my local, The Farthings, but struggled to finish the pint of Fosters I had ordered, as I was not able to swallow it easily, which I thought was highly strange.

Later that night, Janet headed off to bed after enjoying a bottle of her favourite red wine, and I was in my office discussing the upcoming Pax EP with the band online, when out of the blue my mouth started to fill up with blood. I ran into the bathroom to take a look in the mirror at what was wrong, and for the first time I realised that the problem was not in fact in my mouth (not an abscess), as the blood was haemorrhaging from my throat. The flow, thankfully, was not constant, but around every 30 seconds my mouth would fill up with blood, and I knew that wasn't good.
I had used up all the hand towels in the bathroom, and due to the fact Janet had been drinking and was unable to drive me anywhere,

without thinking I posted a message on Facebook asking if anyone I knew would be able to give me a lift to hospital. Keely and Courtney were concerned by the post and started messaging me to find out what it was about, but I don't actually recall debating what was wrong with me. My only concern at the time was to find a way of somehow stopping the bleeding.

I decided to go and wake up Janet, as my options were very limited. At first, when she came around, I think she thought I was being dramatic and over-exaggerating (as always, apparently), but as soon as she visited the bathroom and noticed the blood-filled towels thrown all over the floor, she realised the severity of the situation and called 999. The ambulance took just eight minutes to arrive outside our front door, which I guess is impressive, but at the time it felt as though it was taking forever.

I'm sure it was my first time in the back of one of these vehicles, and I felt every bump in the road, especially with the amount of speed bumps around our way. Once at the hospital, they planned to wheel me straight through to the Resus Department, but surprisingly my bleeding seemed to have stopped, so instead, they took me into a room so that they could carry out the process of triage on me. I understand that folk need to do their job, but it always surprises me that at the time you are feeling your worst, you are expected to fill out a questionnaire.

I remembered visiting the hospital a number of years before with a suspected heart attack, and I recall telling the person who was on reception that I was just about to faint. 'We just need your name and address, and a few more personal details off you, sir,' she said, seconds before my head had hit the floor.

Due to the fact that my bleeding had stopped, they must have deemed my case was not a priority, and they were so busy that they simply wheeled me on my trolley and left me parked up in the middle of the corridor, alongside around ten other trolleys with people all waiting their turn.

Each time Janet attempted to get the attention of a nurse to come and take a look at me, she was repeatedly told they were far too busy, as they only had one doctor in at the time.

After around an hour and a half just sitting there and trying my utmost not to catch the attention of the guy walking up and down shouting and swearing and threatening to kill somebody, Janet decided she would nip back home to collect the car and to grab a few bits. But no sooner had she left the hospital than I found that my bleeding had returned.

I felt bad at texting her to come back, but when she did, the same thing happened again. 'Sorry we don't have the time, we are too busy.'
I was sitting on the top of a trolley in the middle of the corridor, holding one of those cardboard-looking hats which I was collecting all the blood in. I tried my best to get the attention of people walking past, but it was impossible. I couldn't really speak, with constantly having a mouth full of blood, so I resorted to simply waving my hands around.

I had been there for most of the night, when in desperation Janet walked over to one of the staff and asked if somebody could please come and see to me, as I had been bleeding for a pretty long time now. The member of staff was halfway through explaining the same speech we had already heard several times, when she suddenly stopped and asked Janet if she happened to have a sister called Julie. *Charming*, I thought, *what a time to be discussing your family tree.* But luckily for us, all of Janet's family had worked for the NHS, and this woman knew Julie from her time there as a midwife, and had obviously noticed the family resemblance.

'Don't worry,' she said,' I will try and make sure you are seen to now.' It was a relief, and normally I would not be into nepotism or trying to jump a queue (unless up the Cav, or at a gig), but I was pretty desperate for attention by this stage, so willingly accepted her offer of help.

I remember a porter wheeling me through to Resus, and a guy asking me if I had ever been put to sleep before. Dying to crack a joke regarding a bottle of Pernod, I decided that maybe it was not the best time to start trying to be funny, so I replied, 'Have I heck.' I explained that normally I would feel faint and sick at the sight of a hospital ward, and certainly a needle. He told me not to worry and explained that they were about to put me under, and that it would only take about 20 minutes.

Without sounding too far-fetched, those could actually have been the last words that I ever heard, because it took four surgeons and five-and-a-half hours on the operating table to try and stop the bleeding. While this was going on, Janet and Emma were sitting in reception, not having a clue what was going on.

After the op, I ended up in a Critical Care bed, and the next thing I remember was groggily waking up the following day and noticing a little chap at the end of my bed, in a white coat, and remembering where I was.

'It was touch and go, Mr Eastwood,' he said, and explained that they had struggled to locate exactly where the bleeding was coming from, as it was so deep into my throat. He told me they had given me two pints of blood, due to the amount I had lost, but explained that luckily they had managed to stop the haemorrhaging and save me. I simply mumbled, 'Cheers,' and stuck up my thumb. This was extremely good news that he was telling me, even though I felt like I had been dragged through a hedge backwards. But in circumstances like this, there is usually a 'But...', and in this particular case my 'But' was that he told me they had found cancer.

The only people in the room when he told me this news were him, me (obviously), and the incredible nurse Ashley who was looking after me. Within seconds of hearing this life-changing information, I think I fainted for around twenty seconds. Once I had come back round, I asked if someone could please contact my wife and daughter, as I needed to let them know.

Little did I know that the consultant I had seen at Beardwood and who had given me that pointless nasal spray prescription, was the very same consultant that had just managed to save my life in the operating theatre. And he was the same consultant standing at the bottom of my bed, telling me one of the worst things, if not the worst, I had ever been told. I mean, as far as Tom Chance moments go, this one has to be up there.

I didn't know then that both Janet and Emma kinda knew before me, as the consultant had told them the previous day that they had found something, and Janet told me she had known. She also told me that she had almost put her foot in it with him. She was telling him everything I had gone through and was in the process of saying, 'And this so-called expert from Beardwood...' before he interrupted her, and said, 'Yes, Mrs Eastwood, that guy was me.'

I spent two nights in a Critical Care bed, along with tubes, monitors, a catheter, and regular bed baths, and I have to say that the people who looked after me were absolutely amazing, and in my opinion went above and beyond what I would have expected anybody to do. Nurse Ashley had shared that earth shattering moment with me, was there when I fainted, and supported me throughout – something I will never forget.

Despite my phobia about hospitals, when you find yourself in a position where you are that ill, all your fears go out of the window, and you basically let anybody do anything to you, because you trust that they know what they are doing. Also, you recognise and appreciate when folk are being extremely nice with you, and when all the trauma is over, those are the moments that you remember – certainly for me, anyway.

Moving from Critical Care onto another ward was like leaving first class for economy. I really don't mean that in a disrespectful way, as I know they were extremely busy and I am sure they were doing a wonderful job, but where I felt like I was given care 24/7 in my first bed, it felt like that had all changed to somebody just peering through the window of our ward to check if we were still alive. To me, it felt like I was part of a scene from the sitcom *Only When I Laugh*, but I have to add, without the laughing bit.

In my room there were five other males, who I believe were all suffering from some sort of throat cancer, but judging by their scars and their war wounds from the operations they had already had, I felt the luckiest out of the lot of us. When I was first told that they had found cancer in my tissue, I must admit I was a little surprised at being told I had a tumour in my throat, because I would never consider myself to have been a big drinker and had never smoked a full cigarette in my life. But what surprised me even more was how on earth, after two visits to the doctors, two visits to my dentist, including a private clinic, having check-ups, X-rays, and a camera up my nose, nobody at all spotted that something was wrong.

After a night on this ward with my fellow sufferers, they let me go home, which I was glad about. But I was given an appointment to visit the ENT Clinic, so that they could give me a proper diagnosis once my test results had come back. My appointment to determine my future (maybe) was on 17th May, and I had tickets to go and watch my old mucker Pete Doherty at the Albert Hall in Manchester that night. So I planned to attend my hospital appointment, then shoot off over to Manchester in time to watch the gig.

I had already been for my scan, where they put that coloured dye through your body, but I found that horrendous and naturally I had fainted within minutes of it ending. Now I was off to ENT so that I could get my results. I wasn't looking forward to it, even though I wanted/needed to know.

From the minute I stepped foot into the consultant's office, I found him to be a little harsh. He told me to sit up straight in my chair while he was examining me, but his tone made me feel a little like a schoolboy rather than a patient. What followed, I have debated with Janet for the past four years plus. He told me that my cancer was Stage 4 (the worst), and that they couldn't operate as it was wrapped around some vein, or something like that.

This meeting had been pretty negative up until now, and I remember saying to him, 'What is the worst scenario?' and he asked me what I meant. Probably due to nerves, I told him, 'Well, if I have 30 minutes left to live, I need to make sure that it's a good 30 minutes (being facetious).' But he just shrugged his shoulders and replied, 'A couple of weeks.'

Two weeks! Two weeks! I hadn't realised that things were that bad.

Whatever the consultant said to me after mentioning those two words, did not register, and it hit home that I wouldn't be going to see a Libertine that evening. What I do remember is meeting some of my best friends, one by one, that teatime at the Royal Oak pub at the end of our road.

If I was sharing that news all over again, would I do it differently? Yes probably. But when you are told something like that, I don't believe you go through a rational process; you simply deal with the situation the best that you can. Naturally, I explained to our Emma how my appointment had gone, and as always she kept the conversation positive, urging me not to give up on things just yet.

My conversation in the pub went along the lines of 'They reckon I may have two weeks to live, but that is the worst scenario, which I am not prepared to take. I mean, I have been working all this time on the Pax EP, and I am not prepared to miss being there at the end, as I don't trust anybody else with it. Also, I love life and have too many ace plans for the rest of the year, so I am going nowhere.'

I met Sarah and Jez, and they were clearly upset by my news, which I did feel bad about. And I rang Keely and Courtney, as I wanted to tell them myself. Janet called up some of my other friends, as there was only so many times I could go through that story, and my voice was pretty shot. And I ended up giving my Mr Doherty tickets away to some friends, Ainsley and Stacey.

The part that Janet has always contradicted me on, and pulled me up about (even today), is the fact that he told me 'two weeks'. Her version of events is that he shrugged his shoulders, and basically said, 'two weeks, two months,' meaning, *I can't play God, I haven't a clue*. I am not saying that wasn't the case, but she was not in my shoes, and I was the one he was saying it to. Not expecting him to mention only a couple of weeks (as a scenario), I admit I was so shocked at the time that I didn't hear a single word he said after that, but I feel should be excused. Also, I can only tell my story to the best of my memory, and whichever way you looked at it, by the time they found something, I was Stage 4, so it really wasn't very good.

The meeting I had the following week was a little more positive, but initially I struggled even making it into the room. As we walked out of the lift on the ENT floor, I almost fainted at least three times, and needed to sit down. Once inside the room, I was a total wreck, and struggled to even lift my head up. At one point, I was told that I needed to toughen up if I was to stand any chance of beating it. The cancer consultant told me that because it wasn't caused by alcohol or tobacco, we had a chance of fighting this, which is what I wanted to hear. But he explained that it would mean me having to go through weeks of treatment, which he warned would not be easy.

Janet and I were then ushered into another room at the end of the corridor to have a chat with the Macmillan nurse, so that she could answer any questions that we might have. The only thing I remember from that meeting, totally shocking me at the time, was when she actually told us how I had got the cancer – something I had never thought I would ever find out.

Janet was pushing her for some information, and reluctantly the nurse explained that I had personally contracted it via the HPV virus. I had never even heard of this before, even though Janet had, and when she explained that it was in fact a sexually transmitted disease, I almost fell off my chair.

Human Papillomavirus is a very common group of viruses, apparently, and some types can cause genital warts or cancer. The virus is spread by sexual skin-to-skin contact with somebody who has it. The virus usually has no symptoms, so folk don't even realise they have it, and depending on the type of HPV you have, it can linger in your body for years – in some cases, decades. In most cases, the body can produce antibodies against the virus, and most strains go away permanently without treatment – just not mine.

So basically, my situation was down to a sexual relationship I'd had, possibly over 30+ years ago, and when I was at a low ebb and my immune system had been shot at (maybe six days in a field at Glastonbury), the virus had turned into cancer. WOW! I literally couldn't believe what I had been told. Out of all my mates, I certainly hadn't felt I was the one who had slept around.

Once we arrived home, Janet told me that when I left the room the consultant had told her that he didn't think I would cope with the treatment, based on the reaction I had shown that day.

Due to the damage to my throat that the five-and-a-half-hour operation had caused, my treatment had to be planned and pinpointed, once the wounds that I already had were given time to calm down. The hardest thing for me was being told that I was Stage 4, and that without treatment my worst scenario might be only a matter of weeks (my version, not Janet's), but I was going to have to wait five weeks before my treatment would even start!

My mate Waker had survived Stage 4 lung cancer and warned me what to expect. I recall the day before I was due at Rosemere (Cancer Foundation) in Preston, to have my radiotherapy mask fitted.
I went for a walk with Mark around Lammack and Pleckgate, and he gave me the heads up about how absolutely horrendous the

dreaded mask had been, in his opinion. Mark told me that he had panicked when they put the mask on him, and at one point had insisted they get him out of it, but it hadn't taken long for him to realise that the more he refused to wear it, the more times he would be asked to try. He explained that apparently at least two people per year chose to die rather than wearing the thing, he had been told, but that was never an option.

The following morning, I travelled over to Burnley Hospital with Janet to have my feeding tube fitted, as I was informed that once my treatment kicked in, I wouldn't be able to eat, I wouldn't be able to drink, and at some stage I wouldn't be able to talk, which I am sure was a blessing to some people.

To my surprise Burnley Hospital was reasonably quiet, especially on my ward, and I gave my obligatory speech to the nurses about how very squeamish I was, and how there was a pretty good chance that I would faint at some stage. The procedure itself happened without me even feeling it. One minute they put a cloth under my nose, which must have had some sort of solution on it, and what literally felt like a matter of seconds later (may have been longer) I came round to find that a rubber tube had been placed in my stomach. I have no idea at all how they had managed to do it, but to be honest, I think that I prefer it that way.

If I had seen that happen to somebody on TV, I would have no doubt said, 'No way could I go through something like that.' But knowing that I didn't really have an option if I was going to stand a chance of fighting this thing, I was willing to simply just let the professionals do what they needed to.

I stayed the night on the ward, and then my friend Sarah drove over to pick both of us up and take us to Preston, for my appointment at Rosemere. Even though I had heeded Mark's warning, it was still touch and go as to whether or not I was going to cope with it. The best way I can describe it is that I was asked to lie on a bed and told to close my eyes while they put what felt like a wet, warm dishcloth over my face. I was asked to keep completely still until it had set, and Hey Presto, my mask was ready. It slightly resembled some sort of fencing mask, and even though it was covered in minute holes, it covered the whole of my face and didn't even have a mouthpiece for me to breathe through. We were sitting in the waiting area when some staff member walked past carrying a similar mask, and I remember the shock on both Janet and Sarah's faces when I pointed this out.

Once home, we received delivery of my new source of food in the form of these flavoured plastic protein drinks. I made the mistake of attempting to drink some of one, and I can assure you that it tasted nothing like the flavour that was written on the side. It was awful.

Being fed in this way took a bit of getting used to, and initially I relied on Janet's patience to make sure it was done right. I had to slowly fill up one of the plastic syringes I was given, then just lie back and wait until I had a cold feeling in my stomach and I could see it slowly going down the tube. We would do this three times each day, and I tried to see the positives. It would certainly save on the weekly shopping bill, as all the goodies that usually found their way into our shopping basket would be not required for the foreseeable. Also, at the time I weighed 16-and-a-half stone, which was far too heavy, so I reckoned losing some weight would surely be a good thing.

My treatment consisted of 30 sessions of radiotherapy, which I would have at Rosemere, Monday to Friday for six weeks. I would also have chemotherapy sessions every Wednesday, for the same time period.

On the actual day my treatment started, I came up with the idea of writing a blog – not for anybody to be able to read at that stage, but as a way of recording my thoughts and feelings at the time. Pretty much as soon as I started it, I felt too ill to carry it on, which was a shame, and over the weeks I forgot that I had even started it. Months later, I happened to stumble across it in my inbox, and what surprised me was it had felt as though it hadn't been written by me at all, but by somebody else. I guess when you find yourself going through some kind of trauma, the way in which you think and act is different from the norm. I have decided that the best way of representing that situation, is to include my first, and only, entry in exactly the way it was written at the time, mistakes and all.

My name is Pete Eastwood, not Peter (Mum), Pete. (My choice.)
I have lived a charmed life, yes, I was given away after 5 weeks, and yes, I have never owned a bike, but I have lived a charmed life, up to 5 weeks ago that is, where I probably had the unluckiest 24 hours of anyone ever.

So, I have decided to do a blog of My situation, and at this stage, I have no idea why.

Is it for My family? to help them understand what I am going through fighting this horrible disease.

Is it for friends and strangers? to offer advice on different aspects of the fight, or the cancer treatment.

Or is it purely for Myself? to catalogue my happenings, as this news was certainly a game changer.

At this stage I have no idea why I am doing it, I just am.

Monday 13th June 2016.

So today is the big day, the day My cancer treatment finally starts. It's funny when you write the word cancer, and you actually have it, it seems to affect your senses a lot more and makes you think. My daft rule I have given Myself is, never write the word with a capital c, as that is My little way of showing it little respect and keeping it down. Stupid yes, and the fact that I Am so terrible at grammar anyway, means folk who know Me will just think it's Me doing poor English.

How do I feel about this day the 13th June, well it's a double edged sword I must admit.
Before today, part of Me (50 per cent) felt less anxious in a way that I wasn't having horrendous side effects, which I had been told about so many, many times, and I didn't have daily hospital visits to undertake. Going back a couple of months, just the sight of a hospital ward and the very thought of anything needle related, would start Me off feeling faint and dizzy. How things have changed.

The other side of the thinking coin is, the fact that after My first CT scan results, my worst scenario without treatment was maybe, a few weeks/months to live, so yes part of Me had felt anxious and baffled as to why on earth (knowing this) experts would take 4 to 5 weeks to even start the fight, and begin My treatment, so at least now something is happening towards the cause.

Also, one of My best friends Waker, who has recently come out of the other end of this c battle, told Me that from the minute your treatment starts, you will feel a whole lot better, by the fact the experts are treating and fighting it, not just meeting each week to discuss how much it is growing and spreading, so I suppose it is safe to say the latter scenario is My chosen one.

I'm not sure if anyone has noticed but by the same strange thinking about the c word, I have also chosen to write the word Me or Mine, or My, with a capital M, to highlight a sight of importance and power over my enemy word. Yes, I am mental, but that is just how the way I think.

Anyway, it's Monday morning and My first Radiotherapy session is due to start at 2.45pm and based on the fact that the individually made monster mask you have to put on for this procedure, is without a doubt the most hideous experience of My existence, this I was not looking forward to.

I mean call Me soft but being screwed to a bed in a mask that barely even leaves room to breathe, is not My idea of fun. But stay positive Pete, My battle starts now.

Of course, I was anxious during the car journey, and of course Janet and Emma did their best to calm Me down and support Me.

We finally found a space to park on Rosemere car park and went to give My name in at reception.
I didn't really know what to expect but was happy just to follow the experts lead and do whatever.
I mean, yes, the mask is vile, (even though a very important tool in wiping out the small c) but what's 5 minutes.

When you are a patient at Rosemere, you receive a small card (like a loyalty card) which allows you to get free tea and biscuits, and as per norm, it is Janet that takes them up on their very kind offer.
I stick to my daily bottle of water that barely leaves my left hand.

We give My name in and are told I have machine 7 today, so we head for the correct area.
After a short wait My name is called out and I am taken into a small dressing room, where I am asked to replace My PG (Pretty Green) shirt for the hospital gown and told they will return shortly.

The dressing room was pretty small and basic, and for some strange reason reminded Me of the dressing room in Chelsea Girl back in the day.
For one, I didn't make a habit of hanging around female dressing rooms, just seemed to be dragged down on Saturdays with a girlfriend at the time.
And two, it looked nothing like the dressing room in Chelsea Girl, just My weird mind again.

The Hospital staff (who I have already forgotten the names of) returned after a few minutes and knocked on the door. The door I had left the room via, was on the opposite side, and all I could think of was Mr Benn. Maybe I would step out of the room and find Myself in Africa, without having cancer, or maybe I was just hoping.

Reality soon struck, and I was led to machine 7. There were 4 staff who were all very friendly and supportive, so My faith was in their capable hands, until the bombshell they dropped informing me that I would spend 15 minutes under the dreaded mask today, not 5.

Panic set in and trying My best not to act like a quivering wreck, (and failing) I questioned this shocking news. They kindly explained that for the first 3 days, My treatment would also consist of a scan first, to make sure the correct area is being targeted, hence the time increase. I said cool, but thought OMG, I removed the gown and lay on the bed, and suddenly realised that My music playlist would only last for about 6 minutes, so how could I cope.
They fitted the mask, and it was even tighter than I remembered. It literally pinned My head and shoulders to the bed, pressed that tight against My face, that it really was a fine line between coping and not.

The rule is that if you feel you need the mask removing at any point, you raise your left hand (as you can't talk while wearing it) and somebody will rush into the room and quickly remove it. Pete don't be so bloody soft, this is not a scenario of choice and it's on for a reason, and this action would only lead to me having to wear it more.

I raised My right thumb to indicate I was fine, (what a laugh) and My very chosen and selective playlist kicked in.

The Day 1 Playlist consisted of My bands (Pax) upcoming EP taster, (which only lasts 1 minute 43 seconds anyway) Warning Call, which is the new mint tune from Chvrches, and My favourite song off their last album, High Enough To Carry You Over. That's it, and was no way going to entertain Me for the next 15 minutes.

All of a sudden, the scan machine around My head started making strange noises like something from Dr Who, and the staff tried to reassure Me while talking Me through the procedure, before leaving the room, leaving Me with just my mask and My music.

The hardest thing I found was not even having enough space in the mask to even lick My lips, as My mouth was getting increasingly dry, which in turn stressed Me out. You literally spend every second concentrating on breathing and forcing yourself not to give up, and the rest of the time zooming in on your selected tracks.

Having music really does help, but sure enough, the final track finished (a lesson learned) and left Me with the Dr Who sound affects for a little longer.
The next thing I knew, the staff returned to the room, told Me how well I had done, and more importantly removed My mask. Wow, My first session was over, I thanked them all, (even though I couldn't remember anybody's name) put on My gown, and returned to the dressing room.

Janet and Emma were waiting patiently, asked Me what it was like, said well done, and we headed for the car. I just wanted to get home, and hopefully watch the Euros.

What shocked Me was is how sore My throat was straight after My first session. I honestly thought it would take a few sessions before the pain would kick in, but I was in agony, that much that I felt I was going to faint on the car park.
It was decided there and then that tomorrow, My meds would be coming with Me, and timed to be taken straight after treatment, as surely this would help.

That was all I managed to write at the time, as I guess that all my energy was put into simply trying to cope every day, but at least it reveals exactly how I felt on that first day.

BUT I'M DIFFERENT NOW

Every day was like Groundhog Day, as we would get up at the same time and drive over to Preston for the day's session. My chosen daily track list had increased to five songs, selected from my iTunes, and having the music to concentrate on was a godsend, and I would recommend it to anybody going through the same. A couple of times the iPod dock was out of order, which I was gutted about, but two days out of six weeks is not really something I could moan about.

I didn't know what to expect from my first chemo session. I turned up on time, and after a few minutes in the waiting room, I was led to my bed on the chemotherapy ward. I noticed the bag of solution covered in a black bag, and my task was to simply sit there patiently for hours until the poison had been pumped into my body, and then washed through with water.
The only pain throughout the whole procedure was at the start when they attempted to find a vein, in order to fit the cannula. The problem was that all my appointments were first thing in the morning, when it was cold, so on several occasions the nurses struggled to find a vein. This led to them having to try a number of times, which I hated. But after a couple of weeks, one of them gave me a tip and advised me to bring a hot water bottle to place on my wrist during the journey over in the car, and it really did work.

Sitting in the same spot for around seven hours really was boring, so it was really advisable to take a book to read, or some music to listen to on the phone. Going over in the car every day, I really was on autopilot, just closing my eyes or staring at the floor. The treatment itself was actually doable, but what I disliked was having to sit there and wait until they were ready for me. Sometimes you could wait for well over an hour before you were called to put your gown on in the dressing room. And while Janet was happy to have a brew and sit reading her book, I just got more anxious, thinking about what was about to happen. I would rather turn up, have my treatment, and go away, but I guess that life isn't like that.

On one occasion for my Wednesday chemo session, we arrived at Rosemere around 8am, only to be told that my treatment was not due to start until 9am. I found myself starting to worry and getting hotter and sweatier by the minute, until I eventually fainted. This, of course, was all psychological, as in some ways thinking about it was worse than actually having the treatment in the first place. Anyway, as a result of my very cowardly behaviour, I was given a private room for the day, along with three nurses to attend to my every need – or at least that is what it felt like. So the plan was to do the same thing the following week.

The one thing that surprised me visiting every week was that I never really got to know anybody, like they seem to on the telly. You would imagine that seeing the same people in the same situation on a weekly basis you would form some sort of bond with some of them, but I didn't at all. Maybe it was down to me just being unsociable and concentrating on the matter in hand.

Posting personal stuff on social media is not always a good thing, and depending on what you post, it can come back to haunt you. When I was diagnosed with this illness, I decided to make people aware of my situation. I posted one update on my Facebook wall, as there were still some friends who had been freaked out by my 'Can anybody take me to hospital?' post. It was the perfect tool to update folk, as opposed to having to individually message all my friends and reply to their messages.

To say I was humbled by the response I received is a complete understatement. Almost instantaneously I found myself floored with the positive messages of support and well wishes. Even strangers either left a comment or contacted me, and even though I am sure that they meant well, I must admit I was a little bit freaked out by a couple of them. One told me to have some sort of Sound Vibration Therapy, which I had never heard of. And one lady, who again I didn't know, sent me a pretty long private message, telling me that under no circumstances must I agree to have any chemotherapy or radiotherapy sessions at all, as that would kill me anyway – even though they were my best chance of survival, if not my only chance.

I also received a number of messages telling me to start using Cannabis Oil, as it was widely reported and believed that the different Cannabinoids can reduce the ability of cancers to grow and spread. Depending on what you believe, there is an argument for both sides, but there is far too much information out there for me to include in this book.

Mr anti-drugs takes drugs! Wow! But if needs must. I feel that in a situation of life or death, the rules that you believe in your normal life go out of the window. It's okay to be principled, but I would argue that living is more important, so I looked into getting hold of some.

If you ever find yourself going down this path, you really do need to research all the information and make sure you get hold of the correct stuff from the right person, or it will be pointless. I brought the subject up with my consultant and some of the nurses, knowing that there was no way at all they were about to condone me taking it. But to my surprise, I was told, 'I am not telling you that you can't take it, that is up to you, and we can't tell you that you can, but the advice we would give is wait until after your treatment, as it may interfere with it.' And that was not a risk I was prepared to take.

When Waker went through his chemo, he told me he had been constantly sick in bed for days. My chemo was a back-up for the radiotherapy I was having, so obviously was not as strong. So not only did I avoid all the feelings of sickness, but I also managed not to lose my hair – just.

Once I started to use my peg, it had been obvious the amount of weight I had been losing, which in turn had led to me looking pretty rough. At the time, though, my appearance had not really been my priority, even for a Mod. They didn't mention it at the time, but my best friends told me later that they had been upset by how ill I looked. My voice was becoming weaker, and my weight was going down, as those bottles were designed to keep me alive and not to put weight on. But we had an EP to complete, so even though I did not really feel up to it at times, I would force myself to visit the studio, and I believe it did help me to stay positive.

From the minute Mark found out about my battle, he was really supportive, and I could tell by his face that he was genuinely concerned – something I will always remember.

The fact that Keely and Courtney were mad (in a good way) meant that I didn't really have the chance to mope about, even though I had to endure their daily renditions of the whole of the latest 1975 album, as they were warming up for the day's vocals. With Mark's help, and the girls growing confidence, everything was coming together really well. But on one of my visits, my head was so painful that I just sat against the wall in the corner of the recording room with my head in my hands and my eyes shut. That proved I had been kidding myself, and I knew I would have to give some recording sessions a miss.

One Saturday evening, I got out the small table to put my bottles and syringe on, but as I was trying to feed myself, there was a problem, and for some reason the liquid just wouldn't go down. Janet tried her best to sort it out, but the syringe was still blocked. From the second I was diagnosed, she was a saint in supporting me and doing what was required, but I could tell that she was getting frustrated by this latest hurdle. We ended up ringing the NHS helpline (well, Janet did), who told us we needed to go to our nearest hospital. But what I thought would take around an hour, ended up with me being admitted and spending a week in isolation. I couldn't believe it.

Even though that was the last place I wanted to end up on a Saturday night, or any night for that matter, I felt as though Janet was relieved, as it would mean she would get a bit of a break from being my carer 24/7, on top of going to work.

Initially I didn't know I would be spending the night there, but they were monitoring me due to some issue with my white blood cells. I couldn't get my head around the fact that they would wake you all through the night to check blood pressure, and whether the drip needed changing. At 3.30am, I was taken for a chest X-ray, as they were concerned about something, but I recall standing in a corner next to the X-ray machine, freezing, whilst the two staff members, who were kids, stood staring at their phones and giggling, which I felt was inappropriate.

My room was small and hot, and isolation felt more like solitary confinement. I would walk up and down the room (my cell) every day, in an effort to get some exercise. At this stage I was unable to eat, drink, or talk, and each morning (or afternoon) a different doctor would call into my room with a couple of student nurses as part of his rounds, mumble a few words after looking at me, then leave.
On one particular visit, the doctor burst in and, after glancing at his clipboard, told the nurses I needed an injection in my stomach. If I hadn't already been fully awake, I was now. I knew that he was getting me mixed up with another of his patients, but not being able to speak, I was finding it impossible to make him aware of his mistake and I started to panic.

Another thing I had discovered was that the original syringe they had given me was prehistoric, as the ones they were using on me in hospital, or trusting me with, had the ability to simply push the liquid through, so there was no way of it getting blocked. (Now they tell me!) Being squeamish, when I was feeding myself I would always take my time and push it through reasonably slowly, but on the occasions that a student nurse was carrying out the task for me, they simply pressed it as fast as they could, as they were clearly in a rush, and it would give me a ticklish, cold sensation in my stomach. So I had learnt to indicate that I was okay and that I was happy to do it myself.

The Pax EP recordings had been completed, and Mark very kindly visited me in hospital to bring me a copy. Due to me being in isolation, Mark had been asked to dress up like Murdock from *M*A*S*H* (if you're under 35, Google it), but the fact that I was unable to speak made our communication a little difficult to say the least. I mean, there are only so many times I could wave my hands about in an attempt to be understood, but to be fair to Mark, he did his very best to avoid me feeling uncomfortable.

CHAPTER THIRTY-EIGHT

HAPPY ENDING

When I first started my Night At The Museum Live events, I drew up a wish list of the ultimate four artists (being realistic) I would at some stage really love to book to perform in our magnificent room. The list consisted of Paul Heaton, Tim Burgess, Nick Heyward, and Glenn Tilbrook. I had been a huge Squeeze fan from the second I had seen them live in concert on my Grandma's TV. I had seen Glenn's acoustic show before, and was determined to do everything within my power to book him.

It literally took almost two years of negotiations, but the fact that I hadn't been told no led me to keep on trying. Patience eventually paid off, and I agreed a deal to bring him to the museum on Wednesday, 29th June, 2016.

Even though it sold out in a matter of hours, the problem was that I was in the middle of my treatment, and there was a doubt about whether I would be fit enough to attend, which to me was unthinkable. In fact, I am sure the gig was on the very same day that I fainted, and spent the rest of the afternoon worrying if they would let me out. For weeks I had been really looking forward to the event, and the only thing I could think about was that I really hoped my voice would hold out long enough for me to at least introduce Glenn, as it really was touch and go.

On the day of the event, I spent close to seven hours in chemo, then I went down to have my radiotherapy session, then Janet picked me up and took me home for around ten minutes to put on an outfit befitting a musical legend. Then we headed down to the museum, where she dropped me off. As I walked into the museum entrance, I noticed Glenn was walking around, checking out the old cotton machines on the first floor, so I went over to try to introduce myself and show him to his dressing room.

One of the selling points that I always use when booking for these events is, 'You can perform surrounded by around £40million worth of artwork, and you have an Egyptian Mummy in your dressing room – even Jools can't offer that.' To be fair, that is usually the deal clincher, so I really am blessed.

I found Glenn to be incredibly nice, and Squeeze had literally played the world-famous Pyramid stage at Glastonbury only three days before, so we had a lot to live up to (no pressure). I offered to take him for something to eat, but the problem was that in Blackburn on a Wednesday night (or any night) I was limited for choice as to where to go. Ideally, I wanted to take him to sample The Spread Eagle at Mellor, as that was about the best we had to offer, but there was not enough time.

We ended up opting for O' Neill's Irish pub, about one minute away from the museum, and Glenn ordered fish and chips. When I went to the bar to order and pay for it, I realised they had a half price offer on, so it literally cost less than £3. Now I know that Mr Tilbrook isn't royalty (music royalty, yes), and to be fair on him, he managed to polish it all off and didn't complain once, but I reckon that was the cheapest meal he'd had in a long time.

It was just a shame that I was almost unable to talk, as I would have loved to have chatted with him properly throughout his bargain meal. Luckily, though, he had brought a couple of people with him, which thankfully saved me from those uncomfortable silent moments.

Keely and Courtney were working as Artist Liaison that night, and just before Glenn was due on stage, I asked them to bring him down. He was standing at the stage door with Keely, with the door slightly open, so that he could hear me attempting to introduce him to our wonderful audience. Clive, my photographer for the evening, managed to capture this moment, and it remains one of my favourite ever photographs, due to the expression on Glenn's face, and of course the circumstances. So, thank you, Clive.

Emma had helped to make the stage look special, with fairy lights and sunflowers, even though I knew we could never compete with the Pyramid. By this time, you could just about hear my voice, so it was a good job that I was holding a microphone. I have no idea at all if anybody could understand a word I said, but they could tell that this moment meant the world to me, so it seemed to go down well. I explained that Glenn had been on my wish list from day one, and that it was an absolute pleasure to book and introduce somebody I had watched each week on *Top of the Pops*, as he had been a voice of my generation.

I also mentioned that while I was in hospital, I had downloaded his new solo album, and noticed that there was a song on it called *Peter*, and that the title of his album was called *Happy Ending*, so surely that had to be a sign. The audience erupted with applause, which really meant a lot to me.

Glenn came over and thanked me for my very kind words, then picked up his acoustic guitar, and from the first chord strummed he gave everybody in the room a masterclass in music. His set was incredible, and I loved every single minute. I had hinted to him that my favourite Squeeze tunes had been *Vicky Verky*, *Some Fantastic Place*, and *Goodbye Girl*, and to my delight, he made sure he played all three – in fact, dedicating *Vicky Verky* to me, had made my night (year!). I was sitting at the front with Sarah, who told me on the first day we met that she loved Squeeze, and she was loving it.

This was the first of my events that my work colleague Linda had attended, so she had chosen well, along with Jamie, whose friends had travelled from London to be there. Glenn's voice and his guitar playing were outstanding, and everybody was treated to two full hours of hit after hit. It was really such a special event for me, the museum, and the people of Blackburn who had been lucky enough to purchase a ticket.

Glenn must have thanked me at least seven times, telling me he had really enjoyed the experience, which really meant a lot, and he took the time to meet and greet everybody, signing autographs and posing for the obligatory selfies.

Patience had most certainly been a virtue on this occasion, and for every reason it still remains my favourite, and most special, gig I have ever put on. I purchased a copy of *Happy Ending* on vinyl, and Glenn kindly signed it for me. What was also really nice was that I received an email from his wife, saying how much he had enjoyed the experience of performing in our magnificent museum. She also asked if I would let her know how my treatment went, which was kind, but it was safe to say that if it didn't work, she wouldn't be hearing from me again.

What I had been most relieved about was that my voice had just about managed to allow me to introduce Mr T. And sure enough, the following week it disappeared completely.

The hospital gave me a gadget around the size of an iPad, called a Boogie Board, which enabled me to write everything down on a screen. But even though it was a help, I found it pretty frustrating to be writing my conversation down as fast as I could, feeling that the other person was bored waiting (my thoughts, not theirs), only to find that they couldn't actually read my scribble anyway, so I had to start the whole thing again.

I remember Janet went to pick up Keely and Courtney, to bring them round for a band meeting, and even though I couldn't speak a word, the catch-up lasted two hours, which amazed me. It was a good job they never ran out of things to say. Emma used to come over from Manchester and play Beatles Monopoly with me, and even though I was pretty ill, she told me that she didn't just let me win out of sympathy.

That summer I remember sitting in our garden, next to my beloved palm tree, and being shocked at how thin my arms and legs looked in my t-shirt and shorts. I had gone from 16-and-a-half stone down to 11 stone something in just a matter of months. When people visited me around then – Paul, Bullinge, Waker – I am sure they must have been shocked at how rough I actually looked, even though they never let on, at the time.

Every treatment session felt like a milestone, and we would knock them off the total amount that I was due to receive. My cancer consultant, who was always friendly and upbeat, told me that he didn't want me to go through my final two sessions of chemotherapy, as he felt it would be too much for me. But without realising what long-term effects each session might bring, I was adamant that I intended to carry on and see it through right to the end. I wanted to give myself the best possible chance of surviving this. Luckily, he got his way in the end. And even though a work colleague, Sue, very kindly bought me a Trilby to cover up any potential hair loss, I ended up never really needing it for that particular reason.

When I look back at photos from the NATM event with Glenn and me, it always surprises me how thin I actually look. But I had lost over five stone. I managed to get through my six weeks of treatment, and was relieved to say the least after my final radiotherapy session in July. My consultant told me that I would have to wait another six weeks before I would learn if it had worked or not, as my throat needed time to settle down to be able to give a more accurate reading. He also informed me that my next three weeks were going to be hell, and he was not wrong.

When I look back now, three weeks is not really that big a deal in the grand scheme of things, but while you are going through it, it feels as though it will never end.

CHAPTER THIRTY-NINE

F... CANCER, LET'S DANCE

The last thing I want to do is to only highlight all the negatives from my experience, but those first few weeks after treatment were tough, for sure. I obviously couldn't talk, or eat or drink, but the steroids I had been given prevented me from going to the toilet and even sleeping. It isn't until you find yourself deprived of sleep that you realise that there is nothing worse.

Because of the nature of my cancer, my tongue was permanently covered in some sort of disgusting gunge, and even worse, at night my mouth would constantly fill up with what I can only describe as yellow treacle. Every few minutes throughout the night, I would use towels and kitchen roll to do all I could to extract it, as it really was vile, and certainly the worst thing I have ever experienced. But it seemed to be never-ending, and meant I would get zero sleep.

I moved into Emma's old bedroom to enable Janet to at least grab some much-deserved rest, and I can't even remember how long I went with no sleep at all, but remember wondering how I could actually function during the day. I absolutely dreaded going up to bed each night, knowing what was about to happen once I lay down. And I can honestly say that those never-ending hours throughout the night in Emma's bed were the most isolated and loneliest I have ever felt. At its worst, I dared to ask myself whether it was worth it or not, but there is only one answer to that question, and that is 100% YES.

I was told that this discomfort would only last for a couple of weeks or so, and then things would start to slowly start to ease.

And even though I initially wondered if they were right, to be fair, everything they told me throughout was spot on. Things did start to improve, meaning that there was light at the end of the tunnel.

For obvious reasons I had very little energy or strength at first, and remember fainting for three days in a row. The first couple of weeks I struggled even walking from the settee to the chair (next to each other) and ended up just shuffling across on the floor. I really didn't want to sit and watch TV all day but admit getting into *Deal Or No Deal* and *Bargain Hunt*, during the time I was off. (Rock 'n' Roll, eh?) It's a bit like when Jez told me that the main thing he used to watch whilst he was serving time in prison was Formula One (not for me), and even now, he will never miss it.

I knew that to start building up a little more strength, I would at some stage need to attempt to eat something, but the thought seemed far-fetched as I hadn't used my mouth for that long. I was advised that I might need to learn how to swallow again, and that in some cases I might even lose a part of my tongue (in some cases, all of it). I was also warned that I would lose 80% of my taste once I started my treatment, but that if I was lucky, I would hopefully see the majority of it slowly return.

The one thing that is undeniable throughout my illness, from day one, was the incredible support I received from Janet and Emma. They knew that to stand any chance of me staying strong to get through this, they would need to be strong – in front of me, anyway. I can't even begin to imagine how I would have coped at the time without their 24/7 care, support, and positivity, and knew how lucky I was to receive this blessing. I have always wondered how folk who are not this lucky manage to get through an illness like this, but I guess they just do. I really do feel for them.

I used to really look forward to Janet arriving home every day from work, and would notice even if she was only a few minutes late. And I was always excited when I was told that Emma was coming over from Manchester for our convalescent Monopoly challenges, even though I felt lousy and didn't win them all. Janet told me that Emma had been *her* rock, and had kept positive and supported her throughout, although she admitted that she hadn't known herself how she was managing to cope behind the scenes.

Emma would clearly spend hours researching and reading up on what were the best things for me, and one time I remember forcing myself to try one of the ultra-healthy smoothies she made me with ingredients like kale and spirulina. Even though I tried my best to force some of it down, knowing that she meant well, the minute her back was turned I would look for the nearest plant pot to pour it into. It was really disgusting.

They would make sure that I went on my daily exercise walk to help me build my strength up, even though the majority of the time it was a mission, and I didn't feel up to it. We would walk over the local fields and back along Royal Oak Avenue, and I recall walking with my head down, hoping that we wouldn't bump into anybody I knew, because I was aware that I looked terrible. Those walks, though were vital to my recovery, and even though I would do all I could to try and get out of them on some occasions, I was always glad afterwards that I had made the effort.

Once I started to feel a little more like having visitors, Linda from work would call round and bring me some ice lolly sticks that had been recommended by her friend, who had gone through the same thing. My mouth was constantly dry, and when I was in hospital they would give me these small dab sticks to suck on gently, which really was a relief. I managed to bring a few home with me, and the lollies would help in the same way.

On 28th August, my good friend Tony in Manchester was finally making an honest woman out of his partner Kay, and we were invited to the wedding. Other than best friends, I hadn't really seen anyone up until that point, and even though I knew that I wouldn't look my Mod best by any stretch of the imagination,

I really wanted us to go and help them celebrate their big day. This would be a big step, but I was determined to make it happen. I also felt it would be really good for Janet, who had been stuck in the house for months caring for me.

I was back to resembling Norman Wisdom again, as my suit was about three sizes too big. Smith kindly gave us a lift over to Manchester and dropped us off at this pretty cool hotel called Aparthotel' where the ceremony, meal, and night do were taking place. Even though it was Tony and Kay's big day, they had put a lot of effort and thought into making us feel as welcome and comfortable as they could, in the circumstances, which I really did appreciate. And it showed what a lovely couple they were.

We shared a table with our friends Ian and Ally, and also The Tapestry (Manchester's finest). I must admit that I was dreading the uncomfortable scenario of the meal because, not being able to eat, I would simply have to sit there and do all I could to divert the attention from my plate.

During the months at home not being able to eat, I would find myself staring at the TV screen whenever an advert was shown advertising a meal or any type of food (apart from onions). Also, when Janet was eating her tea, even though her chosen dish wouldn't normally be my meal of choice, actually smelling the aroma of the food was the nearest I would get to a meal.

However, at the start of the wedding meal, as they were serving the leek and potato soup, I was encouraged to at least give it a try. On paper, I could not envisage that this would be an option, but not wanting to come across as a wimp, and due to the fact that it really smelt nice, I found myself picking up a spoon and slowly taking a few sips. This might not seem like a big deal to most people, but it was an absolutely massive step for me.

Janet had read on the Macmillan website that if you didn't push yourself to start eating again as soon as it was physically possible, the longer you left it, the harder you would find it. And in some cases, folk had taken up to a year. Each morning, I would attempt to eat some cereal, but I really struggled, and it would regularly take me around an hour and a half to eat just a quarter of a Weetabix.

Because I was unable to taste anything, the texture of some foods was horrible – none worse than chocolate, which in normal circumstances I loved. As the weeks went by, things started to improve, and eventually I found myself eating more and more, which was a huge relief. My daily walks became less of a mission, and I was even okay for friends to visit me at times.

It was the 20th September, 2016, and not only was it my birthday, but it was also the day I was due to receive my results at the hospital to confirm whether my treatment had been successful or not.
When I was initially told about the severity of my situation, after it had (sort of) sunk in, my initial thought was, *I really hope I get to experience another Christmas.* I have always loved Christmas, as do most people, and especially since Emma Leah arrived on the planet. I have always done everything I could to make it as magical as possible for her. I remember one Christmas Eve when she was little, staying up until 3.30 in the morning, attempting to build the Fisher Price kitchen we had bought her.

Last year, we got her an original 1960s' cocktail bar, from Guernsey, including all the original Babycham figures and beer mats, a pineapple ice bucket, and a large selection of glasses from that time. And even though this was the benchmark of Christmas presents, it really was a mission trying to keep it hidden from both Emma and Janet for five days.

Even this year (2020), I still put out the carrot and mince pie for Rudolph and bought Emma a present for every year that Jesus had been alive – and she is almost 28. Janet regularly tells me that her work colleagues can't believe that she has never wrapped a single present up for Emma (birthday or Christmas) in the past 27 years, but it is true. I have done them all.

Janet eventually told me that she had discussed with Emma at the time how could they possibly have Christmas if I popped my clogs and wasn't there to sort everything, and they both agreed that they would have to go away, if that happened.

During those first few nights following my diagnosis, I remember thinking about Christmas, and also lying in bed with Janet discussing the worst scenario. But at no stage do I ever remember thinking that the worst was going to happen and that I would lose my life. I mean, I had been far too busy doing stuff that I loved to start giving up now, even though in the back of my mind I was aware that it could be an option.

I think the thing that I found the toughest was the day I spent with Emma going through all my passwords for my Macs, and talking her through my beloved vinyl collection, pointing out to her which were the limited editions and rare finds, in case she inherited them earlier than planned.

Throughout my journey, on the whole I managed to stay positive and concentrate my attentions on the things that I had looked forward to and the plans that were in place. I purchased a drawer full of upcoming gig tickets to help give me extra things to look forward to, thinking that, at worst, I could always give them away.

When I was stuck in isolation, I used to come up with Pete's Joke of the Day and posted them on social media. I found them funny, but judging by the response I received, it seems I was the only one, as folk ended up begging me to stop. Also, friends would post 'Pete's Positive Playlist' each day, consisting of relevant music videos and ones they thought I would like.

I tried to make sure that anything I posted stayed positive, as at no stage did I (or have I) ever felt sorry for myself or questioned, 'Why me?' (after all, 'Why not me?') People around me would appear to be extra nice in respect at what I was going through, and some of the well wishes (if not all) blew me away, realising that folk would actually spend any time thinking about my situation.

I received a video message from The Gramotones just after they had performed at the Isle of White Festival, sending me their best wishes, mentioning that I had given them one of their first ever gigs, and saying that they loved me.

I also received a video from an upcoming band called April from the same festival. They had played my NATM event, and they told me they knew I would beat cancer and get through this, with all of them shouting, 'We believe!' which was extremely nice of them.

And there was a video clip from David from The Ragamuffins (who I had also booked) from a festival he was at, where he had got every person in the room to jump up and down singing 'Get well soon, Pete', which left me speechless.

It was my birthday, and I was sitting in the ENT waiting room at Blackburn Hospital, about to be told my fate. The nurse called us in to my consultant's office, and I received the greatest birthday present that anybody could ever wish for when he told me, 'Mr Eastwood, I am happy to tell you that it looks like your treatment has been successful in getting rid of your tumour.'

I discovered that it wasn't until you reach five years of recovery that they would use the term ;cancer-free;, but the fact that my treatment had been successful was exactly what I had been hoping to hear, so I couldn't have been happier. I made sure that Emma was the first person I shared my incredible news with, and am sure I put her mind to rest knowing that Christmas had not been cancelled.

To most folk's dismay, my voice started to improve, along with my taste, and even though I was aware that it would be a long recovery and that certain things would never be the same again, I was now in a position to start living my life again. And I knew I couldn't afford to waste this second (third) chance.

After telling Emma, and also my mum and brother, I thought long and hard about whether to post something on social media or not. But I guess these are the times that we live in, and how else was I going to tell all of the kind folk who had supported me throughout?

Facebook it was then, and to this day I am overwhelmed and humbled by the supportive, positive response I received from my post. There are no words to describe the impact that every single person who gave up their time to post a comment had on me, and the difference that they made to my recovery and keeping me upbeat. I recall a lad I had sort of known, messaging me that it made his day listening to his phone ping every few seconds, for hours, in response to what I had announced.

I was now on my way back to being in the land of the living, and talking, eating, drinking, and sleeping. And the whole of the way through my experience, what the medical staff had told me would happen did happen. When I asked Linda how her friend had been getting on – the one going through a similar situation – she told me that he was dead, but she had failed to mention that rather important information all the times that she was offering me recommendations, based on what he was going through.

One of my pet hates has always been getting caught in the rain and ending up getting completely wet. But while I was in hospital, I promised myself that if I managed to get through this, I would never moan about the weather again. I lied, as I most certainly still do.

For anyone reading this chapter about this terrible illness, I am merely telling my experience and how I felt at the time, as that is all I can do. I have tried not to exaggerate, as I am an individual, but every person is different and would no doubt experience something different to me. The last thing I wanted was for this book to be about cancer, but it is a story that I simply couldn't leave out.

What surprised me the most was that soon after my consultant gave me that amazing news on my birthday, at a time when I should have been feeling over the moon, I actually felt unbelievably low. I know that no doubt sounds strange, and at first I couldn't explain it to myself, but Waker told me the same thing. All I can put it down to is survivor's guilt, as I once read about someone who survived a plane crash but struggled to cope with the fact that he had lived, whereas others had not.

I never asked myself the question of 'Why me?' regarding the illness, but I did wonder why I had managed to get through this when so many others hadn't. I never feel sorry for myself – why would I? I have had a mint life. But I certainly questioned if I was worthy of hanging around. There is one thing for sure, if I had survived cancer, I had to be able to justify this blessing by becoming a better person and doing more to help others.

The other issue I had not banked on was the long-term effects that chemo and radiotherapy would have on my body, as I have ended up with a fair number of symptoms from my treatment. The radiotherapy on my throat meant that my saliva glands would be damaged, meaning that I would have to carry a bottle of water with me everywhere (including in bed).

On the day I was given my results, my consultant asked me how much alcohol I would normally drink throughout the week. I explained that I had never been a big drinker, but admitted that I visited my local, and venues, on most days of the week due to my work in music, and told him I would usually drink about two to three pints of lager per day, during the week.

He replied that in future, at most, I would be okay to have two pints per week, but on separate days. When I asked him for a timeline of how long this rule would need to be abided by, I was told for the rest of my life, if I didn't want it to return. I always said that I loved a beer, but if a doctor ever told me that I wouldn't be able to drink again, then I would obviously take his advice and stop. But I never envisaged that it would actually bloody happen!

Apparently, the chemo damaged the nerve endings in my hands and feet, which results in me being freezing in those places when it is only remotely cold.

I have always been paranoid about how dodgy my voice now sounds when I am chatting to folk, but they always assure me that they didn't feel it was that bad.

At the end of the day, no matter how many symptoms I have ended up with, I would have chosen that over the alternative and will certainly never moan or complain about having them – unlike the rain – and I know for sure that I am, and always will be, the luckiest person in any room.

As far as college went and my job, apart from Linda, I don't really remember hearing from anyone other than the odd email from HR reminding me to send in my sick notes. But to be fair, they carried on paying me (in full) for the majority of the time that I was off, even though it was probably the law anyway.

I remember receiving an email from HR within the first month of being off, regarding the redundancy pool that we had all been put into. It used the words, 'We will have to tread carefully now,' based on the fact that I had cancer. I even recall feeling guilty about the amount of time I had been off, and messaging Linda something along those lines. but she simply went mad and told me not to be ridiculous, as I was seriously ill.

What did blow me away was when Harris, one of the students I had been mentoring at college, had called up the Pretty Green Clothing store in Manchester and explained to them that his teacher was fighting cancer. They told him he could choose any jacket he wanted for me. Harris chose well, and he contacted me to say that the class had sorted me out a cool green parka to cheer me up and keep me positive throughout my recovery. It was extremely nice of him, but surprised me because I was always telling him off. A couple of years ago I was standing on the platform at Salford Crescent, when I noticed Harris on the passing train waving at me. He seemed chuffed that I was wearing that very parka he had kindly sourced for me. (Good lad!)

In total, I was off sick from my job for a whole year, and when I finally returned, I was told that I now had a different job, in a different building, with a different team, because the Year 11 Project had now been closed. The person responsible for this decision at the time was apparently quoted as saying, 'We are not here to babysit young people anymore.' But whichever way you look at it, you will always need to find provision for young people who feel that the normal school way of learning is not for them (like me), or the young people who have found themselves not having the best of starts in life, through no fault of their own, babysitting or no babysitting.

To be fair, the team I joined were really nice, and I couldn't complain about the building. My new office was in the old Victoria building, which in my opinion is probably the best building in Blackburn, and where I had studied photography (kind of) in 1980. Also, on paper, the job sounded pretty similar, because I would be still mentoring young people (on paper).

HR arranged for me to have an assessment meeting with a couple of ladies from Occupational Health, who recommended I have a phased return to work, and told me that I would be meeting them each month at first just to see how I was getting on. I never heard from them again.

On the 18th January, 2017, our daughter Emma was due to fly to India with her friend Jessie. They had plans to explore the country and travel for the next few weeks, having daily adventures and discovering a new way of living. I was gutted that, for the first time, we were not going to be with her on her February birthday, but I acknowledged that it would be a wonderful experience for them both.

The issue was that on the same day she was due to fly out, I was given an appointment at Burnley Hospital to have my peg out, and I wasn't looking forward to it. I wasn't sure what the procedure would be, which is probably a good thing, but was hoping that it would be similar to having it fitted, when I had been knocked out for a matter of seconds to be spared all the gory details. I was wrong.

I was asked to lie on a bed and told by the doctor that it might hurt a little. he then proceeded to simply rip the peg out of my stomach as hard as he could, and at the time it felt like a part of my stomach had gone with it. 'Might hurt a little' was the planet's greatest understatement. Now I know that most people reading this will think 'Pete, don't be soft', as it is well known that the majority of males are pretty soft when it comes to medical procedures, so I was perhaps just being dramatic. But let me tell you this, the pain I felt when my feeding tube was ripped from my stomach was like no other pain I had ever experienced before. Thankfully, it only lasted a matter of seconds.

I had gone months without being allowed to have a bath, and still had to wait another few more weeks for the hole that this procedure had made to heal. I was relieved that the peg had finally gone, even though it had contributed to keeping me alive, and I was now the proud owner of (seeming to have) two belly buttons, which is a war wound you simply have to accept (no big deal).

People's kindness has always amazed me in times of need, and throughout this experience I have been blown away by the support and kind offers of help, as well as being totally humbled that so many people had cared. Birchy would always be on hand to take me to the hospital for my monthly check-ups, if Janet was unavailable. And Dave even painted our bedroom, for free, which was hugely appreciated. Friends visited me with gifts, and told me that they would be there if I needed them. People would send me daily positive, and sometimes, funny messages, which helped to keep me upbeat, and on some occasions it was partial strangers, and even people who I least expected, who showed me kindness.

Being honest, some friends (and family) were relatively silent at the beginning of my struggle, and some people who I had expected to contact me, hadn't. But I do realise now that cancer is a very powerful word, even with a small c, and I appreciate that folk handle it in different ways, which is fine by me. You certainly won't find any judgement here from this Mod.

During all the time I was ill, I don't remember at any stage suspecting that I might in fact have cancer. It never entered my head at the time, but it is funny looking back, in an attempt to try and work out how long I might have had the tumour, remembering certain instances. We had been for a. meal to the Spread Eagle at Mellor with our friends Mark (Waker) and Karen, and Craig and Tracy, to celebrate both Mark and Craig receiving the all clear, and surviving Stage 4 cancer. I must have had it then, because I recall struggling to swallow my food and having to ask the waitress at least four separate times if she could bring me an extra gravy boat to make swallowing easier.

When me and my mates turned 50, I went with Waker, Karl, Bullinge, and Ste S on a long weekend to Ibiza. Needless to say, a fair amount of drinking took place during our stay, and I wonder if I had the tumour then. But I guess I will never know.

There is no doubt that having that length of time off work affected my confidence, along with being paranoid about my voice when talking to our students. But it really was good to try and get back to some kind of normal and it was great to actually see people again. I remember that the first class I was supporting in, I received a round of applause from the students, after the tutor told them that I had fought the disease.

At first, I feel as if I would mention the 'c' word constantly, and I am sure that I came across as though I was wearing it as a badge. But at no stage have I ever wanted any sympathy; it is simply my way of getting through it the best I can. After all, mine is a positive story, because I am here to tell the tale.

For the first year I had to visit Blackburn ENT Clinic every four weeks for my check-up, which consisted of my consultant feeling and looking into my mouth, squeezing and feeling my neck, and putting a camera up my nose and down my throat (which certainly makes your eyes water). But the worst aspect of it was when he put on surgical gloves, and proceeded to shove his fingers as far as he could towards the back of my throat, leaving me backing up and almost on the floor, fighting the best I could to avoid throwing up. Granted, this experience is not what you would describe as pleasant, but as long as he kept telling me at the end of the appointment, 'It's looking good, Mr Eastwood,' it was certainly fine by me.

On one occasion, Janet was in the room whilst I was having the camera shoved down. As she is not squeamish, she stared at the screen that was showing what the camera could see (something I never did), and she realised that the tumour that had been in my throat had been massive, which made it even more baffling how nobody had spotted it at the time.

On each of my visits I used to push my luck and ask if at some stage I'd be okay to drink more than two lagers each week, but to my disappointment I have repeatedly been advised, no, even though no explanation is ever given no matter how many times I ask.

At the beginning I found my consultant to be a little harsh. He came across as negative, and to my dismay on one visit he even told me that if it came back, there was nothing they could do. But I appreciate that having to deal with this situation every day, he has obviously become hardened to it, and it didn't take long before I actually grew to like him. After all, he keeps giving me the news I want to hear, and to be fair, once he got to know me a little better, he was a lot friendlier, and we even shared a joke at times.

I was really missing my live music, as it had been months since I had attended any gigs or events. Just before my treatment ended, I kidded myself and attended a Public Image Ltd concert at King George's Hall, thinking I would be able to handle it. But after about three songs, and almost fainting several times, I simply rang Janet and asked her to pick me up.

The Pax EP had been completed, and Mark's contact who had mastered the Coldplay album, kindly offered to master our new tunes, after Mark sent them to him and he liked them. I had promised them that I would sort out a limited amount of clear vinyl EPs, and was proud to make it happen.

On December 13th, 2016, the EP launch for Pax and the Scarlet Field took place at The Castle Hotel in Manchester, and it couldn't have gone any better. Granted, on the whole the room was packed out with all of their family and friends and a fair few photographers, but I think it is safe to say that both the band and the audience really loved the evening.

From the minute I had committed to being involved with the band, I was involved in every aspect of their development. But during my recovery, they chose to go and record their new tune at Sugar House Studios in St Helen's. Keely's boyfriend Owen had recently recorded there with his band, Violet Youth, and had ended up getting signed, performing a handful of gigs in China not long after. I can't remember if I was in hospital at the time when Pax went in to record, or if I was stuck at home, but I was really surprised that they didn't contact me to update me on how they were getting on for around three days, even though they must have known that I was mad keen to find out.

As I was now fully trusting any gut feeling I had, I called a Liz N Lil's band meeting the following week to discuss how I felt. I thought (for the first time) that they might have lost a little bit of faith in me, and maybe thought that somebody else could have a better chance of taking them to the next level. It even crossed my mind that perhaps the studio, or even someone else, had told them that they didn't need a manager – or not me, anyway – and convinced them that this was the case.

To be fair, that is only how I felt; they never indicated or mentioned anything of the kind, but I really did feel that something had changed (maybe my lack of confidence). Before we met up, I thought long and hard about whether I was fit to carry om giving them 100%, as it was always all or nothing with me, and that is what they deserved. But being realistic, there was no way I could attend every gig up and down the country, even if I booked them. At the meeting, I discussed my concerns and, rightly or wrongly, it was agreed that I was going to stand down as their manager, which really made me sad, but my recovery had to be a priority from now on.

My next NATM event was yet another cracker, and even though it had taken me the best part of two years to get my man (again), I was ecstatic to secure the services of none other than Mr Haircut One Hundred himself, and the nicest man in music, Nick Heyward. Nick had been on my wish list from day one, and I had refused to give up on the chance of one day bringing him to our museum, even if the date we had agreed on was in fact my and Janet's wedding anniversary.

I had seen Nick back in the day with his band at Lancaster Polytechnic, when we had managed to blag our way backstage. I had watched him perform at Kendal Calling in the Tim Peaks Diner with Tim Burgess, and also attended his fantastic show at

The Cavern in November 2016, as part of his Calling Captain Autumn Tour. But on that occasion, around four songs into his set, standing at the front had taken its toll and I had ended up watching the rest of the gig from the back of the room, leaning against the wall.

Prior to The Cavern show, I attended A Celebration of The Jam with my friends Craig and Tracy at the Liverpool Echo Arena. Even though it had been a given that Paul would not be attending the event, it was partly organised by Paul's sister Nicky Weller, who had just brought to an end her acclaimed Jam Exhibition, which had delighted fans young and old (and us), finding a home in the Cunard building throughout that summer.

There had been plenty of speculation about whether or not The Jam's drummer Rick Buckler would show up, as his original drum kit was set up on the stage, covered by a large cloth, which undoubtedly added to the suspense. But based on the fact that Rick had told me that the last time he had spoken to Paul was back in 1983, one year after the band split up, I found it highly unlikely. And I was right. From The Jam arrived on stage, so at least we had Bruce there to carry the flag, and to my delight they invited Mr Heyward on stage to perform his version of *The Modern World*.

I have always kept up to date with Nick's solo recordings, which I love, and was now about to bring Captain Autumn to perform to a handful of lucky people in our magnificent Victorian Painting Gallery.

Janet and I made sure that we had sourced everything that we could to meet the requests of Nick's rider, and the event itself went better than any of us could have imagined. Nick had recently released his latest solo album, *Woodland Echoes*, and with his son taking over from Blake on the sound desk, Nick absolutely enchanted the audience with all the expected favourites, *Love Plus One, Blue Hat for a Blue Day, Favourite Shirts, Take That Situation*, and of course, *Fantastic Day*, along with a preview of his new compositions. Our wonderful audience sang along to all the well-known lyrics and contributed to making the event one of my favourites ever.

16trh June, 2017, might have been our wedding anniversary, but Nick had helped to make it extra special for everybody by his performance in our small Lancashire town. After his set, he hung around for at least another hour, meeting every single person that had stayed, and signing every item that they were holding. That simply confirmed my belief that he is the nicest man involved in the music industry. In fact, I'm sure we had to throw him out in the end, as it was way past midnight, and the museum had a curfew of 11.30pm! So I politely thanked him for everything, and hinted that we needed to lock up.

Support on the night came from Dantevilles, from Manchester, and the very talented James Holt from Bolton. I first met James at a music conference in Manchester, when he came over to me, introduced himself, and gave me one of his CDs. I have always tried to make the time to play any of the music that folk kindly send me, or pass on to me, and I recall putting on James's CD one afternoon in my office and thinking, *WOW! I certainly can't ignore him.*

Nick's visit to Blackburn was also special in another way, which only added to my determination to book him. My art class school friend Mick had a sister called Penny, who was a huge fan of Nick back in the day, and I am sure Mick told me that Nick had actually written to Penny at that time. Janet had worked with her at BT, but tragically, Penny ended up losing her life to cancer, which was beyond sad. From the moment Mick heard I was keen to book Nick, he told me the story about Penny and her love for him, and said that if I managed to get him he would invite a couple of his sister's friends. So, not booking him wasn't an option.

Once it had become clear that I was going to hang around a little longer on this planet, I remember saying to Janet that we needed to visit The Seychelles. I had spent the majority of my life wanting to visit this magical land, and now I had been given a second (third) chance, I was not prepared to put it off any longer. I have always said that there is no point in saving up for a rainy day, as it rains every day around here. Emma had absolutely loved her three months exploring around India, and even though she was invited to join us, she felt uncomfortable so soon after some of the sights she had seen whilst on her travels.

On July 3rd, 2017, and around 43 years after I had seen those wonderful images in my Grandma's magazine, Janet and I boarded a flight at Manchester Airport for a 24-hour journey to the Indian Ocean. It was finally happening. We had to change in Dubai and were blown away by the size of the airport there; it was huge. In fact, it was so big that we almost missed our connecting flight, and had to jump on one of those golf buggy-type things to get to the correct gate just in time for take-off.

We arrived in The Seychelles and then had to get a couple of ferries to our island of choice, La Digue. The ferry was frightening, as the water was so choppy that I spent the majority of the journey leaning over a table with my head in my hands – along with a fair few others – listening to Janet telling me, 'We are going to die', every few minutes. (Slight exaggeration, I felt.)

I knew from the minute we arrived at our hotel that we had made the right choice, as I reckon it was the nicest on the island. Our room was massive, and set in the middle of tranquil, palm tree-laden gardens, and was by a country mile the most luxurious one we had ever stayed in. I understood that Emma did have a point regarding the poverty and hardship she had witnessed on her travels, but I felt as though Janet and I both deserved this, based on the horrible months we had just endured.

There were hardly any cars on La Digue, just bikes, which was perfect for me. I have always felt that cars ruined any view. We visited the world-renowned Anse Source D' Argent beach, which hosted the stunning rock formations I had seen in those photos all those years ago. But only I could visit the world's most photographed beach and drop my camera into the sea, destroying the photos I had already snapped (another Tom Chance moment).

We loved La Digue, and if nightlife, fine dining, and saving money were not your main objectives when booking to go away, I would strongly recommend the experience. Another item had been ticked off from the top of my wish list.

In order to have a family holiday with Emma, which I really wanted after her wonderful support during the time I was ill, that August we booked to visit Santorini in Greece. The island boasted world renowned views and sunsets, and even though we all enjoyed our stay there, I found the heat a little uncomfortable at times, and massively struggled with the ultra-cruel practice of using donkeys (still) to carry overweight and heartless holidaymakers up the mountainside. It really upset me watching some overweight, uncaring (in my opinion) Greek bloke holding a stick, treating animals so badly, and the selfish, thoughtless tourists giving him Euros because they were too lazy to actually walk up there themselves, like we did. Tradition or no tradition, they need to stop this practice, or I won't be hurrying back there anytime soon.

On the flight back, we experienced the worst turbulence we had ever known, by a mile. And you know it isn't good when your fellow passengers start to pray and others are crying. I remember turning to the lady sitting next to me, and saying, 'Don't worry, I have just survived Stage 4 cancer, and I am not about to die in a plane crash. So we'll be fine.'

Even during my recovery when I had hardly left the house, I still managed to have one of my Tom Chance moments. We received a letter from a Janet Smith at the council, informing us that somebody had complained about overgrown bushes at the end of our garden, saying that they were obstructing the path for people walking by. Being honest, this wound me up, and initially I ignored it, but I did wonder if it was the same Janet Smith that had flashed her bra to us in the Lakes.

Several weeks later, we received a follow-up letter, telling us that if we didn't trim them in the next seven days, we would need to pay a few hundred pounds for the council to send someone to sort it.
I was still pretty weak at this stage, so Janet asked Fred to call over with his hedge trimmers. Fred came round, and I made the effort to go outside and help him clear up all the branches, knowing that at least now both Janets would be happy.

Even though I don't bet on horse racing any more, the Grand National was on TV, so to make my afternoon more interesting, I had chosen a horse based on its name. About a quarter of the way into the race, my horse was actually winning and, proud of our afternoon's work, I glanced through the window to admire the result of our hard graft when I noticed that the house across the road was on fire. Smoke and flames were coming through the roof, and if we hadn't trimmed the bushes literally 30 minutes beforehand, I wouldn't have even noticed it.

I knew this wasn't good, but my dilemma was that my horse was winning, so I could either wait until the race was over, or miss the race and attempt to save the day. Obviously, I did the right thing and called 999, and within minutes three fire engines appeared on the road – one of the firemen working on the blaze was my good friend Dave. (What were the odds on that?) I am pleased to report that the firemen safely put out the fire and nobody was hurt, but my horse didn't win. And I couldn't help wondering what would have happened if we hadn't cut those bushes when we did.

The very sensible decision had been made to move Confessional from April back to September (16th), and I felt I had booked my finest line-up to date. Cabbage, who were one of the most talked about new bands at the time, were booked to headline, and even though I had agreed a fee with the band only to be flatly turned down by their agent, She ended up calling me back the following day, apologising, and telling me that their manager had agreed for them to play the event, which was a first. Apparently, the band had told their manager that they wanted to play and had agreed a fee, and luckily for us he agreed with them, and contacted the agent. (Artist power.)

Even though I was comfortable that I was booking one of the hottest new bands around – something I always aim to do – I was aware that they definitely wouldn't be everyone's cup of tea. But then, who is? However, on the night they were brilliant, and even folk who had not liked them up until that point came over to tell me how much they had enjoyed them. What was also really special to me was that both Joe and Lee from the band messaged me to say it had been one of their top three favourite ever gigs. And when you consider that they had played everywhere in the UK, and even as far away as Russia, it really was a compliment.

I think that one of the reasons artists enjoy playing my events is that we don't ever use a barrier to separate the audience from the stage, even though I am always aware that this could be a risk, especially booking a band with a reputation for creating a mosh pit. I do tend to prefer the more Rock 'n' Roll aspects of a live show myself, and even though my cameramen Clive and Derren were knocked and shoved all over the place during Cabbage's set, I am pleased to report that yet again there was zero trouble, and the pair managed to snap some truly magnificent photos of the event.

Other acts that performed that year included the incredible She Drew The Gun from Liverpool, and Amber Arcades from the Netherlands. I had seen Amber Arcades at The Trades Club in Hebden Bridge, my favourite venue, and after their set I had gone over to their merch stand to tell their lead singer Annelotte, all about Confessional. As soon as I showed her some photos showcasing how amazing it had looked at previous events, I knew that she was interested.

She Drew The Gun had released one of the best songs I had heard for a very long time in *Poem*, and I was delighted to be able to book them. Theirs still remains one of my favourite Confessional performances to date, along with Cabbage.

The Beat Chics DJs (our Emma and Natalie) ended the event, and I recall a couple of people coming up to me at the end to tell me they had travelled over from Manchester, and hadn't realised that events of this standard happened in Blackburn.

During my stay in isolation, I had promised myself that once I got through it and was fit enough, I planned to throw a celebration event, or party, to acknowledge a positive outcome. I came up with the name 'F... cancer Let's Dance' – nicking the idea from The Selecter track *F... Art Let's Dance,* if I am being honest.

I didn't just plan to have a do, but also wanted to give something back by raising some money for Rosemere Hospital, which no doubt saved my life.

My good friend Craig had also survived Stage 4 cancer. In fact, he had actually been through more than anybody I knew yet somehow remained positive throughout, and he really was an inspiration. Three lifelong friends all surviving Stage 4 was really something worth raising a glass to, and there was talk of all three of us having a joint celebration. But at the time, Mark and Craig felt it was maybe a little too early for them, so I went ahead and organised mine.

I came up with the idea of having an auction, and spent months trying to source a large amount of mainly music-related memorabilia, in an effort to raise some money. Yet again, people were unbelievably kind and generous in supporting my cause. Claire at work painted me a magnificent picture of David Bowie; Elton John's office donated two free tickets for his upcoming stadium tour; Paul Weller signed a couple of his books – thanks to his drummer Steve – along with a signed *All Mod Cons* album;

local festival Beat Herder kindly donated a ticket; Gazza signed a book and a photograph for me; and I also offered signed prints from the likes of Dylan, The Libertines, Oasis, and the main man himself, Mr Nile Rodgers. Blackburn Rovers donated a signed footy, and Howard from Take That generously donated two premium seated tickets for their upcoming stadium tour, as my friend Tony had been in the same class as him at school and had kindly mentioned my cause.

The difficult thing for me was choosing an available date for the event, as my year was more or less booked up (as always) with gig and event commitments. But I eventually managed to narrow it down to only two, to avoid clashing with anything else.

June 17th, 2017 was finally decided on – the night after I had hosted Nick, and the venue of choice was Blackburn Northern (Ex) Cricket Club, just up the road from us. Due to my family's involvement in the venue over the years, it was a no-brainer really, and I certainly couldn't have found anywhere more relevant to stage the event.

Being an event manager, I was fully aware that not everybody I wanted to come would be available or would be able to make it, but when friends Craig and Tracy told me that they would be away on that date, I was absolutely gutted to be honest. I even thought about trying to change the date to one where they could have both made it, but in reality I knew that wasn't really an option. It had taken weeks to narrow it down to this date, and I knew that if I started changing it again there would be other family and friends in the same position, so with a heavy heart I stuck to my original.

Ever since Liz N Lil's Tea Room had opened in town, I had found the owners Sherone and Sonia to be unbelievably friendly and supportive of anything I was doing. We had all our Pax band meetings there, and they were always lovely with the girls. When they heard about my event, they insisted on providing the catering at no cost to me, which blew me away, and they offered to provide freshly cooked food for over 100 people. I couldn't get over their kindness.

On the afternoon of the event, Emma and her friends Vicky and Georgie spent hours decorating the room with some really cool prayer flags that Emma had brought back from India, only to find that when we went back that evening, their efforts had been totally wasted. Some jobsworth behind the bar had actually taken them all down, claiming it was against their Health and Safety, even though the person I had booked the venue through had watched the girls put the flags up. I went mad and ended up telling him exactly how I felt, with it being a charity event to help raise some funds for a cancer hospital, but my rants fell on deaf ears and he wasn't prepared to budge.

Before the event started, I received a text from my mate Waker informing me that both he and Karen were ill, even though he had seemed fine enough at my NATM event the previous evening. I really was upset by this. I mean, the two people I had known for the majority of my life, and who had experienced a similar thing to me, would be missing, and I really did feel down about it.

Matt Abbott travelled up from London to host the auction, which saved me from talking for hours, and the entertainment that kicked things off came from my friends Ian H and Johnny V, David from The Ragamuffins, and the very talented Seamus McLoughlin. And they were all wonderful.

The auction itself went down a storm, and even though it carried on for a lot longer than I had expected, we managed to sell almost every item, which was what I was hoping to achieve.

Paul, my mate from The Live Lounge, donated an absolutely massive 4K Ultra LGTV, and I couldn't have been happier when my friend Strang's raffle ticket number was picked out, enabling him to take it home. To be fair, he was also pretty chuffed.

The support I received from friends old and new was humbling, and I even managed to dance to a few of Smith's Mod classics with the same folk I had danced with in the old days, which was special. We successfully got over another problem when Mr Jobsworth behind the bar told us that, due to Health and Safety reasons, we were unable to use their kitchen (he was obsessed), so Janet ended up warming up all the portions of lasagne and potato pie back at our house. After all that, the event was a great success.

I would have liked the auction to have taken less time, giving folk longer to dance (or try, in my case), and it felt as though something (or someone) was missing, but I celebrated the fact that I was still around, with people I had thought the most of, and managed to raise a massive £4,522 for Rosemere in the process. So, FcLD.

A Paris Match.

She said YES. (16.06.90.) (Simon in the background far left, on his best behaviour)

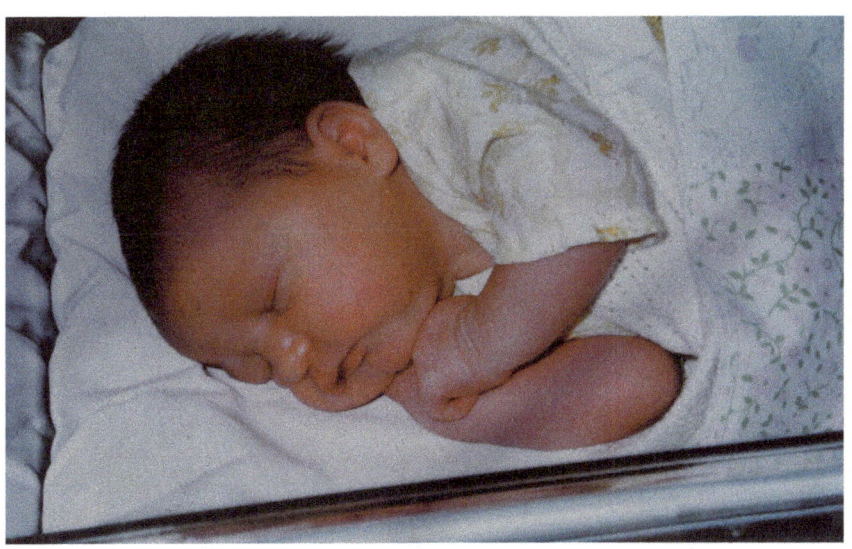

Emma Leah Eastwood (24.02.93.)

Emma at Cafe Mambo, Ibiza. (One of my favourite photos of my Daughter)

With Bullinge in Soho, before the Style Council concert at the Royal Albert Hall.

I love this photograph I took of Faded Image at the Polish Club in Blackburn. (Ash, Kev, Rooster, Kershy, Kipper)

The Stiffs back together again for their 2005 reunion gig at King George's Hall.

The Torrents outside The Cavern on Matthew Street.
(Neal, Swanny, Austin, Joss)

The Tapestry performing at The Live Lounge, Blackburn.

Just qualified as a PADI Open Water Diver,
with my Diving Instructor Clive.

Visiting the Holy Grail of music, Abbey Road Studios.

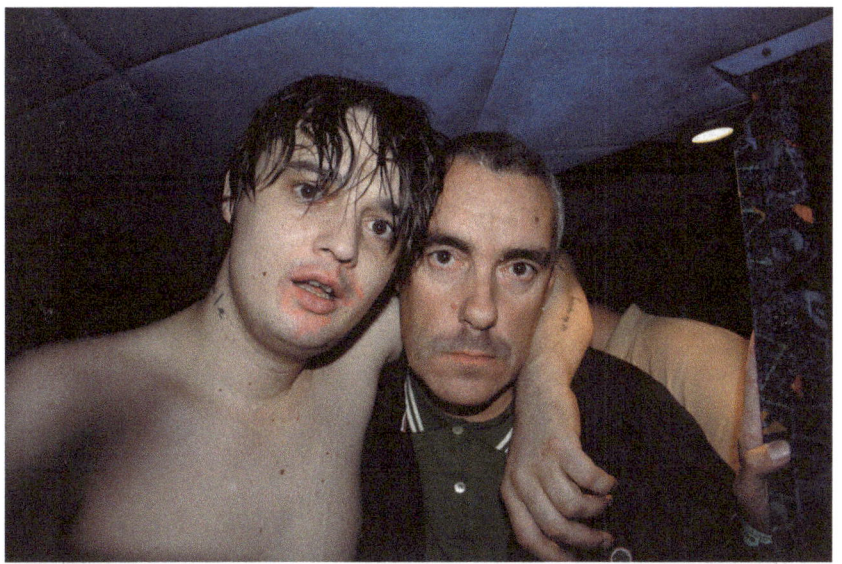

With Pete Doherty after his Blackburn show on Thursday 24th August 2011. (He is the one covered in lipstick marks)

Glastonbury 2010 watching Stevie Wonder, with Carrie, Beth, and Sarah.

Got Lucky, meeting musical legend Nile Rodgers in Liverpool.

With Glenn Tilbrook from Squeeze,
at Blackburn Museum and Art Gallery.

Team Eastwood in Ibiza 2018.

CHAPTER FORTY

A DIFFERENT KIND OF BIRD FOR ME

If 2017 had been a massive step forward in my recovery, 2018 continued to offer a wide range of magical lifetime experiences. And this time I managed to tick two boxes off my life goals' wish list.

My NATM 8 event took place on 24th May, 2018, and I still regard it to be my finest booking and best line-up for this event to date. I came across a young singer/songwriter called Jade Bird, and thought she would be perfect to perform in the museum. I knew that Jade was going places, based on what I had heard and seen from her footage, and knew that booking up-and-coming artists was all about the timing. Getting them just before they broke through was key, and after a couple of negotiations with her agent, I signed a contract to bring her to Blackburn.

I managed to book the fabulous Karima Francis, and Molly Warburton as support, and even though the majority of our audience (if not all) hadn't heard of Jade at the time, the event sold out in advance, based on its reputation.

Jade had a slight Country edge to her music, and it is always great to showcase something new, but I remember watching her at soundcheck, playing keyboards (that Reidys had kindly provided), and thinking, *WOW!* She told me that she had been playing them since the age of eight, which was pretty impressive.

I really was proud of this line-up, and everyone proved me right. Molly was brilliant, Karima was quality, and Jade was superb and absolutely rocked the room. She had a wonderful personality and a fabulous talent, and the reason I consider her to be my finest booking is that I have always strived to book an artist who nobody (or most) in the room has ever heard of, knowing (or predicting) that in a matter of months everyone *will* know who they are. And I feel I achieved that on this occasion.

Jade was only 20 when she performed in our museum, and hairs still stand up on the back of my neck when I watch the footage of her performing a cover of Kate Bush's *Running Up That Hill* from our event. I remember telling her in the dressing room that she was going to have an amazing life (which she deserves), and I've had the pleasure of watching her go from Blackburn Museum to a crowd of around 150 people (at most), to performing at The Deaf Institute (maybe my favourite venue in the city), to a sell-out show at Manchester's Ritz. Next month, Jade is set to perform at the famous RCA Studios in Nashville, where she has recorded her upcoming second album with multi-Grammy Award winning producer Dave Cobb. So I would like to think that at some stage, somebody local will mention her in a conversation along the lines of 'Do you remember when she played Blackburn? I was there.'

The following month saw me, Janet, and Emma, return to my beloved Ibiza, and more specifically, Café Mambo, for the sunsets. This trip was special, because the day I finished my cancer treatment, Emma gave me a star-shaped card she had made which read, 'Well done on finishing your treatment. (You did it.) It will all be worth it when we are chilling with cocktails in Ibiza.' Proving her correct, with a pina colada in our hands at Café Mambo, I made sure that we captured the moment.

On 20th July that year, I put on my NATM 9 event, and was excited to have booked the original New York Dolls guitarist Sylvain Sylvain. Risa, one of the people that had attended my previous event with Jade, was a lifelong friend of Syl's, and was not only a musician herself but had actually attended the same school in New York as The Ramones and Simon and Garfunkel. So she really knew her stuff. Thanks to the wonderful help Risa gave me, I managed to bring the musical icon to the museum, to not only perform a number of his back catalogue, but to also share with our audience some of his crazy stories from the book he had just published, *There's No Bones In Ice Cream* – the story of the New York Dolls.

Joe and Eoghan from Cabbage were our special guests on the evening, offering the normally raucous Cabbage tunes in acoustic form for a rare occasion. Syl brought with him fellow musician and actress, Alison Gordy, who was perhaps best known for her collaboration with Johnny Thunders as part of his back-up band. I found both Sylvain and Alison to be delightful, but remember panic setting in as his soundcheck went way over time, and we had been keeping everybody who had arrived at that point in the bar area, next door to the main room. But no matter how many times I politely explained to Syl that we needed to start letting everybody in, he simply carried on rehearsing until he was happy with the sound. To be fair, he had been a New York Doll, so who was I to argue?

The Cabbage acoustic set went down well, and (again) even folk who had told me that weren't really fans of the band loved it. During Sylvain's set, I watched in horror as Alison fell backwards off the stage, and I was sure she must have really hurt herself. But in impressive showbiz fashion, she simply got back up, dusted herself off, and just carried on as though nothing had happened.

Syl treated us to *Trash, Personality Crisis*, and *Jet Boy*, which encouraged one of those magnificent audience participation moments. And he performed 12 of his tunes in total, alongside sharing tales of the band's early life in New York, which the crowd enjoyed. The audience loved it, the artists loved it, and then Syl and Alison moved through to the bar area to meet folk and sign the books they had purchased.

Sylvain wrote in my book 'Super Thanks for Everything', and in my comments book, 'I had such a great time. Let's do it again soon.' It really had been a pleasure to be able to bring such a musical icon to our town, and I was proper chuffed that he had enjoyed it. But sadly, his comment regarding 'Let's Do It Again Soon' would not be possible. As I have been writing this chapter, it was announced (on 13th January, 2021) that Sylvain Mizrahi (Sylvain Sylvain) had passed away in Nashville at the age of 69.

I was really upset by this terrible news, and even though I knew he had been battling cancer for the past two-and-a-half years, it was still a shock. People were posting photographs of our event (including me), which was really special, but reading the comments from people that had known him or were lucky enough to meet him, it was pretty obvious that everyone remembered him as a gentleman and such a lovely guy, which is not a bad legacy to leave.

CHAPTER FORTY-ONE

FAB

July 25th, 2018, was without a doubt the best afternoon of my life (outside my family), and proved yet again that 'If you don't ask, then you will never get'.
I saw a post from a friend that I knew through working in music, Wendy, who was ultra-lucky enough to have been invited to LIPA (Liverpool Institute for Performing Arts) to listen to a talk by none other than their ex-pupil Sir Paul McCartney. I hadn't been aware that Macca was even due in the city, and even though I am not really a jealous person, I was on this occasion. I recall messaging Wend as a joke, saying that I might head over in an effort to stalk the ex-Beatle, but as I don't do barriers, the more I thought about it, the more it seemed like a good idea.

I tried to think about who I knew that also loved Paul and would be mad enough to join me in my quest, and when my friend Jon messaged me that he had in fact got the day off work and was up for it, I knew that it was happening (fab).

Naturally, Janet thought I was mad, but my friend Tony messaged me that if I had managed to meet Nile Rodgers, then anything was possible. And I agreed. I didn't have too many things left on my wish list, as I have been extremely lucky to have experienced the majority, but meeting Paul McCartney was certainly at the top.

It was a boiling hot day, and I recall saying to Jon on the drive over there that there was a really good chance we would end up simply standing in the sun for hours, just staring at the building and, at most, catching a glimpse of his silver car flashing by, for all our efforts.

We stood at the back of LIPA, listening to the security guards chatting to the very keen crowd, and at that point our chances looked pretty slim. I happened to mention to Jon that I had only ever visited the front of the building before with Emma, and suggested we give it a try.

Once at the front of the building, it was clear that was where everything was happening, so it was a decent decision. But watching folk queue up, hoping to get in, what became apparent was that: one, you had to be a student there, and have your student ID pass to prove it; and two, you had to be holding your invite to the event. They were so strict about entry that they turned away a student who was holding their invite but had unfortunately forgotten their student ID (very harsh).

What amazed me was how many people had travelled and simply shown up on the off-chance, obviously hearing about who was in town. We were talking to a couple of ladies who had flown over from Spain, and also a guy who had come all the way from Los Angeles, which really was impressive.

Jon suggested that I tried to blag it past the security team, but it just didn't feel right, and I explained to him that I wasn't as confident since my illness. So I suggested we should just hang around but, importantly, that we should act as though we deserved to be there and not appear to be desperate.

The incident that led me to thinking that we should at least give it a try was remembering watching the illusionist Derren Brown on TV when he collected on a losing bet at the races, due to his absolute confidence at the time. He went over to the course bookies window, and gave his ticket in, only to be given it back with the words, 'Sorry, sir, this is not a winning bet.' He then very confidently asked the lady to please check his slip again, as he was sure it was a winning slip. To my amazement, she proceeded to apologise to him, then handed him a hand full of cash.

I knew that I didn't have the capability to put the security people under a spell, and I also counted that were nine people watching the door. (Nine!)

It was 1.55pm, and I knew that the last entry was at 2pm, but just before I made a decision on what our last-minute move should be, to my astonishment the main guy on the front door spotted me, called me over (keep calm, Pete!), and asked if I had a pass. I explained that I had worked in music and had been invited by a friend who was already inside. He just looked at me and asked if I had any ID on me. 'Of course,' I replied, lying.

This gentleman who I was about to love forever, told me, 'Ok then, make your way inside.' No words can possibly describe my excitement at that moment, so I won't try and find any! I simply nodded to Jon to come over and join me, knowing that I hadn't yet made it fully inside, and worrying about my lack of ID.

Jon confirmed that he had his driving licence on him, so he was okay, but all I had in my pocket was a battered old Santander bank card, so there was only one thing for it. With Derren Brown at the front of my mind, I simply took out my bank card, held it above my head, and with the swagger of one Liam Gallagher, proceeded to walk past the nine-strong security team working on the door, with my friend Jon following behind me.

Once we were inside the LIPA building (Paul and George's old school), we were escorted to our seats in the balcony, which were more or less the last empty seats in the room. We both sat there, beyond excited and both wondering, *How in all the world did this actually happen?* Wendy, who was sitting on the main floor, had spotted me and no doubt thought the same, and I waved at her with probably the biggest smile on my face ever.

Imagine the scene, two Beatles fanatics from Blackburn, Lancashire, who knew that we now claimed to have more than 4000 holes, had managed to blag our way into the Liverpool Institute. We were a matter of feet away from the two chairs on stage. Jarvis Cocker from Pulp would be sitting on one of them, asking the questions, and the guy who wrote *Yesterday, Blackbird,* and *Here There and Everywhere*, on the other one. And to top it all off, George Martin's son Giles was doing the sound. It really felt like we were dreaming.

Unbelievably, I almost blew it from the start. Even though we were told that there would be strictly no photographs or videos, me being me decided to risk it. I needed some proof of what was happening. But within seconds of starting to record it on my phone, they pounced, and it was made very clear to me that it would not be worth risking it again.

Even Jarvis seemed a little nervous in the presence of such musical greatness, and the hour flew by with tales of Paul's early school days at our venue, and song writing sessions with John. Jarvis thanked him, and I was just about getting my head around how amazing the afternoon had been, when the unthinkable happened.

Just when we thought that things could not get any better, they did.
Paul stood up from his chair, told us that he had a surprise for us all, and I watched with open eyes as the curtains behind him rolled back to reveal a drum kit, some amps, and his band members waiting for him to pick up his bass. Jon and I looked at each other in disbelief. *Was this really happening?* We were in a room in Liverpool, with 200 people at the most, and Paul McCartney was just about to play a secret gig for us all. Does life get any better?

The next hour was magical, and Paul enchanted us with his 11-song set, which included, *I've Just Seen a Face, San Francisco Blues* (cover), *Every Night, From Me to You* (apparently the first time he had played it live since 1964), *Mrs Vanderbilt* (Wings), *On My Way to Work, Love Me Do, Confidante, I Lost My Little Girl* (first time since 2003), *Midnight Special* (cover), and ending the best live gig I have ever attended with The Beatles' *We Can Work It Out.*

What we had witnessed was very special, and the fact that we were a matter of feet away from the stage was the absolute icing on the cake. Not wanting to leave the building in a hurry, I found myself just slowly wandering around after the show and bumping into Jarvis. Under normal circumstances, Jarvis would have been the main celebrity in the room, but on this occasion he also seemed just happy to be there. I explained that I hated asking for selfies, but as he was Jarvis Cocker, how could I not? Then I wandered over to Giles Martin at the sound desk, and asked if he would sign my ticket. I found him to be charming.

After John and I eventually both prised ourselves out of the building and massively thanked the guy on the door for the experience he had given us, we walked across the road to have a pint in the pub made famous by The Beatles, Ye Cracke, and to try to let what we had experienced sink in. No sooner had I taken a couple of sips from my drink than I received a message from Wendy, informing me that Paul was now on his way to The Cavern.

During his question-and-answer session at LIPA, he had hinted that he would be doing a (another) secret gig in the city the following day, so it made sense that it would be The Cavern and that he would be visiting the venue to start to sort things out. Needless to say, we left our pints and made our way as quickly as we could over to Mathew Street.

There was a busker strumming his acoustic guitar at the top of the road, next to the John Lennon statue, and I remembered advising him to start playing Beatles tunes as Macca was on his way. Once inside The Cavern, I actually stopped everybody on their way out, explaining to them that it might be worth hanging around a little longer as a Beatle was on his way. But no matter how much I tried to convince them, they really didn't believe me. As it turned out, we were unable to hang around for too long, so I have no idea if he ever did show his face.

Paul ended up playing The Cavern the following night, but tickets were like gold dust, and you had to have been standing outside the Arena first thing that morning to stand any chance of ending up with one. I was gutted that I had missed out, but felt that I shouldn't be greedy, as I had already attended a secret performance by him the previous day. Even though I hadn't actually met Paul, it had more or less been the next best thing, and I had a photo taken next to a life-sized cardboard cut-out of him to send to my mate Tony.

What I did find funny though was when ITV were filming outside The Cavern and interviewing the lucky folk who had managed to bag themselves a ticket for the show. There in the background was a certain Scouse busker, strumming songs by the Fab Four.

As if that wasn't enough excitement for one year already, the following month I found myself ticking another of the things off my wish list, when I visited the holy grail of musical venues, in Abbey Road Studios in London. Very few people have the pleasure of venturing inside, unless they are lucky enough to record there. I spotted an advert online that for the first time a handful of people would be able to attend a studio tour and lecture, and I knew that I simply had to be there. Initially, I had sorted it for me and Emma to go, feeling that she would hopefully love it – I certainly knew I would. But just before we were due to go, Emma found out that she might have to work, so I ended up inviting my mate Strang to share the experience with me.

What was hilarious was that once we arrived, near the front of the queue, just outside the building, was my good friend Derek and his family. Not only did I not have a clue that he had been planning to attend, but now he was actually ahead of me in the line. After I got over the shock of him actually being there, Derek explained to me that week after week, when we had been having a beer together in The Drummers Arms, he had listened to me harping on about visiting the world-famous studio. But he hadn't had the heart to steal my thunder and admit that he was attending.

What a magnificent afternoon we all had, spending time in Studio 2, and finding out about the equipment, along with the recording techniques that were used by John, Paul, George, and Ringo. I couldn't believe that the exact same pianos used on the recording of *A Day In The Life* were actually still there for us to enjoy and appreciate.

We naturally had a photo of us taken on the legendary steps leading up to the control room, and had the opportunity to venture inside and told about all the musicians who had used it. All in all, our trip down South was wonderful, and even though I would have liked Emma to have been with me to experience it, I knew that Strang had loved it, too. So I chose well.

I can just about cope with people who say that they don't like The Beatles, as music is about personal taste (even though theirs must be terrible!). But to say they are rubbish and overrated, simply proves a lack of knowledge, as the Fab Four changed the music industry forever, in every way.

On Saturday, 8th September, our fourth Confessional took place, and it was certainly eventful. Yet again, we had worked on the festival for months, and yet again, I felt I had booked my best line-up to date. We had the theme of 'Out Of This World', so it was Kev's job to work out how we (he) could build a rocket and the UFO I had asked for.

I booked a band from Glasgow called The Ninth Wave, who had impressed me at Kendal the previous year. And I had Welsh Indie Rockers Trampolene and Manchester-based Pins to headline, having seen them a couple of times live. Being honest, though, the act I was the most excited about was acquiring Dexy's legend Kevin Rowland to end the event, spinning some Soul classics on the decks and hopefully joining in with them if he was in the mood.

Who would have thought back when I was pulling some shapes to *Geno* back in the 80s, in a sweaty club (Friargate Youth Club), that one day I would be booking the main man himself and putting him on in my hometown.

As with our previous three events, the weeks leading up to it were full on, and we found ourselves spending longer and longer in church, preparing it for that year's congregation. The night before the event, it was all hands to the pump as usual, but unusually my mate Smith failed to turn up, which worried me slightly. On the morning of Confessional, there was still no sign of him, and his phone was turned off.

I had always booked Smith to DJ my events, and it was unlike him to be missing and not helping out. The event was starting at 2pm, and when it got to 12.30pm, I had a funny feeling he was not going to show. I couldn't have an event without a DJ, and it was far too late in the day to cancel, so I was starting to get extremely stressed. I asked my mate Birchy if he could pick Kevin Rowland up from Manchester, as I trusted him not to ask him for a selfie or an autograph and to stay professional at all times, even though I planned to do both at some stage in the proceedings.

What was funny was that afterwards, when I asked Ian what Kevin talked about during the journey, he hilariously replied, 'Nothing. I think he thought I was an Uber driver.'

Ian brought Kevin to the church so that I could introduce myself and show him his dressing room. I explained that we weren't quite ready for his soundcheck yet, but arranged for Ian to take him to his hotel and promised I would call him as soon as we were ready for him. I had already dropped off some of Kevin's rider at his hotel room that morning, and was buzzing to have such a well-known artist involved in Confessional.

Time was running out and still no word from Smith, so I made the executive decision to ask another DJ that I knew if he would be okay to do it. There is absolutely no doubt that Ainsley saved the day, for which I was extremely grateful, but I was wound up and stressed and it was not long off us letting folk in.

From our very first event, Keely and Courtney had been involved in Confessional and worked as Artist Liaison on the day, but even they hadn't turned up. That just added to my stress, even though stress was the last road I could afford to go down. They eventually swanned into church just as we were opening, and due to how wound up I was and the fact that the rest of the team had been working for hours, I remember taking them into the dressing room and having a right go at them. It was totally out of character and they had never seen me like this. And even though I still feel that I had a point at the time, I really do regret handling it in the way that I did, on the day.

I seem to remember my mate Derek stood in at the last minute to help with their role (as always), and the event itself was amazing. The only other questionable moment was when our headline band, Pins, invited everybody on stage towards the end of their set, and my sound guy Blake went mental with me (not so sound) as he felt as though his equipment was getting damaged. Other than that, everybody had yet again had a fabulous time dancing the night away in our magnificent church.

Everybody but Smith that is. He eventually rocked up around 3.30pm (an hour and a half after it had started) clutching his bags of CDs, but unfortunately out of his head (on something), declaring, 'Okay, I'm here.'

The one thing I was distraught about, and do blame Smith for, is while I was full on trying to deal with my lack of DJ problem, I completely forgot to give Kevin a call, and I was horrified when I looked at my phone to find missed messages and voice calls from the man himself. The one time I had the opportunity to work with Mr Rowland and I had come across as unreliable, which I certainly was not. But to be fair, Kevin was cool about it once I explained. (But still.)

2019 saw Janet set off on a cruise with her sisters, leaving me home alone. And then we both headed over to Switzerland, and I fell in love with the place. Switzerland had never been a destination on my radar, but when I was a child, my Grandma Edna and Grandad Jim had visited the country and had a painting of one of the lakes hung up in their living room. What inspired me to step on a plane was that I kept seeing these magical photos on Instagram of a place called Grindelwald – apparently the most Instagrammed destination in the world – and I knew that we had to visit. It was a little like when I saw the images of the Seychelles all those years ago.

We were not disappointed, as it turned out to be the most beautiful place we had ever been. From the minute we arrived in the country, the views were stunning, and even the trains were on another level (few levels) to what we are used to – double decker, clean, modern, and on time. So, the opposite of Northern Rail.
Yet again, we sat in First Class by mistake and were asked to either pay a fair bit of money extra, or move into our designated level. To be fair, their Second Class was a lot better that our First Class, by far. At one point in the journey the views out of the window were incredible, revealing wonderful lakes surrounded by snow-capped mountains. To my astonishment, all the people sitting in our carriage were just staring at their phones! I don't care if they lived there and witnessed that view every day of their lives, I just found it to be really sad. But I guess it's just a sign of the times, which is even worse.

Our hotel was about 20 seconds away from the train station, and every morning I used to stand on our balcony and simply stare in amazement at the view of the Eiger mountain, directly in front of us. No matter how many times I did this, I was simply blown away by the view and never got used to it.

If it is nightlife you are after, then Grindelwald is not for you, but if you enjoy magnificent views of snow-capped mountains, ski slopes, and beautiful log cabins for miles in every direction you happen to look, then I highly recommend you boarding that plane. And I for one can't wait to return.

August that year saw me stage NATM10 – an absolute milestone of which I am proud. I booked The Blinders (acoustic), who were one of the most talked about young bands around and were certainly going places. Italian singer/songwriter Julia Bardo, and Millie McLeod from Clitheroe, made up my line-up. The Blinders were used to playing raucous shows, and to agree an acoustic set was rare for them and would most certainly be a treat for our audience. After our first couple of gigs in the Victorian gallery, it was clear that we would only be able to host acoustic acts and not full-on electric bands, as there was far too much expensive art in the room to risk anything happening. When The Blinders showed up carrying electric guitars and amps, I panicked, imagining that Rebecca would pull it, as this was against what we had agreed. But I had a word with their sound engineer and pleaded with them to make sure it was stripped back. And to be fair on them, they kept to their word and their set was fantastic.

Their lead singer Tom told me afterwards that he actually loved the experience, as it was a total change for them. He explained that normally at their shows, the audience would be jumping up and down, going mental, so playing for an audience who simply sat and listened to them was a pleasure.

Julia was in a hotly tipped band called Working Men's Club from Todmorden who I had booked to perform at that year's Confessional, but she informed me at the museum that she was leaving the band to concentrate on her solo career. So this gig at the museum was extra special, as it was one of the first solo gigs that she played. Julia has recently signed to Wichita, the Cribs' old label, so hopefully her future is looking bright.

At college I had been asked to mentor a young student in the Music department who told me he was in a band called Northern Sports Club. I was in Clitheroe with Strang, watching his son's band The Ruby Tuesdays, when I recognised the name of the band that was supporting them, so hung around to support my student. They were really good – a lot better than I had imagined – but I was absolutely blown away by their lead singer, Millie. I thought her tone was amazing, and with a bit of a jazz vibe it was a welcome change from the norm. After the gig, I introduced myself and told her that I would like to book her for my next event.

As soon as I started booking for NATM10, Millie was the first name I wrote down to play the event.
Just before the museum show, someone told me that it was going to be Millie's 21st Birthday the day after the gig, so just before the sound checks, I legged it over to Marks and Spencer to buy her a cake, and then called at the market to buy her two helium balloons. I felt it was a nice touch; I mean, you are only 21 once.

I purchased four balloons in total – a 2 and a 1 for Millie, and a 1 and a 0 to place in the bar area to celebrate staging our 10th event. I placed Millie's just inside her dressing room, along with the cake, and when she arrived I proudly pointed out to her the effort we (me) had made, only for her to turn around and say, 'Thank you, Pete, that is really kind of you, but I am in fact 20, not 21.'
Feeling pretty stupid, and in an attempt to save some face, I quickly thought of damage limitation, and recommended that she take the 2 from the dressing room and collect the 0 from the bar on her way out, but I am sure she still thought I was mad.

The following month saw us stage our fifth Confessional, but this time we ran it over two days – Friday night and Saturday. I had chosen a rainforest theme and remember Kev's response when I told him I wanted a waterfall. It was far too rude to mention in this book. Kev being Kev, though, called me a couple of days later, and I was thrilled when he told me that he'd had an idea, as always.

I ended up booking 19 acts in total, and it really was my best line-up to date. If I didn't feel confident of improving on previous events, then I couldn't see the point of putting in the effort.

I had been determined to book a 100% all female line-up for our Friday night. But The Blinders, who were booked to play on Saturday, were offered a gig in London with The Specials on the same day, so who was I to deny them that experience? They ended up headlining our Friday instead.

More and more festivals are repeatedly announcing more or less male-orientated line-ups year after year, when there are a lot of female acts and artists out there, who are just as good if not better. Also, for some reason, they tend to all book the same old bands for every event, as though it is easier for them.

I have always given myself the rule of never booking the same act more than once for the same event, even though at times I would love to. I consider it to be lazy booking, highlighting a lack of imagination, effort, and knowledge, but that is just my take on things. I have always been proud of my line-ups and by the fact that I book a fair number of female acts. I mean, why wouldn't I? I have never booked an act just because they are female; I book them because they are talented and exciting, and long may that continue.

I had watched Manchester band Witch Fever more or less from the start, and witnessed them getting better and better in their live performances. I was slightly worried about putting them on in a church, but I knew that I had to, and they didn't disappoint. The Blinders almost blew the roof off the church, and the Saturday night really did belong to Red Rum Club from Liverpool. I still get a buzz off watching the footage of the crowd singing and dancing in the pews as they performed *Would You Rather Be Lonely?* It really was wonderful.

International Teachers of Pop ended our 5th Confessional with a Synth party, and everybody went home happy.

To actually be in a position where I can put on events in a museum and a church is a blessing (no pun intended), but it is only ever made possible with the support of a number of people. Without Rebecca and her wonderful team, I would never be able to bring such magnificent artists to perform there. I can honestly say that I have loved every act and performance that I have booked for them, and having a like-minded, music-loving audience really does enhance the experience.

I remember being with Emma at a Sound City conference in Liverpool, and we were just making our way over to one of the lectures, when we noticed a young singer performing at the top of the stairs. She impressed me so much at the time that our lecture went on the back burner. After she finished, I went over and explained that I put on special events, but she probably thought, *Yeah, alright, they all say that!* – but in a Scouse accent. The singer was called Esme Bridie, and I was chuffed to bits to book her to perform at our museum, feeling that she would go down a treat.

My only concern was that Esme had a delightful, delicate voice and mesmerising tone, and I worried that if our audience talked through her set, she wouldn't be heard. As it turned out, I had no cause to worry; on the night you could have heard a pin drop. Our audience was so respectful, and Esme sounded beautiful. I remember being so impressed that I got on the mic to thank them, and Esme told me she had loved it and was blown away by our crowd.

I feel extremely lucky to have staged Confessional festival for five years running in our church. The support of our local councillor Phil is what puts me in a position to make it happen, but it would also be impossible without the efforts and support of the fabulous team that I rely on each year to make my vision into reality. I feel I have got to know some really special people over the years through being involved in these events, and for this I will always be grateful. I now have a pretty young team supporting the more experienced people like Kev. I brought in Courtney, who is actually best friends with my niece, Beckie, so I remember her as a toddler. Connor and Beckie are my new

Artist Liaison, and Beckie's mum Helen and sister Heidi help on the arts team. Also, in 2019 I secured the services of Nicola as our Project Manager for that year, to help chase up possible funding, as she had experience running The Ramsbottom, Head for the Hills festival. And we have the ever-reliable Jason, who is our building manager every year, and who never lets us down.

I really do think the world of everybody who helps to make such a positive thing happen in our town, and hope they know how much I appreciate their efforts. It also means the world to me that Janet and Emma get involved, and even though I have always hoped that my brother would now and again show his face, to see what I have achieved, I guess it just isn't his thing.

Growing up, I always tried to model myself on Mr Paul Weller, taking photos to the hairdresser and buying my shoes from the same shop on Carnaby Street as him. I certainly didn't put any effort into looking like Ian Brown.

As I was walking into Kendal Calling site, a couple of festival-goers outside their tent shouted, 'Oi, it's Ian Brown!', obviously taking the mick. Later that afternoon, a couple of girls came over to me asking if they could have a photo with me, which was extremely strange. But when it happened again, I started to get pretty freaked out. What was even stranger was when I went into Tim Peaks' diner to purchase a drink, and as I was about to pay for it, the man behind the counter said, 'You're a musician, aren't you?' It didn't matter how many times I told him that I wasn't, he absolutely refused to take any money off me, insisting that I was. So in the end I just went along with it.

Not long after that, the comedian Russell Brand played Blackburn at King George's Hall, and as I was purchasing tickets, Janet made me promise not to get tickets near the front. She said she would die of humiliation if he actually spotted us in the crowd and turned any attention on her, so I did as I was told.

BUT I'M DIFFERENT NOW

We were sitting midway back so that she felt safe, and around halfway through his routine, he managed to climb off stage and began heading in our direction. (You couldn't write it, even though I just have.) I hadn't noticed the look of horror on Janet's face at the time, but Russell continued to shove past the packed-out crowd and made his way over to us, and ended up sitting on my and Janet's knees. He was looking in Janet's direction, so I thought I had got away with his attention, when all of a sudden he turned to face me and declared to the audience, 'It's Ian Brown's dad!' (How old does he bloody think I am?!)
Janet found it hilarious, the audience found it hilarious, and just in case anyone was struggling to see it, the incident was shown live on a giant screen on the stage. The following day, I was just about to go into M&S for my lunch, when I heard a voice shout from across the road on Northgate, 'It's Ian Browns' dad!' It took months for me to live this down.

Back at work, I was struggling more and more, as I was spending less and less time supporting students and spending the majority of my time attempting to complete what I considered to be meaningless paperwork. There is a reason why I have never applied for an admin job, it's because I am bloody rubbish at it. My main problem was that I had been struggling with my short-term memory since I had returned from my very long absence, and it had got to the stage where I was dreading going in

I had reduced my hours to two-and-a-half days and then to two, but even though I had spent the past two years telling anybody who would listen that I felt I was letting my team down, because the paperwork side of things was just not for me, and my boss kept telling me they would find me a more appropriate job role, nothing every changed.

Things actually came to a head on 23rd September that year (2019), when I was pulled up about not doing my paperwork quickly enough. Even my previous manager had asked me why I was putting myself through all this when I could just simply concentrate on my music, which is what I was good at – her words, not mine. I ended up taking her advice and walking out of college, and never going back. I was not prepared to let my team down, especially Linda, and I was not prepared to be carried by them.

My mum was ill at the time, and my health was always going to come out top over the chance to earn more money, so after nearly 18 years of working in education, I made the decision to retire.
If I hadn't been as ill as I had been, then I am sure I would have never considered this luxury, but I had been given another chance to make the most out of life and, the truth be known, I had far too many records to play, far too many books I wanted to read, and far too many beaches I wanted to visit, to waste my time doing paperwork. So that was it.

I was not saying that I was never going to work again, but I was going to be careful to choose something I was passionate about, and maybe even volunteer somewhere at some stage in the future.

We spend our lives dragging ourselves out of bed at some unearthly hour every morning for some moron in the government to raise the retirement age to 67, when it should have been reduced. Well, I am sorry, but all work and not enough play makes Pete a dull boy. So, 55 it is then.

CHAPTER FORTY-TWO

'WHAT IS THAT DADDY, A PLATE?'

Being able to drink hardly any alcohol would certainly save me some money, and for as long as I could still afford the latest vinyl releases, along with a selection of concert tickets, I reckoned everything would be fine.

I knew I had a problem when it came to buying vinyl, along with clothes, but to be fair I always have had. From the minute I started receiving any spending money or earning a fiver a day on Pat's chicken farm, a chunk of my funds has always gone on record buying. From Punk singles to Beatles rarities, to more recently limited coloured vinyl, I have always been obsessed. Unfortunately, I had about 80% of my record collection nicked from my flat at Mill Hill, and spent decades attempting to replace them all.

In 1982, the year The Jam split up, we were introduced to a little round silver disc, and initially I was taken in by the hype. The compact disc was hailed as a revolution in music and was co-developed by Philips (up the road from me) and Sony, to store and play digital audio. I remember purchasing *True Blue* by Madonna, and *Making Movies* by Dire Straits on CD, before I even had a CD player. But even though I have hundreds in my collection, I could never fall in love with them in the way I have with vinyl.

The arrival of this new shiny product meant that most people were starting to sell their record collections, if they hadn't already done so when they got married. In some cases, people had even given them away (as if). Luckily, even though I fell into the trap of spending my money on this cheap looking disc, I had no desire to get rid of mine.

I have no idea what photographers must have thought at the time, but I can't believe they were enamoured, as a 12inch square LP cover is the perfect canvas to showcase their image of choice.
I felt this was lost on a CD, and most of the time I struggled to even read the sleeve notes on the accompanying booklet. When you pick up an album, it feels as though it is the perfect size, and how it should be. It provides such enjoyment, going through the routine of carefully taking it out of its sleeve and holding it in a certain way, and the smell of it. Selecting side A, and placing it perfectly on the turntable, selecting the speed, lifting the needle, and slowly dropping it at the start of the correct spot in the grooves. Just that experience alone is enough to win me over, but added to that, the piece of art actually plays.

I know folk always argue that the music sounds warmer on vinyl, and to me it really does. The analogue format, made of polyvinyl chloride, was the main vehicle for the commercial distribution of Pop music from the 1950s until the late 1980s. In the 80s there were more than 2,300 independent music shops in the UK, but by 2009 only 269 remained, which was shocking when I think about the hours I spent in them growing up, and the education they brought me. By the turn of the millennium, CDs were partially replaced by streaming services which, at the risk of sounding old, is really not my thing. I mean, folk only download their songs of choice. I know that sounds ideal, but imagine not hearing the whole album as the artist intended you to hear it! It just isn't for me. I remember watching an interview with Richard Hawley, who said he had woken up one morning in cold sweats, wondering where his music actually was, as it felt invisible to him.

In 2007, a campaign to save the record shop from becoming extinct started, called Record Store Day or RSD, and it has been an annual event ever since – to my bank manager's dismay. The plan is to celebrate the culture of the independently owned stores, and it brings together fans, artists, and a limited number of specially pressed records, coloured vinyl, live recordings, one-off releases, which are only distributed to the stores that participate.

Every April, I set my alarm (Janet) for some ridiculously early hour in the morning, and with my mate Mick, who is as crazy as me, make our way over to my local record shop to join the queue. Some people in the queue have been there for a few hours, and in some cases over a day.

You pray that it won't be raining, though it is usually freezing, and you see the usual suspects every time. About 7:30am, the shop owner rocks up, looking warmer than you and as if they have had more sleep than you, and proceeds to hand out much welcome brews and bacon butties to everyone, which to be fair is good of him, even though he is just about to empty your wallet.

At 8am, you are allowed into the shop one by one, in the order you were standing in the queue, and given permission to choose just five items – not the same vinyl more than once. If you want any more, you are told to go and re-join the line.

One year, the band, Temples, brought out a really cool looking patterned picture disc, and I was determined to get it. The problem was that I had mentioned this to some people in front of me in the queue when they asked me what I was after. The shop only had five copies of this sort after vinyl, and the guy in front of me picked up the last one. I didn't know the guy and he had never heard of the band, but he told me that I had bigged it up so much that he'd decided to give it a try.

That taught me a lesson, and it was the last time I revealed my list to enthusiasts queueing up. At the end of the day, I did shame him into selling it to me, even though it had been a mission.

In 2017, even though I was still recovering from my treatment, I was determined to still write my want list and go along. My mate Mick, who also loved vinyl, kindly drove us over to Clitheroe, Townshend Records, in his van, and by the time we arrived it was around 7:30am and I was 11th in the queue. After about 15 minutes standing there freezing, I ended up fainting on the pavement, as I was still extremely weak. Mick kindly ran off to his van to get me a chair to sit on, and when I came round, I thought that this would at least get me to the front of the line (every cloud). I was wrong, and just to prove how competitive vinyl lovers are, they made sure I ended up back in 11th place in the queue. So not even cancer could get me in any sooner.

I am glad to report that from 2007, vinyl sales started to pick up, and more and more music stores began to open up again. Figures show that vinyl sales in the UK have been growing for the past 13 years in a row, and in 2020 showed the highest sales since the early 90s. I am still that person that if my favourite artists release their record in red, white, and green vinyl, I will attempt to collect the lot. Nothing gives me more pleasure (well, almost nothing; playing them is slightly better) than visiting a record shop of choice – Action Records in Preston, Townshend Records in Clitheroe, Drumbeat Pete's in Chorley, or Hebden Bridge Records, run by my mate Dan – having hours to spend fingering through the racks in an attempt to find some gem I have been after for ages, or simply discovering something new, and chatting to like-minded people in the store, exchanging tales of limited editions or 'did you get that one in pink?'.

This will always be my chosen format, as I suppose it is what I grew up with. Nowadays, folk have the option of all the streaming platforms like Spotify and Apple, and even though I am sent links to them on a regular basis, I flatly refuse to sign up to any of them. For as long as they continue to rip off musicians, then you can count me out. I know I am a record label marketing manager's dream, as I purchased an album in the 70s; had it nicked from my flat, so bought it again; then bought it on CD in the 80s; then again on MP3 in 2001; purchased the re-mastered issue in 2008; and the blue, red, and yellow version in 2017; and in 2020, I ordered the signed, dinked version. So now I have purchased the same LP a massive nine times. They must love folk like me.

Records never let you down, and I even enjoy the sound of static and the frequent crackling you get in between songs. I am proud of my record collection, and there is no doubt at all that when I finally pop my clogs (not yet) Emma will be the very proud owner of one of the best collections around. Well, around here anyway.

CHAPTER FORTY-THREE

TOP TEN

Nine Nine Nine (999) was the first live gig I attended, and ever since that fateful night, I have spent a large part of my life attending live concerts, music festivals, or anything that gives me that fix for a live performance. And I have been lucky enough to have seen the majority of bands and artists I have ever liked. Obviously, I would give anything to go back in time to be in the audience when The Beatles performed at The Cavern, and that footage of them singing *Some Other Guy* remains my favourite footage of all time; I never get bored of it.

I would have given anything to have witnessed Nat King Cole or Frank, from back in the day, or attended Amy in an intimate venue, The Who at the Railway Hotel, Ziggy playing guitar, or The Kinks in their heyday. But seriously, I can never complain. I have been blessed to have attended my fair share of magical performances, and if I was asked to list my Top 10 attended gigs of all time, it would be difficult because I have attended so many over the years. (I wish I knew how many.)

Paul McCartney in Manchester has always been cited as my favourite, as it was the second time that I had seen him, after the first was ruined by a greedy head. I had taken Emma with me, which was her first time witnessing a Beatle, and the night was perfect, with the highlight for me being when he performed one of my favourites, *All My Loving* on the guitar he originally wrote it on. The only one that could match that, was when I somehow managed to see him at LIPA, as it was an intimate secret set and was truly magical.

Watching The Jam in Paris would definitely fight for a third slot, as it was my first time abroad watching my band from back home. Also, The Jam playing my hometown (X 3).

Dancing in a field watching The Specials at Glastonbury is certainly up there, as it was early evening when the sun was going down and was very special (no pun).

And also the Arctic Monkeys there in 2007.

Having the pleasure of seeing Rodriguez (*Sugar Man*) – first in Manchester with Emma, and then at the Royal Albert Hall with both Janet and Emma – was a wonderful experience. Except for the guy sitting next to me who kept repeating, 'I can't believe I'm sat next to a Mod.' He was clearly more excited than me about this revelation. And 'Searching for Sugar Man' is still the best music documentary I have ever seen.

The absolute legend that is Stevie Wonder headlining Glastonbury in 2010 will always be one of my favourites, as it really was everything that I had hoped it would be, and more, and I knew that I would probably never get the opportunity to see him again.

The Black Lips in Liverpool was unreal, as I had never heard of them at the time and thought they were a new band. I recall posting, 'WOW, this band are going to be massive', which was quite embarrassing as they had actually been together for ten years at that point, but I absolutely loved the gig and it was certainly my kind of chaos.

Talking about chaos, the Dustins Bar Mitzvah reunion gig in Islington, with Simon and Helena, is one I am so glad I attended.

Also, The Coral at Kendal Calling, listening to them perform the *Butterfly House* album, was one I'll always remember.

Dexy's at Liverpool Cathedral in 2013 was epic.

Along with The Enemy in The Guardian Lounge at Glastonbury in 2007.

And I suppose the final selection on my list would have to go to Buzzcocks at King George's Hall (not Drumstick Gate), or The Cribs at Gorilla in Manchester in 2017, as part of their four-night residency at the venue.

I also have to include Juliette and the Licks at Sheffield Leadmill in 2006, when she stage-dived and landed on top of me, nearly knocking me out. She and her band were so amazing live that I went to watch them three times that week, which is a personal record.

Also, I would have to mention Oasis at Maine Road in 96.

Nowadays, I still go and watch as many of my favourite artists and bands as often as I can, and also spend a huge amount of time checking out new and up-and-coming talent. It always gives me a buzz when I see something in a band at the start of their career, that not necessarily everyone else in the room sees, and they then go on to bigger and better things.

I saw a young band from Stockport called Blossoms in 2014 and remember thinking at the time that they were by far the best new band I had ever seen. After their set, I went over to Tom, their lead singer, and said, 'I know it won't really mean anything, as you don't know me, but I spend my life watching up-and-coming bands, and you are without doubt the best I have ever seen.' He shouted the rest of the band over and repeated what I had just said, but I really meant it. Their confidence, musical ability, Tom's swagger in between songs reminding me of a very young John Lennon – I thought they were the full package.

A while later, I was in the bar having a beer with Tom and his brother in Night and Day, and he told me that he did not think they had made it yet, just before their first album was released.

Since then, I have seen them sell out the Ritz, watched them perform on the Pyramid stage at Glastonbury (on TV), and was at their homecoming concert at Edgeley Park, Stockport, when they performed to a massive 13,000 fans in 2019. So I think it is fair to say they have made it now.

CHAPTER FORTY-FOUR

TOUGH TIMES

I had more time on my hands after leaving college, and had a stack-load of music autobiographies waiting to be read, and naturally albums to spin.

Up until several years ago, I was never someone who would read a book. In fact, one book took me two years to get round to finishing, and even though *The Magic Faraway Tree* probably still remains my favourite ever read (even though I wasn't the one reading it at the time), these last two or three years I have enjoyed making the time to read – even though most are music-related.

Around July 2019, my Mum started to feel ill, but she had been housebound for years and refused to visit a doctor or even go to the hospital. She was getting worse and, after a lot of persuasion by Janet, Fiona, Robin, and me, on August 4th she was admitted to Blackburn Hospital and diagnosed with the dreaded cancer.

This awful disease had ended my Dad's life, my Uncle Bill's, and attempted to end my own, and now that word had reappeared again. My mum was 85, and told us she wouldn't be having any chemotherapy. To be fair, I didn't just respect her decision, I actually agreed with her – which was rare.

After my dad passed away, Mum moved from Lammack to a bungalow on Openshaw Drive. But not long afterwards, she had a nasty fall at a car park in town, which knocked her confidence, stopping her from leaving the house. It was upsetting to see her gradually give up on all the things she had loved. Her beloved baking was no longer an activity, and it seemed as though she stopped inviting visitors to call from time to time.

After a few days in hospital, she was sent home for a day, but then re-admitted again. We were told by the nurse that she was now terminal, and in their opinion, only had a matter of days to live. She was taken to a care home in Oswaldtwistle, where we visited her most days. What was so sad was that she told us that she had had enough. She had outlived all her friends and my Dad, and on 12th November, 2019, she peacefully passed away in her sleep.
I am not sure how I feel about seeing both my Dad and my Mum dead, or if that is something that a son or daughter should never see, but at the end of the day it was my and Robin's responsibility, and something that most people must go through at some stage or another.

The hardest part for me (as it was with my Dad) was contacting Emma and breaking the very sad news to her. As always, she put on a very brave face and was there when we needed her, offering her usual amazing support, but I knew deep down that she was devastated. She was always extremely close to her grandparents, as they spent so much time with her in her early years, helping to bring her up and giving her fond childhood memories.

Whilst my mum was ill, she told Janet that she still had the outfit that I was wearing the day they picked me up as a baby from Billinge Hospital. We searched her house several times, and even sent Emma up into her attic a couple of times, but there was zero sign of it, which I was gutted about. I couldn't get my head around why she would throw it out.

The funeral was at Pleasington on Friday 22nd and then over to the Millstone in Mellor, which I feel my Mum would have approved of, being posh and all that. As with my Dad's funeral in 2001, I took comfort from everyone who made the effort to turn up and pay their respects. The majority of my close friends attended – Nicky, Bullinge, Waker, Birchy, and even Jez put in an appearance. From my Unilab days, my friends Sarah, Martin, and Ste k attended, along with my old works manager, Colin and his wife, which was nice. Janet's mum and Fred, and all her sisters were there, along with Emma's best friend, Fallon. I am not too sure how my Mum would have felt about Jez attending her funeral, but it really meant the world to me and Robin, seeing everyone there to pay their respects.

Even though we don't have many family members left any more, it is always a treat on the very rare occasions we do meet up, even under sad circumstances. Anne and Terry from Lancaster had travelled down, along with Mary and Adrian and his wife. Jean made the service at Pleasington, and my Aunty Marion had been there throughout.

We found my mum's old recipe book, and after studying it for a while, Janet tried her hand at following it to make some of her famous Fudgerydoos, which was a nice touch, and delighted my friends, especially Birchy. Margery would have been proud.

It would be a lie to make out that me and my Mum were really close, especially in her final years, because she ended up being really negative about everything, and everyone, which I struggled with. However, there is no doubt at all that she couldn't have wished for better daughters-in-law than Janet and Fiona. I reckon my Mum felt that marrying Janet was my greatest (if not only) achievement, and she was certainly right, because without that event taking place, Emma would not be here.

After I left the college in September 2019, my plan was to spend more time in 2020 putting on my events. Glastonbury was booked, along with Sound City. The Confessional line-up had been boxed off, along with a theme and a number of ticket sales, and on top of having a drawer full of upcoming gig tickets and talk of a family holiday to Barbados, I actually felt that it could be the best year yet. Little did I know.

On the 11th January, 2020, the first death was reported of a 61-year-old man from Wuhan in China, from an alleged new deadly virus that was transmitted from animal to humans. Twelve

days later, it had caused 18 deaths worldwide, and by 15th February, 1,666 deaths were recorded, including the first reported in Europe – a Chinese tourist in France. The more we listened to the news, the more worrying this virus was becoming. On 23rd March, the UK was placed into its first national lockdown, and to be fair, I feel we have more or less been in some kind of lockdown ever since (up North).
Total deaths at that point had reached 15, 436, and had been reported in 167 countries.

Even though the reason we were doing it was not good, for maybe the first time in their lives, people were being forced into changing what would have been the norm and experiencing a new way of living. I hadn't wished the illness on anyone, but I did take a number of positives out of the first lockdown and embraced some of the changes, as I am sure most of us did. Due to there being less cars on the road, pollution levels fully dropped, and I have never noticed birds singing like that before – from the moment I awoke, until fairly late in the evening – and I loved it.

Emma and I went on more or less daily walks up Mellor, taking photos of every type of blooming flower you could think of. They really were beautiful, and I also noticed how friendly people had become. Normally you would go on a walk, and the odd person might say hello or nod their head, but now every single person we bumped into or happened to walk past would say 'Good Morning' or 'Good Afternoon', or even more. We were all in the same boat, and were just happy to see another human being.

We are lucky to have a garden, and I am sure that if I had been stuck in a flat or a house without that luxury, it would have been a lot harder to get through lockdown. For once I put in some time and effort into making our garden look nice, and our regular trips to Barton Grange Garden Centre certainly helped, if not in the wallet.

The first lockdown was when I actually came up with the idea of writing this book. I would get up reasonably early each day, and spend hours in our summerhouse at the bottom of the garden, surrounded by flowers for inspiration, going through pen after pen and on the whole just scribbling memories. Today's date is January 25th, 2021, and we are now in our third national lockdown; the current death figures worldwide are 2.13million, with the UK reaching 97,939.

When I decided to put pen to paper and attempt to write my memoirs as something positive to focus on to help me get through all this, I gave myself a set of rules:

Don't write anything too inappropriate that I wouldn't want my daughter or family to read, even though I am sure they have heard worse.

Don't write anything that might lead to any of my mates getting divorced, or in trouble, for things that might have happened in the past.

And don't preach on about politics, even though I have pretty strong views on the subject. Nobody is interested in how I feel things should be happening.

The one thing I will say is that as this virus has taken over the world, it is a no-brainer that for as long as humans continue to abuse animals and treat them in the way that they do, it is inevitable that things like this will continue to happen.
For some strange reason, the powers-that-be, have waited almost a year before any sort of investigation has even started to determine the source of the virus. It is strongly believed that a live market in Wuhan, China, is where it began, and some experts claim that the probable source of transition may have originated from bats. I have even read that it may have been a pangolin.
Bats have lived on our planet for the best part of 52 million years, and pangolin 80million. What blows my mind is that humans rocked up around 6 million years ago, and instead of respecting the living creatures that had been here a hell of a long time before them, they think that it is fine to start abusing them and throwing

their weight around. Well, it clearly is not, as karma has shown time and time again. Eighty million years calling this planet their home, and now the pangolins are the most trafficked mammal in the world. What is wrong with people? Rant over!

Apart from the odd occasion when restrictions were slightly lifted, for the past ten months I have more or less stayed at home every day writing my memories and nipping out for a daily exercise walk. The last two gigs that Janet and I attended were Bryan Ferry and Elvis Costello at the Palace Theatre in Manchester in March 2020 and February 2021, and I still have no idea when I am going to be attending my next live performance.

Like everyone, my lifestyle has changed dramatically. I have gone from going out on a regular basis, attending gigs in different towns and always seeing people, to watching artists strumming online, and only ever really seeing the window cleaner once every two weeks when he calls to collect his money.

I have no desire to catch COVID-19 and have done all I can to stay safe and keep other people safe, but I feel I have experienced enough in my life for two lifetimes, so I am sure a bit of time off will do me no harm. Yes, all my events are on hold, and yes, my drawer full of gig tickets have now been postponed for the second time, along with the cancellation of our family holiday to Barbados. But it is other people I feel sorry for, and there is no doubt at all that this pandemic is affecting people's mental health in a massive way.

Now I know that we haven't been called up to go and fight in a war and certainly, in my case, it's a matter of 'Pete, stay at home, play your records, read some books, and maybe do some writing, in between Netflix series', so no major hardship, but everyone handles things in a different way. Some elderly people will be lonely and confused, whereas young folk will have all their plans on hold – as do we all. Everything in 2020 was cancelled and now at the start of 2021, nothing has changed. In fact, things are worse.

I think of my nephew, Matt, who can't even go to school to see his friends and get an education. I think of my other nephew, Matt, who is the drummer in a band, for whom things seemed to be taking off and then stopped. I feel for students who have planned for years for their life at Uni, only for them to never see a physical tutor and just be locked away in their dorms.
But most of all I feel for the medical staff and all the frontline workers who are doing everything they can to help others and to keep folk alive. I don't understand why the priority has not been to determine the source and do everything within our power to make sure it never happens again. And I am bored with all the Bill Gates' conspiracy theories. But folk are entitled to their opinions, and I will hold my hand up if they are proved right. I just can't see it myself.

I am angry at all the very selfish people who have been ignoring all the guidelines and doing their own thing without a thought for anybody else. I don't like wearing masks and am not even arguing the case of the effectiveness of them, but you have a choice. And if there is a chance that you might be protecting others, you do it, and do the right thing, in my opinion. Social media and all the fake news is enough to drive anybody crazy, and certainly contributes to folk feeling low. But like I tell my friends, the secret is to simply get through this the best way we can, and at the end of the day, yes, the world has gone crazy, but we are still here to tell the tale.

I know for sure that my Mum would not have handled this very well, and it has been a blessing that she didn't have to go through it.

CHAPTER FORTY-FIVE

AND IN THE END

After my mum passed away, I went through a box of old black and white family photographs that I found in her attic, some dating back to as far as 1906. I have always loved photographs and knew we were lucky to discover these. They really are incredible, and I learned stuff about my family that I didn't have a clue about. Some of them had information on the back, which was a godsend, and some had been left blank. I spent weeks studying and researching these wonderful finds and discovered family members I never even knew existed, which was exciting. I also saw my parents in a completely different light.

A few of the photographs featured William Brandwood Burrows, who was the youngest of the five sons of my Great-Grandpa Robert Burrows, who lived on Holland Street in Blackburn. He was an Officer and pilot in the Second World War, and in September 1939, he joined the RAF, receiving a commission at Christmas in 1940.
Apparently that Christmas was the last time my Grandma Edna had 13 family members around her dinner table in Roe Lee Park, as in July 1941, William went out on a bombing expedition on the Monday, and on the following day his parents received a telegram saying that he was missing and presumed dead. It was discovered many years later by our family that Bill had been shot down in a wooden plane mine lying in the Keel Canal in Germany.

I posted one photo per day on relevant Facebook pages, such as Memories of Blackburn and the Talbot Archive, and was amazed when folk left comments that they had known my Mum and Dad years before. Someone even posted that my Grandma was the only person in Roe Lee Park to own a phone, and that people used to call round to use it (which is mad).

I felt that it is a massive shame that I did not have the chance to discuss these magnificent finds whilst my parents and grandparents were alive, and that was my main inspiration for writing this book whilst I still have the opportunity. I say book, but it is really a collection of my life memories. There might be a book in it; that is down to others to decide. I haven't written it for other people, though. I have done it for me, and maybe as something to leave Emma, even though she might think worse of me after reading it!

When I think back about becoming a dad at 29, even though it was the best thing to happen to me – despite what Mary said all those years before – I didn't have a clue how I would handle it. I clearly remember the very first time I took Emma out in her pram, and we went to Roe Lee Park, where I had grown up. I was sitting on a bench at the top of the path (not there now), and I know it sounds stupid, but I remember thinking we were only borrowing her, meaning that everything you have in life – possessions, land, etc – you don't really own anything. It's only for a period of time whilst you are here.

In Emma's case, I meant that in the natural progression of things, we would pass away before her, and my love for her was so strong that I was trying to get my head around the fact that I wouldn't be around forever to be there for her, look after her, and protect her, all the way through life. That is how my mind actually works.

She was a delight during her time at nursery and did us proud (as well as herself) whilst at school. She was made Prom Queen in her final year, and voted the pupil most likely to become famous, which she found funny. She did amazingly well to get her degree at Salford University, and I can never believe our luck that she didn't do the things that I did when growing up (disrespectful behaviour, and parties at every opportunity).

The biggest thing that upsets me in life is that my Dad did not stay around long enough to witness what a beautiful young lady she has turned into, inside and out. He idolised her, as did my Mum, and he would have been so proud (maybe he can).

Behaviour is learnt, and despite the fact that my Mum would constantly point out my faults to Emma and highlight the things I did wrong (in her opinion), the principles and morals that Janet (and hopefully me, too) taught her, has helped her to develop into what she has become. She could have chosen dancing on tables in Benidorm – not that there is anything wrong with that – but instead her choice was to go and explore India and volunteer in the Himalayan mountains for a week whilst she was there. From volunteering at a local food bank, to now managing an Oxfam shop in Manchester, we really couldn't be prouder of her. I will be the first to admit that my legacy to Emma has not been teaching her too much academic stuff (i.e. maths and English), as I tended to leave that to Janet and my mum and dad. But it is safe to acknowledge that her deep love of music (recorded and live) has mainly come from one person, me, and I couldn't be happier about that.

I consider myself extremely lucky and blessed that I regularly attend live gigs with my daughter, and on the whole we love the same bands. We share a mutual love of The Beatles, and our favourite current band is The Cribs. She helps and advises me with my events, and even nicks the odd band t-shirt off me when she is visiting home. Even though I did grow to appreciate Nat, Frank, and Dean, I could never imagine doing any of that with my Dad, so I really am very lucky.

When I was ill with cancer, there was no way it was an option for me not to hang around. I mean, if Emma decides one day that she wants to settle down, I will need to be here to vet her chosen partner for at least a number of years, so I am going nowhere.

They say that behind every great man is a great woman, and even though that is certainly not how I would describe myself

(self-praise and all that), I would 100% describe Janet in that way. June 16th, 1990 was without a doubt the best decision of my life, and anyone that knows us would definitely agree wholeheartedly. I have always said that no way would any other human on the planet put up with me, and I know that Janet really hates it when I say this, but it really is true. I really chose well.

Janet should take the credit for how Emma has turned out, and she has always been there to support me, like a rock. I always see her as some sort of Wonder Woman, as not much seems to faze her or get the better of her – apart from pigeons.
I feel our relationship has stood the test of time because we haven't lived in each other's pockets and have allowed each other to do our own thing. We didn't get rid of our individual friends, which is so important, and we didn't get rid of our interests (why would you?). And having been married for 31 years this June, it proves that we must have done something right.

I would certainly not describe myself as normal, and usually attempt to go against the norm. I would like to think that's even down to the clothes I wear (not always fitting in). I was probably the only person on the planet to walk out of *Star Wars*, when it was first been shown at the cinema, but I feel I enjoyed *Confessions of a Pop Performer* a lot more anyway.

That also includes the effort I have put in over the years in explaining to Janet why it is not an option to have a mirror over our fire, like everyone else. Just because your grandparents, your neighbours, and your friends, choose to hang a mirror in the same place in their homes, doesn't mean that we need to do it. In fact, I see that as a very good reason not to. 'Oh well, it makes the room look bigger.' No it doesn't. It just looks like you are copying everyone else.
When I used to attend Bogart's nightclub in Darwen, one of the walls was covered in a massive mirror, and I didn't think, *Blimey, this club looks a lot bigger than I imagined*. But being honest, I did think they had an extra room on the times I was drunk.

I am pleased that Emma knows her own mind and that she values being an individual. Where she differs from me is that she doesn't look up to people in the music industry (in general), and thinks they are special or any different from us. I will never forget the time when she was helping to run a vintage shop in Manchester, called Junk. A young lad walked in and started to chat her up in an American accent. He told Emma that he and his dad were over from California, as his dad was playing a couple of gigs. Emma no doubt just imagined that he would be playing a pub, but in fact he was performing at his two sold out shows at the Bridgewater Hall.

I remember receiving a text from her asking if I had ever heard of someone called Burt Bacharach, to which I replied, 'Yes, of course. He is one of the most important people in music.' And she explained that she was currently chatting to his son, Oliver, in the shop. She told me that he was going to call in the following day to see her again, and I messaged her that no matter what, she had to marry this guy (imagine!). But Emma, being Emma, had in fact booked the following day off work. (True story.)

She is not impressed by people with money or flashy cars and, like me, finds conversations along those lines one of the biggest turn-offs. I'll always treasure the memories of when I used to take her to Blackpool (as my family had done with me, when I was a child). It was an annual tradition to visit the Pleasure Beach, in order for us to go on the Ghost Train, the Monorail, and then the beach. Recently it has been on the news that the Monorail was destroyed in a fire, and when Emma heard about it, she was gutted.

I also consider myself to be extremely lucky to have a group of mates that I met in the first year of secondary school, and despite the fact that we all have separate lives, different beliefs, and different interests, our friendship has until now lasted the best part of 46 years. And rarely a day goes by when we don't communicate in some way.

Nicky is still working for the Environment Agency, and Simon for the NHS. Bullinge finally left the Post Office after over 36 years' service, lasted a week at another job, and then went back to work for the post. Ste H is still delivering letters, and Jez is still Jez, and to be fair, is currently employed. Karl is working all the hours he can at BAE, and Waker has retired, bought an RV, a puppy, and a guitar, and is making the most out of life. When Birchy left the Army, he spent a year and three months working as a housekeeper/security at Freddie Mercury's old house, and told me that even Freddie's two cats had their own websites. He then worked in Armed Response and is currently still in the London Police.

As for Covid, we have no idea when these pandemic restrictions are due to end. It really is like living in an episode of *Black Mirror*, and I am desperately missing live music (attending and putting it on). I look forward to the time that we see it return, in some form, but I am sure that things will never quite be the same again.

The only option musicians have these days is to stream their live performances online, to a virtual or invisible audience, and to be fair some have been pretty decent. My favourite has to be a number of weeks ago when Andy Crofts, The Moons/Paul Weller, was playing a set from his house. He was halfway through his set when his family apparently returned home earlier than expected. This resulted in his two young daughters barging into the room and attempting to jump on him, then running around the room, jumping up and down and shouting – all this while he was live on air, and in the middle of his performance. But the best part was when his partner Tara shouted from the hallway, 'I thought you were doing the hoovering!' Absolutely brilliant, and one of my highlights in lockdown for sure.

I have enjoyed writing this book and my memories, and in some way it may have been a little therapeutic. Going over the moments in my life, good and bad, has enabled me to address the things I am not proud of, as well as reliving special moments. My Dad would never have believed I would end up passing a degree, working almost two decades in education, putting on my own events, and writing a book.

Who would have imagined that the artists I had watched on *Top of the Pops* would be the artists I would end up working with one day. I have shaken hands with Frankie Valli, discussed Les Dawson with Johnny Rotten, had tea with Glenn Tilbrook, and lunch with Steve Craddock and James Walsh.

I discussed Rovers with Pete Doherty, and talked about cancer with Nile Rodgers, chatted with Nick Heyward about Santorini, and basically had the time of my life.

I can't pretend cancer hasn't changed me, but I can now go for the majority of the day without bringing up the word in my head. At the time I described it as a lonely disease, because it felt that even if you were in a room surrounded by your friends and family, you tended to feel isolated and on your own. I still feel low for a matter of seconds, and still don't look forward to going to bed at night, but it really is a great leveller. And the times when I do find myself starting to feel a little down or fed up, it literally lasts for seconds, as on every occasion I think, *It could be worse.*

At the end of the day, I am here to tell the tale, and this August will be five years cancer free, and hopefully they will actually use those words. I appreciate every day (minute), and know that I am always the luckiest person in any room.

One of the best pieces of advice I have tried to take on board and thoroughly subscribe to, is from Billy Connolly when he said, 'Don't be beige.' I can be accused of being a lot of things, but I think that being beige is not one of them.

As far as we know, we have one life, so surely you would want to make the most of it. I believe everyone is scared of dying, even if they say they aren't, and find it beyond strange that my parents' generation would barely mention the deceased after they had gone. I would rather folk slagged me off than never mention me, as though I had never existed.

I try not to have too many regrets looking back at the things I have done over the years, because that was me at the time, and I would like to think I have learnt from those experiences. I am nobody to offer advice, but if I was pushed, I would say, 'In a world where everyone has a mirror hanging over their fireplace, be the one that doesn't.'

There is no doubt at all that discovering that old box of family photos in my Mum's attic changed the way I actually saw Mum and Dad, particularly the photograph showing my Dad as part of a football team (who knew?) and the photos of my mum in the 50s and 60s, glammed up in her trendy outfits. If I was given the opportunity to have acted in a different way at times growing up with my parents, then of course I would have. But that is not possible.

And if I had the chance to say something again to my Mum and Dad, yes, I would say 'Sorry, I know that I messed up from time to time.' Then I would add, 'BUT I'M DIFFERENT NOW!'

Life Goals with Emma Leah, drinking cocktails at Cafe Mambo.

ACKNOWLEDGEMENTS

My eternal thanks and appreciation to my wife Janet and my daughter Emma Leah, for putting up with all my endless obsessions and crazy ideas, sometimes on an almost daily basis. And for their continued support and understanding. I love you both to infinity.

My close-knit group of lifelong friends, who between them have shared in my life experiences and unusual situations, and no doubt taken the blame for some of my mad schemes and actions.

Linda Sharples, who agreed to help me in typing up my extraordinary long memoirs, and all her efforts in helping me achieve this.

Front cover design courtesy of @Theseasicksailor.

My eternal gratitude to all the amazing medical staff at Rosemere Hospital in Preston, and Blackburn Hospital, helping to save my life in 2016 and enabling me to carry on living my best life.

John, Paul, George, and Ringo, for changing the planet for the better, and setting the benchmark that will never be rivalled.

Paul Weller for his inspiration.

Remembering Mum and Dad, Margery and George Eastwood, my Grandma and Grandad Edna and Jim Burrows, my Uncle Bill Burrows, and my birth mum, Kathleen.

Also remembering my good friends Dave (Kershy) Kershaw and Craig (Rooster) Dunston.

DON'T CRY BECAUSE IT'S OVER; SMILE BECAUSE IT HAPPENED.

www.ingramcontent.com/pod-product-compliance
Lightning Source LLC
Chambersburg PA
CBHW062024290426
44108CB00025B/2772

www.ingramcontent.com/pod-product-compliance
Lightning Source LLC
Chambersburg PA
CBHW062024290426
44108CB00025B/2772